ERNEST NEWMAN

H. T. PARKER

SIR CLAUDE PHILLIPS

PITTS SANBORN

PERCY SCHOLES

EDITH SHACKLETON

G. BERNARD SHAW

RITA SHELL

HANNEN SWAFFER

SIR RICHARD TERRY

FRANCIS TOYE

A. B. WALKLEY

OBSERVERS OF THE OBSERVED—SOME CRITICS

We are indebted to the many public and private sources which provided portraits of the critics reproduced on the endleaves. Specific credits are as follows:

Heywood Broun (Courtesy of Newspaper Guild of New York.)
Richard Capell (Courtesy *Daily Mail*.)
Sydney Carroll (Coll. Mrs. Neate.)
Herbert Farjeon (Coll. Mrs. Farjeon.)
Hubert Griffith (Coll. Miss Griffith.)
Percy Hammond (Courtesy *Chicago Tribune*.)

Ernest J. Hopkins (Courtesy of *San Francisco Examiner*.)
Horace Horsnell (Coll. Frank Wells, Esq.)
P. G. Konody (Courtesy *Daily Mail*.)
H. T. Parker, by Vandamm
Sir Claude Phillips, by Sir Max Beerbohm (Courtesy Wallace Collection.)
Edith Shackleton, by Edmund Dulac (Coll. Miss Shackleton.)
A. B. Walkley, by Sir William Rothenstein (Courtesy The Trustees of the Estate of Sir William Rothenstein, Sir John and Mr. Michael Rothenstein.)

DIAGHILEV OBSERVED

BY CRITICS

IN ENGLAND AND THE UNITED STATES

1911–1929

DIAGHILEV
OBSERVED

BY CRITICS
IN ENGLAND
AND THE
UNITED STATES
1911–1929

NESTA
MACDONALD

Dance Horizons, New York & Dance Books Ltd., London

Library of Congress Catalog Card No. 74-81411
ISBN 0-78127-051-X
Dance Horizons, 1801 East 26th Street, Brooklyn, N.Y. 11229

ISBN 0-903102-14-5
Dance Books Ltd., 9 Cecil Court, London WC2N 4EZ, England

To
the memory of
SERGE DIAGHILEV
and the wonderful artists
he gathered together

and for
MARY CLARKE and FRANCIS FRANCIS
who made this book possible
and
PIP DYER
who understands Diaghilev

CONTENTS

CONTENTS

ILLUSTRATIONS

1909 – 1914

1915 – 1917

(Illustrations on the following pages are all by courtesy of
the Archives of the Metropolitan Opera – 145, 146, 147
148, 153, 158, 165, 175, 177.)

1918 – 1921

1924 – 1929

PROLOGUE

This book – which started as what might, for convenience, have been called a "Press Review," – originated when, on re-reading *Theatre Street*, I noticed that 1971 was the sixtieth anniversary of the first appearance of Diaghilev's company in England, and suddenly realised how little was known about this visit. Almost the only thing I could recall, though familiar with many books on Diaghilev, was that the house lights were up during the Coronation Gala, and that the jewels on the Maharajahs' turbans dazzled! Little else.

Curiosity aroused, I investigated contemporary accounts in the British Museum Newspaper Library. The resulting wealth of discoveries turned into a series of four articles, which appeared in a magazine in 1971.

Reading old newspapers is compulsive: once hooked, it became impossible to stop. All sorts of fascinating detail, not only about the ballets, but also about the social background, leapt from the columns. So, too, did unrecorded interviews with Diaghilev and with Nijinsky, and reports of other matters in which the latter was concerned. It became impossible to limit the scope of the book to reviews of performances alone.

The contemporary reports, written by observant journalists immediately after each performance, were uncomplicated by accretions of legend and second-hand judgments. Sometimes, these eye-witness accounts belied the accepted versions, which had become consolidated in the re-telling of the tale. They certainly amplified them.

Not only did the style of the critiques alter with the years, but so, too, did the critical standpoint. Most obvious of all – *Le Sacre du Printemps*, which stunned audiences in 1913, was viewed differently when, re-made, it appeared again in 1921, and accepted by the time it was shown in what proved to be the last season, 1929.

The plan followed was to go through all the normal daily and Sunday papers which reached the breakfast-tables. *The Times* covered the seasons consistently – other papers more sporadically. Only one critic followed their fortunes from 1911 to 1929 for the same paper – Richard Capell, of the *Daily Mail*. Of course, many reviews were anonymous, and some names which might have been expected to turn up do not appear at all, because they wrote for specialised journals, and what they had to say has been quoted before.

Following a hunch that there might be items about the social scene in weekly magazines such as *The Lady* and *The Queen*, I found, in addition, a rich vein of observation and criticism. Odd clues led to a diversity of other reviews. After the war, *Vogue*, arbiter of taste, discussed the ballets and allied arts, though, then appearing fortnightly, it did not offer immediate "notices."

Although only six of the sixty ballets had their "world premières" in London, the company gave more performances here than anywhere else, and it seemed reasonable to follow all its

Serge Diaghilev:
Serge
Lifar
p.260

seasons in this country. (Lifar described the "stupendous, deafening applause" at the great Gala at Versailles in 1923 as "comparable only with our London triumphs.")

The normal routine was for the company to perform in Paris in the early summer, then in London, and then, after holidays, to visit other countries, such as Germany and Spain. From 1911 onwards, the early months of the year were spent in Monte Carlo, both performing and preparing new ballets. The Riviera was the magnet for the rich and leisured of the whole world during its "season," at that time, of course, in winter. In addition to possessing a delightful and suitable theatre for ballet it also had wonderful facilities for rehearsals, and for scene-painting and the maintenance of the enormous impedimenta of the company.

I also found many references to the two North American sorties of 1916 and 1916-17, about which relatively little had been included in existing books. It became obvious that there must be far more material about these tours – if I could only reach it. American "readers" helpfully addressed my queries to friends in the States, and the Xerox copies mounted.

Through the kindness of Francis Francis, I was given the opportunity to go to New York and Washington, and burrow for myself. I returned with some hundreds of Xeroxes of "clippings," especially from the Dance Collection of the New York Public Library. What was unexpected was to find reports in American papers dating from the Ballet's earliest appearances in Europe, and also much about Nijinsky, which filled in gaps in the great dancer's tragic story.

The original intention had been to select Press notices, from the "front of the house," alone. There were, however, some stories to do with the creation of certain ballets which were not generally known, but which could add to the enjoyment of discussing these works. So, although they came from memoirs written later, the "contemporary" rule was broken for them. Then, too, if some of the stories in the cuttings, especially those about Nijinsky in America, were to be understood, it was necessary to put them in perspective by reference to known and stated facts, without making the book a complete assemblage of all the existing histories.

As the book took shape, I decided to eliminate repetitious statements by starting each season with a "Playbill," giving the new productions, the repertoire, and the members of the company and conductors. Owing to the fact that the spellings of transliterated names could vary, not merely from season to season, but even three times in the same programme, this piece of detective work may not be without flaws, but it proved extremely interesting to me to see how many of the *corps de ballet* stayed in the company for many years, thereby maintaining its cohesion, no matter which of the star dancers were with it at different periods. Jennie Walton most patiently checked the lists for each season, and brought order into the selection of the most acceptable spellings – and Boris Skidelsky, of the Royal Opera House Archives, was the arbiter.

References are in the margins, the unidentified cuttings (mostly from the New York Public Library's Dance Collection) signified by three asterisks. There are only two anecdotes, one concerning Nijinsky, which have arrived by oral tradition.

The most difficult thing of all was to decide how much previous knowledge could be assumed in readers, for, if the aim of printing the new material were to be fulfilled, it would be essential to leave out much that is already available, otherwise the book would have had to be published in several volumes! Feeling that it was unlikely that it would be read by anyone to whom the whole subject was unknown, and the names of the great dancers, musicians and designers – and also the plots of the ballets – a complete novelty, I decided to let them arrive in the Press accounts, simply, as the story unfolds.

Having collected reviews running into four figures, it would obviously be impossible to quote them all, or to give them in full, but I have tried to select alternative opinions, and have been scrupulous never to distort the tone of a notice in extracting its more trenchant phrases.

A word here about the spelling of names. All Russian names started in a different script; they were adapted and spelt phonetically, with many variations. In some of the programmes, as I have already said, although presumably these were provided by Diaghilev's own staff, the variations were extraordinary and many barely recognisable. Diaghilev signed some letters like that, with a 'v," – appeared on many programmes as "Diaghileff" – and sent a wedding-present to one of his dancers with his visiting-card, on which it was spelt "Diaghilew." He removed syllables from some difficult names, such as Miassin and Spessivtseva, (which he simplified to Massine and Spessiva,) to make them more easily dealt with by Western tongues and pens. There seems to me to be no reason to discount these simplifications, nor to try to impose one standard form for each person. Spellings, therefore, vary, just as they turned up. Sometimes, the less common spelling seems to impart a special nuance in a given situation.

Cyril Beaumont, one of the greatest friends and admirers of Diaghilev and the Ballets Russes, (friend, too, of so many members of the company,) wrote a delightful book, full of personal observations and recollections – *The Diaghilev Ballet in London* (1940.) Whilst it would be impossible to thank him adequately for all the tips he has given me and the questions he has answered, he does not feature as a critic, for he did not review the Diaghilev Ballet.

When I started work on this book, I asked Anton Dolin to be a help. From America, he sent me an article which had appeared in an American magazine in 1953 – *The Diaghilev I Knew*, by Igor Stravinsky. This fascinating account came, I felt, with a double pedigree, since both writer and dancer had known Diaghilev and his work so well. Nothing could have been a greater help, and I am very grateful for it.

So many people and institutions have helped by answering questions and sending copies, that it would be difficult to thank them all in this introduction. It would, however, have been impossible to have put it together without the constant help of George Nash, Tony Latham, and the staff of the Enthoven Collection, and the Librarians in the Reference Libraries of the Royal Borough of Kensington and Chelsea, and Westminster, and the Westminster Music Library. Miss Genevieve Oswald, Curator of the New York Public Library's Dance Collection, gave me invaluable help, not only during my stay in New York, but over certain points that arose later.

Illustrations presented a challenge, for, naturally, the best photographs of the most famous dancers in their most famous rôles have also been the most frequently reproduced. Having been generously lent some interesting rarities by friends, in addition to my own modest collection, it suddenly occurred to me that there might be some good prints, instead of poor quality newspaper reproductions, in the archives of the Metropolitan Opera House, which had handled all the Press matters for the company on its war-time tours. Playing this hunch, I wrote and enquired, and eventually received a long list. I cannot adequately thank Mrs. Peltz, the archivist, who gave permission, and Mrs. Pressey, her assistant, who, going in when she was really on holiday, let me have rough proofs of the collection – (thanks, too, to Peter Rosenwald, who had them taken.)

It would have been ridiculous to have contemplated selecting the illustrations for this book without co-opting Pip Dyer, whose encyclopaedic knowledge on this subject is unrivalled. We had already been brooding happily over my earlier "finds." When tiny proofs arrived from New York, some being absolute treasures, we decided that the early ballets should be largely represented by these pictures from the Met. They show the original costumes clearly, and also many of the lesser artists, and should prove interesting as, having been buried for so long, they appear almost as if for the first time. (Picasso made famous drawings from some of them.)

Not only would I like to re-iterate my gratitude to Pip Dyer, but also to the late Madame Sokolova, Madame Tchernicheva, and Stanislas Idzikowski, all of whom struggled with identifications. "Idzi" also allowed me to reproduce a number of rare photographs from his wonderful collection.

Lady Epstein spent hours hunting for the drawings made by her late husband, Sir Jacob Epstein, and Sir Cecil Beaton also kindly allowed me to reproduce a drawing.

I am also very grateful to a number of collectors who have allowed me to reproduce drawings from their collections – each one I approached about a drawing I knew, promptly offered others, as well! I should like to thank the busy people in art galleries – Messrs. Hartnoll and Eyre, and the Fine Art Society, and Richard Nathanson, – for their help, and also Julian Bar-ran, of Sotheby's, for his constant help, and Felix Hope-Nicholson and all the collectors whose generosity is acknowledged with each item.

I should also like to thank Rennie Voase, who translated photographs of Diaghilev's childhood home and his wartime base into drawings which evoke the style of living to which Diaghilev was born.

The Editors of all the newspapers and journals in which I found material ought to be thanked by everyone who is interested in the Diaghilev Ballet – past Editors for the space they gave it and the splendid writers who covered it, and present Editors for their interest in my attempt to show the contemporary view of the company. I should also like to thank Condé Nast Publications Ltd. for permission to quote copyright material from *Vogue*, and also for their beautiful photographs of *Ode*.

In spite of so much description and, in modern times, so much exposure, both Diaghilev, the man, and "Diaghilev," the concept, the *Ballets Russes*, remain a fascinating enigma, discussed not only by lovers of ballet itself, but by others who, though their artistic interests lie primarily in other directions, recognise that his taste and flair indirectly affected their lives. *Avant-garde* though he was, Diaghilev did not ruthlessly discard the old, but took the best of it, added to it what he found that was new, set fresh standards of art appreciation, made the esoteric fashionable, the fashionable familiar – and, eventually, accepted.

Chelsea, S.W.3.
1971 – 1974   N.M.

Money matters crop up at various points in this book.

The value of money had already deteriorated between the pre-1914 era and the 'twenties: a glance at old guide books and theatre programmes will show how the price of hotel rooms, meals, and travel had risen—factors which contributed to the rise in the price of theatre seats.

In 1971, I asked bank experts to give me equivalent values for figures which were mentioned in the text. I have decided to leave those equivalents in although, in the years since then, the arithmetic has altered violently. The great rise in the cost of fuel oil in 1974 affected the whole world. The rate of inflation varies from one country to another, with but one aspect remaining the same—no one can keep pace with it. Therefore, conversion to approximately 1971 values seems comprehensible.

April 1975.   N.M.

DIAGHILEV OBSERVED

BY CRITICS

IN ENGLAND AND THE UNITED STATES

1911–1929

1872 – 1929

"The Diaghilev home was one of the most brilliant and intellectual in Perm. Indeed, it was Perm's 'Athens.' There, artists, musicians, and the most cultured progressive inhabitants of the town congregated for private theatricals, balls, concerts or recitals of chamber music... The Diaghilev house was a large, magnificent mansion at the end of the main street... Indeed, it was like the palace of some feudal prince. Inside, too, all was luxury and wealth."

(O. Vassiliev, in SERGE DIAGHILEV, by Serge Lifar.)

THE BALLROOM FAÇADE

[Rennie Voase, 1974.]

SERGE DIAGHILEV

Although well known, the facts of Diaghilev's life and career must first be summarised.

Sergei Pavlovitch Diaghilev was born on March 19th, 1872, in the province of Novgorod, where his father, an officer in the Imperial Guard, happened to be serving. His mother died a few days after the birth. Two years later his father married again, a charming woman who created a happy family life wherever she was. After spending the next few years in St. Petersburg, his father's debts forced a move to the family estate at Perm, where Sergei (then about ten years old) enjoyed childhood and adolescence in a large, affectionate, music and art-loving household. (His cousin, D. Filosov, wrote later that "Diaghilev, like all the Diaghilevs, reacted to music, to all art in fact, with his *entrails*, emotionally, even sentimentally".) He grew up in love with Russian art and steeped in Russian history.

Lifar
p.13

In 1890, aged eighteen, he returned to St. Petersburg, and then made a "grand tour" of Europe with that same cousin. Diaghilev fell in love with Venice, and under the spell of Florentine art, which he for ever regarded as unsurpassed. In 1899, he wrote: "One must climb the pinnacles of Florentine art to pass judgment on contemporary art."

Lifar
p.30

Back in St. Petersburg, he took a degree in law, and also studied music (especially composition) at the Conservatoire. He was not considered sufficiently talented to warrant continuing with serious musical studies – yet, many years later, the composer Nicholas Nabokov was to write that "he knew more music, and more *about* music, than many an erudite musician . . . Diaghilev had the gift of detecting, after one incomplete and cursory hearing, the quality of a piece of music."

Old Friends
& New Music:
N. Nabokov,
pp.65-66.

Diaghilev's life in St. Petersburg became centred on the activities of a group led by the painter Alexandre Benois. They dreamed of revitalizing Russian art. Amongst them were Leon Bakst, the painter, and Walter Nouvel, a musician (who later excelled in explaining European music to Russia.) Though not, at first, the most active of members, Diaghilev made an impression. In 1893, he and the same cousin made a second European journey, endlessly visiting museums and seeing every possible work of art. Diaghilev also showed a great flair for finding and recognising antique furniture. His purchases looked very effective when they were installed in his flat, and were much admired.

He began to plan exhibitions of modern painting. In November, 1898, the first number appeared of a journal called the *Mir Isskustva* – "*The World of Art.*" Diaghilev was its Editor and moving spirit, and the Princess Tenisheva its financial backer. "Diaghilev, in the course of six years," (its life-span,) "gave a new direction to the public taste," said Vladimir Polunin, (then a student, subsequently a distinguished scene-painter,) when he wrote about it some years later. "He overthrew the old gods from their pedestals and set up new ones, whose names were hitherto entirely unknown, but afterwards became of international reputation.

Continental
Method of
Scene
Painting:
Polunin &
Beaumont
1927

"This magazine had for us Russians another important meaning; it led, for the first time, to our closer acquaintance with the artistic achievements of Europe about which we had desultory notions, often of a negative character . . .

"It was his usual practice to visit the studios of artists whose work interested him, and select, as an omnipotent autocrat, not what the artist wished to be shown, but what he, Diaghilev, considered suitable for a projected exhibition."

This picture of Diaghilev in his twenties would probably stand for him throughout his whole life.

In 1899, Diaghilev was given an appointment in the Imperial Theatres, and, in 1901, made a great success of editing the *Imperial Theatres' Yearbook* – though he extravagantly spent twice the budget in order to achieve the standard of perfection he required. He was entrusted with the production of the ballet *Sylvia*, but, after a farrago of scandals and intrigues, was dismissed by the Director, Prince Wolkonsky, "without leave to appeal." This awesome phrase meant that he could never again hold an official appointment – yet, very shortly afterwards, the Czar attached Diaghilev to his personal household. In later years Diaghilev was to describe himself by various curious semi-official designations, which were always being quibbled about behind his back.

In 1905, having made long journeys and tremendous searches throughout his vast country, Diaghilev arranged the splendid exhibition of Russian Historical Portraits at the Tauride Palace in St. Petersburg. (This palace subsequently became the Duma.)

Next, in 1906, he organized an exhibition of Russian Art in Paris, at the Grand Palais, for which Bakst, whom he engaged for the work, designed ravishing settings. (Gontcharova and Larionov, both then aged 25, accompanied them. The exhibition formed part of the *Salon d'Automne*, showplace of the younger, *avant-garde* painters since 1903. In 1905, a great sensation had been caused by the "*Fauves*," including Matisse and Derain, both of whom Diaghilev was to call on many years later to design ballets.)

In 1907, he introduced Russian music to Europe in a series of historical concerts, again in Paris, conducted by Nikisch and startling the audiences with the magnificence of Chaliapin. Admiration for Diaghilev's work led to his friendship with the great leader of Society and art, the Comtesse Greffuhle, and with Madame Edwards, wife of the immensely rich owner of the newspaper, *Le Matin*, – "Misia," friend and patroness of artists, who later married, as her third husband, the Spanish painter José-Maria Sert. The influence of these women was of incalculable value in all his subsequent projects, and they dipped deep into their pockets in support of his enterprises.

In 1908, Diaghilev took a magnificent production of Moussorgsky's opera *Boris Godounov* to Paris, with Chaliapin in the name part. Diaghilev combed the antique shops of Russia, buying up old sarafans (tunics,) Kokoshniks (head-dresses,) and shawls, so that it was almost entirely dressed in authentic period costume. An arrangement had been made with the Paris *Opéra*, by which all the scenery and costumes were to remain its property. This seems an extraordinary idea, in view of their expense. Some years later, the *Opéra* sold the whole production to the Metropolitan Opera of New York, where it was first given in 1913.

In 1909, Diaghilev returned to Paris, this time with a mixed season of opera and ballet – with which this book, or any book on twentieth century ballet, really begins.

His collaborator in these and subsequent seasons in Paris was the impresario, Gabriel Astruc.

Despite the sensational success of *Boris*, the *Opéra* authorities refused Diaghilev the theatre in 1909. So – typical of the man – he transformed the shabby old *Châtelet* into a sumptuous mock-opera-house, in a mere five days. It was as if he had waved a wand and uttered an incantation. Seats were re-covered, aisles carpeted, walls painted, cherubs gilded. For his opening nights, he gathered together the smartest and most cosmopolitan audiences the capital had ever known, and made them part of the spectacle. The most important theatrical managers and patrons of the world were there, and, somewhat naturally, these managers were fired with the desire to show his company – or, not comprehending the difference between performing in a grand whole and the giving of recitals, to try to tempt his stars with huge money offers which could never have been accepted.

This season truly changed the face of the world in everything pertaining to the arts: music, the pictorial arts of scenic and costume design, and dance or movement. Though it might seem as if one ought to have qualified the word "arts" with the adjective "theatrical," it was to happen, in the future, that Diaghilev's choice of composers and painters, young and unknown, whom he presented to the world, was to make their fame for them.

Following upon this memorable season, Diaghilev collected a company in 1910, which performed for about two weeks in Berlin, and then had its second season in Paris. At the end of 1910, he told his friends that their work was already strong enough to warrant forming a permanent company, which could work together the whole year round, creating new ballets and visiting different cities. His company subsequently performed triumphantly all over Europe, in England, and in South America. Its visits to North America, long desired by the Chairman of the Metropolitan, Otto Kahn, had proved impossible to arrange between 1910 and 1914. The tours which eventually took place, in 1916 and 1916-17, did so under wartime difficulties which had cut off many of the company's dancers. These tours were quite different from anything it had experienced before, and their story emerges vividly from the American press.

The *Ballets Russes de Serge de Diaghilev* lasted for twenty years, ending with his sudden death in 1929, at the early age of 57.

The art of Russian ballet was new to Europe when, thanks to Diaghilev, it first erupted in Paris. Most especially sensational were the fine male dancers. What he presented – sadly, never in Russia itself – was not the traditional ballet of the Imperial Theatres, though his dancers needed to have that splendid training behind them, which they could adapt to the modern conceptions of the art.

Imperial grandeur remained the surface, but, inside Russia, revolutionary ideas had been stirring for years, albeit ignored by the Emperor. Revolutionary artistic ideas were already infiltrating and refreshing the Imperial ballet itself – a peaceful revolution, growing in the collaboration of the friends who became Diaghilev's creative innovators, his "Committee." They met with constant opposition from those in authority, and the criticism and doubt of the conservatives amongst critics and audience.

In addition to the artists and musicians, there was the pivot of the new movement in ballet – Michael Fokine, who had graduated from the Imperial School in 1898. He wished to enlarge the vocabulary of the art by casting off the shackles of its late nineteenth-century conventions, which had been developed and then stereotyped under Petipa. Fokine wished to give each ballet its own correct style, to use new forms and combine with painters and musicians so that each ballet would be a coherent work of art, to eliminate conventional arrangements which did not progress the dramatic action, to use the whole body and devise steps to convey meaning instead of the formal "mime," and to make not only the bodies of his dancers expressive from head to foot, but also the movement of the whole ensemble. These requirements he formulated as his *"Principles."*

Fokine's dancers were of the younger generation, themselves frustrated by the hierarchical system of promotion and seniority within the Imperial Theatres, and denied the opportunity to take over important rôles, which remained the preserves of the established stars. Anna Pavlova admired Fokine's ideas, and danced in his early compositions. She came to the rescue and took over the part of Armida for the first performance of *Le Pavillon d'Armide*, at the Maryinsky, in 1907. Fokine created *The Dying Swan* for her. Pavlova, however, limited the type of music to which she would dance to the more conventional works.

Fokine found his ideal exponents in Tamara Karsavina, five years younger and four years junior to Pavlova, and Vaslav Nijinsky, five years younger still. Individually wonderful dancers, these two together – being perfectly matched, not only in height, but more importantly, in their inner poetry and music – became probably the most miraculous partnership in the history of the dance. Together, they took Europe by storm, and created a legendary magic.

Karsavina, who had graduated in 1902, was at her peak, having developed her full confidence and stature as an artist by the time the European seasons started. Though it had not been

Diaghilev's intention that she should be the star of his first Paris season, this did, in fact, come to pass. On the opening night, in the final *divertissement*, *Le Festin*, (a collection of numbers to music by various Russian composers) she and Nijinsky performed Diaghilev's adaptation of Tchaikovsky's "Blue Bird" *pas de deux*, and brought the house down. Diaghilev had reversed the sexes, so that the male was a Prince, and the female the bird. Bakst had designed breathtaking costumes, Karsavina's being a miracle of flaunting flame-coloured plumes. Diaghilev had called it *Oiseau de Feu*. This led to its being re-named *Oiseau d'Or* the following year, when Diaghilev needed its earlier title for Stravinsky's new ballet, and yet again, later on, *L'Oiseau et le Prince*. Later still, and with new costumes and setting, again designed by Bakst, it was to emerge as *La Princess Enchantée*, indicating that the female was not truly a bird, but under a spell. Finally, this famous *pas de deux* reverted to its original Petipa form as *The Blue Bird* in *The Sleeping Princess* and its shortened form, *Aurora's Wedding*.

As an interpretive artist, Karsavina's range was outstanding, for she could excel in lyrical, poetic, romantic, tragic and witty rôles in the modern idiom as brilliantly as she had done when ballet remained closer to its classical origins. She charmingly acknowledges that she and Diaghilev occasionally had a "formidable row," but they loved and respected each other, found solutions, and made it up with flowers and laughter.

Diary of Vaslav Nijinsky 1918-19

Fokine found the perfect male dancer to interpret his ideas in Vaslav Nijinsky, who had graduated in 1907 at the age of nineteen. Diaghilev must surely have seen him dance at the Maryinsky, but it was not until 1908 that Nijinsky's protector, the Prince Lvov, introduced them. Diaghilev fell in love with Nijinsky, who later dubbed the introduction his "luck." Diaghilev was homosexual, but Nijinsky's inclinations may be said to remain equivocal. Though he later professed to loathe Diaghilev, he also said that he had accepted him as a lover. They did not live together, Vaslav continuing to stay in his mother's flat. Diaghilev was obsessed by Nijinsky, and surrounded him with every luxury – but also saw to it that his valet accompanied him everywhere.

Only one contract was ever signed between them, and this may have been done before the two men actually met. In 1908, planning for the first season in Paris, Diaghilev worked out the dancers he required, and gave the details and contracts to Serge Grigoriev to complete. All the contracts were signed within a week. This document was sold at Sotheby's on October 15th, 1963, fetching £380. The catalogue entry states it to be for May and June 1909 in Paris, to be dated October 10th, 1908, St. Petersburg, and to be signed five times by Nijinsky. (He was to receive a fee of 2,500 francs and a second-class rail ticket. The pound was then worth approximately 25 francs, so that £100 in 1909 would represent about £700 in the early 1970's. Incidentally, the only contracts ever signed between Diaghilev and Karsavina were sold at the same time. There was, of course, no London season in 1910. Karsavina herself was always under the impression that there had only ever been one contract between them, that for 1909, and that subsequently, all their arrangements had been a matter of mutual trust.)

Nijinsky was a genius of the dance. These early seasons in Paris saw the flowering, as if by a miracle, of all the necessary protagonists of the revolution in ballet. Fokine created his finest works in the early Diaghilev years. Though, after the *pas Hongrois* in *Le Festin* in 1909, he never danced a truly virile rôle, Nijinsky gave the male dancer revived status, lost since the days of Vestris. Tamara Karsavina was the ideal ballerina, who could adapt her perfect training to the modern aims.

In 1911, Nijinsky was dismissed from the Imperial Theatres, and thenceforward became completely at Diaghilev's disposal, heading the newly-formed permanent company.

In 1912 and 1913, Diaghilev promoted his ambitions as a choreographer, quarrelling with Fokine as a result.

The progress of ideas was shattered in the autumn of 1913, when Nijinsky suddenly married, and was dismissed.

Without Diaghilev's organising ability and protection, Nijinsky, though he proudly itched for independence, could not cope with the management of a company. He attempted to run a season in London in 1914, but it collapsed in nervous breakdown and financial disaster.

The Property of a Lady

from the papers of Serge Grigoriev, Régisseur of the Diaghilev Ballet

483   DIAGHILEV (SERGEI PAVLOVITCH) AUTOGRAPH CONTRACT IN RUSSIAN WITH NIJINSKI for the Russian ballet season in Paris of May to June 1909, 2½ *pp., folio, St. Petersburg,* 10 *October* 1908, signed five times by Nijinski

*** Under this contract, which relates to the famous first season of the Russian ballet in Western Europe, Nijinski was to receive a fee of 2,500 francs and a second-class rail ticket from St. Petersburg to Paris.

484   DIAGHILEV (S. P.) One autograph contract, *Moscow,* 1908, and one typed contract, *St. Petersburg,* 1912, with Fedor Ivanovitch Chaliapin, in Russian, 5½ *pp., folio,* signed several times by Chaliapin   (2)

*** The contracts are for Chaliapin to sing in *Boris Godunov, Pskovitanka* and *Khovanshchina.* The contract of 1912 provides for a fee of 140,000 francs, of which 15,000 francs was to be paid in advance. Chaliapin was to receive 4,500 francs after the first act of each performance until payment had been made in full.

485   DIAGHILEV (S. P.) A COLLECTION OF FIFTY-FOUR CONTRACTS AND DRAFT CONTRACTS with dancers, conductors, etc., who worked for the Diaghilev ballet, mostly in Russian, but a few in French and one in English, some autograph, a few signed by Diaghilev, all signed by the dancers or other members of the company in question, 1908-1926, covering the period of Diaghilev's great pre-1914 tours, the war period in Barcelona and South America and with a few of later date; also A.Ls.s. of Karsavina, Lopokova and Bolm   (*a collection*)

*** The collection includes contracts with Karsavina (for the Paris season of 1909 and the London season of 1910 and three later contracts), Pavlova, Fokina, Khoklova (Madame Picasso; five contracts—the last broken at Barcelona on 4 June 1917 by Khoklova's refusal to accompany the company to South America), Mordkin, Volinin, Smirnov, Egorova, Sokolova, Cecchetti and Madame Cecchetti, Bolm (2 contracts and 19 additional conditions agreed with Bolm in 1911; there is also an acknowledgement of a loan of 6,000 roubles from Baron Günzbourg, which Bolm evidently raised on the strength of his contract), Lopokova (4 contracts and the *procès verbal* of an agreement between Lopokova and Diaghilev in Buenos Aires in 1917), and Alexandre Benois (2 contracts, the first for designs for Stravinski's "Nightingale"; the latter contract has some pencil drawings of sets by Benois on the back).

The file copy of Sotheby's catalogue indicates the detailed bargaining which went into Diaghilev's contracts with dancers, and records the prices at which the hammer fell as eager bidders battled to acquire them.

As a boy, Nijinsky had never made any real friends in the Imperial School, nor did he in the company. He spoke little, and in a disjointed manner. One side of his nature had a personal sweetness, but the other side could exhibit arrogance and violent temper.

In 1917, after the North American tours, he performed with Diaghilev's company in Spain, and went on another tour to South America. His behaviour was becoming more and more erratic. In 1918, he lived with his wife and daughter in Switzerland, and became even more strange. In January 1919, at the age of 31, he was pronounced incurably insane. Once this was established as a fact, the tales of curious incidents in the past all fell into place. All that has been written about him subsequently has, naturally, been written in the full knowledge of this tragic fact. The contemporary stories which, inevitably, have a prominent part in this book, were written without any idea of such a conclusion. The glory of his career as dancer and interpretive artist, and the originality of his ideas as a choreographer, enshrined him as the darkness of his affliction shrouded him.

Nijinsky's marriage left many gaps in Diaghilev's life, and led to the promotion of the career of a youth whom Diaghilev discovered in Moscow later in 1913 – Leonide Massine. Massine became his third choreographer, creating many ballets of note, which may be described as "*genre*" works. He, in his turn, married, (having been dismissed in 1920 when Diaghilev noticed signs of a courtship,) and was succeeded as choreographer by Nijinsky's sister, Bronislava. She dealt with contemporary themes, and also created *Les Noces*, a masterpiece to music by Stravinsky, in which she penetrated not to the primaeval world, but to ancient peasant rites in Russia.

Nijinska was followed by a younger dancer who had managed to get out of Russia, and whom Diaghilev re-christened Balanchine. Only four years of his career were passed in the Diaghilev stable, but in them he produced ten ballets, amongst them his *Apollon Musagètes* and *Le Fils Prodigue*, both works of deep feeling and great beauty.

After Massine and his first wife had separated, Diaghilev accepted her back into the company, and subsequently engaged Massine to devise additional ballets.

Last in the line of his choreographers was the young Serge Lifar, who, having been helped to stardom as a dancer by Diaghilev, had his first ballet, *Le Renard*, produced in what was to prove the company's final season. This took place at Covent Garden, where, for London, it had all begun. The season was successful artistically, full of vigour and promise.

Only a few weeks later, Diaghilev died in Venice. Long obituary notices appeared in hundreds of papers, not only in capital cities, but in surprisingly remote places which the ballet had never visited. But his *Ballets Russes* could not continue without Diaghilev. They had danced their course.

Throughout its twenty years, one man stayed at his post – Grigoriev, the company's *régisseur*. This office is untranslatable. It is far more than "Stage Manager". In addition to the normal duties of that office, he oversaw everything about the practical side of the company, from contracts to pay-days. He dealt with cast-lists for programmes, took rehearsals, and assisted in the re-mounting of revivals, in which his prodigious memory was invaluable. Exceptionally tall and handsome, he was naturally always cast in majestic and dramatic parts, such as the High Priest in *Cléopâtre*, and the Shah's brother (and sometimes the Shah) in *Scheherazade*. He kept meticulous accounts, and was discreet and uncommunicative. He was undoubtedly Diaghilev's right hand, and in that hand he carried an oil-can. He married the beautiful Lubov Tchernicheva, who, starting as a very young member of the *corps de ballet* in 1909, became one of the principal dancers. She never missed a single one of the seasons in London.

Grigoriev's book, *The Diaghilev Ballet, 1909 – 1929*, which came out in 1953, gave balletomanes a considerable history for which they are all grateful. Owing to the lapse of time, there are a few errors in dating, trifles seen against the importance of the book. (Where reference is made to it in this book, its long title is omitted, and it is simply stated in the margin as *Grigoriev*.)

Another stalwart was Maestro Enrico Cecchetti. Born – in a theatre dressing-room – in 1850, he had settled in St. Petersburg, and in 1909 became Ballet-Master to Diaghilev's company. He maintained the standard of dancing, and performed all the older parts, his genius as

Michel Fokine, by V. Serov.

Leon Bakst.

Serge Grigoriev.

Alexandre Benois, by L. Bakst.

Vaslav Nijinsky, by V. Serov.

Tamara Karsavina.

Gabriel Astruc, by Sem.

Enrico Cecchetti.

Leonide Massine.

Serge Lifar.

Bronislava Nijinska.

George Balanchine.

Boris Kochno, by P. Tchelitchew.

a mime finding outlets in rôles such as the Charlatan in *Petrouchka* and the Astrologer in *Le Coq d'Or*. He codified his teaching methods and technique, ran a school in London for some years, and returned to Milan as Director of its Academy of Dancing in 1923.

The question of financial backing was the bugbear of Diaghilev's existence. Before anything in the world of the theatre can be put to the test of a "First Night," money has to be paid out in abundance, for costumes, scenery, music, props, advertising, printing, and so on, not to mention travelling and salaries and the hire of halls during the weeks of rehearsals. When Diaghilev started, he managed to raise support from wealthy individuals in Russia, the promised subsidy from the Imperial purse having been withdrawn. In France, Gabriel Astruc, his fellow impresario, advanced money on certain occasions. As everything always cost far more than was expected, there was always trouble about its reimbursement. Diaghilev had many rich friends in France, who gave him considerable sums – notably Misia Edwards and the Comtesse Greffuhle. In England, before the first World War, his backer was Sir Joseph Beecham, father of the conductor Thomas Beecham, and his path was smoothed by the Marchioness of Ripon. His Russian friend, Baron Gunzburg, produced money like a conjuror's bundles of ribbons out of his invariable top hat. Highly lucrative private engagements kept his principal dancers happy, so that he paid them less regularly than the *corps de ballet*.

After the war, Sir Oswald Stoll, Managing Director of the Coliseum in London, kept the company employed, and there were powerful friends to help out in addition. Round about 1925, the need for really large sums led to negotiations with Lord Rothermere, proprietor of the *Daily Mail*. With his backing, the company had a most successful season in the summer of 1926 at His Majesty's, and later that year gave a "popular" repertoire, at reasonable prices, at the Lyceum, and created a delightful and very English ballet, *The Triumph of Neptune*.

When, in 1928, Lord Rothermere suddenly withdrew his support, Lady Juliet Duff, daughter of Lady Ripon, came up with a brilliant idea and saved the situation at this moment of crisis. Instead of fruitlessly trying to find one rich backer, she whipped up a number of guarantors for a modest sum apiece. The ballet's own "fans" thereby saved the threatened season.

After the triumphs of the first six years, the ballet struggled for survival in war-torn Europe. Diaghilev struggled to keep its remnants together, paternally concerned to keep his dancers employed, and artistically concerned to keep them inspired to continue to create. It crossed a U-boat-ridden ocean several times, and in North America found itself treated at one moment as a top-flight opera event, and at another as just part of show-biz.

A North American booking had been discussed ever since the original Paris season, but, when it finally took place, Diaghilev behaved in a totally abnormal manner, incurring great hatred amongst the staff of the Metropolitan Opera, under whose auspices the tour was run. The story of these visits, as it unfolds from the newspapers, is something quite outside the mainstream of the history of the *Ballets Russes*. Nevertheless, looking back in 1947, a member of that staff who had travelled with the company on tour, Merle Armitage, balletomane and collector, was to write that "the visit of the Russian Ballet, misunderstood at the time, really had a profound influence on this country."

Dance Memoranda
M. Armitage:
1947

From 1918 onwards, the company spent long periods in London, its seasons being highly successful and influential. Artistically, Diaghilev had turned to Paris for inspiration, in painting and in music, producing ballets which were more and more *avant-garde*. In 1921 came the attempt to return to Imperial Russia, with the full-scale production of *The Sleeping Princess*, a financial disaster not only for Diaghilev but also for its backers, largely owing to his reckless extravagance in repeating the search for perfection which had led him to overspend the budget for the *Imperial Theatres Yearbook* – but this time, without an Imperial purse to pay up.

New dancers came into the company, from Russia and from England itself. Though overshadowed by the legendary Karsavina and Nijinsky, they were undoubtedly stars in their own right, and in their own idiom. Yet at no time did Diaghilev ever discard classical ballet; instead, he mixed his programmes skilfully so that old and firm favourites carried along the new surprises.

Some of these ballets of the 1920's are dismissed in a line or two by many writers. If one studies their plots, listens to the music, and looks at photographs, it strikes one that, in fact, Diaghilev did then just about everything which is now considered to be *avant-garde* – everything except dancing in the nude or to electronic sound. It would be an entertaining exercise to set down in one column each of Diaghilev's innovations, and beside it, a work of recent years which has tried to claim a "first" for some feature, but which, indeed, is only faintly matching up. As the notices show, there was far more content in even the most seemingly trivial of Diaghilev's experiments than is generally credited.

What was Diaghilev, the man, really like?

Merle Armitage said, "When I first saw him, it occurred to me that here was a Russian version of a more muscular and dominant Oscar Wilde . . ."

There is a vivid description of him as he was in 1925, from the pen of one of his "finds" – Vladimir Dukelsky, who composed serious music under his real name, and lighter works for musical comedy and revue under the pseudonym of Vernon Duke.

Passport to Paris
V. Duke:
1955

"In walked a man of an appearance so remarkable that it will be hard to give the reader a faithful pen-portrait of him. Sergei Pavlovitch Diaghilev was a big man – slightly over six feet tall – broad and big-limbed, but not corpulent; his head was enormous, and the face – a world in itself; you hardly noticed the rest of his body. The still-abundant graying hair was parted meticulously on the side and displayed the oft-described patch in the middle – no crafty coiffeur's trick but, from all accounts, something of a birthmark. When I first gazed at Diaghilev's face, I thought instantly of a decadent Roman Emperor – Caligula, perhaps, – although Diaghilev was allergic to horses among other things; then the Tartar in him – possibly Genghis Khan – or even a barbarous Scythian, became visible – and lastly, what he really was: a Russian *grand seigneur* of Alexander III vintage. The eyes had a piercing, mocking intensity about them, softened by unusually heavy lids, and he was fond of closing them slowly, as if persuaded by some unseen Morpheus, but only for a moment; they were soon peering at you again, not missing a thing. The mouth was cruel and soft at the same time, the moustache even more close-clipped than Valitchka's, (Nouvel) the smile irresistible and oddly feminine. Sergei Pavlovitch carried monocles in all his pockets and had a habit of dropping one into his left hand, producing another with the right and screwing it into his eye languidly, making a lazy chewing motion with his mouth the while, as if munching spinach." (Cyril Beaumont said that Diaghilev used the monocle as a weapon of intimidation!) "He was well, although not conspicuously well dressed, and wore his Davis dinner jacket as if it were a dressing-gown. His voice seemed monstrously affected at first – the Imperial page's voice of aristocratic St. Petersburg – but you soon knew that he must have, too, been born with it. Diaghilev spoke French superbly, and English adequately."

Vera Newman, widow of the critic Ernest Newman, who was to indulge in many a battle with Diaghilev after the war, described his voice as "not *black* velvet, but *brown* velvet".

But – in any language – Diaghilev was possessed of one asset, which mostly – though not quite always – transcended criticism and opposition even from those with whom he had little *rapport*. He possessed irresistible, magnetic charm, when he chose to exercise it, with which he could persuade people, bend them to his will, and implant in them the feeling of the greatest satisfaction in having yielded to it; in fact, the satisfaction lay in having been considered worthy of having it turned upon them.

facing page: Diaghilev in his maturity.

"Conversations with a dozen men who knew Diaghilev will produce twelve different versions of him," said Merle Armitage.

Igor Stravinsky, Diaghilev's first "find" in the realm of music, is perhaps one of the dozen best fitted to describe his character.

Atlantic
Monthly:
November
1953

"Nineteen years of close collaboration, of affection and mutual friendship, enable me to draw a portrait far more accurate than the characterizations of some writers of questionable impartiality who knew him but slightly . . .

"I met Diaghilev in the autumn of 1909 . . . From all that I had heard of him, I imagined him haughty, arrogant, and snobbish. To tell the truth, I found, after I met him, that the reputation people had given him was not entirely without foundation. He had many unsympathetic traits – which, however, were not the essence of his nature ... . I think the term 'Russian *barin*' characterizes Diaghilev's nature and explains his amazing activity as the inspirer, promoter, and organizer of a long series of artistic events . . . It is only by understanding the nature of a cultured *barin* such as used to exist in Russia (a nature generous, strong, and capricious; with intense will, a rich sense of contrasts, and deep ancestral roots) that we can explain the character and originality of Diaghilev's creations, so different from the average artistic enterprises. Apart from his intelligence, his culture, his extraordinary artistic flair, and his sincere enthusiasm, he possessed a will of iron, tenacity, an almost superhuman resistance and passion to fight and to overcome the most insurmountable obstacles . . . He displayed characteristics of the enlightened despot, of the natural leader who knows how to drive the most unyielding elements, at times using persuasion, at others, charm. His passionate devotion to the cause he served and to the ideas he was then promulgating and his complete disinterestedness and lack of personal ambition in all his enterprises won the hearts of his co-workers. Working with him, they realized, meant working solely for the great cause of art.

"Like all great personalities, Diaghilev had devoted friends and at the same time violent enemies . . . What he detested most was banality, incompetency, and lack of *savoir-faire*.

"Even in his most prosperous periods he never spent money on himself . . . he never saved any money. Had he wished to do so, he could not have done it, as his undertakings always cost more than they made. Everything he did was idealistic. Commercialism was entirely foreign to his nature.

"He was extremely obliging. I never remember him refusing a service to anyone . . . and they were asked of him very often. The well-known Russian hospitality was deeply rooted in him. When he had money he loved to keep 'open house,' and then his companions were indeed numerous. It would be difficult to count the number of people who took advantage of him . . . How often he came to the aid of friends, relatives, and even people who were not close to him, but he never spoke of these things, and as, in most cases, the people themselves never mentioned them, these facts remain unknown."

Of his part in the enterprise he created, Stravinsky said:

"Diaghilev knew how to create around him amazing activity and an artistic atmosphere that was like an electric current which stimulated all his associates into work, sharpened their fantasy, and made any task worth doing. One forgot effort and fatigue. Carried away by this fever of work, one became intoxicated with the sense of participation in a creation pure and disinterested.

"As a result those among Diaghilev's co-workers who had left him dramatically would always feel a nostalgia for his laboratory, for that perpetually boiling cauldron of work: and fascinated by its irresistible charm – forgetting griefs and grievances – they were always ready to return. As for Diaghilev, though his fits of temper could be terrible for the moment, he never held a grudge, and when his friends and artists returned to him, he always took them back as if nothing had happened."

With this description of Diaghilev's nature, must come understanding of the emotions which led the composer to wish to be buried near him, where both could hear the same music as the waters of the lagoon lap the walls of San Michele, cemetery of their beloved Venice.

Igor Stravinsky, by M. Larionov.

Sergei Pavlovitch Diaghilev could not dance, could not compose music, could not design scenery and costumes; yet he composed pictures with dancers who moved; he found artists of brilliance, many young and little known, gave them a large canvas and brought them to prominence; he found old music and commissioned new for his pictures to dance to. In one department of theatre craft, however, he was personally the supreme master – in stage lighting. He knew how the same scene could be changed from brilliant to sombre, from exciting to menacing, from dawn to dusk, according to the subtle combinations of lights he threw upon it.

So, too, does any given performance have different significance for different people in the same audience, according to the light each personally turns upon it. A work which is a rosy dream of poetic romance in the eyes of one observer, can seem an orgy of fearful lust to another of a different outlook. In such a way did the works created under the spell of this great magician, this Maestro, evoke different reactions from different beholders – those fortunate mortals who lived at the right time to "observe" Diaghilev.

1908 – 1910

LONDON COLISEUM,

CHARING CROSS.

| Managing Director | ... | ... | OSWALD STOLL |
| Manager | ... | ... | DUNDAS SLATER |

WHIT-MONDAY, MAY 16th, 1910
AND UNTIL FURTHER NOTICE
TWICE DAILY AT 2.30 and 8.0 P.M.

THE FAMOUS RUSSIAN DANCERS:

Mdlle. TAMARA
KARSAVINA

Mdlle.
BALDINA

And M. THEODORE
KOSLOFF

Who made so striking a success at the Chatelet
Theatre, Paris, and the London Coliseum last year

AND

Mdlle. ANDERSEN	Mons. TARASOFF
,, ADAMOWITSCH	,, GERBER
,, CHEREPANOWA	,, GOTSCHITOWSKY
,, DAMACHOWA	,, KOTROWSKAIE I.
,, WICHNIAKOWA	,, KOTROWSKAIE II.
,, MALTSCHANOWA	,, ALEXIS KOSLOFF
	,, TSCHOUKOFF

ALL FROM THE IMPERIAL OPERA HOUSES
:: OF ST. PETERSBURG AND MOSCOW. ::

Karsavina's second season at the Coliseum, in 1910.

RUSSIAN DANCERS IN LONDON BEFORE DIAGHILEV

Before Diaghilev's company eventually arrived in London in 1911, the special qualities of the Russian dancers of the Imperial Theatres had already been recognised by perspicacious managers always on the look-out for promising acts for the flourishing music-halls. Some account of the dancers who brought London the first whiff of the Russian ballet must precede the advent of the great company under Diaghilev.

After the triumphs of the Romantic ballets of the 1830's and 1840's, and their delightful ballerinas, ballet in England had degenerated into a formula of large-scale spectacles, full of complicated stage effects, in elaborate productions with large numbers in the *corps de ballet,* mainly at the Empire and Alhambra theatres. The male dancer had become subservient to the female star – indeed, sometimes a stalwart girl in *travesti* supported her, like a "Principal Boy" in pantomime. True, much work went into these productions, and in 1889 George Bernard Shaw, then a music critic, wrote that "At one point in my chequered career I made a point of seeing every ballet produced at the Alhambra in order to study one of the most remarkable artistic institutions of the time. The virtuosity of the principal dancers was the result of a training of a severity and duration unknown among singers . . ." It was a period, however, when the *milieu* for dancing acts was far removed from the social pinnacle of the Opera. One cannot picture the great hostesses, white-gloved and covered in jewels, subscribing for boxes and entertaining grandly in either of those theatres, which were far more the haunt of the male "Promenaders."

The Empire had been the shrine of Adeline Genée, the exquisite Dane, from 1897 until she left on her first American tour on January 1st, 1908.

Her departure left a serious gap, and in 1908, a London agent journeyed to St. Petersburg, the fame of whose ballet was well-known, in search of a replacement. He approached Lydia Kyaksht, a young *première danseuse* at the Maryinsky Theatre, and offered her £40 a week – riches in comparison with the relatively modest salaries paid to members of the Imperial companies. She accepted the offer for one month's engagement, which led to a further offer. Not only was Petersburg reluctant to part with one of its charming young dancers, but in addition, the Tsar personally disapproved of the music-hall as a setting for any dancer trained in his school. Eventually he permitted her to take unpaid leave for a year, during which she attracted an adoring public in London. Moreover, her salary was increased to £75 a week. In 1909, won over by her success, and her desire to stay on in London, the Tsar gave her leave to resign from the Imperial Theatres. Simplifying the spelling of her name to "Kyasht," she remained the attraction of the Empire for over five years.

Kyasht was, therefore, the first of the Russian dancers who, having been trained during the last years of the era of Petipa, but having begun to feel the impact of the novel ideas of Fokine, had come to dance in London. Working in the conventional idiom of the Empire, she impressed the public with her own art and personality. In 1908, she arranged for Adolf Bolm to come over and partner her – so that he was the first of the spectacular Russian male dancers to be seen in London. Her brother George also appeared with her.

Lydia Kyasht and Tamara Karsavina had been sworn friends all through their years in the Imperial School, so possibly Kyasht's descriptions of London may have helped Karsavina to select an engagement to dance at the Coliseum immediately after Diaghilev's first Paris season in 1909, during which she was besieged with offers of contracts by managers from many lands. Reports of the wonders of the Russians' season were appearing in American newspapers in the summer of 1909, and, indeed, it is from *Musical America* that this story of Sir Oswald Stoll's journey to Russia is culled: "Since his return from St. Petersburg his enthusiasm has bubbled over in the London press. 'I happened to look in at the Maryinsky on a Sunday night when a grand ballet, *The Lake of Swans,* which extended well over three hours, was being given, with Madame Karsavina in the principal part. Throughout the whole time you could have heard, but for the strains of the orchestra, a pin drop, so hushed was the attention of the spectators. Never have I seen such exquisite and beautiful dancing.' "

Musical
America
June 1909

Before 1909, small groups of dancers had visited cities outside Russia during their holidays. Pavlova had made several tours. In the summer of 1909, she was engaged, for an enormous fee, to dance at a private party in London at which the Countess of Londesborough, aunt of the Sitwells, entertained King Edward VII and Queen Alexandra at St. Dunstan's, her home in Regent's Park.

Diaghilev's Paris season ended on June 18th, and on June 20th, the Coliseum programme announced: "FORTHCOMING ATTRACTION – THE RUSSIAN DANCERS – FROM THE IMPERIAL OPERA HOUSE, ST. PETERSBURG. RECENTLY THE RAGE OF PARIS AT THE CHATELET THEATRE."

The troupe accompanying Karsavina consisted of Maria Baldina, of her own year, and a brave array of men – the brothers Theodore and Alexis Kosloff, Georges Rosay, of the same year as Nijinsky, Leonide Leontiev, Kremnev, and Orlov.

The
Stage
1.7.09

On July 1st, the following "notice" appeared in *The Stage*: "Naturally the principal attraction in the current bill is the appearance of the much-heralded and 'much-boomed' troupe of Russian Imperial Dancers, who, if reports are to be believed, have created something approaching a sensation in Paris by their work. They were originally billed to appear in an Egyptian love-ballet, but this arrangement was cancelled, and very wisely too, for they are seen to better advantage in the short selection of dances which they now present than they would be in a scena. In three of the dances, *Hopak, Pas de Trois,* and *L'Oiseau de Feu,* the three artists taking part – Mlles. Maria Baldina and Tamara Karsavina and M. Theodore Kosloff – are attractively attired in Watteau costumes. For the remaining item, *Danse des Bouffons,* in which the men appear, costumes in keeping with the subject of the dance are worn. The display is dainty, clever, and interesting throughout, and should be sufficient to fill the Coliseum for the whole length of the engagement, for it is certain that nothing better of its kind has been seen here. Another dancing item is that of Odette Valery who returns with a new scena, entitled *Delilah,* in which she depicts the emotions of the mistress who has sold her master with her usual skill and success . . ."

This example shows the kind of "notice" normal at that time – and by inference, the kind of dance act too!

It would appear, moreover, that the repertoire was hastily concocted from items in the ballets just given in Paris – the *"Danse des Bouffons"* probably being that which was so loudly cheered in *Le Pavillon d'Armide,* though no one mentioned having seen it before when the Diaghilev company eventually arrived in 1911. As there was no time for preparations, one may surmise that Diaghilev helped by lending Karsavina the necessary costumes, though probably stock Coliseum backcloths would have been pressed into service.

Tamara Karsavina and Theodore Kosloff included her great success from the first Paris season in their repertoire at the Coliseum. Their costumes for the Tchaikovsky *pas de deux*, at that time called *Oiseau de Feu*, were simplified versions of those designed by Bakst for Karsavina and Nijinsky. (*The Tatler*, 14th July 1909.)

The *Daily Mail* had been more glowing:—

EXQUISITE PERFORMANCE IN LONDON

Daily Mail 29.6.09

"A new sensation is provided for London by the appearance, which began last night, of the famous Russian dancers at the Coliseum. As light as gossamer and of an exquisitely turned elegance, these Watteau figures, both shepherds and shepherdesses, go through a wonderful series of figures with a smiling ease and a delicate refinement which are irresistible in their dainty charm.

"It is the old classical school dancing which they illustrate, but raised to such a pitch of dexterity and grace which has never been surpassed here in our generation, and never equalled except by Mlle. Genée. Everyone will want to see these artistes, who have aroused Paris to such frenzied enthusiasm, and judging by the furore of their reception last night they will have a like popularity in London.

"It is hard to say which was applauded most vigorously, the delicious *'pas seuls'* of Mlles. Karsavina and Baldina, or the characteristic Russian steps or the quaint evolutions of a little company of buffoons. All the women are of a fragile prettiness which makes instant appeal, while their figures are rounded and supple, showing no trace of the over-development of muscle so often noticeable in dancers of the severely-trained ballet-skirt order. The reports of their excellence led us to expect rare pleasure from their performance, and we were not disappointed."

So started the association between Tamara Karsavina and the London Coliseum, never to be broken throughout her career. Her own version of this first visit to London, in *Theatre Street,* may be said to "make a good story of it," for she writes of knowing no one and being unable to converse. In fact, reading this one thinks of her coming as a soloist, without even a partner, let alone a group of friends. Her tears and loneliness were assuaged by her devoted manager, Marinelli, when he had a brainwave and brought a number of puppies for her to choose a companion. Then, one evening, as she was having supper in a restaurant near Leicester Square after the performance, Loulou, the chosen one, begged a tit-bit – and so introduced Karsavina and Genée. The visit was not quite as solitary as it has seemed to be. Its success was undeniable: Sir Oswald Stoll extended the contract, and of his own accord doubled Karsavina's salary – and, presumably, those of the whole troupe.

News of the high salaries and vociferous audiences in London undoubtedly started a gold-rush. 1910 saw Pavlova and Mordkin engaged by Mr. Alfred Butt for a sixteen-week season at the Palace Theatre, where they were supported by a small company. At the Empire, Lydia Kyasht, partnered by Adolf Bolm, had started a new number on March 21st, called *Les Papillons de l'Orient,* and inserted into the Tokyo scene of a production based on Jules Verne's fantasy *Round the World in Eighty Days.* On May 5th, they appeared in a whole series of new numbers which Bolm arranged, under the title *The Series of Dance Ideals.*

Whit-Monday, May 19th, 1910, was the date of one of those classic clashes of first nights for which ballet is by now notorious. Not only was it the first night of Karsavina's return to the Coliseum, but also of the first appearance of Olga Preobrajenska, (who enjoyed the high rank of 'Dancer of Honour' at the Maryinsky.) With a company of twenty dancers, she gave a shortened version of *Le Lac des Cygnes* at the London Hippodrome. In addition, Pavlova introduced a new number into her repertoire at the Palace on the same night, dancing as Diana the Huntress, hunted by Mordkin, in a costume designed for her by Bakst.

The atmosphere was heavy-laden with that especial sadness which seems to follow the death of a monarch, for King Edward VII had died on Friday, May 6th. The papers were naturally full of information about the funeral arrangements: concert programmes were altered to include every possible "Funeral March." On the same page as it printed criticisms of Preobrajenska and of Pavlova's *Diana, The Times* devoted one-and-a-half columns to the consideration of evening dresses suitable for wear during the period of Court mourning.

The Times 17.5.10

The Times 20.5.10

National Film Archive

The funeral processions on Friday, May 20th, were filmed by a number of operators, mostly in black-and-white. One colour version was shown on the Bioscope at the Palace Theatre the following day, and a longer edition the following week. No copy remains: few would have been made, as this process, *Kinemacolor,* could only be shown where special, and expensive, apparatus was installed. This process had been in use since 1906, and was probably killed by the outbreak of the war. It was certainly a great attraction. How many of the public went to watch the Funeral on the Bioscope, and came away determined to see Pavlova again?

The Stage 5.5.10

In 1910, Karsavina was sufficiently ambitious to present a potted version of a full-length ballet. An advance notice announced it as *Les Sylphides,* to Chopin's music, having obviously heard of this work from Paris, but in fact the half-hour item shown at the Coliseum was something quite different. The Programme Notes gave the story of *Giselle.* They called the ballet "*Gisela, or La Sylphide."* The music was, indeed, that of Adolf Adam, but the choreography was stated to be that of Petipa, with *mise-en-scène* by Theodore Kosloff. As the two acts of *Giselle* appear to have been mingled, one can only wonder just what of the Romantic ballets of those names the Coliseum audience actually saw. (The programme is reproduced in facsimile.)

Daily Mail 17.5.10

The *Daily Mail* limited its remarks about *Gisela.* "The classical *Les Sylphides* with its pathetic tragedy, gives Mlle. Karsavina an opportunity to display her art. It was however, a relief to turn to the lighter fare of the second part of the Russian programme, with its wonderful colours and its combination of exquisite movements and music."

The Stage 19.5.10

The Stage complimented Mr. Oswald Stoll on re-engaging the principals who had so delighted the public in 1909, and doubling the size of the troupe. "People will flock to the St. Martin's Lane house to see the short divertissement which follows the ballet. We make a special

PROGRAMME.

"GISELLA,"
OR,
"LA SYLPHIDE,"

Music by - - ADOLPH ADAM.
Dances arranged by MARIUS PETIPA.
Mise-en-Scene by - M. THEODORE KOSLOFF.

Gisella (now a Sylphide) ... ... Mdlle. TAMARA KARSAVINA
Queen of the Sylphides ... ... Mdlle. MARIA BALDINA
Albert (a young Count) ... ... M. THEODORE KOSLOFF
Hilarion (his Friend) ... ... M. ALEXIS KOSLOFF
Les Sylphides ... Mdlles. ANDERSEN, MALTSCHANOWA,
ADAMOWITSCH, CHEREPANOWA,
DAMACHOWA & WICHNIAKOWA

DANCES.

1. Entry of the Queen of the Sylphides   Mdlle. BALDINA

2. Variation   ...   .   Mdlle. BALDINA

3. Entry of the Sylphides   ...   Mdlles. WICHNIAKOWA,
CHEREPANOWA, ADAMOWITSCH,
DAMACHOWA, MALTSCHANOWA,
ANDERSEN

4. Dance of the Sylphides   ...   ...   Mdlles. BALDINA,
CHEREPANOWA, ADAMOWITSCH.
DAMACHOWA, MALTSCHANOWA,
ANDERSEN, WICHNIAKOWA

5. Entry of "Gisella" ...   Mdlle. TAMARA KARSAVINA

6. Entry of Albert and his Friend Hilarion   THEODORE
KOSLOFF and ALEXIS KOSLOFF

7. Dance (Gisella & Albert)   Mdlle. TAMARA KARSAVINA and
M. THEODORE KOSLOFF

PROGRAMME, continued—

8. Bacchanale   ...   ALEXIS KOSLOFF, Mdlles. BALDINA,
CHEREPANOWA, ADAMOWITSCH,
DAMACHOWA, MALTSCHANOWA,
ANDERSEN, WICHNIAKOWA

9. Adagio (Gisella & Albert)   Mdlle. TAMARA KARSAVINA and
THEODORE KOSLOFF

10. Variation   ...   ...   Mdlle. TAMARA KARSAVINA

11. Finale   ...   . ENSEMBLE

For Argument see back page.

There will be a slight interval between the Ballet and Divertissement to allow for
necessary changes.

DIVERTISSEMENT

1. Trepak (Grotesque Peasant Dance)   ...   ...   MM. GERBER,
   Music by Anton   GOTSCHITOWSKY, KOTROWSKAIE I.,
   Rubinstein   KOTROWSKAIE II., TARASOFF

2. Pas d'Orange   Mdlle. BALDINA, M. THEODORE KOSLOFF
   Music by Gerro.

3. Czardas   ...   Mdlle. DAMACHOWA, M. ALEXIS KOSLOFF
   Music by Grossmann.

4. Songe d'Amour   Mdlle. ANDERSEN, M. TSCHOUKOFF
   Music by Meyer-Hellmound

5. Danse Russe   ...   .   Mlle. MARIA BALDINA

6. Pas de deux "Danse de la Fee Dragee," from the
   Ballet "Casse Noisette"   ...   Mdlle. TAMARA KARSAVINA
   Music by Tschaikowsky.   and M. KOSLOFF
   Costumes designed by Dimitri de Gunzbourg.

7. Indian Dance ...   Mdlle. ADAMOWITSCH, M.M. GERBER,
   Music by Minkus   TSCHOUKOFF, GOTSCHITOWSKY,
   KOTROWSKAIE I., KOTROWSKAIE II.

AUGMENTED ORCHESTRA.

Karsavina's version of *Giselle* at the Coliseum in 1910.

point of the divertissement purposely, because half an hour's performance of ballet in semi-darkness is apt to become tedious, however good the performance may be; the difficulty of following the artists in the subdued light and the strain upon the eyes consequent thereon are hardly calculated to give the best enjoyment . . . *Gisela* is a rather tedious affair. The fact also that the dancing is reduced to a minimum while pantomime occupies the greater length of time also detracts somewhat from its value as a turn pure and simple of a music-hall entertainment, though artistically the ballet may be considered to be of a very high order. Seven short dances are introduced, especially prominent being the admirable work of Mlle. Baldina, as the Queen of the Sylphides, and Mlle. Karsavina as Gisela. M. Kosloff's facial work in this is distinctly good, and a neat and effective number performed by a graceful bevy of Sylphides deserves high praise . . ."

When Olga Preobrajenska presented *"Swan Lake"* at the London Hippodrome in 1910, the rest of the bill consisted of acts such as were typical attractions in the London music-halls to which these pioneers came.

Daily Mail 17.5.10

Preobrajenska's truncated version of *Swan Lake* at the London Hippodrome did not fare too well. True, the *Daily Mail* said that "to Tchaikovsky's passionate music, the story of the flight of the birds, the discovery of the Princess, the declaration of mutual love, and then the passing away of the birds, and the sorrow of the Prince were all expressed with a tenderness and refinement not looked for as a rule in ballet."

The Times 17.5.10

"One can see," said *The Times,* reminding its readers that this work had been composed in 1877, "how Tchaikovsky must have broken through some of the formalities of conventional ballet, appealing more to the minds of his exponents . . . The ballet is in two scenes, lasting an hour. First there is the Festival at the Prince's castle, beginning with a defiant Mazurka. The Prince, whilst entertaining his friends, is summoned to the Palace to meet his bride; of course he refuses to go, and the guests make the Preceptor, who brings the messages, tipsy for his pains. An orthodox *Pas de Trois,* a lively *Czardas,* and a *Pas de Deux* were all danced with the kind of finish and ease which effectively conceals the art. Special mention must be made of Mlle. Schollar. The scene ends with a Torch Dance, and a flight of swans, which entices the Prince to take his arquebus and go after them to the lake with his friends. Once there the swans appear as damsels – guarded, when transformed, by an owl 7 ft. high with vast wings, which he flapped when there was room. Mlle. Preobrajensky evidently has the whole technique of ballet-dancing at her fingers' ends, or rather at the tips of her toes! and added to this she is an artist in mime. She is able to traverse all the most difficult passages of her art with a freedom and accuracy which makes her effects quite complete . . ."

The Stage said that "the grace and elegance which characterizes the whole performance stamp it at once as one of the most beautiful spectacles which have been witnessed in London, and one never excelled so far as the music halls are concerned." But – ". . .it is not until the second scene that Mlle. Preobrajansky and M. Georges Kiashkt dance, and even then, their performances are all too short." The orchestra, which had been increased to 45 players, earned itself high praise. Included in the bill (described as containing "hardly a laugh this week,") was Yvette Guilbert; at the end of the run, a notice describes the illusions of Chung Ling Soo, the Chinese Conjuror, who might well have been the inspiration, years later, for the Conjuror in *Parade.** The Stage 19.5.10

Sir Oswald Stoll generously released Karsavina to dance with Diaghilev in Paris; during her absence, Baldina and her companions gave a longer divertissement. "Very amusing and quaintly rendered is *Le Chat et La Chatte,* from *Sleeping Beauty,* in which Mlle. Anderson and M. Alexis Kosloff impersonate cats, and engage in what may be a love episode 'on the tiles . . .' The magnificent work of the whole company makes their performance one which can be seen and enjoyed again and again." The Stage 9.6.10

Karsavina's return from Paris was given a notice in *The Times,* which remarked that "the performance continues to attract large audiences, and pleases as much as ever." And all through the same season, at the Palace Theatre, under the management of Mr. Alfred Butt, Pavlova and Mordkin had performed nightly, and given innumerable special matinées. The Times 5.7.10

The Times wrote this up in April: "Appearing first as Columbine, the lady exhibits an astonishing power of dancing and whirling on one toe, and the gentleman almost equals her even in a branch of the art generally left to the *première danseuse.* In Rubenstein's *Valse Caprice* the eye is captured at the outset by the colouring and fashioning of the costumes, the nymph especially floating in a cloud of the airiest fabric which ever held together. The bacchanalian dance also was a triumph for the costumiers as well as for the dancers; not less a triumph, but more, because the dresses never distracted attention from the poetic motion of the revellers. The revel, it should at once be added, is not very bacchanalian; and it leaves an impression that the dancers could hardly be ungraceful if they tried. The welcome given to Mlle. Pavlova and M. Mordkin was as warm as it was well-deserved; and it was rightly extended to Mlle. Eduardova, M. Monahoff, and their eight companions, who approach in varying degrees the supreme distinction of their leaders." The Times 19.4.10

"For some time past," said the *Morning Post,* "there has been a rage for stage dancing at the London music-halls, and the Palace has produced some of the best of the dancing. But nothing that has been done before, not the barefoot dancing, not the writhing Apache dancing, nor the violent waltzing, has been so good in quality as this . . . Everything she does is done perfectly. Her earliest essay is in the short-skirted, pointed toed, twirling style, which was driven out of England by the skirt-dances of the 'Eighties and has only been revived of recent years. In these she is clear, definite, and absolutely correct. Later on she has dances which are more expressive, Rubenstein's *Valse Caprice,* a *Bacchanale* of Glazounov, and a *Spanish Dance.* They are all dances expressing coquetry, and they are all performed with the assistance (or the partnership) of a male dancer, M. Mordkin. At the end of the last dance, which finishes on a diminuendo, Mlle. Pavlova and her company had to appear before the curtain over and over again, and even after all hope of an encore was gone the clapping and the shouting and the flower-throwing went on . . . The Palace management has secured a turn which will certainly uphold and increase its reputation for having the best of everything." Morning Post 20.4.10

---

*There were many such performers to be seen in music-halls everywhere, and their nationalities were various. Chung Ling Soo, for example, was really William Robinson, an American, who made his London debut in 1904, and died spectacularly on the stage of the Wood Green Empire in March, 1918, killed by a bullet in his own act. The assumption of Chinese robes, sufficiently voluminous to conceal rabbits, ribbons, and all the paraphernalia of the trade, was a device inherited from the seventeenth century.)

Anna Pavlova and Mikhail Mordkin in a Russian dance. The first to partner her on her extensive tours, Mordkin was also the partner who left the greatest impression, especially in the United States.

If, once upon a time, the music-halls had been ground untrodden by the sheltered ladies of Society, 1910 must have been the red-letter-year in their diaries. Lady Diana Cooper's mother, the Duchess of Rutland, had not cared for traditional ballet, but had fallen for Maud Allan, the Canadian who danced barefoot and in scanty classical garments, in a repertoire which was considered slightly *risqué*. Lady Diana Cooper (Lady Diana Manners in her youth) related their adventures in her book, *The Rainbow Comes and Goes*. "She (my mother) sent us weekly to watch and learn, in spite of the number finishing with 'Salome's Dance' – considered scandalous, for she was all but naked and had St. John's head on a plate and kissed his waxen mouth (a business later forbidden on the Covent Garden stage, where a dish of gravy was substituted.) My mother was untrammelled by convention.

"The Russians were the next to explode on the Palace Theatre stage." (In fact, they were at the Coliseum.) "Karsavina and Baldina, with a little *corps de ballet*. Again my mother forgot her prejudice against blocked toes and tutus and we would stand every Saturday behind the circle, not believing that the legendary Pavlova could outshine such glory. Of course she did. Pavlova was a leaf, a rainbow, a flake, an iridescent foam, her bones of music made. Secret and unsocial, even when she sprang toe-first out of baskets of roses at the most extravagant private parties, she never let us meet her in the flesh."

Pavlova's audience grew and grew, as did that of the other Russian dancers. Though purists poured scorn on those members of the Imperial Ballet who lent themselves to appearances in music-halls, these artists certainly showed the delights of great dancing to thousands who might never have ventured near classical ballet on its own.

A very long article appeared in *The Times,* entitled "IF PAVLOVA HAD NEVER DANCED." Starting with a whole column of dissertation on Mrs. Siddons, Pepys, Galsworthy, Shaw, and many plays and players, the writer embraced all Russian dancers under the symbolic umbrella of Pavlova's name. "The most artistically important and most stimulating thing in the past theatrical season has not been an 'intellectual' play, or any play at all, but the dancing of Pavlova and the Russian Dancers."

The Times 18.7.10

The writer of this then-anonymous, frequently-quoted essay was none other than the redoubtable A.B. Walkley, Drama Critic of *The Times* from 1899 to 1926. One can only say that if *he* felt that way about it, then no one could possibly argue with *him.*

ALHAMBRA.—MLLE. GABY DESLYS, OUR FLAG, MDLLE. BRITTA SISTERS ATHLETAS, THE POLAR STAR, CHAS. BARON, etc. At 8. Managing Director, ALFRED MOUL.

EMPIRE   LYDIA KYASHT and Adolf Bolm in DANCE IDYLLS. "HULLO, LONDON!" and Varieties. Evenings, at 8.   Manager, Mr. H. J. Hitchins.

COLISEUM.—TWICE DAILY, at 2.30 and 8 p.m., THE FAMOUS RUSSIAN DANCERS, KARSAVINA, BALDINA, and KOS-LOFF, supported by Company of 13 Star Dancers from the Imperial Opera Houses, St. Petersburg and Moscow, MISS CECILIA LOFTUS, and All Star Co. Boxes (four persons), £1 1s. and 10s. 6d. Seats 6d. to 5s. Children under 12 half-price to Fauteuils, Balcony Stalls, and Royal Circle afternoons only. Box office, 10 to 10. 'Phone, 7,541 Gerrard.—Managing Director OSWALD STOLL.

PALACE.—ANNA PAVLOVA, MICHAEL MORDKIN, RUSSIA'S GREATEST DANCERS and CO., MARGARET COOPER, CLARICE VANCE, ALBERT WHELAN, PROCLAMATION CEREMONY, etc., on BIOSCOPE, etc. EVENINGS at 8. MATINEE, FULL PROGRAMME, SATURDAYS and TO-DAY, at 2. SPECIAL MATINEE WEDNESDAY, at 3. Managing Director, Mr. ALFRED BUTT.

LONDON HIPPODROME.—Daily, at 2 and 8. Mlle. YVETTE GUILBERT. The Famous Diseuse. 20 of RUSSIA'S ACKNOWLEDGED GREATEST DANCERS, including Preobrajensky, Scholar, and Kiakscht in Ballet divertissement, "Le Lac des Cygnes," composed by TSCHAIKOWSKY. Raymond Phillips' WIRELESS CONTROLLED AIRSHIP, PRINCESS BARATOFF, HENRI LEONI, and All Star Co. Boxes 1 to 4 guineas. Seats 1s. to 7s. 6d Children under 12 half-price to all parts (except amphitheatre) at afternoon performances only. Box Office 10 to 10. Phone, 650 Gerrard.—Man. Dir., Oswald Stoll.

MASKELYNE and DEVANT'S MYSTERIES, St. George's Hall, W. Daily at 3 and 8. Special Programme, including Animated Pictures of Events in the Life of his late Majesty. Mr. Maskelyne, Mr. Barclay Gammon, and Mr. Devant at every performance. 1s. to 5s. 'Phone, 1,545, May.

Londoners could choose the Russian dancers they would see from this amazing list – plus Ekaterina Geltzer and Tikhimiroff, who were at the Alhambra at about the same time. (*Daily News*, 16th May, 1910.)

One week, the "Theatres" advertisements showed all four of these dancers in a single column. The capacity of the theatres where they performed, though apt to vary slightly as rows of seats were sometimes removed for special shows, added up to an astonishing number of seats. The Coliseum had about 2,900 seats, the Empire, London Hippodrome, and Palace something like 1,200 apiece, and the Alhambra about 1,800. In the variety bills, many of the audience were there to see quite different artists, but even so, during those peak weeks, something like 8,000 seats a night were sold. Who filled them? How did they get there? Private cars were still rarities; there were cabs, and splendid buses which ran cheaply and late. Of course, there were many more residents in the West End itself than nowadays, and these naturally tended to be people who liked the entertainments offered in a capital city. The impresarios paid high fees, and competed briskly for the great "draws," and they certainly regarded Russian dancers with favour as amongst their best "attractions." The Empire, offering long ballets with a permanent star, had its steady public. Pavlova and Karsavina packed their theatres. The Alhambra had several visits from yet another Russian dancer, Ekaterina Geltzer. Only Preobrajenska's company failed to captivate.

Daily News 16.5.10

At the Palace and Coliseum, people started to drop in just for the ballet. An audience had been created for Diaghilev by these pioneers.

1911

ROYAL OPERA, COVENT GARDEN

JUNE 21st - JULY 31st

FIRST PERFORMANCES IN ENGLAND

June 21st:
    Le Pavillon d'Armide
(Tcherepnin, Fokine, Benois.)
St. Petersburg, 25.11.1907.

    Le Carnaval
(Schumann, Fokine, Bakst.)
St. Petersburg, 1910.
(Diaghilev Company) Berlin, 20.5.1910

    Polovtsian Dances from Prince Igor
(Borodin, Fokine, Roerich.)
Paris 19.5.1909

June 24th:
    Le Spectre de la Rose
(Weber, Fokine, Bakst.)
Monte Carlo 19.4.1911

June 27th:
    Les Sylphides
(Chopin, Fokine, Benois.)
St. Petersburg, 10.2.1907 (as *Chopiniana*)
Paris 2.6.1909

July 7th:
    Cléopâtre
(Arensky, Taneev, Rimsky-Korsakov, Glinka,
Glazounov, Moussorgsky, Fokine, Bakst.)
Paris 2.6.1909

July 20th:
    Scheherazade
(Rimsky-Korsakov, Fokine, Bakst.)
Paris 4.6.1910

COMPANY

Astafieva S., Baranovitch I., Baranovitch II., Biber, December, Elpe, Fedorova S., Fokina, Frohmann M., Gashevska, Gonsiorovska, Guliuk, Heine, Julitzka, Kandina, Karsavina, Khokhlova, Klementovitch, Konietzka, Kopetzinska, Kulchitzka, Larionova, Lastchilina, Maicherska, Nijinska, Reisen, Sazonova, Schollar, Tcherepanova, Tchernicheva, Vassilieva A., Vassilieva M., Wassilievska, Will, Yakovleva, Yezerska.

Alexandrov, Bolm, Bromberg, Cecchetti, Christapson, Dmitriev, Fedorov, Frohmann, Gherassimov, Grigoriev, Gudin, Kobelev, Kotchetovsky, Kremnev, Kussov, Larosov, Lastchilin, Leontiev, Mashat, Maslov, Molotsov A., Molotsov S., Nijinsky, Ognev, Orlik, Orlov, Oumansky, Petrov, Ponomarev, Rakhmanov, Romanov B., Romanov V., Rosai, Semenov, Sergueiev, Toboiko, Varjinsky, Yanliel, Zailich.

CONDUCTORS

Tcherepnin, Beecham.

THE CORONATION SEASON

Firmly billed as "The Imperial Russian Ballet," Diaghilev brought his company to London as one of the greatest attractions of the glittering Coronation season. It was to alternate with opera, and two orchestras were engaged – that which was to play for the Ballet being provided by Mr. Thomas Beecham. The billing is of more than passing interest. Previously, the European ventures had been called *"Saison Russe,"* and *"organisé par M. Serge de Diaghilev."* Yet, for those periods, he had borrowed dancers (and stage staff) from the Imperial Theatres.

Late in 1910, Diaghilev had called his "Committee" together in St. Petersburg, and told them that the time had come to form a permanent company, and give their own creations all the year round, instead of recruiting dancers afresh for a few weeks at a time. They would require financial backing, and, for the success of the enterprise, top stars. The question of the ballerina settled itself easily, for, as Karsavina had recently been officially granted that status at the Maryinsky, she had the right to group the performances required of her there at her own convenience, and would therefore be able to fit the two commitments together. Nijinsky had no such privilege, for he was still a junior in that rigid hierarchy. However, having worn a too-revealing costume and been accused of causing offence to the Dowager Empress (something which she subsequently denied,) he was summarily dismissed in January, 1911. This left him free to join Diaghilev.

The new company – under its old title – performed for the first time in Monte Carlo in April, 1911. Preobrajenska, one of the older established favourites at the Maryinsky, àdorned it. It went to Rome in May, and thence to Paris in early June. Its new title had been used in February, in the advance announcements of the London season – only three weeks after that dramatic dismissal. Certainly, there is no air of Imperial disapproval in this fact. It could not possibly have been purely at Diaghilev's whim.

It might be as well to describe briefly the England to which "The Imperial Russian Ballet" came. For the first time since the 1860's, she had a monarch under forty. King Edward VII had been over sixty when he came to the throne in 1901, and, owing to a sudden attack of appendicitis, his Coronation had been cancelled.

England had a Liberal government, under Mr. Asquith, and was absorbed by Lloyd George's National Insurance Act, the Parliament Act, Home Rule and the Suffragette Movement. This government put through many radical reforms, one of which was the payment of a salary to Members of Parliament. In modern times, comparisons are often made between the earnings of popular entertainers and Prime Ministers. This initial salary, £400 a year, was the same as the fee paid to Pavlova when she danced at a private party. (Worth about £2,800 in 1970 money, but with income tax at a very low rate, this was not by any means a poor figure.)

House of Commons Library

27

Society was wealthy, extravagant, and culturally focussed on the opera. Many young people were "finished" in Germany, and musical education was naturally geared to appreciation of the great composers of the eighteenth and nineteenth centuries. The rich bought their clothes in Paris, and wintered on the French Riviera. Undoubtedly, the excitement engendered by the advance publicity fell upon a land where many people in Society had attended performances of the ballet in Paris and Monte Carlo. The Marchioness of Ripon, who enjoyed the personal friendship of Queen Alexandra, and was on the Committee of Covent Garden, had been working hard to ensure that the visit would be made under the right auspices.

The preliminary announcement called forth a letter to *The Times* from an unexpected quarter – Sir George Scott Robertson, M.P. The son of a wealthy pawnbroker, born in Southwark in 1852, he had retired early after spending his working life as an administrator in the Indian Medical Services. He had been embroiled in frontier matters concerning the Russians – which probably accounts for his pedantic transliteration of the names of Russian composers and their works.

D.N.B.

The Times 21.2.11.

To the Editor of The Times
Sir,

I trust the programme for the Imperial Russian Ballet recently announced by the Royal Opera Syndicate is still subject to alteration. These dancers are being imported for six weeks at, no doubt, great expense; and it will be almost a disaster if they are not provided with a programme worthy of their powers and the music of the nation to which they belong. The music announced consists of a short composite work by Arensky and Glazounov; a short work by one Stravinski; Rimsky-Korsakov's *Scheherazade,* which was not written as a ballet at all, a short production by the conductor, possibly inevitable, and the dances of the Polovtsi from Borodin's *Kniaz Igor.* So much for the Russian music, but worse is to come. There is to be a thing called *Les Sylphides,* concocted out of Chopin's pianoforte works, and, as a crowning terror, an orchestral version of Schumann's *Carnaval.*

It is true that most of these pieces were presented by the Russian dancers when they were in Paris, but that is no reason why they should be served out to us here . . . I would appeal to the syndicate to give us the opportunity of hearing at least one of the great Russian full-programme ballets, *Mlada,* for instance, or Tchaikovsky's *Nutcracker* or his *Sleeping Beauty* . . ."

This brought a reply from Diaghilev himself.

The Times 10.3.11

A M. le Rédacteur du Times
Monsieur,

La troupe de ballet russe dont je suis le directeur pour l'étranger, et qui est composée en majeure partie d'artistes des Théâtres Impériaux, a été invitée au Covent Garden à la suite de ses succès à l'Opéra de Paris, à la 'Monnaie' de Bruxelles, et à Berlin. Par conséquent il n'y a pas de raison pour remplacer par un autre le répertoire qui a fait ses preuves dans ces trois villes.

Les grands ballets russes ont pour la plupart une musique plus que médiocre, composée par des musiciens de troisième et quatrième ordre, italiens ou allemands aux noms inconnus . . . et des grands maîtres il n'y a que Tchaikovsky et Glazounov qui se sont un peu occupés du ballet . . . Quant à les trois ballets de Tchaikovsky, ils ont été composés il y a un quart de siècle, à une époque où le ballet russe n'était qu'une copie des grands ballets italiens, avec leur style conventionnel, basé surtout sur l'acrobatisme et tout contraire aux tendances esthétiques de la nouvelle école qui vient de triompher en Europe. En outre le *Casse-Noisette* est un ballet exécuté par une centaine d'enfants, élèves de l'école des Théâtres Impériaux, que certainement on ne pourrait trimbaler à l'étranger. Le *Lac des Cygnes,* monté l'année dernière à l'Hippodrome de Londres, n'a obtenu aucun succès; quant à *La Belle au Bois Dormant,* ce ballet interminable au sujet tiré d'une fable française, composé sur des thèmes français, ne possède aucun élément national qui puisse justifier l'idée de donner à Londres cette féerie franco-italienne . . .

Par contre le programme actuel de Londres comporte les grands noms des compositeurs russes tels que Borodin, Rimsky-Korsakov, Arensky, Stravinsky, Tcherepnin, ce dernier le meilleur élève de Rimsky-Korsakov, compositeur de beaucoup d'oeuvres capitales symphoniques, dont les ballets *Le Pavillon d'Armide* et *Narcisse* ne sont pas du tout obligatoires (comme ce du 'conductor,') mais présentent de réelles et éminentes qualités.

Ce qui concernent les *Sylphides* et le *Carnaval*, ces deux petites choses ont obtenu un des plus gros succès à Paris et à Berlin, et ce serait vraiment une raison peu plausible d'en priver Londres simplement parce que la musique n'en est pas russe . . .

En fin de compte, il ne faut pas oublier que Chopin est polonais, donc slave, et par conséquent en tout cas plutôt russe qu'anglais.

SERGE DE DIAGHILEW.

St. Petersburg, le 3 mars.

Enviable postal communications permitted publication of this letter in "The Thunderer" on March 10th. Perhaps this may be considered a reasonable translation:

To the Editor of The Times
Sir,

The Russian Ballet company of which I am the Director for foreign tours, and which is composed in the main of artists from the Imperial Theatres, has been invited to Covent Garden following upon its successes at the *Opéra* in Paris, the *Théâtre de la Monnaie* in Brussels, and in Berlin. One can see no reason, therefore, for changing the repertoire which has already been so acceptable in these three cities, and substituting a different list of works.

The full-length Russian ballets are mostly performed to music of a quality inferior to mediocre, composed by third and fourth-rate musicians, Italians or Germans whose names are completely insignificant . . . Amongst the great composers, only Tchaikovsky and Glazounov have paid any attention to the requirements of ballet . . . As for Tchaikovsky's three ballets, all were composed a quarter of a century ago, at a period when Russian ballets were no better than replicas of the long Italian ballets, with all their conventions of style, based, above all, on tricks of virtuosity, and absolutely the opposite of the aesthetic movement of the new School which has recently captivated Europe. Moreover, the *Nutcracker* is a ballet performed by a hundred children from the Imperial schools, whom it would be quite impossible to trail around on tour outside Russia. *Swan Lake,* which was put on last year at the London Hippodrome, had no success whatsoever; as for *The Sleeping Beauty,* this *interminable* ballet on a subject taken from a French fairy-story, composed on French lines, does not possess the slightest national characteristic which could possibly justify presenting such a Franco-Italian *féerie* in London.

On the other hand, the programme planned for London includes the names of the truly great amongst Russian composers, such as Borodin, Rimsky-Korsakov, Arensky, Stravinsky, Tcherepnin, this last being Rimsky-Korsakov's star pupil, composer of many major symphonic works, whose ballets *Le Pavillon d'Armide* and *Narcisse* are by no means compulsory ('conductor's rights,') but have their own intrinsic and first-class qualities.

As for *Les Sylphides* and *Carnaval,* these two charming trifles were among those most applauded both in Paris and Berlin, which would seem rather an unconvincing reason for depriving London of them just because the music is not Russian . . .

Finally, let it not be forgotten that Chopin was a Pole, – that is to say, a Slav, – and that being so, far more Russian than English.

SERGE DE DIAGHILEV

St. Petersburg, March 3rd.

If this reply did not satisfy Sir George Scott Robertson, at least it silenced him.

In the event, some changes were made from the repertoire as it was originally announced. Neither *Narcisse* nor *Le Dieu Bleu* was ready. The participation of Ida Rubinstein remained in the plan late enough to be printed in the official Covent Garden souvenir programme, though in the end she did not come to London. *Sadko,* also announced in this programme, was dropped, as was the un-named item by "one Stravinski."

The Coronation was to take place on Thursday, June 22nd. A hectic programme of festivities had been arranged, and from the Monday onwards, London was filling up with guests from all over the world, whose arrivals were colourful events in themselves.

Daily
Telegraph
20.6.11

"No fewer than twenty-eight princely and illustrious visitors arrived in London yesterday. Most of them travelled via Dover in two long special trains, and, with their suites in attendance, made a large party. Indeed, never in the history of railways has such an assemblage been seen upon one platform.

"The arrival platform at Victoria Station was closed to the public and temporarily transformed with handsome crimson draperies, entirely covering the outer hall of the station, and a crimson carpet carried the entire length of the platform. The great curtains were looped by means of gold and yellow ropes on both sides of the entrance to the Royal waiting-room, and the rich effect was enhanced by a pretty display of flowers . . ."

On the Monday evening, there was a State Banquet at Buckingham Palace for the Royal guests. The following day, Their Majesties received the Special Envoys and Deputations, gave another State Banquet, and went on to the Shakespeare Ball at the Royal Albert Hall. On the Wednesday, they held more receptions, and in the evening, the Duke of Connaught gave a dinner to the Royal guests at St. James' Palace – thereby preventing them from attending the first performance in London by Diaghilev's dancers, that very evening, June 21st.

A Souvenir Programme had been prepared for both opera and ballet. It started off:-

"It is not too much to say that the Coronation Season at Covent Garden has in preparation for the spoilt and blasé theatregoer a spectacle that should arouse even that pampered individual from his customary apathy."

The writer did not disguise his opinion of the paying audience, many of them season-ticket holders, all totally unsubsidized. He continued:-

"There have been signs and portents for a year or so that we were about to witness something of a revival or even a revolution in the public taste in regard to the classic and beautiful art of dancing. For many moons the sacred lamp became devoid of life. But to their exceeding joy, some three years ago, came some scattered harbingers of the revival, in the persons of certain individual dancers brought by those unfailing judges of the public taste, the managers of the variety houses. The effect of the experiment, if it was an experiment, was instantaneous. The public came in multitudes, took classical dancers and dancing to its heart, and has insisted upon having them ever since."

The writer went on to describe the structure of the Imperial Theatres and Ballet Schools:-

"As in the great Continental armies, so in the hierarchy of the ballet, the same drill, the same encouragement, the identical discipline is enforced upon all, and they may each carry, not the field-marshal's baton in a knapsack, but the chance of becoming a Nijinsky or a Karsavina in their *maillot!*" (Tights.) ". . . And here we must lay stress upon the remarkable fact of the equal pre-eminence of the masculine element with that of the ever-attractive feminine. They possess the same technical perfection, the same grace, the same *'science de la plastique,'* in which their art abides. For three successive seasons these marvellous artists have been the rage of Paris. The connoisseurs and flâneurs of the French *Opéra* have raved over the *'stupéfiante virtuosité, si pleine d'aisance de la troupe la plus riche et la plus homogène que l'on puisse concevoir . . .'* In addition to this rare quality must be reckoned the scenic perfection, the harmonious conception of each scene or tableau, of each colour scheme of costume, of the ordering and movement of the varying groups upon the stage; in short, of all that goes to make each ballet that is presented a separate and unique *chef-d'oeuvre.*"*

How unlike the advance publicity of today – no personal details, no gossip paragraphs. Even the photographs printed were badly chosen, showing dancers who did not come, and ballets which were not performed.

The marvellous troupe itself arrived in London on Monday, June 19th. Diaghilev, arriving in advance, had at first installed himself in the Waldorf Hotel, but moved after a few days to the more fashionable Savoy. The company, numbering 110 dancers, and "quite 200 people independently of those actually taking part in the ballets," stayed in less expensive accommodation in and around Russell Square. To meet the enormous cost, the Covent Garden management announced that, finding that the number of applications for tickets was extraordinary, "the directors will increase the prices for all except those who have already paid for the season."

A semi-public Dress Rehearsal was arranged for Tuesday, June 20th: but there was a terrible snag.

ANXIOUS RUSSIAN BALLET

DRESSERS DETAINED AS ALIENS AT FOLKESTONE

Daily
Mail
21.6.11

"The Alien Immigration Act was put into operation so effectively at Folkestone yesterday that the Russian ballet, which is to make its début at Covent Garden this evening, was unable to give the dress rehearsal planned to take place yesterday afternoon. The dancers were all in the threatre, the scenery was set, the properties and most of the costumes had arrived, but a batch of about twenty people who have charge of the wardrobe were held up as aliens on landing from Boulogne, and were not allowed to proceed to London. The charming ballerinas were astonished that the law could deprive them of the pretty costumes destined to help them to captivate London. They had never been in England before, and knew not what might happen. Would there be no ballet for London?

"Of course, the management of Covent Garden eventually learned what the trouble was. The only people who could pick out the wardrobes for the various ballets were not in London, and M. Serge de Diaghilev, who is in charge of the company, received the following telegram, signed by the immigration officer, Folkestone: 'Dressers for your ballet detained here. Do you guarantee that they will leave this country at the end of their engagement?'

"The directors of Covent Garden at once telegraphed a guarantee to satisfy the immigration officer, but there was no dress rehearsal, and the little group of people in the stalls filed reluctantly out of the theatre as the orchestra started to play and the Russians prepared to go through the rehearsal in ordinary clothes instead of stage costumes."

Possibly owing to the fact that Grigoriev, in a rare lapse of memory, said that "our opening performance was to be a Gala, . . ." the misapprehension that this was so has been largely accepted. Many years later, Diaghilev himself also confused these first appearances at Covent Garden. In fact, the two performances in the week preceding the Coronation Gala were received with hitherto unparalleled enthusiasm.

Grigoriev
p.65

---

*(The writer was Henry Saxe Wyndham, a man of wide culture and charming personality, for thirty-three years Secretary of the Guildhall School of Music. It was said of him that "where many people have only the *taste* for good literature, he has the *palate* for it."

When, in 1906, his "Annals of Covent Garden" appeared, Gabrielle Enthoven teased him at a dinner-party about the number of mistakes. She said he ought to check details by looking up playbills and programmes. He replied that it was difficult to locate them, adding, "Why don't *you* collect them?"

Such was the origin of the Enthoven Collection, later bequeathed to the Victoria and Albert Museum. From this flippant beginning has grown the Theatre Museum, to be housed in Central London in 1975, when the Enthoven Collection and those of the British Theatre Museum and the Museum of the Performing Arts will be joined together.)

"A more sumptuous and magnificent entertainment has never been presented to a Covent Garden audience than that given last night by Russian dancers from the Imperial Theatres of St. Petersburg and Moscow. M. Serge de Diaghilev, who has brought the company together, and the management of the theatre are to be congratulated on the conspicuous success of their enterprise.

Daily
News
22.6.11

"The first ballet presented was *Le Pavillon d'Armide.* When the orchestra began the prelude, under the direction of the composer, people looked at one another in surprise. They had evidently come expecting the jingling tunes associated with the ballet in this country, and found they were listening to a wonderful piece of orchestration, restless, passionate, at times almost poignant, which might have been the prelude to a serious opera. It was the first indication that the ballet, as developed in Russia, is a serious form of art, and not merely a frivolous excuse for showing pretty girls and dresses behind the footlights.

"The scene is entrancing. The glitter of spangles and glare of colour which offend the eyes in most ballets in London were absent, and the combination of exquisite colouring, graceful movement, sprightly, but never banal, music, made a spectacle surpassing in artistic feeling and charm anything yet seen in this country."

Alexandre Benois, author and designer of this ballet, which had been created for the Maryinsky in 1907, had found his inspiration in a mixture of magic and the Court of Versailles. The Vicomte de Beaugency, losing his way, takes refuge in a château, where he is offered hospitality in a pavilion in the grounds. A tapestry (*'Gobelins'*) on the wall portrays an ancestress of his host's, famous for her beauty, in the guise of the enchantress Armida. As he sleeps, the characters in the tapestry come to life. He falls in love with Armida, and under her spell. He dies, and the Marquis-Magician triumphs in his death.

The *Daily News'* critic went on:

"M. Nijinsky has come here with a great reputation . . . In the part of the slave of Armida, he showed that the praise bestowed upon him has not been extravagant. His feats in dancing border on the miraculous; he hardly seems to touch the stage . . . One would think he were supported by invisible wings.

"Charmingly pretty and a miracle of imponderability, Mme. Tamara Karsavina was a delightful vision. She was a pathetic fairy rather than a guileful enchantress."

Daily
Mail
23.6.11

Richard Capell said: "The sylphs and light-footed fauns of the St. Petersburg Imperial Ballet have come at last to London, to the joy of those with imaginations excited by the enchanting dancing of the scattered members of the fantastic troupe already seen here. The spectacle is little less than a revelation."

E.A. Baughan, music critic of the *Daily News,* obviously knew what the spectacle *ought* to comprise, for he said in his review:

Daily
News
22.6.11

"When this ballet is presented in St. Petersburg an additional charm is given to the garden scene by the plash of fountains at the back of the stage, throwing thin jets of water high in the air. It is a pity that the management of Covent Garden were unable to arrange this pleasing feature, and it is to be hoped that they will do so at the gala performance of the ballet before the King and Queen."

As no one records the plash of fountains in reviews of the Gala, one must suppose that this effect was beyond the resources of Covent Garden to provide. (Omitted, too, was the flock of real sheep, with their shepherd, corresponding to those taken on locally in Paris in 1909.)

The second ballet was *Le Carnaval.* Characters of the *Commedia dell'Arte* mingle with the young people at carnival time – they flirt, they tease, they deceive poor Pierrot, they dupe Pantalon, they dismay their elders, the Philistines – all to Schumann's music, and in the pretty costumes of the Biedermeier period, the 1830's.

This ballet was greatly loved, and, according to Baughan, "afforded great chances to the dancers, and Mlle. Elsa Will, the Columbine, danced delightfully with the marvellous Nijinsky, who played the Harlequin."

Morning
Post
23.6.11

"They appear before a curious blue background, clashing somewhat with the quaint dresses of the Thirties," said another critic. "It is practically a draped stage, the blue curtains having a dado of huge white flowers . . . Among the exponents of the characters Mlle. Elsa Will dis-

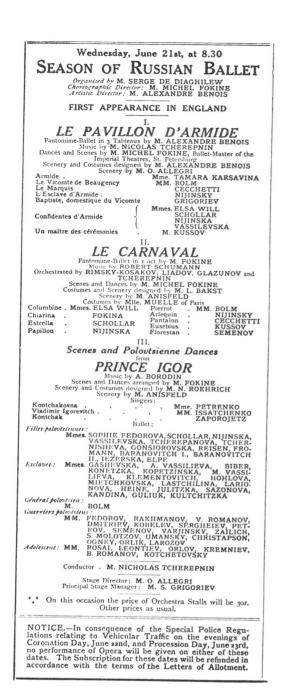

The programme and cast of the opening performance at Covent Garden on the eve of the Coronation.

Sir George Scott Robertson, M.P.

Henry Saxe Wyndham.

played fascinating lightness of style, in which Mlle. Schollar, a most graceful dancer, equalled her . . ." In view of the gloomy prognostications of Sir George Scott Robertson about the music, it is comforting to read here that "The music has been admirably scored for orchestra by MM. Rimsky-Korsakov, Liadov, Glazounov, and Tcherepnin, who have but accentuated its salient features for the purposes of the dancer."

As Elsa Will was the first Columbine to be seen on the London stage, a short biographical note sent by Natalia Roslavleva, the Russian ballet historian, is interesting:

"She was a very charming Maryinsky ballerina of Prussian origin. Born in 1882, she graduated in 1900, and was made a first soloist in 1908. In the summer of 1911, she had leave to go abroad, with pay. In December of the same year, she had an additional two weeks' leave, without pay. From September, 1911, she got ballerina remuneration, probably after her London successes. She was petite, ethereal, had a good technique, and was very popular with the public, though not a great dancer. She remained in the Maryinsky company until she retired in 1928."

The remark to the effect that she had leave to go abroad in 1911 *with pay* in the summer raises an interesting question. If Elsa Will had pay as usual during this season when Diaghilev's company was known as "The Imperial Russian Ballet," what about all the other dancers from the Imperial theatres? If they *all* had leave to perform abroad with him and continued to receive their normal salaries, this would constitute a "hidden subsidy," and would have come from the Tsar's purse.

The third work given on the first night was the *Polovtsian Dances* from *Prince Igor*. Reporting the reaction to this ballet, a now familiar word was introduced for the first time into the English language. (Arnold Haskell was then eight years old.)

Daily
News
22.6.11

"The scene, all red, with a background of radiant yellow sky, was curious, but beautiful, with the beauty of some strange impressionist sunset, and the barbaric dances performed by a crowd of richly-dressed figures were nothing short of amazing.

"Purists in Russia criticised this ballet very severely as being too great a departure from the traditional style of ballet dancing. It was keenly appreciated by the general public, and the reception it met with last night was a foregone conclusion. Judging from the behaviour of the audience at Covent Garden, the Russian term for enthusiasts for the ballet, *BALLETOMANIACS*, will have to be incorporated into the language."

Whatever tricks memory played on those who wrote their stories years later, then either forgetting the two performances before the Gala, or mistaking the conventional decorum of applause at that event for lack of appreciation, contemporary evidence must surely be more reliable. Every paper said in its own words that the house on June 21st was full and enthusiastic. In its Social Notes the following week, *The Lady* said: "The Russian Ballet . . . attracted an enormous audience to the Royal Opera House on the eve of the Coronation, and many extra stalls were needed to accommodate the audience. Its success was instantaneous, and the house was an enthusiastic one . . ." (and this was followed by a list of many notabilities who were prepared to brave both this evening performance and the early morning start for the ceremony.)

The
Lady
29.6.11

In 1926, roughing out an article entitled *Les Quinze Ans,* which was never published in his lifetime, but, having been found after his death, was quoted by Serge Lifar in 1940 in his biography, Diaghilev must have forgotten *Prince Igor's* brilliant reception, for – to suit his own ends at the time – he conjured up a completely different picture. It is this fantasy (which he subsequently worked up himself) which has been turned into history, embroideries accruing with the years.

He pictured an almost empty house, a listless audience, and the "flight of the Dowagers" who, (he said,) numbering about a hundred, (hung all about with diamonds,) left their seats in disgust before the end of the performance and pushed their way out, unable to stand such barbarity. If this had been the truth, surely at least *one* newspaper would have commented upon it? At least *one* critic had his toes crushed?

On the contrary, according to every single daily, evening and Sunday paper account, the *Polovtsian Dances* were a riotous success from the moment they were first seen at Covent Garden, and the audience was reported as applauding wildly. Years later, in America, Nijinsky (who never danced in *Prince Igor*) said, in an interview, that frequently in London a few members of the audience had the bad manners to leave before the curtain fell, but that is a very different sort of exodus from the one Diaghilev invented in 1926, and publicized in 1929, when he wanted to stress the change he had brought to matters of taste in England.

In fact, on the morning after the Coronation, Diaghilev sent a delighted and imperative telegram to Gabriel Astruc:

N.Y.P.L.
Dance
Collection
Astruc
Papers

LONDON 23.6.11.
ANNONCEZ TRIOMPHE SANS PAREIL ARMIDE CARNAVAL IGOR SALLE ELEGANCE INDESCRIPTIBLE

LONDRES A DECOUVERT NIJINSKY FAIT ACCEUIL ENTHOUSIASTE KARSAVINA WILL FOKINE TCHEREPNIN
(*"Tell the Press greatest success ever Armide Carnaval Igor house unbelievable elegance London has discovered Nijinsky welcomed enthusiastically Karsavina Will Fokine Tcherepnin."*)

Pedantry about this matter is not just fussing. London took to the rich fare it was offered without hesitation. The sensational applause became even greater by the following week, when, at second and third visits, the audience was applauding ballets for which it had already an addiction, and dancers for whom it had already great affection.

On that first night, in spite of the need to get some rest before making a very early start for the Abbey or a window on the route, the theatre was crammed. Lady Ripon entertained a party in her box. The Russian Ambassador, Count Benckendorff, was in the Royal Box. Baron de Meyer, who had taken such beautiful photographs of Nijinsky and Karsavina, was among those present. So, too, was the young Countess of Drogheda, a constant hostess throughout the season; she was the mother of Lord Drogheda, for many years Chairman of the Royal Opera House. He was only one year old at the time, and regrets that he was not allowed to be present on this memorable occasion.

On June 23rd, the day after the Coronation, there was a Royal Progress, more or less duplicating the Coronation procession but taking a long route through other parts of London. Lubov Tchernicheva remembered the excitement with which she and many of the company watched it in the Strand, jumping up and down and cheering. Most magnificent of all the sights, never-to-be-forgotten – "The Rajahs! The Rajahs!" The Indian princes stole all the admiration wherever they appeared in their gorgeously rich robes and fantastically glittering jewelled turbans.

The second performance was given on Saturday, June 24th. The apprehension previously voiced at the sacrilege of orchestrating Schumann's *Carnaval* was allayed . . . "One is conquered and won over before a hundred bars have been played."

> Daily Mail 26.6.11

Le Spectre de la Rose aroused the enthusiasm of the immense audience. Richard Capell continued in his review:

"A young girl – the exquisite Mme. Karsavina – returns to her room after a ball. Her room is a delight, with walls of a blue which is brightened to fervent purple in the sky seen through the window, with acid-green trees in the green moonlight.

"She glances tenderly at a crimson rose she holds. Then, as she falls asleep, the 'Spectre of the Rose' – Nijinsky, a singular vision in dull crimsons and purple – enters and dances. He dances and leaps with those leaps of elfin grace which suggest the whole of youth's untrammelled joy. The girl, too, dances in her sleep with the spirit. But day breaks, and with a kiss on her lips he vanishes.

"The spectacle is as exquisite as it is slight."

And in another account:

"M. Nijinsky, as the genie of the rose, danced with extraordinary virtuosity; like Shelley's skylark, he seemed to 'despise the earth,' and he was apparently quite independent of such prosaic affairs as the laws of gravity. Leaps and twirls were as natural a mode of progression to him as tip-toe flutterings about the stage to Mme. Karsavina, and it was all done with such perfect grace that it seemed the easiest thing in the world."

> Daily News 26.6.11

Two reports – and neither drew attention to the final leap!

As the curtain came down, an army of decorators fell upon the auditorium, to the tiers of which trellis had already been fixed, and throughout the weekend, they worked to transform it into a bower for the great Coronation Gala to be held on the Monday night.

On the Sunday evening, all the Ambassadors gave formal dinner-parties. Amongst the guests of the Russian Ambassador, Count Benckendorff, (whose Embassy was reputedly the gayest and most hospitable of all,) was that same Prince Wolkonsky who had once dismissed Diaghilev. Having been in Rome a few weeks previously, and running into Diaghilev in the

> The Times 26.6.11

*My Remin-
iscences,*
Prince
Wolkonsky:
1925

Umberto Restaurant, Wolkonsky said, in his memoirs, that he had gone across and said to him: " 'Sergei Pavlovitch, I have always sincerely admired your work: but my sincerity would not be complete if I did not take advantage of this opportunity of personally expressing my admiration to you.' 'It is so long since we have met,' Diaghilev answered, 'and I am very glad to press your hand.' "

Diaghilev's name does not seem to have appeared in any published guest-lists. It is likely, but by no means certain, that he may have been among the guests invited to a reception after the Ambassador's dinner-party.

Covent
Garden
Archives

Covent
Garden
Archives

There is no need to say that the worst headaches were those of the Box-Office. *Everyone* wanted to attend the Gala. The programme consisted of an act from each of three different operas, and the *Gobelins* scene from *Le Pavillon d'Armide*. Regretfully, one music writer remarked that "No doubt it would be immensely significant if Great Britain could have been represented by an act from a native opera. But what opera by a native composer has shown sufficient vitality to maintain its place, after production, in the repertory?"

"The demand for seats has probably exceeded anything ever experienced by any theatrical management in the world," said another reporter. "The directors were offered £500 for any box in the theatre, and later an American gentleman offered to pay £1,000 to the holder of any box willing to transfer it to him. Neither of the offers has been accepted." Multiply by at least seven for 1970 values.

Covent
Garden
Archives

One plea, however, touched even the frozen hearts of the management: "A letter was received some days ago from a woman in Calgary, Canada, saying that she had been allotted a seat for the Coronation Gala in 1902, and that owing to its abandonment she had been greatly disappointed. She now enclosed a postal order for 21s. for a gallery seat, and hoped she would get it. Mr. Forsyth has had a letter sent her saying that she will find a place reserved for her when she calls. She will be in distinguished company on this occasion in the gallery – for several Peers were very pleased – failing to get better – to secure places there."

It was estimated that the takings would amount to not less than £25,000 for the Gala night.

The
Times
27.6.11

There can be no possible doubt that the Gala presented even more glitter than the Coronation itself – for a myriad bulbs glowed in the newly-installed electroliers, and the house lights remained on throughout the evening. Superlatives flowed from the correspondents:

". . . The culminating point of splendour towards which all the Opera House's operations this season may be said to have been directed . . . a pity we have no Guardi or Longhi to preserve for posterity a lively image of the scene . . . 'Brilliant' is a word that has been hardworked these last few days; but brilliant is the only word for such an event as last night's State performance . . . It was a tiara night, of course . . . it was a night also of the very finest dresses and jewels, of uniforms and Orders . . . Talk, laughter, movement – music that was too good not to be listened to, but not so prolonged as to prevent social intercourse . . . and dancing, the most famous and the most exquisite in the world – London society is still 'brilliant' and knows how to enjoy courtly amusements."

The green trellis was by now covered with "climbing perfumed blooms of every shade from palest creamy-pink to deepest crimson." (But since on a previous occasion the heady scent had proved almost lethal, most of the 100,000 blooms were artificial – though these cost more than the real thing, said Green's, the Piccadilly florists who carried out the work.) "All the imitation roses, which have been modelled with great care, have been made in England. In the Royal box are 5,000 mauve, white and golden-yellow orchid blooms, worth over £200."

Daily
News
27.6.11

"The souvenir programme was printed in colours on rich grained silk – the treatment requiring 20 printing operations. The admission ticket was also an interesting souvenir, and the designs, the colour printing, and the entire production were carried out by Messrs. Finden Brown and Co. Ltd., of the St. Martin's Press."

Morning
Post
27.6.11

Only the *Morning Post* thought the elaboration rather overdone. "Some day, perhaps, an artist will be called in to show what can be achieved with infinitely less pains and at no greater cost by the mere beauty of drapery . . ."

No Gala of modern times could compete with the glories of this one: the sightseers outside

The Royal Box

The Russian Ballet
Scene from
Pavillon d'Armide

In the Stalls

The Highest
Tiers of Boxes

"LE PAVILLON D'ARMIDE" BEFORE THEIR MAJESTIES: SKETCHES AT COVENT GARDEN.
A vivid "Artist's Impression" of the Coronation Gala. (*Illustrated London News.*)

Tamara Karsavina, as London first saw her.

LE PAVILLON D'ARMIDE

Vaslav Nijinsky, as Armida's Slave, by J.S. Sargent, R.A. Lady Ripon took Nijinsky and Karsavina to the artist's studio in Tite Street, Chelsea, for sittings.

had their fill. The Peers arrived in their State coaches, with liveried footmen. The Grenadiers marched up Bow Street to form a Guard of Honour. Beefeaters in their picturesque uniforms lined up outside the Royal box. Her Majesty entered, wearing a rose-coloured velvet cloak, a paler rose dress glittering with precious stones, and the beautiful tiara of crosses and fleur-de-lis. And of course – being England! – during the performance, it started to rain – but the waiting crowds patiently endured.

In the front row of the Royal Box (normally the Grand Tier,) sat the Indian princes. Bronislava Nijinska recalled that she could see "Agha Khan in the front row in a costume ornated with precious stones and strings of pearls."

Letter to Author

Mme. Kirkby Lunn and Mlle. Destinn opened with a scene from *Aida*, and then Melba sang her favourite part, Juliette, by Gounod. After a short *entr'acte*, Tetrazzini and John McCormack delighted the audience in the "Singing Lesson" scene from Rossini's *Barber of Seville*.

Let it be noted, in view of Diaghilev's subsequent tales of a seeming coldness in the audience, that *throughout* the evening, the applause was reported as "muted" – muted by the soft kid gloves worn by both men and women, and by the formal etiquette of the occasion.

The position of honour, last in the bill, was given to the Russians.

"The regal spectacle ended with one of the most enchanting creations ever seen on any stage – the scene of the 'Animation of the Tapestry,' from *Le Pavillon d'Armide*, M. Tcherepnin's ballet – a feast well worthy of the eyes of princes. Both the King and Queen freely used opera glasses, and the interest of the whole company was excited. The pauses after the various dances, meant for applause, were at first silent. As the marvellous ballet progressed there was more and more admiration for the delicious Mme. Karsavina, M. Nijinsky, who seems the incarnation of youthful joy, the astonishing company of buffoons, and the others. With the culmination of the festivities at Armida's pavilion the spectacle closed."

Daily Mail 27.6.11

On her return to Buckingham Palace, Queen Mary wrote in her diary: "The House looked lovely. The music and ballet were both extremely good," and King George put in his note, "It was a very fine sight. The house most beautifully decorated, and the performance excellent."

Royal Archives

The night after the Gala, Diaghilev's company danced again, and presented a fresh work – *Les Sylphides*.

"You have forgotten London by the end of the ballet, *Les Sylphides*," said W.M., for forty years leader-writer of the *Daily Mirror*. (The initials concealed the personality of Richard Jennings, son of a *Times* leader-writer, a man of great culture, a bibliophile of such discrimination that "good enough for Jennings" was a catchword in the antiquarian book trade – a "character" who abhorred whistling boys, such as abounded in newspaper offices – a literary editor who was the first person to publish the poetry of Edith Sitwell, and later to arrange the same thing for Osbert in *The Times* – famous for his world-weary, town-weary musings.) He went on:

Daily Mirror 28.6.11

"The whole of this crabbed world that waits for joy and lightness is crowding to Covent Garden to forget itself in the Russian Ballet. Grim Russia, which most ignorants associated, until the last few years, with caviare and revolution, with Grand Dukes and Kümmel... 'anonymous' Russia has now paradoxically danced herself into the heart of old Europe..."

More eulogies filled other papers – and in view of the horror expressed at the thought of orchestrating Chopin, as well as Schumann, the praise bestowed on the beauty of the result must be mentioned. "How gloriously the familiar music gains when offered in the guise of this charming ballet!"

Daily Telegraph 28.6.11

Two more ballets were added before the end of the season, both exotic, both danced on the last night. Of *Scheherazade*, "concerned with the discovery by the Sultan Schariar of the shameless incontinency of his harem, including his favourite, Zobeide," the *Sunday Times* confessed: "The whole thing rather beggars description; it is at once so daring and so discreet in its expression, so rich and gorgeous but so perfectly harmonious in its colour, so turbulent and yet so graceful in its movement." The beautiful drop-cloth painted by Serov in the style of Persian miniatures, displayed during the Prelude, was so bizarre that it distracted this critic. *Cléopâtre* was to vie with *Scheherazade* for favour.

Sunday Times 23.7.11

As the season ended amidst thunderous applause, especially for Karsavina and Nijinsky, the news that the company was to return in the autumn for six weeks was greeted with rejoicing.

Once most of the ballets had been staged, the company had time to enjoy London's hospitality. Many hostesses were eager to entertain them, most prominent being Diaghilev's friend and sponsor, the Marchioness of Ripon. At her house at Coombe, near Kingston Hill, she had transformed the ballroom, building in it a pretty little theatre. For this she enlisted the help of her next-door neighbour, a well-known interior decorator, Walter Thornton-Smith, (whose nephew, G.B.L. Wilson, is one of this generation's ballet critics, historians, encyclopaedists, lexicographers, photographers – BALLETOMANIACS.) Diaghilev brought Karsavina and Nijinsky down to dance there on several occasions, for one of which Bakst designed a setting in his favourite combination of blues and greens.

The Russian Ambassador's son gave an amusing account of one of these parties:

Half a Life:
Count Constantine Benckendorff

"At Coombe, the atmosphere was different again. It was a villa and there were hardly any house-parties there, but the many functions were attended from Town. It was, I should say, the invasion of the London theatre by the Russians, under Diaghilev's aegis, which first brought me to Coombe. It was marvellous to watch with what poise Lady Ripon used to deal with her only too numerous theatrical guests – a tribe which is notoriously difficult to control.

"It was at Coombe that one evening I partnered Madame Karsavina in a valse; always a very indifferent dancer myself, I was profoundly impressed by the ease with which the tempered steel springs, which purported to be the legs of that small creature, dealt with my not inconsiderable bulk as we swept round the floor with incredible speed, and I hope, grace.

"Lady Ripon had scant support from her husband in her task of entertaining the Russians. Lord Ripon, premier shot in England, cared only for his obligations towards that position; with a large garden party swirling round him, he could be seen practising with two loaders in the middle of the lawn in front of the house, to prepare for the coming shooting season."

It is curious to discover that Lord Ripon was, in fact, a member of The Grand Opera Syndicate.

My First Fifty Years:
P. Poiret

In spite of the many remarks tossed off about the influence of the *Ballets Russes* on decoration and fashion, it is surprisingly difficult to track down references to such alleged influences. "Poiret" is the name that leaps to all lips the moment the subject is raised; yet Poiret insisted firmly that when the Diaghilev ballets arrived in Paris, "I already existed." This is, indeed, true. Poiret had been designing in Oriental styles and Oriental colours for years: a turban and aigrette appeared in Iribe's *Album* of Poiret designs in 1908. It was at the invitation of Margot Asquith that on May 15, 1909, (just before Diaghilev's first Paris season started,) he brought models and showed his clothes at a tea-party at No. 10, Downing Street. (The jokesters promptly re-named this "Gowning Street.") Whilst in London, said Poiret, "I visited the South Kensington Museum, which is full of the treasures of the Indies . . . In particular there was a collection of turbans that enchanted me . . ." He sent for his *premier main,* who came over and spent days copying the innumerable methods of winding turbans. "A few weeks later, we had made turbans the fashion of Paris." The present author has found the collection, stored in the India Department of the Victoria and Albert Museum, to which, with all the other wonderful Indian items, it moved in the 1950's.

Poiret recalled that "it was the period of the first Russian ballets . . . The Baksts, the Nijinskys, the Karsavinas, shone with all their brilliance. Like many French artists, I was very struck by the Russian Ballet, and I should not be surprised if it had a certain influence on me . . . But it must be clearly stated that . . . my reputation was made long before that of M. Bakst . . ."

In the summer of 1911, the elaborate *toilettes* ordered long in advance, and the heavy programme of social engagements, prevented London fashionables from embarking immediately on styles derived from Diaghilev's ballets. They could, however, read about what was being worn in Paris.

The Marchioness of Ripon,
by J.S. Sargent, R.A.

Lady Juliet Duff,
by G. Percival Anderson.

The Russian Ambassador, Count Benckendorff,
by J.S. Sargent, R.A.

Count Constantine Benckendorff.

The
Queen
1.7.11

"I noticed one woman in the stalls" (at the *Opéra,*) "who might have walked out of a seraglio . . . Her dress was all rich silks and embroideries with no shape in it, and her head was wound round with a turban. She was quite an exception, I may mention, as the Eastern style of dress is certainly going out of fashion, and the modes of 1830 threaten to come in. Whether we shall ever get as far as the crinoline I doubt, but more and more one sees signs of the slim waist and the full-flounced skirt." Could this be an echo of the rapture with which *Le Spectre de la Rose* had just been received?

Lady Diana Cooper, asked whether they all rushed out and bought things "under the influence," replied immediately, "Lampshade skirts." This fashion was, indeed, launched in June, 1911, but as a result of Poiret's lavish party in Paris, "The 1002nd Night," for which he designed a gauzy hooped skirt over the trousers of his wife's costume – and was besieged with orders the following day.

Changes in fashion in interior decoration are inevitably much slower to take effect, and, although a few rich devotees followed some of the exotic trends, the war interrupted any natural development. The stencilled motifs of the early 'twenties would seem to have their origin, however, in the scenic work of Diaghilev's collaborators, such as Bakst's frieze for *Le Carnaval.*

The
Times
24.6.11
A long article, from which this is but a small excerpt, went far beyond the realms of mere reporting, into those of contemplation:

". . . Technique is not more the source of the highest pleasure in dancing than it is in painting, in music, or in any other of the arts. It is a channel of communication; it is the means by which the artistic idea comes from the mind of the creator to the senses of the spectator . . ." Anonymous then, the writer is now revealed to have been George Calderon, a delightful man of all-round talent. Son of a former Keeper of the Royal Academy, he had spent two years in Russia, becoming fluent in the language and many dialects, and an expert on Russian affairs, Slavonic history and legend. His death at Gallipoli robbed the ballet scene of his sensitive appreciation.

RETURN OF THE PARLIAMENT BILL

Original caption: *A Vision suggested by a visit to the Russian Ballet at Covent Garden – MM. Nijinsky-Winston, Lloyd-Georgewitch, and Ivan Redmondski receive their old love, Mme. Karsavina Vetoloptoff after rather a poor time elsewhere.*

"Veto-lopped-off" refers to the diminished powers of the House of Lords, which could no longer veto a Bill, but only delay its passage to the Statute Book. Lloyd George had been resplendent in Court Dress at the Gala. John Redmond was the leader of the Irish M.P.'s, who held the balance of power at Westminster. Note the rôle in which he is portrayed! (*Punch*, 26th July, 1911.)

Punch
5.7.11
The Editor of *Punch*, Owen Seaman, went to the ballet himself. Heading his review "TOUJOURS A LA RUSSE," and commending especially the Russians' economy of gesture combined with clarity of mime, he referred to Calderon's article: ". . . There you will learn what makes the difference between British and Russian methods. I am half afraid that in this matter of the ballet we Britons never, never will be Slavs." (Could he have remembered Diaghilev's closing comment in his letter to *The Times*?)

Seaman noticed the "airy exit" of the genie in *Le Spectre de la Rose* – curiously the famous final leap did not attract one single other comment in the British papers. He frankly hated the stencilled frieze on the backcloth of *Carnaval*. His *Punch* cartoonists leapt gleefully at the chance to use the ballet as material for their barbed political jokes.

No future season would ever be able to equal this one for grandeur. In spite of the complicated history of quarrels and dismissals and withdrawals of funds, the liberation of the best dancers argues secret influence, not mentioned by Diaghilev to his colleagues. Since, by convention, reigning monarchs do not attend Coronations, may it not be taken that the Tsar had sent his dancers as a gift to his cousin?

All this time, Anna Pavlova and her partner Mordkin had been performing at the Palace Theatre. There had been constant quarrels between them, including the famous incident of the "slap" on the stage, and these led to a rather mysterious visitation just one week before the Coronation.

Mathilde Kschessinska adorned the coveted front page of *The Tatler* on June 21st, 1911, although her visit to London had been arranged at short notice.

Headlined "MORDKIN'S NEW PARTNER," this small news item appeared: "Although only some twenty-four hours in London, Matilda Kjanski (sic) has held quite a reception of well-known Society ladies who met her in Russia. She has come over from Russia to dance with Mordkin at the Palace during Pavlova's indisposition . . . She is staying at the Savoy, but can only remain in London for a fortnight . . . Madame Kjanski makes no disguise of her wish to make a reputation in London." Daily Sketch 15.6.11

Pavlova recovered from her indisposition at that very moment, and so no such appearance took place. Whether Kschessinska stayed a few days and witnessed the success of Diaghilev's company, is uncertain. (The company had not yet arrived, so perhaps she left before they came, and that could be the reason why no one has referred to it in memoirs.) However, there was sufficient time for *The Tatler* to devote its coveted first page on Coronation eve, June 21, to a charming portrait of her, wearing a little black dress, and reading a magazine. The caption said that she had come for pleasure, but might even dance. Certainly, her desire to "conquer London" must have stemmed from this visit – and behind this desire, most certainly, lay the fact that shortly afterwards Diaghilev was able to purchase the entire production of *Swan Lake* from Moscow, at a modest price, so that, in the autumn, London would have the chance to applaud her as it had applauded her younger rivals.

Between these two seasons, a New York paper was to report "RUSSIAN DANCERS LIKE A PLAGUE ON LONDON STAGE." 1911 had, indeed, been a record year for them. And – as they said in the Souvenir Programme – "The public came in multitudes, took classical dancing and dancers to its heart, and has insisted upon having them ever since." New York Evening Sun 18.9.11

1911

ROYAL OPERA, COVENT GARDEN

OCTOBER 16th - DECEMBER 9th

FIRST PERFORMANCES IN ENGLAND

October 16th: *Giselle*
(Adam, Coralli and Perrot, (revived by Fokine,) Benois.)
Paris, 28.6.1841.
Diaghilev Company, 18.6.10. Paris.

November 3rd: *L'Oiseau d'Or (Le Festin)*
(Tchaikovsky, Petipa, Bakst.)
Paris 19.5.09. (St. Petersburg 15.1.1890.)

November 14th: *Aurore et le Prince*
(Tchaikovsky, Petipa.)
St. Petersburg 15.1.1890

November 30th: *Le Lac des Cygnes*
(Tchaikovsky, Petipa, Golovine.)
Moscow 4.3.1877

REPERTOIRE

Le Carnaval	*Scheherazade*
Cléopâtre	*Le Spectre de la Rose*
Le Pavillon d'Armide	*Les Sylphides*
Polovtsian Dances	

COMPANY

Astafieva S., Baranovitch I., Baranovitch II., Dombrovska, Fedorova S., Frohmann M., Gashevska, Gonsiorovska, Guliuk, Hubert, Julitzka, Karsavina, Khokhlova, Klementovitch, Kopetzinska, Kovalievska, Kschessinska, Kulchitzka, Maicherska, Nijinska, Pavlova, Pflanz, Piltz, Roshanara, Schollar, Stahlko, Tcherepanova, Tchernicheva, Wassilievska, Yezerska.

Bolm, Bourman, Cecchetti, Fedorov, Frohmann, Gavrilov, Grigoriev, Gudin, Kobelev, Kostecki, Kotchetovsky, Kovalsky, Kremnev, Nijinsky, Ognev, Orlik, Orlov, Oumansky, Rakhmanov, Romanov B., Romanov V., Semenov, Sergueiev, Toboiko, Varjinsky, Zailich, Zelinsky.

CONDUCTOR:

Monteux

THREE MARYINSKY BALLERINAS

When Diaghilev's autumn season opened, Richard Capell's first notice began happily, but he pointed out that "victory was a harder task than in the summer, when their ballet-dancing was a novelty to practically everyone."

Daily Mail 17.10.11

Planning the repertoire was a harder task for Diaghilev, beset with problems which he had not had in the summer. Firstly, the season was in full swing in the Imperial theatres. ". . .The directors of these theatres, however, making a great exception in favour of Covent Garden, have allowed the appearance on that stage of several artists to whom as a rule leave to perform elsewhere is not granted." Diaghilev had to keep this goodwill.

The Times 14.10.11

Secondly, possibly after that reconnaissance in the summer, Mathilde Kschessinska, "Dancer of Merit to the Tsar," wanted to "conquer London," and her slightest wish was Imperially granted. Society outside Russia might know nothing of the art of ballet, but it knew everything of the art of gossip. It was an open secret that, in the 1890's, before his marriage, she had been the mistress of the Tsarevitch, as he then was, and that ever since, she had enjoyed his generosity and protection. Moreover, she had for some years been living with his cousin, the Grand Duke André, and they had a son. As a dancer, she would wish to appear as the indisputable Queen of the ballet; how would she wish to be received by Society – and how would Society receive her?

Thirdly, Karsavina, firmly established in London's affections, would have to return to St. Petersburg after two weeks, to fulfil her obligations there. Diaghilev needed a third ballerina, equally able to generate excitement. He needed Anna Pavlova.

Pavlova had not joined his first venture to Paris in 1909 until half-time, because she was already booked to dance elsewhere. (After visiting Prague, Leipzig and Berlin, her tour ended with performances of *Giselle* and *Swan Lake* on May 27 and 28, at the Staatsoper in Vienna. But the poster for the season, by Serov, portrayed her.) As a result of these prior engagements, when she arrived in Paris, she found that Karsavina had already captivated the town. Pavlova's own success in that first Paris season had been outstanding, but she had subsequently formed her own company. Pavlova had been sympathetic to Fokine's ideas and had danced in his earlier ballets, but she drew the line completely at the music of Stravinsky. In 1911, she was due to start a long tour of the English provinces in November, but she agreed to perform for Diaghilev during the earlier part of that month. Not only would she appear in the ballets which had already been danced in London by Karsavina, but also in the spectacular *pas de deux* from *Le Festin* with which Nijinsky and Karsavina had first astonished Paris, but which London had not yet been shown. Kschessinska would have Maryinsky *ballerina* splendour, starting with a *grand pas de deux* whilst rehearsals were in progress for her reign as Swan Queen. No village maidens or oriental slaves for her – but her gift for comedy could be contrasted with the performance of other dancers in the elegant trifle, *Le Carnaval.*

All three would be partnered by Nijinsky.

It is interesting to compare the ages of the leading figures in 1911: the artists Bakst (44) and Benois (40) were the eldest. (Benois had by this time quarrelled with Diaghilev and resigned, but his work remained.) Diaghilev and Kschessinska were both 39. Fokine was 31 and Pavlova 30, Bolm 27, Karsavina 26, Nijinsky 23, and his sister, Bronislava Nijinska, 21.

Diaghilev's decision to open with Karsavina in *Giselle* was bold, but, in retrospect, appears to have been mistimed. London was not ready for the "Romantic Ballet." In the first season, London had been charmed by the *romanticism* of *Les Sylphides*, exquisite and abstract. It had been thrilled by the exotic, especially *Scheherazade*. This was what London wanted again.

In his *Romantic Ballet in England,* Ivor Guest has told of the fervent admiration excited by *Giselle* in the 1840's. "The *Era* recorded that the ballet produced such profound emotion that it had been compared to one of the fantastic creations of Shakespeare." In the 1840's, the critics had discussed every subtle nuance of the plot, and every detail of costumes, lighting, scenic effects, and so on. Above all, "Londoners acquired the habit of comparing dancers in the title-rôle of this ballet very early. Indeed, they were treated to an experience which was denied even to the Parisians, at whose opera house the ballet had been created. There the rôle belonged exclusively to Carlotta Grisi . . . at Her Majesty's Theatre the year after Grisi had introduced the ballet, Fanny Elssler appeared in the same rôle. The contrast between the two ballerinas was most striking. Each played the rôle to perfection in her own individual style, yet how different were their interpretations!"

Karsavina said that Diaghilev set great store on *Giselle* being "re-born" on the stage where it had first been danced, the Paris *Opéra.* She had asked him to have Grisi's dress for the first act copied exactly from the lithograph after Chalon. Yet, in 1910, the revival did not win approbation in Paris.

Possibly, had Diaghilev prepared the London press and public to meet it as romantically as he did himself, telling of its history and of the interpretations of the two 19th century ballerinas, the London audience might have been more intrigued. As it was, they merely regarded it as "old-fashioned," and akin to the story-ballets of the music-halls from which, in the summer, they considered Diaghilev to have rescued the art.

How different it would be now that *Giselle* is once more a "holy ballet!" What queues there would be for tickets, as "balletomaniacs" battled for the chance to compare Karsavina with (as she herself described the older ballerina) "the frail, exquisite Pavlova, who brought back the almost forgotten fragrance of *Giselle* when she danced it at the Maryinsky."

In 1911, the *corps critique* sharpened up its pencils, and wrote out long synopses of the plot; they all thought it meaningless, some going so far as to guy it. Their admiration was reserved for the performances of the stars, but for the ballet itself, tolerance was the best they could produce. The name of the composer foxed Covent Garden's printers, who gave it as "Adams" – an error picked up even by *The Times,* – those who got it right puffing like pouter pigeons in glee at their profound superior knowledge as they listed his other works. All opened in the same vein, however – rapture at the return of their darlings, especially Karsavina and Nijinsky.

Daily
Mail
17.10.11

"Last night, . . . their triumph was not a moment in doubt." As Richard Capell immediately started to cast doubts on *Giselle,* Diaghilev's wisdom in following it with *Scheherazade,* the rave-success, was strategically brilliant. "Were the dancing anything less than perfect *Giselle* would, truth to tell, be a thought tedious. The piece, indeed, is a traditional ballet, and in the summer, the Russians, with their *Cléopâtre, Scheherazade,* and the rest, instilled in us a taste for something different – the *art nouveau* ballet, which has spread broad wings in flight away from and above the old French tradition. . .

"No doubt M. Fokin could have conceived weird and ghostlike measures for the graveyard dance. But instead of a *macabre* vision we see a troupe of charming young women in Taglioni ballet-skirts, whom – and their classical dances – we have already seen in *Les Sylphides.* The dances are nearly all delightful, and the execution is exquisite, but there is this shade of disappointment – the Russians have for the first time done something incongruous. The dances in every other spectacle they have presented here have been part of a harmonious whole. In *Giselle*

Karsavina in the copy of the original dress for the first act of *Giselle*.

we see that even this wonderful troupe of dancers cannot always steer clear of that incongruity which rightly rendered the old ballet a laughing-stock.

"Fortunately, at Covent Garden, there is the adorable Karsavina to look upon – she is Giselle, a vision, fleet of foot, dainty, and truly pathetic."

The Times (represented this time by H.C. Collis, Music Critic from 1911 to 1943,) was of much the same mind: "As a vehicle for the expression of the art of Mme. Karsavina and M. Nijinsky *Giselle* serves admirably. The artless story, with its quaint mixture of human passion with supernatural appearances, matters very little . . . It is no more important than is the plot of an Italian opera of the same date. The dances of the principals are like the arias of the operas, only more so, sufficient in themselves, entrancing in their artifice, and expressive by means of exquisite execution alone. In the first act M. Nijinsky's solo dance was the most conspicuous feature, and was the most warmly applauded . . . The second act . . . presents very much the same picture as that of *Les Sylphides*, which is now familiar. It is less good in that it is danced to the tepid and conventional ballet tunes of Adams instead of the beautifully-poised rhythms of the mazurkas and waltzes by Chopin. But though for this reason they are less musically suggestive the dances are, if possible, even more full of technical brilliancy and variety of execution, and the principals astonished their admirers by their inexhaustible resource."

The
Times
17.10.11

Morning
Post
17.10.11
"The ballet gives wider opportunities to the company than the pieces seen last season, since it includes a good deal of miming and a mad scene, followed by death, in which Mme. Karsavina displayed considerable gifts of characterisation," said the *Morning Post.*

The simple story of a village maiden, wooed by a handsome young lover who turns out to be a Prince playing commoner, and already betrothed, so that poor Giselle loses her reason, and dies, going to join the ranks of the Wilis, (the spirits of young girls betrayed,) who force their betrayers to dance themselves to death too, – thereby giving purpose to every movement in the seeming-similar-to-*Sylphides* second act, – does not seem to have achieved understanding in 1911.

Any tendency to take the "romantic, Germanic" story seriously was de-bunked in the *Daily News*, which gave an hilarious synopsis:–

Daily
News
17.10.11
Saying, "I prefer to give my own impressions," E.A. Baughan wrote: "In the first scene M. Nijinsky makes love to Mlle. Karsavina in the convincing, if a trifle indefinite, language of dancing. M. Nijinsky flew round the stage, and gave me the impression he could quite easily fly into the wings had he been of a mind to let himself go. His poses and flying leaps are as wonderful as ever, so light and yet so strong. His feet spurn the ground. If he were dissected I am sure his tissue would be found to be composed of springs. M. Nijinsky's dancing captivated Mlle. Karsavina, who was dressed as a village maiden down to her waist. She danced piquantly and gracefully, with an animation which set all her body dancing. When this had gone on for some time an old woman, presumably Mlle. Karsavina's mother, interrupted the flirtation. I imagined she was asking her daughter to prance still higher, but the synopsis afterwards informed me that Giselle's mother was warning her that she might become the prey of the Wilis.

"When this warning had been uttered a hunting party arrived, and I gathered that Loys (M. Nijinsky) was other than he seemed. An excited forester, smiling maliciously, steals a sword from Loys' lonely hut, and it was conceivable that the sword was some evidence of identity. Loys tries to kill the forester, and Giselle, after a mad pirouette, falls senseless. In the second act everyone was dressed in white, and a bell tolled mysteriously. There was much more dancing, until Giselle disappeared down a trap-door, and Loys falls senseless to the ground. Before this happened the *corps de ballet* had tried to make Nijinsky dance with them, but he selfishly preferred to indulge in his wonderful solos. The synopsis made this clear, however. It was not selfishness on Loys' part. The *corps de ballet* were Wilis and were endeavouring to ensnare M. Nijinsky. All except he were ghosts. However, the story really does not matter. Both the great Russian dancers were in good form, and the audience was most enthusiastic."

The
Lady
26.10.11
The Lady noticed the opening performance in two different parts of the same issue. "In Society," the social scene came in for attention. An air of condescension and surprise first: "I was quite amazed at the number of well-known faces in the house, which proved once more how full London is. Lady Ripon had lent her box to the Duchess of Rutland . . . Lady Ripon herself was sitting in the front row of the stalls, and on her close coiffure she had a network of gold and jewels, finished by one of those short shaving-brush colonelles of bright pink, which looked very well in her white hair. Her daughter Lady Juliet Duff came to join her mother's party . . . Lady Cunard was another music-lover to be seen, and she was in a grand-tier box with her little daughter Miss Nancy Cunard and Mrs. Raymond Asquith . . ."

Of the performance, however, *The Lady* had grave doubts. "Surely Karsavina never looked so beautiful or so fascinating as in that rich Oriental dress," (in *Scheherazade,*) "and never danced with more suggestive fascination! . . . But the new ballet, *Giselle*, 'left us cold,' and the phrase rather fits the subject, for the second act is a ghostly one, where spirit dancers appear and dance, according to legend, all night in a graveyard."

The *Lady's* Musical Notes turned thumbs firmly down. Remarking that the confidence of the directors of Covent Garden in the favour won by the superb Russian dancers in the summer had left them too optimistic, the columnist said, ". . .The confidence was justified by a well-filled house, but it remains to be seen whether the autumn opera-goers, who are quite a distinct class from the summer ones, are going to take to classic ballet with the same fervour.

"I think it a mistake to try *Giselle* on the opening night," she continued. "Frankly, *Giselle*, whether in summer or autumn, will not do. I do not object to its being Early Victorian . . . The trouble with *Giselle* is not the Victorian story of a peasant hero who is a noble prince in disguise, and of a love-sick heroine, who goes mad in a genteel way; nor yet in its rather watered Gauthier (sic) element of the supernatural; the use of traps and other old-fashioned devices; the white tarlatan skirts and Taglioni wreaths . . . But what we cannot stand at this time of day is the score of *Giselle.* Those 1840 sentimental strains, meaning absolutely nothing, are wearisome to a degree. The little jerky 'tunes' are unendurable. No! *Giselle* will not do!"

She also said of Pierre Monteux, "he does not seem to me to be such a born ballet conductor as Tcherepnin."

The Times was by now adopting an air of cosy familiarity towards the company and its repertoire: god-fatherly criticism of detail was creeping in. It praised the presentation of the second night. "The order in which the three ballets which made up last night's programme were given shows how the Russians are artists as much in the manner of serving their dishes as in the actual preparation of the ingredients . . . *Le Pavillon d'Armide* came first . . . The dancing in so far as it depended on the soloists was as wonderful as could have been desired. The four *confidantes,* too, of Armida, were first-rate dancers." (Piltz, Schollar, Nijinska and Wassiliewska.) "But where the effect depended upon *ensemble* there were many things needing improvement last night. No doubt they will obtain it now that the whole thing has been gone through once; but it is a pity, too, that the pinks and blues and greens of the costumes did not harmonize better with each other and with the yellow-green of the scenery.

"The whole thing whetted the appetite for the gorgeous colouring and riotous movement of *Scheherazade,* in which one would not change the form of a single Turkish slipper or the colour of a waving plume. But instead of juxta-posing these two highly-spiced dishes, which would have made the former seem too tasteless by comparison, Schumann's *Carnaval* was inserted between them. The cool tones of it made exactly the right relief to the other two ballets and rested the eyes which would have been dazzled by too much colouring."

The Times 18.10.11

Both Karsavina and Pavlova had devoted followings. Some rushed from one to the other; some could not bear to see whichever they would have seen second, so devoted were they to their first love. This partisan approach even prevented Cyril Beaumont, a Pavlova devotee of 1910 and 1911, from seeing the Diaghilev Company until 1912. Some of Pavlova's fans felt that Karsavina had had an unfair advantage in appearing in the marvellous creations at Covent Garden.

The *Lady* anticipated Pavlova's advent there:-

" . . . Familiar as London audiences are with Madame Pavlova as a 'turn' at the Palace, they have probably never yet seen her at her best, unless the centrepiece of a mosaic pavement is seen at its best when torn out of its proper surroundings. It is hardly necessary to praise Pavlova at this time of day, but it is interesting to find that there has been a great divergence of critical opinion over her dancing. When she was in Paris in 1909, one critic wrote that she had a very good style, but no great talent, and that her dancing was '*sèche.*' Another said, 'All the essentials of the dance, nobility of gesture, beauty of line, lightness, elevation, have united in her to produce the ideal dancer. She does not dance; she flies; and it is hard to tell when she touches the ground. She produces an effect of having conquered the law of gravitation; of having freed herself entirely from the earth. Her dances are '*des poèmes dansées, des poèsies mimées, des chansons sans paroles.*' " ("Her dances are 'poems in dance, verses in action, songs without words.' ")

The Lady 2.11.11

The *Times* led off after her first night.

"We did not quite get all we looked for when Pavlova was rescued from the music-halls and restored to the ballet. The two parts in which she danced on Saturday gave her no scope. We had hoped to see her as Ta-Hor in *Cléopâtre,* . . . but had to content ourselves with seeing her as a Favourite Slave, (what would ballets be without these favourite slaves always ready to console or to amuse their owners?), a cringing, cat-like, *schadenfreud*-ish person," (full of malicious glee,) "who has nothing much to do with the main train of events. But there are elements in the rôle of Ta-Hor with which Pavlova, with her immense personality, would have worked wonders.

The Times 30.10.11

As a young choreographer, Fokine thought of bringing back the long, romantic *tutu* familiar in prints of Taglioni. Leon Bakst designed this charming costume, garlanded with roses, for Anna Pavlova to wear at a charity performance on February 10th, 1907, in St. Petersburg. With Michael Oboukhov, she danced a Waltz in Fokine's first arrangement to Chopin's music – *Chopiniana*. She must have looked very like this when she danced in Diaghilev's version of this ballet – *Les Sylphides*. (The costume was identified by Roberta Lazzarini.)

"The main thing about Pavlova is that when she dances, the whole of her dances. With others our attention, and their own, is drawn at any given moment to this part or that; the rest is accessory. With Pavlova there are no accessory parts. She dances with her feet, her fingers, her neck (how much expression there is in the various inclinings of her head,) her smile, her eyes, her dress . . . The drama of her successive emotions is perfectly clear; her changes of sentiment are instantly echoed by little thrills and murmurs, even in the inexpressive audience that fills Covent Garden. That roguery of hers is so deliciously feminine in its combination of full-grown intelligence with the mien of childhood. How delightful she is in *Giselle* with her old mother, Cecchetti! It seems impossible that two such expansive people can live in such a very little cottage."

The Times hated the story and suggested correct versions of such legends from Slavonic sources – "far better subjects for ballets than this bewildered bread-and-butter affair." This review is clearly recognisable as having come from the pen of George Calderon, called upon once more for what was considered to be a major occasion, requiring background. *"Giselle, though a big rôle, does injustice to Pavlova's genius. The part exhibits many moods and conditions – love, coyness, fear, anger, despair, madness, death, resurrection; but is all about nothing; there is no sequence or motive. In fact, Giselle is a good subject spoilt. The Wilis ought to be either vampirish and terrible or else plaintive and pathetic. But these are neither one thing nor the other, and pretend to be both. Who could really be alarmed by these nice young ladies in white ballet skirts? we all felt that the forester was a poor, fuddled coward to be so frightened!"*

The *Daily News* felt much the same way about the story, but wrote of Pavlova, "With M. Nijinsky as partner, she enabled one to overlook the weakness of this charming spectacle of broken hearts, insanity, graveyard revels and sudden death. But . . . the extraordinary intensity of Mme. Pavlova's acting in the mad scene lifted the performance to a dramatic significance that seemed almost an intrusion amid the polite conventions of the remainder." Daily News 30.10.11

A report which more closely details Pavlova's Giselle appeared in *The Standard*:

"Were anything wanted to make the Russian Ballet performances more popular than they have been all along it would be the engagement of Mme. Pavlova . . . She has by her previous engagements in London made her name to the man in the street synonymous with Russian dancing. . . The Standard 30.10.11

"One was compelled to ask oneself a score of times: Why was *Giselle* – a ballet which . . . struck us on its recent production as a little slow, not to say tedious – suddenly transfigured into quite a little drama full of poetry, pathos, and romance? . . . Madame Pavlova made one feel that she was that kind of a girl who gives her life with her heart. But we were not prepared for such a wonderful exhibition of counterfeit dementia as that given us at the end of the first scene. It was awful; it was nerve-wracking, and only the dancer's consummate art rescued it from the repulsive. In fact, as we recall this scene in the light of day, we wonder we did not laugh at this piece of tip-toe tragedy . . . But on Saturday the audience was carried away by the dramatic force of Mme. Pavlova's performance, and, though the agony was piled on to breaking point, owing to the undue length of the musical figure, the house was with the dancer, eyes and heart, till the curtain fell, when the enthusiasm was unbounded."

Diaghilev's ballet *Cléopâtre* was developed from *Une Nuit d'Egypte*, which Fokine had produced in St. Petersburg in 1908, to a hotch-potch of music by Russian composers. Unlike most Cleopatra stories, it had nothing to do with Mark Anthony. Amoun, a young and noble hunter, is in love with the Princess Ta-Hor, and she has been promised to him by the High Priests. One day Cleopatra visits the temple. Amoun, catching sight of her, falls wildly in love. He rashly declares this passion in a note wrapped round an arrow which he shoots to her feet. She offers him one night of love, with death at the end. He accepts, in spite of the pleadings of Ta-Hor. As the Queen receives him on her couch, a Bacchanale is danced around it. She gives him the poisoned cup, he dies, and Ta-Hor, distraught, kisses his corpse and falls prostrate over it.

Quite why no one ever seems to have protested at this display of lust and immorality, whilst *Scheherazade*, in which the Golden Slave did not even caress Zobeide, never ceased to excite prurience, remains an enigma. The plot of *Scheherazade* was simple. Egged on by his brother, the Shah Zeman, the King of India and China, Shah Shahriah, left his harem on a feigned hunting trip. Immediately, the wives bullied the Chief Eunuch till he opened two of the blue doors which cut them off from all other males. Two groups of slaves rushed in and the orgies commenced. Mixing bribery with threats, Zobeide, Favourite of the Shah, then forced the Chief Eunuch to open the third door. In leapt the Golden Slave – and when that part was Nijinsky's, he covered two-thirds of the stage in one extraordinary bound. Though lust was expressed in his gestures as his hands modelled the contours of her body, he never actually caressed Zobeide.

The Shah returned: he sought vengeance. Wives and slaves were put to the sword. The Golden Slave perished in a spectacular series of leaps and falls. Zobeide alone remained, pleading for her life with her lord. As he remained deaf to her entreaties, she seized a dagger and slew herself.

The rôle of Cleopatra had been created on the statuesque Ida Rubinstein (as had Zobeide, in *Scheherazade.*) The principal dancing rôle was, in fact, Ta-Hor, – but as there was a *pas de deux* for the two Favourite Slaves, Pavlova elected to dance this relatively minor part.

The *Morning Post* said: "Her daring and abandon illustrated another phase of the art of which she is so complete a mistress," while the *Daily News* observed that "Pavlova and Nijinsky are less important figures in the sumptuous *Cléopâtre,* but their cringing admiration of their mistress was full of subtle by-play, and the veil-dance as fascinating as anything in the production. Perhaps, though, the most vivid impression one takes away from *Cléopâtre,* is the wonderful Bacchanale." (This was one of Pavlova's most admired items in her own repertoire.) Morning Post 30.10.11

Daily News 31.10.11

If *Giselle* was recognised by *cognoscenti* as being a part which demanded Pavlova's exceptional dramatic powers to give it real meaning, then surely *Les Sylphides*, storyless and poetic at the same time, must have given her the finest outlet for the sheer beauty of her dancing. "*Les Sylphides* is as far away from the romantic unreality of magic as from the unromantic of everyday life," said *The Times*. "There is no drama to follow; there is simply pure choreography to watch, and with the orchestra playing some of the most lovely tunes of Chopin and Mme. Pavlova and M. Nijinsky to dance them, one would like to go on watching for the rest of the evening. Whether in a mazurka or the C sharp minor valse or the glorious *valse brillante* in E flat, these two dancers with their swift, elastic steps and fluttering butterfly movements, were so incredibly light and vivacious as to seem hardly human." And then, a new item:–

The
Times
2.11.11

"A little episode from Tchaikovsky's *La Belle au Bois Dormant* was added to the repertory in order that we might see Mme. Pavlova in the dances of the golden bird. Taken by itself it is little more than a display of the virtuosity of the two dancers, Mme. Pavlova and M. Nijinsky, but that is enough to make it memorable, for it includes feats of arms (and still more of legs) which take one's breath away because of the extraordinary control of muscle and limb which they entail.

The
Times
4.11.11

"Here the pointed toe step, which Mme. Pavlova does with an entrancing grace which no one else can quite attain, is used in a new way, with little clawing movements as though only a small thread held her to the ground and she were trying to free herself and sail away into mid-air. As in her famous *Papillon* dance, so in *L'Oiseau d'Or* her art is more suggestive than imitative. She does not copy a bird, but she seems for a moment to partake of its nature ... M. Nijinsky has long succeeded in setting the law of gravitation at defiance, and he makes one exit here which rivals his final one in *Le Spectre de la Rose*. His dancing, too, has new elements in it, wonderful rhythmic patterns of the body which he has not shown elsewhere."

On November 7th, at their own request, King George and Queen Mary paid a private visit to see Pavlova in *Les Sylphides*, *Le Carnaval*, and *Le Pavillon d'Armide*, just before they left for India to attend the Durbar. King George filled in his diary as usual that night: "Madame Pavlova and Mr. Nijinsky certainly dance beautifully."

Royal
Archives

The critics were unanimous in condemning the "passion for cutting which has already robbed *Le Pavillon d'Armide* of all its sense and much of its charm." *Les Sylphides* had also suffered some mutilation. "Surely the management at Covent Garden might give more consideration to that part of the audience which prefers to see three or even two whole ballets rather than four maimed ones?"

The
Times
4.11.11

Pavlova's seventh performance this season, and the last she ever gave with Diaghilev's company, was on Saturday, November 11th, 1911.

"She appeared as Armida, as the chief nymph in the Chopinesque *Les Sylphides*,– surely, as interpreted by this peerless *corps de ballet*, the most enchanting exhibition of purely classic dancing ever seen – and as the Golden Bird.

Daily
Mail
13.11.11

"And she has perhaps never before danced so beautifully. Closer acquaintance with the Covent Garden stage, the orchestra and her fellow dancers evidently had greatly increased her confidence, and things like the dance following the Scene of the Scarf in *Armida* and the C sharp minor waltzes in *Sylphides* were done with a self-abandonment, a 'fine, careless rapture,' that were entrancing.

"After the *Sylphides* – in which, by the way, the excised Prelude has been restored – there was a storm of applause, flowers for Mme. Pavlova, and laurels for M. Michel Fokine, the inspired ballet-master of the troupe, to whom Mme. Pavlova, in an amusing scene, paid homage, handing over to him in gesture, all the audience's applause."

The audience was thrilled to see two such wonderful artists in a single season. Writing with the slight haziness of sixty years of retrospect, Dame Laura Knight said, in *The Magic of a Line*, "This was the season when, for three weeks, Pavlova starred with Nijinsky on alternate nights with Karsavina. All London went half mad with excitement."

Perhaps Lubov Tchernicheva, Diaghilev's faithful dancer for twenty years, made the perfect comparison. "I knew them both," she said, "both wonderful dancers, both wonderful women. But quite different! When Tamara danced on the stage – you never saw anything so beautiful – the most beautiful woman, all warm, wonderful woman. But Pavlova, when she danced – not woman at all – spirit!"

Pavlova

Karsavina

There is some mystery as to the exact costume worn by Pavlova for these three London performances of *L'Oiseau d'Or*. "Decked with resplendent feathers. . ." said the *Standard,* whilst the *Daily Mail,* on the same day, particularized: ". . . a lemon-coloured tutu and orange corsage, and an audacious crest of scarlet and yellow ostrich feathers and so many jewels that the dancing was over before one had fully seen them." This is obviously the same basic design by Bakst as Karsavina wore in *Le Festin* in Paris in 1909. Moreover, there is an "Artist's Impression" of Pavlova in this costume in the *Illustrated London News* for December 2, 1911, just when she had completed her performances at Covent Garden and set off on her first provincial tour of Britain.

The *Daily Mail's* comment about the abundance of the jewelling tempts one to wonder whether Pavlova actually wore her own, pirated, costume – the history of which may be summed up thus:–

In February, 1910, Pavlova included "The Firebird" – (Tchaikovsky) in her repertoire for her first U.S. tour, which opened at the Metropolitan Opera House.

In May, 1910, the Diaghilev Ballet had its first season at the Paris *Opéra*, and obviously, the costume was missed one day, and replaced the next – though Karsavina knew nothing of this. At this time, Pavlova herself was in London, appearing for four months at the Palace Theatre.

In October, 1910, she started her second U.S. tour, again including this number. She must have been reported as wearing a copy of Karsavina's costume, the news reaching the Diaghilev base-camp in Paris.

Apparently, in December, 1910, Mme. Muelle turned tough about the amount Diaghilev owed her – probably when she was sent for to discuss further orders. The riposte must have been an accusation of plagiarism, conveyed to her by one of the other members of the staff. Her angry letters to Baron de Gunzbourg and Bakst are part of the Astruc Papers, one of the treasures of the New York Public Library's Dance Collection.

Pavlova was taller and slimmer than Karsavina. It is hard to imagine that she would have consented to perform in an ill-fitting costume. The original jewelled "collar" might have been appliqued to a fresh bodice: or she might have insisted on wearing her own version. Perhaps one day the question may be solved by the discovery of a dated photograph.

This rare photograph shows her in a similar dress, with a different bodice with low-cut decolletage and the chain-mail basque which correspond with Mme. Muelle's description. It was in the collection of Anton Dolin, and was spotted in *Dance and Dancers,* January, 1950, by Roberta Lazzarini – who, with her husband, has founded a Pavlova Museum in the dancer's home, Ivy House, in North London. The photograph of Karsavina was taken on the 1909 first night. (Collection, Keith Lester.) Standard & Daily Mail 4.11.11

THE LETTERS IN THE ASTRUC PAPERS

Copie d'une lettre de Mme. Marie Muelle à M. Bakst

Paris, le 10 Décembre 1910

Monsieur,

J'apprends à l'instant que M. de Gunzbourg croit que j'ai fait à Melle Pavlova le même costume qu'à Melle Karsavina dans l'Oiseau de Feu, ceci est une erreur très grande pour ne pas dire autrement.

J'ai fait d'après les indications de M. Clustine un costume pour Londres emporté en Amérique, lequel était composé d'une cuirasse en pierreries cousues et d'une jupe de plumes d'autruche.

Cela n'était pas mon goût mais on a commandé, j'ai éxécuter sans sourciller de peur de dire un mot qui les mette sur la trace de ce merveilleux costume de Karsavina. M. de Gunzbourg va jusqu'à soupçonner que le soir où ce costume manquait à l'Opéra c'était moi qui l'avais pris pour le copier. C'est idiot quand j'ai fait un costume je me le rappelle.

Je vous ennuie mais je serais désolée si vous me croyez capable de faire les choses pareilles.

J'ai fait pour l'Amérique un ballet avec des dessins si mauvais que les jolies idées de formes et de couleurs que vous m'avez apprises me revenaient sans cesse à l'idée et j'étais obligée de me retenir pour ne pas copier quelque chose de vos merveilles. . .

Copie d'une lettre de Mme. Marie Muelle à Monsieur Le Baron de Gunzbourg.

Paris, le 10 Décembre 1910

Monsieur,

Je viens d'apprendre que vous croyez que j'ai fait á Melle Pavlova le même costume qu'à Melle Karsavina pour l'Oiseau de Feu, c'est une erreur et je puis vous prouver le contraire, ce costume a été copié sur une carte postale donnée par M. Clustine et fait ainsi: Corsage en pierreries cousues, jupe en tarlatane et plumes d'autruche.

Je pense, Monsieur, que vous ne pouvez croire un moment que j'ai agi d'une façon malhonnête envers vous et M. de Diaghilew et si j'avais voulu refaire le costume de Melle Karsavina moi faisant l'entretien des costumes, il m'eut été bien facile de prendre sous ce prétexte un costume et de le copier, mais je ne l'ai pas fait et j'ai assez de mémoire pour me rappeler ce que j'ai fait une fois pour le recopier sans demander, pas plus que le Ballet pour l'Amérique n'a été fait sur vos modèles, c'est M. Paquereau qui a fait les dessins pour la direction de cette affaire et je les tiens à votre disposition.

Je compte, Monsieur, que vous voudrez bien vous dire que si j'ai insisté d'une façon peut-être indiscrète pour toucher les traites échues, j'étais très génée à ce moment, cela ne peut en aucune façon impliquer l'idée d'un soupçon sur ma façon d'agir vis à vis de la Direction russe ou d'autres directions.

Je pense que ma maison sur la place a acquis une réputation d'honnêteté complète et je ne voudrais pas que vous ayez un soupçon même si petit soit-il sur ma délicatesse.

Translation of a letter from Mme. Muelle to M. Bakst.

Paris, 10th December 1910

Sir,

I have just this minute heard that M. de Gunzbourg believes that I have made for Mlle. Pavlova a replica of Mlle. Karsavina's costume for L'Oiseau de Feu, this is a horrible mistake to say nothing stronger.

Following the instructions of M. Clustine I made a costume for London, which was taken to America, and which consisted of a veritable chain-mail of stones stitched together and a tutu with ostrich feathers.

This was by no means to my taste but it was an order, I made it up without batting an eyelid for fear of putting them on the trail of Karsavina's marvellous costume. M. de Gunzbourg even suspects that on the night when this costume was missing from the Opera, it was I who had sneaked it out in order to copy it. This is ridiculous, when I have made a costume I remember it.

I am sorry to bother you but I should be heartbroken if you were to think me capable of doing such a thing.

I made a ballet for America working on such terrible designs that the lovely ideas of shape and colour which you taught me came back to me all the time as I worked, and I had to bridle myself so as not to repeat any of your wonders.

Translation of a letter from Mme. Marie Muelle to Baron de Gunzbourg

Paris, 10th December, 1910.

Dear Sir,

I have only just heard that you actually believe that I made up for Mlle. Pavlova the same costume as Mlle. Karsavina's for L'Oiseau de Feu, this is quite wrong and I can prove it to you, this costume was specified on a postcard given me by M. Clustine and was made like this: bodice of jewels stitched down, tarlatan skirt with ostrich feathers.

I cannot believe that you could ever think for a moment that I could act in a dishonest way towards you and M. Diaghilew and had I wished to re-make Mlle. Karsavina's costume, as I am responsible for the maintenance of the wardrobe, nothing would have been simpler than to take the costume on this pretext and copy it, but I didn't do so and my memory is sufficiently accurate for me to recall what I have once made and repeat it without going back to the original, moreover, the ballet made for America was not made from your designs, it was M. Paquereau who made the sketches for this work and I have them here and you can come and see them for yourself.

I trust, also, that you will understand that if I was a bit insistent about payment of the overdue accounts, I was extremely upset at the time, and this should not be taken as implying that there is the least suspicion in my actions of any difficulty with the Russian management or any other.

I believe that my business has earned a reputation for complete honesty and I should be most unhappy if I felt that you entertained the least uncertainty as to my scrupulous behaviour.

Mathilde Kschessinska arrived in London a full week before she was to perform. Accompanied by the Grand Duke André, their son Vova, his doctor, and their staff, she settled in to a suite of eight rooms at the Savoy, overlooking the river. That night, the Grand Duke was the guest of the Russian Ambassador in his box. Whether she accompanied him is not clear, for her name was not mentioned.

Daily
Mirror
9.11.11

She obviously took the matter of publicity in hand herself. Certainly she had no qualms about cashing in on her known status. "I feel that I am beginning a new life, a new career; I shall be appealing to a new world next week when I step for the first time on the stage of your historical opera house. . ." The reporter commented: "The unaffected charm of Mme.Kschessinska's delight in seeing her compatriots, who all worship her as an almost exalted personage, was characteristic of a temperament that is essentially magnetic." The *Sketch* stated that "her salon is frequented by Royalty and diplomatists and she has great political influence," but to *The Standard* she had "indignantly denied the imputation. 'Everyone has enemies,' she said, 'and I am no exception to the rule . . . such a report is entirely untrue.' "

The
Standard
9.11.11

The
Sketch
9.11.11

She did not seek to deny the statement that she was the richest woman on the stage. Indeed, she was obviously determined to emphasize this fact, for either all newspaper reporters then wrote precise shorthand, and transcribed it identically, or else she had come prepared with a handout, (thoughtfully translated into English,) for which she ought to have been awarded an Oscar, specially designed by Fabergé but encrusted with precious, rather than semi-precious, stones.

Very similar accounts appeared in most of the papers before her début, but as it is the most complete, the extracts quoted are taken from the *Daily Telegraph*, where an "interview" of inordinate length dead-heated with the notice of that performance.

Headed "A MILLION ROUBLES IN JEWELS," it filled an entire column.

" 'You want to talk of jewels and furs and *chiffons* rather than anything else?' The ballerina was smiling; amusement was in her dark eyes . . . The famous dancer, who is called the richest woman on the stage, is slight and dark, with a little head set proudly and gracefully on her shoulders. She was dressed in close-fitting black . . . A diamond ornament held the frock at the neck, a plaque of diamonds sparkled from an invisible chain; immense diamonds blazed in her little ears, showing under her close-set, dark hair. In her drawing-room there were roses and carnations, for she loves flowers as well as jewels.

Daily
Telegraph
15.11.11

" 'I adore gems!' she cried, as one after another, glorious stones were displayed to the light. 'If you are quite, quite sure that English ladies are as much interested in knowing about my gems and furs and frocks as in seeing me dance, I shall show you a few of my things . . .

" 'A million roubles, my jewels? Yes, I suppose so. I have two sapphires on a chain that alone are worth 45,000 roubles. This is the bandeau I mean to wear on Tuesday night. See how big the sapphires are! the rest of the setting is of diamonds. This great plaque I shall also wear . . .' The light flashed and played, in myriad colours, as she took the ornament from its resting-place.

" 'My presentation from the Emperor of Russia,' indicating a superb decoration forming the two Russian eagles with the Imperial crown in diamonds. Necklaces, bracelets, rivières, pendants – she handles each one. She had the air of one who, though possessing such treasures in abundance, yet had other aspirations as well.

"From a platinum chain like a thread, a ball of crusted diamonds fell lightly, and a tiny watch ticked gaily.

" 'This is a favourite,' Madame remarked. 'It was given me on my gala night in St. Petersburg. I had sixty-three baskets of flowers and twenty-one gifts. The *abonnés* . . .' (subscribers) 'of the Maryinsky Theatre subscribed £1,000 for presents for me. They spent £500 on a tea-table with silver appointments, £250 was paid for my watch, and the other £250 was spent on jewels.

" 'A lot of money, ah! you think so? The ballet in Russia is on quite a different plane from that in England. On Sunday night, the great ballet-night, the Maryinsky Theatre is filled with a gay crowd, the place is ablaze with jewels and uniforms, a sight to be seen! People vie with each other to get the subscription seats, some are held for a generation in the hands of the same families. Russian nobles do not give up their theatre seats, only when they die.

" 'You want to see my furs and frocks, as well as my jewels?'

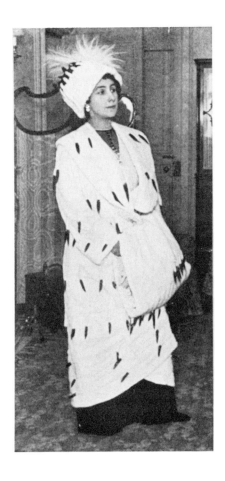

Mathilde Kschessinska was photographed at the Savoy. She is here seen at left wearing the ermine ensemble observed by journalists. In another picture, she had doffed the coat but kept the hat and muff, and her dark dress was decorated with a huge lace corsage. She must have liked the photograph on the right, for she signed it and gave it to a young English dancer, who, as Butsova, became the first soloist in Pavlova's company.

"An attendant threw open one fitment after another, showing serried ranks of garments. A full-length coat of ermine was dazzling in its snow-whiteness, dark Russian sables slipped through her slim fingers as if they had been of the softest silk . . .

" 'Thousands of pounds, my furs? Yes, of course. Furs are costly, you know. Lace is my passion! I buy it wherever I go, and I have quantities of rare pieces. I use some of it on my clothes; I use real lace only on every garment, of course I do! Every little ballet skirt is frilled with real lace, and edged with it; I never wear anything else! . . .

" 'I could talk about lace for ever, and forget everything else!' The ballet-frock worn in *Aurore et le Prince* is rose-petal pink. Flat frills of Cluny lace are held by an *empiècement* of crystal tube beads on net, and the tiny corsage, little more than a belt, is jewelled lace. 'I design my own ballet dresses chiefly, except when they are historical, as in Schumann's *Carnaval* . . .

" 'Gowns, gowns, and always more gowns!' Madame cried. 'You know, I came through Paris, and I got dozens of them. There are many I have not even had on yet . . .' Hats, created in the most entrancing mood of Paris artists, accompanied these marvels of taste and skill.

" 'What do I expect of London? Oh, I am delighted at the idea of dancing at Covent Garden. I think less of my jewels and gowns than of my art, you know. I have won my laurels! I hold the position of Dancer of Merit to the Emperor of Russia. It is a higher title than Prima Ballerina, and was conferred on me by the Board of Direction of the Imperial Theatres. Where have I danced? In Paris and in Vienna. The Emperor of Austria, who had not been to the ballet for a dozen years, honoured me by coming to see me dance. A Russian audience' – and the famous ballerina waved her expressive hands towards the jewels and furs and the rare creations from Paris – 'would not mind all these things in the least. You know, our balletomaniacs follow the ballet, every movement, every expression, as closely as English people do a composition from a great composer. The public are severe critics and ready to say what they think of us. . .' "

And in another paper, there was an additional *bonne-bouche:*

"It appears that Mme. Kschessinska dances but seldom nowadays. In fact, it is regarded as an act of special favour for her to appear on the stage of the *Opéra* at all. She dances only to please the Court, or, as one famous diplomatist in St. Petersburg puts it, 'to conserve the peace of Europe.' The enemies of the Russian Ambassador to France used to say that the greatest triumph of his diplomatic career came when he induced Kschessinska to dance in Paris.

"She tells me that she had been 'greatly interested recently in a wonderful exhibition we had in St. Petersburg to illustrate the history of the theatre in Russia. It was marvellously complete in detail, and I was very proud, and also somewhat amused, when I saw in a great glass case, carefully shrined, a tiny pair of blue satin stays – my first pair, I think – that I had worn when I was eight years old!' "

The Standard 9.11.11

The term "balletomaniacs" which Kschessinska so casually dropped into her conversation must, indeed, have been part of the ballet jargon at home in Russia. It did not get absorbed into its English counterpart until Arnold Haskell re-invented it in the 1930's.

If, in fact, the reporters actually saw the jewels at the Savoy, it must have been during one of their brief escapes from the safes of the London branch of the House of Fabergé, where they were stored. The items wanted each day were brought out by members of that firm, and returned to the safes immediately after the performance or appearance. The *Daily Mirror's* reporter was given a list of the items required for her debut: "I am to wear a string of diamonds and sapphires in my hair, and diamonds alone on my neck and arms, when I dance on Tuesday. I am longing for the day to come and be over."

Daily Mirror 13.11.11

The *Telegraph's* reporter slipped in a question: " 'Madame Pavlova?' (She turned quickly at the name.) 'Ah, if people do compare us they are very stupid. There is no comparison to be made, for we are quite different. Artists must be judged on the merits of their technique and on the power they have to give expression to their own individuality in their art. Thus, you see how stupid it would be to make any comparison between my fellow-artist, Madame Pavlova, and myself. Individuality is the most precious gift of the artist.' "

Daily Telegraph 15.11.11

Kschessinska obviously wished to gloss over that visit to England in June. Now, in November, the *Daily Mail* reported that "Mme. Kschessinska says she sees the great city in a different light from that in which it was presented to her on her first visit last June. 'It all delighted me,' she said. 'I was merely a visitor. Now I come as an artiste, and London is a new world to me. In Russia everyone knows me; here, I am a stranger.' " And, obliterating the memory of June, the suite at the Savoy, the reception, and the Press, she added: " 'I don't believe a soul in London ever heard my name before today.' "

Daily Mail 9.11.11

Kschessinska removed any embarrassment as to whether *she* would be "received" by the simple expedient of being the hostess herself. She gave several parties at the Savoy, to which all the dancers were warmly invited, and one Sunday, the Grand Duke André arranged for a special train and a fabulous lunch, and took the entire company to Windsor. A convoy of landaus picked them up at the station and drove them to the Castle, but, alas, no one had thought to ensure that it would be open. Even to the Grand Duke, its doors were closed. No one minded – it was all such fun.

" 'At home, in Russia, I dance just for the sheer love of my art. I dance when I feel like it, not at stated intervals. When I am to appear at the Opera, I rest all day, just on a sofa, but there is one thing I must always do on such a day, I must myself sew the ribbons on my dancing shoes. I have no fads, no hobbies, only when the summer comes I go away into the silent country to a villa I have built in Finland.' "

The *Daily News* also watched her sewing on the ribbons ("It is my superstition") and obviously led her on about her influence on politics. " 'Isn't that nonsense! I am afraid that I become thoroughly stupid when people begin talking about politics; my art has been my life, and I adore it. I happen to be one of those fortunate people not obliged to earn their living by dancing; I dance for the sheer love of it.

" 'Now . . . I shall be ten minutes late for rehearsal . . .' "

Daily News 10.11.11

The interviewer concluded that he (or she) left with the impression that he had been talking to a very great lady. "Madame Kschessinska's dress and manner have nothing in them reminiscent of the stage."

The
Times
15.11.11

Not surprisingly, the Court column recorded that "there was a full house when Mme. Kschessinska made her first appearance in the Russian Ballet at Covent Garden last night. Among those present were Lady Diana Manners, Lady Muriel Paget, Mr. Alfred de Rothschild," and so on for fifteen tightly-packed lines.

Whatever mirth all this may arouse, it must be remembered that Kschessinska was, indeed, a great dancer in her own style. Karsavina says that she possessed enormous enjoyment in performing, and that the moment she came on the stage, this filled her and communicated itself to the audience. She was considered to be their best mime, and excelled in comedy rôles, such as Lise in *La Fille Mal Gardée*. She had swift and brilliant technical accomplishment, and great determination. She was the first Russian dancer to master the thirty-two *fouettés*, struggling till she learned the trick formerly the secret of the Italian *virtuosi*.

One cannot but wonder what Diaghilev thought of all this. He and Kschessinska were probably the two most self-willed and determined people in the entire Russian ballet. She claimed to have had great admiration for him many years earlier; she had certainly intervened and had his promised subsidy cancelled in 1909. As so often happens, the two were able to respect each other's domineering character.

For her debut, the audience was put into its warmest mood by seeing first its favourite ballet, *Scheherazade*. Then came *Aurore et le Prince*.

It must have been a nerve-wracking moment when the curtain rose and the lace-trimmed frills and the bodice sewn over with real stones became but the appurtenances of a dancer, who must have felt that the audience was composed of lions to whom her partner was about to hurl her. Could anyone at such a moment really believe that such preliminary advertisement would have done anything other than sharpen criticism?

Daily
News
15.11.11

"What would the public say of Mme. Kschessinska if it knew nothing of the sapphires of fabulous size which this famous Russian dancer possesses? if it was ignorant of her friendship with the Tsar; and if it had not been told that she is the wealthiest woman on the stage? Probably that she is a competent dancer of the stereotyped kind."

Daily
Mirror
16.11.11

"The dancing of Mme. Kschessinska is, after all, more important than her jewels; the impression her first performance gives is, on the whole, that she is a dancer of admirable technique with all the points of her profession at her fingers', or rather toes' ends; but that she does not display that added touch of exquisite inspiration shown by Mme. Pavlova."

Daily
Mail
15.11.11

Some critics were better pleased. "She at once conquered everyone by her grace and charm . . . unfortunately the music represents Tchaikovsky at his worst, noisy and vacuous. And the steps of the dances obviously belong to a generation that knew not M. Fokine – they too often verge on the acrobatic music-hall type . . . Rounds of applause greeted her *tour de force* in the Tchaikovsky extract, wherein she danced across the stage on one foot – on tip-toe – whilst, as it were gyrating quite independently with the other." At its second viewing, *Aurore et le Prince*

The
Times
17.11.11

pleased no better. "Even M. Nijinsky leaves one unmoved, and Mme. Kschessinska's share in it is no more than a series of extraordinarily skilful, but often quite unlovely, gymnastics."

The
Standard
15.11.11

It is sad to think that Kschessinska, the first Russian Aurora, chose this particular excerpt for her London début, so that the *Standard* had said after her first night that "the impression left . . . was that her performance was more a question of steps than a character study of any special note . . . we felt that it was technique, and technique alone, upon which she depended for success," whilst acknowledging that the technique was that of a cult "every bit as difficult to acquire as that of any other art."

Daily
Mail
15.11.11

The menu on her first night continued with the exciting *Polovtsian Dances*, and then *Le Carnaval* gave the audience a more agreeable memory of the new dancer to carry home. "London has seen as Columbine Mlle. Elsa Will, Mme. Karsavina, and Mme. Pavlova. The newcomer, in a delicious dress with crimson spots edging white flounces and with cherry bunches in her hair, added one more charming vision to the collection in one's memory. Comparisons would not only be odious but also barely possible . . ."   " . . . In *Le Carnaval*, she won unstinted

The
Times
15.11.11

admiration by her swiftness and lightness of movement, and by her unfailing invention, shown in significant little gestures of hands and shoulders, the raising of a couple of fingers, the sudden withdrawal of a pointed toe, the recognition by the dropping of an eyelid of Harlequin's

Kschessinska's costume for *Le Pavillon d'Armide* was made to the same design (by Benois) as that worn by Karsavina, and originally by Karalli in Paris in 1909. But Kschessinska's jewels were real – the materials look richer – and lace can be discerned through the top layer of the skirt.

coquetting in a corner. M. Nijinsky, too, as Harlequin, was inspired to do perfectly incredible things in less time than it takes to dot the i's in his name."

After her second performance, the *Morning Post* was much more enthusiastic. "*Le Carnaval* . . . provides this most graceful and agile of dancers with the opportunity for the display of the qualities that place her ahead of all the dancers that have appeared since the Russian Ballet began its successful seasons . . . There is so much fascination in her share of the Tchaikovsky ballet that it would be as well to mount the whole work without delay . . ." Morning Post 17.11.11

Next, Kschessinska danced Armida. Whilst this ballet had given great delight in the first season, it had been outclassed by *Les Sylphides* for sheer charm and *Scheherazade* for excitement. "Even with Mme. Karsavina it was still a little dull. Mme. Pavlova displayed her talent by making this somewhat lifeless affair a thing of real beauty and interest. Mme. Kschessinska displays a technical skill which is remarkable, but she has not the personal magnetism of her predecessors. She never makes one forget that she is a *prima ballerina* . . . The Times 20.11.11

The Lady thought otherwise, and, in addition, gave a vivid description of the ballerina's appearance.

"Kschessinska made an excellent impression – a better choice could not have been made. She wore a lovely and original dress. The skirts were the usual half-long, graceful, foamy ones of tulle, but a long overdress of brocade was laced over a front piece of silver tissue to the waist, and then was cut away sharply to the side, forming a long and full coat-shaped back almost to the hem of her full skirts. This brocade was of a gorgeous rich cobalt-blue flowered with coloured bouquets in a branching design, and showed off her graceful, slender form to perfection. She wore ornaments of splendid sapphires set round the square *décolleté*, and sapphires in her ears, whilst over her dark hair a turban of the same deep sapphire-blue was worn, finishing in front with a clasp of sapphires, from which sprang a tall white aigrette. The Lady 30.11.11

"In fact, besides being a finished dancer, she imparts a sense of joyous gaiety which is very captivating."

Roshanara in Oscar Asche's production of *Kismet*, in May, 1911.

left: Princess Serafine Astafieva, niece of Count Tolstoy and sister-in-law of Kschessinska, danced in Diaghilev's company for several years. She appeared as Cleopatra during this season in London. A few years later she took a studio in The Pheasantry, in King's Road, Chelsea, and ran a school whose pupils included Anton Dolin and Dame Alicia Markova, and, later on, Dame Margot Fonteyn. (Dame Anna Neagle took "fancy dancing" classes, to fit herself for a career in musical comedy.) *right:* Sophie Fedorova as the Polovtsian Maiden in the dances from Borodin's opera *Prince Igor*. Bakst and Diaghilev found this beautiful silk, woven in traditional designs, in a market in St. Petersburg.

Diaghilev had found it important to give one of his exotic ballets in each programme. During Kschessinska's reign, he wished to present *Scheherazade.* He came across an unorthodox "find" for his Zobeide this time – Roshanara. She was accorded but few words in notices mainly concerned with Kschessinska – *The Lady,* for example, said, ". . . a very young girl with a slight, almost childish figure, made a fascinating and attractive Zobeide . . ." And in the *Mail,* "The newcomer is an accomplished actress, though she fails to express the pathos and intensity of Madame Karsavina. . ." Daily Mail 15.11.11

Roshanara was only about eighteen, the daughter of an English mother and Anglo-Indian father, brought up in India, travelling all over the country with him on his duties as a government official. She loved Indian dancing, and studied it everywhere. About 1909 she came to Europe with her mother, and attended some dance lessons. She had adopted the name "Roshanara," taking it from a legendary Indian princess of the seventeenth century, who was reputed to have been the first to travel outside her own country. "The name 'Roshanara' is as beautiful as history says the Princess was; its meaning is 'Light-Adorning.' "

Loie Fuller, the American who had created a unique act, with coloured lights playing on yards and yards of chiffon whirling in beautiful space-filling patterns, signed up Roshanara for her company with some kind of contract. When Oscar Asche had put on *Kismet* in London, and it had been running but a month, his "dancer" fell ill, and Loie Fuller lent him Roshanara. She took part in Kismet for a month, from May 22nd, 1911. She was noticed by Pavlova's agent, Daniel Mayer, who said she "ought to be with the Russian Ballet." One way or another, she was engaged by Diaghilev. After the company had departed for Paris, she gave a long interview, ending by saying that she was off to join it. Instead, she joined Pavlova on the English provincial tour which had already started. She later settled in America, gave lectures and recitals, joined Adolf Bolm in his *Ballets Intimes,* and was very friendly with Ted Shawn and Miss Ruth. She never spoke to them of her Diaghilev experiences, the news that she had even had them being a great and complete surprise to Ted Shawn. The Standard 14.12.11 Letter to Author

"The programme of the Russian Ballet has been changed for tonight, according to a last-moment manner so frequent at this house, and so extremely trying to a public anxious to secure seats in advance for any definite performance . . . the public are the only ones who suffer." Daily Mirror 28.11.11

The public was not told that there was a reason for this tiresome alteration in the bill. Kschessinska had insisted on more rehearsals before the first night of *Swan Lake.* This meant that in the changed programme, she had to share the honours with Karsavina, back from St. Petersburg, whose return was welcomed: "Madame Karsavina has floated down to earth again. When the large audience came to Covent Garden last night to welcome her they found her breathing no common air, first in the silvery fantasies of *Les Sylphides* and then in the magic scene with the re-incarnation of the rose she lived and moved in the light of the moon. The slender figures (straight from a canvas of Degas) wreathing dances round her to the strains of Chopin's loveliest tunes form a background which does not need the romantic ruin to evoke the spirit of the music, and both here and in *Le Spectre de la Rose* M. Nijinsky provided a better commentary on what the orchestra was playing than any analytical programme could have succeeded in doing. In *Le Carnaval* he had Mme. Kschessinska for his Columbine, with her droll, dry, minutely calculated steps and her incomparably witty miming. The Times 29.11.11

"*Prince Igor*, with its savagery and its hard, insistent rhythms coming at the end of the evening, made a fine rude awakening from the three delicate dreams which had gone before."

The postponed opening of *Le Lac des Cygnes* finally took place on November 30th. Some thought it was being given in its entirety, but *The Times* knew better: ". . . *Not* in its entirety as a ballet in four acts, but in a truncated version which had the merit of preserving the best of the very unequal numbers that Tchaikovsky wrote at a time when he was in physical suffering and undergoing great mental fatigue. The Times 1.12.11

"Here we leave the green shores of the lake and are transported to the interior of the palace, with crowds of retainers in rich barbaric colouring, organised by a master of the ceremonies who must have sat for his portrait to Ghirlandajo . . ." (Benois referred to them as being "Carpaccio-inspired.") "It is simply a brilliant *pot-pourri* . . . without troubling about any questions of artistic unity. Any dance might be introduced for spectacular purposes, or to show off the technique of an individual dancer, and no one could have been anything but delighted at getting a number from the *Casse-Noisette* ballet (the one with the celesta) introduced for M. Nijinsky into the middle of the revels . . ." (What *did* a man dance to the Sugar-Plum Fairy music?) ". . . Mme. Kschessinska did some extraordinary feats of precisely-calculated design with finesse and a mathematical exactness which suggested a pair of magic compasses controlled by a fantastic philosopher with a taste for humour as well as sense of beauty . . . M. Nijinsky as usual combined skilful and delicate mimicry with astonishingly beautiful dancing. In the second scene he made a radiant figure in cream, gold and orange, with peacock plumes waving in his hair."

Dancing in Petersburg M. Kschessinska 1960

Kschessinska herself has written that, as she had nothing like the success she had anticipated owing to the choice of Aurora for her first performance, she had insisted on inserting a favourite *variation*, to music by Kadletz, into *Swan Lake*. Diaghilev not only agreed, but also leapt gleefully at her suggestion that the Russian violinist Mischa Elman, who happened to be in London, should be invited to play both the *adagio* in the lakeside act, and also this piece, which was always played in Petersburg by a solo violin – usually the leader of the orchestra.

Morning Post 1.12.11

Few members of the company other than the top stars seem to have been mentioned individually in critiques, but the *Morning Post*, which noticed that the swans gliding on the lake "were not real, as in *Königskinder*," mentions "the art of Mlle. Fedorova and M. Bolm, who had an exhilarating *Danse Espagnol* in the second act."

The Lady 7.12.11

Once again, *The Lady* had plenty of precise criticism to offer: "It is a curious jumble of old and new styles; the influence of *Maître de Ballet* Fokine working here and there like restless yeast in the rather heavy choreography of *Maître de Ballet* Petipa, and leaving a good deal of unleavened lump untouched. There is a good deal of work for the prima ballerina, and on Thursday Mme. Kschessinska executed some marvellous technical 'stunts' which commanded admiration mingled with regret that a dancer of such ability should apparently have so little sense of beauty. I have often had occasion to emphasise here that the Russians have rescued classical ballet steps from discredit by making them more fluent, and it is precisely because Kschessinska adopts the bad old staccato methods, giving every step an isolated value, that her dancing does not charm me . . . Nijinsky's performance was exquisite, and his appearance in a 15th century Italian dress a vision of fairyland."

On November 30th, the other ballets were *Le Spectre de la Rose* and *Prince Igor*. On December 2nd, Karsavina danced *Sylphides*, *Spectre*, and, most exciting for London, her glorious success, *L'Oiseau d'Or*, so that the audience could enjoy the experience in one season of seeing both Pavlova and Karsavina dance this with Nijinsky. Kschessinska danced *Swan Lake* again on the 5th, and Roshanara performed in *Scheherazade*, Karsavina not appearing.

The third performance of *Swan Lake* was given on December 7th, and once again, Kschessinska had the lead to herself for the whole evening, giving her success *Le Carnaval* as well. For the last night of the season, Karsavina was left on her own. The huge applause she had received since her return had not been music in Mathilde's ears. There had been formidable rows with Diaghilev in that lovely Savoy suite. Kschessinska's story that Nijinsky was so outraged by the applause *she* attracted that he tore his costume to bits seems most unlikely; Karsavina said that the rage was directed against herself. However, the attitude of the audience could not be altered. Kschessinska obviously made up her mind that she would leave after her final *Lac*, for the last throw-away already shows the cast-lists for the last nights clearly.

The final critique of the season to appear in *The Times* struck one as being written in a familiar style; how useful, in those days, if one had a harmless hobby-horse, to be politically lined up with the Editor of that august journal! Sir George Scott Robertson must have wangled it somehow so that he was allowed to act as critic on the last night, though anonymously:

The Times 11.12.11

"They finished, very appropriately, with the four most popular pieces in their repertory, the *Carnaval*, the *Sylphs*, the *Vision of the Rose*, and *Scheherazade*. If room could also have been found for the Borodin dances the programme would have been complete.

". . . But it is certainly to be regretted that the production of Tchaikovsky's *Swan Lake* was deferred so long, that its very great success has been interrupted by the end of the season . . . we would suggest to the organisers of the ballet that, on their next visit, they should attempt to give us at least a substantial portion of one of the other greater Russian ballets, by preference *The Sleeping Beauty* and Stravinsky's *Bird of Fire.*" (One Stravinski!) ". . . Some more Glinka, too, would be most welcome – say the Mazurka from *Zhisn za Tsarya.*" (Possibly Sir George never liked to confess that his French wasn't up to understanding the points Diaghilev had made in his letter in March. One wonders whether they ever met – and, perhaps, whether the enthusiasm expressed in the *Morning Post* on November 17th did not also have a familiar air about it.) However, of *Scheherazade* he said, ". . . the most splendid – leaves the deepest impression on the memory. It will serve to keep our recollection of these extraordinary artists fresh until they come again."

"The wrench of a painful parting is over," said the faithful Richard Capell. "The sylphs and light-footed fauns who have revealed to us a new art – ballet-dancing resuscitated and transformed from a decrepit bore into an unimagined joy – have gone, and Covent Garden will know them no more until next summer. By way of farewell the ballet performed their four most wholly beautiful pieces with more enchantment than ever. And few indeed of the countless performers of fame who have appeared on that stage have received such homage from a Covent Garden audience.

Daily Mail 10.12.11

"There was thunderous applause at the end of each of the first three pieces, and at the conclusion the audience, from the front row of the stalls to the dark mass of enthusiasts standing at the back of the gallery, applauded, cheered, and waved handkerchiefs for fully twenty minutes. The dancers received many tributes. Among them was a sheaf of flowers and a gold trinket in the form of a ballet-shoe with an inscription for Madame Karsavina, and a huge laurel wreath tied with British colours for M. Nijinsky, which had been subscribed for by frequenters of the gallery."

So ended the only two seasons when Diaghilev could call his company "THE IMPERIAL RUSSIAN BALLET." How did he himself assess the results? He had given London ballets of historical interest without vouchsafing any helpful historical information. He had smothered any mistrust under the comforting blanket of his most successful ballets. He had shown London three very different ballerinas. Had his judgement of them been the same as London's? Kschessinska had London's curiosity, Pavlova (in Diaghilev's ballets,) its amazed admiration, but Karsavina had its heart.

1912

ROYAL OPERA, COVENT GARDEN

JUNE 12th - AUGUST 1st

FIRST PERFORMANCES IN ENGLAND

June 12th: *Thamar*
              (Balakirev, Fokine, Bakst.)
              Paris, 20.5.1912

June 18th: *L'Oiseau de Feu*
              (Stravinsky, Fokine, Golovine.)
              Paris, 25.6.1910

July 9th: *Narcisse*
              (Tcherepnin, Fokine, Bakst.)
              Monte Carlo, 26.4.1911

REPERTOIRE

Le Carnaval   *Scheherazade*
Le Lac des Cygnes   *Le Spectre de la Rose*
Le Pavillon d'Armide   *Les Sylphides*
Polovtsian Dances

COMPANY

Astafieva S., Baranovitch I., Baranovitch II., Biber, Bonietska, Dobrouloubova, Dombrovska, Fedorova S., Frohmann M., Guliuk, Hubert, Jultizka, Karsavina, Khokhlova, Klementovitch, Konietska, Kopetzinska, Kovalievska, Kulchitzka, Maicherska, Nijinska, Pflanz, Piltz, Reisen, Stahlko, Tcherepanova, Tchernicheva, Yezerska, Zaechtelina.

Bolm, Bourman, Cecchetti, Fedorov, Frohmann, Gavrilov, Grigoriev, Gudin, Kegler, Kobelev, Kostecki, Kotchetovsky, Kovalsky, Kremnev, Nijinsky, Oumansky, Rakhmanov, Romanov B., Romanov V., Semenov, Sergueiev, Statkevitch, Toboiko, Varjinsky, Zailich, Zelinsky.

CONDUCTORS

Tcherepnin, Rhené-Baton, Beecham

THE FIREBIRD

The
Times
13.6.12

"The gaiety of Paris is eclipsed. The Russian dancers have deserted her. After providing once again the chief sensation of the season, they winged their flight across the sea that no longer sunders, and alighted on the scene of their English triumphs – the boards of Covent Garden."

Daily
Mail
13.6.12

The Times was as enchanted as every other paper to welcome the Ballet back to London. Curiously, no comment whatsoever seems to have been passed on the change in its description, for it was now plainly called "The Russian Ballet organised by M. Serge de Diaghilev." Richard Capell was "the present writer, who confesses to having witnessed *Le Carnaval* about thirty times here and in Paris, and to have been as fascinated last night as ever."

The
Times
13.6.12

The opening programme consisted of that beloved work, and *Thamar*, the new ballet to Balakirev's music. *The Times* gave details of slight changes in the décor of *Carnaval.* "When the curtain went up last night and disclosed the familiar view of two rococo sofas (red and cream this year instead of red and blue,) the sole note of colour against the green curtains (green this year instead of purple,) a thrill of joy went through the house. The world was once more a world of fantasy, where Pierrot might sob and wave distracted sleeves and Harlequin spin lightning pirouettes before the laughing eyes of Columbine, but where neither tears nor laughter were allowed to scratch more than the surface of our emotion – just enough to tickle our sensibilities, but not to be a charge upon our senses."

Daily
Telegraph
13.6.12

In the *Telegraph*, Madame Karsavina's performance was hailed as "even more accomplished, not, perhaps, technically, but artistically, than a year ago." Richard Capell's thirty viewings must surely have been a record, and given him pride of place for knowledgeability. "M. Bolm, the melancholy Pierrot, was once more eluded by Mlle. Nijinska as an adorable Butterfly. M. Nijinsky – Harlequin – gambolled with elfin humour and demonic bounds. There were the enchantingly pretty Mlle. Piltz (Chiarina) and Mlle. Baranovitch (Estrella) – visions of an idealised 1830. And Mme. Karsavina, the wittiest of fairies, the most pathetic of *poupées*, the airiest and most bewitching of superhuman mortals. But, alas! the blue curtain of the *Carnaval* we knew last year has gone, and green is in its place, a green that quarrels with Estrella's and Chiarina's china-blue flounces. The blue curtain must and shall come back."

Daily
Mail
13.6.12

Only one other ballet was given that first night, the curtain-raiser having been the short opera, *Il Segreto di Susanna,* by Wolf-Ferrari. Karsavina, their charming enchantress, was transformed into the cruel Georgian Queen, Thamar, luring adorers to her bed for a night of love which was followed by death in the morning. This ballet did not quite succeed in captivating "the largest and most brilliant audience of the season." Balakirev's music was conducted by Mr. Thomas Beecham, "warmly received on this his first appearance (as conductor) at Covent Garden in any other season than his own."

Daily
News
13.6.12

In another Chelsea studio, in Glebe Place, Glyn Philpot, A.R.A., painted this magnificent study of Karsavina as Thamar, resting on her voluptuous couch, alert for the signal which would announce the arrival of her prey.

Daily
Telegraph
13.6.12
The curtain rose, "after a portentously long interval," on "a scene in a beautiful castle amid the snows of the Dariol, where Queen Thamar holds a perpetual fête. Lying in front of a large window, Thamar surveys a mountain, the roads, and the river Terek, the turbulent waters of which surround her dwelling." The story is well known – the ballet "a brilliant affair of every imaginable variety of purple and other colours, of Oriental and especially Russian costume, of fantastic rhythms, and grace, of some charm, and of more tragedy. Indeed, Madame Karsavina seems the picture of tragedy, as she rises from one of the most luxurious couches we ever saw, to greet the Stranger, most delightfully played and danced by the clever M. Bolm." The *Telegraph* added that it was a most welcome addition to the repertoire.

Daily
Mail
13.6.12
"Thamar is the Queen, and her chamber is the topmost turret room, with steeply sloping walls of rose-pink brick. Who shall tell the exotic gorgeousness of the garb of her Court," (said Richard Capell,) "the quaint musicians' aspect, or the wild soldiers' frantic measures? Thamar is Mme. Karsavina, lithe in miraculous lilac clothes, and of a dreadful pallor – the victim of her own cruel voluptuousness.

"From her turret she spies a wandering prince. He is haled to the castle. The night passes in a passionate orgy. At daybreak the Queen's caprice is exhausted. The young stranger is stabbed, and drops through a door down from the turret into a torrent. The Queen sleeps, but watchers spy a second stranger. She awakes, and from the turret window waves a rose-red scarf." Thus, as *The Times* put it succinctly, "she signals him to approach, and so – *da capo*!"

Cléopâtre and *Scheherazade* were not, however, ousted from their pre-eminent positions in the hearts of the audience, faithful to their first two examples of Bakst and Fokine combining to thrill them with the exotic. The *Pall Mall Gazette*, which had erroneously awarded these two artists the honour of directing the company, did not like *Thamar* at all. "One is oppressed by the endlessness of this orgy of perverted desire. Somewhere, one feels, in a high-placed castle, ringed round by winds and waters, this horrible woman is waving and waving her scarf for evermore. Perhaps this is an allegory, but it is an allegory not worth the telling. And why are all the dramas of Bakst pitched on the same note? Why is there always this inhuman delight in kisses with a taste of blood? . . . One must say a word, there is no space for more, of the music of Balakirev. M. Bakst has never been more fortunate. It was rich in barbarous colour, it had a throbbing undercurrent, and it rose to passionate heights."

Pall Mall Gazette 13.6.12

Tuesday, June 18th, 1912, should be ringed in red in the diaries of all music critics, for on this date *L'Oiseau de Feu* was first produced in London, and as they wrote of Stravinsky's music for the first time, they were inaugurating an era of writing about Stravinsky's music. This was to become the subject of fearful controversy after the war, thousands of words a week being quilled then about his later works. *L'Oiseau de Feu*, however, met with almost unanimous approval, and with unanimous agreement that here was a composer who had "started something." What a pity, therefore, that whoever reported the new ballet for *The Times* should, on this occasion, so far forget himself as to be confused by the maddening transfer of the name of the ballet from the *pas de deux* in *Le Festin* – Tchaikovsky, of course, – to the full ballet now completed. "The music was by Stravinsky, a young Russian composer who is only known here so far by the dance from this ballet that was given two years ago by Mme. Karsavina and M. Koslov."

The Times 19.6.12

Every paper carried a version of the Stravinsky story. He was described as "a young Russian composer who was originally a pupil of Rimsky-Korsakov, but has settled down in Paris, and is very much in the modern "movement" of that capital. His music is impressionistic in character, very advanced in its idiom, free and varied in its rhythm, and elaborately scored. Its new and subtle harmonies, its delicate broidery, and its unfailing *esprit* give it a charm of its own, and though it is hardly the sort of music that one would expect in alliance with the choreographic art, it fits the action of *L'Oiseau de Feu* like the proverbial glove, and seems to be very congenial to the dancers." The *Telegraph* had already mentioned that, though the name of Stravinsky "figures not in our musical dictionaries, this fact does not argue that M. Stravinsky is unknown."

Sunday Times 23.6.12

Daily Telegraph 19.6.12

Musical circles being familiar with the work of Richard Strauss, several critics chose to try to convey something of the new composer's music by comparisons. "Mr. Stravinsky's music is ultra-Straussian," declared the *Daily News and Leader*, through its new critic, the Strauss expert, Alfred Kalisch, (successor to E.A. Baughan.) "The orchestral effects are amazingly clever, and mirror the action with amazing fidelity. It seems to have no defined rhythm, yet to be the essence of rhythm. One would like to hear it when one has nothing to look at." (Kalisch was not only a critic – he could participate as well. In 1910, Beecham's Opera season at Covent Garden ran into trouble when the censor objected to the text of Strauss's *Salome*. Kalisch re-wrote it, bowdlerizing it; the censor passed it, the cast rehearsed it. At an early stage on the first night, however, Ackté, the Salome, forgot which version she was singing, and reverted to the censored text. As it was being sung in German, and was, anyway, drowned by the orchestra, no one noticed – least of all the Lord Chamberlain, who sent for Beecham afterwards, and, instead of sending him to the block on Tower Hill, as Beecham averred he anticipated, complimented him effusively, and added, "I could not leave the theatre without thanking you and your colleagues for the complete way in which you have met and gratified all our wishes." Possibly their judgment had been tempered by Ackté herself. Unusually, at that period, she was a slender soprano. She had turned to the great couturier Worth to design her gauzy costume, and, instead of disappearing whilst a ballet dancer took over, the normal practice, she had made a rousing success of the *Dance of the Seven Veils* herself. The seventh veil dropped to reveal most of her exquisite torso, which undoubtedly spoke more eloquently than the text.)

Daily News & Leader 19.6.12

A Mingled Chime: Thomas Beecham

Of Golovine's beautiful designs for *L'Oiseau de Feu*, only that for the Firebird herself was unsuccessful. It was worn by Karsavina for the first few performances, in Paris in 1910, when, in the same bill, she and Nijinsky danced their *pas de deux* from *Le Festin* – re-named *L'Oiseau d'Or*. Just as the title, *Oiseau de Feu*, had confusingly been transferred to Stravinsky's new ballet, so, too, was Karsavina's costume – Bakst's glorious fantasy of flame-coloured plumes. In Hoppé's famous portrait, taken in London in 1912, Karsavina's beauty and mystery were captured in the pose which characterized the magical *Oiseau de Feu*.

Kalisch continued his review of *Firebird*:

". . . Whatever else may or may not be said about it, it is certainly the most remarkable and most original of all the things they have done . . . Perhaps its very strangeness may stand in the way of its popularity, but it ought to draw all London.

"It required as many creators as a musical comedy," he went on. "The whole ballet is a riot of rich colour and fantastic movement . . . it is beautiful and bizarre at once. The dance of the bewitched followers of Kostchei, which ends in their all falling prone, is one of the most curiously fascinating things imaginable, with touches of quaint comedy. The dance of the enchanted Princesses is full of the daintiest charm. The scene in which the Prince captures the bird is deliciously original. The harmonies of the dresses and the fanciful colourings and fantastic outlines of the scene defy description."

Daily Telegraph 19.6.12 When it, too, had told the story, the *Daily Telegraph* added that "Of the dancing of all concerned, of Mesdames Karsavina and Piltz, of the great M. Bolm as Ivan, and M. Cecchetti as the Immortal, no praise can be too high."

The Times 19.6.12 *The Times* observed: "The ornithologists will have to add a chapter to the text-books. A new bird – the Firebird – *L'Oiseau de Feu* – has been discovered by MM. Fokine and Stravinsky. She flew on to the stage at Covent Garden last night, disguised as Mme. Karsavina, and after a short delighted flutter fell a prey to the young Prince, Ivan Tsarevitch, (M. Adolf Bolm.) As the price of her freedom she offers him one of her plumes; he accepts it, and she flies off, without a note of song to thank him (for it is a world of ballet and not of opera,) into the soft blue shadows of the night.

Hoppé's portrait showed the Firebird in repose:
Valentine Gross's drawing captured her in flight,
flashing across the stage, delicate hands fluttering,
eyes deeply mysterious. Trial sketches for the
fluttering hands add to the sense of movement.

"It makes a good fairy story," *The Times* continued, "but except for what the bird does there is little dancing of much choreographic merit in it. Some of the miming is expressive, more particularly that of the bird, the young hero, and the god . . . but the dance, at the opening, of the 13 young ladies in their night-dresses was dull, and many of the antics of the buffoons were ugly, though the stage picture as a whole was attractive with the brilliant, huddled, whirling masses centred round M. Bakst's superbly designed bird against M. Golovine's background sketched in somewhat the manner of Vierge."

The *Observer* loved the work. "In comparison with the work of Borodin, Glazounov, Observer 23.6.12 Arensky, Balakireff and others, whose characteristics in ballet-writing are essentially rhythmical in a well-defined and almost conventional way, and provide all the technical necessities for the technical display of the dancer, *L'Oiseau de Feu* would seem to place almost hopeless difficulties in the way of satisfactory execution. It is in achieving this that the Russian Ballet and the wonderful Mme. Karsavina have accomplished a performance that is on a higher artistic level than anything they have yet done, an assertion that is only strengthened by the recollection of many magnificent productions." The *Sunday Times* was of much the same opinion: "Mme. Karsavina – whose staying power and variety were alike exhibited that evening, for she had earlier appeared in *Thamar* and *Les Sylphides* – took the name-part, and quite unforgettable was her bird-like grace and fleetness of movement, and the suggestion of palpitating fear and violated purity with which she shrank from the arms of her captor." The first matinée performance of the new ballet had been given on the Thursday afternoon, and had "a crowded Sunday Times 23.6.12 house, – albeit it was Gold Cup Day at Ascot – showing how eagerly the public seizes every opportunity of seeing these famous dancers."

The
Lady
27.6.12

Daily
News
24.6.12

Though the third new ballet, and the only one with a part for Nijinsky, was not put on until the season had been in full swing for four weeks, interest never flagged. The *Lady* started off the list of Society leaders present on a Saturday night by noting that the Grand Duchess Marie Georgievna was paying her second visit, and that a huge bunch of damask roses was presented to Karsavina after *Le Spectre de la Rose.* Kalisch said that Nijinsky was "even more romantic than before." He added, "The dance is a perfect specimen of a kind of art which belongs to a past generation, and as such annoys the ultra-modern enthusiast for the dance, who takes the art seriously, as much as *La Sonnambula* irritates a Debussyite. Still it remains perfect of its kind, and the audience, which recalled the two about ten times, obviously thought so."

Daily
News &
Daily
Mail
3.7.12

When, on July 2nd, the shortened version of *Le Pavillon d'Armide* was given for the first time in the season, "the observed of all observers were M. Paderewski in the front row of the stalls (as the guest of Lady Ripon,) and Master Anthony Asquith in a pit tier box." The previous evening had seen the very first Royal Command Performance at the Palace Theatre, when Pavlova had danced solos, and also with her current partner, Novikoff.

The
Lady
4.7.12

Earlier on, Admiral and Mrs. Beatty had given a dinner-party followed by an entertainment in the gardens of Hanover Lodge, Regent's Park. "A natural stage was arranged in a clearing between the trees, which were all lit up with little balloons of coloured electric light, and from somewhere behind the trees strong waves of electric light threw a radiance upon the grassy stage, where a charming performance of a pierrot play specially written by Rostand was acted by French artistes. An invisible orchestra discoursed sweet music," said *The Lady.* "Afterwards, when Mme. Karsavina began her dance from *Les Sylphides* to the strains of Chopin's music, the effect the dancers made lightly tripping up that sylvan glade, made brilliant by artificial moonlight, was something really wonderful . . . But quite suddenly, alas! the rain came down, quite a gentle shower at first, which gradually settled into a downpour, and there were some hundreds of ladies sitting in basket chairs without any kind of 'cover' to which to retreat. At first they bravely sat on, hoping for the best, but I saw them with raindrops shining in their hair and obscuring the brilliance of their diamond tiaras when at last they turned tail and fled helter-skelter into the house." Possibly the principal guests, who had included Prince and Princess Louis of Battenburg and Winston Churchill and his brother Jack and sister-in-law Lady Gwendoline, had been on some balcony – or did they, too, have to sound retreat?

The Lady also described a dinner-party given by Lady Ripon at Coombe, for fifty. "The performance was given in the newly-built theatre, when not only did Madame Karsavina and M. Nijinsky dance several of their most effective dances . . . but Mme. Lipkowska, of the Opera, was singing . . . Among the guests at dinner were . . . Mr. and Mrs. John Lavery, M. Jacques Blanche, M. Bakst, Mme. Karsavina, Mme. Lipkowska, and M. Nijinsky," (mentioning here only the artists amongst the Society names.)

The
Lady
11.7.12

The following week *The Lady* described another lavish private entertainment: "The Russian dancers were the *clou* of the evening at the party given at the Ritz by the Aga Khan, when Madame Karsavina and M. Nijinsky were joined by the renowned Parisian dancer Mlle. Zambelli, who came over from Paris on purpose to perform a trio with the Russian dancers, which was as novel as it was effective . . . The ballroom at the Ritz was most beautifully arranged with flowers for this wonderful entertainment. The stage itself had a background of trellis, upon which vines and roses were trailing in profusion; the three round tables at which the Aga Khan had entertained some forty guests beforehand were massed with roses in pyramid form – that of the host was done with amber roses, and the other two were all pink and all crimson – whilst the supper-room, when the entertainment came to an end, was glowing with the beauty of the deep red roses which decked the tables and were massed in the corner, everything being done with Oriental splendour."

The Lady referred to the story that when Rimsky-Korsakov had first heard his pupil's *Firebird*, he had said, "Stop playing this horrible thing; otherwise I might begin to like it!" No such attitudes attached anywhere to the music of Tcherepnin, composer of *Le Pavillon d'Armide* and of the other new work of the season, *Narcisse.* This ballet had been created in 1911, and given then in Monte Carlo and Paris. In 1912, it was Diaghilev's choice for London of a ballet with a classical setting. (London had already been told that it was not to see *L'Après-Midi d'un Faune*, Nijinsky's first ballet, which had created a scandal in Paris in May.)

The
Lady
13.6.12

Valentine Gross turned to the style of Georges Barbier for this subtly-organised study of Nijinsky-Narcisse, in love with his own image, with his beautiful coiffure, his maquillage, his carefully-pleated transparent Chlamys, all reflected back at him in the lake whose distant shore continues the rhythms of the curves of his body.

Narcisse was widely reviewed. "The mythological story of the beautiful youth falling in love with the reflection of himself in the water and dying from the result of his hopeless passion, only to be resuscitated as a flower, is simple enough; but the Russian dancers have woven round this tragic little incident close on an hour's enchanting entertainment. *Narcisse* is, in fact, one of the most charming pieces of this nature that we have yet seen at Covent Garden. This, it must be confessed, is the verdict that follows nearly every new effort M. Fokine puts before us . . . the Russians have the happy knack of going one better each time." The Standard 10.7.12

"BOEOTIA IN BOW STREET" was Alfred Kalisch's heading in the *Daily News*. "It is a singularly poetic production. The scene, with its cloudy purple sky, the rock-hewn images of the gods, rocky bridge at the back with the bright sunshine behind, is one of M. Bakst's triumphs. The costumes are very beautiful and wonderfully accurate reproduction of classic models." Daily News 10.7.12

Daily
Mail
10.7.12

"A glimpse of the antique world, a Theocritean idyll made visible — this is the Russian's new ballet, *Narcisse*. M. Bakst has painted the weeping foliage of an Arcadian grove. M. Fokine has conceived idyllic and bacchanalian measures for the sylvan sprites, the nymphs, the shepherds of the piece. But no scenes of a Regency classicism must be expected," said Richard Capell. "These Muscovites evoke antiquity with new spells. Hence the grotesqueness of the green elves who sport in the twilight; the vivid hues of the bacchantes' lovely garb; the mysterious blue-greenness of this grove sacred to Demeter.

"The entrance of the young Boeotians, come to do honour to the goddess, is a pure delight; this new classicism is truer than the old. The gracious measures of a bewitching Boeotian maiden (Mlle. Piltz) and the superb, delirious dance of a bacchante (Mlle. Nijinska) – these verily bring antique Arcadia before one's eyes, the cortège from a Grecian urn made animate. Then comes the purple-robed, love-lorn Echo – Mme. Karsavina – at whose prayer the scornful Narcissus (M. Nijinsky) is brought to his undoing . . .

"Accompanying these delicious scenes is music by M. Tcherepnin, who is revealed as a composer of unsuspected poesy and fancy. Hitherto he was only known by his *Pavillon d'Armide*. The music of *Narcisse* differs as much from the formality of those pretty strains as does the theme. There was much applause last night."

The
Times
10.7.12

Sunday
Times
14.7.12

The Times was rather more critical of the music: ". . . short reiterated figures which do not flow, together with noisy climaxes, are the chief resources." The *Sunday Times* felt that "the music to the ballet is extremely skilful and interesting. It is free as to design and is full of fresh and charming colour effects, the xylophone and celeste being employed very happily, and a very notable feature is the use of a hidden chorus singing *bouche fermée* passages which seem to voice the inarticulate moods of nature."

At the Fine Art Society's Galleries in Bond Street, a Bakst exhibition was the first of work by Diaghilev's artist to be held in London, and the Society brought out a most luxurious book with fine plates – the English version of Arsène Alexandre's *The Decorative Art of Leon Bakst*. Cocteau wrote notes on the ballets. The de luxe edition (limited to eighty copies) was sold with an original watercolour by Bakst in each copy, price £20; the world edition, limited to 920 copies, cost £5. The photographer Hoppé held an exhibition of his ballet photographs at his studio in Baker Street, the Fine Art Society also publishing an album of them. Tickets for the theatre were at a premium.

Observer
23.6.12

The Bakst exhibition was reviewed by P.G. Konody:

"The most cursory survey . . . cannot fail to reveal how much the Russian Ballet . . . (I am told this advanced form represents a kind of secessionist movement which is not at all typical of the ballet as fostered in St. Petersburg) owes much to the genius and to the poetic imagination of this truly great designer." Seeing a resemblance, especially in drawings, to the work of Aubrey Beardsley, Konody went on: ". . . Endowed by Nature with a taste for beautiful unreality, akin to Beardsley's, M. Bakst frankly adopted the Englishman's language of expression. But M. Bakst began where Beardsley ended. He added to the rhythm of line an equally magnificent rhythm of colour. And . . . he substituted for the rather perverse super-refinement of Beardsley's eroticism the frank sensuality of the East . . . He allows his erotic imagination unbridled play . . . His ideas are poured forth without reference to historical costume plates . . . There is no living artist who could rival M. Bakst's stage designs."

With only seven performances left, Diaghilev put on *Le Lac des Cygnes,* which Karsavina danced for him for the first time. Mischa Elman once again played the solos. The national dances "took the house by storm: in fact, after each act, not only the two principal dancers, but also the chiefs of the combined ballets, were called repeatedly before the curtain." The King and Queen were present. She sat in the normal Royal Box, entertaining the Grand Duke and the Grand Duchess George of Russia. His Majesty sat below in the "omnibus" box, with the Russian Ambassador.

The
Lady
1.8.12

At the close of the season, Baron Gunzburg had enough money left after subsidizing Diaghilev to give a final party at the Carlton, and enough power of persuasion to get Pavlova, Karsavina and Kyasht all to dance for his guests. The papers forecast a spring season to start off the following year.

And in Florence, Gordon Craig, (stage designer and producer, son of Ellen Terry,) brought out a number of his quarterly theatrical review, *The Mask,* (which certainly had no effect on the box office.) Under some seventy pseudonyms, he wrote his stuff and printed and published it and sold it to subscribers. He may be said to have declared his interest when, fulminating against the Russian Ballet, "John Balance" said, "They stole an idea or two from the only original dancer of the age, the American," – (Isadora, of course,) – "and another idea or two from the most advanced scene designers of Europe," – (himself, presumably,) – "and super-imposed all these upon the wirey artificial framework of the old French Ballet. They invited painters of taste to assist them. They knew that some painters who are not very great as painters are only too delighted to air their knowledge of colour and decoration in the more refined atmosphere of the footlights. It gives them a chance . . . Bakst is ugly because of his clumsy sense of the sensual. All his women . . . are drugged and in a kind of sofa orgy. They seem to hate ecstasy and they adore a good wriggle . . . the costumes he puts them in to are mute; they want to speak and cannot; they are the old re-furbished wardrobe of the old Racinet and Sarah Bernhardt, save that these two spoiled us often with stockings, underwear and sleeves, vests and pinafores . . . Many of his designs for costumes have lately been published, but to his eternal undoing photographs of these same costumes have been published at the same time. These photographs give M.Bakst away, for the designs and the photographs are unlike each other, and the stage with which he has merely flirted opens its artificial arms for a last embrace. M. Bakst is dead . . . The stage does not like philanderers . . . and M. Bakst was a philanderer . . . R.I.P."

The Mask Vol. 4., 1912

As the quarterly numbers rolled off the press, so did the curious comments, apostrophizing himself, concealing himself, addressing Djageleff (as he spelt him,) praising Nijinsky but curiously referring to conversing with the latter "in six languages. . ."

There is no doubt that the visit of "the American" to Petersburg in 1905 had helped to hasten the acceptance of new ideas as ballet moved from the nineteenth to the twentieth century: Gordon Craig's affected insincerities had a core of truth in them. But to the London public, the annual visits of the Russian Ballet were now firmly established as periods eagerly anticipated and filled with excitement.

1913 (SPRING)

ROYAL OPERA, COVENT GARDEN

FEBRUARY 4th - MARCH 7th

FIRST PERFORMANCES IN ENGLAND.

February 4th: *Petrouchka*
(Stravinsky, Fokine, Benois.)
Paris, 13.6.1911.

February 17th: *L'Après-Midi d'un Faune*
(Debussy, Nijinsky, Bakst.)
Paris 29.5.1912

February 27th: *Le Dieu Bleu*
(Hahn, Fokine, Bakst.)
Paris, 13.5.1912

REPERTOIRE

Le Carnaval	*Polovtsian Dances*
Cléopâtre	*Le Spectre de la Rose*
Narcisse	*Les Sylphides*
L'Oiseau et le Prince	*Thamar*

COMPANY

Astafieva S., Baranovitch I., Baranovitch II., Bewicke, Bibikova, Boni, Bonietska, Dombrovska, Guliuk, Hubert, Jultizka, Karsavina, Khokhlova, Klementovitch, Konietska, Kopetzinska, Kovalievska, Maicherska, Nelidova, Nijinska, Pavinska, Pflanz, Piltz, Poire, Pozerska, Rambert, Razoumovitch, Schidlova, Tcherepanova, Tchernicheva, Wassilievska, Yezerska, Zulicka.

Bolm, Bourman, Cecchetti, Fedorov, Frohmann, Gavrilov, Grigoriev, Gudin, Ivanovsky, Kegler, Kobelev, Kostecki, Kotchetovsky, Kovalsky, Kremnev, Malignin, Nijinsky, Oumansky, Rakhmanov, Romanov B., Savitzky, Semenov, Statkevitch, Tarassov, Toboiko, Varjinsky, Voronzov, Zelinsky.

CONDUCTORS

Beecham, Monteux, Steimann, Rhené-Baton

PETROUCHKA – THE FAUN

"On Tuesday night," said *The Lady*, "we went to Covent Garden for the first performance of the Russian Ballet, and I heard that there was such an unprecedented application for seats that they were sold out six weeks beforehand! Friends of mine with great difficulty obtained some through a private source for double the money the day before."

The Lady 15.2.13

Beecham had opened this mixed season of Opera and Ballet a few days earlier with *Der Rosenkavalier*, long awaited in London.

On the morning of the first programme of ballet, Richard Capell gave an excellent historical survey of the art since the triumphs of Taglioni and Cerrito, and the other stars of the Romantic era. Heading it "A REVOLUTION IN BALLET," he explained that "the old ballets are still supreme in Russia, where the new 'Russian Ballet,' as we understand it, is looked on unwelcomingly and with distress.

Daily Mail 4.2.13

". . . Previous indications as to M. Fokin's share in this renascence, which to the London spectator would otherwise have been conjectural, were furnished by the Ballet's performance here on a few occasions, of spectacles of an earlier era. Such were *Gisella*, *The Swan Lake*, and *Aurora and the Prince*. In spite of fine passages, such as the national dances in *The Swan Lake*, one felt the usual spell relaxed. The music was found insipid, the motives of the pieces weak, their development diffuse, and the actual dancing – though beautifully executed as ever – monotonous and not seldom stiffly acrobatic."

Capell also discussed the part played by the painters in the newer ballet: "Of course the greatest of these is Leon Bakst, author of the peacock-coloured harem of *Scheherazade*, of the temple in *Cléopâtre* with its monstrous orange columns, and how many other strange and superb visions, all triumphs in the fearless use of the fiercest hues and in exquisite and curious detail."

"Here, then," he remarked later, "we have the twin lords of colour and motion, Bakst and Fokin. The authorship of the plots and scenarios is more obscure. Part is, too, the work of MM. Bakst and Fokin, and part may be ascribed to M. de Diaghilev."

It is curious that the name of Alexandre Benois did not occur once in that whole long column – Benois, who, in addition to designing them, was the author of the "book" of *Le Pavillon d'Armide*, (Diaghilev's opening ballet both in Paris in 1909 and London in 1911,) and of *Petrouchka*, about to have its London première that very evening.

In 1913, London was to see all three of Nijinsky's ballets to date – so much more revolutionary than Fokine's as to make his seem merely evolutionary. If the new ideas of Fokine were anathema inside Russia, what new word could have been coined for the reception Nijinsky's experiments would have been accorded there in 1913?

The season opened with *Petrouchka*. The scene is the Butter Market held in the great Admiralty Square in St. Petersburg, about 1830. An old magician has set up his booth, and displays the three animated life-size puppets he has created. There is a Dancer, and her rival swains – Petrouchka, the ugly clown, and the brilliant, flamboyant Moor. The Dancer prefers the Moor to the pathetic Petrouchka, but Petrouchka has been endowed with a degree of human suffering, and bursts into the Moor's gorgeously decorated cell just as the Dancer is about to succumb to the Moor's charms. The Moor kills Petrouchka. The horrified crowd is being soothed by the Magician, who shakes before them a sawdust puppet; but just as the Magician is demonstrating this to be but a doll, the ghost of Petrouchka appears on the roof of his booth.

The
Times
5.2.13
All the critics gave long expositions of the plot, which they found very mystifying. *The Times* summed it up: "The old Showman glides in and calms everyone with a gesture. 'That? Why, He's only a puppet. Look at the sawdust pouring out of the cut in his throat!' It is all horribly *macabre* and extraordinarily effective. There are a few dull moments in the Moor's show box and one expects a longer glimpse of the puppets before the final scuffle, but the whole thing is refreshingly new and refreshingly Russian, more Russian, in fact, than any ballet we have had. The atmosphere of the crowd on a sunny day and at the end of the tragedy in a gathering snowstorm is skilfully differentiated from the human . . . The orchestration is very brilliant throughout, a piano, xylophone, and celesta being employed as well as the usual orchestra. The ballet was very favourably received, though the house seemed a little puzzled by the newness of it all . . ."

The
Lady
13.2.13
Perhaps it was to consecrate this Russian-ness that Lady Cunard, Thomas Beecham's admiring patroness, was observed wearing a very beautiful Russian diadem with her dress of blue and gold brocade.

Observer
9.2.13
The *Observer* thought the work "entirely inaccessible to judgment by old or ordinary standards. It is supremely clever, supremely modern, and supremely baroque. The attempt to insinuate a certain sense of actual humanity into curious puppets playing the inevitable and commonplace drama of three, under conditions that remove all semblance of reality from their actions, is successful only in so far as the imagination can rise to the occasion."

Observer
9.2.13
Similar communings about the plot in many papers seem to be pure padding: the comments about the music had far more validity, for the public had no doubts at all about *Petrouchka*– the public loved it. "The agitation, the ebullient despair of the soulless Petrouchka is depicted with mercurial lightness; the provocative Dancer through her tragedy to delightfully inconsequential phrases; and the actions of the valiant Moor, with his wooden scimitar, receive a calm and sarcastic comment from all sides of the orchestra, which approaches absolute genius as an example of characterisation. . . The score is tremendously difficult, despite the simple thematic material, and a word of praise is certainly due to the unnamed pianist for a very brilliant and entirely characteristic accomplishment that would have done credit to the most expert pianola."

Daily
Mail
6.2.13
The *Daily Mail* had interviewed Stravinsky after the first night, and quoted him as saying, "The Beecham orchestra is marvellous. I suppose my two ballets are about as difficult in their way as any music in existence. They have never been better played in France, Austria, Germany or Hungary than by this orchestra. My admiration for the English band is enhanced when I carry my memory back to past performances of *Petrouchka*. One orchestra, which is very widely regarded as the finest in Europe, gave endless trouble. Oboists and trumpeters declared their parts to be unplayable, and, indeed, performed them as if they really were."

Daily
Mail
6.2.13
Diaghilev himself was in expansive mood and equally enthusiastic about the British orchestra. "I was so delighted with the experiment of using an English orchestra at our last Berlin season that after our return from South America a year hence I have arranged for the Beecham orchestra to tour with us in Russia. This, by the way, will be our first introduction to the Russian public. It is not generally known in the west that only four of our spectacles, and these the earliest, have ever been presented in Russia; and even these have been done in a more conventional way there than here." (These were *Le Pavillon d'Armide*, *Les Sylphides*, called *Chopiniana*, and *Cléopâtre*, called *Une Nuit d'Egypte*, all given at the Maryinsky, and *Le Carnaval*, which had been hurriedly created for a charity performance.)

The pathos of Nijinsky's interpretation of the name-part in *Petrouchka* is as clearly expressed in the simplicity of this pose as in the more passionate portraits.

PETROUCHKA

Valentine Gross's drawing of Karsavina, with her woman's eyes and face on her doll body, conveys the enchantment of her creation of this rôle—which she danced again in the last season of the Diaghilev Ballet.

77

Shortly after this, however, the theatre which had been booked in St. Petersburg – the Narodny Dom – was burnt down. As no other could be found, the whole tour had to be cancelled. The visit might have been merely postponed, but for the historical events of the outbreak of war in 1914, and the Revolution in Russia in 1917. So, though those Russians who travelled to Europe attended performances, the Russian public at home never had a glimpse of the ballets worked out on the new ideas. The old "story" ballets retained their hold, providing an escape to beauty.

Meanwhile, Diaghilev's earlier favourites were still delighting huge audiences in London.
Daily
Mail
14.2.13
"The *Fire Bird*, which is the pure sublimation of fairy pantomime, was given at Covent Garden last night to a large audience which must have been entranced to a man, if there is any power at all among us of appreciation of the most delicate loveliness of dancing, music and stage setting," was a typical comment.

Totally different was the next new work – the previous year's Paris sensation, *L'Après-Midi d'un Faune*. American newspapers had, from the first, reported the Paris seasons lavishly. The scandal and rumpus attaching to this work in 1912 had given them tremendous scope.

Pittsburgh
Gazette
5.6.12
"WICKED PARIS SHOCKED AT LAST"

had shrieked the *Pittsburgh Gazette* in letters an inch high.

"HOW THE BALLET OF THE FAUN (MORE STUPID THAN WICKED) HAS SET THE FRENCH CAPITAL BY THE EARS, AND THREATENS TO COST THE GREAT SCULPTOR RODIN HIS PALACE FOR APPROVING IT."

"Even Paris has been shocked, and now all Paris is talking about the shocking performance that has shocked it. It is the sort of discussion that delights Paris inexpressibly.

"It might be supposed that Paris was beyond shocking, but the miracle has been accomplished and everybody marvels at it."

This was followed by a rather inaccurate account of the ballet itself, and a more accurate one of the editorial storm which it had provoked. The sculptor Rodin's letter in its defence was quoted in full. The howls of moralists that he should be turned out of the Hôtel Biron in which the French government had installed him (free of rent) were faithfully reported. This paper alone gave about 163 square inches to the story – and columns all over the United States titillated readers, the majority of whom would never see a Russian ballet in their lives.

In 1912, Diaghilev had given an interview in which he had discussed both the new ballet which Stravinsky was composing for him, and the Debussy work. Asked, "And are we to see
Daily
Mail
18.6.12
L'Après-Midi?" he had temporised, replying : "I cannot say definitely – I cannot say because I do not yet sufficiently understand the English public. Are they or are they not in a position to appreciate this little piece? Can you or anyone tell me? The music is Debussy's, the scene is M. Nijinsky's own invention – it represents the furthest step we have taken yet in the development of ballet. In the *Faune* actual dancing is almost dispensed with – it is supplanted by a new plastic art. If we are to give this piece we must have the moral support of London artists and art-lovers, for it is a work that offers no concessions whatever to the Philistines. In Paris we were fortunate in having the enthusiastic concurrence of the sculptor Rodin. As for the London production – it is still an open question."

A few days before it was eventually to be shown in London, the *Pall Mall Gazette* scooped an interview with Nijinsky. This was probably due to Edwin Evans, who became the paper's Music Critic in 1912, and who was devoted to Diaghilev. Bearing in mind the language problems, it was obviously the writer of the article who put the discussion into coherent speech. He must, however, have got the substance right, otherwise it would undoubtedly have called forth a correction or disclaimer.
Pall
Mall
Gazette
15.2.13
"The treatment of ballets of the purely imaginative type is of great importance from the point of view of the producer," said Nijinsky. "One false accent, and the whole decorative value

of the production is destroyed. In the case of *L'Après-Midi d'un Faune*, this is particularly important, and mathematical precision must mark every minute action.

"Whilst I am in London I spend much time at the British Museum, for there I find inspiration from the ancient marbles, the bas-reliefs, the vases, and the decorative themes, for dances, gestures, physical balance, and purity of movement. In Paris, at the Palais d'Automne, the Louvre, and other great galleries, I seek the same inspiration. To be able to give to the world the perfection of the art of centuries expressed by the movements of the dance is my ambition and delight.

"But it is a mistake to suppose that either the plot or the production of *L'Après-Midi d'un Faune* has any suggestion that is incorrect or immodest. It has no story really: it is simply a fragment drawn from a classic bas-relief . . . In Berlin the Police Commissioner, having heard of the absurd cabal against it in Paris, came to the dress rehearsal, and after seeing it, expressed his satisfaction and pleasure at the strange spectacle."

On the same day, the *Standard* had printed an interview with one who was more of an onlooker than a participant in the activities of the ballet, heavily involved as he was with the opera. "Coming from no less an authority than Hugo von Hoffmansthal . . . the following impressions . . . in regard to M. Nijinsky's arrangement of the poem in ballet form . . . cannot fail to be of interest. After paying a tribute to Nijinsky's high qualities as an inventor, a stage manager, and a performer, the librettist says: "There are seven or eight minutes of a severe, earnest, rhythmically restrained pantomime to a piece of music by Debussy, which is well known to all. But this music is by no means the key to this ballet, as perhaps Schumann's *Carnaval* is the key – and a sure-fitting key – to the ballet *Carnaval*. *Carnaval* always seems to flow on as an improvisation on the music. But with the severe inward strength of Nijinsky's short scene,

Standard
15.2.13

In the autumn of 1912, the Diaghilev Ballet had a long season in Berlin, with the Beecham Orchestra. This photograph of a stage rehearsal of *Faune* shows that the work was at that time performed with a stage-cloth, omitted in revivals. "Nijinsky is the leading member of the ballet, and as the most famous male dancer of this generation commands an immense salary," said the caption.
(*The Tatler*, 1st January 1913.)

Debussy's music seems to fade away gradually till it becomes merely the accompanying element – a something in the atmosphere, but not the atmosphere itself. And again, the famous poem of Mallarmé, from which the music takes its title, is not the key; rather do we tend to find this in the verse of Horace: *Faune nympharum fugientum amator*," (Faun, you have a passion for fleeing nymphs!) "which concentrates a bas-relief into four words. This bas-relief is what one finds in the work of Nijinsky – a vision of the antique, which is quite our own, nurtured by the great statues of the fifth century – the Delphic charioteers – the archaic statues of youths in the museum of the Acropolis, with a touch of fate and tragedy in them far removed from the antiquity of Winckelmann, of Ingres, of Titian."

Odes: Book III, No. 18

The falling-away of the music as the strength of Nijinsky's invention increased has been remarked by critics without being in any way related to Horace.

The *Daily Mirror* heralded its arrival in London by saying that "the fuss made over this ballet in Paris was largely a 'put-up' business."

Daily Mirror 17.2.13

In the event, London was able, much more easily than Diaghilev had anticipated, to bear the shock of seeing its idol transform himself into a Faun – half-animal, earthbound, making only one extraordinary leap in the whole work. London applauded so heartily that the whole ballet had to be repeated! Two nights later, Queen Alexandra saw it, and once again, it was repeated.

"Everything that is splendid and barbaric and passionate seems already to have been done by the Russian dancers. Does that mean that we know the whole territory of their art? Not in the least," said Richard Capell, who continued by saying that the poetry and the music "are but two of the sources of the new spectacle in the eight minutes of which are compressed the learning of the scholars and the dreams of the poets of a generation. It is Nijinsky who has gathered together the divers strands in a piece – 'choreographic picture' he calls it, for want of a terminology for this so new thing – which seems the greatest curiosity and also the ultimate refinement of mimic art.

Daily Mail 18.2.13

"The spirit of the piece is remote archaism; the theme, of the strictest economy. A young faun plays his flute on a hillock and tramples on grapes: unperceiving, seven nymphs linger at the foot of the hillock. The faun, with simple, sensuous curiosity, creeps towards them. They flee: but one has lost in her flight a scarf. She timidly seeks to regain it from the odd, wild forest creature, but in vain, and she does not come within range of his brown arms; and goes. The faun goes back to his hillock, caressing the novel, soft, delicious texture of the scarf."

"The beauty of it lies solely in the exquisite grace of the poses which, like the art they copy, keep their grace, although they are stereotyped in stillness," said *The Times*. "On the stage we have beauty of line in the delicately draped figures of the nymphs (and, by the way, the dresses designed by M. Bakst are among his best inspirations,) and we have a similar beauty in the rhythmic curves of Debussy's melodies, but the actual movements of the two have no correspondence. M. Nijinsky as the faun is of course in these circumstances another creature from the M. Nijinsky we have known elsewhere. Save for one leap when he addresses the nymphs, there is no movement to suggest the normal style of his art. Yet his crouching movements, his stiff poses, and particularly his last action when he lies down to dream beside the scarf, are extraordinarily expressive."

The Times 18.2.13

In view of the massive preparation for a scandalously erotic ending, it is interesting that *The Times* should find it so innocent, so dreamy and poetic. It indicates that anyone who chose to read more into that final movement, wanted to.

The *Standard* was one of those. "M. Nijinsky has taken M. Debussy's elusive music and from it fashioned a fantasy which for classic truth rather than beauty ranks with anything M. Fokine has given us. The art of the mime is the art of suggestion, and of suggestion there is unquestionably a great deal in this work." Outlining the slight story, the paper continues: ". . . With becoming modesty the protagonists of the simple life fly from his advances, leaving behind a scarf belonging to the youngest and most beautiful of them all. Then follows the little incident that set Paris talking. If he has failed to grasp the substance, the shadow – or, rather, the scarf – at least remains to him. Tenderly he toys with it, and finally carries his prize off to his lair with some suggestive by-play.

Standard 18.2.13

"M. Nijinsky's spring is said, upon no less an authority than that of von Hoffmansthal, the author of *Elektra* and *Der Rosenkavalier*, to embody the whole faun nature. Possibly that is a

Nijinsky's reverent fondling of the scarf dropped by the nymph made the alleged bestiality of the final moment all the more of a shock and a surprise.

flight of imagination, but it is a very remarkable flight for all that. The morals and manners of faun – to say nothing of his attitude upon the sex question – are scarcely subjects one feels competent to discuss with any show of authority. Whether we regard the scarf incident as a piece of symbolism or merely in the light of a harmless exercise, the fact remains, however, that M. Nijinsky's movements are conditioned by a classic severity of outline, while as an imaginative effort his performance was even more remarkable. The audience received the novelty so cordially that it had to be given again."

The *Sunday Times* was impartial. "So perfect is the feeling that there does not seem to be any convention at all and one was sure that beings whose main function was to exist beautifully would live and move in no other way. M. Nijinsky's Faun was conditioned to its circumstance, but was extraordinarily expressive. There was no movement that was bestial or even ugly, yet the brutish nature of the Faun was subtly but surely conveyed in his stealthy walk, his sudden spring, and his dull, unintelligent gaze." So much for the action: this paper was less pleased with the scenic accomplishment. "For once the *ensemble* of the production did not satisfy. M. Bakst's characteristic scenery, a welter of colour contrasts and impressionistic effects, suited neither the music nor M. Nijinsky's evocation of the beauty that was Greece; something simpler, a background of upland 'in the broad glare of the hot noon,' would have been more congruous."

Sunday Times 23.3.13

The season was exciting enough for *Truth* to report that "Mr. Beecham continues to get capital houses at Covent Garden, but, apart from the production of *L'Après-Midi d'un Faune* on Monday, whose bizarrerie, to put it politely, entirely fulfilled anticipation, repetitions have been mainly the rule just lately – a state of things which, though dull from the chronicler's standpoint, is always one of happy augury so far as the box-office is concerned."

Truth 19.2.13

Before the next new work came a revival, universally welcomed, of the much-loved *Cléopâtre*. In view of the fact that Karsavina and Nijinsky received far and away the largest number of individual notices in reviews, this report is worth quoting: "Chief among the memories it left, perhaps, is the fine realism with which Madame Sophie Fedorova portrayed the despair of Ta-Hor at the loss of her lover, and the terrors with which she anticipates his end, while her final grief, when she falls prostrate over his dead body, was expressed with very rare art." Diaghilev had many magnificent artists in his company, who simply did not have the opportunity to take the leading rôles because those first seen in them had so completely captivated their audiences, which would not let them go. When these early Diaghilev ballets were danced in the repertoire after the war, by a new array of dancers, comparisons were inevitably made by those who had been to the ballet in its first years, and though some could do nothing but sigh for Karsavina and Nijinsky, others gave warm praise where it was due and admitted great performances by the next generation.

Daily
Telegraph
25.2.13

Referee
9.2.13

At the outset of this season, the *Referee* had remarked that "a prominent feature of the productions by the Russian Ballet troupe is the striking difference in the subjects taken for illustration. It is particularly remarkable to anyone versed in the history of the ballet, because for many years previous to the arrival of this company there had been such a similarity in the ballets presented as to induce a feeling of monotony."

The variety of the novelties of this season was indeed striking; the first, a tale of a Russian fair in 1830, the second, an image of classical antiquity, and the third, *Le Dieu Bleu*, in an exotic, pseudo-Hindu-Siamese idiom – with a complicated story by Jean Cocteau, and for which Reynaldo Hahn had been composing music since 1910. Costumed and set with lavish expenditure by Bakst, with Fokine's choreography danced by Karsavina and Nijinsky, it was, nevertheless, universally denounced as a failure. It would seem to have harked back into the too-near and conventional past of ballet.

Observer
2.3.13

Daily
Telegraph
28.2.13

Daily
Mail
28.2.13

"The house was crowded from floor to ceiling," said *The Observer*. King Manoel of Portugal, a devotee, was in Lady Ripon's box, and yet the evening, for once in a way, did not live up to the anticipation. "Four years or so ago this ballet might have been accepted as a new thing. But how can this be now when we know at least something of that amazing personage, Stravinsky? The inclusion of a pianoforte in the orchestra and the sound of its cold, chilly tinkling no longer surprises because so much more importance was laid on it and so much more effect was produced from its chilliness by Stravinsky in *Petrouchka*." "Both the music and the action of the ballet are less wonderful and strange than other pieces, such as the two Stravinsky ballets, provide. Both are by Frenchmen, not Russians, and in both, graceful as they are, one can trace survivals of old conventions rare in the purely Russian pieces," said the *Mail*. Similar comments abounded.

Richard Capell continued: "The Blue God is a benignant deity who together with a fair Lotus Goddess comes to the rescue of a Hindu maid who, guilty of attempting to seduce her lover from a priestly career, has been condemned to be delivered to the strange monsters which inhabit dens below the temple. The appearance of these monsters – fairyland creatures, somewhat lizard-like, and huge, – is one of the greatest moments of the ballet. Another is the appearance of the Goddess (Mme. Nelidova) and the Blue God. Of course it is Nijinsky – Nijinsky in one of his most strange guises. The god is truly blue, a strong azure; the vision is unearthly, and the dance with which he charms the monsters is touched with this singular youth's genius for suggesting the weird and inhuman. Mme. Karsavina's marvellous miming is eloquent of all terror and despair." Even the devoted Richard Capell could do no more for this work.

The
Lady
6.3.13

"M. Bakst has designed some good dresses," said *The Lady*, "notably the Lotus dress, but the whole effect lacks cohesion, and the scenery is unworthy of the artist's reputation. *Le Dieu Bleu* will be remembered chiefly for the beautiful and original performance given by M. Nijinsky. The great young dancer never repeats himself, and as the Blue God he has some postures and steps that recall nothing he has done before . . . but, on the whole, *Le Dieu Bleu* is the least remarkable of the Russian Ballet's productions in this country."

But in this programme, it was followed by *Cléopâtre* and *Petrouchka*, "and so potent was the attraction of the evening that scarcely anyone left before the final fall of the curtain," remarked the *Sunday Times*. Sunday Times 2.3.13

The revival of Fokine's *Narcisse* gave *The Times* the opportunity to contrast the two ballets on themes drawn from classical antiquity; Nijinsky's, "based on a confusion between the convention of linear design and that of human movement. . . *Narcisse* is not conceived in anything but a world of three dimensions. . ." – and the *Telegraph*, though critical of some failures, said that "it is a joyous and beautiful spectacle, and nothing is better achieved by these Russians than the dance of the Bacchantes, exquisitely led by that highly accomplished danseuse, Mlle. Piltz. In point of fact, the production was a complete triumph for this young dancer, who danced straight out from Botticelli's 'Spring,' was full of the *joie de vivre* and as graceful and 'abandoned' as heart could desire." The Times 5.3.13

Daily Telegraph 5.3.13

Diaghilev, in giving some advance information to the effect that, in the coming summer season, which would include both opera and ballet, he would be presenting Chaliapin in England for the first time, also said that on future visits to this country he would adopt a suggestion made by the *Daily Mail* itself, and have the titles of all the ballets translated. (The results were not always felicitous – and, in the end, often abandoned.) Daily Mail 8.3.13

At the same time, Diaghilev had offered a second compliment to his English audiences. He announced that he proposed "on a future visit to produce an English ballet for which Dr. Vaughan Williams is writing music; Mr. Gordon Craig will be responsible for the scenery and staging."

One may deduce that he had settled his difference with Gordon Craig, which dated back to 1911, and which accounted for Craig's diatribes against the Russian Ballet. This had arisen when Craig – who was about to travel to Moscow to mount his production of *Hamlet* at the Arts Theatre – was living in Smith Square, Westminster. Craig arranged a demonstration in the house of his model stage and system of moving screens. Many influential theatre managers and actors were invited. Diaghilev, accompanied by Nijinsky and Count Harry Kessler, a German patron of the arts, arrived late. The demonstration was already in progress, but Diaghilev, in unwontedly ill-mannered fashion, talked loudly to his companions at the back of the room, whilst Craig was describing his methods. Craig suddenly switched on the room lights, and refused to continue the demonstration. Thenceforward, apart from praises for Karsavina, he wrote luridly against Diaghilev in *The Mask*, (as has been shown in 1912.)

Through what agency they "made it up," one cannot tell, but the possibility of a collaboration was certainly discussed by Diaghilev and Craig in 1913, the potential composer being Ralph Vaughan Williams. (In her biography of her late husband, Ursula Vaughan Williams, graphically describing the episode, put it earlier – but it must have been during this year, when Craig had taken a studio in Chelsea for his temporary sojourn in London, not far from R.V.W., with whom he was very friendly.)

"It must have been about this time that a very exotic luncheon party took place," she said. "Ralph had met Gordon Craig and there was some discussion of their writing a ballet together so a meeting was arranged with Diaghilev and Nijinsky at the Savoy. Nijinsky remained entirely silent throughout the meal, while Diaghilev proposed that he should dance both Cupid and Psyche, which was the story Gordon Craig wanted to use. Ralph objected very strongly to this idea. When the party broke up he and Craig walked home together. 'Let me have the music,' said Craig, 'and I'll fit the story.' 'Impossible,' said Ralph, 'you must let me have the scenario and I will write music for it.' 'Impossible,' said Craig, 'just send me the music' – and so they parted. Neither sent anything to the other and the projected ballet became another might-have-been." R.V.W. Ursula Vaughan Williams

The date of the odd incident about to be related is uncertain, but it might well have been during this season, when, between the acclaim he was enjoying with the success of *Faune*, and the struggles in the creation of his two new ballets, Nijinsky might, understandably, have been in a mood bursting to "escape." It is offered just because it is amusing, without documentation or other justification.

Hester
Marsden-
Smedley

The late Basil Marsden-Smedley (one-time Mayor of Chelsea) and his wife Hester served for many years on the Council of the Friends of St. Stephen's, in Fulham Road, which was a Poor Law Institution until 1944, when it became a hospital. Some years ago, they were listening to a bout of reminiscence on the part of a porter, who had been employed there as a lad before the first World War, and had remained to become a senior man.

The porter recalled that one night, a young man had been brought in unconscious – not really ill, but somewhat the worse for wear. This was a frequent occurrence – people often shammed to get a bed for the night. Following the usual practice, he was simply put to bed and left to sleep it off.

One can imagine the feelings of the ward attendants and the inmates when, the following morning, a figure suddenly leapt right over one bed, occupant and all – did the splits in the space, then leapt the next bed, and so on right down the twenty beds on one side and up the twenty beds on the other. Perhaps it was as well that no one could communicate with that figure, which spoke no English – perhaps the art of mime came to everyone spontaneously?

Possibly the young man wrote down some such words as "Savoy" and a name or two, for, according to the porter, a little while later several well-dressed gentlemen arrived in cabs, one of whom said his name was Diaghilev. He extracted golden sovereigns from a sovereign purse, tipped lavishly and distributed largesse, and collected V. Nijinsky, thanking everyone for the care that had been taken of him.

How Nijinsky must have exulted as he gave the slip to Diaghilev's faithful valet, who never let him out of his sight!

During February, the Kosloff brothers and their small company were in the bill at the Coliseum. Rather unwillingly, Diaghilev gave an audition to some of these dancers, and took five into his company. These were Hilda Munnings, (whom he called at first "Muningsova," and later, "Lydia Sokolova," the name under which she became famous,) Doris Faithfull, Anna Broomhead (Bromova, who later joined Pavlova,) and two men, Zverev and Tarassov.

Daily
Mail
19.2.13

The audience, or at least the ladies, were getting to look rather like the dancers on the stage. The *Daily Mail* described the new fashion for "Mephisto" feathers, tall, slender exclamation-marks secured miraculously to a bandeau – remarking that they were less troublesome to those behind them in a theatre than the "sunbursts" they were ousting. Also on the Woman's Page,

17.4.13

later on, the writer went on to the subject of shoes: "The term *Cothurnus* is applied to the Ballet Shoe fastenings that are the fancy for all shoes. Satin ribbon is taken, passed across the insteps and round the ankles, and while in some cases jewels are used as fasteners, in others the ribbon is fastened in a little bow at the back." (Karsavina once told the author that she had started this fashion, having shown her ballet shoes to a Parisian designer and asked him to make her something that tied up like them.)

4.4.13

The same writer had also observed the effects of the Oriental ballets, including the most recent, *Le Dieu Bleu*: "The influence of the Russian Ballet is traceable in many of the fashions of the moment . . . the *bayadère* sash wound several times round the waist and hips is essentially a dancer's toilette attribute . . ."

Daily
Mail
27.5.13

Possibly the previous year the scandals had taken precedence over aesthetic considerations: it was on the ballet's next visit to Paris that the *Daily Mail* reported that "Extraordinary enthusiasm has been aroused in Paris over Nijinsky's new arrangement of the famous *L'Après-Midi d'un Faune*." (New arrangement? Could that mean that Nijinsky had, in fact, re-worked the controversial ending of the previous year?) "The Parisiennes, ever eager to take advantage of new ideas on the subject of dress, are enthusiastic over the classic draperies worn by the 'Nymphs' in this piece; they are deliciously Greek and wholly fascinating. In Paris we find these classic outlines specially interesting because we are entering on an era of accordion-pleated chiffons and muslins."

The perfection of the partnership of Karsavina and Nijinsky is summed up in this drawing by Valentine Gross. In *Le Spectre de la Rose*, Nijinsky guided her steps in a waltz, and Karsavina seemed as if she were dancing in her sleep.

Even audiences dressed to match had to accept the ending of another season: but not without dragging it out to the last possible moment. Richard Capell reported, on the last night, "such demonstrations as are rare indeed in London theatres. After each of the first three pieces there were long roars of cheers and recall after recall, and the audience, refusing point blank to go away at the end of the programme, succeeded in having the last ballet – *Le Spectre de la Rose* – danced by Mme. Karsavina and M. Nijinsky, performed all over again."

Daily
Mail
8.3.13

Toutes les nuits mon spectre rose
A ton chevet viendra danser.

Théophile
Gautier

1913

LE SACRE DU PRINTEMPS

ORIGINAL VERSION

Composer: Igor Stravinsky

Choreographer: Vaslav Nijinsky

Designer: Nicholas Roerich

First Produced: Théâtre des Champs Elysées, Paris
                       29.5.1913

                       Theatre Royal, Drury Lane, London
                       11.7.1913

SECOND VERSION

Composer: Igor Stravinsky

Choreographer: Leonide Massine

Designer: Nicholas Roerich

First Produced: Théâtre des Champs Elysées, Paris
                       15.12.1920

                       Prince's Theatre, London
                       27.6.1921

LE SACRE IN PREPARATION

By far the greater problem, both for Nijinsky and the company, lay in the working out of Stravinsky's new ballet, *Le Sacre du Printemps*, of which it has been said that "No theatre spectacle of this century has stirred up such a fury of excitement. None today is less well known in its visual detail." The composition was so completely original and so difficult; no one – including orchestra and dancers – had ever heard anything like it before. The rhythms changed every bar; yet Nijinsky's idea was to find virtually "a step for every note."

Stravinsky in the Theatre: Ed. Minna Ledermann 1957

Working with them as they struggled to learn strange movements and stranger rhythms was the 24-year-old Marie Rambert. Born in Poland, she had become a dancer, and had then studied Eurythmics for three years under Jacques Dalcroze. Because of her dual experience, Dalcroze suggested her to Diaghilev when he and Nijinsky visited the school in Dresden. Her task was to help to elucidate the difficult music, full of time-changes from bar to bar. Diaghilev did not avail himself of her excellent linguistic powers for other purposes, such as interpreting for Nijinsky to the Press.

So important was *Le Sacre* to prove, so much discussion was it to provoke, so much was opinion about it to change, that it would seem worth while, before recounting its adventures when it was produced, to gather together the statements concerning its origin made by its authors, Stravinsky and Roerich, the interest of Diaghilev, and the ideas of Nijinsky, its first choreographer, so that all the subsequent criticisms may be measured up against those fundamentals.

In his book, *Stravinsky: the Composer and his Work*, Eric Walter White described its inception:

> "The initial impulse that led to the creation of *The Rite of Spring* was derived from a fleeting vision that Stravinsky had in St. Petersburg during the spring of 1910, when he was finishing the last pages of *Firebird*. This came to him unexpectedly, as his mind was then pre-occupied with different things. In his *Chronicle* (1935) he states: 'I saw in imagination a solemn pagan rite: wise elders, seated in a circle, watching a young girl dance herself to death. They were sacrificing her to propitiate the god of spring.' At this stage the vision was not accompanied by any concrete musical ideas. Before leaving St. Petersburg he described his dream to his friend, Nicholas Roerich, who he thought would be interested in it from the archaeological point of view; and on reaching Paris he also mentioned it to Diaghilev, who immediately saw its balletic potentialities . . .

"It was not until the following summer, when *Petrouchka* had been successfully launched, that Stravinsky had time to sketch out the new work. Roerich, whom he had chosen as his collaborator, was not only a painter of considerable talent, but also an archaeologist who had travelled extensively, becoming one of the greatest authorities on the ancient Slavs . . . it was certainly appropriate that he should help Stravinsky with the scenario of this new work."

At this stage in the history of the Ballets Russes, Fokine was the established choreographer. His *Polovtsian Dances* to Borodin's music for the opera, *Prince Igor*, massed and barbaric, were one of the most popular items in the repertoire. Roerich had designed the sets and costumes, (and had even hunted the markets of St. Petersburg for authentic woven cloth, with which they were made.) The idea of going even further back into primitive tribal practices must have seemed a progression from this. The thought of a different choreographer probably never even crossed their minds.

In July, 1911, Roerich was a guest of Princess Tenisheva at her country house. She had been Diaghilev's first patron, providing the money to start *The World of Art*, and had a fine collection of antique costumes. (Immensely wealthy, she also had a house in Paris, and displayed part of her collection there.) Stravinsky joined Roerich in her house, "and in a few days' time the course of the action of the new ballet was worked out, and the titles and order of the different episodes agreed. Roerich also sketched the back-cloths of the scenes, and designed a number of costumes for the dancers . . ."

N.Y.P.L.
Dance
Collection
Astruc
Papers

Stravinsky and Roerich seem to have been of one mind about it, from an artistic standpoint. By the time definite plans to produce the ballet were formulated, Fokine had left, and Nijinsky had been made the company's choreographer. His first creation, as has been shown, was given its première in Paris on May 29th, 1912. On April 18th, 1912, Diaghilev had despatched a feverish telegram to Gabriel Astruc, in Paris – "Have seen article on front page of *Figaro* saying that Fokine is going to put *Faune* on. Nijinsky holding out refusing take part our season Paris have never seen him so firm and intransigent. Have written to Bakst for possible replacement situation more than dangerous . . ." This had been smoothed over, – Nijinsky's ballet was beautiful and original, the "scandal" of its first night was good publicity – he was to remain the choreographer. Of his originality, there does not seem to have been any doubt, but his ability to organise gave cause for concern.

Chronicle of My Life.
I. Stravinsky
(Gollancz
1935).

A composer must surely have some vision of a ballet's appearance in his mind's eye as he works on a specific idea. In the *Chronicle*, Stravinsky said: "Although I had conceived the subject of the *Sacre du Printemps* without any plot, some plan had to be designed for the sacrificial action . . . I joined Roerich . . . and we settled the visual embodiment of the *Sacre* and the definite sequence of its different episodes."

The result was a most definite "Programme."

Part One: The Adoration of the Earth
    Introduction
    'Auguries of Spring' (Dances of the Young Girls)
    'Mock Abduction'
    'Spring Khorovod' (Round Dance)
    'Games of the Rival Clans'
    'Procession of the Wise Elder'
    'Adoration of the Earth' (The Wise Elder)
    'Dance of the Earth'

Part Two: The Sacrifice
    Introduction (Originally, Pagan Night.)
    'Mystical Circles of the Young Girls'
    'Glorification of the Chosen Victim'
    'The Summoning of the Ancients'
    'Ritual of the Ancients'
    'Sacrificial Dance' (The Chosen Victim)

[No. 35.]
The Dance of the Chosen Maiden starts
with convulsive leaps.

Valentine Gross made innumerable
"shorthand notes" of this ballet, and from
them a series of eight drawings of Maria
Piltz as the Chosen Virgin. The musical
references below the six reproduced in
this and the next chapter correspond with
the moments in the great dance. The
details were worked out by Brian
Blackwood and Richard Buckle, and
printed in the catalogue of an exhibition
held in the gallery of Messrs. Hartnoll
and Eyre in 1973. The numbers here
given refer to that exhibition and
catalogue.

Lifar
p.200

At some time during the preparations of the ballet, Roerich wrote to Diaghilev in Paris: "In the ballet . . . as conceived by myself and Stravinsky, my object is to present a number of scenes of earthly joy and celestial triumph as understood by the Slavs . . . My intention is that the first set should transport us to the foot of a sacred hill, in a lush plain, where Slavonic tribes are gathered together to celebrate the spring rites. In this scene there is an old witch, who predicts the future, a marriage by capture, round dances. Then comes the most solemn moment. The wise elder is brought from the village to imprint his sacred kiss on the new flowering earth. During this rite the crowd is seized with a mystic terror, and this our excellent Nijinsky has stylized for us extremely well.

"After this uprush of terrestrial joy, the second scene sets a celestial mystery before us. Young virgins dance in circles on the sacred hill amid enchanted rocks; then they choose the victim they intend to honour. In a moment she will dance her last dance before the ancients clad in bearskins to show that the bear was man's ancestor. Then the greybeards dedicate the victim to the god Yarilo." (Yarilo was the god of Light. There does not seem to have been any idea of portraying this deity on the stage.)

The explanations culminate in the statement Stravinsky made, years later, when asked by Robert Craft what he had loved most in Russia, and replied: "The violent Russian spring, that seemed to begin in an hour and was like the whole earth cracking." This annual magic must, surely, have had some meaning for everyone concerned in the creation of this ballet, accustomed as they were to the violence of the seasons in their native land.

*Memories
and
Commentaries*
(1962)
Stravinsky/Craft

With such ideas, it is impossible to conceive that anyone ever envisaged this ballet in terms of *arabesques* and *attitudes*.

The French title had been thought out by Bakst. It was translated in various forms for the English newspapers. "The Crowning of Spring" – as if it represented the ritual, part religious and part secular, of anointing and coronation, with Spring metamorphosed into a monarch. "The Spring Ritual," "The Spring Rite" – not quite the same thing. Not until 1920, when a second choreographic version was commissioned (partly because no one could remember enough of the 1913 ballet for it to be reconstructed,) was the title consolidated as *The Rite of Spring*.

[No. 36.]
Another attitude, another leap.

In London, Stravinsky gave an interview, which appeared two days before a statement from Nijinsky.

Daily
Mail
13.2.13

He first gave his views on existing music. "There is little that interests me in the music of the past. Bach is too remote . . . Beethoven – there is too much literary thought in his music. Thought so soon grows old-fashioned, but emotion remains the same. I confess to remaining faithful to the fresh feeling and joy of life in Schubert's music. There is something pleasing, too, in Mozart."

He went on: "I dislike opera. Music can be married to gesture or words – not to both without bigamy . . . In any case, opera is in a back-water. What operas have been written since *Parsifal*? Only two that count – *Elektra* and Debussy's *Pelléas*.

"Russian musical life is at present stagnant. They cannot stand me there. *Petrushka* was performed in St. Petersburg the same day as here," (presumably a concert performance,) "and I see the papers are now all comparing my work with 'the smashing of crockery.'

"My new ballet, *The Crowning of Spring*, has no plot. It is a series of ceremonies in ancient Russia, the Russia of pagan days. We are rehearsing it now. It will require 125 rehearsals before it can be produced. The score includes five trumpets, eight horns, and all the wood-wind in families of five."

This detail about the number of rehearsals envisaged is extremely interesting, for it represents *planning*. The impression usually given is that the huge number of rehearsals *became* necessary because the dancers could not comprehend Nijinsky's requirements.

Two days later, in the same interview in which he had given his ideas about *L'Après-Midi d'un Faune*, Nijinsky also spoke about the two ballets which were in rehearsal. "Even now, I am working hard on their production, and spend many hours a day on their arrangement.

Pall
Mall
Gazette
15.2.13

"One is called *Sacre du Printemps* . . . I think it will prove a strangely interesting work. It is really the soul of nature expressed by movement to music. It is the life of the stones and the trees. There are no human beings in it. It is only the incarnation of Nature – not of human nature. It will be danced only by the *corps de ballet*, for it is a thing of concrete masses, not of individual effects.

"The other ballet is a dainty trifle called *Jeu* (sic), and will be danced by Mme. Karsavina, my sister Mlle. Nijinska, and myself . . . The period is in the future. It is a fantasy of the highest description, and already I feel the delight of its interpretation."

[No. 37.]
"The Virgin stands, desolate and still, with hanging hands, before resuming the dance of death."

With two such widely differing expressions of the artistic foundations of *Le Sacre*, it might be expected that there would be antagonistic ideas about its realisation. It does not seem as if the ideas gave rise to strife between Stravinsky and Nijinsky: rather was there worry and concern as the choreography was so difficult, and progress very slow. Stravinsky contrived to travel about and look in on rehearsals as the company moved over Europe. He felt no delight as *Le Sacre* struggled to take shape.

"To be perfectly frank, . . . the idea of working with Nijinsky filled me with misgiving, notwithstanding our friendliness and my great admiration for his talent as a dancer and mime . . . The poor boy knew nothing of music. He could neither read it nor play any instrument . . . The lacunae were so serious that his plastic vision, often of great beauty, could not compensate for them . . . we advanced at a snail's pace. It was all the more trying because Nijinsky complicated and encumbered his dances beyond all reason, thus creating difficulties for the dancers which it was sometimes impossible to overcome. This was due as much to his lack of experience as to the complexity of a task with which he was unfamiliar . . . Seeing that he was losing prestige with the company but was strongly upheld by Diaghilev, he became presumptuous, capricious, and unmanageable."

Chronicle 1935

Stravinsky added that he had no wish to "cast any slur on the fame of this magnificent artist. We were, as I have already said, always on the best of terms . . ."

For the dancers, forced to forget everything they had learned in their rigorous schooling, to poise with turn-in instead of turn-out, to move with primitive gaucherie, when they were accustomed to chiding if grace eluded them for a moment, it was inimical and bitterly difficult. They hated it as counts were shouted at them: they could not hear the rhythms and phrases of the music.

Somehow, it was ready by the end of May. The uproar which greeted its first performance in Astruc's new theatre, the Champs-Elysées, is history.

1913 (SUMMER)

THEATRE ROYAL, DRURY LANE

JUNE 25th - JULY 25th

FIRST PERFORMANCE IN ENGLAND

June 25th:	*Jeux* (Debussy, Nijinsky, Bakst.) Paris, 15.5.1913
June 30th:	*La Tragédie de Salomé* (Schmitt, B. Romanov, Soudeikine.) Paris, 12.6.1913
July 11th:	*Le Sacre du Printemps* (Stravinsky, Nijinsky, Roerich.) Paris, 29.5.1913

REPERTOIRE

L'Après-Midi d'un Faune
Le Carnaval
Le Lac des Cygnes
Narcisse
L'Oiseau de Feu
Le Pavillon d'Armide

Petrouchka
Polovtsian Dances
Scheherazade
Le Spectre de la Rose
Les Sylphides
Thamar

COMPANY

Astafieva S., Baranovitch I., Baranovitch II., Boni, Bonietska, Broomhead, Dombrovska, Faithfull, Fedorova, Guliuk, Julitzka, Karsavina, Khokhlova, Konietzka, Kopetzinska, Maicherska, Maningsova (Also spelt Muningsova – later Sokolova), Nijinska, Pflanz, Piltz, Poire, Pozerska, Rambert, Razoumovitch, Schidlova, Schollar, Tchernicheva, Wassilievska, Yezerska, Zulicka.

Bourman, Bromberg, Cecchetti, Fedorov, Frohmann, Gavrilov, Grigoriev, Gudin, Ivanovsky, Kegler, Kostecki, Kotchetovsky, Kovalsky, Kremnev, Malignin, Nijinsky, Oumansky, Rakhmanov, Romanov B., Savitsky, Sergueiev, Statkevitch, Tarassov, Toboiko, Varjinsky, Voronzov, Zelinsky, Zverev.

CONDUCTORS

Steimann, Rhené-Baton, Monteux.

LE SACRE IN PERFORMANCE

This year Sir Joseph Beecham brought Russian opera to London for the first time, financing the season personally. It opened with a magnificent performance of Moussorgsky's *Boris Godounov*, conducted by his son Thomas Beecham and introducing the marvel of Chaliapin. For the ballet the following evening, there was a very large audience – larger, indeed, than the audience for *Boris*. There could be no mistaking the patroness of this season. "Lady Cunard, in the Royal box, was entertaining a party, herself beautifully dressed in palest emerald green," (her name was Emerald) "with a diamond diadem in her hair, finished at the back with a great bow of sea-green tulle and feathers." As usual, the society columns overflowed. Loyalty was, however, rather strained, for the performance of the ever-popular *Scheherazade* and *Le Pavillon d'Armide* preceded a daring novelty. The intervals were so long that a few days later, the *Telegraph* complained that "as things are at present an evening of ballet is rather an evening of interval, with now and then a ballet. If it be true that the lengthy intervals are necessitated by the fact that the principal dancers have to undergo massage after each dance, is it impossible to arrange the order of the dances so that the same principals do not appear in consecutive ballets?"

Daily Telegraph 26.6.13

The Lady 3.7.13

Daily Telegraph 30.6.13

London had accepted *L'Après-Midi d'un Faune* for its poetry and beauty; it had accepted the controversial ending without the false prudery previously shown in Paris. London was not at all averse to accepting new ideas from Nijinsky. *The Times* printed a report from Paris on the pianoforte arrangement of Debussy's new ballet, *Jeux*, which ended by saying that "melodically it is extremely beautiful – and the whole thing flows with an easy spontaneity which must have made it as delightful for the performers to dance to as for the audience to hear."

The Times 23.5.13

Nevertheless, there was laughter amidst the applause on this first performance in London, and faint hisses at the second. True to the ruling Diaghilev had announced at the end of the previous season, the title was translated as *Playtime*. Diaghilev had then said, "It may be described as a children's flirtation in a park after a game of tennis." Tennis is not quite a children's game. Yet this game was not truly tennis: it bore, in fact, no resemblance to any game described in any Encyclopaedia of Sport. Lawn Tennis, in 1913, was still a gentle kind of social divertissement: it had not yet become the fierce combat into which it developed in the 1920's. In Bloomsbury, tennis parties were regular events on summer Sundays. No lesser luminaries than D.H. Lawrence and Somerset Maugham wielded racquets in company with pretty young ladies of the literary set – and refreshed themselves with tea, buns and lemonade. Probably there was private in-fighting as the young ladies sized up the potential of the young men; perhaps this was the reason for the threesome being distributed as it was between the sexes.

Daily Mail 3.3.13

The Times tried hard to be kind, to praise anything it possibly could. "Some of the symbolism is plastic and here and there are some beautiful poses – notably one of M. Nijinsky when he

The Times 26.6.13

turns his head on one side and tightens the muscles of the neck – but it is confused by being broken into by leaps and bounds and certain swirling movements which seem to have been transferred from the old familiar ballets in the repertoire. Some of the language in which the ideas are expressed is beautiful and eloquent and is really expressive . . . but it is like a language in which the speaker is restricted to a portion of the alphabet . . . Perhaps M. Nijinsky will some day discover and learn the whole alphabet of which at present he has acquired only the partial use; . . . and though we may admire him for attempting to strike out into new paths by inventing fresh conventions, we cannot be insensible to the ludicrousness and the ugliness of much of what he has designed . . . The Valse was one of the best episodes so far as the dancers were concerned, but it only made one long to be able to unbuckle their limbs for them and set them free from the rigid ties by which they were bound. Their faces, too, were rigid, for it is part of the convention that they should express no emotion, and this made one want to have them covered by masks."

Observer
29.6.13
The *Observer*, admitting that the conventions of *Playtime* (almost everywhere referred to as *Jeux*, showing that the difficulties of translating titles were sometimes useless chores,) "test the imagination rather severely," gave this curious new work a little more appreciation. "If one is not concerned, however, with the establishment of the intentions of the three moonlight tennis players, or the significance of the ball, or the symbolism of the vividly startling scenic surrounding (a very effective set, by the bye,) there is an indefinable atmosphere about the whole thing that is full of perverse charm and fascination."

Of all the descriptions and comments, perhaps the most explicit appeared, not in Europe at all, but in America, after the Paris première. This report is interesting not only in itself, but because it indicates that there would indeed be some people, albeit few, whose imaginations were captured in advance of the eventual arrival of Diaghilev's company in America.

N.Y.
Tribune
17.5.13
BY CABLE   PARIS, MAY 17 (N.Y. TRIBUNE.)

NIJINSKI SHOCKS PARIS WITH TENNIS DANCE

EPISODE IN NEW BALLET CALLED NEEDLESSLY MERETRICIOUS

DEBUSSY'S MUSIC FOR PANTOMIME HIGHLY APPRECIATED

"*Jeux* (*Play*) a lyric pantomimic poem, with music by Claude Debussy, scenario by Nijinsky, produced at the Théâtre des Champs Elysées, is a game of tennis set to music and performed by dancers.

"It elicited enthusiastic applause, mingled with half a dozen emphatic protestations against a situation at the close of the ballet that seemed needlessly meretricious. Nijinski, attired in white flannel and with a tennis racquet in his hand, dances in a golden sunset, with sabre-like bounds and with the plastic poses of a faun, all expressive of his devotion to a girl in a white tennis costume. When his gyrations about the tennis court and the shrubbery and trees culminate in a kiss, another girl, also in a white tennis costume, executes a frantic dance, expressive of the paroxysms of jealousy. The triple dance continues and develops feelings which induce both the girls to consent to share their mutual tenderness toward the fascinating dancer. The spectacle closes with a triangular group, in which the gallant tennis champion and the two girls pose in a group forming the letter X.

"A great novelty was this ballet, and the delicious music of Debussy, in which the string instruments in the orchestra predominate, was keenly appreciated. One captious Parisian critic, however, Paul Souday, declared that this Russian ballet is far too rigid and geometrical and is to choreographic art what cubism is to painting."

In London, *Playtime* or *Jeux*, name it as you will, did not attract. Yet, many years later, critics would reminisce about it, as if it had left an ineradicable mark on their memories.

With a backcloth showing London houses, and tennis dresses designed by Bakst and made by Paquin, (and with Nijinsky's impossible costume re-designed by Diaghilev himself,) *Jeux* was the first ballet to attempt to mirror an aspect of contemporary life – something which was to be carried out more fully by Bronislava Nijinska in the 1920's.

The second new ballet, seemingly safe, did not go down well either. *La Tragédie de Salomé* was intended entirely as a vehicle for Karsavina, who had been becoming restive as she felt that recently, "there was less and less left for me to bite on." She was always under the impression that Diaghilev had specially commissioned the music for her; what he had commissioned was re-orchestration for a large orchestra. *La Tragédie de Salomé* had, in fact, been completed in 1907, for Loie Fuller, who gave it at the opening (under new management) of the Théâtre des Arts, in Paris. Her extraordinary treatment was devised solely for one purpose – to display her famous lighting effects. In all probability Diaghilev saw this in Paris and felt that the music was sufficiently interesting to be banked and used some day. Stravinsky greatly admired this work of Florent Schmitt's, and anyone who thinks that Schmitt was influenced by Stravinsky ought to study the dates and read their correspondence, and realise that if there was any question of "influence," it was exactly the opposite way round.

"The piece bears no relation to any other stage *Salomés* of recent years," said Richard Capell. "Eyeing the extravagant production with delicate approval, the spirit of Aubrey Beardsley was, one felt assured, haunting the house last night.

Daily Mail 1.7.13

"The person of the Russian Salomé, as we first see her, when a curtain of tropical foliage parts and she stands in relief against the star-strewn blueness of no terrestrial night, her garb a hood and a prodigiously-trained cloak, comes indeed from one of the pictures of Beardsley, and so do her monstrous Court of ostrich-plumed negroes and the suite of negro executioners. But rather more extravagant than the nature of Beardsley's decoration is the Russian artist's efflorescence of giant vegetation that shadows this scene of Salome's death-dance round the martyred saint's head. (But last night there was no head on the pillar in the middle of the stage that should have borne it.)

"Mme. Karsavina is by nature a fairy, who condescends to be human at times, and at times, as in the erotic torment of the Queen in *Scheherazade*, sub-human. But what is her Salome? A witch, a Lilith, from an Oriental poet's inferno. Merely in the way of endurance, her atrocious dance is probably the most amazing feat in all the annals of Ballet."

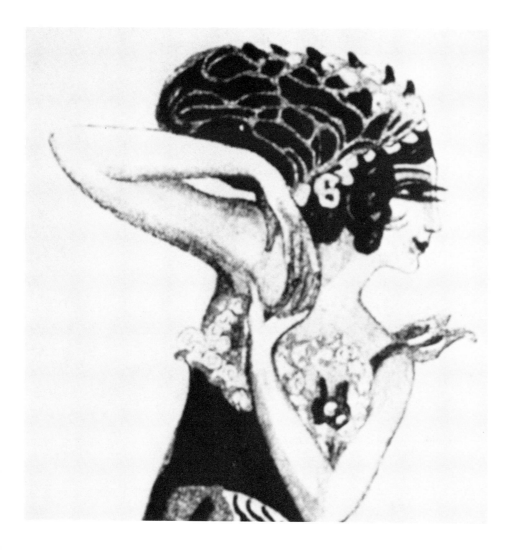

One cannot know whether Soudeikine had been told of the origin of Salome's eyelashes, but in his drawing he gave them full value.

Daily Telegraph 1.7.13 Weird, said the *Daily Telegraph*, weird was the word for it. "Weird, too, one must call Mme. Karsavina's make-up and costume as the protagonist. With blanched face, startling in its pallor by contrast with her mop of raven hair, she presents a striking apparition as she descends a steep flight of stairs at the back of the stage, the long train of the cloak she wears completely covering the steps after she has set foot to the ground."*

The Lady 10.7.13 The *Lady* was firm about this ballet. "There are some people who appear to swallow the Russian Ballet and all its works with open-mouthed and closed-eyed enthusiasm. I have often been enthusiastic . . . but one must discriminate. *Salomé*, the novelty of last week, is worse than *Jeux*, the novelty of the week before. It strikes me, not for the first time, that Paris is not exerting an altogether wholesome influence on the Russian Ballet. At any rate, *Salomé* lacks all those attributes which we have learned to think characteristic of the Russians . . . For once, the choreography was very hesitating and casual. Madame Karsavina appeared to be ill at ease, and the negro slaves and executioners who were her supporters showed a want of '*rapport*' which is very rare in the Russian *corps de ballet*."

---

*The temptation to include an anecdote here is irresistible. The timing – 1966 – was piquant. Great Britain was in the throes of a dock strike, and the newspapers had headed a list of valuable exports which were held up with a certain manufactured aid to beauty, which was, apparently, a considerable earner of foreign currency.

Madame Karsavina was showing the author her whole collection of photographs, telling stories as she went along. As she came to one of herself as Salome, she explained that the designer himself used to paint the stylized rose on her thigh before each performance. "And then," she went on, "for this rôle, I myself invented . . ." and she hesitated for the words. Some note of telepathy brought them from the author. "Not – the eyelashes?" "Yes, that is right – the artificial eyelashes – I had the idea, and asked the wigmaker to make them for me. He did, and so I think I invented artificial eyelashes!"

At last, on Friday, July 11th, came *Le Sacre du Printemps.*

The programme notes (which closely followed Stravinsky's and Roerich's original ideas,) provided a strange contrast with what Nijinsky had said himself – "It is really the soul of nature expressed by movement to music. It is the life of the stones and the trees. There are no human beings in it." By the time the ballet was completed, it would seem that he had had to decide that inanimate objects alone would not suffice.

Before the curtain rose, Edwin Evans (taking a night off from the *Pall Mall Gazette,)* gave a lecture on the new work – but was halted by an impatient house. There was no such demonstration as had attended the first performance in Paris a few weeks before, a modest amount of hissing being considered adequate.

It would be convenient to be able to line up the critiques in neat columns, "for" and "against" – sub-dividing them, "for" the music, "against" the choreography, "for" the choreography, "against" the music, but no such clear-cut classification emerges. Perhaps it makes most sense to list first the comments on the idea behind the new work, then those on the music, and lastly those which try to assess the realisation of these two ingredients in the choreography.

All these comments are dated Saturday July 12th or Sunday July 13th, 1913.

THE IDEAS

The Times
"In *Le Sacre du Printemps* we go back to the beginning of the world, when men were just ceasing to be animals and were coming into their heritage as human beings."

Daily Mail
"It represents some prehistoric Muscovite tribe celebrating at the vernal equinox 'the benignant earth's fertility, the majesty of the great forces of nature, and the mystery of the everlasting stars.'"

Daily Telegraph
"Edwin Evans Jun. . . . explained in a ten minutes' talk ere the curtain rose the purport of the ballet. . . . Precisely how Mr. Evans found all he explained in this whirlwind of cacophonous, 'primitive' hideousness, it is beyond us to conjecture."

The Standard
"The subject – primitive man—is ugly, and his movements are ugly as the ugliest duckling – its symbolism, which, we take it, stands for the immutability of the first cause – equally so."

THE MUSIC

The Times
"It sounds, in fact, as if it had been written as absolute music conceived in varieties of a single mood rather than as programme music, and as though the incidents on the stage had been roughly fitted together and made to synchronize with the music because they happened to illustrate ideas conceived in a similar mood."

Daily Mail
"And the music?

ORCHESTRAL GROANS

"Its savagery is horrific, past belief. Dissonances extraordinary enough have been sought out by other composers of the day to stir our jaded senses with a new thrill. But no one has gone so ferociously to work as M. Stravinsky, and no one has drummed and dinned his dissonances with such maddening rhythmic persistency. And it must be added that all this is uttered by the most outlandish orchestral cries and groans, with masses of wind instruments mainly playing in unaccustomed registers. M. Stravinsky enchanted us a year ago with the fairyland of his *Firebird* music, and then did something utterly new in music with the seemingly artless and mordantly satiric *Petrouchka*. To hear his *Festival of Spring* is the most curious of experiences; but one cannot believe one would ever get it to yield a moment's actual pleasure." (Richard Capell.)

Daily Telegraph
"Whether it is as primitive as it sets out to be we have no notion for it is so much earlier in date than any music of our acquaintance, or than any examples in any history we have read. No doubt it is all very logical, but is not logic the curse of musical matters?"

The Standard
"Everyone should go and see *Le Sacre du Printemps*, if only on account of its bizarrerie and astonishing ugliness – ugliness on the stage and in the orchestra. The thoroughness with which it is pursued in every department is extraordinary, scenic artist, composer, and dancer combining together with marvellous success in accomplishing the general purpose."

Observer
"As a rule the music attached to these performances is of a fine order of art and has done everything towards the general success. On Friday night it threatened to topple a curious and wonderfully conceived stage spectacle entirely to destruction . . . The many present . . . must have been thoroughly disappointed with the perversion of all that is musically artistic which the composer offered as a setting for Nijinsky's ingenious piece of symbolism. If there is a redeeming feature it is an amazing exposition of the possibilities of rhythm, without which, of course, the dancers would have been hopelessly entangled."

Pall Mall Gazette
"As to the music, the less said the better. When one calls it cacophonous, that is the simple truth . . . Some of the rhythms were quite intelligible, and a few melodic phrases here and there stood out generally supported by unrelated harmonies. This, of course, is the new style, and it defies analysis just as it scorns aesthetic charm. But the greatest disadvantage the score presented was that it never suggested 'atmosphere;' it was simply confusion in series."

THE REALISATION

The Times
"The incidents . . . cannot be called dramatic, for they follow each other without much feeling for rational sequence or climax . . . The gestures of the new ballet . . . are more consistently conventionalized than those in *Jeux.* Some of them undoubtedly do express emotion in a primitive way – fear, for instance, and a joy and religious ecstasy – and the general impression is often the impression given one by children at play . . ."

Daily Mail
" 'Cannibal Island Dancing,' someone said, but it was in reality executed by some of our own Aryan ancestors in no tropic clime . . . The dancing . . . is allied to recent manifestations in the other arts, and may perhaps be called 'Cubist dancing,' (according to a recent definition – 'twenty-four dances performed by twenty-four dancers to twenty-four different tunes played simultaneously.')" (Richard Capell.)

Daily Telegraph
". . . and all this primordial, logical business revealed no beauty, save momentarily, when a bevy of maidens posed gracefully and Miss Piltz danced amazingly."

The Standard
"The attempts of the dancers to carry out M. Nijinsky's anti-curvilinear movements were received with a good deal of laughter during the performance and plenty of hissing and clapping at the close – the ayes having it for the most part."

Observer
"The applause that strove for a long time to gain the upper hand of a considerable expression of disapproval and ultimately conquered was evidently a recognition of the remarkable work of the dancers, in particular, the extraordinary *pas seul* of the 'chosen maiden,' Mlle. Piltz, in the second act."

Pall Mall Gazette
"The bearing of the dancers recalled that of the inhabitants of Laputa, who held their heads on one side . . . The movements of prehistoric people were doubtless different to those of the present day, but that seems hardly a good enough reason for making them so grotesque."

SUMMARY

Observer
"THE SOONER M. NIJINSKY HAS NEW MUSIC WRITTEN TO HIS SUPREMELY INGENIOUS AND INTERESTING CONCEPTION THE BETTER. HE WILL BE DOING A GREAT SERVICE TO HIS WONDERFUL COMPANY, WHO CARRY HIS IDEAS TO A PERFECT AND FASCINATING EXECUTION."

The day after the première, the *Daily Mail* gave an interview with Nijinsky. He was reported as having said: 'I cordially say thanks and 'Bravo!' to the English public for their serious interest and attention in *The Festival of Spring.* There was no ridicule of the ballet on Friday and there was great applause. People who say that the piece was hissed cannot know what real hissing is. But the newspapers seem to have been much less sympathetic than the audience. I am accused of a 'crime against grace,' among other things. It seems that because I have danced in ballets like *The Pavilion of Armida*, *The Spectre of the Rose*, and *The Sylphides*, which aim at grace pure and simple, I am to be tied down to 'grace' for ever. Really I begin to have horror of the very word; 'grace' and 'charm' make me feel seasick.

". . . I could compose graceful ballets of my own if I wanted to – by the score. The fact is, I detest conventional 'nightingale-and-rose' poetry; my own inclinations are 'primitive.' I eat my meat without *sauce Béarnaise*. There have been schools of painting and sculpture that went on getting suaver and suaver until there was no expression but only banality left; then there has always come a revolt. Perhaps something like this has happened in dancing."

A few days later, "An Englishman," a regular *Daily Mail* columnist, examined Nijinsky's statements.

"M. Nijinsky, the most highly accomplished dancer of our time, declared on the morrow of his new ballet that 'grace and charm made him feel seasick.' The confession is ingenuous and characteristic. The spirit of the age has gone to M. Nijinsky's head, as it has gone to the head of many other artists. The same lawlessness, the same contempt of order which afflicts the politics of today afflicts also the humanities. The virtue most highly prized is the virtue of novelty."

The article was very long, but this is the essence of its argument:
"A beauty which is sincere, such as the beauty of M. Nijinsky's *Spectre de la Rose*, can never be common or tedious . . . But, says M. Nijinsky, beauty comes easy to me, . . . therefore I must select another aim for my ambition . . . And so . . . he resolves to prove himself a modern among the moderns by the frank assumption of archaism . . . And he does not understand that his return to the primitives is at once arbitrary and irrelevant. The primitives were not angular in form and awkward in gesture because they wished to be angular and awkward, but because they could not achieve the beauty at which they aimed . . . But when M. Nijinsky takes for his model the awkward simplicity of the primitives he does not look forward, as they did, to the goal of a generous hope; he looks back to what they, in the intensity of their fervour, might have confessed a failure . . ."

The season as a whole was considered most exciting. Both opera and ballet were crowded for every performance. But Robin Legge summed up the ballet scene: "To my thinking there was underlying the whole of the new ballets . . . an indefinable something that left a decidedly unpleasant flavour, something artistically almost gangrenous . . . While one could find much to admire in *Le Sacre du Printemps*, with all its primitiveness, the music was surely further removed than any other music from even the semblance of primitiveness, and became the quintessence of all that is sophisticated. However, if there is any truth in the rumour, we are little likely to see this again, since it is reported, with what truth I know not, that that glorious dancer Miss Piltz has been positively forbidden by the medical profession to dance the solo, owing to the detrimental effect it had upon her, the physical strain being overwhelming,"

Daily Telegraph 26.7.13

Rarely prejudiced, the Music Critic of *The Lady* said, of *Sacre*: ". . . Report said before the curtain rose . . . that it was going to whip creation . . . that all previous efforts of Diaghilev ballets were going to be eclipsed. With such stupendous seriousness was the novelty taken up by its creators that Mr. Edwin Evans was sent before the curtain to explain beforehand what it really meant . . . All this did not inspire confidence, for a beautiful work of art ought to be able to reveal itself. If we are allowed to take *Sacre* on its merits, we may accept it and even enjoy it, but all attempts to represent it as inspired truth about the movements of the youth of mankind are likely to alienate us . . . I found it very interesting. There were some charming patterns made by the permutations and combinations of different groups of dancers. There were ideas in profusion. But as a whole I am afraid that it appeals to all that is pretentious in human nature, and so I condemn it as the evocation of a principle. It may be quaint and delightful to see people crawling on all fours, but it is irritating to be told that in that posture they are more 'original' than when walking on foot. It is quite possible to be original in erect motion."

The Lady 17.7.13

At the time, Stravinsky does not appear to have expressed either pleasure or pain at the result.

Though this cartoon by Quiz did not appear until 1925, it shows that Shaw must have given the impression that he would willingly break into a jig at the first notes of the pan-pipes.

Diaghilev usually ensured his backers a good audience by sugaring the pill. *Le Sacre* was given again on July 18th, but so, too, was a great favourite. Not for forty years did a certain contemporary reaction to the exquisite in ballet find publication.

Though by no means a "regular," George Bernard Shaw seems to have attended more often than has been thought to be the case. On July 18th, 1913, he wrote to Mrs. Pat Campbell (his adored 'Stella' –)

10, Adelphi Terrace, W.C.

George Bernard Shaw & Mrs. Pat Campbell: Their Correspondence

I got free from my cares today at a quarter past six: but I didn't dare.
The faithful Prosser glared at me last time for depriving you of your rest and your dinner; and my conscience told me Prosser was right.
I went to the Russian Ballet and consoled myself with Karsavina and Charlotte with Nijinsky. That is how *we* should dance.

G.B.S.

The programme had included *Le Spectre de la Rose.*

[No. 38.]
The Chosen Maiden has been spinning,
as Valentine Gross indicates in the
movement of the skirt.

Not until *The Times* devoted a whole column to a summing-up of *Le Sacre* after its third – and final – performance in London, did anyone really try to describe the *appearance* of the ballet, other than by references to the beautiful back-cloths.

"In the two ballets by Debussy it is safe to say that few people who have witnessed them have been able to hear the music at all; the senses were entirely engrossed by the movements of M. Nijinsky and his colleagues. In *Le Sacre du Printemps*, on the other hand, the functions of the composer and the producer are so balanced that it is possible to see every movement on the stage and at the same time to hear every note of the music. But the fusion goes deeper than this. The combination of the two elements of music and dancing does actually produce a new compound result, expressible in terms of rhythm – much as the combination of oxygen and hydrogen produces a totally different compound, water. Not only does M. Roerich's beautiful scenery also form an important part of the whole, but even the colours of the dresses are to some extent reflected in the orchestration – as, for instance, in the first scene, when a group of maidens in vivid scarlet huddles together to the accompaniment of closely-written chords on the trumpets. Movements, too, are mirrored in an equally realistic way when, a little later on, the dancers thin out into a straggling line, while the orchestra dwindles to a trill on the flutes; then a little tune begins in the woodwind two octaves apart, and two groups of three people detach themselves from either end of the line to begin a little dance that exactly suits the music.

The
Times
26.7.13

[No. 39.]
The first of a series of jumps, in an attitude
reminiscent of a Scottish reel – the instructions
being that it is to be repeated five times.

The same thing is seen equally clearly in the dance of the Chosen Maiden in the second scene,
though as this is a solo dance the effect is less striking and more obvious. As regards gesture, the
convention employed seems to be a treble one. First we have purely ritual movements of a primitive kind, such as leaping on the earth and looking towards the sun; then imitative or realistic
gestures, seen when all the dancers shiver with terror at the entry of the old seer; and lastly
movements of a purely emotional value, neither ritual nor imitative, which can be seen at their
clearest in the dance by Mlle. Piltz already alluded to. These curious jerks of the body and
sideway movements of the head are the modern descendants of the old-fashioned *pirouette* and
entre-chat; and their artistic value seems to be about the same.''

The Times continued:

''What is really of chief interest in the dancing is the employment of rhythmical counterpoint
in the choral movements. There are many instances, from the curious mouse-like shufflings of
the old woman against the rapid steps of the men in the first scene to the intricate rhythms of the
joyful dance of the maidens in the last. But the most remarkable of all is to be found at the close
of the first scene, where figures in scarlet run wildly round the stage in a great circle, while the
shifting masses within are ceaselessly splitting up into tiny groups revolving on eccentric axes. It
is here that M. Nijinsky joins hands with M. Jacques Dalcroze; and it is in this direction that his
theories on ballet are capable of indefinite expansion.''

[No. 40.]
Another stage of the same jump, made with the rhythms becoming more and more intricate.

Turning to the music, *The Times* went on:

'It is through rhythm, too, and rhythm only, that dancing can identify itself with music. M. Stravinsky has made the best use of his opportunities, and utilizes the most amazing and complex rhythms with the utmost skill. He is so pre-occupied with them that he has made no attempt to please the ear. He apparently intends the actual sound of his music to convey nothing more than the idea of something primitive and unformed, and has done exactly what he wanted . . . It seems hardly necessary to consider it as a real foretaste of the music of tomorrow; for M. Stravinsky has already shown himself so adaptable as a composer that his next ballet is no more likely to resemble *Le Sacre du Printemps* than that itself resembles *Petrouchka*."

The Times had started its summing-up by saying that "we are either surprisingly quick or surprisingly careless in accommodating ourselves to new forms of art. The first performance of Stravinsky's *Le Sacre du Printemps* evoked something like a hostile demonstration from a section of the audience; the third and last performance was received with scarcely a sign of opposition . . . The fact remains that London audiences have settled down calmly to a new development of the ballet after a comparatively short acquaintance with it; and now that the Russians are leaving us, it would be well to co-ordinate our ideas before they return with something even more startling."

Well after the end of the season, a letter appeared in *The Times*, coming anonymously from Holland Park.

Sir,

The
Times
9.8.13

A welcome analysis in *The Times* (26.7.13) showed that the admirable novelty in the choreography of *Le Sacre du Printemps* lay in its logical and exhaustive exploitation of the composer's rhythms. In *Jeux*, it was fairly pointed out, the music came through much less. Is it, perhaps, partly for this reason that the not less important nature of the experiment presented in *Jeux* has won so little recognition?

In all previous ballets the inventor has been concerned to account for the circumstances that his dramatis personae dance . . .

This deprecatory attitude towards dancing, this feeling that the appropriate scenario is to be sought in such circumstances as may lend an air of verisimilitude to an unusual spectacle, restricts the art of the ballet . . .

In this important factor *Le Sacre du Printemps* shows no innovating tendency. The spectator has no difficulty in believing that some such scene of ritual dancing actually heralded the coming of many a spring. A London audience would have settled down quite quietly to the news that Maoris do the like to this day. Indeed we, too, might find ourselves thus clustering in groups, stamping the ground and circling in panic, hands to head. But when, in the first dawn of adolescence, we were projected into those first fresh interludes of sentiment – interludes, indeed, inconsequent, with no knowledge of an end, all wonder, hesitation, vague defection, and rapture impersonal – our behaviour was not that of Nijinsky, Karsavina and Schollar in *Jeux*.

"For the first time we are here treated to an employment of dancing as an absolute medium. At one bound the ballet is removed from its time-honoured surroundings of unusual circumstances and is carried into the midst of life as everybody knows it. The dance presents a parallel to emotional experiences without imitating the actions which accompany them in real life. Incidentally, the piece shows Nijinsky once more as an adept in presenting what is young. In *Jeux* the individual is young. In *Le Sacre* society is young. In *L'Après-Midi d'un Faune* – that exquisite piece of sophistication – the earth itself is young.

"The British public (which seldom enjoys the consciousness of pressing to the van in artistic movements) has been commended for its readiness in following Nijinsky's lead in the unfamiliar art of ballet. We owe it to our new reputation that *Jeux* should not have come and gone without an acknowledgment of its importance. For we did rather, it must be confessed, on the first night incline to tell him that people do not wear red ties and that the motions he put before us promised ill for success at Wimbledon . . ."

THE DAILY TELEGRAPH, SATURDAY, MARCH 14, 1914.

VARIETY ENTERTAINMENTS.

COLISEUM, Charing-cross, 2.30 and 8 DAILY.
Change of Programme Weekly.
ENTERTAINMENT DE LUXE by
"STARS" of INTERNATIONAL ART.

ENTHUSIASTIC RECEPTION
AT EACH PERFORMANCE.

GENEE'S
REPERTOIRE
SEASON.

ADELINE
GENEE.
ADELINE
GENEE.

In DIVERTISSEMENT from
"ROBERT LE DIABLE,"
with
ALEXANDER VOLININ
and CORPS DE BALLET.

R. G. HUNTER presents   Supported by
HUNTLEY WRIGHT,   Lewis Fielder, and 'O.
Fred McGuire, and
FLORENCE WRAY, and
in miniature musical play,
"SIMPLE 'EARTED BILL."

CINQUEVALLI, THE INCOMPARABLE JUGGLER.

MALCOLM SCOTT, WILLIE SOLAR,
"THE WOMAN   The dancing success of the original
WHO   London Hippodrome production,
KNOWS."   "Hullo! Ragtime!"

NELLA WEBB, CARLISLE and WELLMON,
The American Disease.   Singers and Composers.

DOROTHY WEBSTER, Contralto,
OSNATOS, Comedy Gymnasts.
FOURTH SERIES OF
BIG GAME HUNTING
IN SOUTH AFRICA
ON THE BIOSCOPE.

NEXT WEEK,
AUSTEN HURGON'S REVUE
"AND VERY NICE TOO!"

COLISEUM—Box-office 10 a.m. to 10 p.m.
Phone 7,541, Gerr. Boxes, two guineas, one guinea,
15s. and 10s. 6d.; Royal Boxes by arrangement;
Children under 12 half-price to
Fauteuils, and Grand Tier Stalls (afternoons only).—
Circle, Balcony Stalls, Orchestra Stalls, Royal
seats, 6d. to 7s 6d. Stalls.
Managing Director, OSWALD STOLL.

PALACE.   PALACE.
There is no stall floor which can show
a braver array of well-dressed folk, and there
is a decided "tone" about the Palace. Daily
Telegraph.

FIRST APPEARANCE of NIJINSKY.

NIJINSKY.
THE FAMOUS PREMIER DANSEUR.

NIJINSKY.   NIJINSKY.

NIJINSKY,   Supported by
Mlle. NIJINSKA, ALEXANDRE KOTSCHETOWSKY,
and Leading Members of the Imperial Russian Ballet.

LES SYLPHIDES.
Last week of

NIJINSKY. "Far more wonderful than
he was at Covent Garden."
"He was his own inimitable
self." "Full of the grace and agility
which have made him the
world's greatest dancer."

LE SPECTRE de la ROSE.

NIJINSKY. "The Triumph of Nijinsky."
"His reception at the end
had something of rapture." "he
seemed inspired." "Last night he seemed

PAS DE DEUX.

NIJINSKY, VALSE CHOPIN.
NIJINSKY and MLLE. NIJINSKA.

NIJINSKY   VARIATION CHOPIN (first time),
DANSE POLOVTSIENNE
DANSE ORIENTALE.   NIJINSKY.

NIJINSKY.

LAST WEEK.
MLLE. ANKA LAYEWA
in Serbo-Croatian Folk Songs.

LAST WEEK
SEVERIN-MARS and IRENE BORDONI,
in L'IMPRESARIO.

"GENERAL" EDWARD LA VINE,
The man who has
"soldiered" all his life.

MATINEES OF THE FULL EVENING
PROGRAMME
WEDNESDAYS and SATURDAYS, at 2.

PALACE.   PALACE
PALACE.   9.15
Overture   General La Vine.... 9.30
Ivy Latimer   Orchestral Selection.... 9.45
Anka Layewa   9.55
Lima Panzer   Nijinsky   10.50
Pauls Sydney   Vicuna Trio   11. 5
                         The Bioscope
Telephone 6,834, Gerrard.
FRED BUTT.

PICTURE PALACES.

WITH CAPTAIN SCOTT IN THE
ANTARCTIC."

WILD ANIMAL AND BIRD LIFE IN THE
SOUTH POLAR REGIONS."

MR. HERBERT G. PONTING, F.R.G.S.,
Camera-Artist with the Scott Antarctic Expedition tells
his THRILLING STORY of the GREATEST ADVENTURE
of MODERN TIMES, and exhibits his COMPLETE MOVING
PICTURE RECORD of CAPTAIN SCOTT'S MEMORABLE
JOURNEY TWICE DAILY, at 3 and 8.15, at PHILHAR-
MONIC HALL, GREAT PORTLAND-STREET, W.

LISTENING to Mr. Ponting's admirable lecture
the other evening, I could not help thinking that
these kinema films were by far the most wonderful of
visible results of Scott's Antarctic expedition. How bitterly,
how gloriously real were these things."—Mr. Filson Young in
the PALL MALL GAZETTE.

THERE is nothing in the theatres of London to
approach this drama. There is no comedy so amusing,
no play so poignant, no tragedy so heartrending, as this tale in
pictures."—Mr. J. T. Grein.

Prices: Reserved Stalls and Circle, 5s., 3s., 2s. 600 unreserved 2s. and seats. At all Libraries, and at the Hall.
Telephone 3,003, Mayfair.

THE EVENING PERFORMANCE CON-
CLUDES at HALF-PAST TEN, thus giving suburban
visitors ample time for returning home.   Business

PHILHARMONIC HALL
is two minutes from Oxford-circus Tubes and Portland-
road Met. Stations. Omnibuses pass the door.
Manager Mr Ponting, Mr. Ben Nathan.

CINEMA HOUSE, 225, OXFORD-STREET, W.
(a few doors from Oxford-circus Tubes).

CONTINUOUS CINEMATOGRAPH ENTERTAINMENT.
Including
THE MYSTERIOUS INN.
DAILY, 1 p.m. to 11 p.m. SUNDAYS, 6 p.m. to 11 p.m.
Prices, 6d., 1s., and 2s. Family 'Box, 10s. 6d.

MAIDA VALE   PALACE.
CONTINUOUS PERFORMANCE, 3-11.
ANNE BOLEYN.
An Historical Romance in Three Acts.
Seats may be booked in advance.
SUNDAYS, 6 to 10.30.   Special Programme.
Adam Tea Rooms. Private Boxes.   Phone, Hampstead, 7,072.

NEW GALLERY KINEMA
REGENT-STREET,
CONTINUOUS ENTERTAINMENT from 2 p.m. till 11 p.m.
A MAGNIFICENT SERIES of SILENT PLAYS,
Including "MIXED IDENTITIES," French Farcical Comedy.

WEST-END Cinema, Coventry-st., Piccadilly, W.
Continuous programme, including, at 3, 6.30, and 9 p.m.,
the picture greater than "QUO VADIS?"
"SPARTACUS.
Booking-office, Regent 2,588.

ELECTRIC PALACE, MARBLE ARCH.
Non-stop, 2 p.m. to 11 p.m., including
"THE ESCAPE of JIM DOLAN."
A Thrilling Drama in Two Acts.

SCALA—BRITISH ARMY FILM, as shown by
Royal Command. Special Edition.   Also Powerful
Pathécolour Drama, IN HIS GRIP, &c.   Unique programme to
be seen only at the Scala, 2.30 till 11.   Gerr., 1,444.

SHAFTESBURY PAVILION, "QUO VADIS," the
nue, W.—LASCA; or, Down on the Rio Grande; the
famous poem, with recitation, by Mr. Nix Webber; also
"ESCAPE OF JIM DOLAN," and full prog.

MUSICAL INSTRUMENTS.

KEITH PROWSE PIANOS.
Overstrung, underdamper action from 20gns. Fully
guaranteed, cash or terms.   Illustrated catalogue of 1914
models, post free.

RECORD PIANO BARGAINS.
Returned from hire and secondhand.   Thoroughly restored and fully guaranteed; Bechstein, 42gns.; Blüthner,
15gns.; Hopkinson, 24gns.; Keith Prowse, overstrung plan ette,
28gns.; Chappell, £35; Broadwood, 20gns.; Cramer, £15; short
grand, Hansen, 26gns.; Haake, 22gns.; Gors and Kalman, baby
grand, nearly new, overstrung, 36gns.; Steins player piano,
65-note, as new, 40gns. of old pianos taken in part payment.
Write for de-criptive list of 100 rare bargains, post free.
KEITH PROWSE (Ltd.), 48, CHEAPSIDE, E.C.

BORD PIANOS.—Illustrated Lists will be sent
free showing prices and rates of hire, on the Three
Years' System, from 15s. per month.   Secondhand
from 10s. 6d. per month.   Ask to see the Auto-Bord' Player-Piano.

BECHSTEIN PIANOS.—May also be had on the
same system, at advantageous prices and terms.
Pianos exchanged.
LIBERAL DISCOUNTS for cash.
CHAS. STILES and CO.
74-76, Southampton-row, London, W.C.

STOCKTAKING SALE
SURPLUS STOCK of GRAND and COTTAGE PIANOS
ordered at exceptional reductions to effect an early clearance.
No reasonable offer refused.
Call or write for List No. 1.
THOMAS OETZMANN and CO. (Ltd.),
ONLY ADDRESS—27, BAKER-STREET, W.

BOYD PIANOS and PISTONOLA PIANOS.
AWARDED FIVE GOLD MEDALS.
For CASH or DEFERRED PAYMENTS.
Full particulars and Illustrated Catalogue Post Free.
BOYD Ltd., 19, Holborn, London, E.C.

PIANOS from 10s. 6d. per month, by leading
makers, on Hire-Purchase. New and Secondhand Pianos
exchanged or repaired.—BERINGER & STROHMENGER.
248, Streatham High-road, S.W. Telephone 4, Streatham.

NIJINSKY AT THE PALACE THEATRE

The water that passed under the bridges between the last night of the summer season of 1913 and the first night of the longer season at the same theatre in 1914 was not so much a stream as a tidal wave.

On July 25th, 1913, no one could have guessed that the Nijinsky who was so wildly applauded was appearing with the Diaghilev ballet for the last time in London.

Diaghilev and Nijinsky left for a short holiday in Baden-Baden. Nijinsky then sailed with the company for its first South American tour. Diaghilev, a prey to terror of the sea, decided at the last moment not to accompany them. Had he gone on that voyage, things might have turned out very differently.

Travelling with the ballet (but first-class, at her own expense,) was a wealthy Hungarian girl, Romola de Pulsky, aged 24. She had seen the ballets when they were in Budapest in 1912. Fascinated by Nijinsky, she had travelled around with the company in Europe, taking private lessons from Cecchetti. Diaghilev allowed her to become a member of the *corps de ballet.*

Nijinsky spoke only Russian and Polish, and a very little French. They had no common tongue, but this did not impede a ship-board flirtation. Nijinsky proposed, or rather, prevailed upon Baron Gunzbourg to propose for him. Despite the consternation of the dancers, who struggled to explain to her the situation existing between Diaghilev and Nijinsky, Romola would not be dissuaded. The marriage took place as soon as they arrived in Buenos Aires.

Nijinsky seems to have been extraordinarily naïf about it. Could he really have believed that Diaghilev would calmly accept his marriage? The latter's biographers have described his rage and chagrin when a cable brought him the news. In the autumn, Nijinsky sent Diaghilev a telegram enquiring the date and place to which he should report for rehearsals. Diaghilev forced Grigoriev to send the reply in his own name – YOUR SERVICES ARE NO LONGER REQUIRED.

Nijinsky and his wife spent the winter in Europe, and early in 1914, he accepted an offer from the Palace Theatre in London to raise a company and give an eight-week season. The repertoire was to include some of his great Fokine successes, and some new works of his own. The troupe was most curiously composed, for there was to be only one other male dancer, his brother-in-law Kotchetowsky. His sister, Bronislava, would be the ballerina, with an all-female *corps de ballet.* Bronislava was already well-known as a dancer, with a gift of elevation comparable to his own. She collected young dancers in St. Petersburg, and he gave them contracts for a whole year.

Though this season was quite apart from the Diaghilev Ballet, its story must be told in order that subsequent events may be comprehended.

Nijinsky's detestation of the idea of appearing in a music-hall was long-founded and obsessional. He was accustomed to the court status of opera and ballet at the Maryinsky. Possibly

Nijinsky and his bride, Romola de Pulsky, leaving the Church of San Miguel in Buenos Aires, on Wednesday, September 10th, 1913, after the religious ceremony, which took place in the evening. Earlier, at 1 p.m. in the City Hall, the civil ceremony had been performed.

facing page: In Nijinsky's new version of *Les Sylphides*, the backcloth was designed by Doboujinsky with silvery tree-trunks which may have been intended to evoke the silver birches of Russia.

T.P.'s
Magazine
May 1911

some recollections of childhood, touring with his father and mother, haunted him. In a pseudo-interview with a former Petersburg correspondent of the *Daily News*, he had said: "I danced with them sometimes in provincial theatres. My first appearance was as a little Chinese with a little pigtail, and that was when I was only six." (This became "a little Japanese, only four," in America.) But in that interview he had said, "One thing I am determined not to do, and that is to go on the music-hall stage. I have had several tempting offers; but, after all, what is money? I think more of my art than I do of money, and I refuse to be sandwiched between performing dogs and acrobats."

Pavlova had been annually at the Palace Theatre since 1910. He must have known that it was a famous variety house.

Nijinsky and Romola, who was pregnant, arrived in London in February. There was trouble because Diaghilev sought to prevent Bronislava from appearing at the Palace, but Nijinsky's lawyer, Sir George Lewis, took the matter in hand, and either Diaghilev backed down or else he lost. But for the first time, Nijinsky had to oversee every detail of the complicated preparations, from which he had always been preserved by Diaghilev. Vladimir Polunin was called in by the scenic designer, Boris Anisfeld, to assist him, and said that "the business was pressing, for only four weeks could be spared for the work, and it proceeded at the rate of fourteen to sixteen hours daily." Costumes, orchestral rehearsals, rehearsals for the dancers – Nijinsky must have been hard pressed.

The ballet was allotted three-quarters of an hour, from 10.5 p.m. until the Bioscope at 10.50. Despite Nijinsky's professions of hatred of the graceful and beautiful in 1913, there was to be no nonsense about the repertoire for Mr. Butt's audience. New versions Nijinsky might make of the attractions in which he had won his reputation, but graceful and beautiful they would have to be.

Daily
Telegraph
3.3.14

For the first two weeks, the programme was to consist of his new version of *Les Sylphides*, a solo by Kotchetowsky, and *Le Spectre de la Rose*.

The notices – excerpts from which Mr. Butt printed in his advertisements later in the week – were rapturous.

"It seems quite fitting that Nijinsky – one may surely drop the prefix – should find a home at the Palace Theatre, the scene of the incomparable Pavlova's many triumphs, and his appearance there last night, his first on the variety stage, was decidedly a feather in Mr. Alfred Butt's cap. The Palace has held no larger audience . . . and the evening brought with it all the signs and tokens of a popular success . . .

Daily
Telegraph
3.3.14

"All the facets of his peculiar genius it is obviously not within the power of a single programme to exhibit. . . . Last night we had *Les Sylphides* in a fresh setting, an impressionist picture of trees and foliage of delicate, ethereal tints, palest greens and indefinable blues, the whole silvered by a crescent moon, whose pale beams were reflected in the waters of a lake forming part of the background . . . The music was different from that which had accompanied the evolutions before. It was drawn, as then, from Chopin, but the nocturnes, mazurkas, and études were not those used in the previous version, and the numbers were chosen from among the less widely familiar of the Polish composer's works. And for this ballet they have been orchestrated, quite simply and with no characteristic note of modernity, by Maurice Ravel. But to most of those present last night Nijinsky, and not the music to which he footed it, was 'the thing,' and in *Les Sylphides* the perfect charm, refinement and grace of his performance made an appeal no less potent than before . . .

"After a quaint little *Danse Orientale* in which Mr. Kotchetowsky (whose clever performance as the Moor in *Petrouchka* will not have been forgotten) danced very nimbly before a background of apple-green curtains, and seemed now and again to turn himself into a Chinese idol, one renewed pleasant acquaintance with *Le Spectre de la Rose* . . . It may be that the famous dancer felt just a little cramped in his new surroundings, and missed, for the purposes of his wondrous flying leaps, the freedom of ampler spaces. But, even so, he was his own inimitable self in this airy, delicate little fantasy, and great was the audience's applause when he vanished, sprite-like, through the window . . ."

The
Stage
5.3.14

At the end of a fairly similar review, *The Stage*, which had kept count, gave a few more details. "M. Nijinsky was called no fewer than nine times on Monday evening, and his season should be one of the most successful under Mr. Alfred Butt's comprehensive management. Mr. Herman Finck's orchestra, it should be added, rendered admirable service, although one could perhaps wish for a little strengthening in the matter of strings . . .

"Also in the programme are Severin-Mars and Irene Bordoni in *L'Impresario*, the Tourbillon Troupe of Cyclists, Lily Hayes, Lena Pantzer, Adler and Arline, Anka Layewa, and the Viennese Trio."

Behind the scenes, there were rows. Madame Nijinsky described her husband's sense of outrage at being asked to go and call upon Alfred Butt in his office. Nijinsky refused. Then, another day, there was an incident when a stage hand made a pass at her, and Nijinsky flew into a violent temper, fell upon the man and knocked him down. Yet another time, when his sister was feeling off-colour, he was so abrupt with her that she burst into tears, whereupon her husband, Kotchetowsky, insulted Vaslav and spat upon the floor behind him, like a Russian *moujik*. It is easy to guess that there must have been many more "incidents." Romola said that they put her husband into a highly nervous state. They probably put everyone else on edge as well.

On March 12th, Butt announced the programme for the second fortnight – which was to include *Carnaval* (though it is hard to see how this could have been managed with only two men,) and *L'Oiseau et le Prince*.

The same day, an exhibition of portraits of Nijinsky, arranged by the Fine Art Society to coincide with his season, received critical attention from Sir Claude Phillips.

Daily
Telegraph
12.3.14

". . . The incomparable Russian dancer – the Vestris of our day – has found many artists ready to depict and to model him in his favourite rôles . . . but few have been completely successful . . . The Society has failed, on this occasion, to produce anything by M. Bakst . . . Rodin, too, if report is to be believed – has made many studies from Nijinsky, and these could not have failed to prove enormously interesting . . . The small collection . . . is well worth seeing, if only on account of the magnificent study in black chalk by Mr. Sargent, who has here depicted his sitter as Armida's favourite slave and dancer in *Le Pavillon d'Armide*. So buoyant in movement, so full of vitality and joy in life, so suggestive of what is highest in Nijinsky's art is this drawing, that it must be ranked amongst the finest things that Mr. Sargent has done in the years of his maturity . . . M. Jacques Blanche portrays the dancer very subtly in an attitude of absolute repose, in *La Danse Orientale* . . . Mr. Valentine Cross (sic), though he cannot suggest all that there is in his terpsichorean hero's dancing of suppleness beneath the strength, is moderately successful in his numerous studies from *Le Spectre de la Rose*. He fails, on the other hand, to evolve not only what here is of sinister force but of poignant tragedy in Petrouchka: of bestial lust in *Scheherazade*, of Italian comedy freakishness in *Le Carnaval* . . ."

"Mr. Valentine Cross" was, of course, Mlle. Valentine Gross. Sir Claude Phillips could not have been expected to know, for the error had been perpetrated in the catalogue.

Monday, March 16th, produced a sensation instead of the anticipated change of programme.

Daily
Telegraph
17.3.14

"A disappointment, keen, swift, and really dramatic, awaited the audience at the Palace Theatre last night . . . The house was full to overflowing – had been filling up steadily, indeed, for well nigh two hours. Artists had succeeded each other, amid general manifestations of pleasure; Mr. Wilkie Bard had evoked round after round of applause . . . the whole auditorium was stilled to expectancy, pending the immediate appearance of M. Nijinsky, who was now due to occupy the stage.

"Instead, however, of Mr. Nijinsky, there appeared – in front of the curtain – Mr. Alfred Butt, who straightway made an announcement that positively struck the audience dumb. But a moment or two previously, he said – in fact whilst Mr. Wilkie Bard had been engaged in singing his encore – he had received a communication by telephone from a distinguished medical man, to the effect that M. Nijinsky had been taken suddenly ill, with a temperature of 103 degrees. At such short notice, Mr. Butt added, it had naturally been impossible to arrange for any substitute; but in the meantime the members of M. Nijinsky's company would present certain dances . . .

"It has already been suggested that the indisposition of M. Nijinsky was wholly unsuspected and unlooked for. The famous dancer had been rehearsing in the theatre with his company all day long – from ten o'clock in the morning until a quarter to eight at night, and there was not the slightest hint of the illness which so suddenly overtook him subsequently. Indeed, there was a disposition in some quarters to think that in the course of his prolonged rehearsal M. Nijinsky had taken too much out of himself, and that his illness was really due to physical exhaustion."

Two days later, *The Stage* filled in some details:–

". . . Mr. Butt said:– 'I heard by telephone eight minutes ago from Sir Alfred Fripp that Mr. Nijinsky is in bed with a temperature of 103 degrees . . . Of course, anyone who wishes may have his money back. The rest of the dancers will perform their part of the programme. I am sorry, but I knew nothing until eight minutes ago.' M. Kotchetowsky gave his picturesque *Danse Orientale*, and Mlle. Nijinska and others distinguished themselves in a short ballet, while other highly acceptable substitutes were forthcoming in Lewis Sydney, with stories and songs at the piano; Evie Greene, with a couple of loudly applauded ballads; and Hetty King, with her popular 'Poppy Show' number . . ." The Stage 19.3.14

The whole company was suspended on the Tuesday and Wednesday. Other variety managers helped out with acts to fill the vacant 50 minutes. Amongst those drummed up were "Vernon Watson, with imitations of well-known artists; Barclay Gammon, with his inseparable piano; and Mr. Fred Emney and Miss Sydney Fairbrother, in the laughable sketch, '*A Sister to Assist 'Er*.'" Daily Telegraph 18.3.14

Mr. Butt exercised his option under the terms of the contract, and as Nijinsky had not appeared for three consecutive days, the engagement was terminated. It is difficult to see what even Sir George Lewis could have done about that, in view of the contract which he had, presumably, agreed. The Stage 26.3.14

The *Era* made some observations:–

"The prospectus is out of the Sir Thomas Beecham season at Drury Lane . . . I am afraid that M. Nijinsky will regret that he is no longer in this social success . . . But independent of the Russian dancer . . . I hope none will be so vain as to be led by a few laudatory Press criticisms to think that they can be a music-hall Atlas and carry an artistic audience on their own shoulders. There are really very few Pavlovas, and as a male dancer has not got quite the same personality and charm, the chance of a success out of the general environment is very small." Era 25.3.14

Certainly, it was widely considered that it was *not* influenza: a cutting in The New York Public Library's Dance Collection, from which, sadly, the identification has been removed, but which is dated April 4th, may have come from an American paper: "It is stated that the illness of Nijinsky . . . is much more serious than is generally realised . . . He is said to be suffering from a nervous breakdown, induced by overwork in the planning and rehearsing of new dances."

Whatever the nature of his illness, the financial loss was in no doubt. Nijinsky had considerable sums in a French bank. Having brought the young dancers out of the Imperial companies, and given them contracts for a year, he paid each one a whole year's salary. The fee for his company had been £1,000 a week, but it was said that he lost £30,000 in the venture. Multiplied to match money values in the 1970's, this was an enormous sum. He acquitted himself most honourably in paying the girls, but possibly this was what led to the institution of an action to recover sums he claimed to be owing to him, the aftermath of which was to come to light later on.

1914

THEATRE ROYAL, DRURY LANE

JUNE 8th - JULY 25th

FIRST PERFORMANCES IN ENGLAND

June 9th: *Daphnis and Chloe*
              (Ravel, Fokine, Bakst.)
              Paris, 8.6.1912

June 11th: *Papillons*
              (Schumann, Fokine, Doboujinsky, Bakst.)
              Monte Carlo 16.4.1914

June 15th: *Le Coq d'Or* (Opera and Ballet)
              (Rimsky-Korsakov, Fokine, Gontcharova.)
              Paris 24.5.1914

June 18th: *Le Rossignol* (Opera and Ballet.)
              (Stravinsky, B. Romanov, Benois.)
              Paris, 26.5.1914

June 18th: *Midas*
              (Steinberg, Fokine, Doboujinsky.)
              Paris 2.6.1914

June 23rd: *La Légende de Joseph*
              (Richard Strauss, Fokine, Sert, Bakst.)
              Paris 17.5.1914

June 26th: *La Nuit de Mai* (Opera with Ballet.)
              (Rimsky-Korsakov, Bolm, Fedorovsky.)
              St. Petersburg, 21.1.1880

REPERTOIRE

Le Carnaval	*L'Oiseau de Feu*	*Le Spectre de la Rose*
Cléopâtre	*Petrouchka*	*Les Sylphides*
Le Lac des Cygnes	*Prince Igor*	*Thamar*
Narcisse	*Scheherazade*	

COMPANY

Baranovitch I., Bewicke, Dombrovska, Faithfull, Fokina, Guliuk, Karsavina, Khokhlova, Klemento-vitch, Konietska, Kopetzinska, Kovalievska, Maicherska, Mamieva, Muningsova (Sokolova), Pflanz, Poire, Razoumovitch, Schollar, Slavitska, Wassilievska, Yezerska.

Bolm, Bourman, Cecchetti, Fedorov, Fokine, Frohmann, Gavrilov, Grigoriev, Gudin, Ivanovsky, Kegler, Kostecki, Kovalsky, Kremnev, Malignin, Massine, Oumansky, Rakhmanov, Romanov B., Savitsky, Semenov, Statkevitch, Tarassov, Toboiko, Varjinsky, Voronzov, Zverev.

CONDUCTORS

Monteux, Cooper, Richard Strauss.

RUSSIAN OPERA AND BALLET

With the sensational collapse of Nijinsky's enterprise right in London itself, there could be no illusions when Diaghilev's summer season opened: there would be no Nijinsky. This had absolutely no effect on the advance bookings.

For his opening night, Beecham netted King Manoel of Portugal and Queen Augusta-Victoria, and the Prince of Hohenzollern, but the same night Queen Alexandra and her sister the Dowager Empress, together with Princess Maud and the Princess Royal, were at Covent Garden.

A fashion writer in the *Mail* was able to say that "inspired by the wonderful toilettes of the Russian Ballet, the designers contrive the most brilliant successes." The Russians were, indeed, the talk of the town, and the town apparently hardly even read political items in the papers. Of course, the Town was not bombarded with vocal news bulletins every hour or so; but the Town appeared to have no interest whatsoever in the trouble brewing in the Balkans. Prince Paul of Serbia's name appeared from time to time in the list of those present in the audience. (Prince Paul was an undergraduate at Oxford: with Lord Cranbourne and another friend, he appeared before the magistrates in June, charged with playing bicycle polo in Merton Street – fined 2/6 each and costs. This, Ascot, and a bomb-scare in Westminster Abbey, completely overshadowed "NEW CRISIS IN THE NEAR EAST – FEAR OF WAR" on the front page of the *Pall Mall Gazette* on June 12th.) Daily Mail 13.7.14

The most important feature of Diaghilev's season was his reconciliation with Fokine, who was not only making new ballets, but dancing in London for the first time. They had quarrelled in Paris in 1912 over arrangements for the first night of *Daphnis and Chloe* and the favouritism being shown to Nijinsky and his first ballet. Now that Diaghilev desperately needed him, Fokine was able to dictate terms. Most important to him was that his wife should be given leading roles.

Daphnis was to be given on the first Ballet night. It was preceded by irate letters to the press from the composer, Ravel, furious because Diaghilev intended to dispense with the chorus of voices. Diaghilev was completely unmoved.

"There was that magnetic feeling about the house that one experiences on rare occasions. The dancing was over the footlights before the curtain was up," was the *Pall Mall Gazette's* description of the opening night. The paper went on: "M. Fokine's choreography strikes a new note. While rejecting M. Nijinsky's revolutionary aesthetic he has not disdained to profit by his plastique. Thus there are many moments in *Daphnis* recalling *L'Après-Midi d'un Faune*, though the progress from one such moment to another is on familiar Fokine lines . . ." Pall Mall Gazette 10.6.14

Richard Capell said that "the new spectacle will charm those who have sometimes complained of the savagery in some of the troupe's shows . . . It is a delicate and exquisite thing, with Daily Mail 10.6.14

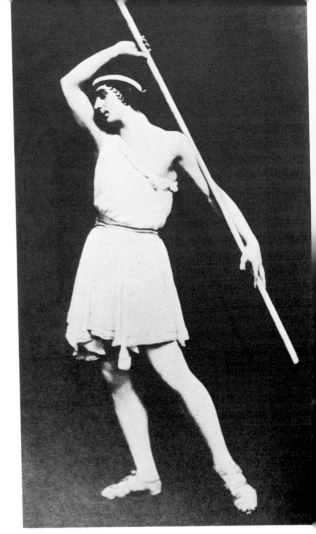

Fokine and his wife, Vera Fokina, in *Cléopâtre*.

Michel Fokine as the shepherd-boy, Daphnis.

M. Bakst leaving his fierce Oriental harmonies for once in favour of the refinement of idealised shepherd life, and M. Maurice Ravel accompanying it all with murmuring music full of faintly clashing dissonances.

"As Chloe Mme. Karsavina was more ingenuous than any other part has shown her. Her dance of supplication in Scene II, to the idyllically bold, bad pirates who have ravished her from Daphnis, has all the charm that can be imagined of her who was the captured Firebird. But perhaps the greatest thing of the ballet is the shepherds' and shepherdesses' final dance of jubilation when the lovers are reunited, thanks to the intervention of Pan – a dance that seemed a miraculous vivication of the garlanded figures of some Grecian urn."

Capell also said that a highly effective new ending had been conceived for *Thamar*, and noted the addition of a movement hitherto excised from the score of *Scheherazade*. "It was a *Scheherazade* without Nijinsky, but that great dancer has not yet been missed, for his successor, M. Fokine, was altogether demonic as the lovely Sultana's negro lover, and his beautiful wife, Mme. Fokina, appearing for the first time as the Sultana, proved herself the adorable Karsavina's equal, which is saying everything."

Most of the early critics of the ballet were really music critics. They were people of general culture, but they had not studied the dancer's technical armament. They knew nothing of the way certain steps were performed, or of the double work with a partner – and were extremely cavalier about the limitations of physical effort and stamina which determine the length of episodes, of appearances, and of intervals as a choreographer plans out his work, or as impresarios plan out an evening's programme. Otherwise highly intelligent people would commit to print absolutely asinine remarks about encores – when the dancers had just completed a physical *tour de force* which would have put a professional footballer on a stretcher – looking cool and graceful, and acting a part, throughout.

Most prolific of critics was undoubtedly Ernest Newman.

Born in 1868 in Liverpool, he started writing articles on musical subjects whilst engaged in business there. These attracted attention by a combination of "solid learning, keen critical insight, and admirable prose," (*Grove*) so that in 1903 he was invited to join the staff of the Midland Institute School of Music in Birmingham. In 1905 he left to become music critic of the *Manchester Guardian*, but in the following year accepted a more tempting offer from the *Birmingham Daily Post*. He was music critic of this journal from 1906 until 1919, when he moved to London – a transition considered by many to be overdue.

Newman was an acknowledged authority on German music, especially Wagner, discussed "nationalism" in music endlessly, and could argue a case putting both sides at great but witty length as no one before or since. During the earlier Diaghilev seasons, he was chained to Proms in Birmingham, but in 1914 he was in town for this first night.

LONDON, TUESDAY NIGHT.

"We are never likely to see the Russian Ballet in the provinces, and a scribe may well despair of communicating any impression of it by mere words to those who have never seen it. Its literalism, its almost mechanical parallelism between music and gesture, sometimes provokes a smile, sometimes jars upon us. But its changeful beauty, and the sense it gives us of witnessing the very apotheosis of youthful strength, grace, and loveliness, make its appeal irresistible." E.N. had much to say about the music of *Daphnis*: "Ravel's music is extremely like Ravel, for good and ill. It has the lightness, the delicacy, the sort of aristocratic blue-bloodedness of the school to which Ravel belongs; but it pays for these qualities in a loss of firmness of the issue and weight of blow, and in a plentiful sprinkling of the perversities and affectations that seem inseparable from music of this type ... Scratch Ravel, I have always said, and you find Chaminade ...."

Birmingham Daily Post 10.6.14

It had been odd for Diaghilev to have produced two ballets with classical settings in Paris, ten days apart, in 1912, when Nijinsky had danced Fokine's *Daphnis* so soon after his own *Faune*. It was odd, in 1913, to have given two ballets which each culminated in a frenzied solo for a female dancer, Salome and the Chosen Virgin. It was not odd for Ernest Newman to deride French music, so renowned was he for his devotion to German composers. He was to have to sit through many ballets to French music in the 1920's, and also to find that the Russian Ballet could visit the provinces.

The *Lady* praised the music and the atmosphere of the ballet. "Nothing the Russians have given us has been more 'classic,' plastically and musically ... It would be idle to deny that Nijinsky is missed. The very fact that Fokine is a designer of ballets and a master of choreography makes his dancing a little over-studied. He not only does the thing; he shows us how it is done. Yet there is much to praise in his work as Daphnis, and the whole ballet is a triumph of his skill."

The Lady 18.6.14

On the second night, the Royal box was occupied by Queen Alexandra and her sister, the Dowager Empress. One wonders whether people who perpetuated the rumour that it was on the latter's account that Nijinsky had been dismissed in 1911, ever noticed her frequent patronage of the ballet in London. Although he was no longer with the company, she had often been present when he was dancing. Would the British Royal family have applauded, or even consented to watch, a dancer who was *persona non grata* with Tante Marie?

Bernard Shaw was also present. He seems to have had considerable appreciation of Diaghilev's part in the enterprise. (In 1930, refusing an invitation to the inaugural dinner of the Camargo Society, he sent Edwin Evans one of his postcards: "Tell them to kick out their press agents and publicity agents, as Serge Diaghilev did. He succeeded by delivering the goods, not by celebrity-hunting and post-prandial speeches ...")

The Times 12.6.14

Papillons was a delightful trifle, set and dressed in the same period as *Carnaval*, with a butterfly-hunt taking place in a garden landscaped by Doboujinski. *The Times* said: "Coming between the wonderful orchestral colour of Ravel and the rhythmic complexity of Stravinsky, we have no shame in confessing a sense of relief at being allowed a brief return to the simplicity of Schumann and the year 1830." In the *Telegraph*: "Pierrot – M. Fokine – is very wary – he

The Times 12.6.14

Daily Telegraph 12.6.14

115

places a lighted candle on the grass and sure enough, in a few minutes the butterflies, lovely yellow and white creatures, are trying to singe their wings at it, and fluttering round as only Mme. Karsavina, Mlle. Schollar, and their companions of the ballet can flutter." Admitted by all to be light-weight, it nevertheless scored an "immediate success," and the *Daily News* said, "The principal charm of the performance, however, lay in the fascinating personality of Mme. Karsavina, who is the incarnation of roguish grace, and dances with matchless agility and fleetness of foot."

Daily
News
12.6.14

The Times noticed that this time Fokina danced Chloe in the Ravel ballet, and that "the fluent grace with which she performed every action gave to the part an incomparable charm. If Mme. Karsavina is technically the more accomplished dancer, Mme. Fokina's personality seems to suit this part better."

Rapturous reports of *Le Coq d'Or* had already been received from Paris.

Madame Karsavina has said that she regarded this ballet as Fokine's masterpiece. In 1902 and 1903, when she had just joined the Maryinsky company, Fokine often used to walk home with her after rehearsals. They sometimes made a detour and "crossed the bridge guarded by stone lions" to amuse themselves looking through the popular prints in a favourite shop. In such prints, Fokine found his inspiration for this great ballet. As Rimsky-Korsakov had written it as an opera, Benois had suggested that singers and dancers should double the rôles. Instead of being hidden, the singers were massed in two great serried ranks flanking the stage, dressed in red, (looking for all the world like Chelsea Pensioners, said the *Sunday Times*.) Natalie Gontcharova, from Moscow, had designed marvellous scenery and costumes.

Sunday
Times
21.6.14

"The wonderful Russians give the critic no rest," said the *Sunday Times*. "*The Golden Cockerel*, both in itself and in its presentation, proved one of the most imaginative and fascinating achievements of Russian art. Its fantastic story, derived from Pushkin, is described as a fairy-tale, but as the astrologer hints in the prologue, there is a strong substratum of satire. It is fairly general in its application to all arrogant and inept authority, but the Russian bureaucracy evidently thought, and probably with good reason, that it was what Mr. Bernard Shaw would call a 'nasty dig' at themselves and kept it off the stage till after Rimsky-Korsakov's death. What is its esoteric objective, however, need not trouble us in the least, for, as presented at Drury Lane, it is just sheer extravaganza, carried through from beginning to end with a whimsical irresponsibility, an airy mockery of conventional ideas, and a childlike zest for romp and grotesquery, to which, unless you are too superior for nursery fun, you will surrender yourself wholeheartedly."

Daily
Mail
16.6.14

"In the middle the play is performed by the ballet troupe. That this new convention should prove so apt is a marvel, but there it is. Thus we have the wondrous Oriental queen who enslaves the preposterous King Dodon enacted by Mme. Karsavina – who surpassed herself in the languorous bare-foot dance in Act II – while the singer of the part was ensconced in one of the tiers to the left." Richard Capell lauded the singer and ended, "The Drury Lane audience has never shown more enthusiasm."

Observer
5.7.14

An interesting letter appeared in the *Observer*:

> ". . . Most people imagine that this method of presenting a work is new. They are wrong, as the following (abbreviated) quotation from Adam's 'Roman Antiquities' (12th Ed. 1835) will show:
>
>> 'Livius Andronicus, who was the first Roman to write a regular play, A.D. 512, and who was also an actor, being compelled by the audience frequently to repeat the same part, and thus becoming hoarse, he asked permission for a boy to sing to the flute, whilst he acted what was sung (canticum agebat), which he did with the greater animation, as he was not hindered by using his voice.'

Q.W.L.T.P., Buckhurst Hill, Essex.

Le Coq d'Or was a political satire dressed up as a fairytale by Pushkin. Silly old King Dodon, bemused by hopeless advice from his boyars, was given a magical golden cockerel, which would warn him of impending danger, by the Astrologer, to whom, in return, he promised to grant any wish.

The country was invaded – the King's sons killed. Then, by magic, the beautiful Queen of Shemakhan appeared, with her tent. The King was completely seduced, though she was a deceiver, and refused to honour his promise when the Astrologer asked for her as his wish. Instead, the King killed him. The Golden Cockerel flew down, pecked the King, and he died. The Astrologer, come back to life, reappeared, admonishing and moralizing.

Fokine said, of this work, "I created a fantasy of subdued Oriental contortions. Parallel with the contrapuntal knitting of the orchestra, I wove on the stage the tender, quivering and, at times, wavy and gliding grace of the Queen of Shemakhan, with the angular movements of Dodon's peasants and warriors." And Cyril Beaumont observed that Karsavina "conveyed that the smiling enigmatic face she showed to King Dodon, with its hint of the exquisite delights in her gift, was only a mask for a sinister purpose . . . Her movements reflected the same mood; those sinuous arms with their languorous movements could strangle as well as caress . . . her beautiful but mocking features dominated the piece, reducing the brilliant figures about her to the level of marionettes which she controlled with the skill of a puppet-master . . ."

Valentine Gross captured all the seduction of the Queen of Shemakhan – Karsavina's favourite part.

The *Lady* also recalled another counterpart: "This experiment (of having the singers dressed alike and massed) was tried years ago, in a slightly different form, by Gordon Craig, but his ungrateful countrymen have apparently forgotten the fact, for they have hailed *Le Coq d'Or* as an innovation." Curiously, for one would have thought that *The Lady* would have liked this

The
Lady
25.6.14

117

colourful and amusing ballet, the paper did not, and dismissed it as "childish rather than child-like."

When, on June 16th, Fokine himself danced Harlequin in *Le Carnaval, The Times* merely made the passing mention that this was the part "which M. Nijinsky used to dance" – no more.

This season was an outstanding success with the public. Not only at Drury Lane, the entire musical scene was filled with stars, and their programmes were pervaded by Russian works. There was a recital entirely composed of Russian music at Queen's Hall, and another at the Bechstein Hall. Amongst the great names listed in one single column advertising concerts were Nikisch, Pachmann, Paderewski, Kreisler, de Lara, Thibaud, Gerhardt, and Arthur Rubinstein. Richard Strauss was given a reception at the Grafton Galleries. A programme consisting of his own music and the *Siegfried Idyll,* performed by an orchestra "the exact size of that for which the work was originally written," was attended by both Stravinsky and Debussy. Strauss played some of his own works, in which "the famous pianist, in his best mood, roused great enthusiasm," and the evening included "fine performances" of *Enigma Variations* and *Tyl Eulenspiegel.*

The brilliance of the Season masked the increasing rumbles in the Near East and the Balkans. (Amongst the Russian aristocrats enjoying it all in London was Prince Youssoupoff.)

The
Lady
18.6.14

An amusing paragraph in *The Lady* conjures up a picture of opera-going – and, presumably, ballet-going – as contemporary manners enjoyed it. "I have just read a protest against the interval, not the interval in general, but the interval in particular which we endure or enjoy in the theatre according to our temperament. If we must have intervals, . . . may we plead that they should be made part of the evening's entertainment? Everyone is growing weary of sitting under blinding electric light for an hour or more (the average total of three intervals) exchanging inane remarks with their neighbours, and pretending to find interest in the sight of familiar people in the boxes. In Germany they go out and drink beer in the intervals. In France they walk in the foyers and corridors. But in England it is still the custom to 'sit it out,' glued to your neighbour, unless the neighbour be a man, when he will use the prerogative of his sex to pass in and out of the stalls, his return generally being made when the curtain has gone up, to the rage of those who want to concentrate on what is going forward on the stage. If you are alone, the long interval is positive torture, unless you can use it, as I saw a lady using it at Drury Lane, in reading '*The Imitation of Christ.*' "

The name of Alexandre Benois had not been given much prominence in England, in spite of his enormous contribution to the early artistic outlook of the group of rebels. It cannot have pleased him if he read the slightly patronising critique of Alfred Kalisch when *Le Rossignol* had its first night, lavish though he was with praise:-

Daily
News
19.6.14

"In *Le Rossignol* we have another fairy tale, with an allegorical significance, and another triumph of staging . . . The scene in the Emperor's palace, with the gold-clad ruler on a very lofty throne, surrounded by courtiers in every conceivable kind of gorgeous robe, is a masterpiece of stage effect. The scene and the costumes place M. Benois on a level with the other artists who have done so much to make the Russian Ballet memorable in the annals of art, and to make Drury Lane the rendezvous of all the distinguished painters in London."

Daily
Mail
19.6.14

Richard Capell said: "The last two little acts (each lasted only 15 minutes) have a restless dissonance that another composer would have needed to dilute in fifty operas. It is all a miracle of ingenuity, fitting the quaintness and the dragons of the scene. The wit of the author of *Petrouchka* is known, and nothing could be wittier and at the same time more extraordinary than the processional march for the Emperor and his fantastic court in Act II." Capell also said that, though this was Stravinsky's first opera, "he is known well enough by his three ballets, of which two, *Petrouchka* and *The Firebird*, are the crowning jewels of the dancers' repertory." (No one brought up Stravinsky's averred dislike of opera from that interview in 1913!)

Daily
Mail
19.6.14

Midas was also shown on the same night as *Le Rossignol.* With yet another classical setting, "*Midas*, music by Maximilien Steinberg, is not in the Russians' most audacious manner," said Capell. "The theme is the musical contest of Apollo and Pan, and the bestowal of asses' ears on the unfortunate Midas whose rustic taste preferred Pan's music to Apollo's. The spirit of the piece is light-hearted. The beauty of the dance of the hamadryads and the Muses can be guessed by those who have seen Fokine's other classical pieces."

"The music is by comparison simple," said the *Telegraph*, "and for this reason, as well as from the fact that the ballet leans well towards the amusing side, *Midas* is certain to maintain its place among the popular favourites." Prophesy ill becomes critics: it was not revived.

Daily
Telegraph
19.6.14

As with some of Diaghilev's other productions, *La Légende de Joseph,* with music composed especially by Richard Strauss, had already been thoroughly "trailed" since its first showing in Paris, and London was eagerly looking forward to this Biblical subject, treated with Renaissance splendour.

The Times had carried a very long exposition of the thought behind the libretto by its author, Count Harry Kessler. The *répétition générale* was reported in several papers, and the première was generously covered. When Diaghilev had mentioned this in 1913 as one of his projected productions, he had referred to it as *Potiphar's Wife,* – an indication that the female would be the predominant character. Its subsequent baptism emphasised the male rôle. The marriage and dismissal of Nijinsky lay between these two titles.

The
Times
9.5.14

On what was to turn out to be Diaghilev's last visit to Russia, he had found the young student, Leonide Massine, in Moscow, and had decided to groom him for stardom. The part of Joseph, the shepherd boy, had been specially tailored to suit his youth and capacity. For Potiphar's Wife, Diaghilev once again wanted a tall woman, and in Paris, the rôle had been allotted to Marie Kouznetzoff, a singer. However, she was not a success in the ballet. (She was singing in the operas in the same Drury Lane season.) So, though she was much shorter, Diaghilev asked Karsavina to step into the high-soled chopines of the 16th century Venetian costume, and Strauss was delighted.

Kessler had said: "This woman is enshrined in a world over-rich, a heavy mass of gold, of beauty, of power, a world splendid but hard, frozen, devoid of mystery. For the first time, when she sees Joseph, she feels an interest in life, curiosity, desire . . . She must fathom it, have him, have his world – this world which is so different from hers; so fresh, so light, so living."

"I wonder what will be the ultimate fate of Strauss's *Joseph's Legend*," said Robin Legge, when it arrived in London. "To judge by what I read the writers are in no sort of doubt whatsoever! It was either damned with faint praise or praised with faint damns, as someone has said." This, does, indeed, sum up the reviews.

Daily
Telegraph
27.6.14

"Seldom has a musical event provoked such interest in London beforehand as that which Dr. Strauss's ballet was able to command. When the great night arrived Drury Lane was packed, and literally humming with anticipation. The fact that the most celebrated German composer of the day should have joined the ranks of those who have supplied M. Diaghilev's ballet with material was felt to be another sign of the cosmopolitan character of this company of dancers . . . Dr. Strauss received a great reception when he appeared at the conductor's desk, and was called at least a dozen times when the curtain had fallen. Every one had something to say about this ballet. Opinions were sharply divided. Some could see no merit in it; others thought it the greatest thing the Russian had ever done. Both parties were right.

The
Lady
3.7.14

". . . The music is a little disappointing . . . The orchestration is the work of a master, but the themes are very ordinary, even to banality. I felt that I was present at a feast where very poor wine was being offered in heavily-chased gilt cups . . . The décor is amazingly fine . . . the raised loggia at the back, with its twisted 'bronzo d'oro' columns, the gorgeously attired guests, the whole atmosphere of a luxury weighing too heavily on the spiritual part of man are wonderfully impressive . . . It is during the second part, when Potiphar's wife returns to the empty hall and endeavours to subjugate the guileless Joseph, that one feels that neither librettists nor composer nor choreographer have avoided vulgarity. There was nothing in the scene to delight the eye or touch the heart. It was curiously inept."

The London dress rehearsal had been a social event. Lady Diana Manners climbed over the backs of seats to a better place. Mrs. Asquith, "in black with a rose-red cloak," was accompanied by her little son Anthony. One wonders how she explained the story to him!

On June 26th, Rimsky-Korsakov's opera-ballet *La Nuit de Mai* was a delightful last addition to the repertoire, the ballet being, as usual, particularly praised for its part in the joint produc-

Leonide Massine's youth and air of innocence were in sharp contrast to the heavy sophistication of the rest of the cast in *La Légende de Joseph*.

Sir Joseph Beecham *(upper right)* and his son *(right)*, who became Sir Thomas twice over – knighted for his services to music before he inherited the baronetcy. They financed this season themselves. Though it must have been an expensive undertaking, they were well satisfied when they read the balance-sheets.

tion. "It is one of the Russians' slighter works," said Richard Capell. The Sunday papers were able to notice both *Joseph* and *Nuit de Mai*, (and also mentioned that, at Covent Garden, the scenery for Boito's *Mephistopheles* had been designed by Bakst. "The appearance of his bold and imaginative work in connection with Italian opera is a portent of new ideals in the conservative world of opera," forecast Richard Capell.)

Daily
Mail
27.6.14

The "Sundays" had much to say about *Joseph*.

"We shall have to revise Beranger's epigram and make it read '*Ce qui est trop bête pour le dire on le danse*' . . . *The Legend of Joseph* presents the Biblical story with frank verism . . . the authors of Strauss's text claim to have treated the story from a symbolic and mystical standpoint and to have raised it from a personal to a cosmic significance . . . Joseph becomes a half-divine figure, apparently without longing of the flesh – 'his gesture when he repulses the woman is a symbol, a mighty inexorable sign,' as the inevitable guidebook tells us – while Potiphar's wife is possessed by no common passion, but 'for her in her satiety only what is divine is of worth.' Buried in presentation, these trimmings occupy a good deal of the first scene, at which, after a banquet given by Potiphar to a party of nobles there is, quite in the fashion of modern days, a programme of entertainment. It is furnished by an Oriental slave-dealer, who submits his human merchandise to the consideration of the magnate and his wife. First he shows a group of dancing women who perform a nuptial dance which, *vide* the guide-book, 'represents symbolically how the Bridegroom on the wedding night unveils the Bride.' Symbolic as the movements may be they actually express a good deal. Then follow a group of boxers and wrestlers . . . Neither of these turns has evoked even a passing interest from Potiphar's consort . . .

Sunday
Times
28.6.72

"The dénouement is quite childish. After Joseph has been denounced, 'something . . . with either boiling oil or melted lead,' after the Mikado's recipe, is brought in for the execution, but a pantomimic Archangel makes an unexpected appearance and carries him off to slow music.

"M. Miassine, who took the part of Joseph, is not a very experienced dancer, but his youthful, ingenuous appearance was a great asset. Mme. Karsavina was Potiphar's wife and danced over the thin ice of this part as only she could do."

And as the public snoozed over the long reports in such small type in the Sunday papers, the Archduke and Archduchess Franz Ferdinand were assassinated in Sarajevo. The papers on Monday were quivering with shock.

But by Wednesday, when the *Telegraph* gave 1½ columns to "PARLIAMENT AND THE MURDERED ARCHDUKE – MOTIONS OF SYMPATHY," this was flanked by a far longer coverage of a boxing-match (described as "not spectacular," though Stone "trained on cigars," and the result was a draw.) On the same page was "GOVERNMENT BANQUET TO FOREIGN EDITORS," beside "TURKEY AND GREECE – HOPES OF SETTLEMENT." An attempt to fly the Atlantic was postponed for ten days; but "for lovers of the ballet, that was a splendid evening of sheer delight which they provided last night." The *Telegraph* invited thoughts as to which the readers would have "liked best," *Daphnis and Chloe*, *Cléopâtre*, or *Le Spectre de la Rose*. The house had been packed, and the *Spectre* was "now danced by Mme. Tamar Karsavina and M. Fokine almost more beautifully than ever before – which is saying much. It was for us all, as for Karsavina, a dream, and a very beautiful dream, a dream of the rose for her, of sheer beauty and grace of movement for us. Karsavina herself was the idealisation of a beautiful dream, so light and fanciful, graceful and poetic was her every action. But no praise could be too high for M. Fokine's charm of movement, which lost nothing whatever by comparison with that of any predecessor we have seen. Indeed, we go so far as to say it was incomparably beautiful . . ."

Daily
Telegraph
1.7.14

It is curious that the review should refer to the creator of the rôle so obliquely. Throughout the whole season, very few papers mentioned Nijinsky by name.

July seemed to pass as another dream. On the 3rd, the *Daily Mail* printed a long letter from a correspondent about the influence of the Ballet on fashion: Joseph Beecham was made a Baronet, and the Tsar conferred the Order of St. Stanislaus upon him. The financier James White (better known as "Jimmy White") proposed to Beecham that he should acquire most of the Covent Garden estate from the Duke of Bedford in what would now be termed a "take-over" of a highly-profitable nature. On July 7th, the *Standard* announced "JOSEPH BEECHAM BUYS THE HEART OF LONDON." On July 14th it was reported that

Rasputin had been stabbed in his home village of Pokrovsky, in Western Siberia.

In 1910, the production of Richard Strauss's opera, *Elektra*, had been reviewed by Ernest Newman in *The Nation*. To put it mildly, he had "panned" it. His review had sparked off a correspondence, extending over several weeks, with George Bernard Shaw – erstwhile Music Critic Corno di Bassetto. When *La Légende de Joseph* came along, E.N. reviewed it for the *Birmingham Daily Post*, (24.6.14.) He also reviewed it for the same weekly as before. This latter review was the pretext for an exchange of letters, ding-donging over seven weeks, which must have given great pleasure to the Editor, H.W. Massingham, (especially if he gave thought to what he would have had to pay for such material as "contributions.") The two music critics indulged in an amusing exercise in literary polemics, far too long to quote fully, far too good to ignore, even though the Diaghilev Ballet, which was the starting-point, was quickly forgotten. This is how it started:-

The Nation 27.6.14	"For some of us the sitting out of Strauss's new ballet the other evening was like attending the funeral of a lost leader . . . for apparently Strauss is not quite dead so far as music is concerned . . . The music of "*The Legend of Joseph*" is bad enough to ruin any man's reputation but his . . . Mr. Bernard Shaw suggested, when he and I were exchanging compliments over *Elektra*, that I failed to see the true inwardness of that work because I could not follow Strauss's new harmonic language; whereby Mr. Shaw simply demonstrated his comical ignorance of Strauss, of modern music, and of me . . . "What will save *Joseph*, if it can be saved, is the splendour of the *décor*, the beauty of the dancing, and, it may be, the quality of the old story and the suggestiveness of the action . . . The Russians, indeed, have done their part of the work magnificently. It is only Strauss who has failed us . . . ERNEST NEWMAN
The Nation 4.7.14	"A gentleman may say that the opening theme of *Joseph* has done service before in "The Minstrel Boy" . . . he may poke a little good-humoured fun if he does not forget Strauss's dignity and his own. But to call the theme the eleventh-fold chewing of a ten-times masticated German standing-dish is not criticism but simple obscenity . . . If *The Nation* could devise some means of printing the opinions which Mr. Newman will have some years hence, instead of his first impressions, your readers would be spared the irritation of being told, at the moment when a masterpiece is being performed, that it is not worth hearing, and learning after the performances are over that it contains quarters-of-an hour of dazzling genius . . . G. BERNARD SHAW (Mr. Newman can (and no doubt will) defend his own taste in music. But we see nothing obscene in his metaphors. *Ed., Nation.*)
The Nation 11.7.14	"It was a voluptuous joy to me to find I had drawn Mr. Shaw again; but his angry letter . . . was a disappointment to me. Mr. Shaw is going off as a controversialist . . . "Before writing about it, I had played through (the work) at least a dozen times . . . and have heard two rehearsals and one public performance . . ." ERNEST NEWMAN
The Nation 18.7.14	". . . As Mr. Newman is not a walking orchestra, I presume he played *Joseph* on the piano . . . Now, . . . if I had played *Joseph* twelve times on the piano and judged the work thereby, it is only too probable that my opinions would have been the same as Mr. Newman's. I conclude that Mr. Newman's accomplishments as an executant bear a melancholy resemblance to my own . . . " 'I wish,' says Mr. Newman, 'Mr. Shaw could make up his mind as to what sort of person I really am in music.' I have. *Sans rancune,* (without malice) G. BERNARD SHAW . . ."

And so on into August, when Shaw allowed Newman the last word.

As, after the war, Ernest Newman was to criticise the Diaghilev ballet – which had so speedily been eliminated from this exchange – first for the *Observer*, and then for *The Sunday Times*, this "contrived controversy," though straying repeatedly from its ostensible subject, has its importance. It gives an idea of the way in which Newman delighted to argue, and is a preparation for some of his·critical attitudes in the 'twenties, when Diaghilev promoted composers whose ideas were totally inimical to E.N.

On July 6th, Fokine outlined his "Principles" in a letter to *The Times,* and on the 7th Karsavina danced *Le Lac des Cygnes,* her "elegancies" winning her the customary praise in the same journal. On the 9th, *The Lady* discussed a performance witnessed before going on to a "*souperdansant*" at the Savoy. After the last performance of opera, on the 24th, Sir Joseph Beecham was dragged on to the stage and disappeared under an enormous gilt laurel wreath; and on July 25th, "the applause showered on Chaliapin and others on Friday was showered equally, possibly even in greater measure, on the glorious Karsavina. Indeed, this queen of the dance must have bowed her acknowledgments for at least twenty minutes, for after each important person had taken a call she was made invariably to come forward again." There was another laurel wreath for Sir Joseph, and some uncertainty as to whether this one came from the galleryites or the company. A good half-hour elapsed between the falling of the curtain on *Petrouchka* and its final fall upon a season unparalleled in the annals of London opera." Daily Telegraph 27.7.14

Sir Joseph's son, Thomas Beecham, gave a long interview. He said that "the most satisfactory feature of the success has been the remarkably ready disposition of the public to welcome musical works of an entirely new character. One result cannot fail, and that is that these Russian works are bound to raise greatly the standard of taste in the theatre . . . As to the cost of such a season, whilst it has been enormous, owing to the large number of novelties, it is impossible to quarrel with the financial results. On nearly every occasion we have been 'sold out.' " Observer 26.7.14

On the same day as that interview and many other end-of-season appraisals appeared, Austria mobilised along the Russian frontier. During that last week, had come the Austro-Hungarian ultimatum to Serbia on the 23rd; Sir Edward Grey's proposal for Four-Power Mediation to solve the Balkan crisis, and on the 24th, the appeal by Serbia to the Tsar. As Diaghilev's company scattered, some going to Ostend and Vichy to give performances, others off on holiday or on the journey home to Russia, Austria and Hungary declared war on Serbia on July 28th. The Times 27.7.14

On Monday, July 27th, *The Times* reported that "All Russia is asking today, 'Is it peace or war?' . . . It is understood that the Tsar has not yet abandoned his cruise to the Finnish Skerries . . . M. Sazonoff (the Russian Foreign Minister) left his home at Tsarskoe and is proceeding to Peterhof to make a report to the Emperor, who is on the point of sailing for the Finnish Skerries with the Imperial Family . . . (Many regiments) were reviewed by the Emperor on horseback, attended by a brilliant suite, including the military attachés.

"A special performance in the Krasnoe-Selo Theatre in the evening was marked by enthusiastic demonstrations towards the officers who were expecting to be called immediately on active service. . ."

On July 30th, Germany "required" Russia to cease mobilisation: not getting its required response, on August 1st, Germany declared war on Russia – and by the 4th of August, Germany had declared war on France, invaded Belgium, and provoked the declaration of war by the United Kingdom.

Diaghilev – having delayed Karsavina's return to Russia by a day in order for her to lend him some money – went off to the Continent. No one could have prophesied then that four years would elapse before he would again set foot in England. At the time, the triumphant ending of the season had no significance. It was Diaghilev's intention to re-assemble his company in Berlin in October.

1915

"...Diaghilev was very happy at this time, living in his spacious villa by the lake, with its marble floors and masses of greenery and flowers..."

(Lydia Sokolova.)

[Rennie Voase, 1974.]

124

AT THE VILLA BELLE RIVE

The company scattered for holidays at the end of that triumphant London season. Karsavina and Grigoriev returned to Russia. No longer part of the company, Nijinsky and his family went on from Vienna, where Romola had given birth to a daughter, to Budapest. There they missed the diplomatic train for Russia, and found themselves interned as enemy aliens, confined under house arrest to her mother's home.

By 1915, Diaghilev had been lent the Villa Belle Rive, near Lausanne, in Switzerland, where he was able to keep the remains of the company in form with regular ballet training, and in hope with creative projects. Money was a terrible problem, for Europe had no engagements to offer. Diaghilev borrowed heavily to pay the expenses of sheer living for them all. One of his biggest loans came from Randolfo Barocchi, a handsome and very wealthy young Italian business man, whose fortune came from a marble statuary works. Not only did Barocchi advance a large sum, but he became so attached to the company that he ended up by joining the entourage in a generally helpful capacity on the management side. (Barocchi had, in fact, been secretary to Henry Russell when, in 1905, the impresario had toured an opera company he named the San Carlo, giving several seasons in North America.) Papers in Private Collection

Once again, negotiations were opened up for a North American tour. They were clinched in Milan, and William J. Guard, Press Officer of the Metropolitan Opera House, under whose wing the visit was to take place, wrote an account of this meeting and a visit to the Villa Belle Rive, which was published as part of the press campaign in advance of the tour.

He started off by quoting from a conversation he had had with Bakst (probably in Paris.) "Is Diaghilev himself going to America?" the artist had asked : "Certainly, Diaghilev is coming." "Then all will be well. It doesn't matter who the principal stars are if Diaghilev is with the troupe." N.Y. Times 9.1.16

It mattered enormously in America, where, as perusal of hundreds of newspaper cuttings has shown, the glories of Karsavina and Nijinsky had been reported in the press even of states far remote from New York and the Met. It was known that these two had a special magic, and were "the best." America just wanted – the best.

However, Guard described the negotiations in Milan. "The modifications seemed very simple. Probably an American ballet impresario and the representative of ordinary theatrical enterprises would have settled the whole business in half an hour in the morning . . .

"How long do you suppose it took to satisfy M. Diaghilev?

"Exactly seven hours – including an hour and a half at *déjeuner*! But I count those seven hours of discussion (not omitting the *déjeuner*) as an episode in life well worth the time it consumed . . . Whilst on one side 'business' was the keynote, on the other – need I say, M. Diaghilev's? – 'art' furnished the tonality.

"What wonder, then, that when he was told in the plain language of American 'business' that he must do thus and so, have his troupe on hand at such an hour on such a date, and see that his scenery is at the theatre on such a moment on such a morning, he almost turned pale with amazement." Described as jumping up from the table not once, but five or six times, – "in fine artistic fury, the one white lock in his thick dark hair dancing menacingly on his broad high forehead" – "Why, if I have to be bothered with all these details imposed upon me in a country I never saw and of which I know nothing, I'll tear up the contract! I won't go! I simply won't go! If you want my Ballet Russe . . . then you must make it possible for me to present it in the only way in which I would think for a moment of presenting it – as perfectly as possible. This is not a 'show' that I am going to take to America. It is an art exposition. But if you don't facilitate my coming, if you are going to hamper me in this absurd way, then in Europe I stay and America will have to get along without my Ballet Russe."

"That is one view of the man," said Guard. An interesting view, one never seen by some of his acquaintances, those to whom nothing but the artistic side was ever displayed. A side, however, clearly demonstrated on the many business documents which exist; a side, at that moment, of brave bluff, for Diaghilev was desperate for this engagement. There was nothing else on the horizon, and between Diaghilev and the horizon lay the company which he was somehow supporting.

The meeting culminated in Diaghilev signing a contract which included his *guarantee* to bring Nijinsky and Karsavina. If it was rash of him to sign a contract including this clause, it was surely equally rash of the Americans to have insisted upon it, for the difficult communications of wartime meant that there was considerable uncertainty as to whether either dancer could be procured, let alone both. They seem to have been in complete ignorance of the fact that Nijinsky had been *dismissed* in 1913, and might not be willing to return.*

Guard continued the same article with a description of the way of life of the company.

"Two weeks later I stopped at Lausanne to pass an hour between trains with Mr. Diaghilev. The cab driver knew his address, Villa Belle Rive. We reached a sort of country lane, and found a charming but simple dwelling house, hidden away in what seemed a little park. It was Mr. Diaghilev's temporary home and workshop, loaned by a rich Swiss banker.

"Here was Diaghilev, the cordial Russian host.

" '*Mon cher ami*, you mustn't leave until tomorrow; in fact, you shan't leave. I want you to see what we have to show.

"Others who knew him have said he is irresistible. I found him so, and speedily changed my plans. So first of all he showed me all over his temporary house and the grounds around it – an ideal spot of several acres, abounding in dates and oleanders, pines and maples, lilacs and roses. Following a little by-path through the miniature woodland, we emerged on a little garden surrounding the smaller villa. 'Here,' he said, 'is where most of the members of my colony live,' and then, leading me within, we visited half a dozen rooms, in each of which I found a young woman or man busy with pen, pencil or brush. All were Russians. One of the women – a striking Slav type – I learned was the grand-daughter of the Russian novelist Pushkin, Natalie Gontcharova, who is designing the scenery and costumes for a newly-composed Ballet Russe; while a tall young painter I found to be another of Mr. Diaghilev's 'discoveries,' Michel Larionov, who is also at work on the decoration for another choreographic composition."

---

*It is hard to credit that there could have been any misunderstanding about Nijinsky's internment, for Gatti-Casazza, Henry Russell, and William Guard were all in Milan together in August, 1915. They attended a charity concert organised on a mammoth scale by Toscanini. The discussion with Diaghilev must surely have taken place then, and Gatti-Casazza, managing the New York end, and Henry Russell, who was put in charge of the transit arrangements for all the properties and the company, must have been the mouthpieces of American "business."

After this, Diaghilev showed Guard the school, where Cecchetti put the girls through a few more turns to let Diaghilev see how they were doing. Then each young woman approached the director and modestly and gracefully extended her hand, which he took with a paternal air, at the same time speaking a brief word of criticism or commendation, which was received with a blush or a smile.

"Then came a private lesson for a young man dancer (Massine) whom M. Diaghilev had recently 'discovered' in Russia. 'That young man is a star already. I have entire faith in my judgment in such matters. I'm keeping him for America to find!' " (Diaghilev here conveniently forgot Massine's appearances in 1914 in Paris and London!)

"With afternoon tea-time arrived on a bicycle from Morges a young man about 30 years of age, keen of eye, prominent of feature, nervous in movement, quick in observation, rapid in speech. The newcomer was introduced to me as Igor Stravinsky, the composer. Later came along Ernest Ansermet, the French-Swiss *chef-d'Orchestre*, whom M. Diaghilev is bringing to America as musical conductor. Two hours passed before we knew it, during which M. Stravinsky did most of the talking, which ranged all the way from the new ballets which are either in embryo or in development, Russian art in general and music and literature in particular. Stravinsky, as I said, did most of the talking (and a brilliant talker he is, so that none objected,) but everyone else had his share, while the '*Maître,*' as they all called M. Diaghilev, with timely question or objection or counter-argument, played with the mentalities of his friends and co-laborers as an organist with the stops of his instrument.

"The discussion was resumed at the dinner-table, and was only terminated when Mr. Diaghilev insisted upon taking the party a thirty-mile motor-ride to the interior of the country. There we found a lonely lake surrounded by hills. We sat on a big log watching the dark water below for nearly half an hour, during which my host hardly opened his mouth.

" 'Time to return,' he said at last, as the full August moon peeped from behind a cloud. It was midnight when we parted at my hotel and I wished him 'au revoir' in New York.

"An uncommon afternoon and evening, I assure you. Certainly some reader will envy me my experience, and would have been willing – as I was – to catch just such a cold in the head, as I did, sitting on that old log and gazing silently on that dark, deep, lonely lake, side by side with the Slavic Sorcerer whose name is Serge de Diaghilev."

Over forty years later, Lydia Sokolova was to write in her reminiscences, "Of all the years we travelled with Diaghilev, those six months in Switzerland were the happiest, and I believe if he had been asked later he would have said the same." Sokolova p.69

Severed from Russia by war and revolution, for the rest of his life he lived from hotel room to hotel room. Sokolova added: "I am sure that Diaghilev was very happy at this time, living in his spacious villa by the lake, with its marble floors and masses of greenery and flowers, and with Massine developing into a brilliant choreographer under his eye."

AMERICA *as* HOST
to the BALLET RUSSE

M. Serge de Diaghileff's Ballet Russe Is to the
Dance What Opera Is to Music, and at Last
America Is to Be Its Host, with All Its Art of
Music, of Dancing, of Color No Whit Abridged

AGAINST BAKST'S BACKGROUND,
THE INCOMPARABLE NIJINSKY
AND KARSAVINA

*"Papillons," below, is a romantic fantasy staged by
Bakst and danced to Schumann's music by Karsavina
(at right of photograph) and a ballet of butterflies.
The photograph was taken at an outdoor rehearsal
at Lausanne, Switzerland.*

Photograph by Ernest Schneider

© E. O. Hoppé

*Lubov Tchernich-
owa has that grace
of dancing and of
beauty peculiar to
the Russians, and
even before the ex-
acting and expert
Russian audiences
she is a favorite.
In "Cléopatre" she
has a leading part.*

*Adolf Bolm is
leading mime and
"maitre des bal-
lets," and for graph-
ically vivid pan-
tomime and danc-
ing he is unex-
celled. In Schu-
mann's "Carnaval"
in which he ap-
pears, he dances
with Karsavina.*

*"Schéhérazade," is colorful as only Bakst can make it, tense with
the music of Rimsky-Korsakov, and sensuous with the dancing of
Karsavina, and of Nijinsky as the black slave. This sketch of the
principals is by Georges Barbier, of Paris.*

VOGUE

December 15, 1915

BACKGROUND TO THE TOURS IN THE U.S.A.

The America of the 1970's has fine ballet companies, many ballet schools, and magnificent collections of ballet material, not only of the Diaghilev period but also concerning the whole history of the dance, in both public and private hands. To this America, the mixed reception accorded to Diaghilev's company makes sad, wry reading – if sometimes very funny. Saddest of all, both for its reputation and for Diaghilev's pride in his achievement, was the fact that the old magic of the partnership of Karsavina and Nijinsky could not be revived. Ever since 1909, America had read of this in its own newspapers. The Press publicity *promised* it; when it did not materialise, America was under no illusions about being offered *Hamlet* without the Prince of Denmark.

The history of these tours may be said to have started right away with the famous Paris *répétition générale* in May, 1909. Gabriel Astruc and Diaghilev had seen to it that important theatrical impresarios were invited, and the Metropolitan Opera had been represented by its Manager, Signor Gatti-Casazza, and Mr. Dippel. The Boston Opera House was represented by its Director, Henry Russell, and his wife. Whilst other members of the hierarchy of the Met. wanted the Diaghilev ballet to perform in America, Signor Gatti-Casazza was against it from the first. There was fierce antipathy between him and Diaghilev, which had serious effects when the tour finally came about. An exchange of telegrams in 1910, when efforts were made to organise a tour, demonstrates the atmosphere of bickering which only became worse with time. Le Figaro
19.5.09

As the Chairman of the Metropolitan, Otto Kahn, greatly admired the *Ballets Russes* and made every effort to show them to America, this must have caused constant friction between him and Gatti-Casazza on this matter, however well they worked together on opera. Kahn did, however, prefer to leave the negotiations in other hands.

14TH DECEMBER 1910   ASTRUC TO NEW YORK
Diaghilev wiring Fokine consider important idea America and London run incalculable risk if we lose Fokine. N.Y.P.L.
Dance
Collection
Astruc
Papers

14TH DECEMBER 1910   N.Y. TO ASTRUC
Diaghilev said earlier he could do without Fokine now says exactly opposite not my way handle business matters such frivolous and incoherent manner.

GATTI-CASAZZA

30TH DECEMBER 1910   N.Y. TO ASTRUC
Diaghilev without our final authorisation engage company we are not committing ourselves.

It can be seen from the tone of such surviving examples that, on the New York side, Diaghilev faced the crotchety opposition of Gatti-Casazza. The latter knew that if he were to accept the company at all, he wanted its stars.

In 1915, America was still neutral, albeit orientated towards the cause of the Allies, and given to immense charitable fund-raising efforts on their behalf. Despite his long years of residence in the United States, his American wife, his cultural interests and great philanthropy, Otto Kahn's German birth made him the target for occasional unwelcome demonstrations. He set about taking out naturalisation papers.

But to Otto Kahn, in fulfilling his dream of showing the Diaghilev Ballet in America, the question was – will American audiences understand the beauty that will be shown them? To his business associates, the question – bearing in mind the enormous expense of transporting the company and its tons of paraphernalia – was would it break even – let alone make a profit?

Of course, this would be by no means New York's first sight of ballet. She had enjoyed the visits of nineteenth century ballerinas, including the captivating Fanny Elssler. Moreover, she had dancers attached to her own opera companies. In the case of the Met., this had started, in 1886, owing to the demands of the stockholders themselves. Some idea of the style of these diversions may be gleaned from a verse, dating from before 1891, inspired by one particular opera:

Story of the
Metropolitan
Opera:
Irving Kolodin

"You advertise *Merlin*
With singers from Berlin,
A full *corps de ballet* and costumes galore;
But I frown without cant, on
One thing, Mr. Stanton,
The ballet shows more than it ought of the corps."

By the time Diaghilev's company arrived in New York, the Met. was already used to its own ballerina, Rosina Galli. A petite but imperious young dancer who had been a child prodigy at La Scala, Milan, when Signor Gatti-Casazza was already its Director, she had joined the Chicago Opera Company's ballet in 1912, and had performed with it in New York. She had also appeared at Covent Garden in 1912, in Wolf-Ferrari's only tragic opera, *The Jewels of the Madonna*. In 1914, she became *première danseuse* at the Met. itself. Gatti-Casazza's marriage to

Giulio Gatti-Casazza.　　Rosina Galli.　　Otto Kahn.

Frances Alda, a soprano from New Zealand, broke up after a brief period, and his relationship with Galli set all tongues wagging. (They did not marry until 1929, when he at last obtained a divorce.) He was notoriously jealous on Rosina's behalf, and his disapproval of the idea of Diaghilev coming to the Met. took on fresh ferocity which was said to amount to the will to sabotage it.

On December 30, 1915, the Met. mounted the Borodin opera, *Prince Igor,* for the first time. Galli starred in the arrangement of the *Polovtsian Dances* made by the Met.'s own ballet-master. She had great success in this part, and the opera was repeated several times during the engagement of the Diaghilev Ballet at the Century Theatre. This naturally roused a wave of loyalty in favour of their own ballerina, and helped to prejudice many opera-goers against outsiders.

America had already enjoyed the art of Adeline Genée, who had visited many parts of the States since 1908, with great success. She had been followed, from 1911 onwards, by Anna Pavlova, partnered by Mikhail Mordkin and others, and supported by a small company. Pavlova's tours had taken her "everywhere," and their story, too, was of great success. Her repertoire was simple and direct in its appeal. Her own exquisite dancing captivated even the Philistines, and Mordkin became their ideal of all that a male dancer should be, splendidly virile, and with technique such as they had never seen before. The entertainment offered was a revelation, but never made her audiences feel inferior or uneducated. Her own performances, her ethereal lightness and bewitching air of fragility, provided the yardstick against which every future ballerina would be measured.

The combination of the arts offered by Diaghilev made far more strenuous demands on the audience. There were so many things to try and take in simultaneously. It required a captivating ballerina to focus the attention. Karsavina and Nijinsky, separately and together, had carried Diaghilev over the hurdles of his experiments in Europe. It is possible that there were other ballerinas who might have done the same for him, but, in wartime, he could not choose. For the all-important outset of this American tour, *faute de mieux,* he backed the wrong ballerina – Xenia Maclezowa, from Moscow, who had not previously been a member of his company.

Until now, the chief sources of information about the Diaghilev company's American visits have been Romola Nijinsky's biography of her husband, published in 1933, a collection of articles about Nijinsky, edited for *Dance Index* by Paul Magriel and published in America in 1946, Grigoriev's *The Diaghilev Ballet, 1909 – 1929*, published 1953, Lydia Sokolova's delightful autobiography, *Dancing for Diaghilev*, 1960, and Richard Buckle's *Nijinsky*, 1971.

Each of these books makes valuable points, but none deals with the American tours comprehensively. Each has a different outlook. Grigoriev, who did not go on the second tour, was the chronicler, mainly concerned with basic events. Romola, the wife, was pre-occupied with deifying her husband. She saw the *Ballets Russes* through a smokescreen of her husband's part in them. The greatness and fulfilment of collaboration with fellow artists in the creation of works of art in ballet, under a presiding genius, escaped her. Moreover, being an amateur, not educated in the discipline of the Imperial Schools, she never acquired the slightest sense of the first rule of the theatre – "The Show Must Go On." The articles collected in *Dance Index* are most valuable, for they include contemporary criticisms by two of the most important American writers, Carl Van Vechten and H.T. Parker. The recollections of Robert Edmond Jones of his collaboration with Nijinsky in the creation of *Till Eulenspiegel* are the experiences of a major artist who worked on a project with him. Sokolova, in 1916 a young dancer who had been with the company for three and a half years, rapidly advancing in her art, was devoted to Diaghilev, who gave her the opportunity to do so. He re-named her, and she Russianised herself very completely, learning the language, becoming engaged to Kremnev, adoring the company and the unity of artistic effort. She had toured in America with a small company before she ever joined Diaghilev, and went on both these visits. Sokolova had joined the company in 1912, in time to take part in *Le Sacre du Printemps*. As an artist, she recognised with sadness the changes in Nijinsky since 1913. She felt that he was not quite the magnificent dancer he had previously been; but, though too young at the time to pinpoint her thoughts, she sensed the tragedy of the breaking-up of his personality.

The reality, as will emerge from the press accounts, was more dramatic – and traumatic – than any of these books has conveyed.

The central figures presented a new version of the Eternal Triangle – two men who had formerly had a homosexual relationship, and a young wife jealous of the influence exerted in the past by the older man – and unwilling to recognise its importance in creating him as an artist.

Sokolova said that "when Otto Kahn insisted on Nijinsky's dancing with us, he could not really have understood the calamity of his previous dismissal."

It is hard to believe that the human reason behind this dismissal had escaped the ears of the entire hierarchy of the Met., men of the international world of opera and the theatre, who had themselves frequently been in Europe during Diaghilev's pre-war seasons. The relationship existing between Diaghilev and Nijinsky prior to the marriage was notorious. Nijinsky would seem to have regarded his monopolisation by the older man as the inevitable price to be paid for the advancement of his ambitions, first as dancer and then as choreographer. That he should have left Diaghilev for another male patron would have been bad enough. To have left him for a woman was unpardonable. Nevertheless, true to his nature, as Stravinsky later described it, in 1916 Diaghilev was prepared to try to make a new, working relationship, and treated Romola with great courtesy. It can be imagined, however, that the strain must have been considerable, and gave rise to magnified clashes over the smallest point.

As for Nijinsky, though he owed everything to Diaghilev, who had presented him to Europe and raised him almost to the status of a god – certainly, *Le Dieu de la Danse* – he was replete with human failings, and had developed touchy pride, a mercenary attitude to his own performances, and ingratitude to an irrational degree.

Long before William Guard was called on to mount a Press campaign for these tours, American papers had carried stories about the Diaghilev company, including vivid accounts of the "*scandales*" attaching to the Nijinsky ballets. Only a few weeks after the event, the episode which led to his dismissal from the Imperial Theatres in 1911 (just in time to be free to lead Diaghilev's newly-formed full-time company) was reported in America from European papers. Here is one version, from one of the American music journals:

N.Y.P.L.
Dance
Collection
***
25.3.11

"Here is young Nijinsky getting into trouble over in St. Petersburg by trespassing on territory on which Feodor Chaliapin, among men, has hitherto held first mortgage . . . Nijinsky, who is a prime favourite, failed to observe the conventions in a recent new production – the name of it is not given, but it was probably *Cléopâtre*, which proved too shocking for a scandalized Milan a few weeks ago – and ventured to make his appearance in a costume so scanty as to offend the susceptibilities of the audience.

"The result was a painful surprise to him. 'First there was a dead silence, then hisses and soon a general uproar,' writes a St. Petersburg correspondent. 'Finally the audience became so menacing that the dancer was forced to leave the stage, which he did amid a shower of missiles.' " One can only wonder at the naiveté of the last paragraph. Did an Imperial audience come provided with tomatoes and rotten eggs? One has always understood that they hurled diamond bracelets at their favourites.

A more plausible story was told in a long article which just preceded the tour:-

The
Theatre:
Late
1915

". . . The truth is that it was merely an incident, perhaps an inevitable one, in the antagonism between the traditional and revolutionary schools of the ballet. For a moment the older school triumphed, and Nijinsky left Russia to undertake the enterprise of the conquest of Europe.

"The pretext which the officials seized upon to rid themselves of the young revolutionary was a detail of costume. Madame Kschessinska, the fixed star in the Imperial firmament, wished Nijinsky to appear with her in one of the ballets of the stereotyped Italian school. He, on the other hand, preferred to take the part of Loys in *Giselle* . . . He carried the day, and the ballet was produced at considerable expense. His costume, a *maillot* of yellow silk, was designed by Benois . . . At the last moment one of the directors objected to the costume, and ordered Nijinsky to change it. The dancer expostulated, and as there was not sufficient time to replace it, the director did not insist . . . At the conclusion of the performance the Dowager Empress told one of the directors that she had never seen its equal. The next day, however, on the pretext that the *maillot* was objectionable, Nijinsky received notice that his services were no longer required. The repentance of the management came quickly, but the dancer declined their request that he should return . . ."

Nijinsky wearing the Maryinsky costume for Loys in the first act of *Giselle*, *(left)*, and *(right)* in the beautiful costume designed for him for the second act in Diaghilev's production.

Apart from the fact that Nijinsky danced on this occasion with Karsavina, the description seems complete. "*Maillot*" in this sense means "tights." This was the beautiful costume which Benois had designed for Diaghilev's presentation of *Giselle* at the Paris Opéra in 1910. The dark doublet and pale tights were worn without the customary intervening "shorts," as can be seen by looking at photographs of Nijinsky in a Maryinsky costume and in Benois' far more glamorous and princely design. If the costume was objectionable without them, then surely it was Benois who ought to have been axed – or else the costumier. It looks more as if the reason was Nijinsky's insubordinate refusal to meet the criticism of one of the directors – which would have led inevitably to dismissal.

In 1915, the Press extravagances poured out.

N.Y. Times 26.9.15

"For six years America has been hearing about the Ballets Russes. Of course there are Russian ballets and Russian ballets" – (a snipe here at a small company which had toured under that title, headed by Theodore Kosloff, organised by Gertrude Hoffman, and presenting pirated versions – bowdlerized – of *Scheherazade* and *Cléopâtre*.) "But there is only one DIAGHILEV Russian Ballet and that is THE Russian Ballet . . . The real Russian Ballet . . . is possible only when it has at its head Serge Diaghilev."

N.Y. Tribune 26.12.15

Just before Christmas, 1915, the Met. put out a Prospectus in its weekly *Opera News*. This stated with optimistic certainty that "for this tour, Mr. de Diaghilev has reassembled his company in full ranks and, as the contract with him specifies, he will bring to America fifty and more dancers. At their head stand Nijinsky and the Karsavina . . ."

Diaghilev may or may not have known that Karsavina, living in St. Petersburg, was expecting a child. All, however, knew full well that Nijinsky and his family were interned. Every possible string was being pulled to obtain his release, but at that time it was still uncertain. Yet, in its own publication, the Met. reminded its subscribers that "by scores and by hundreds, Americans returning from summers in Europe have celebrated the unique qualities, achievements and illusion of the *Ballet Russe*. Its like, they have said truly, the present world does not know."

When the company arrived, without its idols, no comparable skill was devoted to softening the blow. No one claimed the warm sympathy of the American public by telling the truth about Karsavina's "family reasons." And so, in the eyes of the public, a contract was a contract, a contract had been broken, and forgiveness would have to be earned.

In the meantime, Nijinsky's rôles were shared out between Massine, Bolm, Idzikowski, and Gavrilov. Karsavina's creation, the Firebird, was mistakenly given to the newcomer, Maclezowa, and her Zobeide to another newcomer, the opera singer Flora Revalles – protegée of Ernest Ansermet and Otto Kahn – who took on those parts which had once suited Ida Rubinstein. Joining the company in America, Lopokova assumed more of Karsavina's parts, and so, too, did Sokolova and Tchernicheva.

New names crop up in the cuttings, and need explanation here. In addition to Otto Kahn, the Chairman, and Gatti-Casazza, the General Manager of the Met., John Brown, its Business Manager, carried out duties which will show up in due course. Ambassador Penfield was the United States' Ambassador to Austro-Hungary, and involved in helping to obtain Nijinsky's release. On the second tour, the dancer Kola Kremnev replaced Grigoriev as *régisseur*.

As for Diaghilev, once the euphoria which followed the settling of the contract and the advance of enough money to take his company to America had passed, some demon must have got into the man. In Milan, he had won his point that he was not to be troubled with the minutiae of touring arrangements, for which the Met. provided a staff in addition to stage hands, electricians, dressers, etc. No matter what happened in New York City, once on tour, Diaghilev simply refused to recognise them. Merle Armitage, who was the youngest member of that staff, described Diaghilev's attitude in a reminiscing essay in 1947, in a way which most certainly did not come out in the newspapers. This is not a prejudiced account, for Armitage clearly thought Diaghilev to be wonderful; but, looking back, he seeems to have been able to bring a sound sense of humour to his adventures with the *Ballets Russes*.

*Dance
Memoranda
Merle
Armitage*

"Diaghilev found little to admire in America. He detested our democratic ways, intensely disliked our food and found us crude and unsympathetic . . .

The management of the tour, which was under the general auspices of the Metropolitan Opera Company, had been entrusted to an able but cynical showman, Ben Stern. Although Gatti-Casazza, the Italian impresario of the Metropolitan, was hostile to Diaghilev and his project, Ben Stern made a great effort to keep things on a pleasant and harmonious basis. No effort ever achieved less. As Diaghilev and his company had been brought to America through the offices of Otto H. Kahn, Diaghilev assumed that all of Kahn's subordinates, even those in executive positions, were, as in Russia, menials. In fact, he did not acknowledge Stern's existence. As he regarded Gatti-Casazza as his natural enemy, there was only one man whom he recognised. Desiring instructions of even minor importance, Diaghilev always cabled Kahn for advice. And Kahn, during his whole tour, wisely remained in Havana! This brought about unusual tensions and many 'incidents,' and at times actually threatened the progress of the tour."

This makes much that happened in America clearer. It would appear that Diaghilev tried – mistakenly – to use Kahn as if he had been Astruc, part partner, part agent – a man to whom he could relay his imperatives.

One may surmise that Diaghilev used his lack of English as he used his monocle – as a weapon of both defence and offence. It can be no surprise that there are references to Diaghilev as "The Difficult." On the other hand, bearing all those hazards in mind, the company had far more success in the United States than some of the more morose reports would indicate.

The Second Russian Offensive

THE Ballet Russe has been for six years abroad. It was in New York at the Century Theater for two weeks and is likely to remain on the road until April. Apparently, novelty will not be a leading attraction when it reopens at the Metropolitan Opera House—unless its stars, Nijinsky and Karsavina, should be released from Austria, or wherever they may be. But this, we have been assured, is impossible. What of that? We were told that they were coming—and they didn't. Now we are told that they aren't—so they probably *are*. Still, nothing is impossible for a clever manager like Serge de Diaghileff.

SCHEHERAZADE
An Arabian lady-killer at work in the Harem

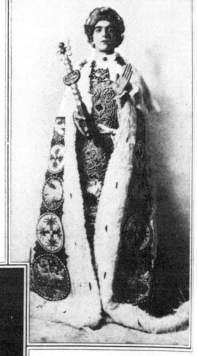

Leonide Massine, as the Prince, in "L'Oiseau de Feu"

Lubov Tchernichewa as she appears in "Carnaval"

Adolf Bolm and Xenia Maclezowa in "La Princesse Enchantée"

Enrico Cechetti and Flore Revalles in "Schéhérazade"

This page, with its rather acid comments, appeared in *Vanity Fair* for March, 1916.

1916

CENTURY THEATRE, N.Y.C.

JANUARY 17th - JANUARY 29th

ON TOUR

JANUARY 31st - MARCH 29th

Boston, Mass.
Albany, N.Y.
Detroit, Mich.
Chicago, Ill.
Milwaukee, Wisc.
St. Paul, Minn.

Minneapolis, Minn.
Kansas City, Kan.
St. Louis, Mo.
Indianapolis, Ind.
Cincinnati, Ohio.

Cleveland, Ohio.
Pittsburgh, Pa.
Washington, D.C.
Philadelphia, Pa.
Atlantic City, N.J.

METROPOLITAN OPERA HOUSE, BROADWAY, N.Y.C.,

APRIL 3rd - APRIL 29th.

REPERTOIRE

L'Après-Midi d'un Faune
Le Carnaval
Cléopâtre
Firebird
Midnight Sun

Narcisse
Le Pavillon d'Armide
Petrouchka
La Princess Enchantée
Polovtsian Dances

Scheherazade
Le Spectre de la Rose
Les Sylphides
Thamar

COMPANY

Andreeva, Antonova, Artska, Bewicke, Bonietska, Chabelska I, Chabelska II., Degelanda (de Galanta), Evina, Faithfull, Kachouba, Khokhlova, Klementovitch, Kourtner, Lopokova, Maclezowa, Maicherska, Nemchinova II., Nemchinova II., Pavinska, Pflanz, Potapovitch, Revalles, Slavitska, Sokolova, Sumarokova I., Sumarokova II., Tchernicheva, Wassilievska, Zalevska, Zamoukhovska.

Bolm, Bourman, Cecchetti, Gavrilov, Grigoriev, Herman, Idzikowski, Karnetsky, Kawecki, Kegler, Kostecki, Kostrovsky, Kremnev, Massine, Nijinsky (after April 12), Novak, Okhimovsky, Oumansky, Pacaud, Pianovski, Statkevitch, Tarassov, Tariat, Voronzov, Woizikowski, Zverev.

CONDUCTOR

Ansermet

AT THE CENTURY

Diaghilev must surely have been thinking of that most glorious of First Nights at the Châtelet in Paris in 1909, when the company's opening performance in New York became reality. *Everything* mattered to him as he aimed at presenting what he considered to be an unparalleled artistic experience – the theatre itself, the audience, and the performance he could offer.

The Century was indeed a worthy setting. "With its broad, shallow galleries, it was far better for seeing these Russian ballets than the Metropolitan would have been . . . the Century floor, re-modelled by the architect of Hammerstein's Manhattan, is now the finest theatre of courtly elegance and intimate effect in the New World," said the *Sun*, so the theatre ought to have pleased him. "Passing in interest any event of the season before or likely to come after, either here or elsewhere, the Diaghilev Ballet last night made its bow. There was no doubt of New York's welcome when the première ended at 11.20 o'clock. More first family limousines turned north for once than all the thousand that left their usual occupants at the Metropolitan, even with Caruso announced on Broadway. The golden Century curtain was held until 8.40 for last comers on Central Park West . . ." (So the audience, too, should have satisfied him.) W.B. Chase, writer of this report, ended it by saying, "If people take the visitors to their hearts as the Parisians did it will be for the same reason. It will be because these performances disclose to them the newest and most pregnant contribution to the decorative as well as the delineative art of the theatre. These are spectacles in which all the spectacular ingredients unite in the dramatisation of a poetic fantasy."

N.Y.
Sun
18.1.16

"If."

What Diaghilev lacked was not only Karsavina and Nijinsky. It was not a professional press campaign. It was patronesses. Here in New York he had no friend to compare with Misia Edwards and the Comtesse Greffuhle in Paris, or with Lady Ripon in England. For all the glitter as the "Diamond Horseshoe" moved over for that night from the Met. – which had surely comitted a solecism itself in putting up the competition of a Caruso night to clash with its own sponsorship of the ballet – he was without the warmth of powerful leaders of Society who were also addicted to his aims.

The audience was led by Otto Kahn and his wife, and included a few of Diaghilev's old friends, such as Baron and Baroness de Meyer and Prince Paul Troubetskoy.

Anna Pavlova, who had been a visitor at rehearsals, was also present. She had just concluded a most successful season at the Hippodrome in New York, which she had announced to be her last in the city for some time, as she was about to leave on another long tour of the West. Of the 3,000 members of the "present world" filling the Century Theatre that night, it is safe to bet that 99% had seen her, quintessence of the Russian ballerina, on their home ground. She would be hard to follow.

"The rattling old piano gave a crash and the ballet came to order. The artists on the side lines whipped out their sketch books, the reporters put on their tortoise-shells and the business of the day began."

"There was another rustle. Pavlova had come in."

A silly row had flared up that very morning. When the *Lafayette* had docked, very early, only one dancer had been up and about – Valentine Kachouba, a pretty young member of the *corps de ballet*. She had posed for photographers, and their caption-writers had done the rest, unwittingly referring to her as the company's "leading ballerina." Maclezowa had been most displeased.

The headlines next day proclaimed enthusiasm, not only in New York papers, but also in those of many distant cities. "BALLET IMPRESSIVE" – "RUSSIAN BALLET A DREAM WORLD" – "BRILLIANT PERFORMANCE – BALLET RUSSE SHINES" – "BALLET RUSSE A REVELATION TO FIRST NIGHT AUDIENCE AT THE CENTURY – WONDERFUL OPENING PERFORMANCE" – "CREATE FURORE BY PERFORMANCE IN NEW YORK – TO BE SEEN IN PHILADELPHIA IN MARCH" – these are but a few samples. The reports were much more critical of detail.

The programme for the opening was so important that, in view of Maclezowa's style, it is really impossible to applaud Diaghilev for the works he decided to present, which were *Firebird, La Princesse Enchantée, Soleil de Nuit, (Midnight Sun,)* and *Scheherazade*. Maclezowa danced both the first two items, for neither of which does she appear to have been in any way suited. *Midnight Sun* might have been given a better build-up had the youth and promise of its choreographer, Massine, been artfully exploited in a country always game to recognise and cherish youthful talent. Special problems attend *Scheherazade,* perhaps Diaghilev's greatest success of all in Europe. It lacked Nijinsky in the rôle of the slave; but in addition, it had a built-in situation of political difficulty in America. It was, however, a vehicle for Flora Revalles. It is hard to believe that, in his heart, Diaghilev could have been satisfied with the show he offered.

Musical Leader January 1916

N.Y. American 18.1.16

Starting with the "exquisitely beautiful *Oiseau de Feu,* which is mirrored with marvellous dexterity in the music of Igor Stravinsky and which is Stravinsky in his most marvellous effects," one writer went on, "Mme. Maclezowa is very skilful on her feet and she has a considerable degree of charm. Her limbs are large and one never gets the sense of flight, elf-like grace or ethereal, spiritual, poetic beauty which the mere presence of Pavlova brought with it." Another said: "What she lacks is the airy grace of Karsavina." The same writer, after much in similar vein, added that "In the foyer, between the acts (and there were two long waits of about half an hour each,) it was very difficult to get a decided opinion from the habitués." On one point they were unanimous. They could not understand why the programme notes outlining the plots had been printed in French.

Complaints about the length of the intervals were frequent. It was not the best of programme planning to have the same ballerina dance *Firebird* and *La Princesse Enchantée* in succession. For the latter, a fussy, overloaded back-cloth had been newly designed by Bakst, together with fresh costumes, in violent reds and blues, instead of either the traditional "Blue Bird" rig or the glorious flame-coloured designs for the version danced by Karsavina and Nijinsky. (As this back-cloth showed huge, tropical vegetation at the sides, though it left the centre clear, with distant mountains, possibly Bakst's idea had been to transform the dancers yet again, this time into "*Oiseaux de Paradis*.") It was denounced the following day as "as classical *pas de deux* of the kind the Diaghilev troupe has given up in Europe, but which its director may think is necessary for New York – a mistake, perhaps, for here we often see Anna Pavlova in that sort of thing, and in that sort of thing Anna Pavlova is incomparable." Globe
18.1.16

"Perhaps the most characteristically Russian of the dances" came next. Stating that "M. Diaghilev and his associates have restored the spectacle to the stage," one writer continued, "As to relative values, *The Midnight Sun* is the most novel of the productions thus far shown, having irresistible appeal because of the feeling of folk life that pervades it and because of its humor." "Many of the costumes were grotesque, as was much of the dancing," said another. "The members of the ensemble danced standing, sitting or lying, sometimes with one leg waving, sometimes prostrate on the floor, their bodies rolling from side to side." Yet another called it "... what in studio slang is conveniently referred to as 'amusing.' The simple arrangement of children's games and national dances, without plot, pleased some and displeased others." The *Journal of Commerce* took one sort of stand on the subject of Larionov's designs: "In this also the new style of stage setting was seen at its best, or worst . . . The colours were as weird as the music and the designs were even more startling than the colours. One of the most noticeable features was a valance across the front of the stage of a vivid red, decorated with great faces of the kind children draw when paper and pencil are first given them." Not all of the reports were as denigratory: the *Sun* thought that "The scene by Michel Larionov is a *tour-de-force* of effective stage decoration." Christian
Science
Monitor
18.1.16

Journal of
Commerce
19.1.16

Globe
18.1.16

N.Y. Sun
18.1.16

The most sensational ballet was held over to the end of the evening. "VIVID BAKST SCENERY AND VARIED BEAUTY OF DANCES GET ENTHUSIASTIC RECEPTION" was a headline. "The famous combinations of Leon Bakst, Russia's master colorist, which have revolutionized fashions in dress and in interior decoration, were daring. The most powerful ballet was *Scheherazade,* the Oriental tragedy of love in the harem. Flora Revalles, as the princess, and Adolf Bolm as her lover, were as spectacular, she in her languid beauty and he in his impassioned fervor, as the Bakst scenery." "Here we found Bakst at his best in his bold use of color . . . the performance was one of splendid ensemble achievement, with Revalles seductive in her mimicry, and the others in the cast wholly competent." Minneapolis
Journal
19.1.16

N.Y.
World
18.1.16

Grenville Vernon, in the *Tribune*, considered the scenic work of both *Firebird* and *Scheherazade* together. "Many a representative of the Metropolitan Opera Company was present last night, and let us hope that when the curtain fell each swore a vow swiftly to engage M. Golovine to paint for them a round half dozen of his sets and to design for them the attendant costumes . . . Yet the scenery of Golovine and Bakst is simple in the extreme; a few painted cloths, almost all of them hung from above, was all – this and the lighting." (In fact, the Met. had seen Russian sets since 1913. It had purchased the wonderful Golovine scenery and antique costumes of the 1908 Paris production of *Boris Godounov*. This production has only been repaired, not replaced, up to 1974.) N.Y.
Tribune
18.1.16

Vernon continued more ominously. "The remarkable impersonation of the negro favourite of Zobeide, Princess of Samarcande, by M. Bolm will render the ballet impossible of production south of Mason and Dixon's line. Even to Northern minds it was repulsive. Yet it is a scene whose Oriental splendor, color, animality and lust will long remain with all who saw it. If it had not been given so wonderfully, so poetically, it would have been bestial. As it *was* given, it was a page of the 'Arabian Nights' most gorgeous imagery."

Vernon was more generous in his overall view of the evening's performances. "In the House of Art there are many mansions, mansions for the classic drama, for the romantic drama, for the music drama. And we who have seen the ballet as it has come to us out of Russia feel sure that we have entered into another chamber whose walls await great masterpieces of the

So much has been written about Bakst's brilliant work for the theatre that it is enough to show this superb example, one of his original designs for a Shah in *Scheherazade*. His fame had spread to the United States before Diaghilev's company eventually arrived there, and his name played a great part in the advance publicity.

Perhaps the best thing one can do is to read Cyril Beaumont's recollection, in 1940, of the scene which first met his eyes in 1912, and try to people it with Bakst's figures in swirling movement:-

"I cannot convey the thrill I received at the first sight of that splendid setting, that great expanse of emerald green curtain, flecked with red and gold, caught up to reveal the viridian walls of Shariar's harem, with those three doors of shimmering metallic blue, and that immense carpet of a burning crimson. From the green and gold ceiling hung two huge lamps of Arabic design, fretted and many-tasselled, which emitted a dull blue light." In revivals in the '30's, copies of the sets, and the lighting, had been but travesties, so that he added, "When I recall what I saw then and what has recently been put forward as Bakst's setting, I am consumed with impotent wrath . . ."

In the U.S.A., once the "scandal" at first attached to this ballet had died down, its gorgeousness was appreciated for itself.

future . . . There is no Anna Pavlova. No Nijinsky – no Tamara Karsavina. Let this loss stand at the debit side of the ledger. Surely the credit list is long enough to cause us to forget? If we have seen greater dancing we have seen no such ensemble, no such perfect wedding of dance, music, scenery and costumes – in short, no such art of the dance."

Globe 18.1.16 "A copy of this piece was presented here by Gertrude Hoffman, and an 'Orientale,' somewhat similar in idea, has figured in the repertory of Anna Pavlova, but not before has the glory of *Scheherazade* in all its integrity been vouchsafed to a New York audience," said Pitts Sanborn.

The World wished to come to a verdict on the eventual arrival of the long-anticipated excitement of the *Ballet Russes*.

The World 18.1.16 "The première over, New York will wake this morning with one query on its lips, 'Just how good is the Diaghilev Ballet Russe?'

"To which one may reply, 'Very, very good.'

"Such apparently was the verdict of competent observers who possess also discrimination for music, which is so prominent a factor in the ballet as the Russians have taught us to know it.

"This must be the verdict too of the unbiased chronicler whose business it is to pass judgement upon achievement of this sort."

If the press reception on the opening night was on the whole more enthusiastic about the Ballet than otherwise, there were undercurrents of a "theatrical-political" nature. "There was, too, in the foyer, talk of some friction between the management of the Metropolitan and that interested in the ballet, on the ground that the Metropolitan people thought that they had quite enough to struggle against with the war and the grippe and business conditions without having an opposition at the Century Opera House made by some of their own people.

"I can fancy that Mr. Gatti and his associates would not view with any particular favor the interruption of their session during the two weeks of the present run of the Russian Ballet, especially as I understand every seat has long been sold, which must naturally detract from their own sales, although, as I said, on Monday night the Metropolitan was crowded to the door-step." (In the *Sun*, W.B. Chase had added that "The Century ballets are drawing the Metropolitan's own subscribers, and they are selling out at almost opera rates.")

As the financial backing came from the Met. and Kahn, it really does seem ridiculous for financial *success* to be an object of dislike by the opposing faction – but such remarks make it clear that if success brought friction, the slightest hitch would mean that it would be wildly exacerbated.

On the second night, *Firebird* and *Scheherazade* were repeated, the other two works being replaced by the *Polovtsian Dances* and *L'Après-Midi d'un Faune*. A few weeks before, the opera *Prince Igor* had been performed at the Met. for the first time, with dances arranged by its own choreographer, and the *Morning Sun* stated flatly that "the Ballet Russe contains no woman dancer of the skill and agility of Rosina Galli." Roerich's lovely setting won praise, however, and the critics hastened on to describe the Debussy work.

The original flare-up of scandal which had greeted the first performance of this ballet in Paris in 1912, all the newspaper exchanges, and the opinions of Rodin, (who defended it,) had been fully reported throughout America at that time. As with *Scheherazade*, notoriety had preceded the sight of the work itself, so that the audience must have been divided in anticipation into those who were prepared to be deeply shocked, and those who thought it would probably not shock them nearly enough to be worth bothering to see. The special style of movement was thoroughly described, but all interest was concentrated on the ending. Massine was dancing Nijinsky's rôle as the Faun.

How much was the way in which the last impulsive action was performed part of the choreographer's design – how much was it left to the interpreter's initiative – how much was it determined by Diaghilev himself? It is impossible to tell.

"The final scene, however, depicts the faun, first looking after the terrified and fleeing nymphs," said one critic. "After a few seconds he picks up a forgotten garment of the nymph and sinks on the mossy bank holding it enraptured. It was daringly suggestive, and those in the audience seemed first to gasp and then to gaze about dazed."

"In its subject matter, it was no food for infants," said *Musical America*. The *Morning Sun*, however, reflected that "M. Nijinsky, the absent star of the company, who planned the spectacle, has treated the subject with insight and a delicate fancy altogether praiseworthy," and *Musical America* added that "of itself it is a highly artistic conception and it is superbly carried out."

The *Tribune* turned on a writer of a cruder stamp. "RUSSIANS' 'FAUNE' NO JOHN WESLEY," enigmatically proclaimed its headline. "A faun being a faun and not the leader of a Methodist revivalist meeting, M. Nijinsky dreaded not to present him as he undoubtedly would have acted. M. Massine, who gave his Goatship last night, expurgated him a bit, but left of his essential nature quite enough to set the audience gasping at the fall of the curtain. We shall not here tell the story. We do not intend to risk prosecution . . . Charming were the young maidens who in M. Bakst's forest attracted the notice of the faun . . . It is not Claude Debussy, but it is stimulating to the eye and to the imagination of the Puritan. We wonder what will be said of it when it reaches the city on the shores of Boston Harbor."

The third evening gave the custodians of public morality a night off. It introduced the enchanting Lydia Lopokova as a ballerina to an American public which already knew her as a

*** 18.1.16

N.Y. Morning Sun 20.1.16

N.Y. American 19.1.16

Musical America 1.16

N.Y. Morning Sun 20.1.16

N.Y. Tribune 19.1.16

dancer and actress. The reasons for her non-participation at the première must remain Diaghilev's secret. Probably by the time she had met him in New York, he was too heavily committed by contract to Maclezowa to include a dancer likely to steal her thunder on the opening night – or, of course, Lopokova may simply not have been free.

Globe
20.1.16
Her appearance in *Carnaval* forced out of the *Globe's* critic the admission that it was "the prettiest thing I have ever seen." "Miss Lopokova was an altogether bewitching and piquant Columbine, and her dancing has lost none of its peculiar charm through her lapse into acting. As for M. Idzikowski, a more graceful and accomplished Harlequin has seldom been seen here. His share of the applause was fully as great as Lopokova's," said another enthusiastic review.

N.Y.
Times
20.1.16
"Mlle. Lopokova's dancing was thoroughly charming and of the kind to make the audience hang on every gesture and change of expression," said the *New York Times,* which does, however, seem to have sensed that it was a "situation" which had prevented her from appearing on the opening night, for he reminded his readers that "oddly enough, this dancer is an old member of the company, who joined it here."

N.Y.
Sun
21.1.16
The *Sun* recalled an advance lecture given by Troy Kinney, in which he had said that "Originality in art is sometimes gained by such a thorough knowledge of a subject that it transcends precedents, thus producing new mediums of expression." To this somewhat portentous statement was pinned an assessment of Bakst's originality as epitomized in Columbine's dress. "According to the above definition of originality, did Bakst have such an intimate knowledge of cherries that he was able to use them as a medium for the expression of his artistic urge? And how did he get this knowledge? Did he ever rob cherry trees? Did he have a weakness for cherry pies? Or cherry lips? Or cherry brandy? Did he ever get the stomach-ache from *too* intimate a knowledge of Royal Annes or Black Republicans? . . . At any rate the man who combined beans and soup, thereby creating the immortal dish of bean soup, must have been an original artist, and so was the man who, combining a 15 cent basket of cherries and a $15 frock, could make a $500 costume."

N.Y.
Sun
20.1.16
The following evening, *Les Sylphides* was added to the repertoire, and the *Sun* explained that "Lydia Lopokova demonstrated what a *première danseuse* should accomplish – she had already shown New York audiences the extent of her ability, even though her support was not comparable to that she is now receiving. But the present surroundings are the first she has had in this city which permit her skill to be revealed without restriction."

The programme for the matinée on the first Sunday included both *Scheherazade* and *L'Après-Midi d'un Faune.* Were they included as a gesture towards those who, living outside New York, preferred to attend a matinée and might not otherwise have a chance to see them? Certainly, the programme had been announced well in advance – and it has already been quoted that the entire two weeks' season had already been sold out. However, amongst the audience who had secured seats for this performance, when they were able to see both these controversial ballets, were representatives of the Catholic Theatre Movement. This had been formed about three years previously with the noble objective, "to uplift the stage." "It was intended to be a play censor for Catholics. Priests were to read the bulletins to their congregations. Members take this pledge; "I promise to avoid improper plays and exhibitions and to use my influence that others do likewise." Up to December 1915, the organisation had recommended 199 plays.

N.Y.
Tribune
25.1.16
It is uncertain whether anyone to do with the Ballet itself knew of the presence of this "Watch Committee" – (though in view of the "Sold Out" notices, one might well ask whether they had been accorded "house" seats.) Sunday's papers stung on other matters: Richard Aldrich, Music Critic of the *New York Times,* contributed a very long article indeed.

No attempt had ever been made to hide the fact that the composer Rimsky-Korsakov's widow had tried to prevent the use of his symphonic poem, *Scheherazade,* for which he had delineated a distinct "programme," and to which the *Ballets Russes* had attached a completely different story, put together by Diaghilev's associates, including Bakst and Fokine, (and, subject of another quarrel, Benois.)

The original "programme" had been: (I) The Sea, and Sinbad's Ship; (II) The Story of the Kalander Princes; (III) The Young Prince and the Young Princess; and (IV) The Festival at Baghdad, the sea, the shipwreck.

Lopokova and Idzikowski extracted every ounce of fun and coquetry from their parts as Columbine and Harlequin in *Le Carnaval.*

Larionov's extraordinary costumes for *Soleil de Nuit (Midnight Sun)* aroused laughter in audiences which found the style ahead of their taste.

N.Y.
Times
23.1.16
"But what becomes of all this carefully wrought musical picturing in the ballet? The music is there: its substance, its character, its quality are not changed. But lo, everything else is changed! The 'meaning' has been completely overturned without a word . . ."

In similar vein Aldrich attacked the use of music by Chopin, Schumann and Debussy – though admitting that, in fact, Isadora Duncan had "undertaken to interpret Beethoven's Seventh Symphony," which no less an authority than Wagner himself had declared to be "the apotheosis of the dance." Aldrich pointed out, however, that this was "a figurative and subjective discussion. Wagner nowhere showed that he ever dreamed of any solitary lady in tights and cheese-cloth draperies taking him up so literally and expounding his vision of Beethoven's meaning by her bodily contortions."

If the Sunday papers gave Diaghilev no rest, Monday was to bring a fresh storm into his tea-cup.

On that day, January 24th, the following letter was made public by John Brown, Business Manager of the Met.: it hailed from the Police Department.

N.Y.
Times
25.1.16
"Serious complaints have been received by this department as to certain alleged objectionable features of the Russian Ballets being performed at the Century. In order to get at the facts the Saturday matinée was attended by witnesses in whose judgment the Department has confidence, and their statements are on hand.

"In order to avoid recourse to the law and assuming that after the objections have been pointed out to you you will correct the same, I am writing this requesting your presence at Judge McAdoo's office, 300 Mulberry Street, at 11 o'clock tomorrow (Tuesday) morning, where you will be joined by representatives of this department."

N.Y.
Sun
26.1.16
The meeting was duly reported: "M. Serge de Diaghilev and the Russians listened with the grave patience and the puzzled amusement with which intelligent folk from Continental Europe have often watched the workings of the censorship of municipal authorities over the American theatre. They were particularly impressed by the abnormal perceptions of some of the protectors of public morals, who discovered 'meanings' that had never occurred to those that had many times set the two pieces on the stage. 'I believe,' said M. de Diaghilev, half-amused and half-perturbed, 'that my mind and the minds of those who planned and executed the ballets are less vicious than the minds of those that made the protest.'"

It was averred that the two pieces had been performed before "two such august and austere matrons as Mary, Queen of England, and Augusta, German Empress," and had been much applauded by them. However, as the paper went on, "The spokesmen of sundry 'vice' societies were arrogant and vociferous until M. de Diaghilev and the representatives of the Metropolitan Opera House, being quiet men of the world, naturally wearied of noisy bickerings and agreed to alter certain items, so that even the agents of the societies in question could not possibly imagine anything into them."

N.Y.
Times
26.1.16
That same night, the *Faune* was again in the bill. "Last week . . . the faun . . . picked up a filmy garment one (nymph) had cast off, and, placing it upon the rock whereon he had been reclining, lay down upon it. Last night the faun placed the drapery gently on the rock and sat gazing at its silken folds. Then the curtain fell.

"When the audience had ceased applauding, after the ushers had carried out huge armfuls of flowers sent to Leonide Massine with requests that they be delivered after his appearance as the faun, M. de Diaghilev came smiling from his seat in the orchestra circle, down the aisle to where Mr. Gatti-Casazza, John Brown, and other heads of the Metropolitan were standing, and said in French, 'America is saved.'"

As another paper put it, whereas "hitherto the spectators have regarded the 'Choreographic Episode' somewhat indifferently, yesterday they applauded it to the echo, recalling the dancers again and again and finally summoning M. de Diaghilev himself." And if Diaghilev actually "took a call" on the stage, this must surely have been the only occasion in the history of his company, for it was something he steadfastly refused to do.

SCHEHERAZADE

Flora Revalles and Adolf Bolm as Zobeide and the Golden Slave.

Zobeide and the Shah Shariah – now played by Serge Grigoriev, who had previously performed the part of the Shah's brother, the Shah Zeman.

Scheherazade presented a different problem. *The Times* ended its report of the meeting by saying that Diaghilev had continued by indicating that "he did not see how he could change it much, since an affair in a harem could not well be made into a pink tea."*

---

*(I am indebted to Miss Kathleen Gordon, C.B.E., for an explanation of this curious expression. About 1915 or so, it was fashionable in America to give "pink teas," also blue, green, yellow, mauve, or any coloured "teas," for that matter. Everything on the table had to be the appropriate colour – table-linen, crockery and comestibles. All the guests had to come clad in the prescribed colour too. These were essentially feminine parties, from which members of the opposite sex were excluded. She remembered going to one in England as a very young girl, when this Transatlantic fashion was tried out by daring friends.)

Serge Grigoriev as the Shah Shariah, his nose altered for the rôle.

SCHEHERAZADE

Zobeide's beautiful costume, worn to effect by Flora Revalles.

"It appeared that it was 'Objectionable' to the champions of public virtue because in Oriental fashion it mingled whites and blacks on the stage. Now they are to be parted. Since there is no such race-prejudice in Europe, the possibility of this 'objection' had only occurred remotely to M. Diaghilev and the Metropolitan."

Nothing, of course, could possibly have been better publicity, not only in the New York press but all over the States. "*SCHEHERAZADE* MILDER," headlined *The World* on the 27th. "Excisions had been made in the harem scene, resulting in a revel of less abandon . . . There was a large attendance, the house being completely sold out."

N.Y.
Tribune
27.1.16

"*Scheherazade* was given last night by the Russian Ballet, with discretion, and probably our American arbiters of taste and morals, the police, were satisfied. Certainly no one else was,"

Nicholas Zverev.

SCHEHERAZADE

Adolf Bolm.

said the *Tribune*, under the heading and sub-heading "TAILORING OF POLICE SPOILS SCHEHERAZADE" – "BALLET STILL FAILS OF MORALITY, BUT SUCCEEDS IN BEING DULL." "*Scheherazade* never was and never can be an entertainment for the young ladies of Miss Prim's seminary . . . By urging upon the negro slaves the desirability of respectful demeanour towards the houris of the harem, the emissaries of our courts succeeded in introducing dullness – they certainly did not succeed in introducing morality.

"A moral *Scheherazade* is about as possible of realization as a continent Don Juan."

In England, such an excitement might have given rise to a memorable "Fourth Leader" in *The Times*: the *New York Times* dealt with it in a Seventh. That extraordinary phrase was picked up: "(M. de Diaghilev) may know a great deal about pink teas, but he is not an authority on harems. A harem scene is not like a pink tea, but it is more like a pink tea than an orgy. A harem is the living apartment or apartments of the ladies and children in a Mohammedan gentleman's household. The etiquette in these apartment differs from that of the apartments of the ladies and children in the home of a gentleman residing in Peoria or South Framingham, Mass.; still, in point of decorum and dullness there is, it is probable, not much to choose . . ." N.Y. Times 28.1.16

Scheherazade and Bakst had for so long been linked in the minds of all who had appreciated this ballet that, amidst the welter of press comment whipped up by this affair, some thoughts communicated by the current Golden Slave, Adolf Bolm, to a little broadsheet published in Greenwich Village, have their own interest from an artistic point of view – not a moralist's. Bolm said that "Bakst had one fault – an immense trifle – his headgear, the hoods, the turbans, the whatnots that he conceives for the heads of his disciples – beautiful? Yes, as only ugly and vulgar things are – but, – But, my friend Leon forgets that in the classic arts the feet should have pre-eminence . . . Some of his designs are purely graphic. From the mind, for the paper. He invents, say, something that he considers decorative, but imagine trying to dance entangled with all the intricacies of Bakst's mind." When asked if America could appreciate Russian art, Bolm replied, "You are not asked to understand Russia. You are asked to feel." Bruno's Weekly 12.2.16

Court Ladies in *Le Pavillon d'Armide.*

Zamoukouska   Kachouba   L. Sumarokova   Khokhlova   N. Sumarokova

N.Y.
Tribune
25.1.16
The novelty of the second week at the Century was *Petrouchka*, which, with *Carnaval*, had made "two ballets to which the late St. Anthony himself would not have objected." Not one paper referred to any colour problem in the love triangle of the puppets. "Petrouchka is one of the most poignant little tragedies New York has seen of recent years. Puppets of fate are we all, the very best of us; and the fate that is ours, is the fate for some of us, of poor Petrouchka and his love. Let us go to the Century, when *Petrouchka* is given again, and recognize ourselves!" This ballet was widely acclaimed as the best the Russians had offered, whilst, towards the end of the week, *Le Pavillon d'Armide* seems to have made little impression.

American
Vogue
March
1916
As he considered the American debut himself, Diaghilev must surely have felt his greatest pleasure at the advent of Lopokova. Not only did she entrance the audiences with her lovely dancing – her great *élévation*, charm and wit – but she was, indeed, an ambassadress, chattering away to the gentlemen of the Press, giving endless interviews in fluent English on every possible aspect of ballet. *Vogue* reported that "beautiful and versatile, this youngest of the stars is their greatest treasure. Idzikowski is the only member of the ballet who speaks perfect English, for since childhood he has felt certain he would one day come to America and in preparation has constantly studied English . . . Bolm . . . is more than half Tartar. He is very proud of his Tartar ancestry and likes to travel in Tartar villages to study the wild dances of the natives. He is a great student of painting and sculpture and wishes to stay here to study these arts as they have developed in America." *Vogue* went on to tell an amusing story: "Last year Bakst was invited to Geneva to meet the one woman (so his friend said) who could wear a Bakst costume as Bakst imagined it, and he met Flora Revalles. Bakst telegraphed Diaghilev to come from Florence, and he came, bringing Bolm. They arranged a private performance, after which Bakst wagered all his royalties on the American tour on Revalle's success, and after the first night at the Century, Diaghilev cabled to Bakst, 'You've won!'."

Courtiers in *Le Pavillon d'Armide*

Zverev   V. Nemchinova   Karnetsky

Musical
America
5.2.16

Whether the New York public had taken the company to its hearts or not, a letter to *Musical America* took stock of the season: "By the aid of Mlle. Lopokova and the police, the Russian Ballet ended its two-weeks' season at the Century Opera House in a blaze of glory, and departed, on Sunday, to attack the moralities of 'The Hub.' Whether 'The Hub' will be able to stand the shock remains to be seen.

"The receipts for the two weeks are said to have been about $100,000, which should leave a pretty handsome profit to those interested, even though it has been stated in some of the official announcements that the enterprise was undertaken 'purely for artistic purposes.' " The writer went on to criticise the programme of the opening night, saying that Lopokova ought to have danced then, and (in his view) the most Russian offering, *Petrouchka*, been given instead of *Scheherazade.* For the rest, he thought he would have preferred *Les Sylphides* to the *Faun*, and thought that had these items been presented, everything would have been quite above criticism. (Of course, *Faune* had not been on the programme for the opening night.)

And so, on Sunday, January 30th, it was into the special train and off to "The Hub" for the huge company which, complete with a whole symphony orchestra, was the largest ever to have had to face the rigours of touring in an American winter.

1916

An advertisement in the programme, The Auditorium, Chicago.

THE FIRST TOUR

It was First Stop, Boston – the Hub itself.

The opening on Monday, January 31st, was given what can only be called a "rave notice." The tone was thoughtful – literary – Bostonian. The critic, H.T. Parker, was one of those who had seen the *Ballets Russes* on summer visits to Europe, and he stated that "the whole ensemble is far more skilful and spirited, better trained and fused, more pleasurable to the eye and more stimulating in illusion than it was in the summers of either 1914 or 1913 in Paris." This was most certainly *not* one of the journalists of whom the *New York Tribune* had been thinking when it had reviewed the Prospectus put out in *Opera News*: "The prospectus bears the imprint of an imaginative enthusiasm, which, seeing that it is to be sent not only to New York, but to those portions of the land where critical balance and reticence of expression are probably considered the marks of an effete civilisation, may perhaps be pardoned."

Boston Evening Transcript 1.2.16

N.Y. Tribune 26.12.15

Parker applauded the choice of *Firebird* as the opening ballet, accepted *La Princess Enchantée* as a necessary vehicle for the ballerina, fell for *Soleil de Nuit*, and then felt able to devote a long dissertation to the controversial *Scheherazade*. "And here, perhaps, is the moment to do two-fold justice to the so-called 'version' that was danced and mimed last evening. Not a few that happened to be looking at it for the first time in their lives said confidently that the 'inherent' sensuality and savagery of the mimodrama had been purged away. It is true that the slaves were nearly white and not black, in deference to an American prejudice unknown to Europe. It may be that the sultanas' fondling of them was a shade less ardent than it used to be on the stages of Paris and Berlin. The plain truth is that the piece and performance have long enjoyed a fictitious reputation on the unctuous tongues of old men and in the shocked whispers of maidens."

The brilliant opening, and the urbane attitude of Boston's principal critic, did not prevent a small insistence on the proprieties. This time, it was reported in a New York paper. "Bare toes on the stage are proper, but any bareness above the very lowest part of the ankles is contrary to Mayor Curley's standard of morality . . . 'The City Board of Censors,' said the Mayor this afternoon, 'talked informally about the ballet and decided that there was nothing irregular or improper about it. But I have instructed Mr. Casey (the local Chief of Police) to request the management to cover the bare limbs. I have no objection to the bare toes.'" This was to be a source of amusement for many a long day.

N.Y. Tribune 3.2.16

Changes in the advertised programme produced the usual protests. It made no difference that these had been necessitated by the sudden rupture with Maclezowa, who, furious at the successes of Lopokova, had walked out – much to the relief of the rest of the company. It made no difference that this meant that the public would see far more of Lopokova as a result – Lopokova, whom it found adorable. In their opinion, Diaghilev ought to have covered himself against the contingency of losing any given dancer. Even Boston did not understand that dancers are not quite interchangeable units.

151

Boston had been promised *Le Pavillon d'Armide*. This ballet had not been greatly liked in New York, but perhaps Boston felt that its seventeenth-century ambience would be more to the taste of its refined outlook. The blame for its withdrawal was placed firmly on the management of the Metropolitan Opera House: ". . . that management has long and warrantably been an object of suspicion to the Bostonian public for music and the theatre. The source and cause of this suspicion is the seeming unwillingness or the singularly besetting inability of the Metropolitan to match performance with promise in whatever it undertakes in Boston . . . already the public is beginning to mistrust, and that mistrust is not soothed by the daily amendment of the announced programme of the Russian Ballet and the appreciable narrowing of the repertory."

Carnaval pleased, and he-who-had-seen-it-in-Europe said that "Mr. Idzikowski was the Harlequin in Nijinsky's stead, younger and lither, nearly as light and fleet and quite capable of most of the ornaments of technical skill or fantastic imagination with which the absent mime adorns the part."

Les Sylphides produced a truly comprehending and rapturous notice. "Lopokova in alternate flashes of technical felicity and girlish charm . . . Tchernicheva with a more opulent grace . . . Vassiliewska with soft flow of expanding line . . . (the *corps de ballet*) in shimmering arabesques, in slender lines, in lightly whirling circles . . . their rhythm, their motion and their aspect seemed no whit less idealised than that of Chopin's music." The *Transcript* did remark, however, that "for the first time in all the dancing of the week, there was reason to miss M. Nijinsky."

Of *L'Après-Midi d'un Faune*, the *Transcript* had no doubts. "The illusion that it seeks is an illusion of a remote and disembodied beauty . . . Hellenic, perhaps, but quite as much of the place and time of Mallarmé and Debussy . . . they visualise in the round and in living being a beauty of line and color that has hitherto been only of inanimate surfaces; and so doing they make more real than reality the beauty of instant and flitting spiritual sensation. Thereby the Russian Ballet has enriched the theatre with a stranger and rarified art that it knew not until the day when *L'Après-Midi* was first set upon the stage."

The ending was reported in another paper: "His treatment of the scarf idly dropped by the nymph was painstaking, deferential." The *Globe* observed that "fauns, whatever their dispositions in Paris or New York, can become docile, tractable and well-mannered in Boston." Possibly this was not only out of deference to Bostonian manners, but also to the guardians of its law – for H.T. Parker had noticed that "conspicuously enthroned in a box at the back of the house sat the three august masters of the pleasures Bostonians may receive at the theatre."

The same writer gave news from New York, which certainly showed the capacity of American audiences for enthusiastically bothering to turn out and attend performances. "With an afternoon and night of continuous opera and all Broadway snowbound at that, the Metropolitan not only hung out the S.R.O. sign twice over yesterday, but also set up the season's top record for one day's prosperity." The matinée, of *Rheingold*, had been at popular prices, but Caruso in the evening had turned it into a $20,000 day.

In Boston itself, the matinée on Diaghilev's first Saturday established a record, for it "filled every seat in the Opera House" – the first time that had ever happened at a matinée. This brought remarks of great sense in the *Transcript*, on the importance of catering for people from out-of-town, and also for ladies, who, it said, had the time to go in the afternoon, but could not turn out at night – (presumably they could not persuade spouses or other escorts to take them in the evening.)

The folly of equivocation in public relations could hardly be more clearly exemplified than in Parker's remarks regarding the apparent gaps in the audiences during the first few days of the visit to Boston. "They are more unwise still when they despatch the Russian Ballet to Boston and wonder that it has not assembled larger audiences there, while they themselves are busily informing New York that, upon its return to the Metropolitan in April, Mr. Nijinsky and Miss Karsavina will join it; that the ensemble will be bettered and the repertory widened." Boston did, however, have one ballet which had not been shown at all in New York – *Thamar*.

"It is tellingly presented. Perhaps too tellingly, indeed, to suit the art form in which it is cast. For the characters in pantomime should never come too near to actually speaking. And the queen and the traveller in this scene, which has been adapted to the music of the Balakireff symphonic poem, seem often on the point of conversing aloud. The same thing occurs in the

Boston
Transcript
3.2.16

Boston
Evening
Transcript
4.2.16

Boston
Evening
Sun
4.2.16

Globe
4.2.16

Boston
Evening
Transcript
4.2.16

Boston
Evening
Transcript
7.2.16

Boston
Evening
Transcript
7.2.16

Christian
Science
Monitor
9.2.16

Leonide Massine and Lubov Tchernicheva in *L'Après-Midi d'un Faune.*

Rimsky-Korsakov adaptation, *Scheherazade*. The leading rôles there, as here, are at times almost oral."

Throughout the entire conspectus of American criticism, this division between "dance" and "mime" was maintained. That the dance should be so telling that, in effect, it spoke was one of Fokine's principles. Dance and mime had, in fact, become one. "Dance," often ludicrously, was considered to be virtually class exercises, and quite distinct, as in the old, outmoded ballet style, from what had once even been taught separately – the "mime." That it needed a trained dancer to move so expressively never seemed to occur to these critics.

The same writer had, however, already said that "certainly the touring company goes to its next calling place with the gratitude of Bostonians . . . It has given ten days of pleasure such as no other group of artists in the world could equal."

The enormous baggage-train set off for a one-night stand in Albany, N.Y. Albany loved it: *Les Sylphides,* the *Faun, Prince Igor* and *Carnaval* enraptured the critic of the *Argus.* Of Lopo- Albany Argus 11.2.16 kova, he wrote that "this mite of a dancer has personality and charm and grace in prodigal measure, and she is the best asset of the troupe." He could see nothing but pleasure in the *Faune,* "for one wondered what possible objection there could be to its fictions." There were a few whispered lamentations, obviously from the travelled, that "the wondrous Karsavina was not in her place." But it was "a great night for Albany and some more artistic history made by Ben Franklin, whose influence with the Metropolitan Opera brought the Diaghilev troupe here."

The company next travelled on to Detroit, where it was to give three performances. "The Detroit Free Press 13.2.16 predominating appeal is to one's sense of the magnificent, the gorgeous and the barbaric," was the feeling expressed after the second performance. Probably the company was tired out with travelling, for *Les Sylphides,* that most elusive of all ballets, attracted some criticism on the opening night for "a distinct falling off from that immaculate perfection we have come to ex- pect of Russian dancers great and small." As for *Prince Igor* – "Of all the ballets given here, it has aroused the most spontaneous enthusiasm. In it, for the first time, the male members of the ballet had their opportunity – and whisper – the male members are near to outshining their associates of the opposite sex." The third programme was considered to be the best, with *Syl- phides*, the *Faun, Prince Igor* and *Scheherazade*. "Strange, that with all Diaghilev's effort to achieve the artistic, this should have been the first logically built-up program of the engage- ment, the first without let-down or anti-climax."

From Detroit, the company travelled on to Chicago, where it was to fulfil the longest engagement of the tour. No one could possibly have anticipated the disaster that was to occur in that city.

The Auditorium held about 4,000 spectators. The usual barrage of advance publicity had informed the citizens of the excitement on its way to them. The great store, Marshall Field, had made an arrangement and, (as announced in the programme) "Simultaneously with the Russian Ballet's appearance here, we are displaying Original Costumes designed by Bakst and worn by the artists in certain of the ballets. It will be interesting to note the influence of these Costumes on women's clothes of the moment – the new Suits, Coats, Frocks, Skirts and Blouses revealing this Russo-Oriental influence in pleasing modification."

One would have imagined that such bait would have tempted the hundreds of shoppers to go along at least once to see their exotic visitors.

The first night was a Benefit. This, for Chicago people if not for the company, invested it with the glamour of a Gala – but with the audience being the performers.

The *Chicago Daily Tribune*, which proudly announced itself on the front page as "The world's Greatest Newspaper," had a circulation of over 300,000 daily, and 500,000 on Sundays.

The headlines on the morrow had a distinct slant.

Chicago
Daily
Tribune
15.2.16

CHICAGO SEES BALLET RUSSE UNEXPURGATED

STRIKING ENSEMBLES OF SERGE DE DIAGHILEV SHOW NO SIGNS OF POLICE CENSORING

AUDIENCE A BRILLIANT ONE

A milk-and-water, highly posed picture of "A Scene from *Scheherazade*," with a lady in a be-trousered tea-gown apparently trying to help a Shah-like gentleman off with the right sleeve of his jacket, and three young ladies in turbans and stage jewellery bent on doing the same with the left – UNCENSORED! – did not look very exciting; Flora Revalles, in a large garden-party hat, smiled graciously at the readers.

"Every seat on the floor and in the boxes had been sold for the evening to the board of managers of the Eli Bates Settlement, who conducted the affair as a benefit performance. As a result, the affair had all the brilliance socially of the first night of the opera . . . about $2,500 was raised by the sale of seats . . . This amount was increased considerably by the activities of a group of alluringly gowned debutantes who invaded the audience in the intermission with valentines and pleas for subscriptions . . . the valentine design was from an original by Miss Elizabeth Cramer."*

*** In another paper, O.L. Hall started a review rapturously. "Here are the radiant Russians, and here is the dance divine." After much eulogy, he said that "they confirmed one's belief in the mighty value of the perfect ensemble."

But that did not satisfy him. He, too, drew that slightly aggravating distinction between sheer dancing and mime. He continued: "But of dancing for the dance's sake there was not enough, of individual greatness there was hardly a hint; of the strong, unwavering appeal of genius at play, like the appeal of Pavlova, there was scarcely a trace . . . Thus the brilliance of high virtuosity rarely lighted the scene . . ."

---

*Thanks are due to Mr. Willis for tracing the explanation of the Benefit: "The Eli Bates Settlement was an eminently respectable Chicago charity, founded in 1876, which operated a workshop and settlement house in a poverty-stricken section inhabited mainly by Italian immigrants . . . Dance was a favourite money-raising benefit for them. There is a record of $4,500 raised by their sponsorship of the Adolf Bolm company in 1920, and a successful opening night of the "Monte Carlo Ballet Russe" – de Basil's company, I presume, – in 1934.
THOMAS WILLIS
Arts Editor, *Chicago Tribune.*"

(N.B. The Diaghilev opening was a success from the point of view of the charity.)

The Chicago Daily Tribune.
THE WORLD'S GREATEST NEWSPAPER

CIRCULATION
OVER 500,000 SUNDAY
OVER 300,000 DAILY

TUESDAY, FEBRUARY 15, 1916.

13

THEIR DEBUT IN MORALS COURT; A NEW PROBLEM

Trial of Three Young Girls with Curious Eyes of Dozens of Men on Them.

HERE IS A PLAIN RECITAL.

BY FANNY BUTCHER.

Monday morning in the city hall. The large corridor downstairs with its impressive gilt elevator doors, its surge eof humanity, the elevator door closing upon that scene and opening upon the crowded dimness of the corridors of the eleventh floor. Men of every class and description waiting to go into court, waiting to see some one who is going into court, or just waiting around.

To get to the Morals courtroom in the northeast corner of the building one has to force one's way through the crowd.

Scarcely More than "Kids."

Three girls, scarcely more than children, dressed quietly with none of the adornment or coloring of the unfortunate who are brought to the bar of the Morals court to answer for their deeds, walked down the corridor and into the courtroom just ahead of me.

With them was a man, not old, but who looked as if he had been suddenly aged. I was watching the men in the corridor and I saw eyes that were ashen glitter into interest when those girls walked by, making it as said to them, but there could be little doubt that those glittering eyes would see those girls again.

In the courtroom they sat to one side and didn't talk, but there wasn't an eye in the room that didn't see them. "Can they be culprits?" I wondered, just as a coarse voice sneered: "Those kids are startin' early."

Neighbors Had Complained.

The police, on a complaint which the neighbors had sent in, went up to a flat on the north side about 1 o'clock Saturday morning, rang the bell, and after a few moments were admitted. The house was dark. One of the girls—the littlest one—was sitting on a couch in the dining room with a boy of about 21, another one was sitting on a couch in the parlor with a man who owned the flat, a widower of 35, and the third girl was in bed with the covers pulled up over her head. A third man had opened the door for the policemen. The policemen found empty beer and wine bottles in the kitchen. Such were the facts.

The three men in the case wanted jury trials. They kept whispering to the girls to take jury trials also, until the judge dismissed the case for a while, so that the girls could be told what a jury trial is.

They had never been arrested in their lives and never had been inside a court and when they understood, they chose to be tried by Judge Uhlir.

Their Stories Told.

Then they told their stories.

The aged young man who had come in with them, and who stood beside them is the father of the littlest girl. She is 17, pretty as she could be, with curly black hair and a smile that would make her breast glad.

"I went to a masquerade for a little while, and then I went over to John's house to a party he had invited me to. I said there were going to be two other girls there and I'd been there two or three times before, and I told mother where I was going. She knew John. He's been over me quite often."

"Yes, he has," the father said. "He's always seemed like a nice boy, and there ...

talked, and played games with Tommy. Then whwen Tommy wanted to go to bed Mr. Jones and I went into the parlor. Tommy sleeps in the alcove off the parlor. Tommy turned out the light, and we were just sitting there when the policemen came. Mr. Jones always has treated me like a perfect gentleman all the time I've known him, and he didn't do a thing Saturday night that wasn't right."

Came from a Small Town.

"And then Susie, 20, pretty as a picture, with blue eyes and a demure little smile, told her story. She lived in a small town and she couldn't find any work there, and so she came to the city. She was living with friends. She begged that she needn't tell their names. They didn't know anything about her being arrested. She didn't know that she was doing wrong, and she hadn't any idea it was so late.

"Frank called me up and asked me if I didn't want to come to a party. I'd been up there before to parties two or three times. Nothing out of the way had ever happened, and I didn't see any harm in it. After we'd all been talking in the dining room for a while, Frank and I walked into the bedroom. I don't know why we did. honest, I don't. We just did. We sat down on the edge of the bed."

Tommy "Turns" Light Out.

"We hadn't been there but a minute when Tommy came by and said 'I'm going to bed. I'm going to turn the light out.' He did, and we were sitting there talking. We hadn't been sitting there very long when there was a knock on the door. It was policemen. Then Frank got up and opened the door. I was so afraid that I jumped into bed and pulled the covers up over my head. I suppose I thought they wouldn't see me or something. Tha's all. We didn't do anything wrong, though."

The policemen admitted that the men weren't under the influence of liquor ...

A Scene from "Schéhérazade"

PHOTO BY WHITE

Flore Revalles
PHOTO BY MISHKIN

UNCENSORED!

Brilliant Audience Sees Ballet Russe in Dances Which Roused Wrath of Police Censors.

ARRESTED GUNMAN MAY BE | STATE SCHOOLS WILL TRAIN

HARD TO BE RID OF HER PRINCE

Judge Not Satisfied with Evidence of Chicago Girl Against Engalitcheff.

New York, Feb. 14.—[Special.]—Supreme Court Justice Bijur, who heard the divorce suit brought by the Princess Nicholas Engalitcheff, daughter of Charles W. Partridge of Chicago, against the former Russian vice-consul at Chicago, on Dec. 24 last and has been considering the case ever since, called the attorneys in the suit before him today and stated that he was not entirely satisfied from the evidence as it now stands, that the suit was brought in good faith.

A. C. Vandiver, who conducted the case for the princess, James W. Osborne counsel for the prince, and Alfred J. Talley, attorney for Mrs. Jane Hathaway, the co-respondent named, appeared in court.

Questions Motive of Princess.

Justice Bijur questioned Mr. Vandiver on the testimony of Mrs. Hathaway, who said that she visited the princess in the latter's apartments at the Vanderbilt hotel, and that the princess told her she was willing to name some one else as co-respondent if Mrs. Hathaway would furnish the name of another woman.

She said the princess told her she knew of a woman who could be induced to testify against the princess for money if Mrs. Hathaway would not suggest another co-respondent.

Justice Bijur also suggested that since the chief witness for the princess was a former maid in the employ of Mrs. Hath-

CHICAGO SEES BALLET RUSSE UNEXPURGATED

Striking Ensembles of Serge de Diaghileff Show No Signs of Police Censoring.

AUDIENCE A BRILLIANT ONE.

In a riot of color, barbaric music, and stirring ensembles Serge de Diaghileff's widely heralded Ballet Russe made its first Chicago appearance at the Auditorium last night.

Three ballets were given—"L'Oiseau de Feu," "Carnaval," and "Scheheerazade." The first proved stately as to its weird setting and dashing as to movement, but aroused only mild enthusiasm. The last two won more spontaneous applause.

No Censoring Evident.

Mlle. Lydia Lopokova, already a familiar figure in Chicago, danced the leading rôles in "L'Oiseau de Feu" and "Carnaval." In none of the ballets was there any particular evidence that the Chicago police censors had interfered with the scheme of things as they did in several instances in New York.

Every seat on the floor and in the boxes had been sold for the evening to the board of managers of the Eli Bates settlement, who conducted the affair as a benefit performance. As a result, the affair had all the brilliance socially of the first night of the opera.

Nets $2,500.

Mrs. Russell Tyson, chairman of the committee on arrangements, reported that about $2,500 had been added to the funds of the settlement by the sale of seats. This amount was increased considerably by the activities of a group of alluringly gowned debutantes who invaded the audience in the intermissions with valentines and pleas for subscriptions to the settlement treasury. The valentine design was from an original by Miss Elizabeth Cramer.

HOLDS BABY FOR BOARD BILL AND BOARD BILL IS PAID.

Mrs. Belle Burroughs Keeps 2 Year Old Boy Until Grandmother Meets Dead Father's Bill.

For two years Edward Friesmeyer had been a resident of the home of Mrs. Belle Burroughs at 1632 Washington boulevard. The most of the time Edward, who is 2½ years old, had spent there with his father, who was also named Edward.

For Edward, the elder, had fallen out with his wife, Mrs. Meta Friesmeyer, and had some from St. Louis with his baby. Then he began to grow ill with tuberculosis, and on Aug. 1, 1915, he died.

Now Mrs. Burroughs and her husband have only one grown daughter. Therefore they had grown fond of the baby. When his mother came from St. Louis, accompanied by the grandmother, Mrs. Bertha Pradler, Mrs. Burroughs refused to surrender the child.

"I want him myself," she said, "and if you just insist on having him, why, I'll just make you pay $100 for his board for two years."

So Mrs. Friesmeyer, through Attorney Eileen H. Markey, obtained a habeas corpus writ yesterday from Judge McDonald. A deputy sheriff served the writ on Mrs. Burroughs, commanding her to produce the child in court this morning.

"I'll pay the $100 if you'll only give him up now," volunteered Mrs. Pradler, the grandmother. Mrs. Burroughs accepted.

So Edward returned at night to St. Louis.

Chicago
Daily
Tribune
16.2.16

The *Chicago Tribune* had reported the first night as an event on the following day, but its first review did not appear until the 16th. Percy Hammond deputised for the Music Critic.

"Mr. de Lamarter, the dancing and music master of this journal, being indisposed or indolent, leaves to my Boeotian fingers the duty of reporting the advent Monday night of the Ballet Russe . . ." He proceeded to enjoy himself, wittily slaughtering the Ballet and the audience indiscriminately. He found the programme, *Firebird*, *Carnaval*, and *Scheherazade*, "an effective distribution of choreographic fairy-tale, harlequinade, and Oriental blood-letting, all of which brimmed with color, music, form and motion. The event (for such it was) marked the annual eleemosynary outing of those devotees of the *joie de vivre*, those keen though scrupulous local hedonists, the patrons of the Eli Bates Settlement. An incongruity at once piquant and meritorious."

According to Hammond, Diaghilev, uncertain as to the probable reception of *Scheherazade* in Chicago, had consulted a *Tribune* colleague. "Miscegenation, no matter how idealised and illegitimate, was pointed out to M. de Diaghilev as not a misdemeanour appropriate to the Eli Bates Settlement or to the community in general, and he wondered what he should do. His continental cunning finally asserting itself, he bleached Le Nègre a trifle at Mr. Whittaker's suggestion and thus skimmed the thin ice of middle west propriety.

"These conventional stories, pantomimed and danced, mean little in my life compared to dancing itself with an accompaniment of music and picture unhindered by the questionable art of the drama," Hammond continued. (There, one may say, wrote a Pre-Fokine Man.) "I believe that what I like are called 'divertissements.' Few of these occur in the de Diaghilev program, which runs somewhat to plots. I mean to say that Pavlova in '*The Swan*' is what you care for and that *Scheherazade* is what you endure with mitigated pleasure . . ."

With tickets at very high prices compared with other shows – inevitable because of the enormous expense of touring a full orchestra as well as a large company – this can hardly have been called encouraging. The Met.'s management had been able to say that the two weeks' season at the Century was sold out in advance. The Chicago promotors can have had hardly any bookings after the opening night. Their anguish can be imagined, for in every town visited, substantial guarantees had been exacted, so that if there were losses, they would not be borne by the Met. They cannot have been best pleased that the city's largest circulation paper should send as its representative a man who wrote that "it is but infrequently that I react to the proceedings of the Ballet Russe," even though he gave a final paragraph full of praise for the settings. "The first ballet was *Firebird*, a pseudo-Maeterlinckian fairy tale in an enchanted forest of wonderful greens and with costumes of lovely pigment and texture, illustrated by the marvelous orchestral dissonances of Stravinsky . . . Then there was *Carnaval*, . . . accompanied by the genial music of Schumann. Finally there was a fragment from the sole and incomparable Arabian Nights . . . told in front of a miraculous Bakst background of sinister greens and the red of oriental degeneracy by comely odalisques, fat, grinning eunuchs, and stately wazirs in a voluptuous debauch of passion, vengeance and massacre. You may not have approved of it, but you were interested. Tomorrow night the sophistication of this primitive frontier will be tested, we are told, by an unexpurgated performance of *L'Après-Midi d'un Faune*."

On another page in the same issue, "Cinderella," who had, apparently, been allowed to go to the "Ball," gossiped away. "The question all day yesterday wasn't 'to be or not to be,' but, did you like it or didn't you? People in general were either powerfully for it, or powerfully bored by it. The first night's performance had a brilliant, but a chilly audience, and there was hardly any response for either the music or the dancing . . . The music . . . proved a most wonderful accompaniment for conversation . . . Lots of people in the audience were talking at the top of their voices during the overture to the *Firebird*, and some of the box-holders, too, were in great form all the evening, Mr. Eliphat Cramer" (who may have been the proud father of the designer of the valentines) "being in especially good vein in a lower box – if only we might all have shared his witty remarks. However, if you like it, that's the sort of thing you like, but *Scheherazade* isn't the sort of thing for Chicago children to take their parents to see . . ."

The second performance (the night before these two comments appeared) was given in a theatre very much emptier than the most pessimistic manager could have expected.

Percy Hammond again reported.

"*The Afternoon of the Faun*" Tuesday night evoked no indignant outcries from the constabulary, though it was presented at the Auditorium with the same luxuriant minutiae that caused the uprising in New York." A glowing account of its languorous beauty might have led one to believe that Hammond was going to extol it – however, – ". . . if it had not been for the final thirty seconds I could have squared the event with the rapturous applause bestowed upon it by many eminently prudent dowagers. This half minute of vicarious nuptials is to be enjoyed only by the virginal, the super esthetic, and the callous. Of these last evening's audience seemed to be composed."

Chicago Daily Tribune 17.2.16

Whether Hammond's articles had any real effect is debatable. The straightforward fact is that Chicago was staying away, in its numbers.

Possibly the management protested to the Editor – or perhaps Hammond could not bear a third night in succession at the Ballet. Friday saw the quill wielded by Kitty Kelly, the paper's kinema critic. "There was picture and here was motion . . ." she said. *Soleil de Nuit* she described as "a jolly commingling of color and motion, with maids dressed quaintly in petticoats shaped like old-fashioned potato mashers . . ."

Chicago Daily Tribune 18.2.16

If it was not murder, at least it was manslaughter. Pictures captioned "Lopokova," but showing the departed Maclezowa, must have helped to mystify those who turned up – but they were few. The ballet was playing, for the first time in its existence, to rows and rows of empty seats.

In the *Post*, Karleton Hackett attacked the *soi-disant* opera lovers and orchestral lovers who could not recognise the wonders being performed by the orchestra – probably they could not hear them through the talk.

Chicago Post 18.2.16

"A week's rapturous attendance upon the programs of Diaghilev's Russian Ballet, registering impressions in well-contented silence, gives me the privilege of adding a postscript to the story of this great episode, which has been chronicled in piecemeal by my colleagues," said Charles Collins. "It has been a revelation."

Chicago Evening Post 19.2.16

However, he went on: "Chicago has chosen to be slightly critical about this benefaction: to call attention to the fact that Nijinsky is not present, and that the company lacks a Pavlova; to observe that it would prefer more dancing and less pantomimic narrative. . . Here we betray a certain mid-Western naïveté – for this reluctance to enjoy in the mood of ecstasy belongs to our civic non-sophistication . . .

"For my part, I do not miss Nijinsky, for I never saw him," continued Collins. "The enchanted music of Stravinsky, the gorgeous color schemes of Bakst, the inspired choreography of Fokine and the orchestral art of Ansermet are too impressive to permit me to worry about Nijinsky; and I am certain that in the curious ensemble dancing of *Prince Igor* there is more of a thrill than Nijinsky could ever impart. As for those who ask for formal dancing in place of the infinitely finer art of Russian choreography, I would not give them *L'Oiseau de Feu* for a wilderness of Taglionis, Elsslers and Genées. . ."

Collins went on, "The nine ballets already given here leave a dazzling impression . . . Never before have so many gifts been assembled in one theatre for our pleasure."

Only one ballet failed to please this critic – *Faune*. "I reject it not on moral but on artistic grounds. I regard it as an imbecile conception . . . completely out of place in this vigorous art . . . neither the beautiful scene painting of Bakst, whose work is here found at its best, nor the artfully archaic costumes of the nymphs, nor the clever way in which the Greek vase theme has been carried out in low-relief pictures, can reconcile me to it. As for the spotted faun, he reminds me of nothing but a coach dog."

Percy Hammond returned to the fray on Sunday. "It appears that we are repaying with but scant contributions of money the disinterested benevolence of the solvent New Yorkers who have sent hither the Ballet Russe . . . we in large numbers remain away . . . The absence of Nijinsky, the tariff of $5 a seat (this last objection from an enthusiastic esthete) . . . have been submitted as causes for the neglect. So we may look upon ourselves as outcasts whilst recalling with pride our interest in Pavlova last summer in the Midway Gardens. There is an essay on the ballet in the Encyclopaedia Britannica which ends with the lament that 'only in an atmosphere

Chicago Sunday Tribune 20.2.16

Karnetsky   Oumansky carrying Mieczkowska.

THE
POLOVTSIAN
DANCES
FROM
PRINCE IGOR

top row: Statkevitch, ..., Evina, G. Chabelska, Pianowski, Pflanz, V. Nemchinova, Oumansky

middle row: Antonova   O. Nemchinova   *bottom:* Herman   Novak

of ceremony, courtesy and chivalry can the dance maintain itself in perfection.' The experience of the Ballet Russe in Chicago seems to prove that sometimes, even in a center of grace and manners, may so imponderable an art fall upon evil days."

"A CRITICISM OF CRITICS OF THE RUSSIAN BALLET" was the heading of a column of comment by "Mme. X." in the same issue. "The question of the moment among the elect is, 'How did you like the Russian Ballet?' If you respond with hyperbolic praise then you are set apart from the common herd; you belong to the Brahmins; you show yourself a true cosmopolite. . . It is an enviable status." Mme. X. compared the modern admirers of the Ballet to those who had applauded Sarah Bernhardt, and "boldly acclaimed her genius to a community that preached against her from every pulpit and fireside as the prototype of the scarlet woman;" and whose immediate descendants "looked thirty years later at Strauss's *Salomé* and recognized and applauded its beauty and art. They are today among those to whom the present performances at the Auditorium give real, acute pleasure. Alas, that their numbers are small. What Mr. Diaghilev wants is quantity, not quality . . .

"It is perhaps too much to expect that an audience of the middle west could and would put itself into a Slavic state of mind . . . But the time will come when those who now decry the various offerings of the Russian Ballet on the ground of propriety will keep as quiet about their attitude as those who once anathematized not only the divine Sarah but all who went to see her."

Mme. X. uttered one practical criticism – (one wonders whether the miscreant was fined!) "In *Scheherazade*, the black was not dense enough nor well put on. It came off on the white arms of the sultan's favorite."

By midweek, Percy Hammond had decided that "if Messrs. Wessels and Voegeli" (the Chicago backers) "ever do me the honour to ask me which of the Russian ballets I like best I shall hesitate a minute, thinking of the *Faune*, and then I shall answer 'Thamar'." It was, however, getting rather late in the day for Percy Hammond's liking of anything to have any effect on the receipts. Chicago Daily Tribune 23.2.16

By the 24th, Karleton Hackett was heading his piece, "RUSSIAN BALLET IS GIVEN 'FROST' HERE." He did not mince his words. "The visit . . . has enabled Chicago to achieve distinction, not to have distinction thrust upon it by adventitious circumstance, but to achieve it by the inherent force of its ineptitude in the arts. The 'frost' which the Russian Ballet has experienced here is already famous and will become historic in the annals of the theatre . . . Since it was decreed by the stars in their courses that we should be unable to rise to this Russian Ballet, it is some satisfaction that we have made the thing so emphatic as to establish a record . . . Last night the audience looked a little better in point of numbers and there was some rather half-hearted, shame-faced attempt at applause during *Petrouchka*. The novelty, *Le Spectre de la Rose*, danced by Lopokova and Gavrilov, did, in fact, really draw applause, which sounded as though the audience were at some familiar entertainment which they understood and rather enjoyed – 'The Follies,' for example . . ." Chicago Post 24.2.16

The State Historical Society has in its possession a complete set of the programmes given in Chicago, bound, and donated many years later by the widow of one of the local impresario-backers, Voegeli. A note dated 16th September 1958, relating to the gift, says in part: "Mr. Voegeli was the first to bring Russian Ballet to Chicago. (Incidentally, he lost his shirt!)"*

A postscript of a different nature appeared on the following Sunday in the column "News of Plays and Players." Pavlova was seeking an engagement in Chicago for the coming April, only a few weeks away, and during the period when the Diaghilev company was due to perform at the Met. itself. "The foregoing paragraph," it opined, "would indicate that Miss Pavlova is not interested in the proposition made to her by Mr. Otto Kahn, the importer of the Ballet Russe, to take the leadership of that organisation for its return engagement in New York, although the Chicago Sunday Tribune 27.2.16

---

*(I am indebted to Dr. Herbert Curtis, of Wilmette, Illinois, who most kindly delved into local records for me, for this revealing observation.)

offer, of itself, would indicate that Mr. Kahn regards her as quite as important as Nijinsky would have been had he and the difficult M. de Diaghilev been able to compose their difference." The paragraph continued, "Miss Pavlova further, through her Mr. Rabinoff, (of Boston,) sends flat denial of a circulated paragraph that she will head the forces of the next extravaganze to be staged in the New York Hippodrome." (But head it she did, for four months.)

What is most interesting, as theatrical gossip, is the broad hint that Nijinsky and Diaghilev *had* differences, and that he therefore might not even dance with Diaghilev's company when – or if – he reached the States. Diaghilev himself never seems to have doubted that Nijinsky would gladly dance again in his greatest successes with many of his old comrades. But that paragraph was followed, a few days later, by another.

On March 2nd the Metropolitan was able to announce that Nijinsky had been released from internment, and would "probably appear with the company when it reaches New York next month . . ." This paragraph is worth noting carefully, in the light of events once Nijinsky had actually landed: it indicates a proper managerial uncertainty of an engagement until a contract had been signed, unlike Diaghilev's certainty that Nijinsky would return to him. But Diaghilev was not up against idle griefs and grievances: he was up against Nijinsky's own character, and moreover, against that of his wife.

The morale of the company must surely have been affected by this dreadful Chicago fortnight. Weeks more of touring lay before them. As they travelled further from New York, would the lack of understanding and the apathy become even worse?

Milwaukee
Discoverer
26.2.16

A shorter journey northwards brought the company to Milwaukee. An article by Lopokova appeared a few days before their arrival, gay, delightful, letting the public in on the secrets of the strain of learning a rôle and the responsibility for collaborating perfectly with the rest of the team. This was ideal for warming the public up. "Mind and body must do wonderful teamwork if our dancing is to carry to the audience the story we wish to impart," she said. (Did "Teamwork" denote the influence of her current fiancé, Baseball Correspondent of the *New York Tribune*?) "So we must realise that the *première* of such ballets as those of Diaghilev, where the dance, music, light and color are in such marvelous harmony, must blend all her powers to make the ensemble perfect." That was a simple, positive statement calculated to help an audience to forget the conception of one star alone. Then Lopokova told them of her excitement as a pupil, when it came to that great night, the graduation performance at the end of school-days. "The ballet was called *The Nutcracker*, and was given at the Imperial Theater. It was a Christmas story, and I was given the principal part. My heart would not keep still. My father, my brother and sister, who are now in the ballet, were in the audience. The music began; the lights blazed; we were on the stage." She said that for many weeks, "there was never a moment that we were not humming the music and doing the steps . . ." Now that the great night had come, "it all seemed so dreamlike, the lights threw a great foglike drapery between the audience and the stage. But we could hear the applause. In a box were the Emperor and so many from the royal court to see our work. In the wings were the teachers and others from the school to help and encourage us. And there were moments when we needed it so. But we did get through it famously, and then all of us passed before the Emperor, who spoke so gloriously of our work . . ."

Milwaukee
News
28.2.16

This charming story must have been worth many official handouts.

An "interview" with Diaghilev himself was printed in another paper on the day they were to open in Milwaukee. He does not seem to have been in communicative mood – forcing himself, perhaps, to produce any response at all, after the Chicago débâcle. The poor, unfortunate reporter was not given much help, and had to fill in his own ideas of Diaghilev "by ear."

"The rich Russian baron was just getting ready to combine breakfast and luncheon in the Hotel Pfister Café, when he amiably consented to be interviewed providing the reporter could speak Italian. After some preliminary skirmishing, the reporter sighed. '*Pas Italienne*.' '*Ah, vous parle* (sic) *Française!*' – and the dapper Russian's brown eyes were aglow with joy and friendliness. "*Si vous ne parle* (sic) *pas trop vite*," pleaded the interviewer. Poor man – just why did Diaghilev, who habitually spoke French, try to insist upon Italian? Not so much, one must suspect, because of a mood but as a device. However, the interviewer must have managed somehow, for he continued: "Anyone who thinks this aristocratic Russian impresario might be nursing a grouch because his spectacular ballet is a losing venture financially ought to see the man. He couldn't be cornered into saying anything uncomplimentary about America or American audiences . . ."

The article continued by detailing the instructions for the large concourse expected for the one performance that very evening, giving all the arrangements for motor cars – "There will be four carriage callers in livery" – and stating that, as the intermissions would be long, the rotunda and corridors would be open for promenading.

The result was much more pleasing than the reception in Chicago. "ALL APPROVE BALLET RUSSE" was the headline. "No small boy at his first three-ring circus ever lamented more bitterly the limitations of possessing only a single set of eyes and ears than did the beholders of the Russian Ballet . . . It was exasperating to realise that . . . he could do little more at a single glance than get a bewildering impression of the most exquisite harmony of beauty in sound, color and movement. Even the trained observer could well demand a four-fold repetition . . . before he could feel that he had really begun to enjoy to the full its manifold beauties – once for the general impression, once for attentive study of the marvelous color effects in decoration and kaleidoscopic groupings, once for the arrangement and execution of the dancing, and once for the sole sake of the music." Milwaukee Journal 29.2.16

Typical, however, of the hazards of touring and performing on varied stages, was the sad experience related by the Curator of the Art Society, Dudley C. Watson. He had had an arena (stall) seat, and bewailed it. "It was impossible for those in arena seats to see the feet of the dancers – half the enjoyment of the performance. I sat about twenty rows back, and occasionally during the toe dancing I saw the feet, all except the toes . . . Had I not seen the ballets before I should have been more disappointed than I was." Milwaukee Journal 1.3.16

"In selecting the four numbers for presentation in Milwaukee the committee of censors was apparently guided by a desire to avoid affronting any Puritanical sentiment which may be abroad in the Cream city at this time. There was nothing shocking or even mildly wicked in dance, posture, costume or suggestion. The costumic disclosures which seemed to be promised by some of the advance pictures were entirely absent. There were grace and beauty and atmosphere; there was sensuous charm, but there was nothing that required the apology of 'art.' " Milwaukee Sentinel 29.2.16

As Milwaukee saw *Carnaval*, *Les Sylphides*, *Midnight Sun*, and *Scheherazade*, – its own choice of programme – it was happier than some other cities, where changes were made. However – even for one night – "Considerable areas of vacant seats indicated that $5 of art does not appeal unanimously to Milwaukee entertainment seekers. The boxes were well filled and the occasion may justly be put down as a brilliant and artistically successful event."

The company moved on to St. Paul; a huge double spread of photographs published there in January had included five of Karsavina and one of Nijinsky. The text had described Diaghilev as a friend of the Czarina, boosted Bakst, and congratulated St. Paul on being able to applaud the ballets before the "Diamond Horseshoe" itself. In the event, St. Paul accepted the company happily, and said that Gertrude Hoffman's version of *Scheherazade*, as given locally several seasons previously, had been much "rougher," while at the same time "it had lacked the wonderful finish and whirl of movement in detail observable in the Diaghilev dancers." ***
16.1.16

"MINNEAPOLITANS ENTHUSE OVER DIAGHILEV BALLET" was a good headline. "The two performances were given before audiences that filled the Auditorium and the criticisms were on the front pages of the daily papers. How seldom does the earnest reviewer get his choice remarks on the front page! The stage settings were incomparable, and the Oriental or semi-Oriental dances brought out the full measure of the Orientalism which underlies true Russian life and art . . . One could not fail to be deeply impressed with the potency of Russia." Victor Nilsson described "all shocks as coming from the orchestra," meaning the originality of Stravinsky's music, "which had been likened for its brisk rhythm and nonchalant exuberance to American ragtime, but there is not in the Washington mint a dollar so bright as this music." He commended the playing of the "Sindbad the Sailor" section of *Scheherazade* prior to the rise of the curtain, "thus avoiding the inundation of the harem scene by the dashing turmoil of the seas." Minneapolis Journal 2.3.16
Musical Courier 16.3.16

It will be remembered that William Guard had described Diaghilev's insistence that he should not be bothered with mundane touring arrangements. That he was absolutely right in this insistence was clearly exemplified by events on the journey to Kansas City, where a matinée and an evening performance were booked for the following day.

Kansas
City
Times
4.3.16

"The artists occupy nine Pullman coaches and the stage settings are in fourteen baggage cars, the whole divided into three sections of a special train. It will come in over the Missouri Pacific Railway. The first section will arrive at 7 a.m., the second at 9 a.m., and the third at 9.30 a.m."

So much for the planning of the military operation.

The first section arrived at 11.30 a.m. Unloading of scenery and costumes took panic-stricken priority over the unloading of the dancers: the latter were divided by onlookers into principals and rank-and-file according to whether they looked as if they were accustomed to handling their own luggage or not. All wore goloshes; and vociferous storms broke out in many languages when the principals reached the Hotel Muehlebach, where the best and most expensive rooms had been allocated to them by the management. All the less expensive accommodation had been fully booked by people coming in from Kansas State and Missouri to witness the performances. "The artists had to take the reserved rooms at prices akin to the prices prevailing for their own ballet."

Kansas
City
Star
4.3.16

Armitage

As if the late arrival were not bad enough in itself, a special problem faced the stage hands here. "We were booked to play the vast Convention Hall," said Merle Armitage, "an oval building without a permanent stage. Therefore, after our late arrival it was necessary to curtain off one end of the great auditorium, instal a gridiron on which to hang the scenery, erect a proscenium arch, and hang all the complicated décor and connect our own portable switchboards and rheostats. Diaghilev insisted that the audience not be admitted until he had completed checking scenery and lights. And it was a rainy day!

". . . As the youngest available member of the staff, I was 'selected' to tell the constantly growing audience that the doors would open soon, and to repeat this at ten-minute intervals . . . After my fourth appearance, they were vocal in the extreme and it was an ominous, howling mob that greeted my fifth and final bow. Friends say I aged perceptibly that afternoon."

Against pleas to get the curtain up on time, Diaghilev remained unmoved. Lighting and other rehearsals were essential. The Chief of Police, Hiram W. Hammil, had appointed Captain Ennis to handle "that Convention Hall Ballet Russe. If he sees anything he shouldn't see – well, he's there."

Not only was he there. He had his own method of dealing with the impresario's name, pronunciation being a topic on all lips that day. He called at the theatre before the first performance. Between the two, he discussed matters with a reporter from the *Star*.

"The show was all right as I saw it – but they'd have tried to put something over if I hadn't seen 'em before it started. I dropped in to see Dogleaf before the curtain went up. Dogleaf, or whatever his name is, couldn't understand plain English, and I couldn't go the Russian . . . I told a fellow" (who could interpret), "This is a strictly moral town and we won't stand for any of that highbrow immorality. Put on your show, but keep it toned down to the decency of a high class city where they don't stand for any monkey shines. What's more, I told him we didn't want to make trouble, but if the show was too rank I'd come right up on the stage and call down the curtain. Well, they took my advice. There were several places where they cut out some stuff lots of people would like to have seen, but I guess they remembered my warning.

"I liked the music fine and I guess the show was all right, but it got above my head at times . . . I never saw anything like it in Kansas City before." And Captain Ennis continued to direct the line of motor-cars.

Pity poor Fritschy, Manager of Convention Hall! The afternoon brought 4,000, and the evening 4,300 – a capacity audience. He beseeched Diaghilev to get on with the performance, as the impresario rehearsed lighting and tired hundreds milled about outside. They poured into the local hotels and bars, into picture houses, and even into other theatres for an hour or so, as still the doors of Convention Hall remained closed. The following day, the *Star* reported that

Kansas
City
Star
5.3.16

"Rumors passed about that Manager Fritschy had borrowed the dagger kept by Flora Revalles for her own tragic demise in *Scheherazade* and was threatening to use it either upon himself or the 'only Diaghilev' if the doors were not opened soon."

Happily, Kansas City appears to have had citizens of generous good nature, who bore no grudge when they finally got in to their seats. "They were very responsive audiences, apparently bringing plenty of imagination to bear on the work of the Russians." "BALLET WON KANSAS CITY" was the verdict.

Whether it was just a case of misunderstanding between interviewer and interviewee, plain language problems, or that bewildered traveller's ailment, "Where am I? Where have I been?" – or just a plain misprint – is uncertain, for poor Flora Revalles was reported as saying, in her dressing-room in the evening, that "we artees, we feel ze so kind appreciation of ze audience zis afternoon," and that "not since they danced in Chicago had she felt so keenly the spirit of pleasure and understanding as she had felt it in Kansas City." Perhaps her style had had a special appeal in Chicago.

St. Louis was delighted with the spectacles, though the *Globe* commented on "chattering conversation which marred the pleasure of those who had come to listen." *Soleil de Nuit* gave especial pleasure here. It was pointed out that when Abraham Lincoln purchased Alaska from the Russians for a mere $7,000,000, (one of the most profitable real estate transactions in history,) the Russians retained the totem pole then in their possession on the western side of the Behring Straits – "and that's the way Serge de Diaghileff and M. Larionow managed to keep these wooden monuments and to bring a painted replica to St. Louis unto our special wonder."

St. Louis
Globe
8.3.16

Oliver M. Sayler, critic of the *Indianapolis News*, hailed the company at its next stop. "The glorious art of Muscovy, now wild, now chaste, won a brilliant triumph last night at the Murat." He was one of the happy and fortunate few who had seen the ballet in Paris and London, and said firmly that it was "up to the mark set in Europe." He wrote feelingly, "What they could do on a perfect stage passes belief, for they are compelled to suffer the handicap of the primitive lighting conditions of the American theatre wherever they go in this country . . . Probably the commonest mistake made is that it is thought to be above the head of the ordinary mortal, whereas the truth is that the ordinary mortal ordinarily is above it, or rather tries to assume a position too strained and unnatural to be able to appreciate its simple unaffected lure . . . If there is a vacant seat at either of the two remaining performances there is just that much joy lost somewhere in Indiana."

Indianapolis
News
10.3.16

Four performances followed in Cincinnati, Ohio, at that time the fifth largest city in the United States. An old German-settled city, priding itself on its culture, it had always centred its interests on its fine Symphony Orchestra.

The advance sales were very good, including large orders from out of town, to see the ballet which, as the *Enquirer* put it, had given New York what that city frankly admitted to be the first real sensation of a decade.

The company had one of its very few free days on the Sunday. "Lopokova took an automobile ride around the suburbs. She stood on the highest point of Eden Park and compared the views across the Ohio river with scenes in her native land." "The stately Flora Revalles went to the Zoo in the hope that she could purchase a baby tiger." "When the mail was distributed, there was great anxiety among the members of the ballet. Everyone awaits the letter from home. But the mail was read in silence . . . 'We do not permit any war talk on the stage,' the director explained. 'We have the same rule that has been adopted at the Metropolitan Opera House. If the ladies or gentlemen wish to discuss war, they must go to their hotels.' "

Cincinnati
Times-Star
13.3.16

At nine a.m. they all went to the theatre to take their accustomed class – much to the astonishment of the reporters. "Imagine, if one can, the summoning of a proud Ziegfeld Follies or a Winter Garden beauty to rehearse at 9 a.m. 'Why pick on me in the middle of the night?' would probably be the answer to the summons."

"Last night the *beau monde* of Cincinnati was very Parisien, very Petrogradien. . . and though Lent precluded any special display of finery, nevertheless the audience had the gala look that always attends many congenial and artistic people assembled together," said the *Enquirer*, following with a very long list of local celebrities.

Cincinnati
Enquirer
14.3.16

On the same page, the Stage Gossip column notes that the audience was "by no means of Music Hall capacity, but before long it was extremely enthusiastic and quite bewildered at the prodigality of the Russians." *Firebird, Spectre de la Rose, Soleil de Nuit,* and *Carnaval* made up the bill, and all were well appreciated. Musical Cincinnati agreed that the orchestration of the Schumann sounded extremely well, "even if the intimacy of the piano piece is missed. But its illustration by the visual introduction of the various characters and episodes which Schumann has marked above the various pieces in his score were so in keeping with the atmosphere of the piece that many will never again be able to hear the *Carnaval* played by a pianist without seeing the despised Pierrot hanging over the footlights or the dainty Columbine and the nimble Harlequin dance and trip merrily . . ." Repeating that in the ensemble it surpassed anything ever seen before, the writer went on, that "in individual dancing the art of Pavlova and the dashing splendor of Mordkin are not equaled in the present instance." Of the orchestra, however, knowledgeable Cincinnati had nothing but praise. "It is a splendid body of men and is extremely well conducted by Ernest Ansermet, who is a leader of many fine qualifications."

With *Petrouchka* in its second programme, "the orchestra covered itself with deserved glory." The riot of colour that was Bakst's *Scheherazade* "came as a shock to our austerity. We have lived among our grays, our blues, our blacks and our whites so long that our eyes wince at the Russian chromatic riot which is offered . . . But after we have recovered from the first shock and liberate the sense of color that has been held in restraint by our time-worn conventions, the effect is that of optic intoxication . . . Latent barbaric sensibilities come to the surface. A respectable Covenanter ancestry of grays is quite forgotten."

Cincinnati
Post
16.2.16

The last performance, a matinée, began with *Firebird* – "a second hearing served to open new beauties both to the eye and ear." *Thamar*, its "fierce barbarity not always reflected in the Balakirev music," was notably presented by Flora Revalles and Adolf Bolm. The *Faune* was described as "one of the most delightful episodes," and the *Polovtsian Dances* gave the visit "a sensational climax, so full were they of splendor and barbaric revelry." Cincinnati said: "Nothing more artistic has been offered here in a generation."

Cleveland
Plain
Dealer
17.3.16

Cleveland, on the shores of Lake Erie, fell victim also to the troupe. "Last night the big theater was filled . . . The great stage, the fact that Diaghileff knew he was able to do his subjects justice for the first time since the aggregation left New York, gave the performers themselves not only an opportunity but an apparent confidence that the audience recognized from the first.

"No fault can be found with the collection of dances for the opening night. There was no one in the audience last night who did not wish he could see the entire Diaghileff repertory."

Musical
America
25.3.16

For once, the big curtain went up promptly. "The season was under the management of Mrs. Adella Prentiss Hughes, acting as secretary and treasurer of the newly-organized Musical Arts Association of Cleveland. This organisation, composed of wealthy music-lovers among the business men of the city, not only raised the large guarantee necessary to secure the Russian Ballet, but is pledged to support other important musical enterprises and to promote the musical welfare of Cleveland. The ballet, its first venture, by its extraordinary success, lends great prestige to the association."

Pittsburgh
Post
23.3.16

Pittsburgh, city of steel – city of tremendous fortunes such as that which had enabled Frick to build up his stupendous collections of works of art, and Carnegie his philanthropic empire – was next on the tour. "Never on the Pittsburgh stage has there been the equal of this assembly of feminine grace which crowned *Les Sylphides* among the dancing beauties of Slavonic ballet. As the curtains rose on that unusual beauty, there was an appreciative outburst from the many present, accompanying the first Chopin strains." Only one work seems to have displeased. "Of all drivelling European crudity submitted to American view the *Petrouchka* pantomime of yesterday afternoon ranks with the worst. The scenic nightmare showed a Benois attempt at Bakst-delirium by enveloping the stage in wash-day blue."

Washington
Post
25.3.16

As befitted the capital, the *Washington Post* announced that the company "comes here with the permission of the Russian Government. There are nearly 250 performers, including a symphony orchestra numbering 80 men. The stage force of the National Theater has been trebled. The advance sales, which are exceptionally large, give evidence of a most fashionable and artistically representative audience." Of course, Washington might be expected to number among its citizens in the *corps diplomatique* a high proportion who had enjoyed the pre-war European appearances.

LE CARNAVAL

Vera Nemchinova and
Vorontzov.

Leonide Massine as Eusebius.

Leonide Massine as Amoun in *Cléopâtre*.

Musical
America
1.4.16
"Tonight will be one of the most brilliant of the late season, with many dinner parties, and winding up with the Russian Ball at Rauscher's in aid of sick and wounded soldiers in the Czar's armies." The President and Mrs. Wilson were to attend the first night. The Russian Ambassador and Mme. Bakhmeteff were, naturally, entertaining a dinner party.

"Social and official Washington turned out *en masse* to pay homage to the Russian Ballet. The President and Mrs. Wilson led the box-holders, their entrance on the first night being heralded by the orchestra playing 'The Star-Spangled Banner' as the entire audience rose and applauded."

166

The following morning, the *Post* reported the wonderful evening.

SUPERB ART OF RUSSIAN BALLET FULFILS
HIGHEST EXPECTATIONS

Washington
Post
24.3.16

"It would have been easy for those who have never visited Russia to have imagined themselves in the Imperial Theatre, Moscow . . . when the curtain rose on *Cléopâtre*, the first of the Diaghilev ballets at the National Theatre last night, for by a happy coincidence, the audience itself presented a most picturesque Slavonic appearance with many of the ladies wearing brilliantly jewelled kokoshniks for the ball which followed at Rauscher's. Entertainers and entertained made a composite picture of rare splendour and striking novelty.

"Following the preludes there vanished with the familiar curtain of the National Theatre all the atmosphere of the theatre of the west. The spectator was at once ushered into the erotic realm of flaming passion and reckless gratification. The scene is an Egyptian temple, with heavy, distended, clustering pillars of angry red on every hand. Preceded by slave girls, there enters Ta-Hor, beloved of the hunter A'moun, who soon bounds upon the scene, and shows his desire in a series of gymnastic evolutions. But suddenly, Cleopatra, the sardonic, sensationsated Queen, is borne into the temple by half a score of attendants. She is taken from a forbidding palanquin, swathed in veils. When she stands revealed in her slender loveliness, there surges through the veins of the astonished A'moun a consuming passion, which whips her body into a frenzy of desire. Hurling from him the adoring Ta-Hor, he wins from the scornful Queen an hour of bliss, while the young women of the temple give themselves over to the sensuous spirit of the occasion in a tempestuous bacchanale. . . At the end of the bacchanale, the Queen demands as tribute for his presumption the life of the amorous A'moun. He drinks the poison cup, and while he writhes in agony, the haughty Cleopatra grants a final boon – a cold, passionless kiss. As he sinks to his death, she glides with angular grace from the scene, accompanied by her attendants, while the forsaken Ta-Hor, entering as the cortège passes beyond the dullyglowing pillars, falls prostrate on the body of her faithless lover."

It is curious that this ballet, *Cléopâtre*, never fell foul of the censorship, as did *Scheherazade*, and was considered a suitable offering for President and Mrs. Wilson. However, the *Post* went on, "The supreme delight of the evening was the infinitely graceful and unsullied *Spectre de la Rose*, superbly danced by Lopokova and Gavrilov. The other items were *Carnaval* and *Soleil de Nuit*."

At the ball, twelve artists from the ballet gave a series of dances, "the center of the room being ribboned off for them."

Of course, the theatre was packed for every performance. One wonders why the Metropolitan had arranged for the Washington visit to come so near the end of the tour.

For Diaghilev, Washington must have been a restorative before the return to New York. It was a return to his old world of cosmopolitan society, staying as the guest of the Russian Ambassador – fêted everywhere.

Next, there was a week in Philadelphia, interrupted by a quick dash to Atlantic City. "What will Philadelphia think of the Ballets Russes," had apostrophised Richard J. Beamish as far back as January, in an article headed "SEX AND THE BALLET RUSSE." When it came to the point, Philadelphia thought as did Washington and Boston, and many other cities – that the company was magnificent and the city's own Opera House (confusingly also named "Metropolitan,") was housing a spectacle worthy of it.

Philadelphia
Press
30.1.16

In spite of Chicago, (and, as has been revealed, it was not the Met., nor Diaghilev, whose shirts went west there,) the tour was a financial success. Otto Kahn planned a longer, coast-to-coast tour, for the following winter.

1916

AT THE METROPOLITAN – BROADWAY

The season which started at the Metropolitan Opera House on Monday, April 3rd, 1916, N.Y. Times 4.4.16 annoyed many subscribers by being made part of their list – they had paid for opera. Possibly in deference to them, the programme was non-controversial, with *Le Spectre de la Rose*, danced by Lopokova and Gavrilov, as the only novelty for New York. It was not a very enthusiastic house; possibly some ballet-lovers, unable to get tickets for a subscription night, had defected to the cinema, for it was also the first night in New York of Pavlova's full-length film, *The Dumb Girl of Portici* – another disappointment, in the event.

Interest was concentrated on the imminent arrival of Nijinsky and his family, who had been N.Y. Tribune 4.4.16 released from internment in Austro-Hungary after superhuman efforts on the part of everyone of influence, including the King of Spain, Lady Ripon, the Pope, and Ambassador Penfield.

How would the reunion between Diaghilev and Nijinsky – the Nijinskys – turn out? Remember what Stravinsky wrote about Diaghilev – ". . . Although his fits of temper could be terrible at the moment, he never held a grudge, and when his friends and artists returned to him, he always took them back as if nothing had ever occurred."

Whether there was ever any hope that this technique could have been applied in the case of Nijinsky alone is debatable. In the case of the *Nijinskys*, it was impossible.

Diaghilev would seem to have done his best. He met them at the pier, with flowers for Romola, and accompanied by officials of the Metropolitan. Nijinsky's attitude was immediately and uncompromisingly expressed in action – he landed his two-year-old daughter in Diaghilev's arms.

Reporters had swarmed over the *Espagne*, and pursued the Nijinskys to their hotel, the Claridge. Diaghilev and Massine, to whom the choreographer's baton had passed, were at the Ritz. That evening, Vaslav and Romola watched *Firebird*, *Les Sylphides*, and *Scheherazade* from a box.

A spate of reports and "interviews" appeared the following day in the press. Speeches of all sorts were written out, ostensibly having come from Nijinsky's mouth. One pompous effort referred to his feeling that it was right that he should appear at the Metropolitan, as he had last danced at the wedding of Kermit Roosevelt, in Madrid in 1914.

As many "interviews" will be quoted, set out in the press as if they had been spoken by Nijinsky himself, it is as well to settle the matter of the language problem right away. The *New* N.Y. Times 8.4.16 *York Times* said that "the dancer talked in French and Russian, and his wife, who is constantly with him and keeps in close touch with his affairs, occasionally added remarks in English. *The gist of what they said was this . . .*"

"The gist" occupied nearly a whole column, in coherent prose. Now, Nijinsky did not speak English, and even in Polish and Russian, was extremely inarticulate, uttering only disjointed, separated words and phrases. Lydia Sokolova, who went on both these tours, says that he sat at such sessions with his head bowed, with Romola beside him. From time to time he would mumble remarks to his wife, in halting French, which she translated, as she spoke English well.

"The gist" of the *New York Times* interview was that Nijinsky wanted his own way in everything and would only appear on his own terms. Leaving aside the question as to where the money would come from to support his family if he refused to earn it, his terms were three-fold: he wanted money, old and new, and the new was to be on a thoroughly Transatlantic scale; he wanted his own ballet, *L'Après-Midi d'un Faune*, removed from the repertoire, as he contended that it was being given without his consent (he had not yet seen a performance;) and he wanted to take rehearsals and restore to the Fokine ballets the true Fokine choreographic touches which he felt to be missing.

In the ensuing months, papers all over the States printed "interviews" with Nijinsky, about his art, his ideas, his life, – and though there are always certain elements that ring true, they bear no comparison with the speech of Nijinsky himself. Romola said, in describing the travelling later in the year, "Interviews for the Press had to be prepared. They were made out in the train and handed to the reporters on arrival. Alterations had frequently to be made in the cast, owing to illness." These alterations do not appear in the press reports.

R. Nijinsky p.278

When they first arrived, there were interviews about the hardships of their internment, statements about the ballets, and others about money matters.

N.Y. Times & Tribune 8.4.16

The headlines in the *New York Times* – NIJINSKY AT ODDS WITH BALLET RUSSE – FAMOUS DANCER SAYS THAT HIS FINANCIAL AND ARTISTIC TERMS HAVE NOT BEEN MET – and in the *Tribune*, – NIJINSKY'S DEBUT IN STRIKER'S ROLE – NOT A TOE WILL EX-WAR PRISONER TWINKLE TILL ANTE IS RAISED – speak clearly for his own attitude, which must have shown in his mien even though the words came from his wife's lips.

The Globe 8.4.16

"To the only man who could interview him in Russian speech, Mr. Baron of the *Jewish Daily News*, the arch rebel related his woes," wrote the *Globe*'s reporter, who had found that "there was war today, real war, in the Russian camp, with the 'pacifists' at a discount this morning. Lawyers and reporters swarmed at the hotel headquarters of Nijinsky . . . Dancers and mere opera directors stood aghast around Diaghilev five blocks below."

Nijinsky told Mr. Baron that he had come, having been released through the efforts of powerful Americans, *expecting* to dance. "Now it appears I have no contract. The company is presenting my special creations, led by other dancers, in versions not authorised. They are belittling me. It is impossible for me to appear unless they withdraw the dances of my repertoire and rehearse them again from the beginning under my direction."

The expression "dances of my repertoire" could be interpreted as including not only his own choreographic creation, *Faune*, but also the Fokine ballets in which he had created sensational individual rôles, and in which not only had alterations been made deliberately, as has been seen, in order to satisfy the American conscience, but also through a gradual process of erosion in the quality of detail since their original conception.

The quotation from the *Globe* went on: "Whether or not the Chairman, Otto Kahn, would find a diplomatic solution of the sudden quarrel between Diaghilev and Nijinsky remained to be shown today. The differences were said to be financial in part. As in the old story, 'Oliver Twist asked for more.' He came on a 'shoestring' and couldn't see that he was getting his share in the golden shower rained on Russia's famous ballet at the Metropolitan."

R. Nijinsky p.259

In her own book, Romola put it that when taken later on the day of their arrival to meet Otto Kahn in his office, "I thought the moment had come for me to explain the situation: that Vaslav would readily dance at the Opera, but not with Diaghilev, as long as he did not pay the amount he owed Vaslav for his past salary."

N.Y.P.L. GA 45/15

An old telegram reinforces the argument that there was no contract on which such a claim could be based. It had been sent by Gabriel Astruc to solicitors in London in 1911:-

"AS FOR M. NIJINSKY, M. DE DIAGHILEV HAS EXPLAINED TO ME THAT, BEARING IN MIND THE TERMS OF HIS FRIENDSHIP WITH THIS ARTIST, HE HAS HAD NO NEED TO SIGN ANY CONTRACTS WITH HIM. M. DE DIAGHILEV ADDED, MOREOVER, THAT IN

ALL THE COUNTRIES WHERE THE COMPANY HAD PERFORMED HE HAD HAD THE CO-OPERATION OF M. NIJINSKY, AND THAT HE HAD ABSOLUTELY NO ANXIETIES ON THAT ACCOUNT." – (Translated.)

But how could Nijinsky have "danced at the Opera" without the company? In solos? And is it to be expected that the intention that he should dance with Diaghilev's company had been omitted from all discussion during the long weeks of the journey across Europe and the Atlantic – escorted by Henry Russell, formerly Director of the Boston Opera, who had acted as Kahn's representative?

"There were those, however, who predicted that the directors would build a golden bridge over which Nijinsky might return to the fold." As he threatened that, unless *Faune* were withdrawn, he could *never* come to terms and dance, withdrawn it was. Globe 8.4.16

Another paper gave this version of the first financial matter: "He (Nijinsky) observes, as the Sicilian day laborer does immediately upon his arrival in New York, that the scale of prices is higher in America than abroad and that in the American theater the exotic artist thrives better than the indigenous plant. . . The imported dancers, from Pavlova to the Dolly Sisters, prosper where Isadora Duncan, Maud Allan and Loie Fuller starved . . ." N.Y. Dramatic Mirror 22.4.16

Diaghilev therefore faced two financial problems. If Nijinsky, announced as the greatest dancer in the world, was to dance, he wanted the same pay as Caruso, the greatest singer. But, in addition, he was also demanding "back pay," amounting to the immense sum of half a million francs. In 1916, this was roughly the equivalent of £20,000 – 80,000 dollars. In the early 1970's, this would be something in the region of £150,000, no mean sum. It presumably related to about six weeks, in Berlin and Paris, in 1910, and to the years 1911, following upon his dismissal from the Maryinsky, 1912, and 1913, until his dismissal in the autumn, after his marriage.

Money comparisons are always awkward but perhaps one interesting comparison concerns the receipts for a whole performance in Paris: in 1909, a subsidy was arranged, only to be drawn on if the average receipts of the whole season fell below 25,000 francs a performance. So this claim was for the equivalent of the minimum acceptable receipts from twenty performances – receipts for the entire enterprise.

During those years, Diaghilev had spared Nijinsky all care about money. In *Le Coq et l'Arlequin*, (1918,) Jean Cocteau said: ". . .*Reste Vaslav Nijinsky. Je vous présente un phénomène . . . Rentré chez soi, c'est á dire dans les Palais Hôtels où il campe . . .*" – "Lastly, Vaslav Nijinsky. Allow me to present to you a phenomenon. At home – that is to say in the Palace Hotels where he pitches his tent . . ." Nijinsky had enjoyed the best of everything, even if the money to pay the hotel bills had constantly to be found by the faithful Baron Gunzburg. Diaghilev had paid his bills, taken him on holidays, brought his mother from Russia to Paris to see him dance, provided for all his needs. Moreover, he had negotiated very high fees for appearances at private parties, which had been paid to the artists.

In her book, Romola Nijinsky also said, "In Lausanne, we received word from Sir George Lewis that the lawsuit he had opened against the Russian Ballet to recover the half-million gold francs, which the ballet owed to Vaslav as unpaid salary, had been won in the English courts, but, as Diaghilev was not a resident in any country, there would probably be great difficulty in collecting it." R. Nijinsky p.252

Nijinsky's lawyer, Sir George Lewis, the second Baronet, had an extensive practice in London, and, like his father before him, took on many cases involving members of society and the theatrical profession. From Ely Place, not only did the firm appear in almost every *cause célèbre* tried in London for more than thirty-five years, but both father and son, brilliant as they were, were equally respected for the fact that many cases were kept out of court "by adroit handling . . . to the benefit of all concerned." That was said of the father: in an obituary notice of the son, much the same was said: ". . . Many cases were prevented from coming into court by the skill and tact with which matters of extreme delicacy were handled." D.N.B.

Owing to the lapse of time, there are no records either in the High Court or any solicitor's office which enable it to be stated with any certainty precisely what form the English proceedings took and how they were concluded, but there was almost certainly no public hearing. Solicitor's Journal 13.8.27

No matter what Diaghilev's attitude to the claim, one fact was absolutely certain when he was faced with it in New York; he simply had not got the money, nor any part of it.

R. Nijinsky
p.260

When Romola explained the affair to Otto Kahn, he asked her to send the judgement over to him. A friend produced a young lawyer, Laurence Steinhardt, of the firm of solicitors, Guggenheim and Untermeyer, who was to take over all Nijinsky's legal problems. Romola said that "in a short time he was quite at home in all the complicated mediaeval intrigues of the Russian Ballet, and within three days settled the case in which so many eminent lawyers had failed during three years. The fight was not easy, as Diaghilev, King's Bench Division's judgement or not, did not want to recognize that he was indebted, and when he finally did, refused to pay . . .

"After three days, Steinhardt arrived with a contract with the Metropolitan for eleven performances, and the arrangement that every week Diaghilev had to pay a part of his debt to Vaslav through the Metropolitan, from the amount he was supposed to receive after the troupe's expenses and salaries had been paid."

N.Y.
Telegraph
10.4.16

As but three weeks remained of the current season, and no decision about a second tour had been reached, the arithmetic here seems optimistic. Diaghilev mused that "3,000 dollars a week for a dancer seemed an inordinate sum." (Even this large sum was not, however, as much as Caruso commanded. Years before, Gatti-Casazza had already paid the singer 2,000 dollars for each of 68 performances in a single season: Caruso had himself set a ceiling of 2,500 dollars, realising that it was essential that his appearances should earn extra revenue for the Metropolitan, and thereby help its general finances.)

Under the "*Striker's Rôle*" headline, the *Tribune* gave its version of the events:–

N.Y.
Tribune
8.4.16

"It has taken only two days of Broadway, ample food and New York's bright lights to transform Wassily Nijinsky, the greatest living male dancer, from a man who was glad to escape from an Austrian concentration camp into a discontented artist demanding the homage his art should command and several times as big a salary as Diaghilev is willing to pay . . .

"On arriving here, the dancer repaired to his hotel, seated himself in his room, and awaited the arrival of the Ballet Russe officials with the contract that he had pictured would be brought to him by a reception committee . . . He waited all of Wednesday, without results. Likewise Thursday morning . . . but (Diaghilev) sent a man named Brown to represent him . . . Moreover, the contract included the figure that Nijinsky describes as ridiculous . . ."

Opera
Magazine
May 1916

A suggestion in *Opera Magazine* added a detail omitted from other accounts of these negotiations: "He (Nijinsky) was immediately approached with a spectacular offer by the vaudeville interests, and with this weapon in his hand he held up the directors of the ballet until he had been promised his own price. Meanwhile the operatic subscribers waited impatiently while more than a week of the season passed."

Sokolova
p.78

On the Sunday, April 9th, Sokolova wrote a long letter to her mother. On this matter, she said: ". . . Nijinsky is here and is making a lot of fuss – won't appear without tons of money, saying in the papers horrid things about the ballet. You know just how they always turn around on those who make their names for them."

N.Y.
Tribune
9.4.16

That same day, the *Tribune* gave another long column to the latest news. "Peace, ineffable and profound, broods once again over the Russian Ballet. (Nijinsky) had flatly declared that he would not dance were he not given a salary approximately that of Mr. Caruso, and in return had been threatened with deportation . . . It seemed to require more diplomacy to get Nijinsky to dance than it did to get him out of the hands of the Austrians and across the big water. Also more money . . . Relations between the United States and Austria-Hungary are delicate enough . . . suppose the Nijinsky incident should strain them still further, and to the breaking-point? The honor of our State Department may also be involved, for the dancer's release had been obtained only to enable him to keep an engagement at the Opera House . . . and there is still another angle on the situation. What if Austria should demand this deportation because her good nature had been abused by this statement which Mme. Nijinsky made to the newspapers on her arrival . . . Mme. Nijinsky is by birth a Hungarian, and the fact that she comes from a family of patriots and state officials adds to the ire aroused in some fiery Magyars by what they considered the almost treasonable calumnies contained in the newspaper interviews . . ."

Whilst making it clear that it was Romola herself who talked to the press on their arrival, telling a harrowing story of privation and distress during their internment, this vexatious matter gave great offence in certain quarters in America. The interviews had included such statements as that "... he was billeted in the home of a minor Austrian official and suffered many discomforts... he was not allowed to talk with anyone, and the house was so narrow that there was no room for him to twirl round on his feet to keep himself in practice for dancing... The landlord was so poor that he could not give them enough to eat, and Mrs. Nijinsky could not get milk for the little baby girl Kyra..."

N.Y.
Times
6.4.16

Similar stories, with slight variations, had appeared in many papers. The *Tribune* had continued its Sunday article:-

"The notion that Nijinsky and his wife suffered any hardships is not only scouted, it is hooted at as wild and arrant nonsense... Nijinsky ought to have had influence enough... to have made his imprisonment easy; and so it was, say Hungarians who have had news from Budapest. 'He was not even asked to report to the authorities, and that I can prove,' said one of them yesterday.

"The interviews have been clipped from the newspapers and sent to Budapest..."

By the following day, the *New York Times* was able to announce that "Waslav Nijinski, the Polish dancer, and the Ballet Russe have signed articles of peace. After the small army of lawyers representing both sides had met in conference and had come to an agreement, John Brown late last night issued a statement declaring officially that the differences had been adjusted..."

N.Y.
Times
10.4.16

There can be little doubt that "adjustment" had meant one thing – that Otto Kahn had paid up from his own pocket, though his biographer, Mary Jane Matz, (*The Many Lives of Otto Kahn*, published by Macmillan, N.Y., 1963,) could not find a record in the Kahn papers at Princeton. He obviously preferred to camouflage this generosity. She did, however, discover that it was through the intervention of the Comtesse Greffuhle that Nijinsky's release had been secured. "In a letter to Kahn she (the Comtesse Greffuhle) refers to the 'difficult negotiation' and to her having been 'fortunate enough to secure the help of an August Personage whose Gracious interest in this affair overcame every difficulty.' In a cable this anonymous benefactor is '*Le Grand Personnage*'. It could scarcely have been anyone but Franz Josef, since the combined efforts of ambassadors and cabinet ministers had proved ineffectual."

Nijinsky finally reached the stage of the Metropolitan at the Wednesday matinée. On one point everyone was united – he was a dancer such as none had ever seen before. He appeared in *Spectre* and *Petrouchka*.

As so often, the *rideau* had been delayed – but for an unusual reason. A letter had been handed to Flora Revalles as she arrived at the theatre. As she opened it, a highly perfumed white powder flew up in her face. "At once visions of poison and vitriol flashed across her mind and, letting out one piercing scream, she collapsed in a faint." It was, in fact, from a slightly deranged admirer, and perfectly harmless. "Another theory, however, was advanced by the friends of Nijinsky, who hinted darkly that the whole affair was engineered by the female dancer to distract attention from the *débutant*."

Musical
America
***

As for the long-awaited performance of Nijinsky, which might well, after such bally-hoo, have been expected to fall flat – the headlines told their story. "NIJINSKY DANCES INTO GLORY HERE" (*The World*), and "NIJINSKY PUTS NEW LIFE INTO BALLET RUSSE" (*N.Y. Times*), were echoed in all the papers. The *Times* most especially noticed little improvements in *Petrouchka*, which it applauded: "By little touches in stage management the story was made easier to follow. Among those that come to mind quickly were those concerned in the first dance of the three puppets, where the showman's manipulation of them was more clearly suggested, and in the entrance of the bear. The prominence the music gives the latter incident was formerly somewhat obscured by the crowding of the stage. Yesterday the bear was visible to the audience as soon as he appeared, and the sudden ponderous voice of the orchestra music was thus immediately explained."

N.Y.
Times
13.4.16

The same critic felt, however, that in *Spectre*, "a super-refinement of gesture and posture amounted to effeminacy. The costume of the dancer, fashioned about the shoulders exactly like a woman's *décolleté*, with shoulder-and-arm straps, even helped to emphasise this, as did certain technical details of the dancing, such as dancing on the toes, which is not ordinarily indulged in by male dancers."

N.Y. Tribune 13.4.16

"At the conclusion of the *Spectre* the audience rose to Mr. Nijinsky. It applauded and cheered for nearly ten minutes, and kept the dancer and his fair partner (Lopokova) in constant appearance before the curtain . . . He lacks the virility of Mikhail Mordkine, but as a dancer pure and simple, as an interpretive artist, as an original personality he stands alone."

There is no mention in any paper of the "shower of rosepetals" with which his appearance was said to have been greeted. It might have arisen from a stage effect which, apparently, had been added to the ballet at the Metropolitan. On the opening night, Lopokova was subjected to such a shower. The ending originally performed had been that the young girl "looked affectionately at her lover's gift, a red rose, and pressed it to her lips . . . She fell asleep . . . The rose slipped through her limp fingers and stained the floor." But the ending described at the

Brooklyn Eagle 4.4.16

Metropolitan was that "the girl really awakes to find the rose-petals showering at her feet, where her lover had been kneeling." Perhaps this was exaggerated as a tribute to Nijinsky, and continued as he took his calls.

Globe 13.4.16

Pitts Sanborn quoted a colleague as saying that "*Le Spectre de la Rose* would have been something for the tongues of angels, not of men, had Nijinsky had as partner Pavlova or Karsavina. The pretty and graceful lady that did share with him the brief ballet was so clearly of the earth that this reflection, ungallant as it may seem, was forced on the observer. The whole affair was simply too swift and heady for her, as it would be for any living dancer one can think of save the two just mentioned."

He remarked also that ". . . Later on Nijinsky was seen in the title rôle of *Petrouchka*, which he carried from its doll-like beginnings of the puppet to appalling tragic heights."

Musical America 22.4.16

Musical America listed briefly some of the comments already given here at greater length, and also these others:–

"Mr. Nijinsky's debut was a success, though he scarcely provided the sensational features that this public had been led to expect of him. (*N.Y. Times.*)

Mr. Nijinsky showed himself a stage artist of refinement, taste, direct method and conviction. (*The Sun.*)

See Nijinsky as Petrouchka and you will never forget the experience. The more you dwell on his portrayal the more it will haunt you. (*The Press.*)

That Mr. Nijinsky is effeminate at times is obvious. But quite apart from that he is a great artist, probably the greatest whom the present generation has seen here. (*The Herald.*)

He dances with a bodily rhythm no man has ever shown Americans, and every movement of head, limbs and torso, as well as his facial expressiveness, has a meaning that is well-nigh perfect. (*The World*)

While the effeminate quality, almost inseparable from the male ballet dancer, is quite visible in Nijinsky, he has at the same time a certain masculinity of strength and rhythm which counteracts the other impression. (*The Evening Post.*)

In addition to quoting the verdicts of many papers, *Musical America* had a good deal to say on the subject itself. One of Lydia Sokolova's observations finds corroboration there – for she says,

Sokolova p.77

"Nijinsky's dancing, however, had deteriorated: he had grown heavier and looked very sad." *Musical America's* own comments noted the change in his appearance:–

Massine, Lopokova, and Bolm
in the principal rôles.

Pianowski, V. Nemchinova and M.
Chabelska as the Rich Merchant
and the Gipsies.

PETROUCHKA

A Coachman.

Lubov Tchernicheva as the Chief
Nursemaid.

Pianowski as the Rich Merchant.

"Nijinsky is unquestionably an amazing dancer. He is said to have been nervous last week, partly because of the naturally disquieting effect of a début, partly because he had not danced in a long time. Later performances will, therefore, probably present him in a more favorable light. But he revealed in his first dance his great technical facility, the agility of a deer, an exceptionally subtle rhythmic sense, great vitality and suave bodily grace. His far-reaching leaps as he entered the window and circled about the room and his volant exit were calculated to stir even the phlegmatic. The rest of the dance impressed one somewhat less and at moments Mr. Nijinsky seemed a trifle heavy – a condition conceivably due to temporary causes. Yet, if possibly a shade more airy of motion than the warmly remembered Mikhail Mordkine, it may be questioned whether he will exert so lasting an effect, wanting as he does the bold virility of the latter. Except for his legs, which are as palpably muscular as those of an athlete, Nijinsky's appearance, bearing and manner disturb by a most unprepossessing effeminacy – an element as forcibly apparent in the airs and graces with which he acknowledges the favour of the audience as in his evolutions . . ."

Musical
America
22.4.16

N.Y.
Times
13.4.16

The company introduced another work strange to New York at the evening performance – *Thamar*. "Pictorially the piece is without question the most gorgeous thing Diaghilev's people have thus far exhibited; but the plot and music scarcely suffice to raise a ripple of interest. However, it barely plays over fifteen minutes, so there is no danger of boredom, particularly as the eye feasts on Bakst in the very fullness of his colorful splendor. In nothing else has he attained such ideal correspondence of scenic character and order of attire. The color scheme is deep, dark red, relieved with green and old gold, and the forms, proportions and perspectives stir the imagination like visions out of the Arabian Nights." After describing the setting, ("the sense of altitude being marvelously conveyed,") the writer seems to have missed out a bit on the point of Thamar's nymphomania, for he says that, after much dancing, "Then for no apparent reason the knight is stabbed to death by Thamar and his remains are unceremoniously consigned to the convenient waterfall in back. Thamar returns to her couch and agitates her scarf in invitation to her next would-be lover and dancing-partner." Revalles and Bolm were pronounced "excellent" by the *New York Times*.

Musical
America
22.4.16

"Nijinsky appeared again on Friday and Saturday nights. Laboring under no such stress of nervousness as the previous Wednesday, he created a correspondingly greater impression and the audience, which grew magically in size, fell into the very ecstasy of enthusiasm. For a time the depression and melancholy which have sat enthroned at the Metropolitan since the ballet took up its abode there were dispelled. On Friday night the star of the company appeared in *Sylphides* and *Carnaval*. All the best qualities of his dancing at his début – the amazing rhythm, the ethereal suppleness, the airy grace and floating motion – were noted once more, though not without that effeminacy of manner mentioned above. But the pictorial features of the *Sylphides* were noticeably improved through Nijinsky's skill as a stage manager."

Continuing by praising his Slave in *Scheherazade* – now Moorish, not negro – in which he "caught the huge audience by his wild abandon and impassioned action" – *Musical America* discussed his *Princesse Enchantée*. "As one spectator observed, he seemed not to touch the stage more than ten times during the whole ballet."

With such comments, not only on his wonderful personal performances, but also on his galvanising effect upon the company, subsequent events are understandable, especially when coupled with the extraordinary way in which Diaghilev had behaved in America.

***

Nijinsky's appearance in a ballet new to America, *Narcisse*, was postponed from the 20th to the 22nd. There had been so many changes in the advertised programmes – Bolm had hurt a foot, Lopokova had been ill – that when poor John Brown was asked for the programme list for the ensuing week, he replied, "Next week – I'd be satisfied if I knew what we'll do tonight." When Zverev had been called upon to deputise for Bolm in *Prince Igor*, "Treasurer Brown again made a speech from the stage. His oratorical power has led to offers this summer for the political campaign."

L. Sumarokova   Zalewska   Potopowicz

Antonova   Artska   Khokhlova   Bewicke

From this Press photograph of a group in *Les Sylphides*, taken in New York in 1916, Picasso made a drawing the following winter, when he was in Rome with Diaghilev.

Narcisse pleased some and displeased others – to the point of the giggles. "It is really the costume rather than the acting of Nijinsky that inspires irreverent giggles. With his golden curls, white pinafore, and immaculate nether garments, from which a pair of exceedingly healthy legs protrude, he looks like a living advertisement for the best food for infants," said Sigmund Spaeth in the *Mail*. "Giggles at the climactic moment were plentiful criticisms at the Metropolitan Opera House last night. Mr. Nijinsky, in short, succeeded in being offensively effeminate, but at most he succeeded in being nothing else."

N.Y. Mail 23.4.16

N.Y. Tribune 23.4.16

That such remarks ran through the notices can be seen from an unidentified cutting, which looks as if it had come from one of the Press journals.

***

"Ten thousand thanks and more yet to whoever wrote the *New York Sun's* account of Nijinsky's appearance in *Narcisse*. I suspect it was W.J. Henderson. The impersonation of Narcisse seemed to be congenial to Mr. Nijinsky, who robed it in feminine graces, leaving him with little wonder that women delighted him not. One could hardly help repeating Gilbert's line, 'What a most particularly pure young man this pure young man must be.'

"It was to laugh, as the French say. Such a lovely costume! A nice white shimmy and a nice white knee skirt, and such dear little white unmentionables underneath!"

N.Y.
Times
23.4.16
Evening
Post
24.4.16

These and other derisory notices were balanced by those, such as that in the *New York Times*, which said that "all things considered, *Narcisse* is one of the most individual and charming numbers in the repertoire of the organisation," and the *Evening Post*, which presented both points of view, spoke of ". . . the great Nijinsky, in the rôle of the beautiful Greek who is turned into a flower after falling in love with his own beauty. His whole conception of Narcissus is of a youth with a marked touch of the feminine – a note emphasised by his make-up and costume, the latter being far more womanly and modest than some of the women dancers, whose costumes might well be censored. Undoubtedly this is a wholly defensible interpretation of the character, quite in accordance with ancient Greek ideas. It must be added, however, that there was no lack of virility or force in Nijinsky's dancing, while his marvellous grace and agility are as striking in this as in his other rôles. His acting at the last, when he adores his own image, was marked by great ability and restraint. But his subsequent appearance in *Le Spectre de la Rose*, with Lydia Lopokova, pleased his audience much better . . ."

The derisory notices must not be taken too seriously, for obviously the New York public acknowledged that Nijinsky transcended all the excellent male dancers they had already seen, and they recognised his artistic merit as the productions, which had been kept rehearsed by Bolm and Grigoriev throughout the wearisome tour, leapt into freshness and additional charm as he revived Fokine's detail. New York, public and management, showed this clearly in the desire to have him dance for them again, and Diaghilev seems to fade a little into the background.

The Nijinskys led a busy life socially, and occupied much of their time giving "interviews" which the Press turned into long articles, some grave, some gay.

Musical
America

On the serious side, there was to be his book on notation. "My detention abroad on account of the war gave me the chance I needed to begin writing it. But the project had been germinating in my mind for years . . . I cannot yet make public the system I have devised. But I may conscientiously say that it is superlatively simple and lucid and analagous to musical notation." After discussing this at length, the dancer went on to describe another project.

"It is likewise my ambition to further in some respect the establishment of conservatories for the dance in all countries. At such institutions should be taught all those arts of which the dancer has need. The modern ballet is a highly-organised form dependent for its effect through the balance and co-ordination of musical, scenic, and choreographic elements. And the modern dancer must be electrically sensitive to all of these. He must be a thorough musician and an actor; he should, if possible, have a knowledge of painting and the principles of pictorial art. I am confident that the future will see such establishments in every country . . . Every nation should sooner or later develop such an art for itself and colored by its own distinctive traits of individuality. And it should be built upon the dances of the people quite as the symphonic literature of a country grows out of its folksong. In the short time I have been here I have noted characteristics in the American people that should inspire and vitalise a national type of ballet."

Even removing the gloss of the journalist who turned this into an article, there is an interesting point of difference between Nijinsky's thoughts, as expressed in it, and those of Diaghilev, who never wanted to found a school anywhere.

Another magazine carried an article entitled "HOW I CONCEIVE MY ROLES." A sentence in brackets states that "this is the first and only interview authorised in America on the subject of his art by Warslav Nijinsky, famous Russian dancer. It was obtained, translated and written by Isabel Goodwin. – Editor's Note."

"One must be as a changing chameleon in the varying rôles one enacts! Like the 'Coat of many colours,' one must be prepared with shades to enhance one's meaning – in the morning, perhaps, a boy, at noon a creature sans sex, at night a full-grown man, as the characters vary – they vary often enough! . . . The meaning should never be lost sight of. The music materially aids, and so do the scenery and costumes, but they are only a part. Of course, the dancing counts for much, but the idea must be seized. Its expression naturally follows.

"For instance, in *Narcisse*, a mythological poem, the rôle is idealised. The beautiful, slender youth, in love with his own graceful image, is in the dawn of manhood, the first sweet flush of life. What could be more natural than to enter into his spirit, to return to the days of one's youth? This is my rôle in *Narcisse*,. Beautiful dreams of boyhood! I have them here, all here!" and Nijinsky tapped his forehead. "There is no virility here, only a boyish pureness. That is the way in which *Narcisse* should be danced. Effeminate it is not! For, even in adolescence, a boy is not like a girl. True, he is not yet a man, any more than she is a woman, but there the resemblance ends. His thoughts and desires are different, therefore his movements are different!"

A long paragraph followed about a rôle he never danced, that of A'moun in *Cléopâtre*. (It is here mysteriously named "Anthony." Nijinsky always danced the Favourite Slave.) More faith can be placed in his thoughts about *Spectre*. "In the dream of a pure young girl, just awakening to womanhood, one idealizes her fancy. Half asleep by the fireside, after an evening of triumph, she weaves for herself a hero, half mortal, half immortal. With the notes of the last lovely waltz from the ball she has left still ringing in her ears, she dreams and nods, by the embers. And then the dancer appears. To the exquisite *pas de deux*, I, who enact the hero, must float upon her vision! *C'est 'le spectre de la rose.'* As such, one can scarcely be human. One has no sex, no form, in the girl's imagination. Just the 'Specter of the Rose!' A half shaped dream, awaiting the breath of love to transform it into being. What purity of conception, what real finesse of treatment! For I believe in the fine and prefer the delicate movement. The muscular type is well, in its own athletic way, but I prefer the more subtle, *à la Slav*, I suppose one will say . . ."

On the other side, there were the social activities and the more lurid tales of the swarms of females who wrote love letters or sought him out in other ways. The very day after his arrival on the *Espagne*, the *New York Journal* had published a long story, put together by Nixola Greeley-Smith, which started off, "In London four secretaries were kept busy ten hours a day answering his love letters. Ladies of the highest aristocracy had hysterics during his dances. For in the fervor of their applause London women tore bracelets from their arms and rings from their fingers, to fling them upon the stage." Four secretaries answering his love letters in London? This story, much longer and amplified in details, appeared in one of the Sunday's, too, and probably in many syndicated papers. "Nijinski, of course, feels that a man of his standing as a dancer cannot cheapen himself by making the acquaintance of women not worth knowing. His secretaries are persons of wide social knowledge. They read each letter and throw into the wastepaper basket those which are obviously worthless . . . To a very few he replies with in own fair hand . . . It is, in fact, a 'MAIL ORDER LOVE TRUST,' controlled by Nijinsky, the first of its kind ever heard of . . ."

N.Y.
Journal
7.4.16

***

The memoirs of the four secretaries have never been heard of. Nor have the letters written in his own fair hand as yet reached Sotheby's.

"He has won the reputation of being as good a letter-writer as dancer. Some of his admirers win the privilege of an invitation to his famous midnight suppers. Others are permitted the colder joy of attending a large afternoon reception . . ." The article went on to mention that there were alluring invitations to shady bungalows up the Thames and cosy cottages in St. John's Wood!

"What is it in Nijinski that exercises such an extraordinary fascination? His charms appear to lie entirely in his figure. His face can hardly be an attraction, unless there are some women who love ugliness. He is really a Kalmuck by descent . . . He has the high cheek bones, the broad flat nose and the thick lips of the Mongolian race."

In the autumn, the *Modern Dance Magazine* noticed that he walked about the streets of New York unrecognized. "He resembles a half-grown Cossack without a beard, and in New York he might pass for a shipping clerk or a plumber's apprentice.

"He looks like a rough person. He is about five feet eight, slim and angular; he has the small Slavic nose, small, black, almond-shaped eyes – a druggist expects to put Nijinsky Almond Cream on the market – prominent cheek-bones, a large mouth and narrow chin. His hands are big enough for a working man. His feet are plenty large enough to support considerably more bulk than the weighing-machine would register for him. There is nothing notable in his style, but he wears a fur-lined coat.

"Nijinski talks business mostly in Polish, gossips in Russian, rests up with small struggles in French, and thinks mostly in rubles. The little English he has picked up does not interfere with his dancing at all."

*The
Tragedy
of
Nijinsky
A. Bourman*

Mrs. William K. Vanderbilt, Sr., (the millionaire's second wife,) had arranged to open her famous house on Fifth Avenue, with tickets at $25 each, to raise money for Venice. "Fully $5,000 was cleared," said one report, the attraction of the evening being twelve tableaux in which society notables posed as replicas of twelve famous paintings. Baron de Meyer had arranged the tableaux, and amongst those taking part in them were Otto Kahn's débutante daughter Maud, Mercedes de Acosta, and many other famous names. The last tableau was of Carpaccio's "Gondolier," portrayed by Nijinsky. It must have been at this party that the episode recounted by Anatol Bourman took place. According to him, Nijinsky said that Mrs. Vanderbilt wanted him to dance with her, but that he had said he could not, as she was not a professional. "But Mrs. Vanderbilt was delightful. I consented. We did a gavotte together before her guests and she gave me ten thousand dollars!"

***

*N.Y.
Tribune**

The season closed with Nijinsky dancing at both the matinée and evening performances "thereby permitting some semblance of brilliancy." There had been one drama when he had run a nail into his foot, but fortunately without serious effects. There had been another over *Faune*, which had to be withdrawn again. There had been a row because, at that last matinée, Nijinsky was to dance only *Spectre de la Rose*, and "as his reported rate of pay was $1,000 a performance, and this lasts eight minutes, it will earn him over $125 a minute, or a fraction over $2 each second: even Caruso singing his best, never got that for every tick of the watch."

The papers summed up rather depressingly. It seemed unfair to dwell on the miseries of the four weeks at the Met., with constant changes of advertised programmes; but the subscribers had had hardly any Nijinsky performances, as these had been reserved as bait for open nights. There was no sympathy for Diaghilev – all blame was placed on him.

*Boston
Evening
Transcript
28.4.16*

"THE HAPPY END OF A HAPLESS TOUR," headlines in the *Transcript*, started off a long article. As to whether the company would return – "The Metropolitan Opera House will not again . . . surrender to it a full four weeks of its regular season . . . Outside New York, the financial losses have been heavy, since nowhere, except in Boston and a 'one-night-stand' or two, did the ballet attract paying audiences." But – more intimately – "There have been endless bickerings between the representatives of the Opera House and M. de Diaghilev, as exacting as he is unstable; the unbusinesslike methods of the Russian director, with his repeated failures to fulfil his agreements, to assemble the promised dancers, to produce the promised ballets, the intrigues and the jealousies, old and new, that keep the company in continuous and seething discord, have disgusted the little group of business men who financed the tour. For good and for all, they – and the Metropolitan Opera House – are done with the Russian ballets . . . If managers have learned wisdom, so also has the Russian director, who at bottom is as observant and intelligent as he is stubborn and capricious. If he has learned nothing else in the past four months, he must have discovered that the American stage and the American public are not European."

*N.Y.
Telegraph
1.5.16*

Diaghilev conducted the final *politesses* agreeably, especially towards the orchestra. "Saturday evening, at the close of the performance, the Russian impresario called all the men together and, in a little speech couched in French, told them how greatly he appreciated their efforts to make his work a success and thanked each man individually. He then presented them with a floral wreath eight feet high . . ."

*The
Graphic
20.7.29*

The upshot of the rows was that in July, Otto Kahn invited Nijinsky to be the Director of the company on a return visit, and the condition was made that Diaghilev – and his closest collaborators – were not to accompany it. However, during what was to turn out to be his last season, in London, in 1929, Diaghilev, in a long magazine interview, described how, in 1916, Kahn, dismayed at the lack of Karsavina and Nijinsky, had said that for success, an average of £800 a night was necessary in box-office takings. "At the end of twenty weeks Mr. Kahn and I sat down to make up our accounts. He was much more cheerful than before; in fact, joy radiated from his expressive countenance.

" 'This is not a success,' he said, 'it is more than that. It is a thousand dollars above the success mark.'

"The box-office returns for the twenty weeks showed an average of £1,000 a night. In New York alone we made £20,000 in two weeks. No ballet has ever before scored such a financial success in America."

The company set sail for its first visit to Spain, (with outstandingly happy results both in friendship and inspiration.) The Nijinskys and Flora Revalles stayed on in America for the summer, and Vaslav started to work on his next ballet. The possibilities on his horizon were discussed:–

"On the other hand, Mr. Nijinsky departs not into Spain, tarrying in New York and as mute about the future as Mr. Diaghilev himself. As some say, he will wait patiently and shrewdly on this side of the Atlantic in the hope to impose himself again upon the company at the same costly terms that he demanded and received for his occasional appearances at the Metropolitan. As others suggest, he believes that he can interest some American Maecenas in a great venture of his own, raising a rival ballet to Mr. de Diaghilev's and exploiting himself as dancer, producer and new theorist of plastic and rhythmic suggestion as in *Jeux* and *Le Sacre du Printemps* in his final year as the dominant member of M. de Diaghilev's troupe. As others conjecture more plausibly, what the managers call 'the personal success' of Mr. Nijinsky for a fortnight past, will tempt one or another of them to carry him up and down the United States, with a little company and a few simple ballets, like *Le Spectre de la Rose*, as 'the newest sensation of the dance.' Yet Mr. Nijinsky's one such venture by himself, in the London that had flocked to watch him in Mr. de Diaghilev's setting, was far from fortunate." Boston Evening Transcript 28.4.16

As for the so-called "scandals" of some ballets – the paper said:–

"Quietly, (*Scheherazade*) and all other pieces of the repertory have been restored to their European form. For the censors and all the other arbiters of our pleasures long since forgot the Russian Ballet, and, after the manner of their species, went on to other hysterics, harassing and advertisement."

SIR GEORGE LEWIS, BT.

1916 – 1917 *UNDER THE DIRECTION OF VASLAV NIJINSKY*

MANHATTAN OPERA HOUSE, N.Y.C.,

OCTOBER 16th - OCTOBER 28th, 1916

FIRST PERFORMANCES IN N. AMERICA

October 16th: *Sadko* (New Version)
                  (Rimsky-Korsakov, Bolm, Gontcharova)
                  This version, San Sebastian, August 1916

October 23rd: *Till Eulenspiegel* (Première)
                  (Richard Strauss, Nijinsky, Robert Edmond Jones.)

CONDUCTORS

Monteux, Goetzl

ON TOUR

OCTOBER 30th, 1916 - FEBRUARY 24th, 1917

1916

Providence, R.I.	Bridgeport, Conn.	Atlanta, Ga.	Wichita, Kan.
New Haven, Conn.	Atlantic City, N.J.	New Orleans, La.	Kansas City, Kan.
Brooklyn, N.Y.	Baltimore, Md.	Houston, Tex.	Des Moines, Iowa
Springfield, Mass.	Washington, D.C.	Austin, Tex.	Omaha, Nebr.
Boston, Mass.	Philadelphia, Pa.	Fort Worth, Tex.	Denver, Colo.
Worcester, Mass.	Richmond, Va.	Dallas, Tex.	Salt Lake City, Utah
Hartford, Conn.	Columbia (?)	Tulsa, Okla.	Los Angeles, Cal.

1917

San Francisco, Cal.	Oakland, Cal.	St. Louis, Mo.	Grand Rapids, Mich.
Buffalo, Mo.	Spokane, Wash.	Nashville, Tenn.	Chicago, Ill.
Portland, Ore.	St. Paul, Minn.	Cincinnati, Ohio	Cleveland, Ohio
Vancouver, B.C.	Minneapolis, Minn.	Dayton, Ohio	Pittsburgh, Pa.
Seattle, Wash.	Milwaukee, Wisc.	Detroit, Mich.	Syracuse, N.Y.
Tacoma, Wash.	Indianapolis, Ind.	Toledo, Ohio	Albany, N.Y.

CONDUCTORS

Monteux, Heidelberg

REPERTOIRE

L'Après-Midi d'un Faune	*Narcisse*	*Scheherazade*
Le Carnaval	*Le Pavillon d'Armide*	*Le Spectre de la Rose*
Cléopâtre	*Petrouchka*	*Les Sylphides*
Firebird	*La Princess Enchantée*	*Thamar*
Midnight Sun	*Polovtsian Dances*	

COMPANY

Artska, Bonietska, Chabelska II, Degelanda, Faithfull, Frohmann M., Kachouba, Kostrovskaya, Kourtner, Lopokova, Maicherska, Nemchinova I, Nemchinova II, Pazerska, Pflanz, Potapovitch, Revalles, Slavitska, Sokolova, Spessivtseva, Sumarokova I, Sumarokova II, Wassilevska, Zalevska, Zamoukhovska.

Bolm, Bromberg, Gavrilov, Herman, Jazvinsky, Kegler, Kostecki, Kostrovsky, Kovalsky, Kremnev, Maximoff, Nijinsky, Okhimovsky, Pianovski, Statkevitch, Tariat, Tehumakov, Voronzov, Zverev.

TILL EULENSPIEGEL

Though the other Directors of the Metropolitan may not have been equally enthusiastic, a second visit, including a long "coast to coast" tour, was planned, "no longer directly allied with the Metropolitan Opera activities but instead as a personal artistic enterprise of Chairman Otto Kahn," said W.B. Chase. Romola said that "even if a deficit were involved, he did not mind, as he wished to educate the American public." Kahn truly wished to show the ballets to far more towns than had seen the company during the first tour, and to make it up to those who had missed the promised great stars by presenting Nijinsky himself.

N.Y.
Evening
Sun
29.4.16

R. Nijinsky
p.265

It is curious that Kahn, who had known Diaghilev since 1909, should have failed to appreciate the different qualities of a director and a star. Once Nijinsky had taken the stage at the Metropolitan, and his wonderful performances and magnetism had affected the majority of the audience, if not all, Kahn was certain in his own mind that Nijinsky was indispensable – that Diaghilev was not – and that Nijinsky must be allowed to have his own way. Against all advice, the decision was announced in July by Laurence Steinhardt, Nijinsky's lawyer, that "This arrangement will give to Mr. Nijinsky absolute control . . . and will centralize authority over the ballet in the hands of one individual."

There was an up-to-date touch in the remark that "the Nijinsky family is having trouble in finding a summer villa that is for rent," but they seem to have had a happy holiday. They eventually went off to Bar Harbor, on the coast of Maine, having bought a car, and enjoying the journey through lovely country.

Before they left New York, there had been a most important introduction: Nijinsky and a young American designer, Robert Edmond Jones, met in a New York drawing-room.

Obviously unable to believe that Karsavina could not be tempted to leave Petrograd, as it was by now called, the trusty William Guard set off on the arduous journey to that far-off city, confident that he would manage to fetch her. An exponent of "positive thinking," he must have felt that if he believed it hard enough, he would pull it off, for the report in a New York newspaper said, firmly, that "When Waslaw Nijinsky takes his place at the head of the Ballet Russe . . . his dancing partner will be the famous Thamara Karsavina . . . Mr. Guard hopes it will be possible to bring her here so that the real Ballet Russe may at last be seen here . . . With the dancer at the head and Mme. Karsavina as his assistant, the Ballet Russe is expected to make the same impression here it did in the cities of Europe."

***

Guard was also charged with the task of trying to find Fokine and bring him too. "There were various explanations for his absence (last season.) He was said to be in the Army, he was said to be afraid of the American climate, which, after Russia, seemed dubious. At all events he will in all probability assume all that part of the direction of the ballet which does not fall to Nijinsky." Once again, there was the astounding, the naïve assumption that a ballet company could be run in such a way because it looked good on paper, without reference to personalities or to history. The breach between Diaghilev and Fokine in 1912, the promotion of Nijinsky as choreographer, and the bargains of 1914 between Diaghilev and Fokine, cannot have been understood for such a preposterous suggestion to have been made.

In the same article, Flora Revalles was reported to have aspirations beyond the ballet. "Now Mlle. Revalles thinks the time has come for her to lift her voice in song again, and she has selected the stage of the Metropolitan for that purpose. Until Mr. Gatti-Casazza returns from Europe she may indulge these ambitions so long as she wants to." The writer did not add that the summer "close season" was upon New York. Gatti-Casazza was indeed urgently seeking singers, and Max Rabinoff was about to sail for Europe in the hope of engaging a successor to Pavlova for the Boston Opera Company. (He was pursuing Ida Rubinstein.)

Some time during the latter part of the first tour, Lydia Lopokova, having broken off her engagement to the gigantic American sports-writer Heywood Broun, had quietly married Barocchi, Diaghilev's financial saviour of the previous year, but the marriage was only made public in August. He was now to manage the company.

The opera subscribers who had been so annoyed in April were to be safe twice over, and able to experiment with visits to the ballet free from any sense of disloyal defection from the opera – or of being done out of what they had paid for. Not only was the ballet season to take place in Oscar Hammerstein's newly acquired and re-decorated Manhattan Opera House – formerly called the Lexington – but also, it would all be over and gone before the Met.'s season opened on November 13th (with Bizet's *Les Pêcheurs de Perles*.)

| Robert Edmond Jones | "I am going to set down as carefully as possible my recollections of this great dancer and choreographer . . ." |

So begins Robert Edmond Jones' account of his work with Nijinsky on the ballet *Till Eulenspiegel*.

> "Not all of my story is pleasant. It is a story . . . of two differing cultures, unexpectedly and violently thrown into contact with one another. In the ballet *Till Eulenspiegel*, the artistic approach of Old Russia and the artistic approach of new America met and fused for the first time in theatre history . . . it fell to me to bear the full brunt of the initial impact of the Russian temperament, to take it, so to speak, head on. Certain details of this experience seem to me in retrospect not unlike the custard-pie scenes in an old Mack Sennett comedy.
>
> "I shall set down my story in a series of pictures, like the 'flashbacks of a cinema . . .'"

Robert Edmond Jones discussed the first meeting in New York:-

> "I see . . . a small, somewhat stocky young man, walking with delicate bird-like steps – precise, a dancer's walk. He is very nervous. His eyes are troubled. He looks eager, anxious, excessively intelligent. He seems tired, bored, excited, troubled. I observe that he has a disturbing habit of picking at the flesh on the side of his thumbs till they bleed. Through all my memories of this great artist runs the recurring image of those raw red thumbs." (Sokolova was haunted by them, too.) "He broods and dreams, goes far away into a reverie, returns again. At intervals his face lights up with a brief, dazzling smile. His manner is simple, ingratiating, so direct as to be almost humble. I like him at once . . .
>
> "I realise at once that I am in the presence of a genius . . . he and I are struggling to communicate our ideas to each other in extremely halting French. I sense, however, a quality in him which I can define here only as a continual preoccupation with standards of excellence so high that they are really not of this world . . .
>
> "Another picture – I am accepted – I am a happy boy this day – and I am sent to Bar Harbor to collaborate with the maestro on the creation of the new ballet . . . He practices hard and long during the day . . . In the evenings we work together until far into the night. And how we work!
>
> ". . . Nijinski's energy, his ardor, his daring, his blazing imagination, by turns fantastic, gorgeous, grotesque, are a source of continual astonishment and delight to me. The maestro is at

my elbow. I draw. He watches, criticises, exhorts. Together we map out the design for the front curtain – a huge sheet of parchment emblazoned with Til's device of the owl and the looking-glass, all blurred and worn, like a page torn from a long-forgotten manuscript of the Middle Ages. The market place of Braunschweg begins to take shape in front of the brooding black mass of the cathedral. We fill the square with flaunting color . . .

" . . . Another picture: we are in New York . . .

"The scale model for the setting is finished. The designs for the costumes are likewise finished and approved. Now comes the first difficulty, the first signs of friction . . .

"In this country, when scenery is to be painted, the various 'drops' and 'flats' of canvas are stretched on frames . . . which hang . . . In Russia, however, the method of scene painting is quite different. The drops and flats are simply laid flat on the floor and the painters, wearing carpet slippers, roam about over them carrying great pails of color and long-handled brushes, like brooms. Nijinsky, quite naturally, wishes the setting for *Til* to be executed in the Russian manner, *sur planché*. But alas! There is no one in New York who knows how to paint in this style . . . Nijinsky orders the work stopped at once.

"The next picture shows the maestro riding toward the scenic studio in a taxi with me . . . We go up steep narrow winding stairs to the scene loft . . . The paint frames hang from cables . . . Underneath the windows stand rough wooden cabinets . . . on which are arranged dozens upon dozens of white china *pots de chambre* filled to overflowing with colored pigments . . . Nijinsky gives a wild look about him . . . He mutters something unintelligible . . . We shout with hysterical laughter. The tension is broken. '*C'est vraiment très heureux,*' the maestro says with a giggle . . ."

On September 18th, forty of the dancers disembarked, William Guard and his wife returning from Europe with them. There would be just over three weeks in hand before the advertised first night, October 9th, when the excitement of the evening was intended to be the première of *Till*. (Nijinsky had demanded five weeks of rehearsals, but Diaghilev had engagements in Spain and could not release the company sooner.)

Grigoriev and his wife, Lubov Tchernicheva, Massine, and Idzikowsky, stayed in Europe with Diaghilev. He decided that they should spend the winter in Rome, where they concentrated on the creation of new ballets, notably *Les Femmes de Bonne Humeur*, Diaghilev's first ballet to Italian music, *Contes Russes* and *Parade* – Jean Cocteau and Picasso joining them for some weeks to work on this novel Cubist conception.

In New York, the rest of the company rehearsed the repertoire, and learned *Till*. (There was also supposed to be *Mephisto Waltz*, to music of Liszt, planned by Nijinsky during his internment, with Robert Edmond Jones named as designer in the Met.'s lists.)

Thanks to an account which came out in the *Chicago Herald*, it is possible to "attend" a rehearsal in the Grand Central Palace.

Chicago Herald 1.10.16

"It is a solemn occasion. One lone chorus man, obviously an American, is standing by a large pillar. Occasionally he tries a fantastic dance step. Soon another man arrives, cane in hand, obviously a Russian. He greets the other with a solemn handshake and passes into a dressing-room . . .

"By fifteen minutes after three o'clock – the rehearsal was called for three – girls and young men begin to file in . . . By half past three the dancers emerge . . . Everything becomes hushed . . .

"A young man, less than the average height and rather slight in appearance, has come into the room. His costume is similar to that of the other men – blue trousers which end half-way between his knees and his ankles; white stockings, light dancing shoes and a sport shirt. It is Nijinsky.

"There is little in his face – except that his eyes are very bright – or in his bearing to distinguish him from the others. Without speaking to anyone he goes to the piano, where an accompanist is seated, and picks out a few bars for her to play. As she plays it he buries himself in it, runs his hands through his hair, slowly, but otherwise remains perfectly still. She repeats the music. Unaware of everyone present, he goes through the movements of a dance. He has got what he wanted and he claps his hands for the chorus to assemble.

"... Thereafter, while the solemnity continues for a while, everything is in motion. Nijinsky is everywhere, seemingly, at once. He is all energy. As soon as the rehearsal begins no doubt is left in the mind of any watchers as to his identity.

"The ballet is *Til Eulenspiegel*... Richard Strauss's symphonic poem turned into a dance. Nijinsky has conceived the whole transformation. There is little discussion. His directions are few. Everything he illustrates by personally going through the movements which he has invented for the chorus. He throws off all the dignity which is generally associated with stars. Hand in hand with the dancers he demonstrates his steps. Each individual receives his personal attention. One little girl in blue, more graceful than the others, he singles out and with her he dances a *pas de deux* as an example. Then one by one, wherever it is necessary, he gives individual instruction. And how the girls do dance when he is their partner!

"There is no discussion of any kind. There is no explosive word, no back talk. Everything emanates from one mind. It is Nijinsky alone who talks, he alone who instructs. His method is not that of the spoken word, but of demonstration ... Since he is a master of pantomime why should he talk when silence and a demonstration are just as effective?

"Occasionally he stops and has the pianist play a few bars of music while he himself runs his fingers through his hair thoughtfully, searching for inspiration. On the second time he invariably has the right idea ...

"So for temperament of a troublesome sort, which is thought to be synonymous with Russian Dancer, there was only once evidence of it. Some one began to saw a board in an adjoining room. Nijinsky stopped operations, threw up his arms.

" ' *C'est impossible,*' "he called two or three times and two men ran–not walked–to have the disturbance ended. Then everything was tranquil and the dancers continued at the same mad rate.

"... At one point Nijinsky was being carried upon the shoulders of several men and it was necessary to pass under a large beam. He avoided hitting it only by ducking his head unceremoniously ... The third time he had one of the chorus men take his place while he directed things from below. So embarrassed was the substitute that he forgot to duck his head.

"After that the rehearsal progressed with less restraint. The gay mood of the dance caught the dancers. There were French and American girls in the chorus, and even the Russian proverbial sadness could not restrain their spirits ... The new things, the things which were difficult to learn, seemed to attract them the most. And whenever the director danced with one of the girls to show her a step or to demonstrate something to those who were watching she was so happy and could not help showing it."

The more experienced members of the company were worried by the slow progress.

Richard Strauss's music was already familiar to concert-goers, but a dramatic difficulty had arisen about this.

N.Y.
Times
27.9.16

"The smoke of battle rose over the reserve trenches occupied by the Russian Ballet at Grand Central Palace, where it is preparing for its final advance on the Manhattan Opera House, due to occur on October 9th ... It turned out to be a skirmish between Pierre Monteux, the new French conductor, who had landed here the day before, on one side and all the embattled Russians and Americans on the other ... As a French conductor, he absolutely refused to conduct works written by alien enemies." Not only was *Till* on his list, but also Schumann's *Carnaval* – constantly in the repertoire – and *Mephisto Waltz*. This program was overcome by the engagement of Dr. Anselm Goetzl, who was to conduct for *Till* – and did, in fact, take some performances of *Carnaval* also.

The construction of the scenery provided the next drama. Owing to a stupid miscalculation, it had been built too short for the stage; but there was plenty of time left for ingenuity to find a remedy.

A rehearsal had been called on stage for October 3rd. Robert Edmond Jones described the events of that afternoon:–

"I sense an obscurely hostile atmosphere in the theatre . . . I am escorted to Nijinsky's dressing-room . . .

"The maestro is waiting for me in a flame of rage. Torrents of Russian imprecations pour from his lips. The open door fills with frowning alien faces. He lashes out with an insensate blind hate . . .

"Presently Nijinsky pauses out of sheer exhaustion . . . The rehearsal begins, belated and listless . . . Suddenly there is a cry. The maestro stumbles and falls. He has sprained his ankle. He is carried moaning and cursing to his suite at the Biltmore Hotel. 'Your scenery is so bad,' a dancer says to me, 'that when our maestro saw it he fell down . . .

"I am a very discouraged boy indeed . . ."

Nijinsky's injury caused far more consternation than scenic problems. He was X-rayed, and to everyone's relief had not broken any bones in his foot, but doctors treating a bad sprain forbade dancing for "some weeks."

By Friday, October 6th, the advertisement in the Theatre column of the *Tribune* announced:

N.Y.
Tribune
6.10.16

The following day, Robert Edmond Jones was told by the theatre management what was wrong with his scenery.

> "First, it is too shallow, and second, it is not high enough to give the effect of crazy exaggeration the maestro had visualised. The first defect is remedied by the simple expedient of placing the setting farther back on the stage. The second problem is not so easily solved. After a consultation (I can never forget this half-hour!) it is agreed that a piece of canvas ten feet high is to be added at the base of each of the two flats which represent the houses of the town, and that this space is to be painted with an impression of foliage in broad shades of ultramarine . . ."

The postponement of the opening night was a horror for the Box Office; the "opposition" at the Met. must have run out of "I-told-you-so's." The company certainly did.

The slightest injury to a star dancer always starts rumours ending a career. Amongst the anxious enquirers was Anna Pavlova, who, according to Romola, sent the most lavish flowers of all. Despite her earlier disclaimer, she had succumbed to the blandishments of Charles Dillingham and had taken over the second half of "The Big Show" at the Hippodrome. She was giving a shortened version of Petipa's *Sleeping Beauty*, with a full company expensively costumed by Bakst, and, moreover, at the far lower Hippodrome prices. She had opened in this on August 31st, and even the "acts" at the Palace Theatre in London were pale beside the lion-taming and other "Big Show" attractions in the same bill. Lopokova's jilted ex-fiancé, Heywood Broun, though officially the Sports Editor and Baseball Correspondent, had worked overtime on the night-shift to report *this* first night for his paper:

N.Y.
Tribune
1.9.16

"For the first time, beauty has invaded the mammoth playhouse . . . it is interesting and at times enchanting, but it is not a thing of joy in its entity . . . It lacks coherence. Pavlova, however, delighted the audience. This great dancer had not all the fire which she once possessed, but her art flames as brightly as ever. It is a pleasure to watch Pavlova dance, since you can applaud her without being told when. Then, too, we have always admired her art because she is the only toe dancer in the world who has not fat legs." (Note the Editorial "We".)

Pavlova's choice of the "Vision" scene did not convey enough of the familiar and beloved story of Perrault to please children. After a few performances, it was decided to add more glitter to Bakst's costumes, which were sewn over with sequins. Not even this could ginger up enough response in a "Big Show" audience, and after a few weeks, Pavlova reverted to her normal divertissements. She was well aware of the lack of interest in her ballet by the time Nijinsky's projected appearance was to take place, and must have wondered how it would affect her.

Postponement of the opening date by a week was not only a matter of a breathing-space, an extra week in which Nijinsky could complete the as yet incomplete ballet. The programme for the opening night would have to be altered. It was decided that Bolm's new version of *Sadko*, which had been shown in Spain during the summer, was to be given on October 16th. The company had to rehearse this, and whilst Nijinsky was unable to continue his practical method of demonstration, he held costume calls in his hotel, and personally taught each dancer the make-up he required.

Robert Edmond Jones continued the story:–

"Nijinsky lies in bed, *maladif*, drenched in pathos . . . The little room is crowded with the entire ensemble, fully dressed in their costumes for *Til* . . . Now begins a scene compared to which the earlier scene in the dressing-room at the Opera House seems but the remote faded echo of an old refrain. This one is good. The maestro really puts his heart into it this time . . . Shoes are wrenched from the feet of the *coryphées*, necklaces are torn from their throats and shattered into fragments against the wall. Unbelievable insults are hurled at me . . . Here I am, with one of the world's greatest artists shrieking at me. There is no escape. There is no hope. This is the end.

"Then something happens inside me . . . As I look about me at the gaily costumed crowd I know with a definite inner conviction that this ballet will be a success . . .

"Another picture: A week later. The dress rehearsal . . . The curtain is up. On the stage stands my setting – my setting, mine! – remote, complete, fully lighted, all glowing with jewel-like blues and greens . . . It is exceedingly beautiful . . .

"The palaces of Braunschweg tower up out of burning blue dusk into a haze of violet and rose . . .

"The relief from the strain is too great . . . I faint dead away."

N.Y.
Times
17.10.16

N.Y.
Commercial
Bulletin
17.10.16

This must have been one of the rare occasions when scenery and costumes were all complete well before the first night, but the ballet itself was not. However, despite the postponement, the 16th "had all those pleasant earmarks of a 'smart' opening night." The programme consisted of *Les Sylphides*, *Le Spectre de la Rose*, *Scheherazade*, and *Sadko*. "Judging from the audience last night and the enthusiasm it displayed, interest in the Ballet Russe has not waned. Rather has it increased, for not even the Metropolitan last spring could have shown a better or more appreciative audience. It would seem that the ballet is sure of a large patronage during its run. The demonstration was the more remarkable because Waslaw Nijinsky, undoubtedly the greatest male dancer in the world, did not appear . . ."

Sadko (a Russian fairy tale) tells the story of a poor wandering singer from earthly regions, who wins Volkhowa, the daughter of the Czar of the Seas and holds the Czar and his entire submarine court in thrall by the power of his music.

MADEMOISELLE DORIS AND ADOLF BOLM IN "SADKO"

The premiere of which was given at San Sebastian in August and was one of the brilliant events of the season. The marvelous richness and picturesque quality of the accessories and the extraordinary grace and symbolism of the dances met with an enthusiastic reception. Rawlins Cottenet, a director of the Metropolitan Opera Company, was an interested spectator, and Madrid and Paris sent special representatives.

This page appeared in *Harper's Bazaar* in December, 1916. The article described the plot – mentioned the fact that the Princess's ladies-in-waiting were mermaids – and said that "Everything is carried out with simplicity, the realism always stopping at the right point, and over its face the veil of the mythical and symbolical drawn. . . . The Princess, Mademoiselle Doris, is gorgeously clothed in a scaly garment of gold, and Bolm, the Prince Charming who has met such a happy fate in his shipwreck, is clothed, without consideration for the weather, in gorgeous red and gold . . ."

N.Y.
Commercial
Bulletin
17.10.16
"Volkowa has endowed him with the power of catching fish with scales of gold, and with the wealth thus secured, he undertakes a voyage which is interrupted by her father. The King demands a victim to be thrown into the sea, and Sadko, realising that he must sacrifice himself, dives in. At the bottom of the ocean Sadko sings a hymn, glorifying the realm of clear waters. The King, charmed by the music, bestows on Sadko the hand of Volkowa, and the nuptials are celebrated by a grand Fête in which all manner of marine monsters take part.

"The set is most striking. Great fish of bright colors hang above the heads of the dancers, devilfish sway back and forth in the submarine foliage and the dancers are dressed as goldfish, sea herbs, sea horses and flowers, while some represent the currents. All the movements of the dancers bear out the idea of marine life as they sway about like swimming fish and waving plants. The colors were gorgeous, the costumes being mainly red and green, against a background of grey-green. Mlle. Doris and M. Jazwinsky were the principals with M. Bolm." Mlle. Doris – Doris Faithfull – was tall and lovely. She remained in America, and was lost to the ballet after these tours.

Musical
America
19.11.16
Musical America reported the first night: "The Ballet Russe appeared to be better, fuller, more persuasive, and more compelling than ever. The program opened with a familiar number, *Les Sylphides*, . . . but new steps and postures seemed to have been added . . . The spectacle aroused no end of enthusiasm . . .

"A wonderful stage picture is *Sadko* . . . A novel and charming effect is the final bit, when a large shell, in which are Sadko and his lady love, rises to the surface of the waters . . ."

W.B. Chase, of the *Evening Sun*, had reported Bolm's sessions spent in the Prince of Monaco's maritime museum, observing details of fishy movement. Someone wrote to *Musical America*: "Now, I happen to have visited this particular museum, which I did not find anything extraordinary . . . It is not as good . . . as some we have had in this country, and it is not in it for a minute with the wonderful museum in Naples. However, if Bolm went down into a few tanks to find inspiration for the 'whirling dances,' it was probably cheaper than going to the gaming tables, not far off at Monte Carlo, where he would have met an entirely different crowd." The

Evening
Post
17.10.16
Post described it as "picturesquely presented, and well executed, winning much applause from a large audience which filled every seat in the house, as well as the 'standing-room.' " (The same writer had heartily condemned the opening number of the evening, . . . "which proved to be as dull, stupid and uncalled-for as it did in the bigger house. Why *Les Sylphides* should be so often inflicted on patient patrons of the Ballet Russe is inexplicable, for the old-fashioned commonplace dancing it exhibits has not a moment of real artistic interest . . ."

N.Y.
Evening
Sun
16.10.16
If the opening night was a success, it was a success born out of strain. W.B. Chase had written before it: "If Nijinsky is present tonight he will most likely be behind the scenes. The premier male dancer limped into the theater for the first time since the accident to his foot and halted a rehearsal early today.

" 'Who is the stage manager here?' he demanded. 'Who orders the curtain up without waiting for us?'

"The Russian Ballet was dumb before its chief. The curtain went down, and stayed down until Nijinsky himself gave the word to go on. An unofficial surgeon to the troupe diagnosed the latest trouble among the members as 'chip on the shoulder' in its most virulent form."

It still remained to get *Till* ready, and with such outbursts and behaviour, everyone must have been on edge.

If the management was worried, the members of the company must have been even more so. The costumes were wonderful:–

Sokolova
p.89
> "They alone might have made a success of the ballet, if Diaghilev had been there to exercise control," wrote Sokolova. "The minimum of progress, however, was made with rehearsals . . . Nijinsky would appear and disappear. As ever, he had great difficulty in explaining what he wanted, and sometimes it was clear that he did not know himself. As . . . the first performance drew near, we all became extremely nervous at the ballet's sketchy state; no proddings from Kola (Kremnev) could make Nijinsky work faster or show signs of realising the seriousness of the situation."

It must have been during this period that, according to Grigoriev, Barocchi started sending a

Nijinsky's ankle must have healed by this night, for not only did he perform the incredible agilities of *Till:* leaving *Le Spectre de la Rose* to be danced by Gavrilov – with Lopokova – Nijinsky also ("contrary to programme," said one notice,) gave his dazzling performance as the Golden Slave in *Scheherazade.*

MANHATTAN OPERA HOUSE

Sole Management......MORRIS GEST

DIAGHILEFF'S

BALLET RUSSE

Management......................... ...Metropolitan Musical Bureau

Week Commencing Monday, October 23rd

REPERTOIRE

Monday Night, October 23rd, at 8:30—

LES PAPILLONS

Ballet in One Act by M. MICHEL FOKINE
Music by ROBERT SCHUMAN
Orchestrated by M. N. TCHEREPNINE
Scenes and Dances Composed by M. MICHEL FOKINE
Rearranged by M. ADOLF BOLM
Scenery and Costumes Designed by M. DOUBOUJINSKY
Scenery Executed by M. M. G. GOLOV

PERSONNEL

A YOUNG GIRL...........................MLLE. LYDIA LOPOKOVA
PIERROT.....................................M. ADOLF BOLM
A YOUNG GIRL...........................MLLE. LYDIA SOKOLOVA

MLLES. PFLANZ, BONIECKA, WASILEWSKA, ZALEWSKA, Galanta,
Nemtchinova, Soumarokova, Slawicka, Mieczkowska, Dimitrieva,
Chabelska, Artska.

EULENSPIEGEL (World's Première)

Ballet comi-dramatic by WASLAW NIJINSKY
Music by RICHARD STRAUSS
Choreography by M. NIJINSKY
Scenery and costumes designed by ROBERT E. JONES
Scenery executed by DODGE AND CASTLE
Costumes executed by WILLIAM ADLER

PERSONNEL

TILL...M. NIJINSKY
FIRST CHATELAINE....................MLLE. REVALLES
SECOND CHATELAINE.................MLLE. DORIS
THIRD CHATELAINE....................MLLE. PFLANZ
A CLOTH MERCHANT...................M. KREMNEFF
A SHOE MERCHANT.....................M. KEGLER
A CONFECTIONER.......................M. PIANOWSKI
A BAKER.....................................M. KOSTROVSKY
AN APPLE WOMAN......................MLLE. SOKOLOVA
FIRST STREET URCHIN.................M. SVEREFF
SECOND STREET URCHIN..............M. KOSTECKI
THIRD STREET URCHIN.................M. KAWECKY
FOURTH STREET URCHIN..............M. OCHIMOWSKI
FIFTH STREET URCHIN.................M. WORONTZOFF
ONE OF THE PEOPLE....................M. GAVRILOW
A RICH CITIZEN..........................M. STATKIEWICZ
HIS WIFE....................................MLLE. BONIECKA
A POOR CITIZEN.........................MLLE. ZAMOUHOVSKA
FIRST POLICEMAN.......................M. TARIAT
SECOND POLICEMAN....................M. MAXIMOFF

Professors, Judges, Priests, Hangmen, Soldiers, etc.
Time: Middle Ages.

Entr'acte Symphonique

CAPRICIO ESPAGNOL...................... RIMSKY-KORSAKOW

I—Alborada. II—Variazioni. III—Alborada. IV—Scena e
canto gitano. V—Fandango Asturiano.

Grigoriev
p.124

spate of telegrams to Diaghilev, in Rome, asking advice – and then a telegram arrived from Nijinsky, asking Grigoriev to travel to New York immediately. With Diaghilev's agreement, he refused.

Sokolova
p.90

"At the dress rehearsal we got through the first act pretty well. Nijinsky danced gaily and without concern for the future. At the end of it, though, we were terrified, because there was really no more ballet – just a few scrappy bits, under-rehearsed. At this point arguments broke out. Nijinsky and Romola got into a car, went back to their hotel and refused to see anyone. The dress rehearsal stopped in the middle.

"Otto Kahn and the management of the Metropolitan were naturally aghast. Poor Kremnev, who was almost in tears, could say, 'I tried to warn you, but you wouldn't believe me.' A conference was held, and the company was called together. It was explained to us that the theatre was sold out and that a postponement was out of the question . . . So the rest of the afternoon flew by as we did our best to piece together what we could and fill in the gaps. It was agreed to tell Nijinsky that everything was wonderful, that his ballet was fine and that he had nothing to worry about, so long as he knew what he was going to do himself in the second act."

(This must have meant "part," as there is only one act. The epilogue, which this would seem to be, does, in fact, occupy only two pages of the score.) Poor Sokolova, whose rôle as the Apple Woman was most important, suffered so greatly in all this worrying time that she wrote, when mentioning that Romola said the ballet was danced throughout the tour, "If this was so, I have no recollection of it." In fact, what the dancers put together must have worked, despite a slight hitch in the stage machinery on that first night. The ballet was, indeed, performed later in all the bigger centres, and was a tremendous success everywhere.

Some conductors have taken Strauss's music at such a pace that it has been "got through" in fifteen minutes. Nijinsky had it played at a tempo which made it last for about eighteen minutes

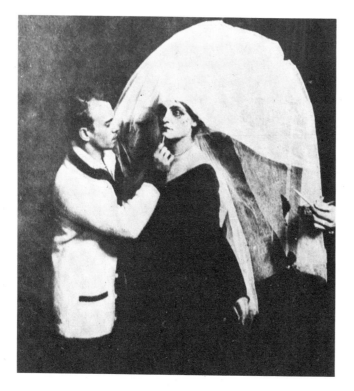

Nijinsky making up Boniecka
as the wife of a Rich Citizen.

Lydia Sokolova
as the Apple Woman.

Robert Edmond Jones' setting photographed on the stage, where the colours were "all glowing with jewel-like blues and greens . . ." The cobblestones of the market-place of Braunschweg can be clearly seen in the stagecloth.

– one paper gave it twenty-one. Into that time was packed a series of incidents which would have made a full-length ballet in other hands.

"Upon the rise of the inner curtain which displays Till's coat of arms, of owl and mirror, the public square of a mediaeval Brunswick is revealed, with the houses tumbling about the streets and the great cathedral looming black and terrible in the background. The town is out, late on an autumn afternoon, bent on business and pleasure. The apple-woman is there, and a vendor of bread who carries his wares upon his back in a basket as tall as himself. Merchants . . . stroll about . . . There are some noble ladies, with hats six feet high and trains that reach half-way across the public square. In and out of the crowd snoop two diminutive, but fearsome, policemen, seeking some wrongdoer in the body politic. And round about are the rabble, the social scum, the comrade brothers and sisters of Till . . . They dare not touch or desecrate property or respectability, in the persons of apple-woman or châtelaine. This is left for Till, the hero-leveller, who capers clad in light green, close-fitting clothes, which are so good that he must have stolen them." Till knocks over the apples and bread, and his friends eat gratefully. Disguised as a nobleman, he makes love – then laughs as he reveals his beggar's weeds. He lectures the learned professors . . . As the rabble raise him on their shoulders in triumph, soldiers and judges enter, capture Till, try him, and as he refuses to recant, they hang him. As Till is swung high on the gallows, there is a scuffle – and he appears again, immortal." Boston Transcript 24.10.16

The *Transcript* continued: "It would be a little presumptuous to praise, not to speak of analyzing, Nijinsky's miming after a single view of it. It was a flash of vivid characterization, too absorbing to permit of critical attention. However, it was so surprising that one had hardly recovered before the brief story was over. This fluid and human characterization, softened by the dancer's art and heightened by the actor's genius, is not a part of the Nijinsky we have known . . . Analysis might show that this is the same art which Nijinsky has shown of old, cleverly moulded to a new end. But it seems more likely that a new part of his genius has found expression." This was signed H.K.M.

193

The Three Chatelaines—Doris, Revalles and Pflanz—in the midst of Robert Jones' mythical market-place

One of the bakers in "Till Eulenspiegel"

Nijinski's Masterpiece, "Till Eulenspiegel"

WE are chiefly indebted to the European War for Mr. Nijinski's wonderful production of his ballet "Till Eulenspiegel." At the outbreak of hostilities he was in Buda Pesth. Being a Russian subject he was promptly interned, and kept a prisoner there for over a year. Although he had, before the outbreak of the war, conceived the idea of composing a ballet for Ricard Strauss' music, it was not until his internment in Buda Pesth that he had sufficient time to devote to the study of his subject. During his captivity in Hungary he was able to make a most careful study of documents pertaining to the old legend, and he had also several consultations on the subject with Ricard Strauss, the German composer. From the engravings of Albrecht Dürer, and others of that period, he conceived the scheme for the marvelous scenery and costumes which, lately, Mr. Robert Jones so successfully executed. And it was at Bar Harbor, last summer, that Mr. Nijinski completed the choreography of the ballet. So that, when he arrived in New York in October, to meet the artists of the troupe, he was able immediately to put the ballet into rehearsal. Thus it took him over two years of almost constant application before the work was ready for production. "Till Eulenspiegel" is, without question, an indubitable advance over anything that the Russian ballet has yet done in America in the development of their art.

An original design by Robert Edmond Jones for the costume of one of the three Chatelaines.

facing page: The fantastic steeple hennins tower taller than their wearers in this page from *Vanity Fair,* December, 1916. The photograph shows the wonderful cut of the costumes, (made by William Adler.) Their fate seems to be a mystery, as no trace of them can be found in the various storerooms of the Metropolitan Opera. It must be presumed that they have been destroyed in one of the fires to which such stores are subject.

Despite the fears in the afternoon, it would seem as if almost everything "came right on the night." The ballet was a tremendous success. All the critics thought that Nijinsky was superb, and the scenery and costumes breath-taking. "How Nijinsky shot a scarf of flaming hue through the puppet crowd of Brunswick burghers, literally wound a stageful of people around his little finger, seemed a matter from the realm of legerdemain," said W.B. Chase, (but it was not a scarf, but a shop-keeper's bale of cloth, flicked with the trick of a fairground performer so that it encircled the crowd and returned to the sender.) "His spirits never flagged – nothing did in fact – except Flora Revalles' wonderful train of seventy yards of silk brocade, or the attendant queens' top hats, taller than themselves, flaunting streamers of twenty-nine yards more."

N.Y.
Evening
Sun
24.10.16

Robert Edmond Jones somehow managed to watch the performance, through a haze of nervous terror.

> "Now the final picture . . . I hear a crash of applause, fierce and frightening. The little figure in green begins its leapings and laughings. There is the scene of wild love-making, the confutation of the scholars, the strange solo dance, swift as the flash of a rapier, the hanging of the corpse on the gibbet – and last of all, the apparition of the ghost shooting upward through a foam of tiny lanterns, like a moth veering above a sea of fireflies . . . Then the triumph, and the cheering . . . Nijinsky and I bow together, hand in hand. He is all smiles . . . he murmurs, "*C'est vraiment très heureux, très heureux . . .*'
>
> "I never see him again . . ."

Fifteen curtain calls – Nijinsky insisting on sharing them until he was forced to take one alone . . . The old German story of the prankster, to whom attached all the earthiness of the proletariat, "smelling of garlic," had completely delighted New York's sophisticated first night audience. Robert Edmond Jones had multiplied the fun and grotesquerie with his sensational costumes, magnifying every feature in brilliant caricature. From all the newspaper accounts, it seems to have been a wonderful work which one sighs in desire to have seen. The *Tribune*, true, had eyes more hawk-like than those of the rest of the press: "The climax was reached, however, in the end, where, like Strauss, Nijinsky brings Till to the gallows . . . The epilogue, however, which by a recurrence of the opening music declares Till redivivus in the hearts of his German admirers, seemed a bit beyond the capacity of the choreographer." (Did the writer guess – or was he in the know?)

N.Y.
Tribune
24.10.16

The *New York Times* said that "without attempting to go into details of the scenic, costume and lighting effects of the ballet, it is enough to say that they form one of the most impressive exhibitions to be seen on our stage today. As for the chorus movements, M. Nijinsky has furnished abundant proof of his genius as a stage director . . . the members of the company have been drilled in strange posturings and queer little movements that constantly pique the interest and remind you that you are in the midst of a mediaeval fantasy."

N.Y.
Times
24.10.16

"After the performance Mr. Nijinsky said: 'Robert Jones is a greater color artist than Bakst," reported one unidentified paper.

***
24.10.16

With such brilliance as Nijinsky obviously achieved – with the aid of the company, for it would seem that he had worked out Till's rôle completely in his internment, but had never mentally particularized theirs – this ought to have become an outstanding item in the repertoire.

In April, Diaghilev had apparently taken no interest when Vaslav had outlined his projected ballet. Yet – had he seen it for himself – would he not have thought it worthy of his ideals? Everyone in the company who is in print on the matter has applauded its conception and the work of Robert Edmond Jones: as the music of Richard Strauss already existed, they just accepted it without nationalistic prejudice. It was the horror of their worry as the choreography developed so slowly which made them dislike the ballet and wish to put it out of their thoughts.

After *Till* – which was given a second performance later in the week – even *L'Après-Midi d'un Faune*, with Nijinsky himself as the Faun, was an anti-climax. (So, too, was the arrival of Spessitseva and Margaret Frohman, who joined the company on the 24th.) The *New York Post* thought that "unless this work has been greatly changed as to action, it is difficult to understand

N.Y.
Post
25.10.16

why it should have been hissed in Paris, unless it was because the Parisians were bored by its dullness ... His impersonation has not been censored, as was that of his predecessor last winter, and he repeats the finale which was objected to last year; but the censoring seems now but a tempest in a teapot." The *World,* which claimed to have been previously amongst those shocked censor-mongers, now reported the performance as "refined, artistic, and masterful," and one at which no one could take offence. The *Transcript* printed a report taken from the *New York Sun,* in which it said that "there was nothing in his acting to bring the blush of shame to the cheek of modesty. But it was full of significance and rich in that special art of Mr. Nijinsky, which is subtle in its inflections and intangible in its grace." Earlier in the month, announcing that Nijinsky would dance his famous rôle, the *Telegraph* had given an interview with him about it. "He insists that the proper conception of the Faun is a spiritual one, and neither material nor physical, He gets his inspiration from the Debussy music, he says, 'and the dominating feature in the portrayal must be mental and spiritual.'"

N.Y.
World
25.10.16

Boston
Transcript
27.10.16

N.Y.
Telegraph
2.10.16

Nijinsky's one week of appearances also included *Petrouchka,* but his foot was not yet strong enough to risk *Le Spectre de la Rose.* It is odd that Nijinsky never seems to have had any possessive attitude to this,possibly his most famous and individual rôle of all.It was regularly danced by Gavrilov; Nijinsky seems to have felt quite indifferent to parts created for him by Fokine, whereas his attitude to *Faune* was not at all impersonal.

On the same day as the notices of *Till* were in every paper, the *New York Times* carried a statement from E.L. Bernays, "who is associated with the American management of the Ballet Russe," to the effect that Waslaw Nijinsky had been ordered by the Russian War Office to return to Russia and report at once for military service, "under penalty of being considered a deserter." Certainly, the last day of preparation for the première of *Till* could not have been more inopportune for such a demand to have been delivered. His biographers have put the event later, after the tour was well on its way, when it is obvious that the matter was raised again, having been parried in October. He had to leave the tour and go to Washington for a couple of days, and others danced his parts. At this juncture, however, the statement continues that "the dancer was released upon his promise that he would not bear arms during the war against the Central Powers. The ballet management holds that for Nijinsky to return to Russia and enter military service in view of his promise would bring up a point of international law that might involve this Government, and such representations will be made to the Russian Government in the hope that it will nullify or at least modify the order of its War Department."

N.Y.
Times
24.10.16

Not until the Thursday, when *Till* was repeated, was a paper able to report that "The Ballet Russe sold out the theatre last night."

N.Y.
Tribune
27.10.16

The company was full of foreboding as it left New York on its four-month tour.

1916 – 1917

SERGE DE DIAGHILEFF'S
BALLET RUSSE
ARTISTIC DIRECTION
WASLAV NIJINSKY
MANAGEMENT
METROPOLITAN MUSICAL BUREAU

City..............................

Date............ Nights...... Mats........

Theatre.............................

Manager.............................

Attraction Preceding.................

Attraction Following.................

Orchestra Call.......................

STAGE DIMENSIONS

Wall to Wall........	Curt. to B. Wall......
Bet. Girders..........	To Girders.......
Pros. Opening........	To Fly Floor..........
Current..............	Sets Lines............

MOVEMENT OF COMPANY

Next Stand........................

Co. Leave................. R. R.

Cars Leave.......................

Crew Leaves......................

Co. Arrive Next Stand.............

Cars Arrive Next Stand............

HOTELS

	SINGLE	DOUBLE	PLAN
....			
....			
....			
....			
....			
....			
....			
....			
....			
....			
....			

STAGE LIST
House management is to supply the following
extra Stage hands :

....

....

Theatre Orchestra is composed of the
following instruments :

....

....

....

House management is to supply the following
Extra Musicians :

....

....

....

BAGGAGE CONTRACT

Address Transfer Co............

Telephone,.............

CITY.................................

The......................., Transfer Company hereby agrees to haul the scenery, properties and baggage of the.................Company from depot to the.................and hotels and boarding houses, and to return the same to the depot of departure when required by the manager of said Company at any hour of the day or night, (agent's fare and baggage free) at the following rates.

Scenery, per load, round trip, $.

Trunks............cents each, round trip;

And the said Transfer Company further agrees to deliver the said property in as good condition as when received to provide ample men and wagons to do the work expeditiously and satisfactorily; to give the necessary assistance in unloading and in loading the said Company's car and to furnish tarpaulins to protect scenery and baggage in case of snow or rain, or to claim no compensation for such services as enumerated above.

We hereby agree to furnish.........carriages to be at the depot on the arrival of.........

and to return to the depot when wanted for the sum of $.........

....

HAUL AT..............

MEN CALLED AT THEATRE AT..........

....

DATE,............................191....

(Signed).........................

For Transfer Company

PRICES		
	NIGHT	MATINEE
......Orchestra ......at	......	......at .....
......Orchestra Circle.at	......	......at .....
......Orchestra Circle.at	......	......at .....
......Balcony........at	......	......at .....
......Balcony........at	......	......at .....
......Balcony, rear...at	......	......at .....
......Gallery........at	......	......at .....
......Gallery........at	......	......at .....
......Boxes........at	......	......at .....
......Boxes........at	......	......at .....
......Loges........at	......	......at .....
......Gen'l Admission.at	......	......at .....

FREE LIST TO BE AS FOLLOWS

Press...., Bill Boards...., Lithos...., Total....

I agree to the above scale of prices and free list.
I have received all necessary Line, Light, Scene and Property Plots, Newspaper Notices, Advs. and Programme Copy,.........Frames and.........Cuts.
Understand Company will arrive from

...........................at................

and will have Orchestra called at...............and will share on extra expenses as scheduled opposite.

....

Manager

BILLS TO PAY

....	....
....	....
....	....
....	....
....	....

NEWSPAPERS

....	.... Critic	
....	....	"
....	....	"
....	....	"
....	....	"
....	....	"
....	....	"
....	....	"
....	....	"
....	....	"
....	....	"
....	....	"
....	....	"

EXTRAS

Extra Advt._____

OPPOSITION

_____

_____

_____

_____

_____

_____

REMARKS

_____

_____

_____

_____

_____

THE NIJINSKY TOUR

A comprehensive form, for every detail of the arrangements, from the stage dimensions to the prices and "Free List," had been mailed to each city on the itinerary – about fifty, coast to coast. Each had specified its own choice of ballets in advance, as well as putting up financial guarantees as before.

The dramas of the presentations were to prove far less poignant than the human drama behind the scenes, as Nijinsky became progressively more and more "difficult." This belongs properly to the biographies, and not to this "front of the house" view. Understanding of these affairs is necessary, none the less, if the sometimes puzzled remarks of the reporters are to fall into place. Suffice it to say that Nijinsky was quite incapable of running the complicated business of such a tour. He remained convinced that he should have overall control, and that such matters as changing the advertised programme could be at his whim, regardless of the fact that each town had made its own choice of the ballets it wanted to see.

Most trying of all was the fact that Nijinsky became a prey to the influence of two members of the company, Kostrovsky and Zverev, who preached Tolstoyan philosophy to him, and persuaded him to become a vegetarian, and to try out democratic theories. The vegetarian diet did not suit him, and the democratic theories, which tempted him to allocate parts so as to give other dancers "a chance," disappointed audiences who were expecting to see the great Nijinsky himself.

No matter what names appeared on the programmes, Nijinsky frequently would not dance – refused at the last moment to dance – and then Gavrilov or one of the others would put on his costume and make-up, and just take his place without any announcement. A set of programmes with pencilled emendations was kept by Grigoriev in the scrapbooks which are now in Stockholm, but it is doubtful whether even these give an accurate account of Nijinsky's own appearances. Gavrilov's widow produced this information, and many a time the newspapers mention the fact that the show began at least half-an-hour late, without being able to offer any hint as to the reason.

It is no wonder that the company became more and more unhappy as the tour progressed. It would be profitless to attempt to cover every city – to repeat endlessly the reactions, mainly very similar, to the various items in the repertoire. *Till* was performed in the bigger centres – Boston (2), Philadelphia (2), Los Angeles (2), San Francisco (2), Oakland, Cal., St. Paul (2), Chicago, Indianapolis, St. Louis, Cincinnati (where Monteux, according to the programme, consented to conduct it,) Cleveland, and Pittsburgh (2). That makes eighteen plus the two in New York, which agrees with Grigoriev's calculation. It was a tremendous success everywhere, and, of course, Nijinsky and no one else danced Till. (Memory is a curious thing. When asked how on earth they transported those enormous steeple head-dresses, without a moment's hesitation

199

Lydia Sokolova replied, "Oh, they had special boxes made to take them – huge long boxes, like coffins!")

It may be said as a generalisation that the charming ballets charmed, but the erstwhile "shocking" ballets no longer shocked. As Romola said, press handouts were prepared during each journey, and the unfortunate local journalists struggled to make sense of the advance lists they had received and things which simply did not match them, programmes being constantly changed without warning. Local typographers struggled with fatigue as they spelt out the difficult names. The stage staff struggled with the endless succession of different theatres. The audiences, though variable, were often small. A few comments and stories may be more intriguing than a long recital.

R. Nijinsky p.278

Providence Journal 31.10.16

In Providence, Rhode Island, to the disappointment of the audience, Nijinsky, still nursing his ankle, danced only *Faune*. However, the programme went without a hitch, and gave great pleasure.

Springfield Union 4.11.16

In Springfield, Mass., the reporter re-told the story of Ralph Waldo Emerson and Margaret Fuller, who, when watching Fanny Elssler, tried to evoke in words the thoughts inspired by perfect dancing. They sat silent for a long time. "Margaret Fuller, so full of the beauty of the dance, was at last moved to words. 'Ralph, this is poetry.' 'Margaret, this is religion.'"

For Boston, it was a return visit. The curtain rose late, the intervals were long. *Till* and *Thamar* and the other "story" ballets were dubbed "mimodramas," and considered to be something quite separate from dancing or "ballet." *Till* was tremendously appreciated. The attention to detail in every production seen on the previous visit was noticed to be now much finer. The sheer beauty of Spessitseva's pure classical dancing was duly admired. When, for the first time, he danced Petrouchka, Gavrilov was so successful that he was voted the "man of the evening."

Boston Evening Transcript 8.11.16

Musical America

It would appear that Boston had completely surrendered to the mania for the ballet. "In the shops meek-faced housewives in sober and godly raiment are trying on scarves *à la* Bakst, *Chapeaux* Revalles, evening gowns *couleur de faune* ... By Tyl, we were bewildered. Similarly puzzled were we by the flat, archaic beauty of *L'Après-Midi d'un Faune*. Though we had eyes, we saw not that one of the greatest living creative artists had opened for us the door to an art greater than any of which we had ever dreamed – an art primeval, eternal, unbearably beautiful ... At present Boston likes Bolm better than it likes Nijinsky. His *Sadko*, exquisitely conceived and exquisitely mimed, was one of the notable ballets of the week."

N.Y. Sun 2.11.16

As the company had left New York, a report had been taken up by the *Transcript*. "To provide for the eccentricities of sixty-five temperamental Russian dancers is not a job to be coveted. No matter what it is, the salary is not half enough ..."

Other managements had their troubles, too. Nijinsky was awarded bad marks in Boston which ought, one would think, to have been applied to the tour organisers instead.

N.Y. Telegraph 16.11.16

"An outburst of artistic temperament on the part of Nijinsky, the dancer, delayed the installing of *Hip Hip Hooray's* ice plant on the stage of the Boston Opera House, but, due to the energy of R.H. Burnside and his assistants, the artificial ice was in place in time for the scheduled first performance of the big spectacle in Boston on Monday night. The Hippodrome management was desirous of installing the ice plant long before, but Nijinsky, who was occupying the theatre with the Ballet Russe, kept the workmen off until Saturday night by an injunction. Naughty, naughty Niji!" Possibly it might have been more accurate to have said, "Naughty, naughty Charles Dillingham" – for how could the ballet have been expected to perform *Scheherazade* on ice?

Toledo Times 12.11.16

A sardonic version of the story that Russia wanted Nijinsky to return and join the army appeared on November 12th. This was printed in a large "Box," with outlines, in the centre of an even larger article headed "WAR AND MOTHER-IN-LAW TROUBLE MOST BEAUTIFUL MAN IN THE WORLD," which gave a lurid version of the tale of animosity in Romola's home in Budapest. "The facts of the matter, which are too grave to be humorous, were not learned from Mr. Nijinsky ... It was Mrs. Nijinsky who sorrowfully and reluctantly told the tale ..."

There were one-night-stands in smaller towns before the company arrived in Washington, D.C., for a second visit. "Returning to Washington without the potent lure of novelty or the insidious appeal of sensationalism, Diaghilev's Russian Ballet was seen at the Belasco Theatre last night by an audience . . . perhaps more representative of the true lovers of the choreographic art than the capacity audiences which witnessed the initial offerings of the famous Ballet in the Capital with explosive enthusiasm in the spring . . . Washington Post 21.11.16

"Curiosity and expectation centred in Nijinsky – fully realised, for this supreme artist epitomised all the grace of absolute ballet dancing, while in *Carnaval* his characterisation was a most enjoyable example of glorified comic pantomime." (The first item was *La Princesse Enchantée*, which he danced with Spessitseva.)

"The most spontaneous applause of the evening was reserved for the stirring, barbaric *Polovtsian Dances* from *Prince Igor,* in which Bolm achieved a noteworthy success.

"Tonight there will be programme changes. Instead of *Mephisto Waltz, Dieu Bleu,* and *Sadko,* the programme will be *Les Sylphides, Carnaval,* and *Cléopâtre.*"

This sample is typical of the infuriating chaos permeating the organisation of this tour. The three works which had been announced would *all* have been new to Washington – and yet that city did not even have *Sadko. Le Dieu Bleu,* which, despite the beautiful and spectacular costumes and settings, had been a failure in Europe, was never performed in America at all.

On the lighter side, the Washington papers produced two gems; "endorsement" as a method of supplementing salaries is no new thing, and an advertisement appeared in one paper, stating that "Lydia Lopokova, Star of the Ballet Russe, writes from her apartments in the New Willard to the Juelg Piano Co., expressing appreciation of the Behning Piano installed in her suite." In the other, it was said of *La Princesse Enchantée* that it was "enhanced by the scenery and costumes designed by Leon Bakst, whose mastery of line and colour won him a Nobel prize." Washington Evening Star 21.11.16

Till was given in the first and last of three performances in Philadelphia, and the paper said: "What took place on the stage had about it all the fantasy, exaggeration and unbelievable qualities which characterize the various tales in the ninety-two histories which have been written about the character . . . it is merely a series of steps and posturings, in which the star reveals a mimetic power which is remarkable and emphasizes the truth of the assertion that 'speech was given to man to conceal his thoughts.' " Public Ledger 24.11.16

Richmond, Va., though foxed by those wretched handouts about works not shown at all, was overwhelmed by the Bakst costumes for *Cléopâtre.* "Set in the court of the Sapphire Queen of the Nile, . . . it affords Flora Revalles, the brilliant mime who is seen in the rôle of Egypt's famous Queen, an opportunity of wearing the most sensational gown in the entire wardrobe of the troupe. It consists of yards upon yards of veiling swathed round the form of the dancer. In the course of the melodrama it is required that the queen divest herself of a portion of her garment. This is done by two beautiful handmaidens who circle about the statuesque beauty much as children circle about a maypole." Times-Picayune 26.11.16

Houston was enthusiastic, but nevertheless, the audience dwindled after the excitement of the first night. Houston Post 6.12.16

Dallas, Texas, had one performance, Nijinsky dancing only in *Carnaval.* Of Bolm's performance in *Scheherazade,* the critic, who seemed to have seen the company in Europe, said, "Bolm's *Nègre* is indescribably wild and violent. It is not the servile pride and servile adulation with which Nijinsky savors the part. It is rather the physical frenzy and fury of an animal that devours in caress. His whole being, his every movement, quivered with the zest of release and animal passion . . ." (It was also observed, plaintively, that instead of the backcloth by Doboujinsky for *Sylphides,* which they had been promised, they were shown the *original* by Benois instead.) Dallas News 8.12.16

In Fort Worth, "Fires had been burning in the big Coliseum since daylight Friday morning, and the huge auditorium was comfortably warm" for the first performance. "The crowds received swift and skilful handling, both from the traction company, which provided a quick and adequate car service, and the large corps of ushers from Texas Christian University." In return for all the excitement of such preparations, Fort Worth saw *Cléopâtre, Carnaval, Faune,* Fort Worth Record 9.12.16

Spectre and *Scheherazade,* if the amended programme is to be believed. In this case, an exceptionally full and attractive programme was offered – but in some places, the ballets were shorter and fewer, and the intervals very long. Many towns which had two or three performances reported a drop in the size of the audience after first nights.

Kansas
City
Star
12.12.16
Convention Hall was once more the scene of the performances in Kansas City, and this time Nijinsky danced *Carnaval* and *Spectre* for them on the first day, and *Sylphides* and *Faune* on the second. An advance paragraph said that "it will be a relief to Kansas City audiences to know that *Scheherazade* will not be produced this season. Nijinsky, who is personally managing the production, has decreed that *Scheherazade* shall not be given where there is a lack of illusory stage effects." They were able to enjoy *Cléopâtre* on both nights, and *Thamar* and *Faune* on the second – sufficiently strong meat, one might suppose.

Des
Moines
Register
16.12.16
Des Moines rejoiced in a brilliant performance, but "the audience which saw the Russian Ballet was small, when the accommodations of the auditorium are considered, but from the crowded conditions of the second balcony it is certain that the Coliseum could have been filled at something less than $3.50 a seat. Des Moines people evidently do not yet think in large denominations where entertainment is concerned."

Rocky
Mountain
News
18.12.16
The arrival in Denver, Colorado, of the enormous trains (six twelve-section drawing-room coaches, two drawing-room Pullmans and seven baggage-cars – including two specially rented from an Eastern rail-road to accommodate the 68-foot drops,) was three hours late. "The Russians were hungry, and, artists that they be, Manager R.G. Hernden testifies that their appetites are in no sense ethereal." Fifty taxicabs were waiting, but the language problem defeated friendly relations.

"Even Waslav Nijinsky himself, who keeps two servants for the sole purpose of attending to his little needs, and who said something in French which the attendants said meant he was enormously hungry, did not get away to suit his pleasure. At the last moment Nijinsky decided to change his hotel, and the servant who had rushed off in a cab to make arrangements for his chief, found himself with the wrong key for the wrong room . . .

"The Russians were keenly disappointed at the late arrival, because they had planned to take a scenic trip to Colorado Springs, leaving Denver tonight. Manager Herndon was busy last night making arrangements for this tour today, as the visitors intend to make the most of Colorado grandeur while here."

This paper gave the numbers of the entourage – "an orchestra of fifty-two, a stage crew of twenty-one, an executive staff of nine and fourteen principals and the *corps de ballet*." It added, "The Denver program . . . will be the most generous of the tour so far. There will be an extra ballet every night, with Nijinsky dancing twice."

Rocky
Mountain
News
19.12.16
The following day, the paper reported on the attendance. "The boxes were filled with members of the exclusive set and in all parts of the parquet were the fashionables seen, intently watching the graceful dancers." It was a full-dress occasion, and the writer described many gorgeous evening wraps which might have come straight out of the pages of American *Vogue.*

Sara Farrar reviewed the performance rather than the audience: "The art of the Russians has become familiar to Denver thru the genius of Pavlova and her troupe, and the present organisation is superior only in numbers and in the magnificence of its pictorial features. There is none among them that reaches the heights of the incomparable Pavlova unless it be Warslaw Nijinsky, and it is impossible to compare the feminine and the masculine dancers. Some prefer the delicate art of the woman and others enjoy the more virile style of the man . . .

"Warslaw Nijinsky, outstanding figure, who is the directing genius of the ballet, is also the outstanding figure of the dance. One feels his greatness in his stillness and repose as much as in his swift flights and bounds . . ." This was Miss Farrar's reaction to *Les Sylphides*; next came the thrilling *Polovtsian Dances*, and then – "After what seemed an almost interminable wait strings began to murmur the Tchaikowsky music that announced the *Princesse Enchantée*. Leon Bakst's marvelous gift for color and line gave the setting for the enchanted ones. A towering forest of flame-colored palms drooped over the prince and the princess while behind a deep blue night melted into a deep blue pool.

"It was in this spot designed by the color magician that Nijinsky and Lopokova were most wonderful. The magic of their twingling feet and hands that trembled like dewdrops were the most extraordinary performance of the whole evening. Nijinsky floated and bounded, it seemed, as no thing of flesh and blood could, and departed, flashing high thru the air. Lopokova, too, seemed to hang like a star trembling in mid-air as she executed her wonderful pirouettes . . ."

The reporter found the performance sometimes "almost overpowering." But – "The Auditorium is a large place to fill and there were many bare spots in it, but practically all of the downstairs seats were taken and a number of the boxes and the centre of the balcony was filled."

It was in Denver, too, that one member of the entourage suffered a traumatic accident.

It has already been mentioned that Randolfo Barocchi was very handsome, and wore a particularly idiosyncratic beard, large, spade-shaped, like an Assyrian – of which he was inordinately proud.

Being settled in one place for several days, Barocchi found time to go to the barber's. Soothed, no doubt, by the relaxed atmosphere, he fell asleep. To wake – clean-shaven!

If Cyril Beaumont, who related this story, remembered correctly, the ensuing nervous collapse resulted in at least three days shut up in bed in that special train!

It was at about this point, in December, that the Metropolitan Musical Bureau, desperate at the inadequate attendances, tried to whip up enthusiasm by putting out a news-sheet called "THE DIAGHILEV BALLET RUSSE COURIER." In view of the refusal to have that great man in the same continent as Nijinsky, it seems tough to trade on his name in this way; the mystery is that anyone could ever have imagined that this ridiculous piece of unspeakable vulgarity would sell a single seat. Headed "Vol.1, No.1," this issue was to be the only issue. "Cuts, mats, feature stories, photographs, frames, prospectuses, window cards, three sheet posters will be furnished free upon application," it said encouragingly.

It stated in a box on the front page that the cost of transporting the company on this tour was $500,000. It announced exhibitions of sketches and fashion, which were supposed to be preceding its arrival in each town, including "ribbon exhibits showing how the colors have been utilized in this accessory of feminine apparel, Bakst combs showing designs and colors of the ballet . . ." and so on. (Large, wide combs, not as high as "Spanish combs," were a fashionable adjunct to the coiffure at this period.) A suggestion that the ballet should be filmed brought a letter repudiating the idea as too expensive. "It would necessitate bringing the entire organisation to Los Angeles, and any aggregation of dancers that can play to $100,000 in two weeks would most assuredly demand all the money I have, my right eye and left hand, in addition to any hopes that I may have for a future life, in return for their services – THOMAS H. INCE."

Columbia gramophone records had been cut of some ballets – that was a good paragraph. But what is to be made of this? "Mlle. Revalles almost caused a panic at the Copley Plaza Hotel (in Boston) when she walked calmly into the lobby with the snake draped about her fingers like so many rings . . ."

Nijinsky's first visit to a football ground was reported.

Flora Revalles' desire to become a naturalised American citizen was discussed. On one page, Nijinsky was stated to be staying despite the "Little White Father's" call to arms, and on another to think that "a man of genius" is under the same obligation as any other to fight when called upon. The refusal of Monteux to conduct German music had full coverage.

The worst was a double column headed "BAKSTERICAL LAUGHTER." One horrible pun followed another. "Ladies, consult the Ballet girls if you wish to become thin. They give Sylphides (Sylph-feed.)" There were many more. This effort must have been just a waste of money. Re-hashing the silly-season stories was, apparently, meant to provide fodder for local papers. Fortunately these appear to have kept their heads and concentrated on reporting.

The mystery is the greater because such an approach would seem totally foreign to the nature of the Met.'s own Press Agent, William J. Guard, a brilliant, sophisticated, resourceful, witty, newspaper-wise man. Gatti-Casazza had wrested him from Hammerstein, "a man of daring and imagination. So was Guard, his indispensable propagandist, whose creative temperament matched Hammerstein's in its quicksilver responsiveness and understanding." In his later life, said John Briggs, he became a Dickensian figure (and prodigious drinker.) But Irving Kolodin

Requiem for a Yellow Brick Brewery: John Briggs

The four sides of the one and only number of the *Diaghilev Ballet Russe Courier.*

stressed that he was "at once the aristocrat and the business-man. He looked more like an artist than any singer or conductor, with his slender frame and face, the waggling goatee, the spats, Windsor tie in red, pink, black or plaid according to mood, the pink striped shirts, the flowing cape and top hat . . . easily the most noticeable figure on opening nights . . . Kind to the tyro, unforgiving to the fake, Billy Guard cast an air of civilised Bohemia over his realm, spiced with the wit of his native Limerick . . ." One can only imagine that the *Ballet Russe Courier* had been produced without his knowledge or consent. It does not seem to have stemmed from the imagination of the man who spent a day with Diaghilev in Milan, and another at the Villa Belle Rive. Possibly he had returned to Europe, whence he had reported on political matters in 1915.

The Story of the Metropolitan Opera: Irving Kolodin

Christmas Eve fell on a Sunday, and was spent travelling on to Los Angeles. The paper which said that "the President of the Salt Lake Railway loaned a private car to take Mr. Nijinsky . . . and an extra baggage car, decorated in the holiday colors, for a Christmas Eve party," omitted to mention that the said President was none other than Otto Kahn himself.

Los Angeles Examiner

Los Angeles, and warm sun, cheered the company and they gave an opening performance described as "overwhelming" by the critic Otheman Stevens, who confessed that he had run out of adjectives fit to describe it. He was thrilled by *Till*, "which made me wonder whether I had really been on the water wagon for six months." Right up front in the stalls was none other than Charlie Chaplin. "Everything went with added charm and increased zest after the first quarter of an hour, for Charlie Chaplin had been waited upon by a full dressed committee of artists and taken to the stage, where he was the welcome and adulated guest of the other artists; they had all heard of him and seen him, some of them while in the trenches, so that Nijinsky, Revalles, Lopokova, all of them, kowtowed to him, and I shouldn't be surprised if someone kissed him; foreigners do that when greatly enthused."

Los Angeles Examiner 26.12.16

Randolfo Barocchi.

W.J. Guard.

It is a pity that Charlie waited over fifty years before setting down his recollection in an autobiography, for when he came to it, he had forgotten facts and made mistakes about them, whilst giving an *impression* of Nijinsky which corresponds completely with the accounts of members of the company. Chaplin thought he hadn't seen the ballet until the matinée at the end of the week. He remained under the illusion that it was Diaghilev himself who had greeted him, and nonchalantly offered to put on *Faune* specially for him. (It was probably the polyglot and now clean-shaven Barocchi, and *Faune* was given on the Tuesday only.) Nothing is easier than to mix up programmes after a mere week, let alone fifty years. Charlie's impressions of the other artist are more valuable. During the week, members of the company visited the studios, and Chaplin found himself made dreadfully uncomfortable by the presence of a sad Nijinsky, watching him at work from behind the camera – Chaplin said that he ordered that this should not be loaded with film, as he was so put off. There is a rumour that Chaplin himself shot a bit of film of Nijinsky on one such occasion, but no certainty about this.

What seems in character with Nijinsky's detachment from the requirements of a performance is Charlie's story of an episode in the latter's dressing-room. Chaplin does not say in what language they conversed, but that Nijinsky, summoned for his "music," refused to budge, preferring to stay with him. "Let them play another overture." Chaplin professed himself shocked.

***
San Francisco
3.1.17

The financial arrangements for the tour are clearly demonstrated in the report from the next stop that "William J. Greenbaum has to pay a round $25,000 for the services of the Russian Ballet before he can pocket a single penny of profit. But he has small room for anxiety. There was not a single vacant seat in the Valencia Theatre last night, and the artistic success of the enterprise was so signal that I regard its financial success as a thing assured," said Redfern Mason.

***
San Francisco
5.1.17

The critic Ernest J. Hopkins began his first article: "That well-worn phrase, 'THE GREATEST SHOW ON EARTH,' will have to be taken away from the sawdust ring and given to the Diaghilev Ballet Russe. Other ballet productions have had truer tragic art, or a finer quality of classic humor, or a purer and higher mastery of the dance. But none has had a more spirited ensemble or richer costumes or more gorgeous scenery or more miraculous lights. Never has San Francisco seen a more brilliant show." He could be capable of a critical comparison – "You might set the *ballon* dancing of Nijinsky against that of Mordkin and feel that the latter's place in memory is fairly safe . . . and of course Lydia Lopokova, charming as she is, could not be expected to sweep away a public trained to the peerless Anna."

Hopkins also gave tremendous praise where few remember to apply it.

"Oh, these lights! The name of the chief electrician ought to be printed on the program in red. What the sets and the costumes only began the lights completed and transfigured. The stage was made to appear a mile deep, or a mere shallow strip. Each costume became not one color, but many; in the course of the progress from front to rear of the stage each single costume would change its hues like a sunset. Such effects are indescribable; they must be seen and felt to be understood. It is worth mention that the overhead 'borders' were entirely discarded and the footlights were used wholly for color, while the principal illumination was thrown from the sides. But there were subtleties in the mixing and mingling of the colored rays which could not at all be analyzed and which thrilled with their romantic beauty. There is nothing in the range of stage mechanics that has half the artistic possibilities of the electric light; and the Diaghilev Ballet has almost, one would think, attained the ultimate." How greatly it could have helped Diaghilev on the first visit, had such understanding of the importance of his magnificent lighting "plots," which needed rehearsal in every new theatre, been truly comprehended. So often – as in Kansas City – he had to earn hatred by his insistence on being an immovable object and resisting the irresistible force of the desire to get the curtain up.

San Francisco
5.1.17

After seeing *Scheherazade*, *Till* and *Les Sylphides* on the third night, Hopkins chose a curious word to describe his feelings. "The Diaghileff organisation very frankly sets forth the dance in its decadence," he said. He continued by explaining that, as everything goes in cycles, the early purity of an idea is invaded by commercial interests, which vulgarise what they have sought to emulate; then the public falls away, "and such effects soon reach their limit, as unrestrained stimuli always do, and decadence is plunged into night. There will be no post-Diaghileff ballet – there could be none. What could out-do such gorgeousness? . . . Adeline Genée or Anna Pavlova could have danced in a bare-walled barn with a greater totality of beauty. But Genée has retired, and Pavlova cannot dance for ever; there are no successors."

Happily, Ernest Hopkins was mistaken in his predictions.

The sunshine of California and the love of outdoor sport gave rise to another of those "interviews" with Nijinsky. In this, he decried the desire to win which is inherent in competitive games. "In football, for instance, which I have frequently watched with interest for a few moments, the contestants think only of the ball and how they can secure or retain it. In dancing one has to concentrate the mind on the muscle in use . . ." "Nijinsky said he had frequently studied, with profit to himself, athletes and industrial workers in the more active callings, such as the building of sky-scrapers. He has possibly received useful ideas and suggestions from their actions, but immediately the figures began to repeat their motions mechanically he had seen enough and was tired." "From a football point of view," continued the writer, R.C. Baily, "Nijinsky is probably an All-American half back – gone wrong." San Francisco ***.1.17

This recalls the suggestions as early as 1913, which appeared then in many papers, that Nijinsky wished to make a large-scale ballet of "sports." "THE DANCE OF THE ROCKE-FELLER AT GOLF!" "THE MOUNTED BALLET IN A POLO GAME AND THE RHYTHMIC SWIVEL SIDE-STEP AND SWAT OF THE 'BALLET DU BOX!'" But it would take another Wagner to compose the music for an affair of gorgeous Amazons in the crunch and scrap and rough and tumble of 'THE BALLET DU FURORE DU FOOTBALL!'" N.Y. World (by cable from Paris 16.5.13

Flora Revalles was revealed as possessing unsuspected talent. "Mlle. is French Swiss and was born in Geneva and learned to swim in the blue waters of the great lake. Only the other day in the Adirondacks, she demonstrated her speed by winning a race to an island."

By now, it was time for the company to start the trek back. A reporter in Spokane thought that the musicians looked at the audience assembling "as if trying to see some faint family resemblance between the Spokane audience and the Diamond Horseshoe of the Metropolitan." He also said, of *Cléopâtre*, "It is the age-old allegory, the story that the movie fans know by heart, the age-old plot of the wages of sin, etc., Circe and the Vampire." But Spokane was most certainly deeply thrilled by what it saw. "All the way out might be heard people scheming to rob the butcher or the baker to find money to see the dancers again tonight!" Spokane 20.1.17

On January 22nd, 1917, the *New York Times* announced that arrangements had been almost completed for Otto Kahn to assume American citizenship.

Minneapolis, having a return visit, was furious to find that only one item was new to it – *La Princesse Enchantée*. But "this number won a pair of results which must surely be described as unusual. It evoked a burst of real enthusiasm from a Minneapolis audience and drew forth an encore from Nijinski. Since the niggardliness of Nijinski with encores has become a national proverb, and the niggardliness of our audience a local proverb, it must be conceded that the evening was not altogether devoid of the element of the unexpected." Minneapolis Tribune 22.1.17

There were, however, other elements of the unexpected that made the writer less happy. "The performance last night made it clear that the Russian conception of a program is a strange and wonderful thing. Once again the bill was arbitrarily altered without an announcement of any sort. The result was that a large proportion of the audience was meditating on the beauties of *Prince Igor* while *Scheherazade* was being enacted, and another large percentage of it was endeavouring to find the wickedness of *Scheherazade* in the racing, plunging, barbaric dances of *Prince Igor*. Such a procedure may have its humorous aspects but it is altogether indefensible; the audience did not come to be needlessly tantalized and confused. Five numbers in all were played, including the Rimsky-Korsakov symphony, and this is the quaint chronology in which they appeared: One, Five, Four, Two, Three. Perhaps the Slavic numerals run differently from the numerals of Western countries; but in that event our visitors ought to acquaint themselves with our system when in our country; their own way madness lies."

Minneapolis
Tribune
22.1.17

H.T. Parker had come over from Boston, and wrote, after this performance: "... Mr. Nijinsky is no contented technician of the dance, superlatively as he may exemplify the older virtuosity in such a piece for the display of it as *The Enchanted Princess*, or, in a measure, the quasi-idyllic *Phantom of the Rose*. He was schooled in it for nine years, as is every Russian dancer; he practised it for years afterwards in the Imperial theatres of Petrograd and Moscow before a public more expert and insistent with these technical felicities than any other in the world. He still makes use of them daily in mimed impersonation and graphic suggestion, remote, indeed, from the ends for which the older French and Italian ballet masters designed them. They conceived the art of the dance as self-contained, self-sufficient, absolute, reward enough in its own agilities, graces, subtleties, for those who practised and those who watched and applauded it. Obviously, it asked little of the mind; it gave as little room for the play of the spirit. Yet for the dancer and the mime of these later and newer days, who would ply his intellect and set free his fancy and feeling in all that he undertakes, this old virtuosity provides often the apt and ready means ... The alertness, the patience, the dexterity, the endless quest for exactitude of the older virtuosity have their uses in the new freedoms. In itself it may be no more than a relatively paltry goal; yet, without it, the dancer and the mime of these days lacks his tested tools."

St. Paul
5.1.17

If first-night houses were good, those on subsequent nights seem so often to have been much smaller. "LEGS PRICE COMING DOWN HERE," shrieked a headline well in advance of the return visit to St. Paul. "The range of prices is designed to fit the smaller size in purses, which is now in vogue."

By this time, Chicago had realized what it had missed by staying away on the first tour; a single matinée was arranged, after which a telegram was despatched to the *Toledo Blade* by Press Representative Wells Hawks – a Met. man.

"CHICAGO JAN. 28. Turning away twice the capacity of the theatre, the Ballet Russe played and scored a brilliant success at Cohan's this afternoon ... The famous dancers appeared before one of the most fashionable audiences of the year. The street was blocked for an hour with motors filled with theatre parties. Nijinsky was cheered to the echo and called before the curtain a score of times ... Probable return matinée will be arranged after the Southern tour ..." And, indeed, it was.

Indianapolis
30.1.17

Indianapolis produced a run-down on Nijinsky's day – presumably a bright thought in varying the handouts. "Nijinsky gets up at 7 a.m. and eats a very light breakfast. Then he takes a little spin in his car, which he drives himself." (Another writer had said that his chauffeur drove the car from town to town, so that it was always waiting for him – presumably, where longer stops were to be made.) "He rehearses for three hours with the pianist, practising muscle scales." After an enormous luncheon, with wine, which he liked, came correspondence. "In London Nijinsky had to hire four secretaries to answer his mail and acknowledge the flowers and gifts he received from admiring women" came out again.

Post
Louisville
5.2.17

Louisville, also a return visit, reported that "it can be positively stated that there is no field of modern art that has not been touched by the Russian ballet and the influences around it," and discussed Matisse and modern French painting, and Stravinsky and modern music.

Cincinnati
Times-Star
7.2.17

The return to the musical Cincinnati brought out a more critical assessment than on the first visit. The curtain went up half an hour late, and, as so often, there was complaint about the long intervals. Cincinnati prided itself on the punctuality of its own orchestra! The cause of the delay in starting on this evening is not clear, but there must have been some real crisis about the conductor, for here, and here alone, Monteux took the rostrum and conducted *Till Eulenspiegel*. Cincinnati felt him to be as good as anticipated – "*hors ligne*." In view of the fact that his reputation for conducting Stravinsky was so great, Cincinnati was regretful that no work by that composer was scheduled for either programme. Nevertheless, though the writer remarked that "the novelty of the Ballet Russe has somewhat passed away," he pronounced the verdict that "Nothing more marvellous than the stage picture of *Till Eulenspiegel* has been offered on any stage."

After the final performance, "Discussion will narrow down to the artistic verity of Nijinsky's ideas concerning the ballets and mimes in which he participated." The writer felt that in *Spectre de la Rose*, "one immediately understood not only his fame, but his equipment for attaining it," and that had it been given on the first night, there would not have been an empty seat after. Of *Faune*, after a dissertation on Etruscan art, the writer felt the verity to be much less. Obviously, this discussion was taking place in the finest possible atmosphere – that of a good restaurant over an after-the-show-supper. "The discussion waxed so hot that at one moment it was threatened to refer the verdict to no less a person than Nijinsky himself. But when that athletic young man was discovered contemplating another version of his faun, a lunette in the supper room of the Sinton, it was decided to allow him to draw additional historic details from another phase of art. If one were to name the celebrities who assisted at this discussion a delightful episode would be revealed." Indeed, this delightful episode evokes the atmosphere of the seasons in Paris and London.

Cincinnati
Times-Star
8.2.17

In Detroit (although *Sadko* was not performed,) a cartoonist, having fun with the repertoire, drew a fish half out of water, captioning it "Russian Caviare in its Original State."

Detroit
Free
Press
10.2.17

Toledo, whose *Blade* had carried stories of the Diaghilev Ballet since it first came to Europe, reaped its reward with a single performance at its Valentine Theatre on February 12th. "Exceptional charm and unappeasing brevity characterized the performance . . . Three numbers . . . constituted the entertainment, which began late and was concluded by ten thirty."

Toledo
Blade
13.2.17

Reading between the lines, this may well be guessed as being one of the occasions when someone else had to make a hasty stand-in appearance, for the paper went on: "Waslav Nijinsky, declared to be Russia's supreme dancer, appeared . . . only in *Les Sylphides,* the second and most artistic number of the evening. Nijinsky, the embodiment of grace and agility when in motion, proved lacking in personal appeal or charm when in repose."

As for the rest of the programme, Toledo thought that, for *Scheherazade,* "the Bakst scenery and costumes were unique and attractive, but in no respect luxurious or pretentious . . . *Prince Igor* was a commingled arrangement of fantastic war dances, very very quaint, very lively and very pleasing, but not very interpretative. The scenery and costumes of Roerich invested the number with kaleidescopic splendor. The music was faultlessly and impressively presented."

Chicago, having come to regret its earlier boycott, did indeed have a second matinée, forecast after the successful visit in January. Of Nijinsky, a reporter said that "his leaps were long undulations, apparently without effort – his *entrechats,* to use the argot of his profession – in the Dickens' novels they were called 'pigeons' wings' – were marvels of swift, twinkling deftness . . . 'Twas pity the show was given in too small a theatre." ('Twas pity, too, that he got the argot mixed up, for 'twas not Charles Dickens, but Washington Irving, who used this term to describe a different ballet step.)

***

By this time, Nijinsky's behaviour must have been becoming unbearable, although, so far from being curtailed, as has been said, the tour had actually been extended for a week longer than the original itinerary given in the *Opera News.* Romola herself said that, the influence of the Tolstoyans having advanced dramatically, she told her husband firmly, when they were in Chicago, that he would have to choose between them and her, and that she had decided to return to New York. This departure, in fact, took place a few days later, from Pittsburgh, on February 18th, the day the company arrived in that city. But between Chicago and Pittsburgh, lay a two-day return visit to Cleveland, Ohio.

R. Nijinsky
p.289

Pittsburgh
Telegraph
18.2.17

"The theater was almost filled with people who literally devoured the music and dance festival." Favourite item of the evening was *La Princesse Enchantée* – but something happened which must have been noticeably odd. "This dance gave the full opportunity to each dancer of making a direct appeal to the audience and it happened last evening that Nijinsky rather ungallantly took the encores away from the lady.

Cleveland
Plain
Dealer
17.2.17

"The audience admired Nijinsky, but it wished to deliver a personal tribute to the woman, Lopokova, even if it appreciated right along that the man was the better dancer. This little bit of feeling on the audience's part had the effect of spurring Nijinsky on to better and better dancing – but not to letting the audience recognise the lady alone. And, together with a few other things, helped to make the audience hard towards the performers. They invited it – and got it." This report repeated the complaint that Nijinsky refused to let them applaud Lopokova alone, and also – as on other occasions – the fact that the continuity of the evening 'dragged.'

"It seemed that the dance company danced when it wished, and the audience could ponder the price it had paid, and wait for the Ballet Russe to get good and ready." The writer, Charles Henderson, was so huffed that he even described the attitude of some of the ballet's "subordinates" as "contemptuous" of the audience. Certainly, the atmosphere in Cleveland was charged with storm.

Cleveland had so greatly enjoyed the company's first visit that this time, some enthusiastic and hospitable patrons of the art had arranged a splendid soirée in a private mansion. Merle Armitage still remembers the extraordinary event of that evening – an event so extraordinary that one may surmise that it was this which finally precipitated Romola's departure, though she diplomatically said that it was necessary for her to leave and start the preparations for the return to Europe.

Merle
Armitage

The story is curious and tragic.

". . . The entire company attended a supper party given in a fashionable suburb. All evening while the guests enjoyed fine food and vintage wines, Nijinsky remained alone. Wearing an old grey suit, a shirt without a collar, and brown unpolished shoes, he sat in a corner seemingly preoccupied with contemplating the two walls. Among the guests at this gay affair was the distinguished pianist, George Copeland, a celebrated Debussy interpreter. At approximately 2 a.m., the hostess insisted that he play, and Copeland went to the piano. This was the prelude to an amazing, satyr-like performance. As Copeland began his own arrangement of Debussy's orchestral *L'Après-Midi d'un Faune*," (which had not been presented in any of the three programmes in the theatre,) "out of the corner came the sulking Nijinsky, the movement of his muscles plainly visible despite the comically ill-fitting clothes. The guests drew back and gave him the floor.

"It is one thing to see Nijinsky in make-up and costume, aided by the entire *mise-en-scène* of the Ballet Russe, and quite another to observe him closely in the cruel flat lighting of a drawing-room, without a single theatrical accoutrement. Yet, the impossible disadvantages of time and place could not entirely negate Nijinsky's tremendous powers of communication. When he had finished that poignantly erotic performance, Nijinsky furtively retired to his corner, and without a word or gesture resumed his solitary meditation. The guests, greatly moved, departed subdued and silent."

Pittsburgh was a great city with a number of theatres. In the most conventional of ballet traditions, their managers succeeded in arranging a clash of dance companies both times. In 1916, Ted Shawn and Ruth St. Denis had a booking for the same dates – and in 1917, Theodore Kosloff and his "Imperial Russian Dancers" were in the variety bill at the Vaudeville in the same week. Reviews of the two companies were printed in adjacent columns.

Pittsburgh
Post
20.2.17

N.Y.
Telegraph
23.3.17

However, "Long awaited, Waslaw Nijinsky came to Pittsburgh last night . . . and scored a personal triumph." Pittsburgh must have enjoyed the first visit, for this time, it had made a specially inspired effort to create a delightful and festive atmosphere, by decorating the foyer of the Pitt Theatre with prints from the Paris seasons. Moreover, the management had redecorated the dressing-rooms, with fresh, colourful cretonnes. For Nijinsky, there was a deep purple, with a splash of yellow – "looking like a sunset over a row of mosques." This was intended to harmonize with his costumes for *Scheherazade* and *Cléopâtre*. For Lopokova, the colour-scheme was pink and white, and for Flora Revalles, Nile greens, and – shades of Elinor Glyn! – a tiger rug, "that might have come from Cleopatra's barge." (It was reported that her snake had made the entire tour without complaint.)

Pittsburgh
Dispatch
19.2.17

Pittsburgh
Post
21.2.17

The utter impossibility of relying on the programmes as either printed or amended, so far as Nijinsky's own parts are concerned, was demonstrated in Pittsburgh. Grigoriev's filed programme casts him as the Slave in *Scheherazade*; the papers said that "a vivid demonstration of his unusual histrionic gifts was given in his portrayal of the chief eunuch . . ." The same report, however, went on to say that "in comparison with last night's performance, the performance last year, with Leonide Massine as the Faun, was a poor thing, aping the Greek, but catching nothing of the classic and the pagan spirit. As Nijinski presents it, *L'Après-Midi d'un Faune* expresses the abstract beauty, the pure pagan feeling, which inspired Greek art, and which Debussy has put into his music. The angular grace of the figures created the effect of remoteness – not stiffly, but with an underlying plastic quality that served to emphasise the suggestion of pagan desire." But – though *Till* was given twice – attendances were small.

On the Sunday, a party of the dancers made an expedition to see Niagara Falls, and as usual, Lopokova, by virtue of her five years' residence in the States, acted as guide and interpreter.

The last appearances were at Rochester, Syracuse and Albany. Syracuse was given *Scheherazade, Les Sylphides* led by Lopokova and Nijinsky, and *Thamar.* The company was received with rapture. "Pavlova, Mordkin and Nijinsky – here is the great Russian triumvirate. And the greatest of these is Nijinsky – perhaps because he is the most recent comer to the American stage, perhaps because we are already tired of Pavlova, and perhaps because we have not seen Mordkin for several years.

Syracuse
23.2.17

"Linked inseparably to Nijinsky's name is that of Leon Bakst. It is more than art. It is art to the hundredth power. It is life. It exhilarates, intoxicates, carries you away from the world. It is a form of hashish if those who have tried the drug are to be believed."

Syracuse
***
23.2.17

What would seem to be the last American "notice" appeared the following day, and first of all, harked back to the morality argument: "New York accepted *Scheherazade* but baulked at *L'Après-Midi d'un Faune,* which was not on last night's programme. If *Scheherazade* is a sample of the emotions which may be aroused by the Russian Ballet, and the *Afternoon of a Faun* goes it one better, one can readily imagine why the latter was barred from production on the American stage. One expects these things of foreigners and in a foreign land. The old lady with qualms who shudders at it in Syracuse would be enthusiastic over the identical performance at, let us say, the *Opéra Comique* in Paris, or, going lower, the *Moulin Rouge* or the *Dead Rat.*

"Every member of the company is an artist.

"Nijinsky – it is absolutely impossible to describe the grace, the perfection, with which he dances. The most tremendous thing is that his soul seems to be so wrapped up in it that he forgets the audience, that he has no care for the applause which directly accompanies and follows his efforts.

"There was a brilliant house to greet the dancers. The sense of art is not yet lost in Syracuse."

Printed on the same page as the previous day's advance news of the advent of the ballet, were headlines which told of the harsh reality of the world in February 1917.

Syracuse
***
23.2.17

LLOYD GEORGE ADMITS U-BOAT DANGER
13 MORE SHIPS SUNK IN STARVATION WAR
BRITAIN ADMITS FOOD CRISIS
PRESIDENT WILSON CONCERNED AT FOOD CRISIS
BALLET RUSSE SCORES SUCCESS

The final programme was given at the Harmanus Bleecker Hall, in Albany, on the evening of Saturday, February 24th, 1917. Bolm having been out of the company for some months, owing to an injury, the men were still having to share out rôles. The ballets given were *Cléopâtre,* (in which Nijinsky did not perform,) *La Princesse Enchantée,* which Lopokova and Nijinsky danced together, and *Scheherazade,* in which, if the printed programme is to be believed, Zverev danced *Le Nègre,* and Nijinsky appeared as the Chief Eunuch.

Only a few weeks later, in April, 1917, America entered the war.

Certainly, this second tour had lost money. Otto Kahn had never thought that it would do otherwise. He believed in the necessity for patronage of the arts. With so many glowing notices and the comprehension of the superlative quality of the Diaghileff Ballet Russe which was offered by a nucleus of public and critics, he had, in truth, accomplished his objective. A start had been made.

HARMANUS BLEECKER HALL, ALBANY
SATURDAY, FEBRUARY 24th, 1917
AT 8:30 O'CLOCK P. M.

By Arrangement with Metropolitan Opera Company

SERGE DE DIAGHILEFF'S

BALLET RUSSE

Artistic Direction, WASLAW NIJINSKY
For "Sadko" and "Les Papillons," ADOLF BOLM
Management, Metropolitan Musical Bureau

ARTISTS

MMES.	MESSRS.
Janina Boniecka	Adolf Bolm
Ekaterina Galanta	Alexandre Gavrilow
Lydia Lopokova	Ivan Jazwinsky
Vera Nemtchinova	Nicolas Kremneff
Sophie Pflanz	Waslaw Nijinsky
Flore Revalles	Mieczyslas Pianowski
Lydia Sokolova	Nicolas Zverew
Alexandra Wasilewska	

AND CORPS DE BALLET

Symphony Orchestra Conducted by M. Pierre Monteux

Serge de Diaghileff's Staff

Business Manager..........................M. Stanislaw Drobecki
General Stage Manager......................M. Nicolas Kremneff
Technical Director.........................M. Edwards S. Fennell
Chief Machinist.......................M. Michel Tschaoussovski

LOCAL MANAGEMENT OF BEN FRANKLIN

PROGRAMME

CLEOPATRE

Choreographic Drama in One Act
Dances composed and arranged by M. Michel Fokine
Scenery and Costumes designed by M. Leon Bakst
Music by M. A. Arensky
Incidental Music

(a) Prelude by M. S. Tanejeff (b) Arrival of Cleopatra by Rimsky-Korsakow (c) Veil Dance by Glinka (d) Bacchanale by Glazounow

PERSONNEL

Cleopatra...Mlle. Flore Revalles
Tahor..Mlle. Lydia Sokolova
Amoun..................................M. Alexandre Gavrilow
Favorite Slave of Cleopatra............Mlle. Alexandra Wasilewska
Favorite Slave of Cleopatra........................Nicolas Zverew
High Priest of the Temple................M. Mieczyslaw Pianowski
Bacchantes.......................Mlle. Sophie Pflanz; Mlle. Galanta
Servants of the Temple—Mlles. Potapowicz, Kurtener, Zamouhovska.
Grecian Women—Mlles. Boniecka, Pajewska, Doris, Kachouba, Chabelska, Sumarokova 2.
Grecian Men—MM. Zverew, Jazvinsky, Worontzow, Herman, Kostrovskoy, Statkiewicz.
Silenes—MM. Ochimowski, Tariat.
Pas de Deux Orientale—M. Zverew, Mlle. Nemtchinova 1.
Egyptian Women—Mlles. Zalewska, Slawicka, Mieczkowska, Sumarokova 1, Nemtchinova 1, Nemtchinova 2.
Egyptian Men—MM. Kostecki, Kegler, Kawecki, Maximoff.
Syrian Musicians, slaves, attendants of Cleopatra, people, servants of the temple.

———

Violin solo...Frederic Fradkin

———

LA PRINCESS ENCHANTEE

Music by M. P. Tschaikowsky
Scenery and Costumes designed by M. Leon Bakst
Choreography by M. Petipa

PERSONNEL

Princess.......................................Mlle. Lydia Lopokova
Prince...M. Waslaw Nijinsky

The programme of the last performance given by the Diaghilev Ballet in the U.S.A., at Albany, N.Y., on February 24th, 1917. A point of interest is the evidence that Nijinsky did, indeed, take the part of the Grand Eunuch, at least on this occasion.

No. 3. SCHEHERAZADE

A Persian Fable in One Act by MM. Leon Bakst and Michel Fokine
Music by Rimsky-Korsakow
Choreography by M. Michel Fokine
Scenery and Costumes by M. Leon Bakst

PERSONNEL

Zobeide, Princess of Samarcande.................Mlle. Flore Revalle
Le Negre, Zobeide's Favorite.....................M. Nicolas Zverew
Shariar, King of Indes............................M. Jazvinsky
Schah-Zeman, his brother..................M. Mieczyslas Pianowski
Le Grand Eunuque...........................M. Waslaw Nijinsky
Odalisque...........................Mlle. Alexandra Wasilewska
The Sultan's Wives—Mlles. Pflanz, Boniecka, Slawicka, Doris, Kachouba, Chabelska, Zamouchovska, Sumarokova 2.
First Slaves of the Harem—Mlles. Sokolova, Zalewska, Mieczkowska, Pajewska, Galanta, Nemtchinova.
Negres—MM. Worontzow, Kawecki, Kostrovskoy, Statkiewicz, Kegler, Herman, Bromberg, Tehumakow.
Second Slaves of the Harem—Mlles. Potapovicz, Kostrovskaja, Artska, Kurtener, Sumarokova, Nemtchinova.

———

Violin solo...Frederic Fradkin

———

METROPOLITAN OPERA CO., INC., EXECUTIVE STAFF

Manager ....R. G. HERNDON
Business Manager............................FRANK T. KINTZING
Director Publicity..........................EDWARD L. BERNAYS
Press Representative.............................WELLS HAWKS
Technical Director..........................EDWARD S. FENNEL
Mechanical Director in Advance.................WILLIAM J. CASEY
Treasurer..................................FREDERICK A. HAHN
Assistant to the Manager.......................PHIL BARUCHSON
Manager Orchestra............................H. H. HEIDELBERG
Secretary...................................DAILEY PASKMAN
Master Transportation.............................HARRY BOHN

1918–1919

COLISEUM THEATRE

SEPTEMBER 5th 1918 - MARCH 29th 1919

FIRST PERFORMANCES IN ENGLAND

September 5th: *The Good-Humoured Ladies*
(Scarlatti, Massine, Bakst.)
Rome 12.4.1917

October 31st: *Sadko*
(Rimsky-Korsakov, Bolm, Gontcharova)
San Sebastian, August 1916
Earlier choreography by Fokine,
Paris 6.6.1911

November 21st: *Midnight Sun*
(Rimsky-Korsakov, Massine, Larionov.)
Geneva 20.12.1915

December 23rd: *Contes Russes*
(Liadov, Massine, Larionov.)
Paris, 11.5.1917

REPERTOIRE

Le Carnaval	*La Princesse Enchantée*
Cléopâtre	*Scheherazade*
Papillons	*Les Sylphides*
Polovtsian Dances	*Thamar*

COMPANY

Allanova, Andreeva, Antonova, Cecchetti J., Clark, (later Savina, also Massina), Evina, Grantzeva, Grekulova, Istomina, Kostrovskaya, Lopokova, Mascagno, Matriunina, Mikulina, Muravieva, Nicolaeva, Olkhina, Pavlovska, Petipa, Potapovitch, Radina, Slavitska, Sokolova, Tchernicheva, Wassilievska, Zalevska,

Cecchetti, Fernandez, Gavrilov, Grigoriev, Idzikowsky, Jazvinsky, Kegler, Kovalsky, Kostecki, Kostrovsky, Kremnev, Lukin, Mascagno, Massine, Novak, Okhimovsky, Pavlov, Ribas, Statkevitch, Stepanov, Whitworth Jones, Woizikowski.

CONDUCTOR

Defosse

THE HIPPODROME, MANCHESTER

APRIL 7th - 19th, 1919

REPERTOIRE: All the ballets mentioned above.

RETURN TO LONDON

The Times welcomed the Russian ballet back in stately terms: "It is good news that M. Diaghilev has brought a large number of ballets with him; if they are all as good as the two he introduced to Coliseum audiences yesterday, London will have little cause to complain." The Times 6.9.18

Diaghilev had performed another of his miracles. He had arrived with a fine company, complete with a star new to London – Lydia Lopokova, of captivating charm. But instead of the glamour of an Opera House, they were to give one ballet as the centrepiece of the variety bill at the Coliseum, and twice daily at that.

The war dragged on: the Russian Revolution had taken place in October, 1917. The Imperial family had been murdered in July, 1918. For the majority of Diaghilev's company and friends, this meant severance for ever from their native land.

In 1917, the dancers who had been on the second North American tour joined Diaghilev in Rome, performing there and in Naples, and working on new ballets. Then they went to Paris for an early summer season – back for the first time for three years, except for one charity performance. During this season they presented the Cubist ballet, *Parade*. After this they returned to Spain, where they were joined by Nijinsky and Romola.

Once more, a South American tour was arranged, though with many complications. Diaghilev did not travel with the company. During this tour, Nijinsky's behaviour became more and more difficult, so that, (writing many years later,) Grigoriev said that he had felt that they were witnessing the end of the brief, meteoric career. A practical disaster was the destruction of the scenery for *Le Spectre de la Rose* and *Cléopâtre,* when a spark ignited one of the baggage trucks in a tunnel. The men in the company pushed the burning wagon apart from the others, thereby saving the costumes, without which they could not have performed. Such was the sad end of Bakst's greatly admired set with the huge Egyptian columns, and the delicate Biedermeyer bedroom which had been created with such love.

Once again the ballet returned to the Iberian peninsular, dancing not only in Madrid and Lisbon, but in small towns all over the place, until there were no more bookings left, and, but for the generosity of King Alfonso and Queen Ena, the dancers would have starved. Even so, Diaghilev had kept the creative instinct alive.

Diaghilev managed somehow to go to Paris and, from there, arranged this Coliseum booking with Sir Oswald Stoll, who gave him the money to bring the company from Spain to England. By herculean efforts, Diaghilev managed to get the enormous quantity of scenery and costumes conveyed across battle-torn France, at a time when nobody else could have ensured the arrival of a box of chocolates.

A great sadness hung on this return to London, however, for Lady Ripon had died in 1917. Her personality, her enthusiasm for beauty, her friendship and influence, were hard to replace. Her daughter, Lady Juliet Duff, became Diaghilev's ally in her mother's stead.

Society flocked to the Coliseum, but no longer with quite the elegance of pre-war days. On the other hand, the ballet could now reach a far wider public.

Diaghilev established himself at the Savoy, and sent a telegram to Vladimir Polunin, who was "digging potatoes in the Chiltern Hills." Scenery had to be painted; the first item was a set to replace Bakst's unpopular 1917 design for *Les Femmes de Bonne Humeur*. Polunin, helped over the English by Cyril Beaumont, later wrote a short book in which he described his work and adventures with Diaghilev, whose drive and initiative he endlessly admired.

Polunin

"Diaghilev clearly showed that the success of this ballet would enable his company to rise to its former eminence," said Polunin. "All the difficulties of finding a studio, procuring canvas and other materials (by no means easy at this period) were quickly surmounted, thanks to Diaghilev's untiring energy and his gift of inspiring all those with whom he came into contact. The studio, at the top of the fruit baskets store at Covent Garden Market, became the repository of Diaghilev's scenery, and there my wife and I worked uninterruptedly for over two years.

"To transfer a design by Bakst into suitable proportions for the stage proved to be a difficult task, for he often painted his effective designs with more regard for their pictorial effect than for the use of the scene painter . . . The nearest houses of the back-cloth would have looked so small that the heads of the dancers would have been on a level with the roofs . . . On the other hand, if the buildings were to be of normal size, the top of a tower would have been cut off by a sky-border.

"Diaghilev immediately decided that the tower should be 27 feet high, and he was right; the sky-border did not spoil the effect and the nobility of the tower gave the proper dimensions to the surrounding buildings. He . . . chose another type of fountain instead of that depicted by Bakst, which was not to his taste . . .

"Diaghilev's views required that the tone of the sky should be altered; Bakst's 'inky' tone, as Diaghilev termed it, was to be changed to a pure Italian blue . . . Diaghilev then remarked that the watercolour blotches in Bakst's design had not been reproduced by us. But, on wiping the portions in question with a sponge, we achieved in his presence a perfect imitation of the effect in the design. Diaghilev was so pleased with this process that he always remembered it and requested its application in other cases. When, at the dress rehearsal, everything was in its right place, Diaghilev said to me: "Thank goodness, at last I have a scene in accordance with what I wanted.""

Reserving his first novelty for the evening, Diaghilev opened at the matinée with *Cléopâtre*. The Bakst scenery having been destroyed when fire broke out on a train in South America, he had, when in Paris, commissioned a fresh back-cloth from Robert Delaunay – an audacious choice, as this painter's "orphist" style, with very brilliant colours and crisp shapes, was far removed from the splendour of Bakst's universally admired original setting. Tchernicheva was the Queen, and the welcome was terrific – but appreciative. "Probably the finest compliment that could be paid to the ballet is that, with a huge audience such as that which filled the Coliseum, there was not a sound as the action unfolded itself. Drury Lane or Covent Garden could not have behaved itself better."

The
Times
6.9.18

Observer
11.9.18

The Good-Humoured Ladies was different from any ballet shown before the war. "The merry adventures are unfolded with a rapidity of action that only perfect precision can sustain, and it is this precision with which every gesture is linked to its accompanying musical phrase that is the secret of this remarkable feat of stage production. A movement out of place would be a catastrophe, but it never happens, and the result is not only a very brilliant work of art, but a most exhilarating entertainment. Wordless wit is not easy of accomplishment, but Massine's choreography has attained to it.

"The new *première danseuse*, Mme. Lydia Lopokova, takes the part of Mariuccia, the soubrette, and plays it with irresistible charm. Leonide Massine, not content with devising the whole, sustains a part with easy grace, and in Stanislas Idzikowski, the company has another dancer of quaintly expressive movement."

Karsavina had been enthroned as the Queen of Hearts in the great pre-war seasons at Covent Garden and Drury Lane. Lydia Lopokova might, in Russian ballet nomenclature, be designated Queen of Hearts II, her reign being mainly at the Coliseum. One of Cyril Beaumont's most affectionate friendships in the ballet world was with her, and she gave him this photograph of herself as Mariuccia, the pert maid in *Les Femmes de Bonne Humeur*, signing it with the nickname she gave herself for him, "Petrograd."

Goldoni's plot goes like this:–

Young and old are preparing to enjoy the fun and flirtations of carnival time in Venice. The elderly Marquise Silvestra prinks; her lovely niece, Costanza, decides to test the fidelity of her betrothed, Count Rinaldo, by sending him a letter purporting to come from a mysterious lady who is mad to meet him. She says she will wear a pink rose in her hair. He keeps the rendezvous, but four ladies arrive in turn. All wear pink roses – and blue masks! But all four disdain him. Rinaldo finds himself landed with the Marquise, fooled by the back view of her fashionable dress. Mariuccia, Costanza's maid, invites her admirer Leonardo to supper, and they are joined by Battista. There is much merriment, and in comes the Marquis di Luca, another of Mariuccia's admirers. Trick follows trick, until the poor old Marquise's wig is knocked off, and youth laughs cruelly at the discomfiture of age.

The
Times
6.9.18

There was special notice for "the veteran, Enrico Cecchetti, who arrived in the morning, after travelling night and day, to play the part of the old beau with his own indefatigable spirit . . . Few who saw his capering and his mimicry would have imagined that he was well over 70 years of age. He is indeed a master of his art.

"If one can imagine a farcical comedy played at the speed of a cinematograph film, and then accentuate the pace, one can get a fair idea of this wild revel of 18th century Venice at carnival time . . ."

The
Lady
12.8.18

The *Lady* was back again. "Here we are experiencing the truth that a fine organisation does not die because its personnel changes . . . An Italian has orchestrated the cameos from Scarlatti with good effect, although the introduction of a spinet on the stage missed fire, owing to its sounds being quite inaudible at the Coliseum."

Observer
11.9.18

Massine's study of the paintings of Pietro Longhi and other artists had enabled him to create a ballet of which the *Observer* could say: "Not only has the Russian Ballet sustained its reputation, but in defiance of circumstances, it has treated us to an artistic event of the first importance."

The orchestra was under the direction of Mr. A.C. Boult, and "incidentally, a Stradivarius was in Mr. John Saunders' hands, perhaps for the first time in a music-hall."

For the Coliseum, it had been a considerable business risk to import such an expensive company for one-third of its programme. For the ballet, music-hall seemed like a come-down. In fact, both sides found that it worked marvellously. The Coliseum's 2,200 seats were practically sold out. Ballet-lovers soon got the habit of dropping in for that alone, but of course they paid the full price. The dancers were able to relax into a steady routine, a great relief after so many years of a nomadic and uncertain existence.

The
Times
7.9.18

By early September, it seemed as if the war would drag on for ever. The *Times'* critic had ended his first review by saying that "they brought back memories of days when one could think of something else besides war." Side by side with the critiques, so often printed on the Court page, were lists of casualties.

Vogue
October
1918/2

Vogue – already an institution in America – had started a London edition in 1916, coming out twice monthly. It did not "notice" first nights, but frequently pin-pointed trends, and in due course, gave particular attention to ballet's component arts. (Curiously, it never seems to have printed an article on the Russian Ballet's alleged influence on fashion.) As the ballet returned to London, *Vogue* said: "The Coliseum repertoire is significant. It invokes memories, but it does not point to a future . . . The tradition is still there . . . But we are not moved to say that this is the Russian Ballet. We can only say that this is the sort of thing the Russian Ballet used to be. In place of Nijinsky, who made choreographic history before our eyes, we have M. Massine, who administers it as a routine . . ."

If Diaghilev was incapable of resting on the laurel wreaths so frequently bestowed, here was the spur from the audience, certainly from the "stalls," – the spur to present modern ideas to the post-war world. Gone with the monarchs, the corset, the sweeping skirts and elaborate coiffures, the great hostesses in their boxes, the mansions – the servants – was the literary tradition on which pre-war ballets had been founded, given fresh "twists" by the Russian Ballet. The musical discords which had startled pre-war audiences were losing their power to shock. Diaghilev was to go much further in his search for the new than even *Vogue's* contributors could accept straight away. But the message was clear – go forward, not back.

No one has described the mood at this time better than Sir Osbert Sitwell, in the opening chapter of *Laughter in the Next Room.* It is sacrilege to quote only extracts. Osbert Sitwell had first seen the Ballet in 1912, and had become a devotee.

On November, 11th, treading unbelievingly, Sitwell, Diaghilev and Massine left the Coliseum together, and watched the crowds celebrating in Trafalgar Square.

". . . It seemed to me most happy that Diaghilev and the new great dancer . . . should dine at my house" (in Swan Walk, Chelsea,) "on the night of the Armistice: most fitting, for several reasons; chief among them . . . that the return of the Russian Ballet to London had constituted

Thadée Slavinsky as the dandified Count Rinaldo—
by Elizabeth Polunin.

Massine's choreography for every detail of
the supper-party – bringing in the props,
laying the table, offering the menu, serving
the dishes, and getting to work on them
with knives and forks, – all performed at
lightning speed – was a masterpiece of
ingenuity in the use of the classical
repertoire of technique. All had been
concocted in a merry atmosphere; under its
influence, when time was short and there
was still much to be done, Picasso helped
Bakst out by painting all those props for
him – furniture, tableware, and a menu.
What, one wonders, happened to those
objects?

Lubov Tchernicheva as Costanza — the moving
spirit of the Good Humoured Ladies.

a private and sole omen of peace. Then, too, I hold that the music that floats idly through the head to form a kind of personal climate of the mind, is of consequence to every artist, affording him the background rhythms and colours and tones . . . How much, for example, one would give to know what airs Leonardo or Michelangelo sang to himself at various times while he worked . . . So (without putting myself on these heights) throughout the early years of my adult life, I had become a devoted adherent of the Russian Ballet, and in consequence, during the two winters I had spent in the trenches, the music that came to my rescue – apart from the current and most vigorous American dance tunes – . . . had all been gathered by my subconscious mind, as I had sat in 1912, 1913, and 1914, watching the ballets I grew to know so well . . ."

In 1918, Osbert Sitwell welcomed a fresh start, with Lopokova and Massine.

". . . These two famous artistes led the Ballet into its second Golden Age, with such superb creations as *La Boutique Fantasque* and *Le Tricorne*, though *Parade* was, in essence, the most tragic and the most original of the newer spectacles."

Criticism was more patchy than before; newspapers were small, many of the critics were still at the wars, – some, like George Calderon, would not return. A new generation of critics was starting to look at the Ballet.

The
Times
6.9.18

When *Carnaval* was revived on September 12th, *The Times* said, "The exquisite charm, the gay yet touching appeal of it are as strong as ever, whatever changes may have taken place in the cast. We missed those two perfect sofas which used to sum up the spirit of the ballet; there are two sofas now, but they are not *those* sofas. On the other hand, we do not remember anything in the costume of the previous production so lovely as the orange-red velvet coat worn by M. Massine as Eusebius. These are small matters; but the Russian Ballet is not one to neglect small matters . . . If M. Stanislas Idzikowski as Harlequin is not Nijinski, . . . he is delightful in his impudent humour. They are all delightful – none, certainly, nearer to the perfection of delightfulness than Mme. Lydia Lopokova as Columbine. Mlle. Sokolova as Papillon is another on whom one must dote . . . the whole production is as potent to charm as it used to be in the tranquil old days."

The
Times
17.9.18

Diaghilev did not neglect the classical ballet which remained ever the foundation of his company, and which was maintained under the watchful eye of Cecchetti in the daily class. *La Princesse Enchantée* brought the house down on September 16th (and every time they danced it.) "Mme. Lopokova and M. Idzikowski seemed to have borrowed each other's virtues to add to their own; the woman had strength and the man grace," said *The Times*.

The
Times
11.10.18

In October, *The Times* had reported that "the season seems like continuing indefinitely, for M. Diaghilev's company goes from one success to another. Last night the repertory was further extended by a revival of *Scheherazade*. It was a strange contrast to pass from the surroundings of the glorified fairground of Trafalgar Square to those of the Persian harem, as imagined by M. Bakst; equally strange also to go from the realities of today to the voluptuous make-believe of a dim past; but it is these very contrasts which are drawing such packed houses to the Coliseum."

The
Lady
7.11.18

Not only *The Lady*, but also the audience, were back on form for the next first-night. "The production of *Sadko* was responsible for the attendance last Thursday evening of many well-known lovers of ballet of the Russian variety, and picturesque headdresses were notable in the boxes. Baroness d'Erlanger had a Byzantine headdress of metallic tissue and upstanding leaves . . . Lady Juliet Duff was wearing a black velvet picture gown, and Lady (Arthur) Paget had a black tuft in her hair, and a long black velvet wrap, with a deep ermine collar, over a black dress . . . The charming and all-too-brief *Enchanted Princess* made a greater appeal than the new production, with its denizens of the world under the sea in bizarre posturings."

The
Times
4.11.18

"Fishiness, scaliness, greenness, wetness, underwaterness – do we dare it? – Shelleyness. Queer, finny movements, a little grotesque in detail, extraordinarily watery in the whole," said *The Times*. "Only in such *disjecta membra* of language can one describe the wateriness, the pulsing, throbbing, deep-sea hush of *Sadko*." "The human musician so charmed the Sea-king's daughter that she drew him down under the waves . . . Once there he started playing his harp till the finny Court had to dance to it. How oddly, how madly, how waterily they jigged! There was the great Sea-King himself, with his huge green beard and his splendid robes and crown, bobbing it up and down and round and round . . . It is a fascinating little ballet, at once comical and exquisite; and we devoutly hope that it will get more than the three performances of last week."

Observer
3.11.18

There is an amusing touch, for modern times, when artists jet about the world and perform in London one day and Sydney the next, in noticing the speed with which the Armistice was followed by a development in travel accelerated by the war. "Within a very short time we are to have an air passenger service between London and Paris; indeed, tickets can be obtained at the Ritz Hotel, whence passengers will be conveyed by motor-car to the aerodrome." (The first of these flights was, in fact, made in July 1919, from Hendon.) This mode of travel would probably have had little appeal for Diaghilev, but for those of his faithful who could restrain their spirit of adventure, there were two new ballets to be seen before Christmas.

The
Lady
21.11.18

Both were completely "Russian," both had choreography by Massine and designs by Larionov, both were based on old stories and legends. Both were highly successful, though *The Lady* said tartly, of *Midnight Sun,* that "the synopsis of the action printed on the programme is a hindrance rather than a help to understanding what the ballet is about." The ballet, so popular in America, was about the custom in peasant communities of dancing to the sun, which is seen as a god, and which, for about two weeks in June, sinks not at all, but stays to give Northern Russia nights of curious beauty, an iridescent sunset merging immediately into a magical dawn. (In *Le Sacre du Printemps,* primitive Slavs invoked the coming of Spring; in *Soleil de Nuit,* or *Midnight Sun,* their descendants rejoiced in Summer.) Larionov, a painter of the Moscow School, was at his best in these designs, inspired by traditional peasant painted decoration.

"It begins with a kind of overgrown nursery game, which breaks gradually into a formal set of figures, during which the village idiot moves from one to another with helpless hands. Then a large circular audience is formed, squatting, to listen to Mme. Rosovsky singing behind the scenes, in honour, one supposes, or in explanation of the rite – most improper in a ballet, but very delightful – and to watch Mme. Lopokova's lithe little figure interpreting the song. The Sungod appears, accepting graciously his worshippers' homage, and four of them form the wheels of Phaeton's chariot, as he mounts the heavens, with the idiot as charioteer.

The
Times
22.11.18

"The red and gold head-dresses of the women and white costumes of the men stand against a dark blue and green ground. The music is thinly orchestrated, and leads the dance with precision rather than noise. The whole thing is a beautiful example of close construction."

To the Music Critic of the *Daily Telegraph,* it was "a score so full of grace and poetry that one would like to hear more of it than we get in the very short, but delightfully gay, spectacle at the Coliseum. Practically all the music used in the ballet is of the liveliest, and some of it presumably was taken from the arcadian revels in the forest scene in *Snegorouchka.* Korsakov's dance rhythms are invariably delightful and some of those heard in this ballet would set a hermit capering." Sydney Carroll, beginning his series of notices in the *Sunday Times,* said, "Emblematic of Pagan Russia – the savage vitality, the crude colour and design, the primitive exuberance of this village dance thrill the senses and arrest the mind."

Daily
Telegraph
23.11.18

Sunday
Times
24.11.18

Contes Russes – Childrens' Tales – came as a Christmas entertainment, but one quite out of the ordinary. "M. Massine has strung together three old Russian legends in a very ingenious way; the grotesque setting is so quaint and so unlike anything that one usually associates with a childrens' entertainment, the dancing of the whole team is so exhilarating, that one cannot wonder at the enthusiasm which greeted it."

The
Times
24.12.18

"Idzikowsky's remarkable *élévation* was admirably suited to The Cat, and his miming was excellent, especially his sorrow at the death of the dragon. The whimsical manner in which he despondently shook his head, and dabbed his eyes with an orange handkerchief dangling from a trembling hand, used to make Diaghilev shake with laughter," said Cyril Beaumont.

The Diaghilev
Ballet in
London.
C.Beaumont

In January, Diaghilev received news from Switzerland. Nijinsky had been declared insane.

Contes Russes – Larionov's design for The Cat – a rôle in which Idzikowski always made Diaghilev laugh till he cried.

Sunday
Times
2.2.19

In February, Diaghilev arranged a full programme for a gala in aid of Servian charities, which was attended by Queen Alexandra. "The colour, the vivacity, the speed, the grace of their productions are intoxicating," said the *Sunday Times*, "whether one sees the pristine grotesqueries of the *Children's Tales*, the sensuous pirouettings of *Les Sylphides*, or the macaronying masquerade of *The Good-Humoured Ladies*. It is amazing that we have to go to a music-hall to find such a marvellous symptom of the artistic impulse. The dance evidences itself here as ever a living symbol of human energy, joyousness, and beauty, and to M. Serge de Diaghilev and his remarkable company we can but inadequately express our heartfelt gratitude." (Diaghilev sensitively refused the invitation to attend a festive dinner.)

During the winter of 1918-1919, a virulent form of influenza raged the world over – "Spanish 'flu." Diaghilev must have trembled when a vital member of his company fell ill; conductors need special experience to deal with ballet.

The
Times
11.3.19

"The Russian Ballet was nearly involved in tragedy yesterday afternoon. At the last moment M. Henry Defosse, the conductor, was taken seriously ill, and with Mr. Alfred Dove, the Coliseum's musical director, ill with influenza, matters looked difficult. The situation was saved, however, by Mr. Landon Ronald, who showed his appreciation of the work of the ballet by taking his orchestra through the music of *Scheherazade* with as much skill as if he had been conducting every performance that the ballet has given. It was a *tour de force* on Mr. Ronald's part, which the audience was not slow to recognise." *

---

*(Mr. Ronald came of musical stock; his father, one Henry Russell, had composed no fewer than 800 songs, including "Woodman, Spare That Tree," and "A Life On The Ocean Wave." His elder brother, another Henry, bore the same patronymic as their father, Russell. He was indeed the same Henry Russell who had toured the San Carlo Opera Company, and had been Director of the Boston Opera House from 1909 to 1914, when its finances collapsed. Otto Kahn, who dreamed of an operatic empire, a circuit, in the United States, and was a patron of the Boston house, came to Henry Russell's aid when disaster struck, and sent him money for his personal expenses. On this money, Henry Russell and his second wife, Donna, lived in the Palazzo Orsini, in Rome – hence his usefulness, in 1915 and 1916, as "the Metropolitan's agent." Curiously, his younger brother's birth had been registered under an invented patronymic, but he achieved lasting fame as Sir Landon Ronald, Principal of the Guildhall School of Music from 1910 until shortly before his death in 1938.)

There were no fewer than 17 curtains on the last night, and amidst the wildest enthusiasm, it was announced that the company would return about the end of April.

The
Times
31.3.19

In the interim, Ernest Newman's prophecy that the provinces would never see the productions was set at naught, for Manchester booked the ballet for two weeks. A Special Supplement of the *Manchester Programme* printed four pages to help its readers understand what to expect: "In England the word 'ballet' is very much misunderstood. It is generally associated with short skirts, clap-trap music, and a series of uninteresting evolutions on the toes. With the Diaghilev company it has a totally different meaning. It is a synthesis of the sister arts of music, poetry, painting and dancing. These four are blended together to form one harmonious whole, in which the component parts softly and imperceptibly merge into one another . . ." There followed a brief description of each ballet. The bookings rolled in.

This time, they had to give one ballet in each of three shows a day. Once again, Lopokova proved herself a tremendous asset not only as a dancer, but also as an ambassadress. Cheerful interviews with her filled columns in the local papers, her English (which she laughingly admitted to having learned in America) making her their natural target.

It was considered "slightly timid" to begin with *Les Sylphides,* but *Prince Igor* was received with the customary raptures. ("A good deal of praise is due," said the same paper, "to Mr. Henry Defosse, the conductor, who, from a miscellaneous orchestra, contrived to get a splendid rhythmical impulse. He has his own technique, has an absolute faith in it, and by its means he bends every player to his will.")

Manchester
Guardian
8.4.19

Manchester
Guardian
10.4.19

It was not, perhaps, until they saw *Cléopâtre* that the audience felt it was really getting some of what it expected. "A more barbaric theme could not easily be found. Beside it, the Salome of Miss Allan that yesterday kept Watch Committees on tenterhooks is a suburban drawing-room performance . . ." But there was enthusiasm for its style: "Here is no matter of twirling, springing, tripping, and gliding . . . but an abrupt emphatic adoption of a kind of lissom stiffness, a clean-cut and almost geometrical style that gives to the fifth proposition of Euclid, Book I., a human interest." And there was a comment from the town of cotton – "Surely never was genius in decoration more economical of material, and yet the result is rich beyond words."

Manchester
Guardian
11.4.19

Manchester could always be relied on to give a practical thought to what lies behind the obvious, and remarked, in the *Programme,* as the second week began, that "Russia has sent us so many brilliant exponents of the modern school of dancing that its ranks must be getting alarmingly depleted, unless its recruiting is as successful as its tuition."

Lopokova's sense of fun provided the papers with some merry paragraphs. "I had a shock in America," she said, recalling the affair in Boston. "A police chief there actually requested, when I did the Bacchante dance in *Cléopâtre,* in future, I should wear trousers, on pain of a veto.

Manchester
Evening
Chronicle
12.4.19

"Our manager – what did he do? Simply told the journalists the comic facts, and heigh-ho! the poor police chief had an unhappy life for weeks. A Bacchante in trousers plagued him in print. Until officially he died of a Bacchante in trousers. At last he resigned his post. At that I was sorry. But what would you? Art has its martyrs; must Philistines be without them?"

1919

ALHAMBRA THEATRE

APRIL 10th – JULY 30th

FIRST PERFORMANCES IN ENGLAND

July 5th: *La Boutique Fantasque*
(Rossini, Massine, Derain)
World Première

July 22nd: *Le Tricorne*
(De Falla, Massine, Picasso.)
World Première

REPERTOIRE

Le Carnaval	*Papillons*
Cléopâtre	*Petrouchka*
Contes Russes	*Polovtsian Dances*
Good-Humoured Ladies	*Scheherazade*
Midnight Sun	*Les Sylphides*
Narcisse	*Thamar*
Oiseau de Feu	

COMPANY

Allanova, Andreeva, Cecchetti, J., Evina, Grantzeva, Grekulova, Istomina, Karsavina, Klementovitch, Kostrovskaya, Kyasht, Lopokova, Mikulina, Nemchinova I., Olkhina, Pavlovska, Petipa, Potapovitch, Radina, Savina, Slavitska, Sokolova, Tchernicheva, Wassilievska, Zalevska.

Bourman, Cecchetti, Fernandez, Gavrilov, Grigoriev, Idzikowski, Jazvinsky, Kegler, Kostecki, Kostrovsky, Kovalsky, Kremnev, Lukin, Mascagno, Massine, Novak, Okhimovsky, Pavlov, Ribas, Statkevitch, Stepanov, Vinogradov, Woizikowski, Zverev.

CONDUCTORS

Ansermet, Defosse.

TWO WORLD PREMIERES

Whole programmes of ballet again – for three whole months. Sydney Carroll said, "I have exhausted my superlatives." And the Drama Critic of the *Observer* – "To see and hear the Russian
Ballet is to find oneself deeply moved; to feel that criticism, in the ordinary sense of the word, is
impertinent. Here is something beautiful – one 'goes down' before it. While it is there before the
eyes and ears one is amused, or thrilled, or frightened, or touched to a deliciously sentimental
sadness, able to enjoy consciously all the varied appeals to the senses and the feeling which this
magical art can exercise. When it is over, one finds itself, as it were, on one's knees, thanking
whatever gods may be for beauty, and wondering, perhaps, what life would be without beauty
and without art." Sunday
Times
4.5.19

Observer
4.5.19

On the same page, Ernest Newman, newly arrived as Music Critic of the *Observer*, began
what was to become a series of exhortations to Diaghilev – in this first case, an exhortation to
which some people wish that Diaghilev had paid heed.

Newman posed the question, "Am I too fanciful in supposing that the ballet will some day
receive an enormous expansion by associating itself with the kinema? . . . Imagine Debussy's
faun drowsily brooding, to that lovely music, in a glade really palpitating under the heat of the
sun, with the leaves really quivering in the faint breeze! Imagine *Till Eulenspiegel*, staged on the
scale of the kinema!"

But his final sentence is a reminder of the stage reached in kinematic technique in 1919, for he
ended: "This sort of ballet would have the great advantage, too, that it could be exhibited in
every town on earth that had a competent orchestra – or the ballet could carry its own orchestra
as an opera company does. Perhaps the idea may fructify one day." Not, however, with Diaghilev.

During May and June, there was a tasteless wrangle in the *Observer*, over the subject which so
completely divided the outlook of Diaghilev and Ernest Newman. As so often, a neat
summing-up was to be found in *The Lady*: "The controversy . . . cannot be described as useful.
Both the protagonists exhibit too much prejudice. M. Diaghilev thinks Beethoven and Brahms
are bores, and that Elgar is a bore because he imitates them. Mr. Newman, angry because M.
Diaghilev ranks Mr. de Goossens, a young English composer of rather freakish music, above
Elgar, retorts by belittling the national Russian school, and glorifying the German composers.
Why cannot people understand that in musical art, as in heaven, there are 'many mansions?'
Because one is interested in and stimulated by the original efforts of the new school, is it neces-
sary to abuse the classics? And because one admires the fine solid constructive powers of the
German composers, is it impossible to recognise the new beauty brought into the language by
Moussorgsky, Debussy and Ravel?" The
Lady
12.6.19

There had, in the meantime, been a spate of letters from correspondents on that subject of an Observer
1.6.19

Derain's sketch for the makeup *(below)*, and Leon Woizikowski, who took the part on from Massine.

Vera Nemchinova seen in Lopokova's original costume as the female Can-Can dancer, when she took on the part already identified with Lopokova, and also danced by Karsavina.

alliance between the ballet and kinema. Newman wrote again on this subject: "I suppose no one has ever yet succeeded in writing an article that some reader or other could not misunderstand; but I seem to have been especially unfortunate with my recent article on 'Possibilities of the Ballet.' . . . I am sure that, like myself, a correspondent would be the first to protest against any attempt simply to translate the ballet as we now have it into the key of the kinema . . . What we both want is a genuine kinema art . . . Most people will agree that at present the kinematograph is almost beneath contempt . . ."

Ernest Newman proceeded for years to exhort, blame, and occasionally praise the ballet. Sometimes he was very acute, and sometimes he displayed his personal prejudices more than his critical faculties. For example, in the same article, he went on:–

"*Cléopâtre* and *Narcisse* reminded us that occasionally the best music does not coincide with the best choreography . . . The bizarrerie of *Cléopâtre,* its sub-erotic suggestions, and the touch of Oriental cruelty in its eroticism, all suit the Russians perfectly; while they are never, I think, at their best in a Greek subject. But Tcherepnin's music to *Narcisse* is ballet-music of the best type, clean and pat to the stage theme, never suggesting the concert-room, and with a piquancy or a poignancy in almost every phrase, so that the spectator's eyes and ears are always piqued in the same way at the same moment . . . Where . . . in *Cleopâtre* . . . is the equivalent of the cruel immobility of the marvellous face that Mme. Tchernicheva shows us as Cleopatra? On the stage the ballet is so perfect as a whole . . . that one feels it to be a pity that the Russians do not cast about for a new musical setting for it."

But even Ernest Newman went down like a ninepin before one member of the Russian ballet: for at last, yielding to the spate of importunate telegrams with which she had been bombarded in Tangier, where her British diplomat husband was *en poste,* Karsavina joined Diaghilev in London. *"La Grande Karsavina* is with us again," Diaghilev said expansively.

226

In criticising something quite different, Newman spoke of "a lack of nervous incandesc- Observer
15.6.19 ence," but went on, "No great art is possible without this incandescence; but some artists have the enviable faculty of calling it up at any moment at will . . . a mere turning of the eyes, a mere quiver passing along an arm, is surcharged with the whole vitality of a very rich artistic temperament . . . You may not be able to analyse the effect she makes on you, still less get to the secret of how she makes it; yet you know, the moment she comes on the stage, that the one genius of this Russian ballet troupe is there . . . no one could see Karsavina for three minutes in *Carnaval* or *Scheherazade* without feeling a new magic in the air . . ."

Diaghilev's policy of having a planned series of orchestral items in the intervals was liked by the more serious members of the audience, but letters and columns everywhere in the Press appealed for the issue of "domes of silence." There is something to be said on both sides – no fun not to be able to talk about what one had just seen, no fun not to be able to hear unusual music properly. This was an idea rather doomed to failure, though he gave the first performances in England of no fewer than fourteen works.

However, the next new ballet, *La Boutique Fantasque*, was no failure. "I can do nothing but Sunday
Times
22.6.19 rhapsodise," said Sydney Carroll, (reviewing it rather late.) "Your doll is the most alive creature on the stage. In the stuffed breast of the marionette there is more feeling than in the most sensitive of human hearts. Construe me that if you can – you lovers of great acting. For what part does imagination play in the theatre? It can animate wood, vitalize metal, and electrify clay. The real dramatic struggle is not in these puppets, alive or dead, but in ourselves.

"*La Boutique Fantasque* lets loose around me a flood of sensations too revolutionary to be tolerable. It makes me feel a child again. I find here revived in their full glory all the delights of childhood, the joyous hours I spent with my toys, the pictures that used to hang on the walls of my nursery – the scraps that I found in my aunt's album, the glad spirit of games and romps, the impossible trees and flowers, my toy mandolin, the houses like dog-kennels, the wonderful paddle steamer, the Italian peasants that whirled in a wild tarantella, the doll kings and queens of hearts and diamonds in their stately mazurka, the little grey snob with a pink bow, the melon seller, the troop of Cossacks, the dancing poodles, brown and white, with their pink and blue ribbons, the can-can dancers, especially the gentleman in the black velvet suit, white spats, patent leather shoes, black curly hair, side whiskers, and the tricky little black moustache."

LA BOUTIQUE FANTASQUE

"...Henceforth I could boast, 'I was there, I saw the first night of *La Boutique Fantasque*...'" So wrote Cyril Beaumont, twenty-one years later. Almost the same words were used fifty-five years after that première when the author was invited to lunch by Edith Shackleton, a critic who was to write about the Diaghilev Ballet, and Gluck, the painter. Every part in this ballet was a perfect blend of observation and interpretation, and its original cast never surpassed. "Those who never saw the Can-Can in *Boutique* danced by Lopokova and Massine will never know that dance as it was, or appreciate how exhilarating it could be," said Cyril Beaumont. The photographs here are, however, of later exponents, – that of Woizikowski to show the make-up, which can be compared with Derain's sketch for it, and that of Nemchinova to show the charming detail in the costume.

The poodles! When the costumes were made, Diaghilev courteously offered first pick to Savina. She chose the brown one, simply because it was smaller. Gluck had been one of the huge audience on that first night. Trying to describe it, she said, "Oh, the poodles! ...you never saw anything like them ...they were the *most lascivious* poodles...!" – at which point Edith Shackleton, who, being by then a great age, had seemed to be dozing, spoke up: "Especially on Saturday nights!"

227

The Souvenir Programme contained a delightful essay which, though unsigned, must have been composed by Diaghilev himself. He first gave an amusing picture of Rossini – who, "having closed his musical career in 1829 with *William Tell*, deserted music, almost entirely, for forty years," and settled in Passy, becoming the centre of Parisian musical life. "This delightful fat gourmand remained seated to the end of his days." His hospitality was notorious, and invitations to his Sunday lunches greatly prized. "At these banquets there was also music. The works of young musicians were performed, and sometimes one by the maestro himself, who prepared for these occasions merry compositions, full of irony, most of which, unfortunately, remained unpublished. The titles of these works alone suffice to show the disposition of their author. We find among them piano pieces, entitled: 'Four Hors-d'Oeuvres; Radishes, Anchovies, Gherkins and Butter, themes in variations.' We discover preludes headed, 'Dried Figs,' 'Here I am, Good-Morning, Madame,' 'Almonds,' 'It is striking twelve, Good-Night, Madame.' From the albums we may take an 'Anti-Dancing Valse,' a 'Funeral as Carnival,' an 'Asthmatic Study,' an 'Abortive Polka,' a piece entitled 'Ugh! Peas!', a 'Convulsive Prelude,' and even a Petite Valse: 'Castor Oil.' In the Russian vein, Rossini composed a Siberian Dance, a Slav March, (which serves as prelude to *La Boutique Fantasque*,) and even a Tartar Bolero, dedicated to the celebrated Russian painter Ivanoff who lived at Rome, and to whom Rossini sends 'un bacio,' in his letter of June 11th, 1848.

"Of these delightful pages which sparkle with satire, and are so little expected from the composer of the *Barber*, having more in common with Chopin, Delibes or Glinka, the music of *La Boutique Fantasque* is composed. The central number of the Ballet is dedicated by Rossini to the composer whom he admired beyond all others at this period of his life, Offenbach. The piece is entitled 'Capriccio Offenbachique. This delightful Parisian Bacchanal, this Can-Can with its amusing false note, dominates all the music of *La Boutique Fantasque*. It is a work full of laughter, redolent of the period, and of its author's well expressed freedom from care.

"The old-fashioned subject of animated dolls: Derain's bustles and flounces, against the background of a paddle-steamer, reviving the period of Edouard Manet, Stevens, and the earlier paintings of Renoir; Respighi's simple orchestration; and Massine's choreography in the manner of Lautrec, these are the elements which have been collected with love and admiration round the delightfully ingenuous music of the gems which Rossini modestly named 'Les Riens,' ('The Nothings,') and which until now have remained entirely unknown even to amateurs.

"I hold myself to be right in doing honour to this composer of genius, and in revealing this absolutely new aspect of his inexhaustible and radiant inspiration."

The writer then considered the design and the designer.

". . . Nearly all that has been seen until now at the Russian Ballet, and that has revolutionized theatrical art, is the application of decorative art to painting. Bakst, Larionov, Golovine were great decorative artists and remarkable costume designers who succeeded in composing a picture by decorative means. They employed strong, brilliant means; they arrived at orgies of Oriental colour, at broad and careless painting which corresponded to the aggregate effect of their decorative conception.

"In the presentation of *La Boutique Fantasque*, the opposite principle is applied. André Derain, the great *fauve*, the leader, with Matisse, of the new French school, is essentially a painter of easel pictures. He is a renovator of the purest French classical painting without being a mere reconstructor. This Italian primitive, in the guise of the modern French movement, is at the same time a great revolutionist in the region of colour. Deriving, like Matisse, from the Impressionists and Divisionists, Derain's point of departure is that at which Matisse ended his quest. Derain has progressed in the direction of conscious colour. He has begun to measure out colour in careful doses. To the bacchanalian splendour of the Russian decorators he has opposed the classic harmony of colour, aided by the well-balanced taste of a Latin deriving from Giotto and Leonardo. That is why, in the harmony of the scenery and costumes of *La Boutique Fantasque*, we are agreeably surprised at the application of this broad view and at the admirable result of his quest of harmonies that are tender and calming."

In 1917, when Derain was driving heavy transport for the artillery at the Front, Guillaume Apollinaire had said that not one of his pictures was to be found in any French museum, though they were already in collections outside France. Derain had a considerable reputation.

Before deciding to invite Derain, Diaghilev had asked Bakst for designs, but had rejected the work he produced. (These drawings are now in Chicago.) And so, André Derain became the first French artist to design for Diaghilev. (Polunin's version of this story was that Diaghilev "could not come to terms" with Bakst. Is it not more likely that Bakst had returned to his Maryinsky doll ballet of 1902, *Die Puppenfee*, and Diaghilev wanted something more up-to-date?)

Derain came to London, as Picasso had done, to collaborate in the realisation of his designs.

"Derain was a man of colossal stature, calm aspect, and endowed with a strong will," said Polunin. "His design, painted in oils, at first glance seemed to me to be so untheatrical that I could hardly conceive how it could be used for the stage. Diaghilev, too, seemed to have some doubts . . . But later on, when Derain himself began to take an active part in the work, often diverging from or rather developing the ideas contained in his rough design as he proceeded, everything fell into its right place . . .

Polunin
p.56

"Derain paid little attention to the accurate rendering of drawing and tones; . . . often altering and introducing new details, he paid no heed to warnings of a technical character, but used such thick colours that he ran the risk of their cracking and peeling off; in fact, this actually occurred in the case of the fruit painted by him into the foliage of some bushes. The flowers at the right window he purposely altered, while those on the other side were left as I had painted them.

"In general, he appeared to ignore all the demands of technique and stage requirements . . . The addition of curtains to the windows and entrance gates, required by the action of the ballet, were reluctantly conceded by him. The pieces of furniture were painted straight on to the walls of the '*boutique*,' but their perspective did not correspond with the normal perspective employed in the general scene. However, the final result was of great consequence, and *La Boutique Fantasque*, which, as Diaghilev declared in his speech at the dress rehearsal at the Alhambra, was more like a restaurant on the Lake of Geneva than a fantastic shop, became the favourite ballet of the London public.

"Costumes, curtains, properties, scenery, all seemed out of key with the general idea of the ballet, but in spite of that what a good laugh we had to the accompaniment of the lively airs gleaned from Rossini's note-books. Particularly humorous in a childlike way was the drop-curtain on which Derain had painted two figures and a hill with a three-cornered hat on it . . . I remember how Diaghilev, Picasso and other visitors, looking at the curtain before it was despatched to the theatre, could not refrain from a smile at the sight of those incoherent figures, double basses, palm trees and flying birds . . . Designer and painters were rewarded by the great success achieved by the production."

Derain's designs were perfect – as was the music.

Finally, the Souvenir Programme discussed the action.

'All that I have said concerning painting may be applied to the principal element in the dancing; the choreography. Fokine was a great decorator. He brushed his dancing with a wide brush, taking great care of certain details which were specially dear to him, and neglecting without scruple the expression of the whole plan of the work. His were always flat panels, painted by an unconscious temperament. Nijinsky, who brought great care to the preparation of his works, was still farther from nature. All that he constructed was a mere fresco, an artistic formula, a vision in two dimensions.

"Massine, whose choreographic mind derives chiefly from the Spanish school, is the exact opposite of his two predecessors. Adopting as principle the absolute perfection of the style of dancing in Spain, which is what is termed in pictorial art a 'miniature,' Massine presents himself as a choreographist in space. He detests the decorative principle, and if Picasso is his god in the art world, it is because Picasso is a 'painter' to his finger-tips. Massine transforms reality in his imagination, but in all that he does he starts directly from nature, which he interprets with a vision that is full of vitality, opposed to all formulae, and perhaps even to all principle."

La Boutique Fantasque was a triumph, hailed as a masterpiece, with Lopokova excelling herself, and Idzikowsky creating one of his personal masterpieces in the rôle of "Snob." The magic cauldron of creation bubbled and gave off delicious aromas of music, colour, interpretation and movement. Diaghilev's production of this work was potent with its maximum charm. No revivals have ever caught it. London flocked to see it, and it remained in the repertoire, a favourite, always a great draw.

Variety
***

And so, London was astounded when, only a few days after the tremendous success she scored in *Boutique*, Lydia Lopokova vanished. "DANCER MAY COST BALLET MILLION," said *Variety*, when the news reached America. The million was in francs, advanced to subsidize a fifteen-week season.

Earlier in the same year, there had been plans afoot for Lopokova to star in a very different sort of stage entertainment in London.

A frequent visitor to the Russian Ballet was Sir James Barrie, whose playlet, *Half an Hour*, was in the Coliseum bill. Denis MacKail, his biographer, said that Barrie, having always been interested and puzzled by the Ballet, now "had an opportunity of studying them at closer quarters again. One dancer, however, was already his friend.

*The Story
of J.M.B.*
(1941)
p.536/7/9

"Lopokova had written to him and asked him to write a play for her . . . Why not? She had acted as well as danced in the United States, and surely the best of all ways to get what you want is to go straight to the point. Barrie was amused – though one may well imagine that such requests had reached him before – and flattered . . . They met, they struck up a close friendship, and almost at once he had another idea. A three-act comedy about the life, or the imaginary and fantastic life, of a Russian dancer. Mlle. Lopokova was to star in it, so he told her, at the Haymarket in the autumn. Triumph of the system of asking for what you want, or in this case, perhaps, of being the right person to ask for it. Yet Mlle. Lopokova was, in fact, even more Russian than he realized, and there would be a surprise and a disappointment in this particular and tantalising plan.

"Mlle. Lopokova – with the new play at least half-written – was suddenly seized with an overwhelming desire to escape from the glare in which she lived. With no warning to anyone she just vanished . . . the play came to a complete standstill. Not that the work was wasted; for presently it would be re-shaped into an affair in one act, with more dancing for the heroine and no spoken words in her part at all, and as *The Truth About the Russian Dancers*, would reach the Coliseum – with Mme. Tamara Karsavina as its star – in the early spring. But this also was unknown yet. Just now, though of course he would have to forgive her in the end, Barrie was feeling distinctly sore with the siren who had started the whole thing. And indeed no one, anywhere in the story, had ever dreamt of playing such a trick on him before."

Polunin and his wife were hard at work all the time.

Polunin
p.53

"One day, Diaghilev came into the studio accompanied by a gentleman of medium height, southern complexion and wonderful eyes, whom he introduced to me as Pablo Picasso. After mutual greetings, Picasso showed me the booklet-maquette of his scene for a new ballet, *Le Tricorne*, and we all began discussing the construction of the future setting. Having dealt so long with Bakst's complicated and ostentatious scenery, the austere simplicity of Picasso's drawing, with its total absence of unnecessary detail, the composition and unity of the colouring – was astounding. It was just as if one had spent a long time in a hot room and then passed into the fresh air.

"The next day I planned out the constructional model according to Picasso's booklet, and the nobility of the tones, the harmony of the composition, the voluntary divergence from the laws of perspective produced an artistic whole even with the absence of colour. Both Diaghilev and Picasso approved my model without any alteration, and the work proceeded in a spirit of exultation.

"Picasso came to the studio daily, evinced a keen interest in everything, gave his instructions regarding the drawing and requested us to preserve its individuality and pay special attention to the colouring. The drawing, despite its deviation from the usual perspective, was set down with mathematical precision. The tones, of which there were four fundamental ones, were reproduced to a high degree of precision."

Polunin found that "in general, Picasso's theories were diametrically opposed to those held by the majority of Russian scene painters." This led to much technical experiment with pigments, and especially to problems to do with the use of pure white and the painting of the sky.

"Diaghilev laughingly transmitted to me Picasso's wish to paint the stars on the sky with his own hand, which he informed me he had granted on the strict condition that no blot should be made. Picasso, putting on slippers, then painted on the back-cloth seven stars and the silhouette of the distant town.

"The drop-curtain having been drawn and the general tones carefully roughed in, Picasso himself set to work on the central portion while my wife and I prepared the colours and helped him in everything. After working on the curtain for more than a fortnight, he asked me to stop him when, according to the demands of the stage (which he said I knew better than he did,) he had achieved the most suitable result. This I did. Diaghilev expressed his admiration to Picasso, embracing him, and thanked us for the execution of the scene."

But little of the quality of such work comes through in photographs or colour reproductions. Polunin added:

"Although this scene had been planned in accordance with the usual lighting, the changes expressive of the passing from day to night, and night to dawn, introduced by Diaghilev, proved to be exceedingly interesting. The scene, owing to the presence of some soft reddish tints, acquired the aspect of a Japanese print which, so far from impairing its beauty, endowed it with a certain unexpected charm.

"The scene proved to be well painted and was not renovated for six years. Only at a still later date, when badly damaged by rain, was it retouched with thick paint by somebody and so lost its silkiness . . . However it remains to the present day one of the most interesting scenes of the Diaghilev Company."

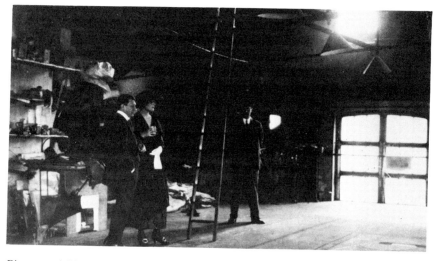

Picasso and Olga Khokhlova married in 1918, and, in 1919, came to London for him to work on *Le Tricorne*. No one could recall the address of Polunin's studio in Covent Garden, where Derain and Picasso worked on their sets with him. In 1974, Massine answered the author's query instantly. "It was just opposite the Gallery entrance of the Opera House." It was the top floor, which is now cut up into small offices, housing, amongst other departments, the Covent Garden Archives. The low ceiling and curved window style show in the snapshot of Picasso and Olga (and an unidentified companion.) The Continental method of scene painting can be observed in the picture of Polunin, *(left)*, the sketch suspended at eye-level, a long-handled broom-brush in his hand to apply the paint.

Woizikowski and Karsavina as the Miller and The Miller's Wife in *Le Tricorne*. Picasso mostly watched Polunin work, but asked to paint the stars himself. Then, for the drop-curtain, he announced his intention of doing the eyelashes, and said that he would bring his own brushes the next day. Massine said that there was much amusement when Picasso was seen in the street, approaching the studio which was accustomed to the sight of brooms in use – carrying two tooth-brushes!

Eventually the ballet was ready.

The
Sunday
Times
27.7.19
"The season of Russian Ballet at the Alhambra is coming rapidly to a close. With its disappearance, one of the few really dramatic thrills in London will go too. M. Serge de Diaghilev wears to the last moment his mantle of triumph. His latest triumph, *The Three-Cornered Hat*, hails from Spain. In conception and workmanship it rivals the other stories from Russia, Italy, France and the Orient, told with such splendour, colour and audacity in poetic motion. The music is marvellous. Tamara Karsavina, Massine, Woizikowsky, distinguished themselves and made us inarticulate with words and approval."

Observer
27.7.19
The *Sunday Times* had been struck dumb by earlier productions. The *Observer* (whilst Ernest Newman remained with it) – never so. "My respected colleague of the *Daily Telegraph*, by the way, could not understand how it gets its title. I am rejoiced," (said Newman,) "to be able to enlighten him: the ballet, like the story on which it is based, is named *The Three-Cornered Hat* because the hat is three-cornered. A careful survey of the stage will reveal this hat on the head of the Governor. Alarçon's Spanish story, of which there is an excellent French translation, (*Un Tricorne*,) is one of the very neatest workings-out of the problem of the eternal triangle. It is upon this novel that Hugo Wolf based his delicious opera, *The Corregidor*. It is not an easy subject to adapt to the stage; it is very hard to represent properly certain flittings to and fro between the Corregidor's house and the miller's house that are vital to the neat cogging of the wheels of the intrigue . . . Even with a previous knowledge of the story I found the action of the ballet a little obscure; . . . The music is full of cleverness, and is always apposite, as ballet music should be, to the gesture of the moment." (Didn't Newman ever realise that a choreographer listens to the music and fits his work to it? This was one of his constant comments, which must have amused Diaghilev at first and irritated him more and more as time went by.) "At present I am not sure that it is quite de Falla at his best; though I shall be willing to retract this opinion if a closer knowledge of it convinces me that I am wrong.

"M. Massine seems to have designed the choreography mostly for himself. It suits his own vigorous style; but I am afraid the more delicate art of Mme. Karsavina suffers in it. In some of the things she had to do" (what were they?) "she suggested to me a racehorse being set to take a coster's cart to the Derby . . . I thought the neatest piece of work in the whole thing that of M. Woizikowsky as the Corregidor. The ballet is an admirable unity so far as design is concerned; there is genius in the way the central motive of rather aggressive grotesque is carried into every detail of the dresses and the miming of the chorus. The drop scene and the background of M.

A rare photograph of the company in *Le Tricorne* – thought to have been taken on tour in Europe.

Picasso I frankly did not like; perhaps it was the gentleman with the bad squint in his calves in the drop curtain that put me out of tune at the commencement."

Le Tricorne was a great hit, and with this ballet and *La Boutique Fantasque* Massine had two remarkable successes, clearly stamped with a style totally different from that of either of his predecessors. Added to *Les Femmes de Bonne Humeur*, he had, indeed, a hat-trick. In all these ballets the classical technique was the basis of his work, but the original creators of these rôles added personal genius to mere technique. The nuances are no longer understood, and revivals never quite make the same mark.

Vogue was interested in the changed aspects of the public by now flocking to the Ballet. Speaking of the transition from Covent Garden via the Coliseum to the Alhambra, *Vogue* said: ". . . We have democratized our imperial entertainment in the way of the English who, as Falstaff noted, never have a good thing but what they must make it common. There is really something a little incongruous in the Russian Ballet serving as a popular entertainment in a country which has begun to rage against wealth and leisure." Vogue August/1 1919

Vogue had much to say about the exotic ballets in whose creation Bakst had played so large a part – "It is useless to pretend that the thousands who throng to see these ballets have the remotest idea as to what they really represent or signify. Most of them, indeed, would be deeply shocked if the pathology of *Cleopatra* or *Scheherazade* were clearly explained to them . . .

"We would like to believe that the success of these ballets at the Alhambra really meant that the public was tired of revue and eager for good music, expressive mimicry, and the decorative art of Picasso. But . . . we have heard too many enthusiasts praise the Russian Ballet who have never intelligently heard a note of good music, or visited any picture show except in Burlington House, not to realize that there is a strong element of aesthetic snobbism in the popular cult of *La Boutique Fantasque.*"

Vogue considered this ballet to be a repetition of the *Petrouchka* formula, without the emotion.

"A party of children and purchasers enter a shop and see some wonderful dolls perform. Two are bought and packed to be taken away. But these dolls are lovers, and the other dolls, when the shop is shut, set them free from their boxes. It is all wonderfully pretty and ingenious; but we are merely watching a troupe of clever dancers pretending to be dolls, and dancing with a quaint automatism. In watching *Petrouchka* we were watching the expression of the very soul of a doll, and the tragedy portrayed for us was all the more poignant because it was the result of doll loves and hates."

1919

EMPIRE THEATRE

SEPTEMBER 29th - DECEMBER 20th

FIRST PERFORMANCE IN ENGLAND

November 14: *Parade*
       (Satie, Massine, Picasso, Cocteau)
       Paris, 18.5.1917

REPERTOIRE

La Boutique Fantasque   *Petrouchka*
Le Carnaval   *Polovtsian Dances*
Children's Tales   *Scheherazade*
Cléopâtre   *Les Sylphides*
Good Humoured Ladies   *Thamar*
Midnight Sun   *The Three-Cornered Hat*
Papillons

COMPANY

Allanova, Antonova, Cecchetti, Edinska, Evina, Grabovska, Grantzeva, Grekulova, Istomina, Karsavina, Klementovitch, Kostrovskaya, Mascagno, Mikulina, Nemchinova I., Nemchinova II., Pavlovska, Petipa, Potapovitch, Radina, Savina, Slavitska, Sokolova, Tchernicheva, Wassilievska, Zalevska.

Bourman, Cecchetti, Grigoriev, Idzikowski, Jalmujinsky, Jazvinsky, Kegler, Kostecki, Kostrovsky, Kovalsky, Kremnev, Lukin, Mascagno, Massine, Novak, Okhimovsky, Pavlov, Ribas, Slavinsky, Slavitzky, Statkevitch, Stepanov, Svoboda, Vinogradov, Woizikowski, Zverev.

CONDUCTORS

Ansermet, Boult, Clark

PARADE

The Ballet was so successful that a third season was arranged, for twelve weeks at the Empire. Not even a rail strike could keep the audience away. Only one novelty was offered – the "Cubist" ballet, *Parade*. The genesis of this ballet has been treated in various books, notably Douglas Cooper's *Picasso: Theatre,* Sir Roland Penrose's *Picasso – His Life and Work,* and Francis Steegmuller's *Cocteau.* (References in this chapter are to these books.)

Brooded earlier by Cocteau, composed in Rome whilst the second American tour was in progress, *Parade* was first produced on May 18th, 1917, at the Châtelet, in Paris. It was considered witty, though there was some uproar at the fall of the curtain. It had supporters as well as detractors. Douglas Cooper pointed out that three years later it was acclaimed in Paris, those who had at first booed it having forgotten their earlier reactions – for by that time, Picasso and his Cubism were accepted.

Parade having, in the first place, been the idea of Jean Cocteau, his conception of the right artists whose style would give it the meaning he had intended, has its own importance. In his biography of Cocteau, Francis Steegmuller said that he showed, in his letters from Rome and his notebook on *Parade,* "a shrewd obsession with those aspects of Cubist painting that best lend themselves to impressive stage effects. His preferences reflect his theatrical flair. In the *Parade* notebook he wrote:

> For the Chinaman, look at Braque
> For the girl, Léger
> For the acrobat, Picasso

– indicating his choice of precisely the three Cubist painters whose work was capable of producing stage magic, a quality that could probably not be associated with the excellent Gleizes, Cocteau's 'first' Cubist. That the chosen painter had to be a Cubist was obvious; Cocteau was still working in obedience to Diaghilev's 'Astound me!' and in 1917 Cubism, though long practised by the original Cubists, was still shocking to everyone else. At various times Cocteau undertook in his writings to give graver grounds for his choice of Cubism for his 'realistic ballet.' He wrote in his notebook: 'Make the dancing realistic like Cubism, which is realistic, which always carefully plans the grouping of forms, and which seeks to render relief, volume, the texture of objects.' But it was the 'Astound me!' that underlay it all."

Francis Steegmuller continued:-

"As for his subtitling the ballet *Parade 'ballet réaliste,'* Cocteau wrote later: 'I have the habit, no doubt detestable, of using ordinary words in a sense that I attribute to them, without explaining myself. Thus I called *Parade* a 'realistic ballet' meaning by that 'Truer than true'; and to be understood I relied solely on the fact that the contrast between this ballet and other ballets, between the word 'realistic' and the unreality of the show, would be evident to the spectators.' More simply, if *Parade* can be called 'realistic' it is because unlike the earlier sumptuous ballets whose libretti were based on myth or folklore or fairy tales, Cocteau's ballet takes place in a Paris street, with street-fair characters, and quite lacks any supernatural touches *à la Petrouchka* . . .''

Brief synopses and criticisms of odd parts of a ballet leave out so much detail that, in the case of this highly original work, it seems preferable to put together the action fully – the action which was summed up in the one word of the title, *Parade*. That it was, in fact, an allegory, may occur to the reader.

Outside a fairground booth on a Paris boulevard, samples of the entertainment to be offered within are shown to tempt the crowd to buy tickets and see more: but they are not tempted – the Managers collapse – it is failure.

For the first time, Diaghilev ordered a special drop-curtain (a practice which he followed for most later ballets.) The audience, expecting something "Cubist," was taken by surprise by it.

Sir Roland Penrose described its impact on London in 1919:-

"There was a sigh of pleasure and relief . . . The curtain was a delightful composition in a style which was only indirectly cubist; it owed its inspiration rather to the popular art of the circus poster . . . The colours, mostly greens and reds, are reminiscent of the tender melancholy light in which the saltimbanques appeared ten years before. In their re-appearance they seemed less soulful . . .''

Douglas Cooper described it as "one of the tenderest and most evocative of all Picasso's circus compositions."

Not until 1972 was the wit underlying it detected. Reminiscent of the "saltimbanques" the figures were indeed – but decidedly less soulful. However, before discussing the drop curtain, the ballet itself, and its reception in London, should be considered.

Sir Roland Penrose continued his description of the ballet:-

"The delightful hopes offered by the drop curtain were to be shattered as the curtain rose. The music changed; sounds 'like an inspired village band' accompanied by the noise of dynamos, sirens, express trains, airplanes, typewriters and other outrageous dins broke on the ears of the startled audience . . . They announced, together with rhythmic stamping 'like an organised accident,' the entry of the gigantic ten-foot figures of the 'managers.' Only the legs of the performers showed beneath the towering machines built up of angular cubist agglomerations . . .

"The French manager carried at the end of a grotesquely long arm a long white pipe, while his other, real arm, pounded the stage with a heavy stick." (Could this have been a caricature of Astruc?) "The American manager, crowned with a top hat, carried a megaphone and a poster showing the word 'Parade.' Both were decked out with forms in silhouette appropriate to their native scenery: the back of the Frenchman was outlined with shapes suggesting the trees of the boulevards and the figure of the American towered up like a skyscraper." (Gatti-Casazza or John Brown? Or an amalgam?) "The third manager was a horse. Its head held high on a long wrinkled neck had the fierceness of an African mask. Two dancers inside its body pranced about the stage with perfect realism. It was not by violent colour that the audience was shocked. The backcloth was in monochrome; it represented houses in perspective with a rectangular opening like an empty frame in the centre. The costumes of the managers, including the horse, were also sombre. Among the other dancers the dazzling Chinese conjuror, with his angular movements, seemed like some brilliant insect."

Then Sir Roland went on to describe the action more fully.

"The Chinese conjuror wore a costume of brilliant yellow, orange, white and black with bold patterns symbolising a rising sun eclipsed in wreaths of smoke: his headdress in the same colours looked like flames or petals of a flower. Cocteau's directions for his miming were: 'He takes an egg out of his pigtail, eats it, finds it again on the end of his shoe, spits out fire, burns himself, stamps on the sparks, etc." Massine must have had plenty of fun working out these tricks, with a double meaning as he also made it look as if he, the performer, were a "mime" taking off a conjuror – a double *tour de force* of which few dancers would ever be capable.

"With the conjuror appeared a little girl who 'runs a race, rides a bicycle, quivers like the early movies, imitates Charlie Chaplin, chases a thief with a revolver, boxes, dances a ragtime, goes to sleep, gets shipwrecked, rolls on the grass on an April morning, takes a Kodak, etc.," continued Sir Roland. Dressed in the hated sailor-suit of schoolroom prescription of the period, this part was gaily performed first, as has been said, by Chabelska in Paris in 1917, then by Karsavina in London in 1919, and later on by Sokolova.

Sir Roland continued: "The other two dancers were acrobats; their tight-fitting costumes were decorated in blue and white with bold volutes and stars, 'simpleton, agile and poor' . . . Clothed in the melancholy of a Sunday evening circus, they danced a parody of a *Pas de deux*," (The character of the female acrobat was added whilst the ballet was in rehearsal, in order that this item could be included, and as Lopokova, who created the part, was dressing, Picasso painted his designs on her tights.)

The tragic content observed by Sir Osbert Sitwell resided in the fate of the Managers.

". . . As they stumped about the stage they complained to each other in their formidable language that the crowd was mistaking the preliminary parade for the real show . . . and for which no one had turned up. Finally their fruitless efforts brought them to a state of exhaustion and they collapsed on the stage, where they were found by the actors, who in turn also failed to entice an imaginary crowd inside . . ."

For the first performance in Paris on May 18, 1917, (when the other ballets that night were *Les Sylphides, Soleil de Nuit,* and *Petrouchka,*) the poet, Guillaume Apollinaire, had written an introduction for the Souvenir Programme, entitled *Parade et l'esprit nouveau.* – (*Parade* and the New Movement.) Apollinaire was a great friend and admirer of Picasso's.

"It described the ballet with enthusiasm and spoke of its significance in the dawn of a new era," Penrose continued. "There was hope that the new movement, which was proving that it could survive the disruption caused by the war, would soon blossom into new wonders. He claimed that the fusion of the designs of Picasso and the choreography of Massine produced a kind of '*super-réalisme*' which heralded the New Spirit." (This was the first time that these two words were assembled, two words which were, by 1920, to become one, '*Surréalisme,*' with its own special significance.) He added that 'the spectators will certainly be surprised, but in the most agreeable way, and, charmed, they will learn to understand all the grace of the modern movement of which they have no idea.'

"Apollinaire was right . . . With each production it won more respect . . . It remained a ballet for the élite and a victory in the campaign of the *avant-garde,*" added Sir Roland.

In addition to Apollinaire's famous introduction, it is interesting to note that Bakst, greatest of Diaghilev's early designers, and whose style could not possibly have differed more widely from Picasso's, also wrote a "generous introductory note" for the Souvenir Programme. "In it he praised the way in which Picasso had discovered a new branch of his art."

London's reception of the ballet was informed with curiosity.

"Satie-Picasso! At the two names in association disciples of ultra-modernity, musical and pictorial, will surely prick up their ears . . . You are to understand that the scene represents a Sunday fair in Paris . . . Various itinerant performers are giving the public a taste of their quality in order to attract them to their show. But their efforts are vain . . . The Parade has failed, and so – curtain.

"The brilliant Russians' latest incursion into the realms of bizarre fantasy carries bizarrerie to the point at which practically everything is left to the imagination. There was Picasso's simple, though defiantly unconventional, art to supply a setting that required no label . . . But the rest was of an oddity so extravagant, a conception so grotesque . . . that without the informing synopsis it would have been impossible to have made head or tail of it.

"On the musical side, the novelty piqued curiosity to no small extent. For the composer is Eric Satie, of whose eccentricities one has heard a good deal of recent years.

"As an arch Futurist – so he has been called – Satie has exhibited in several of his pieces (mostly written for the piano) a sovereign contempt for such foolish conventions as key-

Daily
Telegraph
15.11.19

Sunday
Times
16.11.19

signatures and bar-lines . . . But, whatever his gifts, Satie, to judge, at any rate, from a single hearing of *Parade*, has not found his true vocation as a composer of ballet."

Sydney Carroll thought that "this is craziness with a touch of genius. It is queer, satirical foolery, without beauty, charm or grace . . ." but conceded that "Karsavina, as the naughty American girl, has a parodic pleasantry and oddity."

Considering his pro-German-anti-French-music prejudice, Ernest Newman seems to have been almost too uninterested to bother to let himself go about *Parade*. After a second visit, and saying that if anyone but Diaghilev had put it on it would have been dismissed as music-hall or

Observer
23.11.19

pantomime stuff, he added: "Eric Satie is a feeble French joker in music, or rather in the vicinity of music, for his jokes . . . are mostly in the letter-press that accompanies his amateurish trifles . . . He fancies that he has been humorous when he sets up a couple of pages of inconsequent harmonies without bar-lines, and witty when he has printed a foolish little composition in red ink instead of black."

Newman saw some quality in the performances. "Massine as the Chinese Conjuror gives a performance such as only he could give . . . If it were anyone but Karsavina who was giving us that impersonation of a little American flapper we should say that there are dozens of music-hall performers who can do this sort of thing better, because they are more to the impudent manner born. Of course there is a curious sort of interest in seeing Karsavina at all in such a part, just as there would be in seeing Mr. Asquith as Charlie Chaplin; but the interest is simply the fleeting one of incongruity."

Was Osbert Sitwell the only person to see *Parade* as either tragic or original?

Surely *Parade* was, perhaps more than any other ballet, allegorical. The allegory is in the fate of the managers. Man proposes, God disposes.

The setting against which the performance took place was a Cubist's vision of a Parisian boulevard, the colours soft and luminous, as in the light of early evening. Huge buildings studded with the blackness of rows of stark, plain oblong windows tilted their anonymous façades over a gracious parapet. The proscenium of a fairground booth looked like a child's toy theatre of a different age, tilted in the centre, with thick barley-sugar twist columns and a lyre on the centre of the pediment. There was nothing in the colour to shock. It was entirely a matter of the style. One should imagine oneself to be sitting in the auditorium, watching Bakst's lavish sets for *Scheherazade* or *Cléopâtre*, or his delicate Biedermeier bedroom for *Le Spectre*, or Benois's romantic setting for *Les Sylphides*, to be able to pretend to react with shock to this composition. And so it is time to return to the drop-curtain.

Everyone just accepts the fact that this was "non-Cubist." Has anyone ever asked himself – why?

Faced with a mystery, the detective of fiction arrays the evidence under the headings of Means, Motive, and Opportunity. In this case, there is but one suspect – Picasso. For Means – put the offer of a vast canvas; for Motive – theatrical, artistic, and self-expression – release from the tyranny of the Cubists' code – and for Opportunity, his first visit to Italy, perennial inspiration of artists, with fresh impressions crowding in on him every moment, and the stimulating company of a new group of brilliant friends.

The present writer pleads guilty to having been diverted from her curiosity by the weight of expertise already devoted to the *Parade* curtain. Yet it remained tantalising. Setting out the evidence showed up the gaps. Thinking, "What would they have been doing then?" suggested possible areas for enquiry. Feeling the atmosphere led to a hunt – and the hunt to a source.

When Stravinsky said that "Diaghilev knew how to create about him amazing activity and an artistic atmosphere that was like an electric current which stimulated all his associates into work, sharpened their fantasy . . ." and spoke of "that perpetually boiling cauldron of work," and of its "irresistible charm," one period of which he must have been thinking nostalgically would have been that winter when the base-camp was in Italy. Dates are nebulous, but from those which are clear, a skeletal chronology is put together on Page 242. The most important points to emerge are that Diaghilev made numerous trips to Paris, that there were two visits to Naples, not one, and that the scene-painter Socrate came to work for them in Rome, temporarily deserting his Paris studio.

The disparity of style between the Cubist set and the primitive perspective of the drop-curtain *had* to stem from some change of inspiration. The whole point of having a drop-curtain was to prepare the audience by setting the style. One may imagine that Picasso had proposed something on the lines of his sketch of a Paris skyline – (No. 97 in *Picasso: Theatre,* shown with two preliminary sketches for the set, Nos. 99 and 100.) Why should this view from the studio he left be included here unless it had had some theatrical purpose? It would be logical to precede a Paris boulevard with a characteristic view of the city. *Something* changed this: something different inspired Picasso. Cocteau later said of him, "He's a rag-and-bone man of genius, a king of rag-and-bone men . . . He doesn't only pick up unusual objects with his hands but with his eyes too; they notice the slightest thing, and if you study his work carefully you can always recognise the district where he was living when he painted this or that picture, for you can see the elements that inattentive people don't notice: drawings chalked on pavements, shop-windows, posters, lamp-posts spattered with plaster, treasure from dustbins . . ." The treasure which Picasso used as a crib for the *Parade* curtain can be pinpointed, but it did not come from a dustbin.

My Contemporaries Jean Cocteau (Ed. Margaret Crosland)

In any city, Diaghilev's first port of call would be its opera house or principal theatre. Looking at the *Parade* drop-curtain, one sees masses of huge draped crimson stage curtains, edged with gold bullion fringe, and, instead of the sawdust of the circus ring, the floorboards of a stage. The background is not a view – it is stage scenery, foothills leading to Mount Vesuvius. The "ruins" are stage props, inelegantly lying about between performances. (The wooden chest, on which the Neapolitan Sailor sits, and the "beauty" kneels, bears a remarkable resemblance to the stout wooden chests, $3 \times 5 \times 3$ feet, in which the Diaghilev impedimenta was packed. Several large backcloths, on thin canvas, could travel in a single box, said Polunin.) The group is, in fact, on the stage of a deserted theatre. So next comes the question – what theatre? Well, what theatres were they frequenting? In Rome, the Costanzi; and in Naples, the San Carlo.

Rebuilt in 1817, the San Carlo boasts a permanent painted *"sipario"* – a drop-curtain. Commissioned in 1854 from Giuseppe Mancinelli, surrounded by crimson velvet curtains and draped pelmets, bordered with gold bullion fringe, it spans the proscenium in a vast classical composition showing Mount Parnassus against a blue sky, with Apollo presenting to the Muses the great of Arts and Letters throughout the ages, including Homer, Petrarch, Giotto, Donatello, Machiavelli, Boccaccio, Sappho, and many others. Forty figures in all easily find places in its harmonious scheme. The comparison with the colleagues of the Diaghilev Ballet must have been obvious. (Who knows – possibly the faces in Mancinelli's *sipario* are those of the colleagues of his age?) In addition, the Royal Box, which projects over the centre of the auditorium from the grand balcony, is heavily be-swagged with crimson draperies too. Standing in it, these frame the *sipario* on the distant stage.

The five men who went down to Naples to spend the lull before the arrival of the American contingent (which could not possibly reach Rome before March 20th,) were Diaghilev, Massine, Picasso, Cocteau, and Stravinsky. They all adored Naples. "The Pope is in Rome, but God is in Naples," said Cocteau. They went to Pompeii and all the museums, and haunted the print-shops, and Picasso, in particular, became a devotee of the great Aquarium.

Putting oneself and one's friends into pictures has long been a self-indulgence of artists. Grouping them convivially round a table is a common device. In 1972, Dr. Marianne Martin, Professor of Fine Arts at The New York University and author of *Futurist Art and Theory, 1909-15,* (Clarendon Press, 1968,) was working on a lecture on *Picasso and Futurism.* Scrutinizing a reproduction of the *Parade* drop curtain, she noticed a distinct resemblance between the Clown and Jean Cocteau – as Picasso frequently drew him at that period. Once started off, all but one of the identities came to her quickly. Picasso had indeed done "naughty things," and not only with the personnel, but also with the setting. Dr. Martin realised that he had profited from his visit to the famous Aquarium in Naples to lift the composition for the drop-curtain from a fresco known as "Friends in a Pergola" – one of a series executed in 1873 by Hans von Mareés – merely turning left and right about, and inventively letting Vesuvius be seen through the ruined arch. As for the *Forains,* they were, indeed, less soulful than the saltimbanques of his earlier period.

Dr. Martin spotted most of the identities. The present writer spotted the fun.

Cocteau had been mad about clowns all his life; for him to don their clothes would be to enter, briefly, their world. And what fancy-dress party is complete without its Clown?

Whilst they were in Rome, Cocteau and the seventeen-year-old dancer, Marie Chabelska (who was to be The American Girl in this ballet,) had been running a mock-flirtation. The joke had been fostered by the entire company. So Chabelska snuggled drowsily against the Clown's breast.

Stravinsky (tiny of stature, gigantic in genius,) towered now over the others, converted into the Blackamoor of his own Petrouchka. (The face may be compared with No. 272 in *Picasso: Theatre.*) Since, in profile, his nose would have given the game away, he was shown full-face, only the eyes and mouth betraying him.

Ever mindful of his nationality, Picasso dressed himself up as a *torero* – of course, also a virtuoso on the guitar! There are his beady eyes and stubby nose, and his square-shaped cranium. (In a letter to Stravinsky from Paris in August, 1916, Cocteau had referred to Picasso as "sentimental mandolinist and fierce picador." Surely this must have been brought out in laughter when they were all together?)

In Rome, Picasso, recovering from the death of Eva, had been busily falling in love with one of Diaghilev's dancers, the elegant Olga Khokhlova, of the auburn hair and large chapeaux; and so, being in Italy, he idealized her as a Botticelli-like beauty, with rippling, lighter red-gold hair – his *Primavera,* in a huge Italian straw hat. (For good measure, he gave her also her pearl choker.) The guitarist's serenade might, indeed, be intended solely for her.

The Harlequin is Massine, (of whom Douglas Cooper shows an identified and dated drawing in the identical costume, treading similar floorboards, No. 123.) His nose is here drawn a bit longer than it actually was, but in the sketches, Nos. 114 and 117, the nose is short.)

The Bare-back Rider, (whom Dr. Martin could not identify,) was Lopokova. Funnily enough, the photograph of Lopokova which caught her at the same facial angle is one of those taken in America, and found in the archives of the Metropolitan Opera House. Picasso has transformed the wings of a Sylphide into those of a baroque cherub – perhaps to symbolize her elevation. (Her presence in the curtain and the published sketches – which may not have been the first – show that the composition was not completed until the return to Rome.)

Best and biggest joke of all was the transformation of Diaghilev into a Neapolitan sailor. Diaghilev's famous terror of the sea had kept him on his knees to and fro across the Atlantic, (except when he had deputed his valet to do the praying, at mealtimes; but, according to Ansermet, when they had completed the earlier voyages, and Diaghilev stepped on to solid earth, he had gone down on his knees and prostrated himself completely, in the Orthodox manner, touching the ground with his forehead in thankfulness.) Wittiest of all, then, was this crack. In addition, Picasso gave him the curled and waxed moustachios of Marinetti, leader of those very Futurists whose art he despised and disliked, though he was friendly with them as people.

(Indeed, Depero was instructed to make three costumes for his ballet for 400 lire. These were probably "The Constructions." He had been told by Diaghilev to stop work on *Le Chant du Rossignol,* but, in compensation, given this order, and Bucci an order for about 40 costumes for 1500 – 2000 lire. This information comes from Futurist papers, published in Turin in 1970.)

Dr. Martin described her identifications in lectures given at the Courtauld Institute in London, and at the Futurist Exhibition in Newcastle-on-Tyne, in November, 1972. Once she had spotted it, it was all so simple that one can only wonder why no one had noticed it before. The present writer may, perhaps, be allowed to mention that she had thought the faces "too real" to be mere decoration, even when looking at them in a rather poor reproduction. She had asked an authority whether anyone knew who the people were supposed to be, but had been told that they were just some troupe of circus people. As the clothes have little place in a circus, it still seemed an unlikely solution. About six weeks later, she met Dr. Martin, who explained her discovery. Shortly after this, the author asked Madame Sokolova, who, at first, dismissed it in the same way. However, two days later, Madame Sokolova telephoned saying that it had all come back to her, and that, in fact, everyone had been amused at the time by the caricatures, but that the ballet was given so rarely that this feature had simply gone out of the thoughts of the company. Being backstage, the dancers barely saw the drop-curtain themselves.

By 1917, Diaghilev's company might well be described as *"Forains"* – travelling entertainers. Their massive tours in the United States made them deserve the soubriquet. They were not, however, *circus* people in the group in the curtain. What Picasso turned his friends into, was people dressed up – dressed as for Carnival. What circus includes a blackamoor, a Spaniard with a guitar, a Harlequin from the Commedia dell'Arte, a sailor who looks as if about to dance a hornpipe, and a lady of fashion shading her complexion with a sun-hat, and wearing a pearl choker (frequently photographed, though not in the picture shown for comparison.) One clown does not make a circus, even with the aid of one bare-back rider and a mare and foal. Rather is the spirit Neapolitan – that of Carnival – and delightful.

Picasso is alleged not to have shown the influence of this trip until the early 'twenties, when he painted massive women. In fact, he obviously couldn't wait to get to work – pushed the painting of the set aside when they returned to Rome, and set to work on this with Socrate and the Italian assistants. (When, in 1919, Polunin was asked to look over the scenery and drop-curtain for the London performance, Picasso complained to him that the set had been very badly painted in a rush in Paris, and that the paint had come off on the dancers' costumes.) He turned to the lack of perspective of the Primitives, and to the heads at a twisted angle of so many early Italian paintings – but, as usual, he transmuted it all into something completely his own.

Unquestionably, Picasso's genius dominated the production. It did, indeed, mark the advent of a new outlook in scenic design. Massine's choreography matched it, and when, in 1919, Karsavina performed in it, she brought in her own sense of fun. But, writing about it years later, Karsavina herself said of this work: "As always, Massine was consummately ingenious, but *Parade* projected so far into the topical as to strip it of ballet's essential virtue – its own creative material. It came nearer to an imitative art. I had the part of an American flapper, filmstruck, imitating Charlie Chaplin and thriller stunts. I enjoyed the part as it was tremendous fun."

But for Karsavina, Diaghilev's outlook seemed ominous so far as her own career was concerned. "*Parade* sounded the alarm, and what I knew of Diaghilev's plans for future productions gave me very little hope. And then appeared a caricature by Dulac. It represented me as a puppet, wound by a cubistic manager. The caption read: 'The wrong turn.' Dulac wrote to me, begging me not to take offence; the caricature was meant as a protest against using an artist in a way derogatory to her talent . . . Dancing Times February 1967

"I steeled myself for the breakaway, fearing that my classical training might go by default. Diaghilev came to discuss the matter with me. The sting of this meeting has never completely left me – not that either of us got cross, as in some tiffs we had had before. Those would be followed by reconciliation and celebration, with a good seasoning of tears and embraces. This time the issue was not personal. From what he told me, I understood that to build a production round an individual dancer was, in his opinion, a hazardous policy; that at the present time, classicism would shackle ballet from contemporary trends. He sweetened the pill by saying, "No one could fill your place in what has been and what could be achieved by progressive ballet.

"We came to a compromise. I was to give him some stated periods of service and to the end I remained his guest dancer."

The upshot of this discussion was to encourage Karsavina to conduct her own seasons, with a small company at the Coliseum, and with a partner on extensive tours.

She continued to perform her old parts in that current season, and it was noted that "the steady crescendo of beauty and intellectual power that has been noticeable in Karsavina's dancing as she recovered her health came to a climax in her miming of the part of Ta-Hor . . . She filled the part with the nervous intensity that is the secret of her genius, an intensity that, and as is always the case with great artists, fills not only her speeches, as it were, but her silences." Observer 26.10.19

In November, the *Sunday Times* reported that "But four weeks remain of the delightful season of Russian Ballet at the Empire, and then the vast site on the north side of Leicester Square is committed to surely the most ambitious scheme of pleasure palace building involving probably a million, and certainly many months, ever undertaken." Sunday Times 23.11.19

PARADE - A CHRONOLOGY

1915 - 1916
Cocteau's idea to create ballet about fairground entertainers. Diaghilev (D.)
interested, not committed. Ballet to be "Cubist" – *dernier cri*. Cocteau (C.) and
Satie worked together on *Parade*.
Picasso's mistress, Eva, died Jan. 1916. Picasso (P.) depressed. About May, 1916,
D. and P. met. D. possibly visited P. in Rue Schoelcher.

AUGUST 1916.
D. and P. met again, D. liked ideas. C. persuaded P. to design *Parade*. P. worked
well with Satie, brought fresh ideas (better.) C. accepted them.

OCTOBER 1916
D. in Paris, P. moved to Montrouge.

DECEMBER 1916
Stravinsky (S.) ill in Switzerland. D. visited him, suggested S. conduct own works
in Rome in spring.

JANUARY 1917
D. again saw P., must have approved rough sketches and model of set.
Jan. 9th. P. wrote letter to D. stating terms as they had agreed them, 5,000 francs to
design curtain, set and costumes, plus 1000 if he went to Rome. Letter looks as if
written at D.'s behest, to be shown to potential backers.

FEBRUARY 17, 1917
P. and C. left Paris for Rome, joining D., Massine, Bakst at Hôtel de Russie.
Joined there by S. Worked hard for 2 weeks, completed designs for costumes and
set. Italian costumiers at work on new ballets: Socrate came from Paris, date not
shown, to paint Bakst scenery. (Ref. *Giornale d'Italia,* April 14th). Company could
not arrive from U.S. until about March 20th. D. took Massine, P., C., and S. to
Naples. March 10th, P. sent postcard from Naples to Gertrude Stein. S. said he
spent two weeks in Naples.

MARCH - APRIL 1917
Returned to Rome around March 20th. Rehearsals and scene-painting both in
great hall of Palazzo. P. must have said painting of set could wait, and started on
drop-curtain instead. Photo w. Socrate and Italian-faced assistants sitting on it,
part done. Marie Chabelska remembers walking on it in Rome. (Dr. Martin.)
Bakst troubled. Socrate's time spent on P.'s drop-curtain. P. "helped Bakst out" by
painting props for *Femmes de Bonne Humeur* for him. (Massine told Author.)
Ansermet said Sert also in Rome, his ballet's scenery being painted or altered by
Socrate.

APRIL 1917
P. wrote to Gertrude Stein from Rome: before performances started, as no mention
of them. Obviously great friends with dancers: had been given Chinese things
bought in San Francisco – possibly by Lopokova. Décors to be painted in Rome.

LOPOKOVA

ROME, COSTANZI THEATRE
Tues., April 10.	*Sylphides, Firebird, Las Meniñas, Midnight Sun.*
Thurs., April 12.	GALA – *Firebird, Femmes de Bonne Humeur (Première,) Petrouchka* (Suite of music only,) *Fireworks, Prince Igor.* Stravinsky conducted own works.
Mon., April 16.	5 p.m., popular prices: *Sylphides, Femmes de Bonne Humeur, Las Meniñas, Firebird.*

NAPLES, TEATRO SAN CARLO
Wed., April 18.	*Sylphides, Firebird, Las Meniñas, Midnight Sun.*
Sat., April 21.	*Sylphides, Firebird, Femmes de Bonne Humeur.*
Sun. April 22.	Performance (ballets not listed.) Series curtailed.

FLORENCE, GARDEN OF VILLA LA PIETRA
Mon. April 30.	One performance, ballets not listed.

MAY 1917
Rehearsals in Paris. Set for *Parade* painted, hurriedly; possibly because drop-curtain
being finished first.

PARIS, CHÂTELET THEATRE.
Fri. May 11.	CHARITY MATINEE – *Les Femmes de Bonne Humeur,* (first Paris performance,) and *Contes Russes (première,) Firebird, Prince Igor.*
Fri. May 18.	*Parade (première,) Les Sylphides, Midnight Sun, Petrouchka.*

The faces in the Picasso curtain above may be compared with the corresponding portraits beneath. On the left, the fresco, "Friends in a Pergola," in the Aquarium in Naples, may be compared with a reversed version, with the main features of the composition outlined.

STRAVINSKY

KHOKHLOVA

COCTEAU

PICASSO

DIAGHILEV

MASSINE

M. CHABELSKA

(*left*) The auditorium of the San Carlo, in Naples, with the "*sipario*" painted by Mancinelli in 1854, and (*below*) the whole of Picasso's drop-curtain, showing clearly that the group is on a stage. The crude drawing of the figures is reminiscent of decoration in popular theatres in Naples.

(*right*) Edmund Dulac's cartoon of Massine appeared in the weekly publication, *OUTLOOK*, in November 1919. Karsavina was his subject after her success in "*The Truth About The Russian Dancers*" in 1920. Dulac's title is not quite as apt as her own version of it! Both were exhibited at the Leicester Galleries in June, 1920, at the same time as the show of Laura Knight's sketches of the Diaghilev Ballet.

Apparently there was no pictorial record of the colour of Picasso's 1917 set for *Parade*. When the Joffrey Ballet wished to revive the work in 1973, Edward Burbridge copied the drop-curtain, and made a "realisation" of the set from a photograph in monochrome. (*Picasso: Theatre*, no. 428.) He repeated both for London Festival Ballet in 1974.

To his vision of the window-studded facades of apartment blocks such as are to be found in Paris from end to end of the Nord-Sud Picasso had added the fruits of his Italian journey in the architecturally monstrous joke of the proscenium of the booth, and an Italianate balustrade. In preliminary sketches—presumably those shown to Diaghilev in Paris—the buildings totter at alarming angles, the proscenium is edged with scallops as if cut out of card, the volutes of the pediment are without the focal lyre—and there is no balustrade at all. (*Picasso: Theatre*, Nos. 99 and 100.)

Whereas the drop-curtain stands out as a single item in theatrical design, the set, so revolutionary then, but which no longer shocks, was an innovation which has had many successors, and was more important in terms of theatrical history. (Photo courtesy London Festival Ballet.)

AN ATTACK OF CUBO-VORTICITIS.
(M. Leonide Massine.)
SOME HOPES OF RECOVERY.

"THE TRUTH ABOUT THE RUSSIAN BALLET."
(Madame Tamara Karsavina.)
THE WRONG TURNING.

1920

ROYAL OPERA, COVENT GARDEN

JUNE 10th - JULY 30th

FIRST PERFORMANCES IN ENGLAND

June 10th: *Pulcinella*
(Pergolesi/Stravinsky, Massine, Picasso)
Paris 15.5.1920

June 22nd: *Le Astuzie Femminili* (Opera-Ballet)
(Cimarosa/Respighi, Massine, Sert.)
Paris 27.5.1920

July 16th: *Le Chant du Rossignol*
(Stravinsky, Massine, Matisse.)
Paris 2.2.1920

REPERTOIRE

La Boutique Fantasque	*Midnight Sun*	*Les Sylphides*
Le Carnaval	*Papillons*	*Thamar*
Contes Russes	*Polovtsian Dances*	*Le Tricorne*
Good-Humoured Ladies	*Scheherazade*	

COMPANY

Allanova, Antonova, Bewicke, Boni, Cecchetti J., Edinska, Evina, Forestier, Grabovska, Grantzeva, Grekulova, Karsavina, Klementovitch, Komarova, Mascagno, Matrunina, Mikulina, Nemchinova I., Nemchinova II., Pavlovska, Savina, Slavinska, Slavitska, Sokolova, Tchernicheva, Wassilievska, Zalevska.

Addison, Bourman, Cecchetti, Grigoriev, Idzikowski, Jalmujinsky, Jazvinsky, Kegler, Kostecki, Kremnev, Lukin, Mascagno, Massine, Mikolaitchik, Novak, Okhimovsky, Pavlov, Ribas, Slavinsky, Statkevitch, Stepanov, Woizikowski, Zverev.

CONDUCTORS:

Ansermet, Morin.

AUTUMN PROVINCIAL TOUR

Bournemouth:	November 3-6	Leeds:	November 13
Leicester:	November 9-10	Liverpool:	November 15-27
Nottingham:	November 11	Birmingham:	November 29,30,
Sheffield:	November 12		and December 1.

CONDUCTOR:

Edward Clark.

RETURN TO COVENT GARDEN

The ballet left London for Paris, where, to Diaghilev's great delight, it had been booked for a series of forty performances at the *Opéra*. In spite of an orchestra strike, work continued on the new ballets which were to be given in Paris, and which London was to see when, on June 20th, 1920, it opened once more at Covent Garden itself. The first night was a "special," according to *The Lady*. " . . . They had a perfectly splendid reception – in fact, quite an ovation – and were called for again and again as the curtain fell. Covent Garden was packed from floor to ceiling, and I was not surprised to hear that there was not a vacant seat anywhere." That night, Massine added another to his string of successes – *Pulcinella*.

The
Lady
17.6.20

Richard Capell was back and rejoiced:-

"This is a company less of entertainers than of artists, whose choice is less the exploiting of old triumphs than the chase of the new idea. Nine years ago the acme of grace and harmony was already reached. *Pulcinella* is different. It is a comic view of the human puppet show. It looks through the spectacles of the 18th century's dry fun and crackling wit. It is related to the Venetian piece, *The Good-Humoured Ladies*. But these inexhaustible folks have invented a fresh sauce. The 20th Century has ingeniously added a little more than occurred to the 18th, just as Stravinsky's music carries on suggestions started by themes of Pergolesi."

Daily
Mail
11.6.20

Picasso had designed a set which, as Cyril Beaumont said, " . . . a cubist study in black, blue-grey, and white, admirably conveyed with a remarkable economy of means a moonlit street overlooking the Bay of Naples."

Richard Capell gave the essence of the story: All the girls love Pulcinella, alike the fine young ladies (Tchernicheva and Nemchinova,) and the charming contadina (Mme. Karsavina.) Why? Pulcinella (M. Massine) is simply a masked pierrot, in a pierrot's baggy garb. The young women's sweethearts cannot explain it. What fellow could? The fact remains, in 1720 or 1920, when a Pulcinella comes along he always gets his own way.

"The fellows of 1720 decided that a quick end by a rapier was best for Pulcinella. He falls; and while the women mourn, the plain man thinks that now his turn may come. But Pulcinella is of course not really dead. And the curtain comes down on the rejoicings over his resurrection – rejoicings, that is, on the part of everyone but the plain man.

"There is the idea, and a multitude of details garnishes it. M. Massine expresses a rich rogue in spite of the mask on his face. Mme. Karsavina, the country lass, is allowed the one natural touch in the puppet comedy. As for the music, an impossible project has somehow been carried out. Sometimes it is old Pergolesi plainly enough and sometimes M. Stravinsky undisguised, but M. Stravinsky may well defy us to say where one begins exactly and another ends."

Criticisms of Stravinsky's work might defy Richard Capell – but not, of course, Ernest Newman. Receiving an offer of a higher salary from the *Sunday Times*, he had written earlier in

Sunday
Times
13.6.20

247

the year to J.L. Garvin and asked leave to withdraw from the *Observer*. The transfer was made for what his widow described as "a delightful season for E.N.'s début with the *Sunday Times*." (This Grand Season for ten weeks at Covent Garden had opened with opera. Of that, E.N. wrote: "Anything, we said, would be better than this eternal Puccini idiom, of which we have really had so much lately that I, for one, do not want to hear any of these operas again for a couple of years.")

He was relatively brief about *Pulcinella*; "I prefer to wait until I hear the new Diaghilev ballet *Pulcinella* again before I attempt to discuss it at any length. It is difficult at a first performance of an unknown work of this sort to concentrate on both the choreography and the music." (A sensible point.) ". . . Purists will tell us that Stravinsky has no right to re-make Pergolesi in his image. It may be so; but as we cannot prevent him, the only thing to do is to see how well he has done it, and accept it if it is done well.

"The case for or against the re-arrangement of old music is different from that for or against the re-touching of old pictures. To paint over a picture is to destroy the original for all time; but a hundred re-touchings of a piece of old music leave the original as accessible as it was before. . . . We enjoy the parodist in art; why should we not enjoy the semi-parodist that Stravinsky is here – the later worker who is not maliciously bent on guying the original, but only on giving it certain humorous turns that the music will bear quite well . . . Pergolesi and Stravinsky, of course, do not mix. Perhaps that is just the secret of the charm of this music. We are never taken in; the smile on Stravinsky's face puts any thought of injury to Pergolesi out of the question. It all seems pure *gaminerie* on Stravinsky's part; but as *gaminerie* it is mostly first-rate."

The *Observer*, where Percy Scholes succeeded him as Music Critic, did not sign its review that day. "That Stravinsky's adaptation and re-scoring of Pergolesi is not carried out in the spirit of self-effacement goes without saying. But somehow the lapses from Italian melodious purity into unadulterated Stravinsky do not jar, as Massine's wonderful choreography follows the changes with such understanding that the dancers – the perfect ensemble – seem to take the lead, and the orchestra merely to follow their spontaneous movements. The whole ballet-opera is as bizarre as the intersecting houses and sky-planes of Picasso's scenery. The opportunities given to the dancers are unique. And yet *Pulcinella*, whilst given a warm reception, failed to arouse the storm of applause like that which burst forth when the curtain descended on *Contes Russes*."

The *Sunday Times* continued, "There can be no doubt that the atmosphere of Covent Garden is particularly congenial to the Russian dancers . . . Somehow they are animated by quite a different spirit which gives new life and sparkle to things that had become almost stale and flat . . . Very remarkable is Roerich's new setting for *Prince Igor*, which obtains a degree of barbaric splendour thoroughly in keeping with the wild strains and turbulent movement maintained throughout the whole ballet. The drop scene is a triumph of decorative painting applied to stage purposes."

Just before the next new production, Diaghilev gave an interview which explained it. "The opera-ballet we are going to give is *Le Astuzie Femminili*, which may be translated freely as *The Wiles of Women*. It had its origin in the composer's experiences in Russia. In the year of the French Revolution, 1789, Cimarosa went to St. Petersburg and took the place of his country-man Paisiello as director of the Italian theatre. He conducted there for three years, composing much music during that time, and seeing many things, amongst which may be included the Russian peasant dances.

"It was on his way back to Italy in 1792 that he produced *The Secret Marriage*. Two years later, in Naples, he brought out the opera we are going to produce at Covent Garden. It is a typical comic opera of the eighteenth century, in three acts. There is the usual kind of intrigue, and the vocal numbers, which are in the style of the period, include a love duet and a laughing trio.

"The story winds up with a wedding, and when it is a question of celebrating the wedding the last line of the libretto is, 'And now let us have a Russian ballet.'

"To me, already head over heels in love with the eighteenth century Italian music, this final appeal was irresistible. I have put in this ballet at the point at which the libretto indicates it, and have supplied in the second act other dances that are required. Where Cimarosa goes on with

Observer
13.6.20

Observer
20.6.20

Igor Stravinsky,
by Robert Delaunay.

the wedding music he makes use of a tune called 'Kamarinskaya,' a dance which no doubt he saw the peasants dance at weddings in Russia. Forty years later Glinka, the father of modern Russian music, used the same tune for an orchestral fantasy which is looked upon as the starting-point of the modern Russian school.

"The first scene is an eighteenth century interior, influenced by the Chinese importations which one met with in palaces such as Aranjuez. The second is a colonnade in a garden. A tree in the centre looks like a tree of coral and has been much discussed. The third scene, in which the ballet takes place, is a broad terrace with a panoramic view of Rome. The costumes are a trifle ahead of the date, being those of the opening year of the nineteenth century.

"And this leads me to tell you another reason that impelled me to produce this work. I am of the opinion that the principles of choreography are equally applicable to the action in opera, and I wanted to put this theory to the test and show how it could be done. So the action in this opera has been invented and directed by M. Massine.

"When the singers were called together for the first rehearsal, I told them that, whilst every singer naturally knows how to sing well, none in all their experience ever learned to make good movements.

"In order, in fact, to get really beautiful movements it is necessary to study them for about ten years, but as there was no time for that they were instructed to make as little movement as they could. If the characters have to fight a duel they of course fight it; if they have to make love they make love; but all superfluous gesture is cut out . . . At first, when this idea was put them, the singers were a little at sea. It meant setting aside part of the very training which a certain kind of operatic artist receives. But with youth and enthusiasm on their side they soon accommodated themselves to the new idea."

The *Observer* continued, "M. Diaghilev's library contains every work that has been printed by Cimarosa, Paisiello and Pergolesi. Whilst collecting it he found an orchestral score by Cimarosa called *L'Italienne à Londres*, the scene of which is laid in London, 'in the café of Miss Fanni.' Cimarosa, it seems, intended to come to London, but being prevented by illness, wrote instead this '*opéra bouffon en trois actes.*' 'Some day,' said M. Diaghilev, 'I hope to produce it in London.' "

This recalls an amusing episode related by Vera Newman. Once, in Paris, E.N. had instructed her to seek out Cimarosa scores, which he was collecting. She found nothing, and later in the day the Newmans bumped into Diaghilev, who laughed heartily, telling them that he had already bought up every single score of Cimarosa in Paris.

Morning
Post
23.6.20

Astuzie was a tremendous success. The *Morning Post* said, "The music is of extraordinary freshness. Its melodic contour is original and attractive and the style has immense individuality. The dances reveal M. Massine, their designer, in a most imaginative mood, in which he completely matches the fertile inventiveness of the deviser of the wonderful dresses. The Tarantelle and the *pas de deux* between Mme. Karsavina and M. Idzikowski take their places as part in a whole that constitutes an artistic triumph. The production was received with emphatic approval, well indicating that M. Diaghilev has discovered the real way to make masterpieces of the past acceptable to the present-day public."

Daily
Mail
23.6.20

Richard Capell gave the story: "The opera tells of a rich heiress, the rich merchant her guardian would have her wed, and the young tenor whom by woman's wiles she wins. She and this lover evade their elders in Carnival time in Cossack disguise, and this disguise gives to Cimarosa an excuse for the introduction of Russian dance tunes – and to the Russians an excuse (if they needed one) for handling Cimarosa. They have handled him freely – abridged him, re-scored and transposed – but he triumphed, so his ghost should rest well content. Next to the triumph of this exquisitely neat and sparkling music comes that of the 'production,' which gave us opera singers in a frame, so to speak; not merely singing, but looking and moving beautifully in their parts."

Percy Scholes was not so convinced.

Observer
27.6.20

"What was it that made the advent of the Russian Ballet so great an event?" he apostrophised. "Not, surely, the exhibition of a technique polished to the last gleam, but the use of that technique with a really artistic purpose. Taglioni, we may assume, had technique of the highest kind, but a Taglioni ballet must have been very different from, and artistically very inferior to, what the Russians have shown us. Briefly, the Russians have made of the ballet an expressive art; they have given us not merely beautiful movements but emotions. Now I may be quite wrong, but I think I see a hardening and conventionalising process at work which will some day destroy the art and call for some reformer to build it up afresh . . .

"I know it is difficult to look at things with a fresh eye, but try next time you go to Covent Garden to imagine that you had never before seen a ballet and ask yourself whether everything you see satisfies either your sense of beauty, on the one hand, or your desire for emotional expression on the other.

". . . Leaving generalisations and coming now to *Le Astuzie Femminili*, in particular, I think I see in this evidence of the artistic thoughtlessness which lies behind such defects as I have mentioned. Take the scenery, for instance. In that first scene really of artistic value? In it the designer, Sert, has for some reason elected to depict on one flat canvas, floor, ceiling, and three sides of a room – (five surfaces in all,) and has done it in such a way that the whole thing is grossly out of perspective. The floor slopes, the ceiling slopes, the whole thing looks wrong. What is the point? Of course, it is quaint – but is quaintness a sufficient excuse? The scenery of *La Boutique Fantasque* is quaint, but it is also satisfying. Merely to be quaint or outrageous is in itself surely nothing. Things artistic must be either expressive or beautiful or their existence is unjustified . . . What I cannot understand is deliberately ugly and anti-realistic scenery which keeps the mind occupied all the time in putting its perspective straight and re-arranging its clashing colours so that they may not hurt the eye so horribly."

Scholes then referred to Diaghilev's interview the previous week, and his idea that choreographic design should be used in producing opera. "Observe the broad generalisation. Not

"CIMAROSIANA"

LEO.P DOWD.

"And now let us have a Russian ballet!" The wedding-guests assembled on a lovely terrace overlooking the panorama of Rome's skyline – by moonlight – with lights seemingly twinkling in the windows far away, for tiny apertures had been cut in the back-cloth, as in eighteenth-century prints which could give day and night effects in magic lanterns. Dressed in their best – (in full-dress uniform, or in the long frock-coats and top hats of the early nineteenth century – the ladies in gowns already losing the high-waisted Empire look) – they were entertained with the divertissement which was given alone, after that first year, re-christened *Cimarosiana*. This "Artist's Impression" by Leo Dowd shows Vera Nemchinova and Stanislas Idzikowski in the *pas de deux*. The details show more clearly than in the photographs – including even the "Wedgwood" plaques decorating the male dancer's costume.

merely this piece, but opera in general is affected. No longer is opera to be drama set to music, (or, better, permeated by music;) it is to become merely a branch of the art of ballet . . . These Russians have a ballet obsession. They are forever sacrificing some other art to ballet . . ."

Scholes added, ". . . the little band of six '*artistes du chant*' (what a mixture of languages they give us on a Covent Garden programme!) is excellent. You imprison them in a new convention, and they sing as well as ever – like caged skylarks!"

What mysterious grapevine conveyed the attitude about to be struck by the critic of one leading Sunday paper to his opposite number on the other, so that his stance would be diametrically opposite? Ernest Newman gave *Astuzie* a "rave" notice: hard ever to find another as enthusiastic from his pen. "Since *La Boutique Fantasque*, M. Diaghilev has given us nothing for which we have so much reason to be grateful to him for as *Le Astuzie Femminili*. I hear that some of my colleagues have been a trifle condescending-like towards it. For my own part, I have enjoyed nothing so much for a long time in the theatre. Sunday Times 27.6.20

"There must be a good deal of eighteenth-century light opera that is worth reviving, (Mozart by no means exhausted the vein), and apparently it is to M. Diaghilev that we must look for the revivals, for only he, with his thorough methods of preparation, and his equal understanding of all the elements of a production, can deprive us of any excuse for condescension towards these old works. This rippling, sparkling music should be the delight of the town. The new principles of gesture and movement that Massine has gone upon for the opera singers deserve more detailed consideration than I can give them today: briefly, no gesture is made that is not necessary and pertinent. The acting thus wins a curious and paradoxical repose as well as animation. Massine's ballet (that follows the opera) is one of the most beautiful creations of the extraordinary young genius; it has the quiet harmony that one or two of his later inventions, brilliant as they have been, have lacked."

Dancing
Times
February
1967

Dressed like a pair of Jacob Petit figures of highly imaginary Chinese-ness, Karsavina and Idzikowsky danced a *pas de deux*. "In our pagoda hats we looked like *bibelots* that any collector might have contentedly put on his mantelpiece. I wish this precious little masterpiece of Massine could be revived, and that Stass (Idzikowsky) could be seen in it," Karsavina wrote in 1967. The critics who seized so knowingly on Diaghilev's explanation of the occurrence of 'Kamarinskaya' in the score probably did not know that, as she told us, "it describes the highly indecorous deeds of a moujik from Kamarinsk . . . but familiar as the tune was, it could only be hummed: the words not being for polite ears. In the opera, however, the swift rhythm became a processional tempo. The powdered hussars and ladies in panniers gracefully performed their steps, bowed and curtseyed. Diaghilev enlightened me, explaining that Cimarosa was the Master of Music at the court of Catherine the Second."

The
Times
9.7.20

Possibly as a compliment to the King of Spain, on one occasion only Diaghilev gave *Le Tricorne* in the same bill as the opera, *L'Heure Espagnol*. *The Times* said: "The performance of the ballet seemed more wonderful than ever, not only as a display of virtuosity by M. Massine, Mme. Karsavina, M. Woizikowsky, and the others, but in its realisation of the possibilities of music and movement as the complement of one another . . . The artists who took part in Ravel's opera could scarcely be expected to reach the same level of ensemble in their different art, and the feeling that the whole was lacking in *élan* may have been partly due to its following a performance of such perfect finish as only the Russians can give, and partly to the fact that, after a preposterously long interval, some of the audience began to think it was time to go home when the clocks, the mechanical toys, the lovers and their lady had played half their tricks, and before the intrigue had reached its climax."

*Two or
Three
Muses*
M. Sert

Daily
Telegraph
15.7.20

Observer
11.7.20

There were two exhibitions in London art galleries that summer, relating in different ways to the ballet. At Agnew's, "Two Decorations and Some Sketches," by José-Maria Sert, were on show. The decorations painted for Lady Ripon (of whom Misia Sert said, "I think she is the only person in the world whom Sert presented with one of his murals,") were described by Sir Claude Phillips: "The finest decorative ensemble in the present exhibition is eccentrically styled 'Balkanerie 1915.' It is a modernised rococo design, of a rare decorative beauty, carried out in a kind of silver-and-black camiaeu with a perfect unity that even the strong accentuation of certain episodes fails to disturb . . . it is the best, if not the most sensational, work of the kind that Signor Sert has yet produced."

P.J. Konody was more puzzled: "Whilst his forms are stated with unmistakable representational clearness, his allegorical meaning cannot always easily be deciphered." Having discussed the other works displayed, Konody went on, "All this is painted with inimitable bravura and with a palette as rich and glowing as translucent enamel. Whether this baroque flutter and blazing colour are suitable for the wall decoration of dining-rooms and other apartments in a modern house, is more than questionable. But such considerations need not interfere with the enjoyment of the exuberant vitality and dazzling bravura displayed by the Spanish artist."

The
Queen
10.7.20

At the Leicester Galleries, Laura Knight showed her pictures of the Russian Ballet itself. The *Queen* said: "A few critics have decided that a decadence is already in sight. The proposition cannot be accepted without argument. If the ballet veritably be in a state of decay, then we have a very pretty deterioration to study. Undoubtedly a change is taking place. *Scheherazade*, as played this season, is a staid production in comparison with the wild abandon of a few years ago. New stars have arisen. The *mise-en-scène* of Derain and Picasso has never approached the gorgeous imagery of Leon Bakst, first and best of the decorators attached to the company . . . The members of the ballet have scattered . . . The old triumphs can never be repeated . . . The mimic business of the stage is as difficult to paint as the portrait of an actor in character. Mrs. Knight has succeeded where most artists fail . . . Realism on the stage is a mistake, and the artist who paints stage life in a realistic fashion usually comes to grief. Mrs. Knight is too accomplished to fall into such an error. Her incisive and vivid brush knows how to deal with a convention based upon the limelight man and the stage carpenter, the 'dresser' and the box of make-up. She catches a sense of movement and expectancy which is most admirable. From the front of the house, from the orchestra, from the wings, we can study again the *Three-Cornered Hat*, the *Oiseau de Feu*, *Les Sylphides*, and the *Good-Humoured Ladies*. But one ballet is missing. There is no picture of *La Boutique Fantasque*. Will Mrs. Knight kindly give us a record of the dolls, of the man with the barrow, and especially of the two poodles? That solitary bark, the only spoken word in the whole ballet, has always touched my heart."

Ernest Newman's heart had been touched this season; he confessed that he had been playing truant: "Two more hearings of *Le Astuzie Femminili* during the week (the piece has drawn me there when perhaps I ought to have been at recitals) have only deepened my delight in this enchanting little work, and my sense of the complete individuality of Cimarosa as against Mozart." Sunday Times 4.7.20

Le Rossignol, the opera based on Hans Andersen's story, had been given before the war complete with the ballet, and with settings and costumes by Benois. Now Diaghilev had arranged with Stravinsky a much shorter version for the ballet alone, reduced in scope and story, and had re-named it *Le Chant du Rossignol*. Matisse had designed fresh settings and costumes. "The whole thing is played on a simple scene of sky-blue curtains against which The Times 17.7.20 dresses and dance figures can have the maximum of effect, and it need scarcely be said that all this is brilliantly designed and carried out. The nightingale is borne in seated on her nest. She throws aside her mantle of feathers and becomes Mme. Karsavina, who dances the nightingale's song with innumerable flutterings and trills of hands and feet. This dance should be the chief feature of the ballet, but there is something wrong between the dance and its music. It halts and wavers: the nightingale never seems to find her full voice . . ." But though, on the whole, this ballet was not as well received as the earlier novelties, it had its admirers. The *Daily Herald* liked it. "There are no big dancing opportunities but it is full of quaint devices, of curious and Daily Herald 17.7.20 unexpected effects, and consistently remains a fairy tale. It is a fairytale such as one would never have dared to hope to see in the flesh. Who could have thought they would have lived to see the Emperor really walking on the backs of his courtiers – or, death defeated, see his funeral robes turn magically to an indescribable magnificence?

"It was hard to decide between the claims of the rival birds, for if Mme. Karsavina was beautiful as Nature's nightingale, Idzikowsky was almost equally irresistible as a mechanical one."

There was one strange flaw in the adaptation.

"We miss most of all the little maidservant who brought the mandarins to find the nightingale and was the only member of the Court to weep when it was driven away in favour of the mechanical bird from Japan." It seems hard to understand how that opportunity to create a memorable rôle was missed, and it would seem as if this ballet was lacking in that special amalgam of new twists to old stories which was the hallmark of the Russian Ballet. Percy The Times 17.7.20
Observer 18.7.20 Scholes felt that Stravinsky had spoiled his opera. Ernest Newman confessed that the music left him rather bored: "This music . . . being mostly without rhythm, it has baffled even the genius of Massine to invent a satisfactory choreography for it." Sunday Times 18.7.20

What was, at about this period, to test the genius of Massine to invent a satisfactory choreography was Stravinsky's diametrically opposite score, *Le Sacre du Printemps*. Diaghilev had decided that this work ought to be revived. The sets and costumes had been used only seven times; but the dancers who had taken part in Nijinsky's ballet simply could not put it together again. He decided that Massine should start afresh.

As usual, the company went off on holiday as the London season ended, and Diaghilev, as usual, went to Venice. Bookings were proving hard to arrange for the autumn, and remained unsettled. Eventually, a tour of the English provinces was fixed up, to begin in November. The company, which had recollections of the difficulties to be encountered in halls which were inadequately equipped, was unhappy at the idea, but had to agree, however reluctantly.

The tour was managed by an ordinary commercial firm, which handled the matter of advance publicity very poorly. It was not to be wondered at that attendances were patchy.

Bournemouth
Graphic
5.11.20

In Bournemouth, it was reported that "crowds are wending their way daily to the Winter Gardens to see Serge Diaghileff's Russian Ballet and *corps de ballet* of 60 performers . . ." – but the papers did not print any notices at all.

A brief visit to Leicester (which had seen Pavlova, whom it described as the only visitor of the kind to come there before) brought an understanding notice:

Leicester
Mail
10.11.20

". . . Fundamentally, the attraction of watching good dancing is the same as in listening to good music or poetry . . . The Russian dancers prove the claim of dancing to be a high art . . . The English taste does not perhaps care for quite so much in the way of saltatory effort, which seems to be a large feature in Russian dancing; but there is no denying the very high degree of expressiveness and variety attained . . ." But this paper deplored the fact that the audience was not larger, and the *Post* had more to say on that account:-

Leicester
Daily
Post
10.11.20

"The Russian Ballet, with which the name of Serge Diaghilev is honourably associated, has an established reputation in the capitals of Europe, and it is therefore a little difficult to ascribe to the superior judgment of Leicester people the fact that it did not succeed in filling the De Montfort Hall last evening. The fact of the matter is that the education of the provinces has been sadly neglected in regard to that particularly delightful symposium of the arts known as the ballet. It is to be hoped that further opportunities will present themselves for remedying this gap in our artistic experience.

"Last night's audience, if not large, was enthusiastic, and it had good reasons for being so . . .

"Prominent among the ladies were Mlle. Lydia Sokolova, who was quite enchanting as Columbine in *Carnaval*, Mlle. Leokadia Klementovitch, Mlle. Vera Savina, and the only Englishwoman among the principals, Miss Hilda Bewicke." (An amusing touch, this, for both "Sokolova" and "Savina" concealed English dancers, apparently most successfully.)

After one-night-stands in Nottingham, Sheffield and Leeds, a two-week engagement in Liverpool gave company and audience a better chance to become acquainted.

Liverpool
Echo
17.11.20

"The Russian Ballet at Olympia get ahead of Mr. Lloyd George in giving us a new world," said the *Liverpool Echo*. "Although, after all, it is only the old, old world plucked from its grey ashes and set spinning again for us like a top . . . As an exhibition of personal excellence and physical ability only, the ballet is wonderfully stimulating and interesting . . . But who is responsible for the appallingly long and wearisome intervals, and why cannot the orchestra have a little regard to Mr. Edward Clark's unsparing efforts to haul forth ever so little more sound from the mighty array of instruments so conspicuous during the intervals by their absence when we might be most inclined to suffer them?" How can you please everybody? Play *entr'actes*, and half the audience chatters and the other half complains it can't hear – as Diaghilev had found out earlier on.

Liverpool
Daily Post
& Mercury
23.11.20

Liverpool printed another thoughtful and imaginative article about this new phenomenon and its Russian-ness and art; and just as, so often across the years, such thoughts have flooded the minds of spectators as they left the glamour of the Royal Opera House and picked their way through the decaying vegetables littering the market, so did this writer ponder on leaving the Olympia: "Such beauty is heart-warming and inspiring. We came away from the sight of it regretfully and grateful. And when still thrilling from the call of it we find ourselves in the chill gloom of West Derby Road, with its black shiny pavements and the rank odour of the thronged 'fish and chip' shops, we realise what a queer thing civilisation is and how infinite in variety is man."

Birmingham
Post
29.11.20

Sadly, all that could be arranged for Birmingham was a series of three matinées. Ernest Newman had been succeeded on the *Birmingham Post* by "A.J.S.," who wrote a full column giving a most excellent introduction for the visit. He was extremely well acquainted with the ballet: "Two or three years ago M. Diaghilev's company gave a fortnight's season at a Manchester music-hall, with a fine orchestra mainly of Hallé players. Twenty-eight performances were given, and the present writer made a fairly successful attempt to attend them all. Of the memories left by that experience the most pungent today is that of Massine and Tchernicheva in the *Cleopatra* ballet . . . It is unfortunate that the performances are restricted to three; and still

Vera Clark, a product of Stedman's Academy, scored a great success in the stylistically difficult part of the Brown Poodle in *Boutique*. She "danced the Brown Poodle number as you can no longer see it danced today. She was so light, so playful, so delightfully wanton..." By 1920, Diaghilev was promising her bigger parts, and turned her into Vera Savina. He chose the name of the famous actress, Russia's "Sarah Bernhardt" – who, at the age of twenty-five, acted in Turgenev's play, "*A Month in the Country,*" making a great success of the secondary role, and captivating the sixty-one year old author, whose last love she became. They exchanged letters over the last four years of his life, of which his to her remain. Diaghilev said that he chose the Russian actress, a tragedienne, and a brunette, because "Savina," fair-haired, petite, and lively, was exactly the opposite.

Diaghilev concealed the increasing number of English dancers in his company under real or mocked-up Russian-sounding names. Lesser members of the company sometimes had their own names Russianised. His most successful dancers were rewarded with patronymics which he chose from those of real stars of the Russian theatre's past.

Most famous of these adoptions was undoubtedly Hilda Munnings. Joining the company in 1913, he re-named her Lydia Sokolova in time for the first tour in the U.S.A. She was already dancing leading parts. (This name was taken from Eugenia Sokolova, a dancer who flourished in the 1870's, and became a famous teacher after her retirement.) Lydia Sokolova is here seen in *Chout,* the special make-up failing to spoil the wonderful smile.

more so that they are to be given at a time of day when Birmingham is concerned with matters that must needs have preference, I suppose, over even so serious an art as that of the Russians."

Birmingham had been given a list of ballets, but instead it got very little more than *divertissements*. What was the use of reading A.J.S.'s article? "The finest example of the modern conception of the relation between music and gesture is Stravinsky's *Petrouchka*. Technically, I would put de Falla's *Tricorne* in the same class, but to my mind some debasement to music is wrought in the process of unification. All these, Russian, Spaniard and Frenchman alike, have found an avenue of approach to the public through the Diaghilev organisation . . . The Russian ballet is an international institution; but it has almost found a home in this country."

Obviously, A.J.S. himself was dying to see the newer ballets, and the first programme, opening with *Les Sylphides* and then *Carnaval,* did not evoke loving nostalgia; instead, the feeling was that Birmingham ought to have been given something more up-to-date. The *divertissement*, as always, brought great applause for individual dancers, but "Candour, indeed, compels the statement that we have had quite as good a *divertissement* from less famous troupes of dancers, with solo dancing of a higher imaginative beauty than even the best we had yesterday afternoon." The orchestra was thought to be a scratch one: "M. Diaghilev is too venturesome altogether. Even the noble Duke of Plaza Toro never travelled the provinces without a band . . . The least musically sensitive among yesterday's audience must have writhed under the leaden treatment of Chopin's marvellously supple-jointed melody, the discordances alike of tune and rhythm. There was one ecstatic moment, indeed, when the listener might have been forgiven for imagining that a bar or two of Stravinsky had become incorporated with the score . . .

"What, then, did the orchestral failure entail? Frankly, it meant that the life went out of the performance . . . When the music could be forgotten the lovely harmony of the dancers' evolutions, a trifle discommoded as they were by circumstances, had the old enchantment for the eye. These, indeed, as they flit before the eye, make a music of their own – exquisitely orchestrated as the colours mingle one with another – weaving an enticing counterpoint of graceful motion. Tchernicheva and Idzikowsky were yesterday's star solo dancers, but they had fine support from many another . . .

"Were our musical life what it ought to be, the assistance of a permanent orchestra would be available for so important an occasion. Is it too much to hope that another year this may be arranged?"

C.F.M., in the *Mail*, was "approaching the Russian Ballet as a novelty," and recalled that "in the last century there was for a time a flourishing English ballet, but that it became so conventional and formalised that at length it died of inanition." The ballets brought this time were thought to be already "dated," and not by any means the most advanced which Birmingham would like to have seen. "Yesterday afternoon the auspices were not very favourable, but it was possible to perceive an inner light of merit in the performance which nothing could extinguish."

This was a disastrous visit. There was the disaster of giving matinées only, in an industrious city where the menfolk just didn't "take the afternoon off." There was the absolute disaster of the orchestra. There was also a social disaster which simply cannot be explained, only reported.

"In the evening a reception arranged by the Birmingham Centre of the British Music Society at the Queen's Hotel in honour of the artistes of the Russian Ballet was disappointed of their presence through the claims of rehearsals for a forthcoming Paris production. Mr. Leigh Henry, of London, spoke to a large attendance of the society's members on the work of the Ballet and on the musical aims of the Stravinsky school of composers . . ."

And for the final disaster, Serge Grigoriev said that "our financial position was hardly improved by our agent in Birmingham, who made off with the takings."

The company returned to the continent, performing in Paris and Rome.

Lest there be any misapprehension as to the drawing-power of ballet in London at this period, a glance at some other activities in the field will clarify the situation.

After Lopokova's flight in 1919, a friend had introduced Karsavina to Sir James Barrie, and he had been charmed. At that time her English was not as fluent as Lopokova's, and this gave him the inspiration to convert his play into a one-act fantasy in which she would not speak her lines, but dance them. Karsavina devised her own language of mime for the part of "Karissima

Birmingham
Post
30.11.20

Birmingham
Mail
30.11.20

Birmingham
Post
30.11.20

Grigoriev
p.166

of the Ballet," and *The Truth About The Russian Dancers*, "showing how they love, how they marry, how they are made, with how they die and live happily ever afterwards," was produced as the middle section of the Coliseum bill on March 16th, 1920.

Denis
MacKail
p.544

Denis MacKail had more to tell of the story.

"No less than ten typescript versions of this ballet-fantasy, in its one-act form, were discovered long afterwards in the wooden box that had once accompanied the author on his night journey from Dumfries to St. Pancras, and no one would like to say that these had been all. When he took it up again, he had worked on it and polished it, and in the end, it contained the essence of Barrie and the essence of the ballet as well. Charming, ridiculous, light, tender, and touching. An interpretation of the world of dancers as only one author could have seen it. And a very complete entertainment, with acting, dancing, music by Arnold Bax, and décor by Paul Nash . . . The exquisite Karsavina just danced her lines, as she fell in love, married, had a baby, died, and came to life again – all with a dream-like disregard for time and space. Even the ballet fanatics fell under its spell . . . Music meant nothing to Barrie, but he had seen and made others see the Russian Ballet . . . leading a consistent, preposterous and unearthly life played by all concerned, though of course particularly by his new star." (The producer, to whom honour was due, was Gerald du Maurier.)

"A.B. Walkley gave it three-quarters of a column in *The Times* next day, and a whole column – still gloating over the memory – on the day after that. A special and characteristic little success."

Karsavina followed this later in the year with three weeks at the Coliseum, with a small company of dancers.

Pavlova had opened at Drury Lane in April, with a large repertoire. A small group, headed by Adolf Bolm, was in the Coliseum bill the week after the Diaghilev company left it in July, and other lesser luminaries of the dance flitted to and fro in the variety halls. There was certainly an abundance of choice for those who loved the dance.

1921

PRINCE'S THEATRE

MAY 26th - JULY 30th

FIRST PERFORMANCES IN ENGLAND

May 31st: *Cuadro Flamenco*
(Andalusian Dances and Songs, Picasso.)
Paris 17.5.1921.

June 9th: *Chout*
(Prokofiev, Larionov and Slavinsky, Larionov.)
Paris 17.5.1921.

June 27th: *Le Sacre du Printemps* (Second version)
(Stravinsky, Massine, Roerich.)
Paris 15.12.1920.

REPERTOIRE

Le Carnaval	Papillons	Scheherazade
Cléopâtre	Petrouchka	Les Sylphides
Contes Russes	Polovtsian Dances	Thamar
Good-Humoured Ladies	La Princesse Enchantée	Le Tricorne
Oiseau de Feu	Pulcinella	

COMPANY

Allanova, Bewicke, Cecchetti J., Coxon, Devillier, Evina, Germonska, Grekulova, Koksova, Lopokova, Mascagno, Mortonova (Moreton), Slawicka, Sokolova, Sumarokova I, Sumarokova II, Tchernicheva, Zirmunska.

Addison, Augustino, Bourman, Cecchetti, Grigoriev, Idzikowski, Jalmujinsky, Jazwinsky, Koviarsky, Kremnev, Lukine, Mareno, Mascagno, Mikolaitchik, Novak, Okhimovsky, Singaevesky, Slavinsky, Stepanoff, Vladimirov, Woizikowski, Winter, Zverev.

CONDUCTOR

Ansermet

A SEASON WITH COCHRAN

Charles B. Cochran brought Diaghilev back to London in a summer of legendary heatwaves – a summer, however, when Hannen Swaffer was to write that "Covent Garden is closed, Drury Lane is closed, the Alhambra is showing a moving picture, the Palace is a picture theatre. So fashionable London flocks to the New Oxford, only recently a derelict music-hall, and the Prince's, a theatre that the Melvilles, who built it, had given up trying to make a success of, and that scarcely any London management dared to experiment with." The Prince's held 2,000, but the stage was too small for a large ballet company to show to its best advantage. Sunday Times 5.6.21

Controversial novelties were held back, and the opening, with great favourites, was the occasion for wild enthusiasm. "It was an evening of musical gaiety, for Liadov's music to the delightful fantasy of fairy tales which began it (*Children's Tales,*) is extraordinarily vivacious, and Rossini's tunes, arranged by Respighi, simply bubble over with high spirits. Lopokova received a tremendous ovation at the end of *La Boutique Fantasque,* . . . M. Idzikowski is inimitable as the 'snob,' with his geometric poses and his wonderful pirouettes . . ." The Times 27.5.21

There had been important changes in the company since it had left for the Continent in December. At about the time when the choreography of the new version of *Le Sacre* was complete, Diaghilev had noticed that Massine was looking in a more than comradely fashion upon the charming young English dancer, Vera Clark, known professionally as Savina. Massine had been summarily dismissed. Savina had left with him. They married. This dismissal, like the dismissal of Nijinsky, left gaps in both the private and professional sides of Diaghilev's life. On the latter, it left him without a choreographer. He had, however, gained a librettist, for a young man named Boris Kochno had joined his team. On the credit side, he had welcomed Lopokova back, forgiving her behaviour in 1919, when her sudden disappearance would have stranded him, had not Karsavina arrived and taken over the part of the can-can dancer in *Boutique* – a rôle in which Karsavina herself thought Lopokova "unsurpassed."

Sydney Carroll gloated: "The shade of Peter the Great must be, I fancy, lingering in the wings of the Prince's Theatre, watching with greedy, devouring eyes the antics of the Puck-like Lopokova. I do not propose to examine this revival of the Russian ballet in any critical sense. I am content to enjoy it. I may miss Massine. I may regret the insufficiency of the size of the stage and deplore the fact that Mr. Cochran has found it necessary to bring into conspicuous and unescapable prominence parts of his orchestra. The mysterious undulations of *Carnaval,* the pirouettings of Pierrot, Columbine and Arlequin, the graciousness, the witchery, the quaintness of the good-humoured ladies, the ingenuous and primitive hypnotism of *Children's Tales,* the magical fantasy and infantile glory of *La Boutique Fantasque* — these things conduct us into the realms of fairy-land, out of the strife and muddle and murkiness of our own world into realms of beauty, colour, harmony, the poetry of motion and gesture. Sunday Times 29.5.21

Idzikowski made "Snob," in *Boutique*, a very special rôle of his own, dancing it with "the exact precision of clockwork."

facing page: Picasso had been so entranced by Naples that he was Diaghilev's obvious choice as designer for *Pulcinella*. He was also delighted with the "theatre within a theatre" concept of his own *Parade* curtain. Picasso's first sketches for *Pulcinella* were on those lines, and were rejected by Diaghilev – the action was in the streets. With strict economy Picasso brought them out and furbished them up a year later, for the *Cuadro Flamenco*. For this purpose, they were delightful, giving the look of a mid-nineteenth-century theatre proscenium. The boxes with their couples resembling clever rag dolls were completely in key with the natural performers taking part in the entertainment.

"Mr. Diaghilev retains in his splendid company most of our old beloved dancers, and his good fortune in persuading Mlle. Lydia Lopokova to adorn it once more cannot be questioned. The contrast between her art and personality and that of Mlle. Tchernicheva is interesting. Two widely different aims with much the same aesthetic result."

The first new presentation was something quite different from anything Diaghilev had ever shown before – fruit of many happy months spent in Spain, and especially earlier in the same year, when he and Cochran had both been in Andalusia at the same time.

Cock-a-Doodle-do C.B. Cochran (1941)

"By great good luck Diaghilev, after finishing his season with the Russian Ballet in Madrid, came to see me in Seville, accompanied by Stravinsky and Boris Kochno," said Cochran. "Diaghilev and Stravinsky were as inflamed by the Spanish music and dancing as I was, and when Diaghilev urged me to give him another season of ballet in London I made it a stipulation that we should produce a *Cuadro Flamenco,* performed not by the artists of his troupe, but by actual performers engaged in Spain. Diaghilev agreed. And Diaghilev was not easily pleased . . ."

A ravishing setting was devised for the London appearance.

The Times 1.6.21

"The curtain rises on a décor by Pablo Picasso, a satirically sketched theatre interior with a suggestion of 1850 about it that harmonizes skilfully with the painted jackets and broad trowsers of the men and the shawls and flounces of the women who are seated round three sides of a square on a raised platform in the middle of the stage," said *The Times*. "For all the notice they appear to take of the audience, as they sit tuning and strumming upon their guitars, smoothing their skirts or exchanging jests from side to side, they might be shut up in the four walls of a country inn-room. And so, before anything has happened at all, you get the novel zest of seeming to peep through a window at an unacted scene of folk-life.

"Then (you hardly know how it comes about, so rapid it is,) the whole scene changes its spirit. The guitars quicken, the hands begin to clap, and abruptly, without warning or designation, two of the men spring into the middle. The 'Tango Gitano' goes to a sustained tattoo of heels on the hollow flooring that whips the blood like military drums." *The Times* described much more, and felt that "the strong savour of popular life, the barbaric energy and the naive display of passion tend to carry the onlooker away and blind him to the pains and exactitude of the technique. But the technique is there; Maria Dalbaicin's lovely 'La Farruca' is almost academic in its grace. Of the complex threads that make up the charm of this spectacle her sinuous elegance is, perhaps, the most captivating."

Cochran added that "the *Cuadro* proved the box-office draw, and we were sold out every time it was included in the programme." He quoted Sydney Carroll against himself – "What manager but Charles Blake Cochran – adept at the odd and incongruous – would have dared to introduce into Russian ballet such a strange contrast?" Cochran said that Carroll saw nothing in common between the choreography of *Les Sylphides* and what Carroll described as "an amiably energetic concert party from Spain." Cochran and Diaghilev obviously felt alike, that these artists – singers as well as dancers – were of the first quality. Edwin Evans explained that "for many years Diaghilev has held the belief that only two nations dance naturally, Russians and Spaniards. To others the dance is an acquired art."

Pall Mall and Globe 31.5.21

As he had these authentic Spanish dancers on the spot, Diaghilev tried an interesting experiment. He put on the lovely dancer Maria Dalbaicin (whom he had discovered at a party in Seville) in Karsavina's rôle as The Miller's Wife in *Le Tricorne*. "It had been expected that Senor de Falla would conduct, but he wisely left that duty in the experienced hands of M. Ansermet." Chiding the audience for too-ready applause in the middle of the action, *The Times* went on, "The beauty of the Russian Ballet is its continuity; it is also, what London theatre audiences are apt to overlook, as much a musical as a dramatic performance, a thing to be heard as well as seen. De Falla's music is a reminder of this, for in the whole repertory there is nothing in which the music and the action work more intimately together. One wonders how either could have come into existence before the other." *The Times* applauded Dalbaicin's beauty and performance, but it was generally considered that lovely as it was, it did not really fit in with the Diaghilev production.

The Times 3.6.21

Diaghilev gave a long interview. He told with humour of the way in which he had found the dancers in Spain – "It was necessary to settle down and get acquainted with the people before you came to know the very best dancers, and then they might be discovered in the clerk from the wine store or the young woman from behind the counter. Having discovered them, I asked where they had learned to dance in this wonderful way. Invariably their reply was: "Nowhere; we have danced like this since we were seven – like everybody else.""

Observer 5.6.21

The season was almost a sell-out.

"Mr. C.B. Cochran should issue season tickets for the Prince's Theatre; there would be a rush on them on the part of those by whom headquarters of the Russian Ballet are used as a kind of club, and to whom the repetitive business of telephoning for seats night after night has become not a little irritating and abashing," said *Vogue*. The reasons for this repetitive attend-

Vogue June/2 1921

ance struck the journal as being comparable to the desire of children to enjoy over and over again their favourite delights. "Yes, we become children once again at the Russian Ballet, large eyed, hypercritical children; for like children we are content, night after night, to hear the same stories re-told, to see the same stories re-danced; like children we never tire of our old loves; and like children we are absurdly up-in-arms against the least perceptible change in the 'text.' A new dancer may be better than an old one, but we resent the intrusion of the new dancer; we declare with emphasis that he is not a patch on his predecessor, until one day the old dancer returns and we discover our mistake . . .

"It is two years since Lopokova, lyrical of youth and joy, a rhapsody for Heine, as blithe and graceful as Euphrosyne herself, last danced in London; . . . we confess to having feared lest her art should have lost something of its sparkling precision and exuberant enchantment. But Lopokova's technique, if it has suffered any change, has suffered a change for the better. We have never seen – we never expect to see – a dancer with more perfect poise, with more unresisting verve, with a more absolute sense of balance or of time; never a dancer with a more fascinating *diablerie* than she exhibits during the *can-can* in *La Boutique Fantasque,* with a more barbaric abandon than she exhibits when she flings herself into the tornado of *Prince Igor*; never a dancer more incorporeal than is Lopokova, floating like a feather in the breathless air through the tremulous nocturne of *Les Sylphides.* As dancer pure and simple she does not yield pride of place even to the immaculate Karsavina, though Karsavina's tragic miming and cultivated artistry are unapproachable. One slips into that adjective 'unapproachable' when writing of Karsavina, for Karsavina is, one feels, the imperious queen, born in the purple, educated in the best style, versed in the best literature and music, a lady of unimpeachable taste moving in the highest circles, an object for remote adoration requiring that all bouquets shall be presented through her secretary . . ."

Observer
5.6.21

In his *Observer* interview, Diaghilev had also explained the season's new ballet, *Chout – (The Buffoon.)*

"Mr. Serge Prokofiev has started off in a new direction. The only resemblance between Prokofiev and Stravinsky is that both are Russian, and both are living in the same century. Some idea of the story on which this ballet is founded may be gathered from its sub-title, 'How One Young Buffoon Deceived Seven Old Buffoons and a Stupid Merchant.' The scenery and costumes have been designed by M. Larionov, and the choreography is by a young dancer, Slavinsky, after indications by Larionov. In fact, a new principle has here been introduced, that of giving to the decorative artist the direction of the plastic movement, and having a dancer simply to give it choreographic form. Both the setting and the music of this ballet are of the highest modernity and entirely in keeping with Russian characteristic, without the musical themes being derived from folk-lore."

Speaking of the *Cuadro Flamenco,* Diaghilev said that "without effort and mostly without schooling, these Spanish dancers have developed a technique which is as formidable in its own way as that of Pavlova."

Looking ahead, he ended by discussing the event which was, undoubtedly, to be the highlight of the musical season – the coming presentation of Massine's new *Rite of Spring.* "I have just been giving this ballet in its new form in Paris, and it has established as a classic masterpiece a work which eight years ago was so revolutionary that it almost led to broken heads. After hearing it this time several persons said to me, 'Why, it is Beethoven,' to which I replied, 'No, it is better.' "

Diaghilev also talked about the programme of musical interludes he had prepared with great care. Those who preferred to stay in the auditorium during the intervals would hear works by Stravinsky, Prokofiev, Satie, Poulenc, Honegger, Auric, Milhaud, Eugene Goossens, Lord Berners, Bliss, Bax, Roger Quilter, Ravel, Chabrier, Debussy, Borodin, Rimsky-Korsakov, and Balakirev. Percy Scholes remarked that two of Satie's *Gymnopédies,* "beautifully orchestrated by Debussy, would be of great interest." Fourteen works would be heard for the first time in England.

The
Times
21.5.21

The Paris correspondent of *The Times* had reported enthusiastically on the reception there of *Chout.* "It is sure to please a London audience as well as it pleased that at the *Gaieté Lyrique.*"

Chout was devised and designed by M. Larionov. The styles of Russian peasant art this Moscow painter loved (and of which centuries-old examples can be seen in Russia to this day,) he then carried out in a Cubistic manner. The colour was built on fierce reds.

Perhaps he had been absent from London too long; *The Times* itself was not by any means as delighted with this series of waggish episodes of buffoonery. Saying that the material was not really right for ballet, *The Times* felt that "something might have been made of it if it had come into the hands of the artist who devised the *Children's Tales* and *Pulcinella* (Massine.) Unfortunately, it had not such luck, and in spite of the brilliant Cubist scenery and dresses with which M. Larionov has provided it and the equally brilliant and equally Cubist music of M. Prokofiev, it has the effect of a loosely-improvised charade . . . One hardly finds in it a touch of that art which has made the Diaghilev ballet famous throughout Europe and beyond it." The Times 10.6.21

Richard Capell rocked with laughter at the slapstick of it all. "The Chout is the practical joker of the village. His wife joins in the first joke. He pretends to have a magic whip. He will stab his wife dead, and with a slash of the whip bring her back to life. The experiment charms the seven elders, who insist on purchasing the whip (and with what roubles – the size of dinner plates!) Alas – the good women in Act II are duly slaughtered and cannot be revived. The revengeful elders seek out the Chout, but his wife has disguised him as a nursemaid . . . All ends with the whole company, after absurd events, making merry together." Daily Mail 10.6.21

The *Observer* just thought it dull – and babyish. "After the lyric loveliness of *Carnaval* some new art-form had to be found: further progress along the same lines was impossible. But *Carnaval* remains a masterpiece of beauty while the new art-form, as represented by *Chout*, has not yet learned to walk. It can scream very piercingly while waiting for its bottle." Observer 12.6.21

Years later, Cochran recollected that this season was "replete with novelty." Saying that *Chout* had attracted as much controversy, praise, and abuse as the *Cuadro* and *Le Sacre,* he had some interesting points to add about this ballet. Its first performance, conducted by the composer, "was received with enormous applause." (Stravinsky and de Falla were both in the audience.) "Many strange things were said about *Chout,* but perhaps the strangest by an English painter who declared that it was 'Bolshevist propaganda.' At any rate, none of the musical critics came to fisticuffs at the Prince's, as they had done at preliminary performances in Paris." (Now who was right about this – Cochran or *The Times'* Paris correspondent? Or was Cochran confusing it with the 1913 furore about *Le Sacre*?) "I think *Chout* came a little too early, and I, for one, should like to see it again . . . I recall one moment when seven suitors, after shaking seven cardboard swords at seven fathers, spun round on their heels to express their devotion to seven red-haired daughters, who poised passionately on their fourteen big toes."

The most significant event of the season, however, lay in the return of *Le Sacre du Printemps* – now, and for ever, *The Rite of Spring.*

Not a note of the score had been played in public for eight years. It was but a memory or a rumour. Massine's new version had been given in Paris on December 15th, 1920, and accepted, without any recurrence of the uproar of 1913.

For London, Diaghilev decided on a master-stroke. A concert performance was given at Queen's Hall on June 7th, 1921. It was a resounding success. From then on, there was hardly room for news in the papers, so much space was devoted to discussion of *The Rite.*

Observer
12.6.21

"Mr. Goossens' concert was a triumph for conductor and orchestra (a specially-gathered one of his own – incidentally there were four members of the Goossens family on the platform," said Percy Scholes. "An opinion of this work is given, more or less, by implication elsewhere." (Scholes had devoted two whole columns, his weekly music essay on the same page, to what he entitled "THE RITE – AND THE WRONG OF IT.") "I asked Mr. Bernard Shaw (who has been indefatigable in attendance at performances of modern music all the week) to give *Observer* readers the view of our oldest music critic, and he replied: "Mind, I'm not to be understood as condemning it, but – if it had been by Rossini people would have said there was too much rum-tum in it!" Scholes added that amongst the other items Ireland's "very refined *The Forgotten Rite* was given. So in one concert we had the forgotten rite and the unforgettable one." Scholes himself had come down on the side of approval of the Stravinsky work, though he had thrown down a few gauntlets in so doing. He had called it Romantic; he had argued against Edwin Evans' appraisal of it as symphonic. He had demolished in argument the composer's own conception of it as "purely abstract." "Frankly, is not the *Rite* a piece of the most closely written 'programme music' ever composed, and is not all this talk about its 'absolute' and 'abstract' quality more (uncommon) bluff?"

Sunday
Times
12.6.21

Ernest Newman was on precisely the opposite side. He admitted that Goossens gave it a magnificent performance, and that it had all made a great impression, "especially by the rhythmic energy of the parts of it in which the composer gets away from his tiresome little Russian formulae." He claimed that no critic of standing denied Stravinsky's genius, but that his colleagues were so taken up with sonorities that "they were deaf and blind to defects in certain works."

The
Lady
16.6.21

The
Queen
18.6.21

The Lady was enthusiastic. "The performance under Eugene Goossens illuminated much that was then (in 1913) obscure. I cannot imagine that the work could be better played, and I enjoyed it immensely." In *The Queen*, which now began to notice the Russian Ballet far more frequently than it had done, Dr. Richard Terry said, "I attended all the performances in those days, and I well remember how the Stravinsky ballet gripped most of us, despite the derision (not to speak of hisses) with which a section of the audience greeted it. As a ballet, it appeared as a work of complete coherence and cohesion. As a concert item, it leaves one in a condition approaching puzzlement . . ."

The
Times
28.6.21

When, on Monday, June 27th, the ballet was performed, *The Times* reported that "everyone had asked for it. M. Diaghilev had granted the general request . . . Naturally the theatre was very full."

The rôle of the Chosen Virgin had fallen to Sokolova, who has described the creation of the work and its performances with great clarity and immediacy in her own autobiography. *The Times* said: "Mme. Sokolova, the 'Chosen Virgin,' was given a bank of white roses taller than herself. M. Stravinsky got a laurel wreath of equal size, and the whole house roared itself hoarse while the protagonists held their trophies and each other's hands and bowed themselves to the ground. Thus the London public proved its connoisseurship in contemporary art."

Eight brief years.

The Times, going more into detail, said: "There is no drama, no story; only a passionless ritual, in which the men lunge and spar at one another, and lift the women on their shoulders. In the second scene the Chosen Virgin stands in the centre of the stage in a striking pose, the other participants grouped around her. Sometimes they cluster closely and indulge in a curious spasmodic quiver. At last the chosen one deigns to move in a high-leaping, ungainly dance which is at least a triumph of callisthenic skill. The others leave her to herself; her dance be-

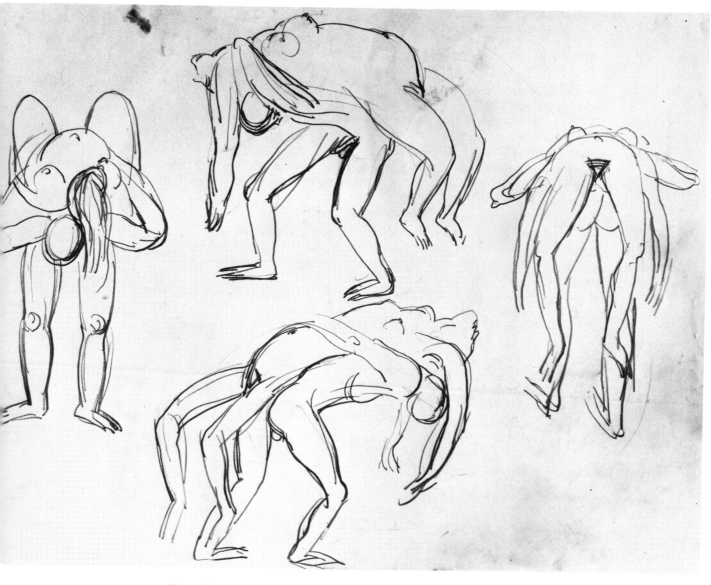

The sculptor, Epstein, made two drawings of *Le Sacre du Printemps* on his return home from seeing Massine's new version this season.

comes more extravagant, till at last she falls to the ground exhausted. That is all that happens, and through it all Stravinsky's orchestra tears its way in ever-increasing harshness."

On his return from this performance, the sculptor Jacob Epstein was inspired to make two drawings of the passage where the men lift the maidens on their shoulders; he stripped them down to the sculptor's framework and drew them in the nude. (It is one of these drawings which Lady Epstein has generously allowed to be reproduced.)

Richard Capell sorrowed: "They have tried something new and this time they have taken the wrong turning . . . they have spoiled a perfectly good ballet . . . the Stone Age of 1913 appeared weird and impressive. The Stone Age, new version, is a bore." (Had he forgotten that, in 1913, he had referred to it as "Cannibal Island Dancing" – quoting something overheard?) Daily Mail 28.6.21

"If Pagan Russia's artistic ideas had advanced to the point suggested by Nicholas Roerich's beautiful dresses, they would never have tolerated the dances which M. Massine has attributed to the period . . . Their fault is that they commit the unforgivable offence of being dull," said the *Telegraph*. ". . . One felt, indeed, quite sorry for Mlle. Sokolova, that she should have been called upon to execute so stiff and ungainly a dance. She did it wonderfully, but one could not help feeling that a Pagan Maiden who devised such a dance richly deserved to be sacrificed." Daily Telegraph 28.6.21

Morning
Post
28.6.21
"RUSSIAN BALLET AT ITS NADIR," said the *Post*. ". . . What the audience saw was not a magic picture but the spectacle of some fifty people in strange garb playing organised games accompanied by uncouth music. Mr. Massine has turned his back on any idea so definite as the ceremonial action which M. Nijinsky fitted to the music eight years ago."

Observer
3.7.21
"H.G." – (Hubert Griffith) said that "the back-cloth is the finest the Ballet has ever had, charging the atmosphere at once with an impression of bleak, wind-swept places, backgrounded by terrifying mountains . . . The motive once admitted, – the idea, as in the earlier Nijinsky ballet, of the Chosen Virgin sacrificing herself in a death dance to the unknown forces of Nature once acknowledged – all becomes significant and clear to understand. It was a strange thing to do on the stage; the stake that was risked was very high. It would have taken very little to make it absurd, but Mme. Sokolova made it impressive." (In reviving this ballet, Grigoriev
p.167 Diaghilev abandoned the first of Roerich's sets, giving both parts before the second, "which represented the ancient Scythian steppe under a lowering black and yellow sky."

The
Queen
9.7.21
Dr. Terry went to see the new version. "But, to my mind, the arrangement of the dances was less illustrative, and carried less conviction, than the production of 1913. When the controversy now raging round this particular piece of music has died down, I think it will be accepted as a work of great originality and power . . . We all thought it incomprehensible in 1913; now we find ourselves sitting down to the piano and playing lengthy extracts from it . . . So it has ever been in music – the daring feats of today are the conventions of tomorrow, and the critics fight the same battle round each one as they have done throughout all generations and in much the same terms."

One wishes that there had been clearer comparisons between the visual differences of the 1913 and the 1921 productions. The costumes and settings were being used again, with the exception of the dress for the Chosen Virgin, which Sokolova had found impossibly heavy. So the designs looked the same. There are hints in different papers of what struck the critics about the changes in the new choreography, but it is at this point that their lack of knowledge of the technique of ballet leaves the greatest blank.

Cochran, the business man, remembered that "although it necessitated a largely augmented orchestra, which, with long rehearsals, was an enormous expense, and meant, moreover, sacrificing four rows of stalls, I was anxious that it should be done, and Diaghilev was grateful for the opportunity. Prices were increased, and on its first night it drew the record receipts for the season."

Even if *Chout* was not to all tastes, many of the favourites were in the repertoire. Once more, a season had to be extended beyond its advertised date. This, in a year of slump in the theatre, demonstrates more trenchantly than words the strength of the support for ballet.

Daily
Telegraph
15.7.21
Diaghilev continued to vary the items in each programme. The *Daily Telegraph* pointed out that "within the brief ten minutes or so that the *pas de deux* from *La Princesse Enchantée* takes there is more sheer dancing than there is in half a dozen of the more modern additions to the Russians' repertory put together. One is not, of course, cavilling at the latter on that account, but it is none the less very delightful to see the old-time graces so deliciously executed as they were last night by Mme. Lydia Lopokova and M. Stanislas Idzikowski. The former, with her ease, her daintiness, and her charm, and the latter, with his admirable finish, completely won the hearts of the audience, which would have had every movement of the dance repeated had it had its way." Theirs was one of the memorable partnerships of dance history. Both were tiny, and well-matched for size – but, moreover, both had superb senses of fun, fabulous coquetry, and the ability to dismiss technique and make their performances look as if nothing was the slightest effort. London could take classical dancing and perfection – when the offering was as perfect as that.

"The Dancing English" had not only Diaghilev's company, but others of their favourites for varying periods during the same season. At the Coliseum, Karsavina had one of her regular engagements for three weeks, with a small company. "Karsavina, Maud Allan and Grock are Sunday
Times
10.7.21 at the top of the Coliseum bill, continuing the association that proved so popular last week," said the *Sunday Times*.

In addition, for one week only, Pavlova – unable to find a theatre – gave a concert-programme at Queen's Hall. For this, the management sent the critic Ernest Newman tickets in the stalls.

"The ways of box-offices are past finding out," he raged. "Presumably a critic is invited to Mme. Pavlova's performances to write about them. But he cannot write about them unless he sees them – though musical critics *have* been known to write about performances they had not heard. The Queen's Hall floor does not slope as a theatre floor does. I found myself in the middle of the stalls, with a phalanx of tall men and women in front of me, and beyond them, the conductor's body reaching, as it seemed to my aggrieved imagination, half-way to the ceiling. It was not wholly a wasted evening, of course. I could see all the dancers from the chin up, and every now and then I caught a glimpse of one of them down to the feet; but under the circumstances, the most I can say is that whenever I did see Mme. Pavlova she was the incarnation of grace and lightness." A chivalrous summing-up.

Sunday Times 3.7.21

It would appear that Diaghilev had the best of relations with both the managements which had given him their West End stages since 1918, for, whilst he was giving this current season in collaboration with C.B. Cochran, a grandiose plan was worked out with Sir Oswald Stoll and his fellow-directors of the Coliseum and Alhambra theatres, which was to take form in the following winter.

C.B. Cochran, by Quiz.

Eric Wollheim.

Sir Oswald Stoll.

1921 – 1922

ALHAMBRA THEATRE

NOVEMBER 2nd, 1921 - FEBRUARY 4th, 1922

The Sleeping Beauty was originally produced at the Maryinsky Theatre in St. Petersburg on 15.1.1890, to music specially composed by Tchaikovsky, with choreography by Marius Petipa.

For his production, Diaghilev engaged Sergueiev, formerly *régisseur* at the Maryinsky, to revive the Petipa choreography. He commissioned some additional dances from Nijinska. The design for the scenery and costumes, and responsibility for the whole production, were vested in Leon Bakst. The title was changed to *The Sleeping Princess.* to avoid confusion with the pantomime.

COMPANY

Allanova, Antonova, Astafieva II., Bewicke, Brianza, Coxon, Dalbaicin, Damaskina, Doubrovska, Egorova, Evina, Gostemolova, Klementovitch, Komarokova, Krassovska, Lopokova, Maicherska, Moreton, Nemchinova I, Nemchinova II, Nijinska, Plotnikova, Poplavska, Rosenstein, Schollar, Slavitzka, Sokolova, Soudeikina, Spessivtzeva (Spessiva,) Sumarokova I., Sumarokova II., Tchernicheva, Trefilova.

Addison, Bourman, Fedorov, Grigoriev, Idzikowski, Jalmujinsky, Jazvinsky, Karnecki, Komissarov, Kornetsky, Kosiarsky, Kremnev, Lukin, Mikolaitchik, Okhimovsky, Patrikeef (later Dolin,) Pavlov, Savitsky, Semenov, Sergueiev, Singaevsky, Slavinsky, Stepanov, Treer, Vilzak, Vladimirov, Winter, Woizikowski, Zverev.

CONDUCTORS:

Fittelberg, Goossens.

THE SLEEPING PRINCESS

"Quant à *La Belle au Bois Dormant*, ce ballet interminable, au sujet tiré d'une fable française, composé sur des thèmes français, ne possède aucun élément national qui puisse justifier l'idée de donner à Londres cette féerie franco-italienne . . ."

It will be remembered that it was Diaghilev himself who, in his letter to *The Times* in March, 1911, had poured scorn on this ballet. This scorn seems spurious. True, he and his original collaborators had expressly sought to break away from the rigid conventions of late nineteenth-century productions – but, with *La Belle au Bois Dormant*, first produced in 1890, and considered to be his masterpiece, the Frenchman Marius Petipa (who had gone to St. Petersburg as *premier danseur* in 1847, and ruled there as *maître de ballet* from 1870 until his death in 1910,) had already done so.

Diaghilev loved Tchaikovsky's music. No matter how he dressed it up or re-christened it, the Blue Bird *pas de deux* was always one of his company's greatest successes, from the moment of its brilliant performance on the famous first night in Paris in 1909, when Karsavina and Nijinsky, in all the magnificence of Bakst's flame and gold, gave the audience the performance of pure classical glory which was the sensation of a sensational evening.

When, in 1921, Diaghilev and Sir Oswald Stoll decided to mount a full-scale production of that very ballet, those earlier remarks were either forgotten or ignored. No one seems to have dug them up and quoted them.

Although only the name of Stoll is ever mentioned on the side of the theatre management, the position ought to be clarified. Sir Oswald Stoll was Chairman and Managing Director of both the Coliseum Syndicate and the Alhambra Company. Each had four Directors, of whom three were common to both.

The Coliseum held approximately twice as large an audience as the Alhambra, and was enjoying a period of great prosperity (to which the Diaghilev company had contributed since 1918.) The Alhambra (where George Robey had reigned for years) was paying much smaller dividends. Stock Exchange Yearbook

So, although it is always spoken about in terms such as – "Diaghilev and Stoll decided . . .," it must have been a majority decision of the Board of Directors of the Alhambra Company to put up a large sum of money, and present a full-scale spectacular Christmas show, in competition with the traditional pantomimes. These normally opened on Boxing Day and ran until nearly April, annually providing secure employment for the acting profession. In them, all the conventions were both expected and respected. There was the Principal Boy, (played by a female,) striding about in tights. There were palaces, kitchens, seashores, mountains, under-the-sea, enchanted forests, the transformation scene, songs and dialogue which had little to do with the story – (but which could be heard in the back row of the gallery!) – and funny knock-about men sending the children into roars of laughter. The familiar Perrault stories, such as *Jack and the Beanstalk, Aladdin, Cinderella, Mother Goose*, and the *Sleeping Beauty* itself, were barely discernible under the mixture of variety turns and "musical comedy" in which they were enmeshed. There were fairies, witches and ogres – and everyone loved the Dame (always performed by a man.) Many a father must have nursed a secret ambition to play her.

The *Sleeping Beauty*, with its well-known romantic story, a lovely heroine, a handsome Prince Charming, fairies both beautiful and good, a wicked witch, richly-dressed courtiers, and mysterious scenic effects which were actually part of the plot, must have seemed ideal to fill the bill as both Christmas entertainment and a work of art as well. With a view to a long run, the Alhambra Company voted to put up the money for scenery and costumes, usually thought to have been £10,000. Diaghilev arranged an immediate christening, re-naming it *The Sleeping Princess*.

No matter what his vaunted scorn for it in 1911, Diaghilev was in love with this ballet in 1921, and threw himself whole-heartedly into the preparations. He gave the design, and responsibility for the whole production, to Bakst, called on Sergueiev, (formerly *régisseur* at the Maryinsky) to revive Petipa's choreography, on Bronislava Nijinska to create some additional dances, and on Stravinsky to arrange Tchaikovsky's music. With such a team, all seemed set for success.

This delightful story by Charles Perrault, together with others including, in addition to those already mentioned, *Puss-in-Boots, Little Red Riding-Hood,* and *Tom Thumb,* first appeared in Paris in 1697, under the title *Contes de Fées.* The idea of making this particular story into a ballet, and its actual libretto, were those of an earlier Director of the Imperial Theatres, Vsevolojsky, who, in 1888, wrote and invited Tchaikovsky to compose the music "if the idea appealed to him."

Era of the Russian Ballet N. Roslavleva

"As described by Vsevolojsky it consisted of a ballet in the style of Louis XIV, with melodies in the spirit of Lulli, Bach and Rameau, and a quadrille of characters from all the fairy-tales of Perrault in the last act . . . While Tchaikovsky did carry it out, following very closely Vsevolojsky's 'book' and, particularly, Petipa's detailed draft of the future ballet, indicating the nature and duration of every dance, in reality he created a work that amounted to a reform in ballet." First performed at the Maryinsky on January 15th, 1890, it was an immediate success, and became a great favourite.

Was this ballet doomed to be misunderstood outside Russia until the Sadler's Wells Company re-opened Covent Garden with it in 1946?

When Anna Pavlova gave her shortened version in New York in 1916, it was performed on a very wide stage. Bakst designed two settings, one with a skyline and the other a conventionally pretty "French patisserie" palace interior. Both were utterly swamped by an ornate proscenium and dark velvet curtains and pelmet, heavily outlined with rigid gold braid around the elaborate scallopping. Pavlova's own costume was also very rigid, with a high-piled white wig dragged up most unbecomingly from her brow, completely destroying any *ingénue* illusion. Her company was augmented with locally-recruited dancers – but despite the sumptuous production, the popular prices at the Hippodrome (in contrast to the high prices for Diaghilev's Nijinsky-led company at the Manhattan, which overlapped for two weeks,) and despite even the magnetism of Pavlova herself, it was nothing like the success she had anticipated. After a few weeks, it was withdrawn, and replaced by her customary *divertissements.*

In 1921, as the number of costumes required for the Alhambra was enormous, Bakst adapted many of these designs. The *ateliers* of Pitoëff and Mme. Muelle, in Paris, could not cope with the whole order, and one act was entrusted to the workshop of Mrs. Lovat Fraser in London – (where alterations to those sent over from Paris were willingly managed at the last moment.) Only the most expensive materials would do, and Bakst and Diaghilev scoured the antique markets of Paris for braids, tassels, and other ornaments, as years before they had scoured markets in Russia for *Boris Godounov.*

The sets which Bakst designed for Diaghilev bore no resemblance to those designed for Pavlova. Inspired by the architectural conceits of the Bibienas, (that extraordinary family of eight who, from the 1680's to the 1780's, designed scenery, mainly for the Hapsburg court, with an original conception of perspective, and in such an identical idiom that all their work might have come from the same hand,) Bakst's settings for *The Sleeping Princess* were of far greater refinement. The Bibienas had discovered a trick by which they could open "even the tiniest stage to hitherto undreamed-of space and loftiness by painting buildings as seen at about a forty-five degree angle ... These restless flights of architecture running diagonally offstage toward undetermined distances revolutionised and dominated scenic design for most of the eighteenth century." A. Hyatt Mayor, Metropolitan Museum of Art, N.Y.

When such designs were drawn with the precision of the Bibienas, they must still have required considerable technical skill for their conversion into scenery; when, as in Bakst's drawings, they were far more impressionistically indicated, the intention of the designer was, indeed, difficult to follow. Vladimir Polunin described some of the problems which afflicted him and his wife as they worked at their share of the sets:-

"The numerous acts of this ballet had been prepared in Paris; some of the scenes were painted there and others in London. Bakst, like a field-marshal, sent out from his headquarters in Paris his instructions to the various studios. Those intended for us arrived by air mail, but his explanations were frequently contradictory ... As Bakst was not present, it was often difficult to fathom his meaning so that the work had to be held up pending explanations. To add to these difficulties it was found that the canvas, which had been purchased in great quantity, was worthless; the priming fell off, while the colours peeled away and changed in tone before our eyes. Polunin p.67

"The fire-proofing with which the canvas had been treated was so strong that it destroyed or altered every tone, impaired the adhesiveness of the medium and absorbed even the slightest moisture in the atmosphere due to a shower of rain. Although each piece was repainted five or six times, which improved the tone for a short while, it was impossible to obtain a satisfactory result ... daily a whitish deposit of unknown origin covered the whole canvas like a hoar frost."

It may well be imagined that comparable difficulties were delaying the work on the other sets in Paris – and adding to the costs.

The working of the stage machinery for Bakst's "effects" was so complicated that the technicians almost came to blows. Diaghilev held costume calls, when each dancer appeared before him in dress and make-up, carrying Bakst's original design protected by talc. The Maestro asked each member of the company to perform a few steps; luckily, in trying things out, it was discovered in time that Vladimirov was so weighed down by one of his costumes that it positively impeded his elevation, and alterations were rushed through.

The £10,000 of the budget was spent long before the opening night. Diaghilev, pressed for payment by *fournisseurs*, had to confess this to Stoll, and ask for a further £5,000. This was produced, though not without disquiet. Still the costs soared, and shortly before the opening date, Diaghilev had to repeat this performance. It was too late for withdrawal – too much money was already committed – and so, however grudgingly, Stoll's fellow-directors of the Alhambra Company produced another £5,000. This doubling of the capital investment must have presaged financial ruin, for the number of seats could never have carried the extra burden, even if the theatre had played to capacity.

Though he must have paid most of the bills to the makers-up, (otherwise they would not have delivered the costumes,) Diaghilev did not pay Bakst for his work on the production. This led to Bakst bringing an action in 1923, and obtaining an injunction restraining Diaghilev from using his scenery. The whole business caused a final quarrel between Bakst and Diaghilev, and ended a friendship which had existed, despite many tiffs, for twenty-five years.

Bakst's detailed, Bibiena-ish design for one of the
sets for Diaghilev in 1921 *(above)*, and, for
comparison *(left)*, the stage realisation of his two
sets for Pavlova's version of *The Sleeping Beauty* at
New York's *Hippodrome* in 1916, for Charles
Dillingham. Some idea of the relatively banal
earlier work can be obtained. Similarly, her much
larger *corps de ballet* is disposed in rigid cohorts, like
those of the West Point cadets who took part in
another turn, or the Mammoth Minstrels in yet
another. (400 – count 'em – 400! – as the
programme says.)

right: Another aspect of the preparations for *The
Sleeping Princess* – last-minute work on the
costumes, as Grace Lovat Fraser adjusts a jacket
in her London workroom. Last-minute it was,
indeed, for some costumes were only delivered
after the performance had begun on the
postponed opening night.

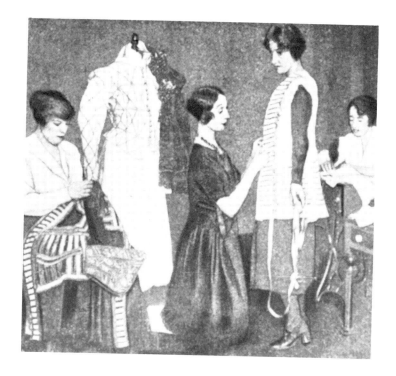

In the rôles of Giselle, the peasant girl deceived – of the Swan Queen, bewitched, held in thrall and released by the love of a Prince, and of Aurora, the Princess awakening to first love, Diaghilev in his time presented the three great ballerina "tests" to London. In St. Petersburg, such long parts would be danced only once or twice in a month: he therefore decided to distribute the performances of Aurora amongst four ballerinas. Not even Karsavina could have been expected to dance such a long rôle without intermission. Yet there, in the casting of this part, lay one of the greatest pitfalls.

Dancing
Times
October
1921
"It is, I believe, no secret that a considerable effort was made to persuade Madame Karsavina to throw in her lot . . . at the Alhambra, but Madame felt that, much as she would have liked to work once more under M. Diaghilev, her husband in Bulgaria had the first claim," reported "The Sitter-Out." He went on to quote from an article once written by Karsavina: "Petipa was exceedingly clever. Nobody knew better than he how to handle individuals and ensembles, but all his ballets appeared to be built on the same formula. An inevitable *divertissement* terminated those which ended happily, and an apotheosis not less inevitable crowned those in which the hero had a tragic end . . . His ballets are too full of marches and processions."

The Sitter-Out continued: "The days of Petipa were the days of virtuosity in dancing, the days of countless entrechats and innumerable pirouettes, and those who know M. Diaghilev well are aware that a production of this nature would be foreign to him."

Diaghilev was always unpredictable. For this production, he strove to recapture every nuance of the Petipa original. Although he himself had castigated those processions and marches as "interminable," Sergueiev was made to revive them in minute detail.

Unable to have Karsavina, Diaghilev engaged four beautiful dancers. Olga Spessitseva, most perfect of classical ballerinas, was to open – (her name shortened, for convenience, to Spessiva.) Four years senior to Karsavina, Lubov Egorova, (Princess Troubetskoy,) who later ran a famous ballet school in Paris, was another. So, too, was Vera Trefilova, who had graduated four years earlier still – in 1894. Widow of the great critic Valerian Svetlov, and a dancer of considerable refinement and the grand Maryinsky manner, she was by now aged 49 – and so horrified when she learned that Diaghilev had engaged her for the sixteen-year-old Aurora, that she threatened to commit suicide if he didn't release her from her bond! London's adored Lydia Lopokova danced some performances as Aurora, and many as the Lilac Fairy.

The rumour that Mathilde Kschessinska, the first Russian Aurora, who had taken over the part from its creator, Carlotta Brianza, in 1890, might return to dance it, came to naught. (She, too, was by now 49.) Vera Nemchinova also danced a few performances.

Great though each of these dancers was, not one was really an ideal Aurora. Some intangible element was missing.

The Prince Charming was to be Pierre Vladimirov, an exceptionally handsome *danseur classique*, who had graduated in Petersburg in 1911.

The complicated preparations led to that most ominous of theatrical set-backs – postponement of the first night. This meant that the tickets for the opening performance all had to be transferred to the new date, upsetting those who had already booked for that night. This is a box-office nightmare. But *The Times* encouraged the impatient: "The public are promised a
The
Times
30.10.21
succession of brilliant stage pictures and beautiful effects, one of the most notable being the growing forest, which rises round the Palace immediately the spell begins to work," it said.

The Sleeping Princess opened on November 2nd, at 8.30 p.m.

The critiques all struck the same note – every one dwelt upon the *splendour* of the spectacle.
Daily
Mail
3.11.21
"Last night's Sleeping Beauty was a young lady at the Versailles of 200 years ago," said Richard Capell. "She is, this new 'Sleeping Princess,' the grandest possible relation of our known Sleeping Beauties of the fairy-book pictures and of the cheerful, vulgar pantomime. This new ballet, which out-splendours splendour, is more grand than vulgarly cheerful, conjuring up as it does before our dazzled eyes all the pomp of dead and done-with kings and emperors – Bourbons and Romanoffs.

"If you ask how, without song or ordinary pantomime fun, Perrault's nursery tale made a full evening's wonder for the West End world, the answer is – by splendour. By the obvious and undeniable music of Tchaikovsky, all banners out, vehement, never at a loss. By an un-

Olga Spessitseva.

THREE AURORAS, AND PRINCE CHARMING

Lubov Egorova.

Vera Trefilova.

Vera Trefilova and Pierre Vladimiroff.

exampled display of that strict, classical dancing before which one gapes with wonder, even if not quite knowing in the rules of the art.

"It is supremely serious within its own conventions, this art; it is as serious for this Princess to dance before her parents in the shortest of pink, flowered tutus and tights as for an operatic princess to sing an aria. It was as serious for last night's Princess, (a wondrous newcomer, Olga Spessiva,) as a concerto for a fiddler, and she did it with all the serious accompaniment of the best fiddler of them all."

But Capell went on: "The major splendour was Bakst's. All the colours of all jewels, of all sunsets, of all flames, are in these stage pictures . . . only babes in the star Sirius can have christenings like last night's Princess, such orange, saffron, and moss-green of the court ladies, such glistening azure and ermine of the royalties' robes . . ."

Daily
Express
3.11.21
"The story itself merely trickles through the maze of scenic splendour, but the appeal to the eye and ear amply atone for the lack of dramatic cohesion," said the *Express*. "Taglioni might have envied Lopokova her series of ovations (as the Lilac Fairy.) A new *première danseuse*, Olga Spessiva – lissom as a veritable fairy – was hardly less triumphant, while M. Stanislas Idzikowski, as a Blue Bird, created quite a furore.

"The demonstration at the fall of the curtain was quite extraordinary. There seemed to be about fifty calls and recalls."

Neither of these papers had thought it necessary to draw attention to hitches in the elaborate production, realising that these would straighten out in time. *The Times*, however, dwelt upon them.

The
Times
3.11.21
"Tchaikovsky's conception of the ballet was very much like the average attitude taken by opera composers towards grand opera before Wagner had turned the world upside down. . . . It begins with the christening to which only the wicked fairy was not invited. Chief of the Good Fairies is Mme. Lydia Lopokova, and with her are half-a-dozen others of the most charming fairies who every stood on the tips of her toes . . . The wicked fairy (Carlotta Brianza) arrived in her coach, drawn by four plump, grey rats, and filled the court with consternation as she told without a word what would happen some day when the princess pricked her finger.

"Sixteen years passed while we listened to the slow movement of Tchaikovsky's Fifth Symphony (in the interval) . . . Next came the scene when, just as four princes were making proposals of marriage, the wicked fairy re-appeared and the spell took effect . . . Unfortunately the 'machine' worked badly, and the cactus which began to spring up round the enchanted castle refused to become the luxuriant crop which it should have been."

But Aurora, though danced with perfection, simply did not "come across." The Prince was meaningless, in terms of stage impact. Both these fine dancers were completely outshone by Lopokova and Idzikowski. The enchantment of an Aurora who can make the most staid audience catch its breath was submerged in the gorgeousness – the splendour.

The Sunday papers were even cooler:

Observer
6.11.21
"With its five acts, with its huge dress-parades, with its half-dozen principal dancers, with its solo dances that can be recalled and encored while the rest of the company are 'left in the air,' it makes a spectacle too endlessly and evenly the same to endure four hours' complete attention," said the *Observer*.

This was small beer compared with Ernest Newman.

Sunday
Times
6.11.21
"In common with some hundreds of other people, I was present on Wednesday at the Alhambra at the suicide of the Russian Ballet. It was buried with fitting pomp; we can say of it as was said of Enoch Arden:

> So passed the strong heroic soul away,
> And when they buried him the little port
> Had seldom seen a costlier funeral.

"That Wednesday's proceedings were costly was evident; no less evident was it that they were a funeral. The Russian Ballet, as an art force, has ceased to be. It almost died last summer of cerebral anaemia, after having become intellectually bankrupt. It has cultivated inanity, off

Vera Soudeikina, wife of the designer, Soudeikine, (and subsequently, of Igor Stravinsky,) made a beautiful Queen, for whom two magnificent costumes were designed. The King (Walter Treer) was a figure of extravagant splendour too.

and on, for some years. It reached its limits, along this line, in *Chout* and the new choreography of *Le Sacre du Printemps*. Human brains could not invent anything more foolish; and if they could, people would not put up with it." Amongst M. Newman's other points were that Diaghilev was now in business in competition with Oscar Asche (producer of the spectacular and long-running *Kismet* and *Chu Chin Chow*) – but that women would flock to it because of the dresses. "But what looked like being a fiasco was saved by the loveliness of the final scene and the series of 'turns' by the old favourites of the Diaghilev troupe and some of the newcomers, such as Mme. Nijinska and Mme. Spessiva."

Vogue
December/1
1921

Vogue began a long article by stating firmly that the dates of Diaghilev seasons in London were red-letter days, to be earmarked in advance in diaries lest such delights as fishing or shooting, or "the unlooked-for catastrophe of a long-planned trip to the Riviera," might clash with a season. But the magazine, likening its feelings for Diaghilev's ballets to a love affair, went on: "It will be so difficult to convince our grandchildren of the authenticity of our romance that it may, perhaps, be advisable not to omit those passages which redound less lustrously to the credit of our terpsichorean gods and goddesses, and to record the occasional lapses of M. Diaghilev from grace. There were *Le Dieu Bleu* and *Sadko*, poor pages out of Christmas pantomimes; *Narcisse* and *Daphnis and Chloe*, no more in the spirit of Greek mythology than the pictures of Sir Frederick Leighton are in the spirit of Aeschylus; *Chout*, a nightmare of impudent, bad boy perversity for which the perpetrators deserved rather to be spanked and put to bed than criticised. Nor, unhappily, should we omit from our catalogue M. Diaghilev's latest effort at the Alhambra – *The Sleeping Princess*.

"It is quite astonishing to find M. Diaghilev, the quondam pioneer, sponsoring this elaborate, long-winded, cumbrous, mechanical ballet of action, constructed on the formal mid-Victorian lines which brought ballet into such low esteem among artists till M. Diaghilev himself appeared upon the scene to show what imagination and originality could accomplish ... Can it be that the abysmal commonplaces of *The Sleeping Princess* are merely a passing reaction against futurism, consequent upon the well-merited unpopularity of *Chout* and the unmerited unpopularity of *Le Sacre du Printemps*? If M. Diaghilev is endeavouring for once to give the public what it wants, we would warn him that only those who themselves want what the public wants ever succeed in this attempt . . ."

After condemning much of the choreography, *Vogue* continued: "Nor could we find comfort in the music of Tchaikovsky, which . . . was dramatically so ill-proportioned that some of the most significant moments of Perrault's story were allotted a mere handful of bars. For example, the awakening of the Princess, which should have furnished the grand climax, had to be scamped because the composer had scamped it in his score, and the kiss which aroused the Princess Aurora from her twenty years of slumber seemed of little more account than a rap on the door and a jug of hot water on a bright summer's morning."

So, though *Vogue* thought that Lopokova, "by dint of sheer dogged perfection," raised the whole ballet to the plane of "her own artistic purity" – "Nijinska, *folle* from the hips upward and flinging herself with a delicious *abandon* in two directions at once, provided an occasional grotesque excitement;" that Woizikowsky and Idzikovsky seized any opportunities offered them, and that Sokolova, Tchernicheva and Nemchinova were "compelled to spend long stretches in tantalising, if masterly, inactivity" – it really just thought the whole thing a bore.

If there was one thing to which *Vogue's* devotees were unwilling to submit, it was boredom; they were the purchasers of the more expensive seats; can one doubt that, reading this and much more, they took that exciting trip to the Riviera instead?

In the article from which some passages have already been quoted, Igor Stravinsky later recalled this first performance, and gave a most moving and intimate picture of Diaghilev's reaction to it all:

Atlantic
Monthly
November
1953

"The time that I saw Diaghilev the most enthusiastic was when – feeling that the moment had at last arrived when he could give to the public a composer whom he had never ceased to love – he produced in London, with unprecedented splendor, Tchaikovsky's ballet *The Sleeping Princess*. I never saw him work with such ardor and love! . . . But a catastrophe took place. At the end of the second act when the actors were meant to sleep, an enchanted forest, with trees and foliage, was supposed to rise slowly out of the ground to hide the background. In St. Petersburg this was wonderfully arranged, thanks to the perfect machinery and competent stage-hands. At the Alhambra, however, the equipment was much more primitive. So, at the beginning of this scene, the audience suddenly heard a great cracking noise, the machinery stopped working, and the end of the act was completely ruined . . .

"Diaghilev was in despair. That night, probably because he had worked so hard and used so much vitality, he had a nervous breakdown. He sobbed like a child and all around him had difficulty in calming him. With his usual superstition, he saw in this incident a bad omen and seemed to lose all confidence in his new creation, to which he had given so much of his soul and energy."

Perhaps *The Queen* and *The Lady* put accurate fingers on the two spots of weakness, other than length (which could, after all, have been adjusted.) Dr. Richard Terry mentioned an artist friend who had said, of the orchestra, "This is just a shade too British. One misses that full-blooded 'pull' in the middle of the bar, in the waltzes." "Untechnically expressed," said Dr. Terry, "but that just hits off what was missing." But *The Lady* said (of a different night) that "in spite of the sprite-like loveliness of Lydia Lopokova, a most adorable 'Lilac Fairy,' there is no definite and magnetic personality in all the vast throng of dancers on the big stage . . . The Princess Aurora is prettily mimed and danced, but Mlle. Egorova creates no genuine sense of dramatic enchantment or choreographic sensationalism . . . Prince Charming is a personable youth, but as he is almost a lay figure it is difficult to measure the talent of M. Pierre Vladimirov. However, it is more than likely that *The Sleeping Princess* will become immensely popular as well as fashionable."

The Queen 26.11.21

The Lady 10.11.21

Amongst those who wrote letters to the papers protesting against what they felt to be unfair criticism of the ballet, were the artists Edmund Dulac and John Lavery. The Dramatic Critic of the *Observer* had said, on the 6th, that though some of the costumes were magnificent, many were no better than a provincial pantomime. Lavery felt that "it is a criticism at once unworthy of the fine work in question and of the critic himself, and liable to prejudice a public otherwise inclined to use its own judgment." Dulac attacked the critics for "their lack of mental suppleness," saying that "This delightful association of seventeenth-century romance and humour with music and dancing of the eighties' has been approached by some in a spirit of hostility which makes one wonder whether it will ever be possible for some minds to break away from the stultifying limitations imposed by personal grudges." He had continued: "The mission of the critic is not to extol what he likes and murder what he dislikes; it is to judge whether the artist has succeeded or not in accomplishing what he set out to achieve. In this instance, M. Diaghilev proposed to show us another side of the wonderful art of his unique company . . . and no one with an average culture and a sense of decency could deliberately associate with the tinselly riot of bazaar Orientalism this most intelligent reconstruction of a fairy-tale presented in the quaint old-fashioned terms of an Italian ballet-master of the Pre-*Scheherazade* days . . ."

Observer 13.11.21 27.11.21

Sunday Times 4.12.21

Observer 27.11.21

Ernest Newman argued with himself. He had already written fiercely against Diaghilev's most *avant-garde* ballets to date. Now, for example, he said, "I have never been able to take M. Diaghilev seriously as a musician . . ." and, in the same article, "I can imagine no limit to the musical sincerities of M. Diaghilev." And again – "My objection to the ballet as a whole was that it showed a decline in intelligence . . ." and later, "My grievance against M. Diaghilev is that he should be wasting so much time and energy on a production which, beautiful as it is as a spectacle, and fascinating as some of the dancing 'turns' in it are, is a decided step backwards for him . . ." However, Newman, and others, said that they would like to see the last act alone "as a delightful *divertissement*," – so that when, later on, Diaghilev did indeed give that act alone, re-christened *Aurora's Wedding*, it may be said to have been "owing to popular demand."

Sunday Times 27.11.21

Was everyone taking it too seriously? When it had been running about a month, the *Daily Telegraph* said, "Frankly, I have been astounded by some of the critical pronouncements upon a production which, in its kind – that is, as an exemplification of all the graces of classical dancing, allied to the arts of music, scene-painting, colour blending, stage décor, and the rest, – must surely excel in beauty and sheer artistic merit anything of its type seen in London in the last thirty years, to take a period covering my own experience."

Daily Telegraph 3.12.21

At the Christening – The Blessing.

Carlotta Brianza, the first Aurora, as Carabosse in 1921.

Enjoying herself in one of Bakst's most wonderful costumes as Carabosse, the Wicked Fairy, was Carlotta Brianza, the Italian ballerina who had created the rôle of Aurora in St. Petersburg in 1890. In a delightful interview, she recalled that, at the end of that first performance, she had appeared before the curtain to take her calls with Tchaikovsky on her right and Petipa on her left, acknowledging the applause from an audience which included the Tsar. It had been so successful that she was given the second performance as a Benefit. "My share was to be half the receipts. That amounted to 20,000 francs" – (probably about the equivalent of £5,000 in 1970's money.) "The Tsar, Alexander III, paid me the great honour of sitting in the stalls in order to see my performance better. It was very exceptional for him not to sit in the Royal box . . . The present production follows that first performance very faithfully, and the part I now play is just the same as it was then." The Times 3.12.21

A Royal visit which had a special air of celebration about it took place on December 12th – for a British Royal Princess was newly-engaged to her own Prince Charming.

"The King and Queen, and as many of their loyal subjects as could conveniently be squeezed into the Alhambra, spent a couple of hours in that region of fairyland which the Russian ballet has made particularly its own. Their Majesties, who were accompanied by the Duke of York, the Queen of Norway, Princess Victoria, Princess Mary, and Lord Lascelles, arrived at Fairyland (by the Charing Cross Road entrance . . .) The Times 17.12.21

"The scene within the Alhambra recalled the palmy days of Russian Ballet, when London was at the feet of the dancers from the Imperial Court and the relative merits of beautiful ballerinas gave rise to fierce controversies. There was all the old glamour and very nearly all the old skill . . . Magic forests appeared from nowhere just at the right moment; Blue Beard's beard seemed to be even more highly coloured than usual; M. Stanislas Idzikovski was more nearly Nijinski than we have ever seen him before; Mlle. Olga Spessiva looked more beautiful than ever; Mme. Lopokova danced her way into everyone's heart with the greatest of ease; and Mr. Gregor Fittelberg had his orchestra under complete control."

The *Star* had added some social detail: "Princess Mary was in very vivacious mood – time after time she would lean forward to Lord Lascelles with some gay comment; and the Queen of Norway . . . shared in these jokes . . . Queen Mary looked particularly charming, and the King wore the air of a father who has done his duty by his eligible daughter. The Star 13.12.21

"The dancers were at their best, Lopokova, bewitching, exchanging such a happy kiss with that laughing pocket Adonis, Idzikowski, in the final scene; and the dark Spessiva, ravishingly lovely."

Writing up their diaries as usual, King George recorded it as "excellent and very well given," and Queen Mary as "beautifully given and most enjoyable." Royal Archives

Whilst such a Gala evening was naturally also House Full, there is no hint in any of the papers that the attendances were particularly sparse, but probably the less expensive seats were sold. One would have imagined that at least during the school holidays, there would not have been an empty seat. The production had been trimmed to more manageable proportions after a few days; still, the late start was hopeless for children. On Boxing Day, four pantomimes had their traditional openings in the West End, and three others in the suburbs. In fact, *The Sleeping Princess* seems to have been attracting far better audiences than most theatres that winter, when, for no explicable reason, but following on the trend of the previous summer, a great blight descended on the West End scene. Hannen Swaffer gave disturbing news: " 'We only had £21 in the house tonight.' 'We had £20.' This is the sort of conversation you heard amongst West End managers all last week Never were there so many Christmas entertainments: never were there so many special matinées. But few people attended them. One play which has only been running for two or three weeks had a matinée on Boxing Day, only to find there were seven people in the stalls and four in the pit . . ." Sunday Times 1.1.22

That week saw the Alhambra crowded once again for an "occasion" – the fiftieth anniversary of the first stage appearance of Maestro Cecchetti, who celebrated it by taking over the part of Carabosse from Brianza – the part he had created at the first performance, over thirty years before. Teacher of all the greatest dancers, "as an artist he is best known in this country for Observer 8.1.22

the rôles he created during his twelve years' association with Serge de Diaghilev ... Every balletomane knows his Grand Eunuch in *Scheherazade,* his Showman in *Petrouchka,* his Marquis in *Good-Humoured Ladies,* his Shopkeeper in *La Boutique Fantasque,* his Kostchei in *L'Oiseau de Feu,* his Pantalon in *Le Carnaval ...*" said Cyril Beaumont. Of his Carabosse, he continued: "Few of those spectators privileged to be present will ever forget that magnificent exhibition of the art of mime. It is difficult to remember how many times the curtain was raised ... Then when the curtain was lowered, a moving scene was enacted upon the stage ... He was embraced and kissed by all, then lifted shoulder-high, and carried in triumph to his dressing-room."

Stock
Exchange
Yearbook
1921

Business ebbed away in January, and the house was poor except at weekends. The running costs for the large company, orchestra, and stage-hands were fantastic. The management must have been forced to dip into its own pocket to meet the wage-bills. It had already signified that the scenery and costumes would never repay their costs by writing off the sum of £12,000 from its productions account, when its books were made up to December 31st, 1921.

Grigoriev
pps. 181/2

Remembering the successes of other seasons, Stoll suggested to Diaghilev – probably more than once – that he should bring over from Paris the sets and costumes of ballets in his repertoire, and alternate "triple bills" with his *Sleeping Princess.* Had Diaghilev agreed to do this, the financial crisis might have been averted, and the losses on the season reduced. But at this point Diaghilev's nerve seems to have broken. His legal training seems to have deserted him. Presumably under the terms of his contract with the Alhambra Company, the costumes and sets for *The Sleeping Princess* would remain their property until the cost was reimbursed. He could have asked for a contract stating that these others were his own property and did not form part of any such lien. Instead, he took the attitude that he dare not bring his other material into the theatre, in case the management impounded it too, leaving him unable to present ballets anywhere at all. He refused.

The Alhambra Company's accounts showed a loss of £23,272 at December 31st, 1921. When that loss is calculated in terms of money in the early 1970's, it becomes the equivalent of about £150,000, even including the receipts from about eight weeks of performances. The decision of the Board that the show must close becomes clearly inevitable. Stoll was forced to announce that it would be taken off in a week's time.

Dancing
Times
March 1922

Weekly
Dispatch
5.2.22

The idea has been put about that *The Sleeping Princess* tailed off lamely: not so. It was packed every night, throughout its last week.

Here is a description of the final performance.

"The fantastic, glittering Russian Ballet show of *The Sleeping Princess* came to an end last night, after 114 performances, and Londoners gave their favourites an amazing send-off.

"The theatre emptied three-quarters of an hour later than usual, and this time was occupied with clapping and a roar of cheering that sounded as if the gallery were full of carnivora anxious to devour the dainty creatures on the stage.

"Dancers bowed and curtsied till they looked thoroughly weary. There was a fortune in flowers for the favourites—for the queenly Tchernicheva and the wonderfully-accomplished newcomer, Trefilova; for the English girl, Sokolova, and for the Spaniard Maria Dalbaicin; for Egorova, and above all, for the charming Lopokova.

"At the end, after the intoxicating mazurka of the wedding scene, there were a dozen curtain calls – then "God Save the King" did not send the people home—then the safety curtain was lowered for ten minutes and the audience kept up a sustained roar for a last sight of the dancers.

"At last Mme. Lopokova came to make a speech in charming English. 'We are touched – we hope to be back soon as very 'good-humoured ladies,' she said.

"But the audience would not go till it had a speech from Idzikowski, who by that time was in his dressing-gown and civilian trousers. He was so hoarse he could barely murmur 'Thank You.'

"The ballet is going next to Monte Carlo."

By February 7th, the Alhambra was showing a Norma Talmadge film, *The Sign on the Door,* thrice daily.

Nicholas Kremnev as the Mandarin – by Elizabeth Polunin.

right: Two English dancers, Hilda Bewicke and Ursula Moreton (Mortonova,) not only danced as The Porcelain Princesses in the divertissement, but proudly boasted that they never missed a single performance.

below: Maria Dalbaicin, the leading lady of the *Cuadro Flamenco,* remained in Diaghilev's company, and performed as Scheherazade in this divertissement.

It seems futile to have prevented the elaborate production from earning money. The mixture of bankers, directors, contracts and temperament combined to immure these exquisite objects, costumes and scenery, in a sleep more profound, and much longer, than that of the bewitched Court itself.

The untimely ending of what had been intended to be a run of about six months was certainly a financial disaster, both for Diaghilev and for his backers. Disaster for his company might have been averted had there been less hysteria; it may be opportune at this point to trace some of the subsequent events.

There was an excellent Paris booking for May and June, and Diaghilev anticipated a visit to Monte Carlo before that. At the moment, he was stranded without an immediate engagement, and without money. London could not produce a loyal friend with a sufficiently ample bank balance to help him out. He called the company together, and told them that until he could arrange a booking, the most he could offer was a flat rate payment of £2 a week as a retainer. This was obviously inadequate. Frightened, and under pressure from other managements, (naturally wanting the stars,) several of his principal dancers accepted other engagements. They included Lopokova, Sokolova, Slavinsky, Woizikowsky and Idzikowski.

Diaghilev could not bear to witness the final performance, and, having borrowed £300 from Hilda Bewicke's mother, left for Paris.

The costumes and scenery were stored under the stage of the Coliseum. Some years later, a tank used for a diving act leaked, and rumour had it that they had all been ruined. This was turned into a diatribe against Stoll, who was accused of rank carelessness in their storage. Many years were to pass before the truth was eventually revealed. Certainly, of the scenery only that for the last act survived, but in all probability the fire-proofing chemicals had rotted the other sets.

Once in Paris, Diaghilev seems to have recovered his equilibrium speedily. He contrived to assemble a company, run a season in Monte Carlo in April, fulfil his commitment in Paris – and put on new works.

Rumour and legend have combined to give the impression that he could not "show his face" in London after the *débâcle*. Every theatrical production is a gamble, and this was neither the first nor the last to cost more than had been anticipated, and end up not paying its way. Only in the autumn of 1972 was a letter produced which most clearly gives the lie to such ideas.

Diaghilev's other London impresario, C.B. Cochran, would appear to have had faith in the capacity of the Ballet Russe to stage a come-back. The text of a letter from Diaghilev, (reproduced in facsimile, and here translated,) shows this. (It was obviously written by a secretary.)

Private Information

Dame Marie Rambert

HOTEL CONTINENTAL, PARIS.
25th February 1922.

Collection John O'Brien & David Leonard

My friend,

Before I left London, Cochran sent Creighton to me with the offer of a season in London on a percentage basis, opening about June 19th.

Will you please be so kind as to see Creighton at once, and get out of him, diplomatically, what percentage is suggested – whether we could get 60% for ourselves, and what weekly takings he envisages. Do this without delay, and let me know the reply at once. (It goes without saying that you would be in on the matter.)

All the best,
SERGEI DIAGHILEV.

From the last sentence, it would appear that the addressee was Eric Wollheim, Diaghilev's London agent.

Dates, dancers, percentages, size of theatre, clash of dates – what ever the reason, this visit did not eventuate, but what is interesting is that it was suggested by Cochran.

Avant mon départ de Londres j'ai eu l'offre de Cochran par Creighton d'une saison à Londres au pourcentage à partir d'environ le 19 Juin.

Voulez-vous avoir l'obligeance de voir Creighton immédiatement pour lui demander d'une façon diplomatique de quel pourcentage il s'agit, si nous pouvons arriver à 60% pour nous, et

quelles seraient les possibilités des recettes par semaine. Faites cela très vite et donnez-moi aussitôt la réponse. — Il est entendu que vous serez intéressé dans l'affaire

Bien à Vous

Serge Diaghilev

Only three weeks after he left London, a day before the last performance of *The Sleeping Princess,* Diaghilev had recovered sufficiently to send this letter from Paris – undoubtedly to Eric Wollheim, his agent. Like Stoll, Wollheim remained faithful to Diaghilev, and continued to act for him in London.

Diaghilev adjusted his repertoire and new works to suit his altered company, and recovered fairly quickly. For the Alhambra, the struggle was far longer. The huge loss in 1921 resulted in a debit balance of £21,344, which was carried forward. Receipts from the cinematograph and variety shows in 1922 improved this to a debit balance of £8,576 at December 31st, 1922 – after writing off a further £2,000 on the productions account for scenery and costumes. But the Alhambra Company passed its dividends in 1921, 1922, and 1923, and shareholders received their first dividend for four years in September, 1924. *Stock Exchange Yearbooks*

The *Sleeping Princess* passed into ballet history: the *Sleeping Beauty* awoke at Covent Garden in 1946. In 1967, following upon the first sale of Diaghilev material at Sotheby's, Baron Thilo von Watzdorf, David Ellis-Jones and Richard Buckle were allowed to penetrate a warehouse on the outskirts of Paris. Dust and cobwebs had settled on hundreds of theatrical hampers, filled with the costumes of many ballets. To their astonishment – having always believed the story of destruction in the flood at the Coliseum – they dragged out a magnificent coat, which they thought must have been for Prince Charming himself, so splendid was it. But no – there were five more like it, and nearly all the three hundred costumes from this production. Only a few can have been damaged, or, more likely, the other back-cloths and scenery. The backcloth for the last act (called Act V by accident in the catalogue, instead of Act IV,) remained with them.

Their splendour was awe-inspiring.

Against that exquisite backcloth (which was purchased for the projected Museum of the Performing Arts,) students of the Royal Ballet School wore the costumes at the resulting sale at the Scala Theatre on July 17th, 1968. Madame Sokolova had made an arrangement of part of the ballet, so that, for a few minutes, a privileged audience could get a faint glimpse of Diaghilev's production, before the costumes which had so long slumbered together were scattered in "lots."

1924

COLISEUM THEATRE

NOVEMBER 24th 1924 - JANUARY 10th 1925

FIRST PERFORMANCES IN ENGLAND

November 24th: *Cimarosiana*
(Cimarosa, Massine, Sert.)
Monte Carlo, 8.1.24.

November 24th: *Le Train Bleu*
(Milhaud, Nijinska, – Scenery, Laurens,
Costumes, Chanel – Curtain, Picasso,
Scenario, Cocteau.)
Paris, 20.6.24.

December 1st: *Les Tentations de la Bergère.*
(The Faithful Shepherdess)
(Monteclair, Nijinska, Gris.)
Monte Carlo, 3.1.24.

December 15th: *Aurora's Wedding*
(Last Act of The Sleeping Princess)
(Tchaikovsky, Petipa, Benois.)
Paris, 18.5.22.

REPERTOIRE

La Boutique Fantasque	*Polovtsian Dances*
Contes Russes	*Les Sylphides*
Midnight Sun	*Le Tricorne*
Petrouchka	

COMPANY

Antonova, Chamié, Coxon, Danilova, De Valois, Doubrovska, Fedorova, Gevergeva (Geva), Ginzbourg, Klemetska, Komarova, Krassnova, Krasovska, Maicherska, Nemchinova I, Nijinska, Nikitina I, Nikitina II, Rosenstein, Sakovska, Savina, Schollar, Sokolova, Sumarokova I, Sumarokova II, Svekis, Tchernicheva, Troussevitch, Zalevska.

Balanchine, Deline, Dolin, Domansky, Efimov, Fedorov, Grigoriev, Hoyer I, Hoyer II, Jazvinsky, Jouraw, Kornetsky, Kotchanovsky, Kremnev, Lapitzky, Legat N., Lifar, Michaelov, Pavlov, Savitzky, Singaevsky, Slavinsky, Strechnev, Tcherkas, Unger, Vilzak, Woizikowski, Zmorslik, Zverev.

CONDUCTORS:

Milhaud, Flament

LE TRAIN BLEU

The Diaghilev Ballet had not committed suicide with *The Sleeping Princess*, as Ernest Newman had averred; it had, however, seriously strained its heart. One might say that it had temporarily passed out. Not until November, 1924, could *The Lady*, faithful admirer, cry triumphantly that "the Diaghilev Ballet is like a phoenix which constantly rises from its own ashes with renewed vigour."

The
Lady
11.12.24

The interim, about thirty-two months, was the longest period that London was without the *Ballets Russes* except during the war. The situation was, however, diametrically opposite to that which had pertained during the war, when dancers had clustered round Diaghilev for safety; they had no alternative. In peacetime, there were other possibilities, and, naturally, other managements wanted the best dancers. To Diaghilev's chagrin, without waiting to see what he could fix up for them, Lopokova, Sokolova, Woizikowsky, Idzikowsky, Slavinsky and others joined Massine, who had formed a company.

Nevertheless, Diaghilev and Grigoriev managed to recruit dancers and took a company to Monte Carlo by the end of March, and then on to Paris as planned. The loss of his dancers could have been a far more lethal blow than the loss of a production, but Diaghilev was always at his most ingenious when in a dilemma. Shortage of funds limiting the matter of new productions, he resuscitated one of Benois' lovely back-cloths for *Le Pavillon d'Armide*, and many of the costumes, and the last act of *The Sleeping Princess* reappeared as *Le Mariage d'Aurore*. The only new works were Nijinska's ballet to Stravinsky's *Le Renard*, and a short opera, *Mavra*, by the same composer. In spite of all the difficulties, the season at the *Opéra* was so successful that Diaghilev was persuaded to move to the *Mogador* for a further three weeks, during which Karsavina came and danced for him.

During 1922, Diaghilev succeeded in making an excellent arrangement for the future. The company was to spend six months of each year in Monte Carlo, dancing in the operas put on by Italians, giving its own ballets, preparing new works and doing the maintenance on scenery and costumes, so necessary to keep the repertoire going. As it always had two months for holidays, this left the four summer months for lucrative engagements elsewhere. Monte Carlo possessed huge studios for scene-painting, and the paint dried much faster than in London – a great help.

With *Le Renard*, Nijinska had established herself in Diaghilev's eyes as a choreographer. Always thinking ahead, he had asked Natalie Gontcharova to make designs for Stravinsky's *Les Noces*, which had been composed in 1917. One day in the spring of 1922, he treated Nijinska to lunch at Prunier's, and told her that in 1917, when they were all in Madrid, Nijinsky and Massine had quarrelled violently as each wished to create the ballet – so that, playing Solomon, he had decided that neither should do it, and had put it aside. He now wished her to undertake it. She was, as she put it, "a-glow with pleasure."

287

After lunch, Diaghilev took her along to visit Stravinsky, and the composer played the score through for her. In writing an appreciation of Gontcharova years later, she described her own reactions.

Gontcharova et Larionov Ed. Klincksieck 1971

"The music stunned me, took possession of my senses, set me pulsing to its rhythms. *Les Noces* seemed to me deeply dramatic, interspersed with occasional bursts of gaiety. These elements found their reflection in me, entering into my soul with the most profound and sincere of Russian feelings; and immediately, at that very moment, I saw clearly the whole picture of *Les Noces*, exactly as I would create the ballet choreographically."

Diaghilev then took her on to Gontcharova's studio.

"There were about eighty designs, beautifully executed in glorious colours, very theatrical and richly Russian. Both males and females were weighed down with great, heavy garments – very long skirts for the women, sweeping the ground, and tall kokoshniks for their heads; the men, all bearded, were shod either in heavy boots or shoes with heels. To my mind, these designs would have been more suitable for an old-fashioned Russian opera than for Stravinsky."

As they left the studio, Diaghilev, noticing her silence, said that he hoped the costumes had delighted her. He was extremely annoyed when she replied that they did not, and said that both he and Stravinsky had approved them. As they were so clearly at variance on this issue, they decided mutually to cancel the project.

Early in 1923, Diaghilev brought the matter up once more. This time, Bronia was in her own little sitting-room in Monte Carlo. She gave this dialogue:-

" 'I have finally decided to give *Noces* in Paris: are you prepared to start rehearsals and create this ballet? How do you see it? You recollect the first scene? We are in the home of the bride-to-be. She is sitting in a great Russian armchair, at the side of the stage, and her friends are combing and plaiting her hair . . .'
'No, Sergei Pavlovitch,' I broke in. 'There should be no armchair, no comb, and nothing like such a quantity of hair!' I seized a pen and a sheet of paper, and immediately drew the girl with many pigtails, three metres long. Her friends were holding out the plaits, making a pattern with them around her. Diaghilev burst out laughing – often a sign of satisfaction with him.
'And what happens next? How are the young girls to comb tresses that length?' he asked.
'They won't comb them,' I replied. 'They will dance on point, and as they dance with the bride, the steps will explain the rhythm of plaiting her hair.' I went on drawing, and set down my ideas for the choreography and setting. Sergei Pavlovitch seemed more and more amused. 'A *Russian* ballet danced on point!' he exclaimed. Boris Kochno, who was with him, listened with great attention.
'What Gontcharova designed . . . was for one of the old operas, not a peasant wedding. I would like the very simplest of costumes, and all the same for everyone.'
'Very well, Bronia,' agreed Diaghilev, 'you start work as you wish on *Les Noces*, and when the choreography is finished, Gontcharova and I will come to see it, and she shall make completely new designs. But start rehearsals at once!' And I did."

Bronislava Nijinska continued her article, giving her ideas about the interpretation of the score in terms of peasant nuptials.

"Chance decided the lot of the engaged couple, who had been chosen by their parents, to whom they were bound in filial obedience. No question of love entered into it. The young girl could know nothing of the family she was about to join, and of the future that awaited her; would she even be loved by her husband? . . . The spirit of the young girl is anxious, deeply troubled, for she is about to leave for ever the carefree life of the beloved daughter of a devoted mother.
"For his part, the young man has no idea either as to how life will work out for him. How can it be possible for two such creatures to feel rejoicing during the ceremonies attending their marriage? Only the parents and friends are happy, for to them a wedding is a matter of festivities, of feasting, singing, and bucolic dancing.

Gontcharova's first design for the Bride in *Les Noces*, in which she wears a costume so elaborately embroidered that one might imagine her mother starting it at birth, like putting down a son for Eton, is in itself charming. It is easy to see how widely it differed from Nijinska's conception of the ballet, and why Diaghilev finally decided to allow her to have her own way, with very simple costumes.

"To present, to bring to life in a ballet the rituals and the reality of such nuptials, seemed to me to require an approach to theatre different from that which I already knew, one in which they would be brought to life and would speak only in the purest of movement. Mime was superfluous to me, stage properties unnecessary."

There is a curious resemblance to some of her brother's utterances at the time when he was preparing *Le Sacre du Printemps*, for she said, "In my conception, the entire company of dancers, like a whole orchestra, would speak as one to indicate the shades of meaning of the choreography."

When Gontcharova arrived from Paris, Bronia explained her ideas, pointing out the necessity to have very simple Russian costumes, in one colour only, and to abjure heavy footwear and heels. "Gontcharova found it hard, at first, to give up her plan – and her husband, Larionov, kept offering suggestions for 'props.' He wanted a wedding-wagon, painted and decorated, and various other devices. "But in the end, when she had watched several rehearsals, Gontcharova fell in completely with my ideas . . . Her costumes and décors, designed with great distinction, corresponded entirely with my choreography."

Although the ballet was not brought to London until 1926, and the English reaction to it was not put to the test until so many other advanced works had been seen, this description of the relationship between Diaghilev and his collaborators is interesting. Nijinska's works for him were so extremely original, and so varied, that it must be enough to say that he had great faith in her. She, for her part, may be said to have adhered to Fokine's principles, finding even newer styles to fit even newer themes.

In 1923, *Les Noces* was such a success in Paris that she was there dubbed "La Nijinska," greatly to her delight. (Diaghilev had already accorded her this title in London in 1921, for her choreographic additions to his *Sleeping Princess.*)

Remarking that, for one fairy-like night, Versailles had woken from its slumber, neither for the occasion of the marriage of a Dauphin, nor for the dazzling of an Ambassador, but as the crowning event of this season, *L'Illustration* commissioned a drawing which shows that, as it said, "Art and Taste combined in this resurrection – the past floated before the eyes."

Atlantic Monthly November 1953

When, thirty years later, Stravinsky described Diaghilev's nature in the article from which some excerpts have already been quoted, he said: "Diaghilev loved splendour, sumptuousness and brilliance. He loved to do things in the grand manner. Unfortunately he never had adequate means to satisfy his wishes. How happy he was when he did have sufficient money! He had extreme pleasure in organizing a grandiose pageant in the Palace of Versailles in the summer of 1923. Diaghilev was given the necessary funds to provide a spectacle in the château's celebrated Gallery of Mirrors to depict the court of Louis XIV . . ."

The French Government had organised a series of events, aimed at collecting funds for the restoration of the Château de Versailles, culminating in this *"Fête Merveilleuse,"* honouring Louis Quatorze and the great artists who made the brilliance of his reign. Gabriel Astruc and Diaghilev were invited to arrange the evening's entertainment.

Nothing could be more difficult than to stage a spectacle in a room 238 ft. long, 35 ft. wide, and 40 ft. high. The magnificence of the setting, with its marble columns, the great mirror panels reflecting the long row of windows, its painted ceiling and huge chandeliers, was as much of a challenge as its dimensions. Diaghilev called on Juan Gris to design a raised stage at one end. His brilliant solution was described in *Le Figaro:*

Le Figaro 30.6.23

"With the collaboration of the Keeper and the Architect of the Château, Juan Gris has created a décor worthy of Mansart. Imagine a great staircase, covered in mirror from St.

Rene Lelong, the artist, gave a vivid impression of the mirrored stage devised by Juan Gris, with its spun-glass embellishments, garlands, baskets, and fountains, at the very moment when Sert's brilliantly coloured, vastly-panniered Infantas of Spain were delighting the fortunate thousand who, for that one night, constituted "tout Paris."

Gobain, and completely embellished with glittering adornments; spun-glass fountains, baskets, hedges, flowerbeds, dazzling swags and garlands – all leading gradually to a stage some ten metres square, on which the ballets were to be performed. In front of all this was a low fountain with mirror representing the water in the basin, and more spun-glass jets, catching the light from the great chandeliers originally installed in the *Galerie*." (The originals had, in fact, been put into store, and faithful copies made, wired for electricity.) Stravinsky said, "The famous Gallery was flooded with light. The jewels of the top ladies of fine society sparkled under it." Stravinsky may not have known it, but it was the very first time that electricity was used in the Château de Versailles. As no more than 1,000 places could be arranged, and "tout Paris" wished to attend, the price of 300 francs – in the region of £30 a seat in terms of 1970's money, and inclusive of supper, does not seem excessive. Tardy applicants received tickets firmly marked, "View not guaranteed." But on the night, said *Figaro*, just as the performance was about to begin, a lady drove up, rattling in pearls from head to foot, but without any sort of ticket. Determined to get inside the Hall of Mirrors, she offered 6,000 francs. On this occasion, (which was, after all, supposed to be raising funds,) money talked. She was admitted.

Le Figaro 1.7.23

Disposed about the staircase and platform, charmingly grouped, were members of the *Comédie Française*, (whose extensive wardrobe must have saved a great deal of expenditure.) The Master of Ceremonies was Daniel Vigneau, a singer from the *Opéra Comique*. With due pomp, after a fanfare by Rameau, he pronounced a text written in the style of the period and announced the ballet, *Le Mariage d'Aurore*. (Boris Kochno made the only appearance of his life on the stage as one of the Heralds, wearing the magnificent costume designed by Juan Gris which was used, the following year, in *Les Tentations de la Bergère*, and which is now the property of the Museum of the Performing Arts.)

A varied programme of songs, recitations, and dances followed, the high spot being the *Pavane*, to music by Gabriel Fauré. The costumes, for the two Infantas of Spain, had been designed by José-Maria Sert, and recalled the period of Velasquez. One can recognise in this part of *Las Meñīnas*, the ballet produced in Spain by Massine in 1916.

Music by Cimarosa heralded the appearance of the Queen of the Night, and then Vigneau sang a song by Lulli, in praise of Versailles. More dances followed – the Court Jesters, and a procession of the characters from Perrault's *Contes des Fées* – including the familiar numbers from the last act of Tchaikovsky's *Sleeping Beauty*, the Danse Arabe, the Blue Bird, Little Red Riding-Hood, the Porcelain Princesses, the Bouffons, and the *pas de deux* of the Princess Aurora and Prince Charming.

That led up to the grand finale, the apotheosis of Louis Quatorze, to the accompaniment of Rameau's *Hymn to the Sun*. *Le Roi Soleil* (impersonated by Anatol Vilzak,) slowly mounted the mirrored staircase. As he ascended, twenty Negro Slaves, his Pages, gorgeously arrayed, spread over the steps and right across the stage the fabulous blue velvet train, thirty-five metres in length, embroidered all over with golden fleurs-de-lis, and bordered with ermine, which Juan Gris had designed. There was deafening applause as *Le Grand Monarque* surveyed his court. Then, exactly as he disappeared through some opening at the centre of the setting, a magnificent display of fireworks was let off in the park outside.

The fireworks continued for about half an hour, as the privileged subscribers made their way to the *Galerie des Batailles,* where tables had been prepared for supper. All the dishes on the menu were given names appropriate to the occasion – consommé *Mansart,* salmon with *sauce Maintenon,* Prague ham *à la Sevigné,* chicken *Vatel,* salad *Trianon,* ices *Lulli,* and some sort of *délices* charmingly called "*les papillons du château.*"

Everyone felt that Diaghilev had excelled himself. For the dancers, using as dressing-rooms Madame de Maintenon's room and the bedroom of Louis XIV himself, it was an unforgettable occasion.

What a pity it was that some of the money put up for the creation of the entertainment could not have been diverted to paying off part of Diaghilev's debt in London, so that Bakst's glorious costumes for *The Sleeping Princess* might have been released to adorn it. Nevertheless, with the sole exception of the grouchy critic of *Le Temps* (who thought the fireworks the best part of all, and wondered why the Russian dancers had been summoned to appear, instead of the native company from the *Opéra* – perhaps the supper disagreed with him?) – everyone else could find only one word to describe it – *inoubliable!* (Unforgettable.) It must have out-splendoured even *The Sleeping Princess.*

Probably the excitement attaching to the use once more of the material from *Le Pavillon d'Armide* helped to effect a reconciliation between Diaghilev and Benois, estranged for so many years. (Benois had remained in Russia after the Revolution, but was allowed to leave in 1923, and settled in Paris.) Diaghilev invited him to design and produce three short operas for Monte Carlo, thinking it a delicate compliment to give French works. He chose *Le Médecin Malgré Lui,* adapted from the play by Molière, *Philemon et Baucis,* and *Colombe* – all composed by Gounod.

In September, 1923, needing fresh blood in the ranks, Diaghilev sent for a pretty young Irish girl who had been dancing professionally for some years, and had recently been with Massine. Born Edris Stannus, she was to achieve fame as Ninette de Valois – spelt, at first, Devalois. About the same time, he engaged another Irish dancer, even younger, who, as a boy, had been one of the pages in *The Sleeping Princess*. (Billed in 1921 as "Patrikeef," he had by now been re-named "Anton Dolin," a name which he, too, made famous.) Though only twenty, he had improved so greatly in the interim under Princess Astafieva, whose studio was in The Pheasantry, in King's Road, Chelsea, that he was now able to take on the arduous responsibility of becoming the company's *danseur classique*.

23rd September 1924.

The carbon copy of a letter from Sir Oswald Stoll
to Diaghilev, September 23rd, 1924.

Dear Sir,

In consideration of your paying to the Alhambra
Company Limited the sum of £30 per week during the seven
weeks that your Company is performing at the Coliseum, and
paying the balance of the agreed amount of £2,000 viz:
£1,790, before any subsequent performances by you or your
Company in London, it is hereby confirmed that no
proceedings will be taken against you for the recovery of
your debt to the Alhambra Company Limited, and on
settlement in full of the said sum of £2,000, the whole
of the production of "The Sleeping Princess" will become
your property. It is also confirmed that the payment of
the said £2,000 will be accepted in full settlement of
your debt to the Alhambra Company Limited.

Yours faithfully,
For & on behalf of The Alhambra Company Ltd.,

Managing Director.

Secretary.

Serge Diaghileff Esq.,

Dolin appeared as Daphnis in Monte Carlo on January 1st, 1924, to considerable acclaim. He also took part in *Le Médecin Malgré Lui*, "an opera with some spoken dialogue, but so charming, so delightful, that one wonders why it has not appeared before the footlights for fully fifty years . . . we must give a special word of praise of M. Anton Dolin, a skilful young dancer, graceful and artistically well trained, whose whole bearing calls to mind a style which, sadly, seems to be disappearing . . ." (This was a comment by Jehan d'Everat in his "LETTER FROM THE CÔTE D'AZUR" to a Paris paper.)   *** 5.1.24

The company travelled to Spain, to Paris, and to Germany. The Paris season was once more an outstanding success, with new works by Nijinska. As Dolin was an expert in acrobatics, *Le Train Bleu* was specially devised to make use of this talent.

So far from being dead, as Ernest Newman had stated, the ballet had acquired new stars and a new choreographer – and, with her, a new lease of life.

Sir Oswald Stoll has been represented as a veritable ogre by some people because, as Managing Director, he had to be the spokesman when the Alhambra Company decided to terminate the run of *The Sleeping Princess*. The truth would seem to be that Diaghilev had few more loyal friends. Just as in 1918 he had been the saviour, so, despite the hysterical disagreements of 1922, it was Stoll who, once again, brought the company to London in 1924. The formula which had proved so successful in 1918 was to be repeated – one ballet in each session of the Coliseum. Terms were set out (as shown in a letter from the Alhambra Company, dated September 23rd, 1924, reproduced in facsimile,) which would enable Diaghilev to pay off his remaining debt and acquire his lavish, beautiful production. It was decided that the amount outstanding was £2,000 (a figure which indicates that some money had been forthcoming out of the receipts during the run, even though large sums had been written-off.) Rumour dies hard. The appearance in the London salerooms of these letters and documents does not seem to have shifted the die-hards from their attitudes. These letters, and the subsequent contracts, tell their own story.

Diaghilev opened at the matinée with the arrangement he had made of the last act of *Le Astuzie Femminili*, now re-named *Cimarosiana.* The reception exceeded all expectations. In the evening, Nijinska's *Train Bleu* had a true London "*Première.*" The libretto of this ballet was by Cocteau, and it was contemporary and chic, dressed by Chanel, a great friend and supporter of Diaghilev's. For some obscure reason, the Blue Train did not go to the Côte d'Azur, but to Deauville – but what would you? All that mattered was that dancers disported themselves on a sunny *plage.* Both ballets were a delight to the critics.

The *Daily Mirror* was thrilled by the dancers.

Daily
Mirror
25.11.24

"No finer tribute to the artistic memories of this brilliant company of artists could have been found than the way in which people rushed to gain admission to these inaugural performances," it said. "Sokolova, with that entrancing swing of the arms, and Dolin, a newcomer, with such a fine balance that he seems able to lean against the air, were the greatest successes of the week. Of the soloists perhaps the greatest impression was made by Mlle. Nemchinova in her *pas de deux* with M. Dolin. Her dancing is extraordinarily dainty and agile, and at the same time expressive." Every paper said similar things about *Cimarosiana* and *Le Train Bleu*, both a delight to eye and ear. Naturally, the greatest attention was focussed on the new work.

The
Times
25.11.24

"Constructed after the pattern of a musical comedy," said *The Times*, "there is only a slender thread of plot which gives scope rather for character work than miming. The scene is a beach at a fashionable seaside resort, the time one of the fine days of the summer of 1924. 'Flappers' and their 'boys' are discovered dressed for bathing-parade, and, in place of the usual chorus of

Anton Dolin as *Beau Gosse.*

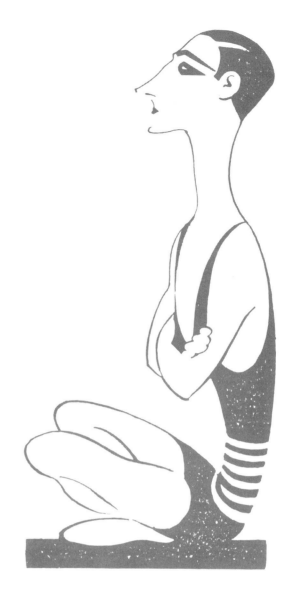

musical comedy, execute a dance founded on the motions of swimming and diving. Enter *Beau Gosse* (a Bright Lad) and Perlouse, who soon dances herself into hiding in a bathing-box. They are followed by a lady lawn tennis champion and a male golfer, (M. Leon Woizikowsky,) a wonderfully Anglo-Saxon-looking athlete. The general merriment ends with some figure dancing in which a human 'merry-go-round' is made with the 'Bright Lad' rotating in the middle.''

Discussing the music, *The Times* continued: "Darius Milhaud has avoided the most modern mannerisms of his school and deliberately written some simple little tunes, some of them, however, punctuated with unexpected pauses that give a touch of Stravinsky to their rhythm. The use of brass and percussion, too, is not as innocent as the simple little tunes might lead the ear to anticipate . . . The Bright Young Things enjoy themselves, but they can laugh at themselves enjoying themselves, with their sun-spectacles and elegant costumes and endless flirtations.''

The *Morning Post* liked it, too. ". . . *les poules* and their gigolos engage in various kinds of acrobatics and other exercises . . . The conventions of the musical comedy, the opening chorus, the waltz, – charmingly danced by Mme. Sokolova and M. Woizikowsky – (which the audience would like to have had repeated,) the intentional inanity of the plot, and the equally intentional irrelevance of the music, are all respected. *Le Train Bleu* is decidedly amusing. One laughs at Nijinska's take-off of Lenglen, and at M. Woizikowsky's plus fours and leisurely drives.''

Morning
Post
25.11.24

In 1913, Vaslav Nijinsky's *Jeux* had been a puzzler; the surface of something to do with two girls and a man in clothes roughly approximating to tennis dress had been but a pretext for an attempt to convey curious undertones of the relationships. Bronia's approach was quite different – the wittiest possible caricature of the manners of contemporary society, overtly displayed, with the twists characteristic of the *Ballets Russes*. (One wonders what the result would have been had Nijinsky ever carried out the idea of making a ballet founded on sports!)

A new generation of stars joined those already established in Londoners' hearts, and there should be no mistake about this – stars indeed they were, attracting their own public, raking in money at the box-office, playing to full houses. "It is as difficult to get a seat for the *Blue Train* as it is to get a seat in the thing itself during the height of the Riviera rush," said one glossy weekly. (The Riviera rush was then a winter one – summer still saw the South of France "out of season," too hot.) A rival referred to the drop-curtain: ". . . Any initial boredom was dissipated by Picasso's strange curtain – representing, apparently, two 'fat ladies' of the Fair, breasts well to the fore, and not exactly where one would expect to find them, rushing over the sands as if in the first flush of ecstasy of being *enfin sans corsets*." (This drop-curtain, actually painted by Prince Shervashidze from Picasso's design, was auctioned by Sotheby's in 1968 and bought for the British nation for the astronomical price of £69,000.)

The Queen thought that "*Le Train Bleu* has a Greek starkness (not, of course, anything like the 'classical' dancing of young ladies with a Chopin waltz and two yards of chiffon,) and it is impossible to imagine more skilful dancing than this, where the effects are unheightened by artifice and the defects unsmothered by glamour of costume."

Herbert Farjeon gave his thoughts on the welcome return of the company. "Our gramophones may now enjoy a well-earned rest. No longer need we solace ourselves of an evening with records of *Petrouchka* and *Scheherazade* and *La Boutique Fantasque*. Once again we can see, hear, taste the thing itself . . . It is good to see that the Russian Ballet, while retaining the best items in its old repertoire, keeps abreast of developments in the other arts, and attempts to interpret the spirit of the times. It is always moving. *The most youthful go-ahead intellectuals cannot dismiss it as a back-number yet.* It is just here that Diaghilev's dancers fail when they leave him and court public favour 'on their own.' They seem to have no initiative, no courage. They can only reminisce. One of these days I shall, no doubt, be shedding a tear over the lamentable disappointment of Anton Dolin, managing a troupe of dancers on his own in some variety theatre. But so long as he remains with Diaghilev, he is likely to afford us the most intense delight."

Bystander
3.12.24

The
Tatler
10.12.24

The
Queen
3.12.24

The
Sphere
6.12.24

Another of Nerman's witty cartoons, which appeared in *The Tatler*.

296

Lubov Tchernicheva and Anton Dolin as Venus and Hymen.—*right:* Vera Nemchinova as The Faithful Shepherdess.

The next new work to be shown was *Les Tentations de la Bergère.* Richard Capell described the plot for his readers: "It is an elegant pastoral of the *grand siècle,* with a Louis XIV marquis exercising his *Droit de Seigneur* over a village maiden. Dismay of the village swain – virtuous decision on the maiden's part – and final triumph of true love, with mythological assistance (Venus and Hymen, two of the prettiest figures of animated porcelain.) The theme is trite, but it has this time fallen into the cleverest of hands. The ballet is made by a succession of happy little touches. Everyone has sought to do what would have been pleasing to the taste of a Saint-Simon, and – what is more – with a perfect knowledge of what Saint-Simon's taste would have been . . . The Faithful Shepherdess was Mlle. Nemchinova, and no wonder the Wicked Marquis (M. Slavinsky) thought her easily the equal of the grand ladies about him." The designs, by Juan Gris, were ravishing. Daily
Mail
2.12.24

Hubert Griffith, a critic who always wrote with complete fairness whether he liked or disliked a new work, had no hesitation about this one. "I cease to lament that the Diaghilev Ballet has no longer its former star dancers with it. *The Faithful Shepherdess* is the third ballet of their present season. It is complete and perfect, and altogether delightful. It proves that M. Diaghilev himself is a bit of a genius, and that it is he who makes the fame of his dancers, not he who has had his fame made for him by them. His old stars have left him, but the new principal dancers who have been promoted, or snatched up from elsewhere to take their places, Mlles. Sokolova and Tchernicheva, M. Woizikowsky, and the new young man from Ireland, M. Anton Dolin, are just as good as any of the former lot, or at least are made to appear so. The perfection of the dancing is still far and away above that of any other company that now comes to London." Observer
7.12.24

"Or at least are made to appear so." Was it not largely in this that Diaghilev's genius lay – in the inspired casting which enabled every and each individual to shine, whether in great parts or small, as a perfect artist in his or her own line? Force of circumstances, especially when touring, sometimes made him ask an artist to perform a rôle for which he or she was not ideally suited. This applied also, on a larger scale, to *The Sleeping Princess.* He did show various artists in the classics, but when it came to producing new works, despite the remarks quoted by Karsavina in 1919, the success was due in large measure to the perfection of the individuals. In his own memoirs, Fokine said, "In general, I would say, however, that I did not create the rôles for the dancers but for the ballet as a unit. But . . . those artists who were selected for the first performance of the rôles were usually best fitted for them." Fokine
(Constable)
p.156

The
Times
2.12.24
Nijinska's range pleased *The Times*. "*The Faithful Shepherdess* has been arranged to selections from the music of Montéclair, a French composer of the time of Louis XIV. This provides plenty of scope for formal dances to Minuet, Sarabande, and Musette . . . We see enacted before a group of courtiers the tale of how a shepherdess resisted the addresses of a marquis and was faithful to her humble lover, preferring his simple gilliflowers and a bunch of fresh grapes to the nobleman's *bombes glacées* and ostrich feathers . . ." *The Times* went on to describe the scene, "a beautiful design of M. Juan Gris, who has rightly found his inspiration in Watteau and his school. Against a delicate grey background the groups of courtiers in mauve, of peasants in green, and of the Marquis and his followers in pale blue and black, made pictures as exquisite as any this company has given us since the production of *Daphnis and Chloe* . . ."

The
Lady
11.12.24
The Lady did not attend the first night, which clashed – as now is, indeed, traditional – with another, the return to London of Nikita Balieff's *Chauve-Souris*, a Russian cabaret turned into a stage performance, compèred in unbelievable English (an integral part of the fun) by Balieff himself. However, when it caught up, *The Lady* said: "The three productions I have seen are all distinguished by that fusion of music, decoration, and movement which Diaghilev alone seems able to accomplish. He has a very able lieutenant now in Nijinska . . . her choreography in *Le Train Bleu* and *The Faithful Shepherdess* is brilliant, besides showing amazing versatility, as in the first she has to design steps and movements founded on modern athletics – swimming, lawn tennis, golf, etc., to tunes of the musical comedy type by Darius Milhaud, while in the second she has to match the formal music with conventional '*closes*' of Montéclair . . . *Le Train Bleu* is the quintessence of modernism in every respect, except perhaps in its polished technique."

With the utmost temerity and persistence, Diaghilev once more gave London Petipa – Tchaikovsky – *The Sleeping Princess.* He gave, of course, only the last act, as in Paris, (and as critics, including Ernest Newman, had suggested in 1921.) This time, London adored it.

Morning
Post
16.12.24
"*Aurora's Wedding* vastly entertained the Coliseum audience, which would have liked to have had every *divertissement* repeated. It certainly affords the many distinguished ballerinas . . . brilliant opportunities for showing off their wonderful technique," said the *Morning Post*. It is odd to think that, years later, Diaghilev himself was to say that "for years the Russian Ballet had not been the classical ballet." It had not been *limited* to being the classical ballet, but never for a single day in the twenty years of its existence was the classical training neglected. Technique had to be perfect – then it could be adapted.

"The choreography of 'The Marquesses,' 'The Three Ivans,' and the variations danced by the Prince Charming – which were amongst the most striking details – was actually the work of the accomplished Nijinska, so that both Petipa and Tchaikovsky play only relatively important parts in this wonderful pantomime . . . But what details! Last night Vera Savina and Anton Dolin captured the house by their dancing in the Blue Bird episode . . . while there was a wild outburst of applause for the dancing of the Three Ivans (Woizikowsky, Slavinsky and Kornetsky,) the verve of whom beggars description . . . The curtain had to be raised and raised again many times at the close before the audience had tired of cheering." (Aurora and her Prince were danced by Nemchinova and Vilzak; Savina, having separated from Massine, had been received back into the company, though Diaghilev had at first said that he would not offer her any star rôles.)

Throughout this season, revivals were greeted with pleasure. There had been *The Times*, reporting that "the *Polovtsi Dances* from Borodin's opera *Prince Igor*, one of the works with which
The
Times
11.12.24

Observer
14.12.24
the Diaghilev ballet first took London by storm, were greeted with a storm of applause as enthusiastic as that of ten years or more ago." There had been Hubert Griffith, writing despairingly, "I propose shortly to give up criticising the Russian Ballet, for truth to tell, I find I can no longer criticise it in any useful sense. . . (If there is a finer and more romantic back-cloth in the world that Roerich's panorama of the tents and bonfires of the Tartar camp, I should like to know it.) . . . When one gets music of Borodin's richness and power, the whirl and fire of the barbaric dances, the splendour of Roerich's setting, all orchestrated and composed into a whole, the three arts blended into something that is both less and more than each. When this happens as completely as it is the genius of the Russian Ballet sometimes to make it do, criticism

sinks back in its seat for a rest. There is nothing like it on the stage, and for the few short moments that it lasts it seems a compensation for all the ills of life."

The *Sunday Times* was temporarily out of the criticism stakes, for Ernest Newman had gone to New York for a year as Guest Critic.

Diaghilev's other newly-recruited dancers, refugees, were also performing in London for the first time. In 1923, at Nijinska's suggestion, he had engaged several of her former pupils from the school in Kiev – the Hoyer brothers, Lapitsky, Unger, and Serge Lifar. Though, at first, Diaghilev had been most disappointed in them, he had taken them into the *corps de ballet*, and one, Lifar, was beginning to assume the aspect of a star.

In the summer of 1924, came four more recruits, trained in Petrograd, (as it was now called,) who had managed to leave Russia on a pretext; Balanchivadze, Efimov, Danilova, and Gevergeva. Shortening the first's difficult name to Balanchine, Diaghilev had immediately re-cognised this particular young man's fine musicality and quality, and though he was but twenty years old, had appointed him ballet-master to the company. Danilova was dancing leading rôles.

Shortly after Christmas, Diaghilev received news of the death of Bakst. Despite their final disagreement, Diaghilev was reported as being much grieved.

The
People
28.12.24

The season was an unqualified success, and on the day before it ended, Diaghilev and Stoll signed a contract for two further seasons in 1925, totalling eighteen weeks. On January 10th, Diaghilev received an advance of £750, and the last night came in an atmosphere of restored confidence.

"The season of Russian Ballet at the Coliseum closed last night with a scene quite without precedent . . . It was the glorious last act of *The Enchanted Princess*, with all the Fairy Tales that have delighted us again and again.

Observer
11.1.25

"When the end came after a short forty minutes, floral tributes without number were heaped upon the wonderful dancers, and twenty times or more the curtain was raised. And then 'Auld Lang Syne' was sung, and afterwards, 'We Won't Go Home Till Morning.'

"It became a question which would last the longer, the roaring cheers of the audience or the raising and lowering of the curtain. The management wanted to get on with their programme. They had 'Sporting Life' to show on the screen, but the audience did not want it. 'Extra Ballet!' they cried. When the management persisted with the pictures they booed and protested. It was 'More Ballet!' they wanted, not the pictures. An announcement was thrown on the screen that 'the ballet will return to the Coliseum in May.' Then the pictures were continued. So were the booing and the shouting for 'More Ballet!'

"Twenty minutes after the ballet was over the principals came before the curtain again, and once more 'Auld Lang Syne' was sung. Still the audience wanted 'More Ballet!' It was now ten minutes past eleven. The orchestra played the National Anthem, lights were turned low, and the stalls began to leave. But in the balcony they were still calling for more ballet, and it looked as if they would go on calling for it either inside the theatre or outside till midnight."

Next day, the company left from Victoria Station in a typical London fog, bound for the sunshine of Monte Carlo. "Diaghilev, grave and mountainous, was hovering between porters, taxis and troupe, and at intervals having a personal quarrel in Russian with the fog. Sokolova, daunted by the gloom, made straight for the carriage, and, retreating into a corner, gazed sadly over her big fur collar. Tchernicheva, bewitching even in a fog-logged station in the early morning, was busy supervising and eager to see that all went well. 'I am in despair at leaving London – of all the places we travel to, I want always most to be here,' she said, first in bad English and then in good French. Anton Dolin, the clever Irish dancer, declared he was glad that a typical fog had come to see them off." And finally – (the latest new recruit) – "Little Alice Marks, the 14-year-old London child who has joined the ballet, was begging her mother *please* not to cry."

***
12.1.25

1925

COLISEUM THEATRE

MAY 18th - AUGUST 1st

FIRST PERFORMANCES IN ENGLAND

May 25th: *Les Biches*
(Poulenc, Nijinska, Laurencin)
Monte Carlo 6.1.1924

June 3rd: *Les Fâcheux*
(Auric, Nijinska, Braque)
Monte Carlo 19.1.1924

June 29th: *Les Matelots*
(Auric, Massine, Pruna.)
Paris 17.6 1925

REPERTOIRE

Aurora's Wedding	*Narcisse*
La Boutique Fantasque	*Polovtsian Dances*
Le Carnaval	*Le Tricorne*
Cimarosiana	

COMPANY

Chamié, Danilova, De Valois, Doubrovska, Evina, Gevergeva, Klemetska, Komarova, Markova, Myers, Nemchinova I., Nemchinova II., Nikitina I., Nikitina II., Savina, Sokolova, Sumarokova I., Sumarokova II., Tchernicheva, Troussevitch, Zalevska.

Balanchine, Dines, Domansky, Efimov, Fedorov, Grigoriev, Hoyer I., Hoyer II., Idzikowski, Karnetsky, Kotchanovsky, Kremnev, Jazvinsky, Lapitzky, Lifar, Michaelov, Pavlov, Savitzky, Slavinsky, Tcherkas, Unger, Vladimirov, Woizikowski, Zverev.

CONDUCTOR

Goossens

LES BICHES

The company was to give the first performance of its Monte Carlo season at a gala on January 17th, under the patronage of the Prince and Princess of Monaco, in the presence of the Duke of Connaught and all the international celebrities fashionably wintering there. The *corps de ballet* selected that day to present Diaghilev with a round-robin, demanding higher salaries. Almost as the curtain was due to rise, only five dancers were in the theatre. Diaghilev went to the Royal Box, and informed the Princess that in place of the two ballets announced, *Cimarosiana* and *Les Tentations de la Bergère,* he would present a *divertissement.* Kotchetowsky persuaded his fellow-dancers that the scandal would ruin the company if the strike were to be continued, and a performance was somehow contrived. Unfortunately, although, as principal dancers, they had not been involved, Ludmilla Schollar and her husband, Anatol Vilzak, had mistakenly stayed in their hotel. Next day, they were summarily dismissed.

This year, Diaghilev had decided to re-engage Massine, but as a choreographer only. He arrived to work on *Zéphire et Flore,* commissioned from a new young Russian composer, Vladimir Dukelsky. The principal parts were given to the "poetic-legged" Alice Nikitina, as Dukelsky called her, and to Dolin and Lifar as the brother winds, Zephyr and Boreas. When he first discussed the project with Dukelsky, Diaghilev had said that he wanted to "combine classicism with Russian overtones." Massine devised a particularly beautiful short *pas de deux* for Dolin and Nikitina, which so delighted Diaghilev that he made them dance it as a "trailer" in another grand Gala, on January 31st. It was described as "*un fragment exquis,*" in a report which added: "*Puis, Mlle. Markova, ageé de treize ans, fut étourdissante de grâce, de légèreté et de talent, dans diverses danses qui lui présagent le plus brillant avenir.*" ("Next, Mlle. Markova, only thirteen years old, astonished the audience by her grace, lightness and talent, in several numbers which forecast a brilliant future for her.") Balanchine had arranged items suitable to her youth, using music by Chabrier and Rubenstein.

L'Eclaireur de Nice 9.2.25

When Dukelsky's ballet had its *première* on April 28th, a critic said that the music "successfully blends classic idiom with a moderate jazz influence in a closely-woven texture and was warmly appreciated." He felt that London would enjoy it.

Continental Daily Mail 30.4.25

After several happy weeks in Spain, the company returned to the Coliseum, intending to give a new ballet on the first evening, as before.

They gave the beloved *Carnaval* at the *matinée.* "It means much to say that the part of Harlequin was taken by Stanislas Idzikowski. Could anyone in the world put such fairy grace and romantic whimsicality into the part? He rises from the ground as if he did not know the word 'weight.' He is light as thistledown. By his art he has conquered all the limitations of this too too solid flesh, and arms and legs and body move as if his most trifling fancy were stronger than earth.

Evening News 19.5.25

AURORA'S
WEDDING

Vera Nemchinova and George Balanchine as the Princess Aurora and Prince Charming.

Alicia Markova and Boris Tcherkas, as Little Red-Riding Hood and The Wolf. This was her first appearance in London with the Diaghilev Ballet.

"So might we speak of Lubov Tchernicheva. With what exquisite grace her arms move! Just so the reeds beneath the stream rise and fall as the current bends them. Her hands twinkle over her head, they move smoothly down and then seem to vanish into light until they are over her head again. And there are half a dozen dancers who give as much delight to the eye and to the imagination." *The Times* also chose to discuss Idzikowski. "This is surely M. Idzikowski's finest part, and one knows no other dancer who can invest it with such whimsical beauty. There is no one else with that idiosyncratic shake of the head, which gives the character its piquancy."

The Times 19.5.25

The new ballet promised for the evening had to be postponed, owing to an injury to Woizikowski, but the audience was more than content to see *Aurora's Wedding.*

Evening Standard 19.5.25

"Again the Coliseum is filled with the most picturesque audience of all assembled in London," said Edith Shackleton, "the stalls orchidaceous, pearly and brilliant-hued, the gallery hand-woven and Spanish-hatted, but all of an equal eagerness.

"There was great warmth in these greetings. Shouts and cheers for Dolin, who, as they say in his own country, was leppin' like a hare in the blue bird part, and who will be a very great dancer indeed when he has got over the solemnity of extreme youth! Chorus of 'What a darling' for little Mlle. Markova, so prettily innocent as Little Red Riding-Hood," (and making her London début with the Diaghilev company.) "Cheers for the English Mme. Savina! Cumulative roars for Nemchinova — not only as a friendly welcome but because her dancing has improved to an enchanting exquisiteness, and she will probably be the rage of the season.

"A lively drop-curtain by Polunin should be mentioned among the attractions of the entertainment." Diaghilev had decided that it would enhance his company's dignity if, during the intervals either side of the ballet, a special curtain could separate it from the variety bill. So St. George slew a great dragon with Russian bravura. The gold size Polunin was forced to use in order to overcome the fire-proofing chemicals turned into a blessing in disguise, making the background glow like the gold of an icon.

The design for the Drop Curtain which Diaghilev commissioned from Vladimir Polunin for the Coliseum.

The
Times
22.5.25

Narcisse was revived, and *The Times* recalled the past. "It was unfortunately one of the least inspired of the pre-war productions of M. Fokine and M. Bakst. Now it seems extraordinarily old-fashioned, like Tcherepnin's music, which must once have sounded very new and brilliant, and proved last night to be a dull collection of the fashionable clichés of Parisian music fifteen years ago.

"How much we have altered, if not advanced, in stage ideas since the ballet was first produced may be judged from the inclusion in what was in its day 'the very latest thing' of those twinkling electric lights at the end and of that preposterous blossom which rises behind the looking-glass pond."

The Times found Tchernicheva, as Echo, extremely graceful – "every posture she assumed was unfailingly beautiful" – and Sokolova a great success as a Bacchante. "M. Theodore Slavinsky looked well as Narcissus, and did not smirk like the last interpreter we saw." (This must have been at the Alhambra in 1919.)

Evening
Standard
26.5.25

The new ballet, *Les Biches*, had a mixed reception. The translated title, *The House Party*, did not really fit its *esprit*. The subject-matter was completely contemporary. Few writers who mirror the contemporary scene are universally applauded. The *Evening Standard* carried an interesting review by Edith Shackleton: "Gautier laid it down that the creatures in a ballet must be those of the imagination only, like fairies or sea-nymphs or satyrs, or at least that they should be fantastically remote from contemporary human life, but Gautier himself now belongs to 'once upon a time,' and we live in a world which has changed so suddenly under our own eyes that we have ourselves become strange, interesting, incalculable – in short, figures for ballet.

"This was well exploited last season by *Le Train Bleu*. Last night . . . the Diaghileff company exploited it again in *The House Party*, which is a sort of indoor version of *Le Train Bleu*, but even more isolated in its modernity, since it has not even the echo of Sparta which was given in the

303

"J'ai un beau laurier de France – qui veut
de mon laurier – à qui faut-il le donner?"
An innocent-seeming song
accompanied a not-so-innocent
number – *Petite Chanson Dansée* – here
performed by Alexandre Danilova
and Lubov Tchernicheva.

No one who saw Lydia Sokolova's portrayal of The
Hostess – satire, not farce – could ever forget its
brilliance. Toying with that rope of pearls,
manipulating her long holder, she is seen here with
Leon Woizikowski, (one of the athletes.)

latter. A blue sofa suggests a luxurious interior, there is a bunch of pink, befeathered girl guests,
three proud men in blue shirts (Woizikowsky, Dolin and Zvereff,) and a supercilious hostess
with pearls and a cigarette holder (Mme. Sokolova,) and a beauty (Mlle. Nemchinova.) They
play childish games, flirt with an offhand calmness, while songs that sound like old ballads out
of tune are sung 'off,' and then the curtain comes down. There is no story, no conventional
composition.

"You may dislike *The House Party* and long for Mozart and Watteau and the graceful
hypocrisies of another age, but you will not be able to deny that Mme. Nijinska in its choreography has marvellously caught the attitudes of the moment, with its bald frankness between
the sexes, its poverty-stricken lack of trimmings, and its self-conscious physical prowess. And in
his music, which seems in part to be thin, childish and ugly, the young M. Francis Poulenc has
caught the restless, unhappy spirit of the present day.

"Mme. Marie Laurencin was not appropriately employed in designing the costumes and
scene of this ballet. The women of her paintings are shadowy, mysterious, wrapt in gentle
dreams, and do not belong to the present century, and though she has worked amusingly
enough – Nemchinova's dark sapphire tunic is a stroke of genius – the ballet has not – and
should not have – a typically Laurencin flavour.

"Nemchinova, dancing in an unexpectedly independent way, which shows that feminism has at last tinged the ballet, had a great success and displayed a great sense of character. So did Sokolova in the hostess part. Her high-shouldered attitudes were especially good. There was great enthusiasm, indeed, for the new production, which is extremely witty and provocative, and on no account to be missed."

The *Morning Post* considered the music "frankly ironical," the choreography "hardly less so." "A charming *Adagietto,* danced by Mme. Vera Nemchinova, gave her an opportunity of showing her extraordinary precision of technique.

Morning Post 26.5.25

"But on the whole *The House Party* seems to us to be a *jeu d'esprit* that is too elaborate to be amusing. The intervention of the chorus singing 'off stage' added little to the atmosphere and a good deal to the noise. One can hardly imagine that *The House Party* will add anything to the laurels of M. Diaghilev's company."

Poulenc (who had probably written the words himself,) attached great importance to the songs, but the English "translation" printed below the stave bears hardly any resemblance in meaning to the French. He stipulated that there should be not fewer than four singers in each voice, tenors, baritones, and sopranos.

The words fit the music perfectly, but as they move between the voices, and are repeated and interspersed by refrains, one can give only a poor idea of their flavour.

In *Chanson Dansée,* as the three young men display their physical beauty, Youth questions Experience – "What is love?" And Experience answers with a warning – "Love is a trap – love is like a cat that puts out a soft paw to caress, and then, without warning – out come the claws. Beware of love!"

Jeu is danced by the same three men, the Beauty, and the ensemble. The song is a parental grumble – "*J'ai quatre filles à marier . . .*" *Four* daughters to get married off – one is reminded of Jane Austen!

Lastly, *Petite Chanson Dansée* – the *pas de deux* for two of the girls – is a song of courtship, of bouquets, of kisses, of impending marriage. Perhaps one can read innuendoes into the seemingly simple words if one wishes to. It seems a pity to leave them out when the composer wished them to be sung.

The Times printed a column-long article attributed to "A Correspondent." ". . . Whatever imitators of, or offshoots from, it there may be, this company maintains even in its least happy moments a unique spirit whose mysterious existence can be attributed only to the inspiration of its director. Like the old conjuror in *Petrouchka,* he makes the puppets dance and must accept responsibility for their caperings." A survey of the Fokine and Nijinsky eras led on to Massine: "Massine's best ballets are little behind those of Fokine." Coming to the present, "A Correspondent" went on: "Their latest choreographer is Mme. Nijinska, who has evolved yet another convention. She has discarded the dramatic ballet and attempts to give us, under the form of divertissements, the atmosphere of contemporary life, or rather of that insignificant slice of it which is lived on the beaches of expensive watering-places, and in the houses of people who make themselves more conspicuous in human society than is warranted by the actual proportion of their number on the whole." Of her "big leaps and quick leg-movements," "angular gestures and sideways motion," the writer said that "These produce some original and delightful effects when they are carried out in concert by several dancers, as in the duet for M. Woizikowsky and Mme. Sokolova in *Le Train Bleu* and in the men's trio and the duet for Mmes. Tchernicheva and Danilova in *The House Party.* She seems to have singularly little invention where solos are concerned, and the success of Mme. Sokolova in the 'Rag Mazurka' last Monday was due to the spirit the dancer put into a burlesque which would have been very feeble if less capably done. Mme. Nemchinova . . . won her applause by her astonishing virtuosity in the classical style, for she obtained little assistance from the material she was given."

The Times 30.5.25

Of the music, the writer said, "The music written for this ballet by M. Poulenc is apt in its ineptitude. It has exploded one's notion that he is the most amusing of '*Les Six.*' . . . In a few years it will sound even more absurd than Tcherepnin's pre-war modernisms in *Narcisse.* One would not follow the example of its creators and devotees in taking this futility so seriously, did one not feel that it marks the decay of an art which has provided some of the most delightful moments in one's theatrical experience."

AN AGREEMENT made this   NINTH   day of JANUARY
1925, BETWEEN SIR OSWALD STOLL for and on behalf of THE COLISEUM
SYNDICATE LIMITED, (hereinafter referred to as "The Management" of
the one part and SERGE DIAGHILEFF (hereinafter referred to as "The
Producer") of the other part.

WHEREBY IT IS MUTUALLY AGREED AS FOLLOWS:-

The Management engages the Producer and the Producer accepts an
engagement to produce and present as hereinafter provided at one
performance every afternoon and one performance every evening (Sundays
excepted) at the London Coliseum, DIAGHILEFF'S FAMOUS RUSSIAN BALLET
formerly known as The Imperial Russian Ballet) for a period of ten
weeks commencing May 25th 1925 and for a further period of eight weeks
commencing November 23rd 1925 at a salary at the rate of £1,200 (one
thousand two hundred pounds) per week of twelve performances upon and
subject to the following conditions.

1.   The Producer shall provide an efficient company of 40 (forty)
competent dancers who shall be to the entire satisfaction of the
Management and shall include the following:- Vera Nemchinova, Lubov
Tchernicheva, Lydia Socolova, Leon Wojzikovsky, Anatole Viltzak, Anton
Dolin, Thadee Slavinsky, Alexandra Danilova, Vera Savina, Nicolas
Efimoff, or artistes of the same value.

2.   The Producer agrees that during the period of this agreement the
Producer will provide, produce and present any Ballet to be selected by
the Management from the following:- "Le Train Bleu", "The Good

17. The salary mentioned in the first part of this agreement being
strictly inclusive, the Management shall not be liable for any further
payment whatsoever.

18. The Management agrees to provide - unless prevented by a strike
of the musicians - an efficient orchestra of not less than forty-six
musicians and necessary supers for the said ballets not exceeding
thirty in number.

19. This agreement is subject to the written confirmation of the
Management.

AS WITNESS THE HANDS OF THE PARTIES:

For and on behalf of THE COLISEUM SYNDICATE LTD. *Oswald Stoll*

The top and tail of the counterpart copy of a contract between The Coliseum Syndicate Ltd.,
("The Management") and Serge Diaghileff ("The Producer") – dated January 9th, 1925,
and initialled by Diaghilev in the margin.

Victoria
& Albert
Museum
(Enthoven
Collection)

Before describing the next new ballet, it might prove interesting to study the terms of the
contract under which the season was running.

Diaghilev was to receive £1,200 for twelve performances weekly. He had to bring two new
ballets for each season, and fourteen more from his repertoire. (This does not seem to have been
insisted upon.) A company of 40 dancers, to be headed by Nemchinova, Tchernicheva, Sokolova, Woizikowsky, Vilzak, Dolin, Slavinsky, Danilova, Savina and Efimov, or artists of the
same quality, was stipulated. He had to provide all scenery, costumes, props, fares, transport,
royalties, dressers over two in number, and indemnify the Management against any sort of
trouble. The Management would provide an orchestra of 46 players and necessary extras
(unless prevented by a Musicians' strike.) If the theatre were to be closed for any reason, Dia-

ghilev would lose £100 for each performance which could not be given. If, on the other hand, he had to substitute one dancer for another, no matter what the reason, and if the substitute's salary was lower than that of the dancer who was "off," then the Management would deduct the difference.

The simplest arithmetic will show that this was a very tough contract. One thing that was a help was that at least the Coliseum paid his agent's commission. When it is remembered that halls had to be hired for class and rehearsals – that the scenery and costumes required constant maintenance – that Diaghilev and his staff had to be lodged – that entertaining was a necessity – it can be seen that Diaghilev still needed financial backers.

There had been an interesting snippet in a Gossip column. Speaking of Diaghilev's financial affairs, this said: "It costs a lot. His regular pay-roll, I believe, is £800 a week for nine months of the year. For the other three, artists draw smaller salaries. Then there are the high cost of production, composers' royalties, and other things.

Sunday Express 12.7.25

"I understand that at the Coliseum he gets about £1,400 a week for his show. It is all a big risk, you see. Only Diaghilev's worship of art could make it go on. One of the company tells me that the higher-paid dancers get about £50 a week, but that it varies according to the exchange."

That extra, but mythical, £200 a week would have made a great difference.

No one seems to have thought it necessary to translate the title of the next new ballet, possibly because the story was adapted from Molière and it might be assumed that everyone had learnt about it at school – possibly because "The Bores" or "The Interfering Ones" might have been discouraging. The libretto and idea came from Boris Kochno, and the ballet was designed by Georges Braque, with music by Auric, another of "*Les Six,*" and choreography by Nijinska. *Les Fâcheux* was a tremendous success. Serge Lifar, who had been given his first important part in *Zephyr* earlier in the year, now appeared in a leading rôle in London for the first time.

"A number of troublesome people appear, always at the wrong moment, to delay the love-making of Orphise and Eraste. Two gossips, a valet, a card player, a dancer, a dandy, a group of people playing shuttlecock, a group of ball players, a group of masqueraders enter and re-enter. Eraste (Lifar) is intrigued into dancing with one, then another; always his advances towards the delightful Orphise (Mlle. Tchernicheva) are interrupted; and when at one instance he does get within whispering distance her guardian enters and orders her off. Of course, it all ends happily, and there is the usual 'tutti' at the fall of the curtain."

Daily Telegraph 4.6.25

Only the music received adverse criticism, and in this case, the rest could carry it. The ballet gave wonderful opportunities for characterisation to all the cast, and laudatory comments on them pepper all the critiques. Anton Dolin created a sensation by dancing on point. "M. Dolin's dance as The Dandy enraptured the gallery, but was only imperfectly visible from the stalls," said the *Morning Post,* but as the critics were unanimous in giving his performance the highest praise, they must have been in the Dress Circle. (A morning paper had said that "A prima ballerina can do two twirls on one toe, and with a male partner's help can do three. Dolin does four solo.")

Morning Post 4.6.25 ***

The Diaghilev genius for lighting would seem to have dozed this time – or else there was a "technical hitch," for several papers referred to this ballet being given "in the dark," and the *Morning Post* indulgently assumed that "Doubtless at the next performance the stage will not be plunged into such Cimmerian darkness."

A gossip paragraph told the story, very sad, of those who would both study and enjoy the arts. "OXFORD AND THE BALLET: I met the other day four Oxford undergraduates who had been 'gated' for the rest of the term for arriving on more than one occasion at their college after one o'clock in the morning. Their reason (which they did not tell the dons) was that they had paid lightning visits to the Russian Ballet at the Coliseum, 'motoring up afterwards quite drunk with beauty,' as one of them described it. Anybody who had seen *Les Fâcheux*, the newest ballet of all, would not blame them. For sheer brilliance of dancing, the performance of M. Woizikowsky as the card-player is unsurpassed. Perfect, too, is the achievement of Anton Dolin as The Dandy."

***

Alice Nikitina and Anton Dolin in *Les Fâcheux*.

Observer
7.6.25

"Everything that the Russian Ballet do these days is gracious and inventive, high-spirited, and full of fun," said Horace Horsnell in the *Observer*. He explained his idea that *Les Fâcheux* had, overall, an all-pervading beauty and an all-pervading truth. For beauty, it had "the stately Tchernicheva (who is also a comedienne,)" . . . and for truth, "it amounts to this; it is a ballet founded on Molière, and it evokes extraordinarily accurately and interestingly the spirit of Molière and the spirit of his century. In England we have not the same tricks. English musical comedies can be founded on stories supposed to take place in ancient Egypt or in China. It makes no difference to them. They never get more than a mile away from Surbiton or Maidenhead. M. Diaghilev employs ultra-modern artists, and they often employ ultra-modern methods, sometimes strangely inverted jazz rhythms, sometimes scenery scrubbed over with a few touches of primary colour. But it makes no difference to the truth of the 'period' ballets they invent. If they are out for modernity, we get modernity, as in *Les Biches* or *Le Train Bleu*. If it is Schumann's *Carnaval,* we get nineteenth-century romanticism in utter perfection. In another ballet we have had *Le Roi Soleil* in all his fantastic splendour. In the present short ballet we have something that, with all its slightness and all its sketchiness, is good enough to be an introduction to Molière. *Les Fâcheux* should be seen."

The revivals were greeted with delight. *The Three-Cornered Hat* was now danced by Sokolova as the Miller's Wife, and by Leon Woizikowsky as the Miller himself. This became one of his finest rôles.

As the Coliseum season ran from May until the beginning of August, it had seemed as if the ballet's customary Paris season would have to be omitted. However, the Coliseum had agreed to an interruption, so the company shot over for one week at the *Gaieté Lyrique.* There they gave six performances in June, including the *première* of another new Massine ballet, *Les Matelots,* and the first Paris performance of *Zéphire et Flore.* Both were rapturously received. Diaghilev also showed his third attempt at *Le Chant du Rossignol,* and this time the choreography, by Balanchine, was satisfying. Markova, as the real Nightingale, scored a tremendous success. At last, Hans Andersen's story had won a permanent place in the repertoire – the Matisse sets and costumes being used again, (but plus the new, white, "pyjama" costume for Alicia.)

After the company had returned to the Coliseum, Diaghilev remained in Paris for a few days. He gave an ecstatic interview on his return:-

"It was wonderful – it passed so quickly that my artists were described as just dancing in and out of Paris, but during those few days they created a sensation as great as any in the past and greater than those of recent years. Several writers called the week the *'Saison de Vingt Ans,'* the season of youth, because most of the successes fell to artists compared with whom poor Auric, already twenty-six, has reached ripe middle age. Beginning with little Markova, our youngest dancer, who is only fourteen, there is Serge Lifar only eighteen, Pruna, the Spanish painter of *Les Matelots* who is twenty, and Balanchine is the same age. Then Kochno, who has done the scenarios of our latest ballets, is twenty-two, and so is Vladimir Dukelsky, our latest composer, and Alice Nikitina, the rising star of the ballet. The week certainly was an apotheosis of youth." (Diaghilev had a happy habit of taking a year or so off a young one's age, as has been seen before. For example, reference books give the date of Lifar's birth in Kiev as 1905.)

Observer 28.6.25

Diaghilev had acquired the habit of introducing Dukelsky as his "third son," the first two being Stravinsky and Prokofiev, and did so in this interview. Young though he was, Dukelsky had already visited America, and had there become a devotee of Gershwin and jazz.

When Dukelsky came over from France with him at the end of June, Diaghilev said that *Zéphire et Flore* was being completely re-shaped. "The music has been revised, and instead of one scene, there are now three, so that the work of Georges Braque has become the most important he has yet done for the theatre."

Dukelsky

Otto Kahn had been in London in May, and had made a statement which, coming from the Chairman of the Met. and an Honorary Director of Covent Garden,was of great interest.

"Jazz is going to be the music of the future," he had said. "I will go further, and say that jazz is going to be the opera of the future. If any composer can come to me with a well-developed jazz opera I will produce it at the Metropolitan Opera House as a national duty." And Mr. Kahn had added. "America has only produced two great national inspirations. One of these is jazz music, the other the skyscraper." In his other personality, as "Vernon Duke," Dukelsky might have taken up that challenge, following on his semi-jazz ballet.

Morning Post 20.5.25

Diaghilev also said, "*Les Matelots* is the most definite success we have had since the war – I decided to present it in London at once, though it has not been announced." He described some points of interest about it.

"We could have run it for a month . . . It is not a ballet, and not a pantomime, but just a play" (he used the word *jeu*) "constructed very simply out of five of the best dancers in the troupe, five back-cloths, and three chairs. I mention these because in one tableau they are as important as the artists. There are also some spoons, which are used after the manner of a performer we saw in a London street." (Diaghilev had sought out this famous busker and given him a contract.) "Massine has achieved nothing so astonishing since the *Boutique.* And the reason why it is so good is that he did it quickly, in one impulse. Sometimes a ballet-master plans, makes changes, and hesitates. Here he has no doubts, no hesitations."

This is an interesting observation. Whilst not an infallible recipe, there is no question but that some ballets which had been brief in labour had had the qualities that endured. *Carnaval— Le Spectre de la Rose—La Mort du Cygne—*(Pavlova's immortal *Dying Swan,*) had all been created by Fokine in swift waves of inspiration. There are on the other hand, some ballets which no number of rehearsals can make come right. That does not mean to say that they should never have been attempted. Some works cannot be fully assessed until they have confronted the audience. Sometimes, then, they can be improved – sometimes, their kindest fate is to be quietly dropped.

For good measure, and to show that he was not unaware of earlier criticisms, Diaghilev added that "Auric's music is dazzlingly orchestrated. If his music was open to question before, this at least signifies his attainment of maturity."

The
Times
30.6.25

The Times described *Les Matelots* thoroughly. "It is in five scenes and has as many characters, three sailors and two girls. The action takes place in any port, and concerns the simple story of a sailor and his girl, who is faithful to him during his absence and is not to be led astray when he and his two friends disguise themselves with a view to testing her. M. Massine has used this plot for the artistic presentation of life in a sea-port, just as in *The Three-Cornered Hat* he made a synthesis of Spanish dance. He has shown a great wealth of imaginative invention, which is very welcome after the pale trivialities recently put before us . . . If the ballet is taken in the light-hearted spirit obviously intended, it is a real success.

"The scenery is by a young Spanish artist, Pruna, and is the best we have seen since Derain's for *La Boutique Fantasque* and Picasso's for *The Three-Cornered Hat*. It is also full of amusing invention – we liked especially the revolving cube which signified for us the departure of the sailors, the loneliness and fidelity of the maiden, and then by the return of the ship on its first surface, the homecoming – and there was some excellent draughtsmanship in the designs, especially that of the drop-curtain.

"The dancers were Mlle. Nemtchinova, Mme. Sokolova, who had one of those grotesque parts in which she excels, and MM. Woizikowsky, Lifar and Slavinsky. They all danced so extremely well that it would be quite invidious to single any one out for special praise. Each one held the stage while he (or she) was on it, and made one think he was giving the best performance of the evening. A word of praise must be given to Mr. Dines, the musician with spoons, one of those men who entertain pit-queues. He added a touch of appropriate colour to the café scene, and was too like the real thing not to be true.

"The music of the ballet is by Auric, and consists of the rather tiresome repetition of trivial phrases which we have come to expect of him. But on this occasion we could forget about it, and on the whole it made a suitable sound for the accompaniment of the dancing. There was great enthusiasm at the end; the dancers were presented with lifebelts (though we would all have leapt in to save them at that moment), and M. Massine and M. Goossens were called before the curtain."

Observer
5.7.25

The *Observer* was less enthusiastic. "It is exactly like M. Diaghileff and M. Massine to have invited an artist 'on the spoons' (used as castanets when dashed rhythmically against head, shoulders and arms) to abandon his kerb-side and to step inside the Coliseum with them to lend a needed touch to the new public-house-cum-nautical ballet they are devising there. The artist is incorporated with perfect success in the ballet, and – in addition to proving that the ballet can take itself with becoming levity from time to time – his engagement is a tribute to a class of performer that I have always secretly admired and enjoyed. The ballet itself is rather a funereal affair, the sort of thing that Ibsen might have devised in trying to write a satyric (sic) comedy about the public-houses of Spitzbergen. The dances of the three sailors are spun out too long, and one particular background against which they take place (colour scheme, red and black) is positively calculated to freeze the blood. There is, however, some of the most perfect dancing in the world from Mmes. Nemchinova and Sokolova, and Auric, abandoning for the moment his pet combinations of piccolos, trumpets and trombones, writes them some deliciously tender music."

Sunday
Express
5.7.25

The *Sunday Express* remembered morosely that the Coliseum orchestra had come in for a great deal of criticism during the previous season – but was generally conceded to be vastly improved under Goossens – by drawing a comparison with the playing of Rossini at which it had been bad. "Yet Rossini's music is simple and straightforward compared with the eccentricities of Auric, which they master completely. Or is it that Auric is so odd that one cannot recognise the wrong notes?"

The photographs on this page show the scenery of the new Diaghileff ballet, "Les Matelots," the designs for which are by Pruna, of whose work an appreciation appears on another page. At the top on the left is Nemtchinova and on the right Woizikovski. Below are Sokolova (left) and Lifar (right)

(Left) This photograph shows the backcloth for the last tableau of "Les Matelots." The two colossal figures, like most of Pruna's work, remind one, in this case perhaps a little maliciously, of Picasso. It is, however, one of Pruna's most personal works. The backcloth is reproduced by courtesy of M. Boris Kochno

A page from *Vogue,* in late July, 1925.

The
Queen
8.7.25

The *Queen* thought the scenery and costumes by Pruna "inspired" – (with a child-like air) – and the whole production provocative and invigorating. In the *New Stateman,* Raymond Mortimer described it as "seductive," and felt that in *Les Matelots,* Massine's style "approached perfection . . . Every movement is unmistakably signed 'Massine.' There is in it wit, satire and good humour, superabundant vitality and continual formal beauty." Going on to personalities, Mortimer continued, "Of the five dancers who appear in *Les Matelots* four who danced superbly are old favourites; and a new one declared himself in Serge Lifar, his ephebe graces going straight to the warm hearts of the Coliseum audience. But they showed their regret that the choreographer was not also an executant, and their perception that the triumph was predominantly his, by the just tempest of applause with which at the end they greeted the appearance of Massine."

Vogue, having survived the calamity of *The Sleeping Princess,* felt at one with Diaghilev's new outlook.

Vogue
July/2
1925

"The Russian Ballet has ceased to be Russian. As a result of its happy exile, it has come to give Western Europe its completest artistic expression. The instrument remains, of course, of Russian manufacture . . . but the tune it plays is a product not of Petersburg or Moscow, but of Paris.

". . . Bakst went to our heads: Picasso got to our brains. And this revolution is in the first place the work of the painters of Paris . . . and the three finest of them, as some of us think – Picasso, Braque and Derain – have all designed décors for Diaghilev.

". . . Among the young painters Pruna is a most remarkable figure . . . And in getting him to design the décor for a ballet, Diaghilev has once more shown his rare sensibility to whatever is at once new and good."

Observer
19.7.25

A ballet event which was not directly connected with Diaghilev's company, and which might have seemed insignificant at the time, was reported in the *Observer.* Its effects were, in time, to prove extremely significant. After a programme arranged by Frances James, at the Scala Theatre, Ashley Dukes, (Marie Rambert's husband, the distinguished playwright,) explained the objective . . . to form a ballet-producing society on the same lines as play-producing societies, and try to bridge the gulf between the Diaghilev ballet and the occasional school matinée. "The idea should certainly be taken a stage further," said the *Observer.*

The
Lady
23.7.25

The death of Satie had provoked rather scathing obituaries; *The Lady* unexpectedly printed an assessment of broad tolerance, worthy of notice. Saying that "Now people are sceptical and doubt the sincerity of the experimenters, branding them as charlatans and mountebanks, striving to achieve a reputation for daring originality by mere defiance of tradition," she thought differently herself. "In *Modern Music,* by Rollo Myers, there is a tribute to Satie which I like to recall now that everyone is throwing bricks at him. The writer claims that his art was governed by a definite philosophy, and that he had a genuine desire for 'simplicity in outline, brevity in statement, and clarity in conception . . . His music has line, and the enormous merit of condensation. It is devoid of trappings and useless decoration, and when it has no more to say, it stops.'"

There was a sensation when, rather than sign a contract for two years, Dolin suddenly left the company and his parts had to be handed round. Like so many of Diaghilev's dancers, he would one day return.

The
Star
25.5.25

Earlier in the season, the Russian Ballet had been the subject of one of those Tuesday pages of wit which made Londoners buy *The Star,* whether they wanted an evening paper or not. "Low and I" had been backstage, and watched a performance to boot. First – the audience – at a matinée. A mannish lady sat beside F.W. Thomas – (the "I" who wrote the words.) "In the park the sun was shining, yet the Coliseum was packed with these adoring ones, who sat through the other turns with kindly tolerance, and wriggled with delight when '9' went up on the number board. Neither Low nor I wriggled to any extent, but we nevertheless agreed *nem con* that *Aurora's Wedding* was a wonderful piece of magic and beauty. Bakst's gorgeous setting of great pillars and broad stairways was the fairy palace of our young dreams, peopled by fra-

SUCH EXHIBITIONS OF FEMININE GRACE AND CHARM SERVE TO SHOW US THE HITHERTO UNSUSPECTED POSSIBILITIES OF THE MISSUS.

" 'Low and I' ranged London wild and free . . ." From 1927, Low ranged the *Evening Standard* equally wild and equally free, and permitted to oppose the paper's own politics.

gile dancers, lovely women and men who moved together like poetry . . ." (Was this not Benois' *Pavillon*, and the programme, as so often, inaccurate?) "Slowly and beautifully the pageant of faery unwound itself; gorgeous negro slaves, dainty maids of honour, china shepherdesses, brave gallants and cavaliers; with Savina of the twinkling toes, Lydia Sokolova who stole my heart away, Tchernicheva who stole it all over again, and Nina Devalois who danced like a wave of the sea . . . On a sudden the audience went wild and hurt its hands applauding, and, like a pair of beautiful kingfishers, there flew on to the stage Mme. Nikitina and Anton Dolin. And 'Ooooooh!' we all said; a half-suppressed gasp, such as one hears at the Crystal Palace when the rockets go up . . ." Perhaps Low's sketchbook was out and he drew the pictures as they "presently withdrew and drank Patsy's very good health in two samovars of vodka, so we did and all, glorybeeski!"

The last night brought the usual vociferous demonstrations. "Enthusiastic scenes – 14 cur- ***
tains –" and so on. "Particularly enthusiastic was the reception accorded Vera Nemchinova, 3.8.25
Vera Savina, and Stanislas Idzikowski, all of whom received presentations. Idzikowski was given two green wreaths and a huge white rabbit, while the two ladies received bouquets. Every seat in the theatre was occupied and in addition, there were about 600 people standing, 300 in the gallery alone. Two ladies had occupied the same seats throughout the entire ten weeks' run of the ballet."

1925

COLISEUM THEATRE

OCTOBER 26th - DECEMBER 19th

FIRST PERFORMANCES IN ENGLAND

November 12th: *Zephyr and Flora*
(Dukelsky, Massine, Braque)
Monte Carlo, 28.4.1925

December 11th: *Barabau*
(Rieti, Balanchine, Utrillo)
World Première

REPERTOIRE

Aurora's Wedding	*Good-Humoured Ladies*
Les Biches	*Les Matelots*
La Boutique Fantasque	*Petrouchka*
Le Carnaval	*Polovtsian Dances*
Cimarosiana	*Le Tricorne*

COMPANY

Barasch, Chamié, Danilova, Doubrovska, Evina, Fedorova A., Gevergeva, Klemetska, Komarova, Lopokova, Maicherska, Markova, Nemchinova I., Nemchinova II., Nicolaeva, Nikitina A., Savina, Sokolova, Sumarokova, Tchernicheva, Troussevitch, Vadimova, Zalevska.

Balanchine, Domansky, Efimov, Fedorov, Grigoriev, Hoyer I., Hoyer II., Idzikowski, Ivanov, Jazvinsky, Karnetsky, Kremnev, Legat N., Lifar, Michaelov, Pavlov, Slavinsky, Stepanov, Strechnev, Tcherkas, Winter, Woizikowski, Zverev.

CONDUCTOR

Desormière

TOWARDS JAZZ BALLET

Pavlova had a four-week season at Covent Garden running well through October. Diaghilev opened at the matinée with *Boutique,* which suited the purpose deliciously. Nemchinova danced the can-can until Lopokova returned, and Idzikowski and Woizikowsky were back in their places as Snob and the male can-can dancer.

The evening had a tremendous air of the "Gala" about it. "Last night the Queen of Spain, most of Mayfair and all Chelsea, headed by Mr. Augustus John, were at the Coliseum..." Daily News 27.10.25

The Field gave its impression of both the Ballet and the bill: —

"It seemed only fitting that one of the most beautiful queens with which England has endowed a Continental throne, should virtually lead the rapturous applause which greeted the return of the Russian Ballet. As Columbine, Mlle. Vera Nemchinova was at her lovely best, for she danced throughout with the very poetry of rhythm. The part of 'Papillon' was danced by Mlle. Alicia Markova with such grace and allure that we did not wonder at the frantic efforts to catch her made by M. Woizikowsky. M. Stanislas Idzikowski is easily the best Harlequin we have seen. The Field 5.11.25

"Besides the Russians there were several extremely good turns in this week's programme. The best of these was certainly Dr. Angelo's Living Jewellery, where lovely young women clad in 'fleshings' posed as the ornamentation in various gigantic bracelets, brooches and combs. There was also the ever-popular Tex McLeod, whose slowness of speech is only less attractive than the rapidity with which he spins his ever-whirling lassos."

There were revivals: *Petrouchka,* which *The Times* thought "poorly played, well performed by Lopokova, magnificently Petrouchka'd by Woizikovsky, indifferently Moored by Zvereff." ("There has not been a better interpreter of Petrouchka since the creator of the part left the company. How often has one heard an audience provoked to laughter by the second scene, where the actor has appeared to be suffering from a stomach-ache!") Nicholas Legat came to dance the Showman. "... Altogether this ballet seems on its re-appearance infinitely the best thing the company has ever done." The Times 30.10.25

The Queen rejoiced at Lopokova's return in *La Boutique Fantasque.* "Unbounded enthusiasm greeted the appearance of Lydia Lopokova ... However marvellous her technique may be, however overwhelming her physical attractions, no other Russian dancer is so beloved by a Coliseum audience as Lopokova, with her entrancing combination of wistfulness and pertness. These qualities make her work in this ballet unforgettable. Who else can be so innocently naughty in the Can-Can – who else so wring our hearts for the sundered lovers as she in that ineffable moment when she is slowly raised on the sticks of the Russian soldier toys and borne from sight? And this week she was dancing at the very height of her powers." The Queen 11.11.25

315

Morning
Post
13.11.25 The forecast that "London would like it" was justified when *Zephyr and Flora* came to the Coliseum. Francis Toye said that "This is one of M. Diaghilev's most successful modern productions . . . Such an essay in pseudo-classicism might well have been . . . presented at the Court of *Le Roi Soleil,* where stories of gods, demi-gods, and the denizens of Olympus (Eighteenth-Century style) were always favourite subjects for ballets . . . (Kochno, Massine, Braque and Dukelsky) have made of *Zephyr and Flora* something essentially modern, without, however, quite forgetting the period to which the conception inevitably belongs. And this is as it should be.

"The actual story of Boreas' and Zephyr's quarrel over Flora amidst the band of Muses – topically gay Muses by the way – is of little importance; it is the details that are everything, and some of the details are very good. For instance, Flora's little dance of lament over her wounded husband is really moving; the mourning procession is most effective, and the Blind Man's Buff dance a sheer delight. They were admirably executed, Madame Nikitina being extraordinarily apt and neat as Flora, and Lifar, as Boreas, with his splendid leaps, conveying an impression of virility that has often been lacking at the Coliseum.

"It would hardly be true to write that M. Dukelsky's music had, except for a certain elegance, even a remote flavour of the Eighteenth Century; but it struck us as by far the most interesting of all the compositions associated with M. Diaghilev's most recent ballets. Perhaps it does not get fully into its stride until the Blind Man's Buff dance, but after and including that it never failed to hold our attention. Here is a young man who, despite the discordant idiom of the times, knows how to shape a musical phrase and conceive a musical idea. Strange though it may appear to many people in the audience, M. Dukelsky has a real gift of tune, and some of his contrapuntal writing is extremely happy."

The youthful pair, Lifar and Nikitina, (whom the former described in his biography of Diaghilev as "a dancer all grace, and the very soul of the music,") were given a great reception.

The
Times
13.11.25 *The Times* liked it, too, and filled in more detail: "The action takes place on Mount Olympus . . . Boreas entices Zephyr into playing blind man's buff and so leads him away from his wife. He then aims an arrow at him and goes in search of Flora . . . The second scene is the interior of a cave . . . whither Boreas has brought Flora. This is the *Scène-a-faire,* at the end of which the heroine, true to her type in such situations, 'swoons.' Meantime the wounded Zephyr is brought to Olympus by the mourning Muses and, after a very beautiful funeral procession, inexplicably revives. The Muses tie Flora firmly to him by the wrist, so that he may not again mislay her, and Boreas is suitably punished for his crime.

"The story, admirably suited for ballet, is treated in a modern style, the dresses being for the most part modifications of present fashions to suit the Grecian theme. There is no fundamental objection to such a treatment of the subject, which has a good precedent in the 18th century idea of classical dress. Moreover, M. Braque has blended his colours with such skill that the spectacle was always beautiful . . .

"M. Massine's choreography is vivid and ingenious. He does not use concerted movements, like Fokine, but gives to each dancer a separate part, so that the effect may be called, in the musical term, contrapuntal . . . Mlle. Nikitina has not appeared in such an important part before, and she acquitted herself with real distinction. Her slight and graceful figure lent great charm to the rôle and her technical accomplishment is worthy of the company's traditions. M. Lifar danced better than on any occasion when one has seen him before . . . As to the music, it is a pleasure to welcome a work which not only avoids mere silliness but shows that the young composer really has something to say . . . The ballet was received with great enthusiasm."

The
Queen
18.11.25 The *Queen* said: "It displays still further the increasing Gallicism of the Russian Ballet, but much as we may lament the Muscovite splendours, it is commendably honest and spirited of these people to show frankly the Parisian airs which they must inevitably acquire in exile if their art is to make new growth at all. Massine's choreography is mostly pure Massine, but shows sometimes that this rare genius of dancing has seen something of Cretan art. Indeed, the Olympus on which the simple tale is enacted is distinctly Mycenaean (why not?) with touches of eighteenth-century theatrical classicism and (again, why not?) a perceptive American accent now and then in the shoulder movements and half-savage energy of his dancing Muses.

Vladimir Dukelsky,
by
Pavel Tchelitchew.

"Thus Flora is an *article de Paris* in an insect-like costume, while others follow the 'smartness' of Knossus – which, after all, was closely akin. Especially lovely are M. Braque's low-toned backcloths, which suggested pale, forlorn seas, awesome caves and happy plains in the most economical manner. It seemed a mistake, though, to have Zephyr's costume and makeup pale and silvery, while that of Boreas had a golden glow which perversely suggested the warm South.

"All the dancing was excellent, and Nikitina had great technical difficulties to overcome in the long part of Flora and overcame them with ease, but I do not think she is perfectly cast in this part. I thought in turn of the wistfulness and charm that certain other dancers in the company might have brought to it, and was not consoled by Nikitina's dazzling technique. Lifar seems to improve with each new opportunity and was a fine Boreas. Massine leaves him at the end in a marvellous Cretan pose which is a superb climax to the ballet. Indeed, one seems to remember poses rather than rhythms on thinking over *Zephyr and Flora*, which is perhaps a bad sign. Tcherkas was an agile Zephyr (a rôle originally danced by Dolin) in a Flaxman hat, and Tchernicheva and Sokolova, without the least insistence on their own recognition as dancers of the first flight, led the queer spasmodic movements of the Muses who wear Mycenian gold masks on the tops of their heads as though they were Watteau hats. A refreshing and delightful affair, very much of our own time, and very well worth doing, though it probably will not last anywhere as long as *Petrouchka*."

317

The mixture of fashionable and theatrical design of the dresses shows up in this photograph of *Zéphire et Flore*.

Observer
15.11.25
Horace Horsnell, in the *Observer*, had an amusing suggestion to make: likening it to the genre of *The House Party*, he said that "had that eclectic coterie ever been prompted to enliven their evenings with a ballet, *Zephyr and Flora* is just the divertissement they would have devised . . . Its pseudo-archaisms made severe demands upon the technique of the company, and their success was more notable than that of the ballet as a whole. . . . The whole affair seemed to me a joke that was taken too seriously."

Unlike some of the critics, he did not care for the music. "I though that the finest achievement here was that of M. Georges Braque, designer of the sceneries and costumes. His three back-cloths had a pure beauty of tone and colour that was the more effective by reason of their lack of theatrical emphasis ... Flora, herself, strangely translated into an artificial flower, was modishly attired to the waist – as for the Champs Elysées; but thereafter contented herself with mere spotted tights. The Muses had chic little porkpie hats and earrings, quite in keeping with the only Olympus they had ever known – one nearer Deauville than Thessaly; their Pierian spring being that of some sparkling spa."

Vogue
December/1
1925
Vogue thought it a delectable "year." "Each ballet that Diaghilev gives us becomes more sophisticated, and those who pretend that the best contemporary painting makes no appeal to the Man in the Street should hear the roar of applause with which the décors of Picasso and Pruna are greeted by the Man in the Gallery ... The décor for *Zephyr* is by Braque, and once more this painter shows a delicacy of taste which is, I think, unrivalled by any living man." It thought the third of the back-cloths, a seascape, of "extreme beauty." But *Vogue* thought that it was "the calculated incongruity of the ballet which makes it so engaging to the sophisticated mind," adding that "Nikitina had danced her way into the heart of the Coliseum public by her performance."

Lydia Sokolova and Serge Lifar
in *Barabau*.

The next new ballet, *Barabau*, was definitely intended as a joke, and appears equally definitely to have been taken too seriously by the majority of the critics.

Diaghilev paved its way by giving another of his interviews to the *Observer*. He said, "We have lived through a period of German and of Russian music, and whilst it was very important, it left out of consideration what one might call the pleasant in music, including laughter . . . Observer 6.12.25

"At present we are passing through a period which is in every respect similar to that of Mozart, Cimarosa and Rossini . . . The German art participating in *Opéra Comique* has found nothing more comic than the *Meistersingers* and *Rosenkavalier*, and as for Russian music, – only one single comic opera, *A Night in May*, by Rimsky-Korsakov, and perhaps one unfinished work by Moussorgsky, *The Fair at Sorotchinsk*.

". . . I am quite certain that we will never see Hindemith or Krenek or Stravinsky or Prokofiev giving us music that is really gay. Their sarcasm frightens one . . . At a time when precious newspaper columns are wasted upon a discussion of the particular day on which Wagner wrote a certain letter, and on which day he was in love or not with his wife, perhaps it is a waste of time to try to devote one's energies to something else. When one is corroded with that point of view, evidently the art of Chabrier, Satie, Auric, Poulenc, Rieti, and the still younger men will appear, as a certain section of the English press has said, banal, vulgar and trite."

Explaining that this was why he was going to present the music of his Italian friend Rieti, based on a Tuscan folk-song, he continued: "No doubt it will be noted that the vulgar people of Florence composed this vulgar song, and that my friend Rieti has written round it some very vulgar music. The best thing I can wish him is that no one will write about him an ocean of commentary, which is so wearisome to the public."

Diaghilev went on: "The scenery is by Maurice Utrillo, a Spanish-French painter, and this may also appear a *mauvaise plaisanterie*. The choreography is by George Balanchine, a *maître de ballet* who is new, and therefore open, as always, to every attack. In this ballet there are only two principal parts; one is played by Leon Woizikowsky, and the other by Serge Lifar. I can modestly express the hope that it will not be said that they cannot dance."

Observer
13.12.25

The following Sunday, H.H. seemed determined not to be blarneyed by the fact that Diaghilev's explanatory interview had appeared in his own paper. He called *Barabau* "M. Diaghilev's latest and broadest joke; real hokey pokey, in fact, wrapped in the gayest of coloured paper. There is nothing neo about it. No need to see it half a dozen times to fathom its subtleties. . . . It calls less for raptures than for the kind of hearty guffaws that hail the too-too-flowing bowl at Harvest Home; and such reservations as one may have are due to the feeling that puppets would possibly interpret its rather sprained ingenuities even more suitably than these highly-trained, wonderfully efficient, admirably adaptable Russians do.

"Its simple theme is suggested by a nursery rhyme, and amounts to little more than bucolic high jinks between a passing squad of soldiers and the lassies of the village. The latter make great play with the more sedentary parts of their anatomy; a form of humour, or gallantry, that the prude may either blink at or swallow as local custom or folklore . . ."

Answering back at Diaghilev's jibe about the dancing, H.H. said: "Bravo, Lifar! Vive Woizikowsky! – with all my heart. Woizikowsky dances Barabau to perfection, and in order to hoodwink the rapacious soldiery, shams death in the most inspired nursery style. Serge Lifar dances the sergeant of the squad – an awkwardly agile, professionally amorous squad, whose manoeuvres are a beautiful bit of burlesque – and maintains thereby a slight but grateful link with the classics which this ballet as a whole seems rather too desperately anxious to break.

"I like Vittorio Rieti's music; more particularly its Mozartian echoes. But though M. Diaghilev's spirited desire to break new ground adds considerably to the uncertainty of life and keeps us wondering and expectant, the unashamed reactionary in me prefers the old. I wonder what you will think about it?"

The
Times
13.12.25

The Times had offered a clearer word-picture of the action: "A funereally dressed chorus of men and women behind a hedge sing '*Barabau, perche sci morto?*' while the gay and genial Barabau, his friends and relations, six soldiers and a sergeant, give an elaborate display of callisthenics in the foreground."

> Barabau, Barabau, why did you die?
> You've wine in your cellar, your bread was not dry.
> And salad you grew in your garden near by.
> Barabau, Barabau, why did you die?

The Times likewise apostrophised.

"The answer to the question of the funereally-dressed singers is that Barabau did not die. But they might ask many questions harder to answer. Why did Barabau ever become the hero of a ballet? Why did Vittorio Rieti . . . think he could compile a ballet 'book' from such slender material as the Italian nursery rhyme affords? Why does M. Diaghilev expend the talents of his brilliant company on the result? Why does the audience talk loudly through the music, remarking how funny it all is, while rarely being tempted to laugh? Why are there about a dozen recalls for every one concerned at the end?"

The Times answered itself – in part. "Diaghilev's ballet is now one turn among many in a variety entertainment. The music is not meant to be listened to, but just to provide a cheerful background to the jumping and stamping contortionists of the stage. Every one is clever enough, every one is grotesque; it all goes with a will. But those who want a laugh should wait for the roller-skating act of Steele and Winslow, which follows the ballet."

Barabau was given at the Coliseum for a Coliseum audience – Diaghilev's own idea. The vulgar slapstick of false noses and padded bottoms may well have been offered to amuse those who came to see the 'turns' in the bill either side of Polunin's segregating drop-curtain. Diaghilev must have looked about him on many a Coliseum night, and given this balletic *Gianni Schicchi* to compensate for the time generously devoted to watching his more esoteric experiments. He did it to bring back laughter – hearty laughter.

One critic who understood this aspiration completely and took it at its face value was Francis Toye. "It would be difficult in writing to give any idea of this delightfully absurd fantasy on a nursery rhyme theme. The comic soldiers, the delicious dance and feigned death of 'the hero,' the impossibly rustic villagers, the impossibly staid and black-clothed chorus must be seen to be appreciated . . . For my part I laughed from beginning to end, and most of the audience seemed to be with me. . ." Morning Post 12.12.25

Toye found the music "straightforward, rather in the manner of early Rossini, with a few (a very few) discords thrown in to make the ballet audience feel at home." He said of Balanchine, whose first whole ballet this was, "What his talents are in other directions it is impossible to say, but he certainly has a genius for inventing comic, and sometimes even rude, poses." And he concluded, "*Barabau* ought to be a great success."

Barabau might be said to have been Diaghilev's "Christmas Number," and though many people actively disliked it, there were enough who laughed with Toye for it to be revived in several later seasons. Lifar said that "Utrillo's sets proved somewhat difficult to adapt to the stage, and Serge Pavlovitch was kept busy modifying them to his requirements. As a result, he became for the nonce a sort of decorator-dressmaker, besides helping in other ways, as, for instance, suggesting that the chorus (of mourners) should be masked by a partition, so that only heads should be seen." The mourners, in black bowler hats and gloves, popped up and down behind that fence, and, according to Lydia Sokolova, "It was obvious that Balanchine was a born choreographer. Leon Woizikowsky was in his element, with long black moustaches, eating imaginary spaghetti, swilling it down with Chianti straight from the flask, doing amazing tricks and dancing on top of an enormous barrel." Sokolova danced her first farcical rôle, and hugely enjoyed the burst of applause which greeted her. Lifar p. 306

After this season, *Vogue* said: "To make an intelligent criticism of a modern ballet you need to have some knowledge not only of dancing, but of contemporary developments in the other arts, music, painting, and even literature. Most notices . . . are written by dramatic critics, a few by musical critics, almost all by writers who know nothing at all about painting. As a result *Barabau,* like most of Diaghilev's recent productions, has had a bad Press. The critics of the leading daily and Sunday papers omitted to mention the name of Utrillo . . . probably they had never heard of him. Yet Utrillo is one of the more important living painters, and a lot of the pleasure to be derived from the ballet depends upon the spectator having some knowledge of his work . . . If in future Press tickets were sent to the art critics instead of to the dramatic critics, the resulting notices should prove very much more intelligent. . . Vogue January/2 1926

"The scene is French, intensely French, as only Utrillo could make it . . . Utrillo expresses the essence of a French town or a suburb as no other painter ever has. He does not go, as the Impressionists did, to the banks of the Seine or the lovely countryside; but to dingy streets, quiet corners of Montmartre barracks, provincial boulevards and undistinguished churches. The little town in *Barabau* makes the same impression on lovers of France as the first cries of the blue-bloused porters at Calais . . . Utrillo's *Barabau* does not poetise life, it stylises it . . . There is nothing pretty about *Barabau* with the exception, perhaps, of young Monsieur Lifar . . . But the general effect is very jolly . . ."

Quot homines, tot sententiae, was never more appropriate as a tag than when considering Diaghilev's later works. The years have tended to consolidate one opinion about each ballet. It must be recognised that there were, in fact, differing opinions about almost every one of them.

Two of the nine masks made  by Oliver Messel for the Muses.

1926

HIS MAJESTY'S THEATRE

JUNE 14th - JULY 23rd

FIRST PERFORMANCES IN ENGLAND

June 14th: *Les Noces*
(Stravinsky, Nijinska, Gontcharova.)
Paris 13.7.1923

June 21st: *Romeo and Juliet*
(Lambert, Nijinska, Ernst and Miró.)
Monte Carlo 4.5.1926

June 28th: *La Pastorale*
(Auric, Balanchine, Pruna)
Paris 29.5.1926

July 5th: *Jack-in-the-Box*
(Satie, Balanchine, Derain.)
Paris 3.6.1926

REPERTOIRE

Aurora's Wedding	*Good-Humoured Ladies*	*Les Sylphides*
Barabau	*Les Matelots*	*Thamar*
Les Biches	*Parade*	*Le Tricorne*
La Boutique Fantasque	*Petrouchka*	*Zephyr and Flora*
Le Carnaval	*Polovtsian Dances*	
Cimarosiana	*Pulcinella*	

COMPANY

Barasch, Bartovska, Branitzka, Chamié, Danilova, De Valois, Doubrovska, Evina, Fedorova A., Gevergeva, Karsavina, Klemetska, Komarova, Lopokova, Maicherska, Markova, Nikitina A., Savina, Sokolova, Stepanova, Sumarokova, Tchernicheva, Trefilova, Troussevitch, Vadimova, Zarina.

Balanchine, Cieplinsky, Domansky, Fedorov, Grigoriev, Hoyer I., Hoyer II., Idzikowski, Ignatov, Jazvinsky, Kotchanovsky, Kremnev, Lifar, Lissanevitch, Michaelov, Pavlov, Slavinsky, Stepanov, Strechnev, Tcherkas, Vladimirov, Winter, Woizikowski.

CONDUCTOR:

Goossens.

PIANISTS IN *Les Noces*:

Auric, Dukelsky, Poulenc, Rieti.

LES NOCES

Diaghilev must have looked forward to his next visit to London with pleasurable anticipation, for this time the company was to be installed at His Majesty's Theatre, under the patronage of H.R.H. The Duke of Connaught, and would be giving whole programmes of ballet for the first time in London since the withdrawal of *The Sleeping Princess.*

"The first night audience – a more distinguished one could scarcely be imagined – felt they had come to a delightful party, where everyone knew everyone else, and the hosts, who were not revealed till the curtain swung back, were beloved by all.

Daily
Mirror
15.6.26

"As beautifully-gowned women filled the stalls the party atmosphere grew. Newcomers smiled greetings to one another and leaned across from the boxes to talk and shake hands. The stalls seemed filled with flowers, for most women wore gigantic posies of carnations pinned to their shoulders.

"Flowers made their appearance, too, very early on the stage, for, at the conclusion of *Carnaval*, the first item on the programme, Lydia Sokolova received a basket of sweet peas nearly as tall as herself. Pulling them out in handfuls she showered them upon the company and threw them over the footlights to the audience.

"The new Stravinsky ballet, *Les Noces*, interested the audience immensely, and evoked many curtains and much subsequent discussion . . . Among those discussing it were Lord Balfour, Mr. H.G. Wells, Miss Poppy Baring, Mr. Noel Coward, the Hon. Stephen Tennant, Mr. Augustus John, Lady Waterhouse, and the Duke of Lenorado. Tiny Lydia Lopokova watched from the front and received an ovation when she crept shyly into her seat. Many striking fashions were seen. One beautiful fair-haired woman wore what looked like a Guard's crimson cloak with a black velvet collar and a silver brocade waistcoat. Lady Diana Cooper was in a pale gold sequin dress matching her golden hair, which she now wears waved and bobbed.

"The Duchess of Rutland, who was with her, brought her umbrella into the stalls, many people having left their cars and walked rather than remain in a queue and miss a moment of the ballet."

And the *Daily Chronicle* noted that "the only people, apparently, not in full evening dress were a few students from Chelsea, who wore lounge suits, with shirts and collars ranging from salmon pink to grey flannel," and in addition to many of the notables noticed by the *Mirror*, spotted the Laverys, Lord Lathom, Nigel Playfair, and Anthony Asquith.

Daily
Chronicle
15.6.26

The Dance had commiserated with Diaghilev over the two losses which the company had sustained – Anton Dolin, who, since his departure, 'had been offered two hundred pounds to make half-an-hour's appearance at Palm Beach," and Vera Nemchinova. "She is twenty-five – she joined the Russian Ballet when she was fifteen . . . Pavlova is among her sincerest and most outspoken admirers . . . the principal fact that the general public remembers about her – in England, at any rate – is that her wonderful legs are insured for £30,000."

The
Dance
27.3.26

The serious matter of the evening was the London *première* of Nijinska's solemn ballet, *Les Noces*. Diaghilev had held this work back, feeling that it was not suited to the Coliseum. This time, he did not give any preliminary interviews such as might have helped London to comprehend its meaning. Perhaps he thought that, once more, shock tactics would promote maximum publicity. He certainly succeeded. The critics were mainly bewildered, and their attitudes were summed up some weeks later by A.H. Fox-Strangways, when he devoted his whole column to it.

Observer 4.7.26

"*Les Noces* stands in a class by itself; so much adherents and dissentients will both allow. Broadly, judging from what one hears, those who dislike dislike the music, and those who like like the thing as a whole: so, as they are talking about different things, there is no real disagreement."

Francis Toye was one of those whose criticisms appeared the morning after the performance.

Morning Post 15.6.26

"It describes the scene of the bride and bridegroom being blessed, the departure of the bride from the paternal home, and, finally, the Wedding Feast. The choreography by Nijinska is decidedly in the modern manner, but there can be no gainsaying the vitality of the movements, and the colour effects, black and white dresses against an austere background, are extremely effective.

"As for the music, I make no attempt to pass judgment on it. Sung by a Russian chorus, to the accompaniment of four pianos and percussion, it is typical of the composer. The rhythms are hammered into one's brain until one hardly knows that is happening. Three in a bar, four in a bar, seven in a bar – the more it changes the more it sounds to me exactly alike! Poor Mr. Goossens, who conducted an excellent orchestra admirably, wore himself out giving the right first beat in the right place, but I wonder whether the composer's subtlety will not always be more apparent on paper than in performance.

"At a first hearing I found the general effect monotonous until the extremely ingenious bell-like chords at the end, played on all four pianos . . . The general impression I received was of one large, noisy blur of sound, exciting, of course, but extremely fatiguing."

Daily Mail 15.6.26

Richard Capell said that, despite its French name, the new ballet was "indeed a Russian ballet, showing that they have not parisianised themselves as much as at one moment we had feared.

"An out-and-out Muscovite affair, this Stravinsky wedding! The service was, as they say, 'fully choral' . . .

"In the scene of the wedding breakfast the rhythms work up to terrifying power, reminiscent of the composer's '*Sacre.*' It is all as though Stravinsky had this time wanted to strip his art bare of all its earlier embellishments and show it as nakedly and brutally as possible. An astonishing intensity has gone to the making of this score, and of course a masterly technique. What Stravinsky has wished, he has done.

"The stage performance, designed by Mme. Nijinska, struck us as hardly on a level of interest with the powerful music . . ."

Daily Telegraph 15.6.26

The *Daily Telegraph* said that "in this latest work the Russian composer follows the plan adopted in *The Rite of Spring*, which reduced music to rhythmic sound, as Andrew Marvell would have reduced existence to a green thought in a green shade . . . There is, however, a difference. Stravinsky's aim is not to soothe but rather to inflame the savage breast. He does not deal in pleasant fancies, but in stern reality . . . On the stage striking effects have been obtained with a colour scheme which is mainly black and white – extreme distances in colour corresponding to sounds at the extreme ends of the gamut.

". . . The music suggested grave reasons for the melancholy of both bride and bridegroom. But the performance was a *tour de force* of virtuosity for all concerned, and the public applauded loud and long dancers, conductor, pianists, and others who contributed to the production."

Nijinska had not travelled to London to revive the choreography, and this exacting task had formed one of the innumerable duties of Serge Grigoriev. Trevor Allen had attended the final rehearsal.

Westminster Gazette 15.6.26

". . . The dancers begin to move to Stravinsky's profoundly piteous music, Felia Doubrovska in the midst of them with pale, earnest face over black tunic.

"But not for long. Grigoriev waves his arms; the orchestra stops; his voice, speaking staccato Russian, darts electrically through the theatre . . . repeatedly Grigoriev's voice thunders into Stravinsky's music. He is concentrating all his dynamic energy and vision on one point; when certain dancers should show a profile, when full face . . .

"Sometimes Diaghilev, the brain, just as Grigoriev is the voice, claps his hands to still that labyrinth of movement. For the most part, however, he sits quiet and impassive behind his pince-nez; one senses a constant, alert telepathy 'twixt him and Grigoriev, gesticulating at the rail . . .

"Then, when the men have to lie back prostrate one over the other, pyramid fashion, Grigoriev's iconoclasm rises to a crescendo. He darts through a door, and on to the stage, man-handles them as though they were cushions, and lays them out one by one, exactly as they should go . . ."

So determined does Diaghilev seem to have been to treat this ballet as an ensemble, that the names of the principals were not even shown on the programme – which obviously accounts for the lack of "mentions" in the notices. The Bride and Groom were danced by Doubrovska (who had created the rôle) and Slavinsky, with Tchernicheva as the Bride's mother, Woizikowsky as her father, and Lifar leading the rest of the dancers.

This pyramid was typical of the concerted movements which both Nijinska and Gontcharova had sketched. P.G. Konody had visited Gontcharova's exhibition at the Claridge Gallery in Brook Street a few days earlier, and had there noted among the items relating to *Les Noces* "a group of dancers that is remarkable for the splendid linear rhythm of the concerted movement." Daily Mail 11.6.26

One of the most decidedly "anti" of the critics was Hannen Swaffer, who wrote "THE TALK OF LONDON" for the *Daily Express*, under the pseudonym of The Dragoman. After admitting that "even the opera at its most magnificent has never seen a more remarkable assembly," he had criticised the performance of *Le Carnaval* as "ragged," offering his guinea stall to any taker for a shilling. But he had continued:– Daily Express 16.6.26

"*Les Noces* filled my cup of bitterness to overflowing. Except for the usual extravagance of the devotees, *Les Noces* – why not call it 'The Wedding?' – was coolly received.

"Its most interesting feature was the pyramidical grouping of the characters. Tom Titt" (the paper's pocket cartoonist) "has designed a similar scene, which, I hope, will one day be staged. The top of the pyramid is Diaghilev; the two women are Sokolova, the dancer, and Ruth Draper . . . and the base is composed of Lord Balfour, Idzikowsky, (who is now as popular as Massine used to be,) and H.G. Wells."

One of Diaghilev's earlier adherents, Alfred Kalisch, wrote vehemently against this ballet. "Some of the elect tell me it is too marvellously clever, but I, for one, can see nothing in it but ugliness and aimless noise . . . It is supposed to represent the preliminaries of a wedding. It is enough to convert intending brides and bridegrooms to celibacy. Daily News 15.6.26

"The élite applauded."

The Times was not impressed, either.

"There are no heart flutterings about the drear ceremonies of this village wedding. If that was the way Russian peasants got married we feel it is no wonder things have happened as they have . . . The bride lives in a house with one tiny window in it, the bridegroom in one with two tiny windows . . . We return to the one tiny window for the departure of the bride, and then are transported to an equally drab scene, with the bridal bed piled with pillows inside a rabbit hutch, for the scene of the barmecidal wedding feast . . . Two double grand pianos, terrible engines of war with a keyboard at each end of them, are banged, thumped, tickled, and titillated by four serious musicians, each one of whom has composed ballets of the modern kind and only consents to perform 'in token of the deep admiration all modern musicians have for the composer.' The Times 15.6.26

"The audience sat and shared in the admiration, all except two people in the stalls who went out in the middle because they could not stand the racket. For our part, admiration was concentrated on the skilful patterning of the figures on the stage, without inquiring what it all meant or whether it meant anything, on the extraordinary energy of Stravinsky's rhythmic invention, which enables him to keep it up, whatever 'it' may be, and on the truly marvellous performance of the ringers. After this *Les Matelots*, music by Georges Auric (one of the bela-bourers of double pianos) was child's play for all concerned."

Daily
Sketch
15.6.26

The *Daily Sketch* was fair and reflective: "Here is once again the Stravinsky of *Le Sacre*. The deadly seriousness and austerity, the primitive savagery and brutality of the music affect one in precisely the same way. One may like it, one may hate it, but it is so immensely vital, so throbbing with life and energy, that one cannot but be moved. It is impossible to pass any kind of judgement on such a work after one shattering performance."

Felia Doubrovska as The Bride in *Les Noces.* The stark simplicity of her dark tunic is in distinct contrast with the very pretty, embroidered dress the design for which appears on Page 289. The immense plaits designed by Nijinska swirl on the floor. The costume seems to give her the air of a nun.

The *Graphic* later reported that "H.G. Wells was stoutly championing the Russian Ballet the other night against criticism of their latest extravagant ventures – which he described as the most wildly beautiful of modern productions. His taste for theatrical fare is scarcely conservative, for I last saw him at the first night of *Lady be Good.* The Graphic 25.6.26

"The Duke of Connaught, who is patron of the season, saw Stravinsky's *Les Noces* from a box. I should dearly have loved to know how far his opinion of the sombre extravagance coincided with that of the novelist.

"Afterwards, however, I had the rare privilege of witnessing the type of dancing which the artists themselves really appear to prefer, for I went on with a party, Idzikowski, Danilova and Woizikowsky, among others, to the Kit-Cat for an hour. Nearly all of them danced quite normally, some of them badly, and one, Jazwinsky, most superbly, as befitted his name."

H.G. Wells might have been overheard championing *Les Noces;* this was, however, no idle chatter, for he took the trouble to write a letter which looks as if he had intended to send it to a newspaper.

June 18th 1926

I have been very much astonished at the reception of "Les Noces" by several of the leading London critics. There seems to be some undercurrent of artistic politics in the business. I find in several of the criticisms to which I object, sneers at the "*élite,*" and in one of them a puff of some competing show. Writing as an old-fashioned popular writer, not at all of the highbrow sect, I feel bound to bear my witness on the other side. I do not know of any other ballet so interesting, so amusing, so fresh or nearly so exciting as "Les Noces." I want to see it again and again, and because I want to do so I protest against this conspiracy of wilful stupidity that may succeed in driving it out of the programme.

How wilful the stupidity is, the efforts of one of our professional guides of taste to consider the four grand pianos on the stage as part of the scene, bear witness.

Another of these guardians of culture treats the amusing plainness of the backcloth, with its single window to indicate one house and its two windows for the other, as imaginative poverty – even he could have thought of a stove and a table; – and they all cling to the suggestion that Stravinsky has tried to make marriage "attractive" and failed in the attempt. Of course they make jokes about the mothers-in-law; that was unavoidable. It will be an extraordinary loss to the London public if this deliberate dullness of its advisers robs it of "Les Noces."

That ballet is a rendering in sound and vision of the peasant soul, in its gravity, in its deliberate and simple-minded intricacy, in its subtly varied rhythms, in its deep undercurrents of excitement, that will astonish and delight every intelligent man or woman who goes to see it. The silly pretty-pretty tradition of Watteau and Fragonard is flung aside. Instead of fancy dress peasants we have peasants in plain black and white, and the smirking flirtatiousness of Daphnis and Chloe gives place to a richly humorous solemnity. It was an amazing experience to come out from this delightful display with the warp and woof of music and vision still running and interweaving in one's mind, and find a little group of critics flushed with resentment and ransacking the stores of their minds for cheap trite depreciation of the freshest and strongest thing that they had had a chance to praise for a long time.

(Signed) H.G. WELLS.

Contrary to some ideas on the matter, this letter did not appear in the press at all. One may surmise that Wells showed it to Diaghilev, who thought of a different use for it. H.E. Wortham, Music Critic of the *Daily Telegraph,* (and subsequently "Peterborough" in that paper,) explained in his music column in Apollo: "Mr. Wells's letter, at later performances of *Les Noces,* was distributed in the theatre during the ensuing *entr'acte,* so that after we had appreciated the ballet on its merits we might know what effect it had had on his imaginative mind. Since, so far as I know it has not been published anywhere, I will quote the concluding paragraph:" (and he did.) Apollo August 1926

Daily
Express
19.6.26

The controversy raged. Hannen Swaffer must have said more than he had written, and coupled Noel Coward with his sentiments, for the *Daily Express* printed a letter from Osbert Sitwell objecting to their witticisms, defending the ballet and Stravinsky, "probably the greatest musician we have seen for a century," and roundly stating that "some of M. Diaghilev's creations have already survived for fifteen years, which is more than can be said for the works of genius turned out at such short intervals by Mr. Noel Coward."

These and many more blasts of invective kept the publicity cauldron merrily a-boil.

Observer
20.6.26

At this point, Diaghilev, as had become his wont, gave a long interview to the *Observer*.

"The first of the new ballets . . . has been rather severely handled by the critics. M. Diaghilev's reply . . . is that they have failed to understand it.

" 'There have been two receptions – that on the part of the public, and that on the part of the Press. The public, which has the right not to understand anything, has nevertheless understood everything; and the Press, which is under the obligation to understand everything has, as usual, not understood anything! . . .

"The Parisian Press, who were grotesquely mistaken over *The Rite of Spring*, – to such an extent that the leading critic found it necessary some months later to recant publicly – did not make the same mistake about *Les Noces*.

". . . If you want anything Russian, I believe that nothing represents Russia more completely than this work . . .

"There is no folk-lore in it, because for many years Stravinsky has been the declared enemy of the exploitation of folk-lore for the purpose of local colour . . . From folk-lore has been retained only the conception of the subject and something in the text, and that the non-Russian cannot understand and can only feel.

"As for the purely musical side of it, I cannot understand how it is the critics have not yet learned the language of Stravinsky, for which there has been plenty of opportunity . . . During all these recent years the English critics have reproached me with presenting works of the operette type with grotesque dances. I have transported them to church and I have given them a Mass, and the result is the same.

". . . A young girl from the gallery, whom I did not know, came to me after the first performance of *Les Noces*, and said that though she could not understand it, she had felt something she had never felt in her life before. I think she very well expressed the feelings of any young girl before and during the wedding. I wish the critics had at least shared that feeling."

Around 1909, when in his twenties, Horace Horsnell had been secretary to H.G. Wells. He did not agree with the latter's view on *Les Noces*.

Observer
20.6.26

". . . *Les Noces* is a plastic fantasia of love at its most dolorous. It is the Valentine's complete antithesis . . . The barely progressive action begins with the blessing of bride and groom; it ends with the epiphany of a many-pillowed bed. An exultant carillon on pianos announces consummation, and the hitherto cold, grey light of the scene is flushed with gold.

"The dancers . . . prostitute Terpsichore in the service of some strange static deity, while the music drills and drills its pitiless plainsong. At the double-ended pianos sit four young and gifted composers – Auric, Poulenc, Rieti and Dukelsky – with awful eyes on Mr. Goossens' brilliant baton, playing like hell, and counting, counting the time like demon metronomes. You watch them fascinated, yet fearful lest they should miss the beat and be whirled into a sausage machine.

"Not that you fail to admire the plaintive beauty of the bride, or to wonder at her miles of braided hair, with which the posturing chorus does everything but skip . . . Oh! I promise you, sensations will not be lacking!"

Back from the United States, Ernest Newman had much to say about it.

Sunday
Times
20.6.26

"*Les Noces* is new to us, though the score dates from 1917. Had the work been first introduced here five or six years ago, what a controversy there would have been about it! How the bright spirits whose business it is to be at least a shade ahead of their duller fellow-mortals would have rhapsodised over it! What warnings would have been handed out to us of the awful fate of 'reactionaries' who cannot recognise the future when they see it! But during the last five or six years a good deal has happened. There is not a moderately intelligent musician anywhere who does not now recognise the absurdity of the high-falutin' claims that were made for Stravinsky in those days. Everyone now sees him for just what he is and what he always was – a Little Master who flamed up to genius for a brief year or two of his life, then declined into a talent, then into a mediocrity, and is now a nonentity. His vein yielded rare metal during those golden years, but the vein was a thin one, and it soon ran out. Whether he will ever strike another, Heaven only knows; but the omens of the last few years are not promising."

Newman went on to discuss the ballet. "It is merely a succession of ugly poses and pyramid-buildings . . . The pianos were played by Auric, Poulenc, Rieti and Dukelsky – a symmetrical allocation of a quarter of a composer to each piano. The agonised expression on their faces would have made, as the execution of Macheath did, 'even butchers weep.' Mr. Eugene Goossens, who conducted, also seemed to be sweating anguish from every pore; conducting *Le Sacre du Printemps* must be child's play to keeping that crew together . . . the percussion, as often as not, overrides the pianos so brutally that, so far as the hearer is concerned, it would be safe for the pianists to play anything or nothing as they chose."

Pursuing his favourite theme of nationalism in music, E.N. also said, "Some of the tunes have the usual Russian piquancy, but musical Europe is already more than a little tired of the moujik and his half-baked brain . . . The whole score, indeed, is a piece of musical atavism . . ."

In complete contrast, *The Lady* was enthusiastic. "The playing on the night I went was first-rate . . . The vigour and freshness of the music made by this simple means must attract anyone who is not hopelessly prejudiced against Stravinsky. The rhythmic appeal is overwhelming. The ballet is the best the Diaghilev company has brought to London for years." The Lady 24.6.26

A note of warning, however, was struck in a letter to *The Spectator*, which may be said to have been endorsed by several of the comments on the opening night's performance of *Le Carnaval*, which was not considered to have been up to scratch: Spectator 26.6.26

> ". . . Stravinsky is here obsessed by percussion . . . Nijinska did all she was required to do with the choreography . . . The dancers were heroic.
> ". . . Incidentally, the new technique which is required to bring these fearful and wonderful ballets to pass is undoubtedly injuring the old perfection, as we saw very well in *Carnaval*. Only Idzikowski seems to be resisting its pernicious influence.
> "I suggest to M. Diaghilev that he should have two separate troupes . . .
> BASIL MAINE.

Of all the critics, perhaps A.H. Fox-Strangways was the least blasé – the one who shared the emotions of that young girl from the gallery.

"The music is the heart-beat of *Les Noces* . . . Observer 4.7.26

"The ballet is a wedding under circumstances we do not understand, only feel. A rope, as it were of the Norns, is wound and unwound by village maidens. Something with a sense of history in it, then, is to happen. The gradual attraction to one another of groom and bride is mimed before us; the village faces cluster and separate and cluster again. The bride is drawn into the circle for their blessing and involved in the coils of the rope until at last she can move neither arm. The two fathers are there, but betraying no emotion . . . Then the wedding dance, a lovely piece of choreography, depending entirely on mass effects, and the bride and groom bowing stately thanks, and it was over . . . Epic; things happen once, and once only, and they can't be undone; the family counts, after all.

"Where does it all come from? We must go back to the music again. It comes from the Caucasus, we guess? But no; it is more likely to come from under the dome of St. Paul's. Stravinsky was there one Sunday morning, and when the bells from Wren's churches began their chorus he was greatly moved, and began busily noting down the cross-rhythms they made, as one gained upon the other . . . Stravinsky's ear is alert to rhythm, and he makes patterns of time as others make patterns of tune, and it is on these patterns that his music is to be judged . . . I have seen only half-a-dozen of M. Diaghilev's two dozen ballets, and of those, *Les Noces* seems to me far the most satisfying; the others are mainly spectacles; this is an experience."

The *Daily Mail* had earlier reported a brief interview with Diaghilev, in which he had ex-

Daily
Mail
16.6.26

pressed himself overwhelmed by the warmth of his reception – delighted with the theatre, and with the orchestra, with which Goossens had worked his customary wonders. Now he was "wondering what London will think of my first English ballet, to be given on Monday next – *Romeo and Juliet.* My anxiety centres round the question of what London will think of the scenic decorations by the young Paris artists Max Ernst and Joan Miró. I am sure it will like the novelty."

Is there any need to say that a Diaghilev/Nijinska ballet made to the title "Romeo and Juliet" would bear only a trifling resemblance to the story of tragic young love and family feud in Renaissance Italy with which readers of Shakespeare are familiar? More important to say that the music had been commissioned from Constant Lambert, a student at the Royal College of Music, and but 20; and that Diaghilev had exerted his famous powers of persuasion, and succeeded in getting Karsavina to create the rôle of Juliet for him, first in Monte Carlo, then in Paris, and now in London. She had told the *Daily Mail* – presumably in the person of the de-

Daily
Mail
18.6.26

voted Richard Capell – "You can say that we 'rag' *Romeo and Juliet.* The whole thing is great fun – for us at any rate. It will give an idea of the spirit of the ballet to say that, when Romeo and Juliet come to the part where they are supposed to die, they decide to do nothing of the sort, but to elope in an aeroplane instead."

Daily
Mail
22.6.26

In its review, the paper gave an outline of the new treatment. "The show is a frolic, a trifle, a sketch. It is like a number from a 'revue' – only raised to an uncommon power by the grace of the lissom young performers and the quick wits that are behind all the Diaghilev shows.

"All the world is curious to know what its stage favourites are like off-duty. The new ballet professes to take us behind the scenes. It sets out to be an informal sort of at-home. Montagus and Capulets have not much to do with it.

"In the second part of the piece the dancers are seen in a series of flashes toying with the idea of a Shakespearian ballet. But the real subject of it all is the charm of the fit, graceful young folk of the troupe as they appear when informally doing their morning drill.

"To give it a shape, a love-affair between the principals (Mme. Karsavina and M. Lifar) is sketched in. At the end there is an elopement – to the dismay of the ballet-master (our smiling young friend M. Slavinsky.)

"Flattering as was this invitation to go so informally behind the scenes, the first part of the action was too slight. But soon came the "Romeo and Juliet" scenes, and they brought a whiff of sweet poetry.

"It was wonderful how Karsavina could, within a matter of a few seconds, give a true glimpse of Juliet, pale and sweet. The young Lifar as swiftly sketched a romantic Romeo in a few love-lorn poses.

"Light-hearted and fugitive as the piece is, there is no sort of 'guying' of Shakespeare. The *entr'acte* (without music) in which the youths smoke and play cards and the girl dancers skip and pirouette idly was one of the amusements of the evening."

Capell added that Constant Lambert, 'the fortunate youth,' had turned out to be worthy of his fortune. "He has written a charming, spritely little score – and latter day enough without any such wild jumps into the future as MM. Ernst and Miró, the painters of the decorative curtains, have indulged in."

The
Times
22.6.26

Looking at Karsavina's performance, *The Times* said that, despite an obviously bandaged knee, she danced with all her usual grace. "The most remarkable thing . . . was the fact that throughout she conveyed the impression that this *was* only a rehearsal and not the first night. That reversal of the true situation cannot have been easily achieved."

Observer
27.6.26

The *Observer* went a little deeper into the machinations – one can hardly call it "The plot." "Karsavina and Lifar appear in mufti and in their proper persons, and they remain themselves despite their Romeo and Juliet aliases. The point of the joke is that they are in love with one another and forget their parts. The scenes they rehearse never completely divert their interest, or ours, from the pretended tumult that agitates them. Thus, while Juliet pirouettes so grace-fully, or dives like a dear little clockwork duck from her balcony into the arms of Romeo, or wakes in the tomb to plunge a mimic dagger into her lovely bosom, the sympathetic laughter their absent-mindedness evokes is barely over before another lapse into amorous forgetfulness arouses it again."

Miro and Ernst designed an unusual balcony for Juliet.

ROMEO ET JULIETTE

The opening of the ballet.

An Explanation of Postal Delays?
"La Pastorale" Ballet.

THE RUSSIAN BALLET TAKES US BEHIND THE SCENES IN A FILM STUDIO: M. THADEE
SLAVINSKY AS THE PRODUCER DRILLING HIS ACTORS.

Daily Mail 29.6.26   June 28th saw another first night, of *La Pastorale*. This had a plot by Kochno, music by Auric, scenery by Pruna, and choreography by Balanchine. "In essence it is a skit on the kinematographic art, and a rather bitter one," said Richard Capell. "A 'movie' troupe invades a riverside meadow on a summer's day, and there creates the very dickens of a din. A telegraph boy (Serge Lifar) who has been playing truant to take a dip in the stream, falls victim to the siren charms of the kinema star (Mme. Doubrovska.) The villagers come in a rage to claim the missing mails. Night falls, and the youth returns to his village sweetheart."

The Times 29.6.26   "The story matters little and is not very clearly told," said *The Times*. "It provides an opportunity for one more display of the new gymnastic method which the company has, unfortunately we think, adopted. The exercises have this time been devised by M. Balanchine. It must be admitted that many of them are clever, notably a dance for M. Slavinsky and the duet for M. Lifar (the telegraph-boy) and Mme. Felia Doubrovska, (the star.) These were amusing and very brilliantly done . . . (but) we found little that was pleasing to the eye in these new caperings of the *corps de ballet* . . . M. Pruna has designed a very pleasing setting. M. Auric's music is the same small beer, with the acid tang, which has been brewed in France for similar occasions in recent years."

Morning Post 29.6.26   Francis Toye commented that "Georges Auric now shares with the composer of 'Fedora' the distinction of having wedded bicycle and music . . . This ballet is supposed to be grotesque and funny. It is not; it is grotesque and dull. At least, so I found it, and so, apparently, did a large part of the audience . . .

"Lifar and Doubrovska gave us one good dance, and Lifar and Gevergeva made a capital exit, while Auric's music exhibits a certain nonchalant virility that is not without attraction. Indeed I thought the music by far the best part of the entertainment; it at least did what it set out to do – which, in my opinion, the choreography failed to do."

LA PASTORALE

facing page: The film actors in historical costume "on location."

right: Felia Doubrovska and Serge Lifar – the Film Star and the Telegraph Boy.

Though Capell did not like it much, he found something to please him in the choreography of all but the *corps de ballet* parts, and he praised Pruna's setting. Though adverse, both these criticisms were offered without rancour. But on the Fourth of July, Independence Day, Ernest Newman had his say:– Daily Mail 29.6.26

"Could we believe our ears at His Majesty's Theatre on Monday night? Could it really be true that some members of M. Diaghileff's audience, usually so all-admiring, so family-partyish, so obsequious, were booing the new ballet? It seemed so, and for many people it must have been as shocking as brawling in church. For my part I was not surprised. M. Diaghileff's faithful followers have stood a good deal from him in recent years, but such a thing as *La Pastorale* is very difficult to stand . . . The trouble with *La Pastorale* is that it is merely feeble and silly. What sort of a composer Auric is the followers of Russian Ballet already know. The music of *La Pastorale* is merely a succession of the commonplace devices of a thoroughly commonplace mind to avoid the stigma of the commonplace." Sunday Times 4.7.26

These remarks did not pass unnoticed. This time Newman had gone too far. Diaghilev acted.

SUNDAY TIMES JULY 11, 1926.

". . . Last Monday morning I received a telephone message to the effect that as my criticism of *La Pastorale* had not pleased the authorities at His Majesty's Theatre the seat usually reserved for me would no longer be at my disposal. It would henceforward accommodate some more worthy occupant, and the place thereof should know me no more. My habitation should be desolate, and my bishoprick should another take. Sunday Times 11.7.26

"Ah! if only M. Diaghileff had sent me tickets for his best things, instead of his worst, what a different tale there would not be to tell! I am asked to *La Pastorale* – the product of the amalgamated geniuses of a Balanchine and an Auric – but not to *The Three-Cornered Hat*, or *Prince Igor*, or *Petrouchka*, or *Pulcinella*, or *Cimarosiana*, or *Thamar*, or the *Good-Humoured Ladies*. M. Diaghileff is in the position of a jeweller with a drawer full of Oriental and other gems who asks an expert (or a supposititious expert) for his opinion on his stock and then shows him a bit of Parisian paste and asks for a public testimonial to it. I could have said some really nice things about such ballets as those I have named: instead of which – I am invited to *La Pastorale*, which I found the most painful of a series of Auricular Confessions."

Ernest Newman went on to mince Wollheim, Diaghileff's London manager, into little tiny pieces for his handling of the Press List for revivals. As Karsavina had danced several of her old rôles, including *Petrouchka*, *Good-Humoured Ladies*, and *Thamar*, he would obviously have liked tickets for these occasions. He does not, in fact, seem to have had treatment any different from that meted out to the rest of the Press which was that they had tickets automatically for premières, and that if they asked, Wollheim would try to give them House seats for revivals.

E.N. had been reading the other notices.

"I am now waiting, in amusement, to see what Mr. Wollheim is going to do about some of my colleagues, whose sins in connection with last Monday's production of *Jack-in-the-Box* and *Parade* must equal my own of the Monday before in quantity if not in quality. I see that Mr. Toye, whom no one will suspect of immoderation, sweeps Satie's music aside as 'imbecile and impotent;' while Mr. Hannen Swaffer says that 'the scenery of both these ballets, if used in a Wigan pantomime, would have been hissed off the stage.' There are only two courses, it seems to me, now open to M. Diaghileff and Mr. Wollheim. They must either cut Mr. Toye and Mr. Swaffer and a few others off their first-night visiting list, or they must restore my name to it. It is not for me to advise them, but perhaps I may be allowed to hint that the former course of action would be the less painful of the two to me."

It would appear that Diaghileff preferred to be merciful to Newman, and spare him the agony of paying further visits, whatever he may have done about the other rebel few.

After the Russian's sudden death, Edwin Evans discussed the Diaghilev – Newman relationship in an article.

Musical
Times
1.10.29 "The knell of romanticism had been audible to the alert ears of Diaghilev before most people were ready to speed its parting, and he was prepared for the phase of hard, quasi-ironic brilliance that was to dominate for a time the greater part of artistic Europe. Naturally this brought him into collision with upholders of the other aesthetic creed, and in particular with Ernest Newman. Their exchange of passes was, and could only be, futile as, neither being willing to concede that the other might have valid reasons for the faith that was in him, they spoke no common language, and the very terms they used meant different things to each of them. There was, however, this difference between them – that whereas Newman was congenitally unable, or at least in his writings never showed himself able, to enter into the spirit of the party opposed to him, Diaghilev's spiritual adventures had been of both kinds, and he was merely impatient that Newman, whom he really admired, had not reached his own conclusions. Newman's opposition eventually took such a form that he and the paper he represented were excluded from the so-called 'press list.'

"I hope it is unnecessary for me to say that the view I took of this incident was the only one a journalist could take, and so far as I was consulted my advice was given accordingly. Had Newman found anything at all to admire, that view might have prevailed, but his anathema was only too comprehensive, and I found myself powerless to avert an incident which would have been ludicrous had it not been lamentable. When, a year ago, (1928) Newman did at last find something to praise in Stravinsky's *OEdipe*, Diaghilev, whose profound admiration for the composer did not extend to that particular work, commented: *'Naturellement! Dès que c'est ennuyeux, ça lui plaît.'* " (Naturally, when it's a bore, he likes it!)

Ernest Newman was a delightful man with hosts of friends in the musical and artistic world. As he never studied the component elements of the Russian Ballet – never even understood the physical limitations and requirements of dancers – so that he could never truthfully have been called either an expert or a suppositious expert – his endless strictures had often given Diaghilev cause for amusement rather than umbrage. When Newman wrote a particularly slashing piece, Diaghilev would invite him to lunch. The two men really rather liked each other, though Evans also said that Diaghilev regarded Newman as "childish."

It seems a pity that Newman, who really cannot be said to have liked ballet except when Karsavina melted him, should have been given the monopoly of those immense columns for so many years. But for the remainder of its existence, the Diaghilev Ballet would never again be reviewed in *The Sunday Times*.

No matter whether the critics were happy or not; there were happy faces in the box-office, and, once again, the season had to be extended. Before the end of the original span, a new Satie ballet, *Jack-in-the-Box*, with choreography by Balanchine, was shown in a special memorial programme, the composer having died in 1925. *Parade*, that ballet for the *élite*, together with piano music by Satie and Stravinsky, played by Marcelle Meyer, made up the bill.

"Satie, (1866 – 1925,) was the spiritual father of the new French Musical school – Auric and the rest – of whom we have lately heard so much," said Richard Capell. "He was a humorist and a *blagueur*, and aspired to be the musical counterpart of the author of 'Alice in Wonderland.'

"The music of *Parade* is full of facetiousness. Parodies of César Franck rub shoulders with foxtrots; and the nonchalant dance of the American Girl (Mme. Sokolova) is to give trans-Atlantic colour – accompanied on the typewriter in the orchestra.

"The music of the new *Jack-in-the-Box* is a collection of small, typically Satiesque pieces in the course of which familiar tunes are quoted. It accompanies the dancing of half a dozen dolls from the nursery toy-box. Derain's dresses and the gracefulness of Mmes. Danilova, Tcherni-cheva, and Doubrovska, and of M. Idzikowsky, gave distinction to the little piece."

Daily Mail 6.7.26

The *Observer* seemed unperturbed by any thoughts of losing its tickets, as in common with most of the other papers, it always "wrote as it felt," distributing praise and blame with wit untinged with malice. "As works of art these two ballets seem to me negligible . . . Our rude forefathers affected stuffed birds; their electric descendants have a similar weakness for stuffed circuses. Each of these pert but hollow little ballets contained choice specimens of the art of Vaudevillean taxidermy. Of the order of charivari, they depend for their effect on the skill with which the soloists dance.

Observer 11.7.26

"*Jack-in-the-Box* owed everything to Idzikowski's *pas de deux* with Danilova. This fantastic couple – a puppet and a blackamoor – suggested two of the more irresponsible members of a Versailles haymaking party trying their hand at a cotton-picking in Dixie, with amours to match . . . The pantomime horse, however, that curvetted through the show, had been rather badly left at the post by that remarkable animal owned and trained by the Brothers Griffiths.

"The more one sees of this variegated entertainment, the more the mood of the moment seems to matter. This latest programme was a pleasant mixture of odds and ends; odds that were new, and ends that were old. The ends – mellow *Cimarosiana*, and the sharp, exacting *Matelots* – had it each time. Sokolova and Woizikowsky danced the Tarantella like twin flames; the square-pushing vivandières and their beaux filled the chorus interludes with gallantry and colour, and it was nice to see Lopokova again. The audience keeps large and lively, and the ex-tension of the season shows how much we like the ballet, novelties and all."

This summer, *Vogue* persuaded its beloved Lydia Lopokova to write an article assessing the newer developments in the Ballet. She found its success at His Majesty's to be the greatest since 1919 – and said that all the dancers felt this to be the ideal theatre for the kind of ballets they were now presenting.

"The Diaghileff Ballet is a puzzle," she said,–"how always it survives and comes up with new life when everyone is predicting its decline. I think the success this year was due more to the richness of the repertory than to any individual ballet, but also because M. Diaghileff is un-fluctuating in his faithfulness to youth – young dancers, young painters, young musicians . . .

Vogue August/2 1926

"For me the *Ballet Russe* begins not with *Carnaval* or *Les Sylphides* or *Scheherazade*, but with the ever exhilarating, incomparable *Petrouchka*, with more flesh and bones than any other of the ballets old or new, the screeching soul of Petrouchka, the mass domination of the chorus at the fair, the trumpet of the ballerina, the religious festival of the Moor with his nut, and, governing all, the musical masterpiece of Stravinsky.

"After *Petrouchka* comes for me *Pulcinella* – the tenderest and most exquisite of the pale colours of Picasso. It is its own lyrical qualities which touch me – the eyes of the onlookers and of the dancers are caressed by the music and by the colours . . .

"Which of the new ballets will live? The more I see *Les Matelots* I like it better . . . It is a *succès*, the most *réussi* of all the new ones – dancing legs performing sea-chanties in such an intimate way that we rollick with laughter and experience the 'sailor-boy and girl' feeling.

"An intellectual thrill was provided by *Les Noces*, for few understood it. I think that

The Russian Ballet Again: Diaghileff at His Majesty's.

IN "THE HOUSE PARTY" ("LES BICHES") : MR. SERGE LIFAR
AND MLLE. NIKITINA.

AS THE GROTESQUE PEASANT IN "BARABAU" : MME. LYDIA
SOKOLOVA — AND HER FALSE NOSE.

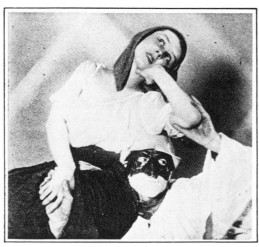

IN "PULCINELLA" : PULCINELLA (M. LEON WOIZIKOVSKY)
AND PIMPINELLA (MME. LOPOKOVA).

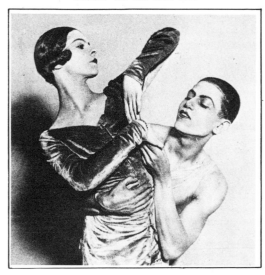

IN "THE HOUSE PARTY" ("LES BICHES") : MLLE. ALICE NIKITINA
AND M. SERGE LIFAR.

"ROMEO AND JULIET" AS PRESENTED BY THE BALLET: MME. TAMAR
KARSAVINA AND M. SERGE LIFAR.

Photographs by Lenare.

M. Diaghileff's season of Russian Ballet, which opened recently at His Majesty's under the patronage of H.R.H. the Duke of Connaught, is enjoying a big success, and is the first repertory season of its kind which M. Diaghileff has presented in London since 1921. "The House Party" (" Les Biches "), a ballet with song in one act, to music by Poulenc, is a favourite number. "Barabau" is a ballet suggested by an Italian nursery rhyme, "Barabau, Barabau, why did you die?" and has book and music by Vittorio Rieti. In it Mme. Lydia Sokolova gives an admirable grotesque performance as the First Peasant. "' Romeo and Juliet' in Ballet Form. Rehearsal without Scenery in Two Tableaux," is an exceptionally interesting production, seen in London for the first time this season. The music is by Mr. Constant Lambert, and the ballet is the first with English music to be given by the Russian dancers. "Pulcinella" is a ballet with songs in one tableau, with music by Igor Stravinsky, from Gianbattista Pergolesi, and has scenery and dresses by Picasso.

The photographers, Lenare, provided all the pictures for this page, which appeared in *The Sketch* during the 1926 season. Sadly, all their negatives were destroyed during the war.

the dancing is the least thing in it. The *Ballet Russe* offers this precious custom of humanity with drab colours, hardly any feasting, although towards the end the voices outburst with drunkenness and the final bells in the orchestra open the door in the imagination towards the great unknown, and everyone is moved without knowing why. It is a way to stir up a highbrow, and that is why I call it intellectual."

Lopokova found it difficult to make up her mind about Balanchine's ballets. "They are never 'stupid,' always 'amusing.' I think that they move along a line of development for dancers, which is necessary, inevitable. They have delicious moments, moving details, novelties which are always refreshing even when they have faults. If, for the moment, the ballet seems to have lost some of its tenderness, some of its soul, that is only to say that it reflects modernity."

Lopokova looked at the current company, and made some very pertinent observations. "Diaghileff's company is remarkable for its lack of affectation, and for this quality above all we must begin by saluting Leon Woizikowsky. The facility of his legs in any dance, his rhythmic precision, his spontaneous interest in every part he takes, and something beside all these merits, something that is attractive and sweet in his nature, make him the muscles of the ballet and win our hearts too. Lubov Tchernicheva, the ever beautiful, there is no fear that she will become less so . . . Sokolova is a strong personality who controls her art from head to foot. These three, with some other old friends, give the company its foundation of experienced, professional knowledge . . .

"The rising sprigs are Serge Lifar and the three coming graces, Danilova, Doubrovska and Nikitina. Danilova has the best dancing legs, Nikitina the best figure, Doubrovska, who might be the best of all if she were not such a harum-scarum creature, the most personality. But in each there is a personal expression, be it an instep or the curve of a throat . . . Lifar is first of all an artist. It is shown by his comedy gifts in *Pastorale* and *La Boutique*, his lyrical beauty in *Les Matelots* and his youthful intensity in *Romeo* . . . His faults last year were inexperience and a certain bodily weakness for the hard tasks which modern choreographs set to the muscles and breathing of the dancers. But this year his dancing has progressed out of knowledge and he is learning to throw out the attraction of his gifts beyond the stage to the audience. He is too nice to be a natural *star*, but I believe this year, that I doubted last year, that M. Diaghileff's judgment has been right once again in discerning where possibilities lay amongst the undeveloped talents of his artists."

Whilst the season was in progress, Chelsea's *New Chenil Galleries*, recently opened as something more than a club, housed an exhibition of the young Serge Lifar's collection to date of original designs for the ballet. Contemporary criticism is interesting, in view of the fact that the augmented collection has, for some years, been considered a prize at the Wadsworth Athenaeum, Hartford, Connecticut.

"It is a somewhat disappointing affair but has a peculiar interest as a demonstration of the very slight material from which the wonders of the Russian Ballet are built up. For it must be confessed that these sketches, so effective in their final form on the stage, can, in many cases, scarcely be taken seriously as framed pictures . . ." (P.G. Konody.) *Daily Mail 6.7.26*

The season was summed up in *Apollo* as "the most brilliant the Ballet has enjoyed in London since the war." Lord Rothermere, its backer, must have been satisfied, for plans were already afoot, in which his influence was felt, for its successor, later in the year. *Apollo August 1926*

Tom Titt's Pyramid (p. 325)  was, alas, never staged!

1926

LYCEUM THEATRE

NOVEMBER 13th - DECEMBER 11th

FIRST PERFORMANCE IN ENGLAND

December 3rd: *The Triumph of Neptune*
(Lord Berners, Balanchine, nineteenth-century designs adapted by
Prince Shervadchidze, Book by Sacheverell Sitwell.)
World Première

REPERTOIRE

L'Après-Midi D'un Faune   *Le Lac des Cygnes*
Aurora's Wedding   *Les Matelots*
Les Biches   *L'Oiseau de Feu*
La Boutique Fantasque   *Petrouchka*
Le Carnaval   *Polovtsian Dances*
Cimarosiana   *Le Tricorne*
Contes Russes

COMPANY

Barasch, Branitzka, Chamié, Danilova, Evina, Fedorova A., Gevergeva, Istomina, Jazevitch, Klemetska, Komarova, Kouchetovska, Maicherska, Markova, Matveeva, Miklachevska, Obidennaia, Orlova, Petrova, Savina, Slavinska, Sokolova, Sumarokova, Tchernicheva, Vadimova, Zarina.

Balanchine, Borovsky, Cieplinsky, Domansky, Efimov, Fedorov, Gaubier, Grigoriev, Hoyer I., Hoyer II., Idzikowski, Ignatov, Jazvinsky, Kotchanovsky, Kremnev, Ladre, Lifar, Lissanevitch, Michaelov, Pavlov, Petrakevitch, Romov, Slavinsky, Strechnev, Tcherkas, Winter, Woizikowski.

CONDUCTOR

Defosse

THE TRIUMPH OF NEPTUNE

If there had been groans about the high prices at His Majesty's, (where pit seats had been sold as stalls,) there can have been nothing but glee when the next London season was moved into the Lyceum, with a top price of 17/- – the front rows of the gallery bookable at 2/4 – and plenty of Unreserved at 2/- and 1/-. The season had a popular air, with nostalgic revivals of many favourite ballets, the low prices aimed at attracting a wider public, and a new ballet which, at the express wish of Diaghilev's backer, Lord Rothermere, was to be very English in every way.

This was not ready to be shown until the season was well advanced; and there were a number of changes in the company, the most notable being that Vera Petrova, a dancer from Warsaw, had been engaged to replace Nemchinova.

Despite the doubts voiced in the summer, the Duke of Connaught cannot have been as dismayed as some of the professional critics at the Ballet's adventurous departures, for he once more extended his patronage to the season.

Francis Toye (who said that "Ballets Russes de Monte Carlo" reminded him of "The Scotch Tea-Shop from Monte Carlo," somewhere in Brittany!) found the opening ballet, *Petrouchka*, which he thought to be the most satisfactory of all in the repertoire, "spirited in its performance." *The House Party* – "anathema to some and a delight to others" – had Petrova as The Beauty: "she danced well, though she did not manage to make us forget Nemchinova's exquisite performance in the same number." *Swan Lake*'s classic requirements showed up the current company, "who have been experimenting too much in modernity to maintain the rigid accuracy and perfect technique indispensable in dancing of this kind." The principal rôles were danced by Danilova, who "was good and looked lovely," and Idzikowski, who "danced everybody else off the stage, a fact at once recognised by the public." Morning Post 15.11.26

Two "Russian" and two "French" works were given on the following night – *Children's Tales* and *Prince Igor*, *Les Biches* and *L'Après-Midi d'un Faune*. This last revival was an event of importance, for it was the first time that Diaghilev had given it in England since before the war – the first time that England had seen any Faun other than Nijinsky.

"It acquired a veil, a patina, from the years between. We were all a little conscious of our changed selves," said Edith Shackleton. The Queen 24.11.26

One critic to whom it was legend and not a memory was Horace Horsnell. "There were anxious hearts at the Lyceum . . . I felt them beating with hope and fear as Debussy's plaintive oboes began to murmur in the darkness. Had Woizikowsky only known the emotional odds laid for and against him, he might have lacked courage to step down from his sunlit rock, and to maintain, as he did, the admirable poise of the faun's plastic trance." Observer 21.11.26

"Seeing his pretty fantasy for the first time," continued Horsnell, "I found it a slighter but not less pleasing piece than I anticipated. For me there were no dreams of past delight to be re-captured or traduced; distance had not lent its deep enchantment to my expectations; nor could I do more than dimly conjecture the ghost of that other faun ever at this one's gilded heels. Yet for all the inevitable comparisons between the past and the present, I do not think that Woizi-kowsky would have been displeased with such comments as I overheard; nor, I am sure, would the ghost of that other, now legendary faun, have been disturbed."

Though *The Queen* complained of the new clear blue backcloth in place of Bakst's original complicated and sylvan setting, *The Times* was content. "The faun, clad in the pagan garb of the woods, and the nymph (Mlle. Tchernicheva, wide-eyed and fearless,) move, and are still, and move again. So do the elusive idea of Mallarmé, the pictorial impressionism of Debussy, and the formal lines of Nijinsky's choreography fuse into a wonderful unity."

For *The Firebird*, Diaghilev had commissioned new scenery and costumes from Nathalie Gontcharova.

The
Times
26.11.26

"One always felt that the original setting and costumes of this ballet missed the full possibi-lities for colour and fantasy provided by the story," said *The Times*. "Mme. Gontcharova . . . has seized her opportunities and provided a wonderful spectacle, in which the grotesque and the beautiful are imaginatively compounded. The one definite fault which struck one about Mme. Gontcharova's costumes was the lack of brilliance in the dress of the Fire Bird herself. Her plumage in the older setting was, at least in recent years, not as bright as it should have been; but Mme. Lopokova, who danced the part last night, was almost sombrely clad. For the rest, the effect of the magnificent costumes against the green-and-gold background of the first scene, and the even greater splendour of the second, in which the background is a successfully formalized Russian city, provide one of the most beautiful spectacles which this company has provided either before or since the war."

During the summer season, Diaghilev had heard music composed by Lord Berners – most unusual of English milords – and had invited Sacheverell Sitwell to write the "book" for a very English ballet. Sitwell had the idea of making a ballet version of the "Penny Plain, Tuppence Coloured" juvenile dramas, and took Diaghilev to see both Pollock's and Webb's shops, where descendants of the original publishers still communed with the woodcuts and model theatres with which their ancestors had delighted generations of children. Diaghilev had never seen anything like them before, and was himself delighted. He arranged for Prince Shervachidze to adapt these designs, (originally by George and Robert Cruikshank, Tofts, Honigold, and the first Webb,) and, in modern parlance, to "blow them up" to stage proportions. The ballet was called *The Triumph of Neptune.*

Daily
Express
4.12.26

Hannen Swaffer, frequently a grim critic of the ballet (and its audiences,) loved this one, and gave a full account of it.

"The scenes include ex-Mid-Victorian ideas of a shipwreck, London Bridge, Fleet Street, a frozen wood, an evil grotto, and an ogre's castle; there is a most entrancing fairy ballet, with flying fairies, suspended on wires, and among the musical effects are the sound of a wind made by bird-blowers, sold at toyshops.

"There is a story of two intrepid explorers, a journalist, and a British tar, who go on a voyage of discovery into the fairy world. We are shown the inhabitants of the sky, and then we see the explorers bidding farewell to their families. But Neptune objects. The travellers are ship-wrecked, and a goddess saves them.

"Meanwhile, at home the sailor's wife is dancing with another lover, while an amateur vocalist is practising 'The Last Rose of Summer.'

"The sailor's spirit returns and, seeing his wife in the dandy's arms, approaches the window with a raised knife. The policemen rush to arrest him, but he is only a shadow.

"Meanwhile, the travellers have reached the ogres' cavern, in which ten ogres seize one of the travellers who is about to be sawn in halves by a two-headed giant when the scene changes.

"At the end, the 'Triumph of Neptune' is shown as an old-fashioned pantomime trans-formation scene, while the sailor becomes a fairy prince and weds the sea-god's daughter."

**THE TRIUMPH
OF NEPTUNE**

Tamara Gevergeva
wearing one of the
Foilstone tunics, with
Serge Lifar – Tom Tug.

This happy conglomeration of typical incidents of the annual pantomimes must have pleased children of all ages.

"Except for the quality of the dancing," continued Swaffer, "you might have seen all this at Islington seventy years ago . . . The theatre was crowded, and although the ballet was so unrehearsed that there was more than one minor catastrophe, the curtain fell amid such enthusiasm that Lord Berners found himself mixed up amongst the dancers, the laurel wreaths, and the bouquets. Then, right at the end, there was a call for Mr. Sitwell, who received from Serge Lifar a small floral token, torn from the many which had been sent to him.

"This is the best ballet since *La Boutique Fantasque*."

Balanchine, the choreographer, had endless opportunity for the display of his wit and ingenuity, which he briskly seized.

Serge Lifar was a great success as Tom Tug, the Sailor, and Danilova as the Sea-King's Daughter. Sokolova was a most unusual Goddess, who danced an unusual version of the Hornpipe in front of the drop-curtain, clad in a marvellous sequinned nineteenth-century foil stone tunic, which Diaghilev had spotted when taken to May's, the theatrical costumiers, in Garrick Street. This inexplicably topped a kilt and was surmounted by a glengarry! The other tunic he had bought at the same time made a resplendent figure of Neptune. They were extremely heavy, and had originally been worn for "walking-about" parts. Poor Sokolova endured great trials as she staggered under the weight in her energetic number.

Lubov Tchernicheva and
Vera Petrova as two of the
Fairies in *The Triumph of
Neptune.*

Just as Diaghilev had cast a London busker for a part in *Les Matelots*, so did he turn in this case to another expert – or, rather, a whole family of experts – to "fly" his artists in *The Triumph of Neptune*. "Flying Ballets" had been a feature at the Alhambra and other theatres (such as the *Grecian*,) in the late nineteenth century, and had become a favourite item in pantomimes. The Kirby family had been "flying" Peter Pan since his first appearance in 1904. J. Raymond Kirby headed the family business in the late 1920's.

"Flying" – rather, *being* flown – was an art new to the dancers. A.E. Wilson gave the secrets away in *The Pageant of Pantomime*. "I have often watched the girls taking their dizzy flights with the grace of swallows on the wing. The chief qualification for a flying ballet girl is a considerable amount of pluck and an inconsiderable amount of weight . . . not more than eight stone. The wire from which each girl is suspended is controlled by one man in the wings. He holds the wire, forming the other end of a human see-saw, and by pulling and relaxing enables the girl to perform her somersaults and other evolutions. Eight stone of aerial dancer is just about as much as any man can safely manage."

There was so much wit in the detail of the "book:" at first, the crowd gathered round a magic telescope, peering at Fairyland. In the Fleet Street scene, two rival newspapers, "The Evening Telescope" and "The Evening Microscope," vied with each other to scoop the news of the voyage. In the "programme notes," (presumably written by Sacheverell Sitwell himself,) the Sailor's escape from the Ogres when they were about to saw his friend in half was described in these terms: "But you mustn't imagine that he deserts his companions through cowardice – not at all – he is a British mariner and would never leave a friend in the lurch. The truth is that he is obliged to rush away and change his costume for the last act."

Swaffer had started his article by saying that "we saw at the Lyceum last night the beginnings of a British Ballet."

342

The *Queen* adored it for itself. Edith Shackleton had this to say about it: "I wish no harm to the customary pantomime which will replace the Russian Ballet at the Lyceum Theatre, but it is a thousand pities that the Diaghilev company could not have been appearing somewhere in London through the holiday season now that their repertoire contains so English-Christmassy an item as *The Triumph of Neptune*, which may be described as essential Christmas pantomime with a quirk. It is a joke, but not an acid joke like *The House Party*. Rather does it give a comfortable sense as of a rich background of Sunday dinners and family festivals, of the solid fat English life of the late nineteenth century. Lord Berners' music recalls wittily all that one ever heard in little provincial theatres in one's childhood; Mr. Sacheverell Sitwell's fantastic tale of a sailor who gets into Fairyland and eventually marries a sea-god's daughter is an excellent device for showing no fewer than twelve sets of scenery of the two-pence coloured sort.

The
Queen
15.12.26

"There is a pleasantly possessive feeling about seeing these scenes again in their giant form – here are those magnificently looped red plush curtains, that curly and cruel storm at sea, that gloomy and impenetrable enchanted wood! Mr. Sitwell's dashing journalists are, I think, an anachronism. In the red plush period Fleet Street was less hungry for scoops and thought less of feeding the early express trains than it does now. His rival journalists are distinctly of the Northcliffian era, in spite of their funny clothes.

"The choreography, quite properly, shows no novelties, but mildly parodies the solemn Victorian ballet. Memorable are a fairy ensemble, a delightfully comic polka in which a 'dandy' (should he not have been called a 'masher'?) takes part, and a Highland Fling for a fairy to dance, in the obliging spirit of all the best pantomime fairies, on the front of the stage while the scenery is being changed . . .

"It is heartening to realise that the Diaghilev productions now contain an item so English as *The Triumph of Neptune*, and it will be interesting to see what the foreign audiences make of it when it is done abroad. One criticism is that the joke is not worth the trouble it makes with its twelve scenes and its innumerable, confused characters and costumes, but it is this ponderousness which gives the ballet its true All-British flavour. A sense of mighty effort going on behind the scenery was part of the joy of the heavy pantomime of long ago. The thing could not have been done simply any more than a Christmas pudding can be made from a few inexpensive ingredients."

The *Queen* made another interesting comment on the move to the Lyceum, which had approximately 3,000 seats. "A new audience was drawn to the popular Lyceum Theatre, which is too big to depend entirely on an art-student gallery and Bright Young People to fill the stalls." The newly-enticed audience certainly had its appetite whetted by a season packed with such a delightful repertoire as it was offered, but, like Christmas itself, all good things had to come to an end. "In Active Preparation," as it said in the programme, was the big event of the Lyceum's year, its Christmas pantomime, traditionally opening on Boxing Day, (twice daily, popular prices, 2/4 to 7/6, all bookable.) Ironically, this year the choice was *The Sleeping Beauty*.

1927

PRINCE'S THEATRE

JUNE 13th - JULY 23rd

FIRST PERFORMANCES IN ENGLAND

June 14th:	*La Chatte* (Sauguet, Balanchine, Gabo and Pevsner.) Monte Carlo 30.4.1927
June 20th:	*Les Fâcheux* (2nd Version) (Auric, Massine, Braque) Monte Carlo 3.5.1927
July 4th:	*Le Pas d'Acier* (Prokofiev, Massine, Yakoulov.) Paris 7.6.1927
July 11th:	*Mercure* (Satie, Massine, Picasso) Paris 15.6.1924, for Comte Etienne de Beaumont
July 18th:	*Le Chant du Rossignol* (3rd Version) (Stravinsky, Balanchine, Matisse.) Paris 17.6.1925

REPERTOIRE

L'Après-Midi d'un Faune	*Contes Russes*	*Pulcinella*
Aurora's Wedding	*Le Lac des Cygnes*	*Romeo and Juliet*
Les Biches	*Les Matelots*	*Les Sylphides*
La Boutique Fantasque	*L'Oiseau de Feu*	*Le Tricorne*
Le Carnaval	*Petrouchka*	*The Triumph of Neptune*
Cimarosiana	*Polovtsian Dances*	

COMPANY

Barasch, Branitzka, Chamié, Danilova, Evina, Fedorova A., Gevergeva, Jazevitch, Klemetska, Kouchetovska, Maicherska, Markova, Matveeva, Miklachevska, Nikitina A., Obidennaia, Orlova, Petrova, Savina, Slavinska, Sokolova, Sumarokova, Tchernicheva, Troussevitch, Vadimova, Zarina.

Balanchine, Borovsky, Cieplinsky, Domansky, Efimov, Fedorov, Gaubier, Grigoriev, Hoyer I., Hoyer II., Idzikowski, Ignatov, Jazwinsky, Kotchanovsky, Kremnev, Ladre, Lifar, Lissanevitch, Massine, Pavlov, Petrakevitch, Romov, Slavinsky, Strechnev, Tcherkas, Winter, Woizikowski.

CONDUCTORS

Goossens, Sargent, Beecham, Desormière.

LA CHATTE – LE PAS D'ACIER

After this Lyceum season the company went to Turin and Milan, (which it had visited before, but not previously giving its performances at La Scala, an ambition of Diaghilev's now fulfilled.) The annual sortie to Monte Carlo was followed by brief visits to Barcelona and Marseilles, and then, as usual, the important Paris season.

There was a real drama the day before the Paris première of *La Chatte*. Olga Spessiva, for whom it had been designed and who had given its first performance in Monte Carlo, sprained an ankle so seriously that dancing was out of the question. Diaghilev turned to Alice Nikitina (herself more than prone to similar accidents,) asking her to learn the part and dance it that night. It was then 4.30 p.m. Balanchine, the choreographer, objected furiously to the idea of such a rushed job, but by some miracle, it was accomplished. Moreover, it was such a tremendous success that the part remained Nikitina's so long as she was in the company. (Markova danced it after her, at Covent Garden, in July 1929.)

The success was so great that Diaghilev decided to give *La Chatte* as the novelty on the opening night of the London season. A totally different disaster occurred this time. Diaghilev arranged for Nikitina to explain it to the audience herself; wearing a black Chanel dress, she came before the curtain and read a little speech which had been written for her by Wollheim:

"Ladies and Gentlemen, I have a sad announcement to make. The Southern Railway has not yet delivered to us a large part of the scenery of *La Chatte*. Therefore I will be unable to dance it for you tonight. But my colleagues will dance for you *Carnaval* instead. But please come tomorrow, when you will see my performance. I thank you."

Nikitina
by
Herself

Observer
28.11.26

"Coming tomorrow" is not such an easy matter as all that in the theatre, for the seats have mainly been sold. Such a postponement presents the box-office with fearful problems. Not only do inveterate first-nighters have to be soothed, but the critics have to be accommodated. Critics tend to like the familiarity of their accustomed seats. They expect seats which give a good view. It is not such a bad thing for them to have less favourable positions from time to time; during the previous season, Horace Hornsnell, twice foiled when he went to see *Firebird*, only to find a change of programme, had also found compensations when he had to be fitted into one of those seats in the dress circle so close to the stage that the wings can be seen. ". . . This enabled me to see the ballet as it were in mufti – that is, without its first-night furore – and to observe, which a detachment of dazzling principals and a new programme seldom permit, minor details that included an unofficial peep behind the scenes. Degas was right; ballet dancers at rest do assume the poses his strange genius never tired of particularising with paint and pencil. From where I sat, little coveys of the *corps de ballet* could be seen clustered in the wings, testing the pliancy of shoes and strappings, and holding still, expectant attitudes Degas himself might have designed. And just before braving the full limelight of the stage, I saw them make the quick, triple sign of the cross."

When *La Chatte* arrived the following night, it astonished, but did not disappoint. Based on an Aesop fable, it had décor and costumes designed by the "Constructivists," Gabo and Pevsner, (brothers who had left Russia, having started a new style of sculpture whence came the soubriquet,) music by Henri Sauguet, a young Frenchman who did not lean towards *"Les Six,"* and choreography by Balanchine.

The Sphere 2.7.27 "More and more, in its modern items, the Russian Ballet is becoming the Parisian Ballet," said a critic in *The Sphere*. *"The Cat* is by Euclid out of Aesop; it is a blend of a nursery tale and a geometric problem. The story is Aesop's fable about a young man who fell in love with a cat and implored Aphrodite to make the animal human. The cat becomes a girl, but just as she is about to return the young man's love, instinct causes her to scamper after a mouse, whereupon the goddess changes her back to her original shape. But the metamorphosis wrought by M. Diaghilev, his choreographist and scenic designers, is wider than that from cat into lady and from lady into cat. They have transposed the young man, his companions, and their background, into a mathematical pattern.

"Aphrodite's temple is built out of celluloid in the form of geometrical instruments. The figure of Aphrodite herself is built up by transparent rotundities that suggest cooking casseroles designed by Mestrovic or Epstein. The young man and his fellow athletes wear enlarged rulers, triangles and circles; they move and leap as though they belonged to a theory of ballistics.

"The effect, besides being novel, is curiously stimulating and the music of M. Henri Sauguet, who does not use modern dissonances, and might be a modern successor to Offenbach, removes the element of the grotesque from too much emphasis. If, however, the principal dancers were less naturally graceful than Alice Nikitina and Serge Lifar, the general outcome of the adventure might seem absurd as well as fantastic."

The Queen 22.6.27 The *Queen* liked it, too. "The choreography and setting are excitingly new. The young man's room has walls of shiny black American cloth and furniture of mica, which give most curious and pleasing lighting effects; and the dances are on new patterns, though they sometimes remind one of the stern Greek exercises of Mr. Raymond Duncan's school."

TWO PORTRAITS BY ELIZABETH POLUNIN

far left: Felia Doubrovska.

left: Alice Nikitina

Alice Nikitina and Serge Lifar in *La Chatte*.

The *Observer* gently stretched its claws: "It is, if you care to say so, an exercise in pure plastique, deliberately devoid of story, which reduces scenery and costume to so artful a minimum that you scarcely notice the absence of either. . . The result is definitely *fin-de-siècle*. The dancers are seven youths, students of no mean academy – the Fifth Form at St. Dynamic's suggests itself – whose studies are diversified by an exotic romance between the Head Boy and the school cat, whom Aphrodite, in answer to his prayers, has changed into a Young Girl. The appearance of a mouse undoes the metamorphosis and puts romance in its place. The girl becomes a cat again. The young man dies of a broken heart." (*The Sphere* had omitted this detail.) "The fascination of this modish trifle lies in its sheer athletics. Serge Lifar is an astonishing technician, who has never been trammelled by what one might call the humanities. Here his technique is seen to perfection. There appears to be nothing set him by the most exacting choreographist that he cannot do, and he does it as instinctively as others smile or pirouette. His dancing, together with that of Nikitina and his six companions, is not only remarkable in itself, but marks a further stage in the ballet's Gallicisation." Observer 19.6.27

This time, the *Morning Post* was represented by "B.M.," who said that the new work was acclaimed with enthusiasm, but was uncertain whether that was intended for the ballet or for its performers. Discussing the music, B.M. made a comparison with some saying of Cocteau's – "Music is not always a gondola, or a race-horse, or a tightrope. It is sometimes a chair." "Well," said B.M., "M. Sauguet has carried out that particular function. His spasmodic score provides something for the ballet to rest upon whenever it appears to be flagging, and there are a few moments when the work eagerly seizes the opportunity to be seated." Morning Post 16.6.27

Nevertheless, this ballet became very popular and found a permanent place in the repertoire.

The
Times
21.6.27
Despite the "rave" notices which *Les Fâcheux* had attracted in 1924, Diaghilev had now asked Massine to invent fresh choreography for it. *The Times* was not impressed: "There are a few amusing grotesques for M. Massine himself and M. Woizikowsky, and a graceful dance for Mme. Tchernicheva, but the total effect was incoherent, and there was far too much rough-and-tumble in the ensembles." More favourable – "Except where he falls back upon his grotesque clichés, he has given the work a new and attractive surface. The dance of Eraste with Orphise (Massine and Tchernicheva) was a beautiful fantasy of symmetrical movement, and the final Masquerade suggests that Massine is at last beginning to solve the problems of group dancing.

Morning
Post
21.6.27

"The dance of the battledore and shuttlecock players is an amusing invention, introducing a back-hand stroke as effective as any to be seen at Wimbledon."

The
Times
21.6.27
The same evening , a tightened-up *Triumph of Neptune* appeared. "A vast improvement of an already good original," said *The Times*. "A new dance has been added for M. Idzikowsky, who in the part of Cupid unites the sailor and the fairy-queen after executing a *pas seul*, which is a burlesque, all the funnier for being carried out with the utmost gravity, of the old school of male dancer."

Observer
3.7.27
The great excitement of the following Monday was an all-Stravinsky programme, conducted by the composer himself. "He had taken up the baton, . . . and in the most businesslike but least showy manner, electrified three of his popular ballets. You should have seen how *Petrouchka* pulled himself together; how radiant was *Pulcinella*; what raptures animated *The Firebird*. It was as though father himself had paid a purposeful visit to the nursery. Every dancer from A to Z was on the tiptoe of form, and the evening (in the happier sense of the term) was a spanking one."

The title of the next new ballet, *Le Pas d'Acier*, was rendered in French in the programme: most of the papers left it at that, the *Daily Express* "freely translating" it as "The Steel Way." A number of ugly variations have been attempted. None ever seems quite right.

Daily
Express
5.7.27
"The first scene presents a picture of rural life, the second a factory in full blast," said the *Express*. "The overture sets one's teeth on edge with its discords, but soon this stridency proves the right accompaniment to the frenzied action on the stage. Massine has created new postures and steps, strange contortions and movements that give the impression of powerful, complicated machinery, pistons working, wheels turning, and intense labour. The effect is stimulating, exciting, at times comic, and on the whole interesting to the highest degree.

"Many will dislike it, it will be over-praised, but no one will be bored by it, and, judging by the tempestuous reception it received last night, it will become a regular feature of the Russian Ballet programme."

Prokofiev's ballet was intended as a tribute to the efforts Russia had made, in the ten years since the Revolution, to build a new industrial nation out of one which was primarily peasant and agricultural. Anticipating "the talkies" and film background music, the music was revolutionary itself, not for the employment of dissonances alone, or hammering rhythms alone, but for its insistence on the rhythms of machines.

Observer
10.7.27
The *Observer* had a graphic description this time from St. John Ervine, instead of Horace Horsnell, who seemed to have had a plethora of commitments that week.

"Mr. Diaghilev not only believes that all play and no work makes ballet a dull toy, but consistently puts precept into practice. *Le Pas d'Acier* is not a ballet that makes love to you, but one that either lifts you up or knocks you down. It might be called 'Hot Steel,' for it reproduces – as only pitiless music, galvanised anatomy, frenzied rhythm, and Massine's exacting choreography can – the dream of an overwrought rivetter who sleeps at his post.

"It is presented in two tableaux. The first, says the programme, 'summarised the legends of the Russian countryside; the second the mechanism of the factory.' And if you think so, why, so they do. The music suggests unfriendly rivalry between massed roundabout organs and a shipyard on full time. Though brilliantly woven, the general pattern of the dancing is difficult for the tyro to disentangle because of its incidental distractions. Chaos, you say at first sight, not cosmos, while appreciating the richness of the detail and astonishing skill and endurance of the dancers.

LE PAS D'ACIER

Alexandra Danilova and
Leonide Massine.

"You see your favourites, whose art in happier circumstances has long since conquered you, fantastically attired as for a grim but impromptu charade. Some wear the uniform of that fabulous corps, the Horse Marines, others are apaches, hoydens, plain girls, hamadryads – what you will; the rest are overalled, mackintoshed, or stripped to the buff, and all strain nerve and muscle to keep time with purposeful cacophony, pace with mechanised frenzy. Great hammers clang and boilers let off steam; the soul of man is but a variant of the fuel force with oil and gas. The result, though perplexing, is anything but dull.

"Perhaps if one saw as much of the ballet as M. Diaghilev sees one would be more eager to welcome such departures from gracious orthodoxy. These 'méchante' novelties do set off, by force of contrast, applause-proud favourites. *The Cat, Les Matelots,* and *Prince Igor,* which followed, seemed simple treats indeed, save perhaps to some of the dancers, into whose souls the iron of innovation appeared to have settled."

St. John Ervine then considered the music more particularly: "Prokofiev's music is good stage music in the first place... it must have been one of the factors which inspired the remarkably good steps and figures invented by M. Massine. It is noisy, but the scoring, though very thick, is yet balanced, and the final effect is not so much one of noise as of continual, deep sound. The climax at the end of the second and last act is finely done, so gradually built up that the listener is carried onward with no sense of effort. The stage action helps here, and this moment is one of the best examples of close interplay between dance steps and orchestral sounds. As regards music pure and simple, one is continually reminded of Stravinsky's *Sacre du Printemps,* beside which Prokofiev's work takes a place, though it does not bear close comparison. There is in Prokofiev none of the subtlety of Stravinsky; it is all more obvious. *Le Sacre* makes good concert-room hearing. It is improbable that *Le Pas d'Acier* would stand that test."

Lubov Tchernicheva, Serge Lifar, Alexandra Danilova, Leonide Massine.

The
Times
5.7.27 *The Times* also found the second part the more interesting. "All kinds of mechanism, from the steam hammer to the most delicate weaving machinery, find a place in this elaborate scheme, in which human beings are the cogs and pistons. The scene is extraordinarily impressive, and even terrifying, as a large factory in full swing is terrifying to the layman. Noise plays a part in producing the effect, and Prokofiev certainly gets from the orchestra an extraordinarily vivid impression of the hum and roar of machines. . ."

The
Lady
14.7.27 *The Lady* had her own thoughts about the new work and its implications. "The efforts of some modern composers to enlarge the range of musical expression have had the result of making us wonder whether the old distinction between 'musical' and 'unmusical' sounds was not purely arbitrary. If we accept the big drum which cannot be tuned to a note, why should we be shocked at the introduction into a score of hammers, whips, and whistles? We must judge these experiments by results. Does the composer achieve something which could not be achieved if he confined himself to the use of instruments of which the modern symphony orchestra is made up? The question has been raised again by Prokofiev's new ballet, *Le Pas d'Acier*. To the 'musical' sounds of brass instruments the composer has added the thud of hammers. The effect obtained is remarkably powerful. If it is objected that it is the musicians' business to make music, not noise, the answer is that the boundary between the two is not easy to define. Noises subjected to the laws of rhythm, as they are in *Le Pas d'Acier*, are justified. To some ears Prokofiev's music sounds 'hideous,' but that may be only because we have set up a standard of beauty to which it does not conform."

One performance only was given of something which could by no stretch of the imagination have been called a "Diaghilev" ballet. It had been commissioned by the wealthy Comte Etienne de Beaumont for one of a series of private charity performances in 1924, *Les Soirées de Paris*. When it had first been given there had been a noisy demonstration by Dadaists, who objected to a Cubist production. Designed by Picasso, it had choreography by Massine.

The Times was not impressed.

"Nothing dates so quickly as the latest thing, and if ever there was any merit in Eric Satie's ballet, *Mercure*, . . . it has evaporated . . . We hardly know which is more outmoded, Picasso's ridiculous contraptions or Satie's music, which harks back to the palmy days of rag-time . . . Half the gods of Greece appeared on the stage, but we doubt if any would have recognised himself, except Mercury, who was at least allowed his winged hat. The three Graces were like music-hall Rhine-Maidens and added a touch of low humour to the dull affair . . . Mr. Diaghilev is to be congratulated on his wisdom in giving only one performance of it. . ." The Times 12.7.27

So far this season, Balanchine had been represented by only one new work, *La Chatte*, and the revival of *The Triumph of Neptune*. The last offering new to London was his version of *Le Chant du Rossignol*, made in 1925 – Diaghilev's third attempt to satisfy himself with a ballet on this theme. The Matisse designs were retained, but, according to *The Times*, "Simplification of the stage mechanism is carried considerably further. The Times 19.7.27

"The aim seems to be the employment of what may be called pictorial gymnastics to give the gist of the story by Hans Andersen which first inspired the music. We get courtiers, first female, then male, indulging in more or less grotesque and angular movements and arranging themselves in conventional patterns without any very clear expressive intention. We imagine that expression is ruled out from the modern technique of the ballet as it is from the modern technique of music. The living nightingale is represented by a young woman in white pyjamas (Markova) who first makes her appearance in a large gilt cage. The cage and certain fluttering movements of her hands are the only indications that she represents a bird. The mechanical nightingale (Woizikowsky) is a clown in a red hat and a costume reminiscent of a well-known advertisement for somebody's motor tyres. We assume him to be a bird because he is brought in and made to gyrate before the Emperor (Grigoriev). There is no song for either save what the orchestra provides. The lady in the white pyjamas pleads and wrestles with one in red tights a military helmet and upturned moustache, who is Death (Lydia Sokolova.) White wins; the Emperor signalises his recovery from illness by throwing down his black robe and appearing in scarlet before a prostrate court.

"There is little else to be said except that if simplification is to be carried out to this extent, precision in the movement seems doubly necessary. The courtiers should not hesitate when they form their grotesque patterns, and the audience should not be allowed to hear someone in the wings snapping his fingers to direct the members of the troupe into their places. The technique of the Russian Ballet used to be above the reproach of amateurishness. It is not so now."

(This note had crept into several of the reviews this season; a study of the programmes indicates that there were new recruits in the ranks. Owing to the habit of concealing their identities under a smotheration of pseudo-Russian names, it is difficult to be sure who they really were except where principals are concerned.)

By now, moving with the times, the magazine called "*The Lady*" had been re-styled. The page which had formerly been headed "THE LADY IN SOCIETY" had become "THE LADY LOOKS ON." From her seat in the stalls, *The Lady* noticed an infrequently-observed member of the ballet ensembles – or rather, members.

"How different in his methods as conductor Malcolm Sargent is to Eugene Goossens. The music and the ballet generally seem to affect him. In *Le Pas d'Acier* he appeared oddly angular in all his movements, and just as if his arms were not jointed at all. In *The Three-Cornered Hat* he swayed his shoulders and nodded his head in quite the Spanish way! I confess I did not notice him in *The Swan Lake*, which, with its curious ghostly grey scenery and girls in old-time white ballet skirts, seemed almost a lullaby after its predecessor!" The Lady 21.7.27

Dr. Sargent had started to get the swing of conducting for the ballet only a few weeks before. He had taken over the Coliseum orchestra for what was intended to be Karsavina's usual spring season there, but which had itself suffered a disaster on the first night, March 21st. She had turned the notoriously ill-omened *Prometheus* legend into a ballet, using the well-known Beethoven music. Just before it ended, Karsavina over-leapt, and ruptured her Achilles tendon. Fortunately, she responded well to treatment, and was able to give her postponed series of performances in May. She herself had been delighted with the effect of his "electrifying baton" on the Coliseum orchestra. His debut with Diaghilev came unexpectedly, when yet another potential disaster threatened this season, as Goossens suddenly fell ill. Urgently summoned by Diaghilev, Malcolm Sargent was begged to conduct *Firebird* and *Les Biches* that very night. "At that time Sargent knew neither score in the professional sense. Nor did he know much about the conventions and niceties of ballet *tempi*, which, as between theatre and concert hall, are apt to differ for the same work. When he reached the theatre a perturbed Diaghilev stopped pacing the stage, flung his arms round Sargent and exclaimed: 'You are my saviour.' 'But,' said Sargent, 'I don't know the scores. The thing's impossible.' 'In that case there will be no ballet tonight,' said Diaghilev in the manner of one announcing the end of the world. Sargent hastened to Goossens's bedside and had a coaching session that went on for six hours. Propped up in bed Goossens . . . hummed salient themes and conducted with one finger while Sargent, following from score, made notes about *tempo* changes and technical pitfalls. There was no time for any sort of rehearsal." Poor Sargent – the dancers fell upon him just before the rise of the curtain, bewildering him with demands to make adjustments for their special numbers – demands impossible even to comprehend, as they were made in a babel of languages. Until Goossens recovered, Malcolm Sargent took the score for each coming evening's ballets home with him, studied them, and had a run-through with a rehearsal piano and a few dancers in the morning. "When the season ended Diaghilev said that he would never forget what Sargent had done for him. Of his feats of conducting virtually at sight, he said, '*C'est une specialité anglaise . . .*' " (Maddeningly, the conductor's name continued to appear in the programmes as "Goossens," so it is not possible to determine how long this went on. However, a friendship had been formed between Sargent and the ballet. He returned in 1928 to conduct for Diaghilev again.)

Malcolm Sargent: Charles Reid

The "Bright Young Things" who thronged the stalls took inspiration not only for their clothes, but also for their fun, from the Ballets Russes. Parties with a theme were "the thing," and the first night of the revival of *Les Matelots* was the excuse for just such a rout. A studio was borrowed "somewhere in Kensington," and *The Lady* told her readers all about the evening, or, at any rate, some of it, in suitably cryptic language.

The Lady 28.7.27

"The revival of *Les Matelots* was celebrated by a terrific party, organised by Miss Allanah Harper, Madge Garland, Miss Olivia Wyndham, and Mr. Martin Wilson, (son of Sir 'Scatters' Wilson.)

"I took a master of industry to see *Pas d'Acier*. I thought it would do him good! It certainly depressed him, but he had to admit its power as the embodiment of the spirit of this age of mechanics.

"You've heard so much about the *Les Matelots* party – Lytton Strachey's wonderful get-up as an admiral and Tallulah Bankhead's impersonation of a naughty little boy in his first white sailor suit – that I won't inflict you with any more of it. But the question, 'Who broke the sideboard?' is still circulating, and I don't think it is known that toward 5 a.m., Miss Allanah Harper said that if her guests wouldn't go home, *she* would. And she did!"

The "Mr. Martin Wilson" of this story, (who later succeeded to the baronetcy,) had a younger brother, Peter – too young to participate in the activities of the "Bright Young Things." Peter Wilson, later Chairman of Sotheby's had the imagination to run a series of sales at which, between 1967 and 1973, hundreds of costumes and the surviving scenery were auctioned off. Before each sale, the costumes were exhibited and their magnificence could be examined. The extraordinary attention to detail, starting with the selection of the materials, astonished everyone. (Periods when the budget was slender showed in this very clearly.) Many have found their way into collections in different parts of the world, and must be an inspiration to theatrical designers.

A serious project for quite a different ballet was under discussion this season. The Blake scholar, Sir Geoffrey Keynes, (brother of John Maynard Keynes, later Lord Keynes, who had married Lopokova, and subsequently became Chairman of Covent Garden,) and his friend, the artist Gwen Raverat, planned an eight-part scenario on the story of *Job*, prepared it in French, and offered it to Diaghilev. Vaughan Williams was composing music for it. With the scenario, Keynes and Mrs. Raverat sent a set of full-size reproductions of Blake's engravings of the story.

"Diaghilev rejected the idea as 'too English,' in which he was quite right, and ' too old-fashioned,' in which he was quite wrong," Keynes noted drily. The book of engravings, however, was not returned, and it was interesting to see traces of Blake's influence appearing in a different Biblical ballet, *The Prodigal Son,* two years later.

One member of the "team" was not the least surprised at Diaghilev's refusal of this suggestion: it was about fourteen years since, at the Savoy, they had discussed another project for a ballet. *("C'est tout ce que je déteste,"* was Diaghilev's comment later, on the *Job* scenario, not the music.) In 1927, Mrs.Raverat received the following letter:

> My dear Gwen,
>   I amused myself with making a sketch of *Job* – I never expected Djag (sic) wd. look at it – and I'm glad on the whole – the *'réclame'* wd. have been rather amusing – but it really wdnt. have suited the sham serious really decadent and frivolous attitude of the R.B. toward everything – can you imagine *Job* sandwiched between *Les Biches* and *Cimarosiana* – and that dreadful pseudo-cultured audience saying to each other 'My dear, have you seen God at the Russian Ballet.' No – I think we are well out of it. – I don't think this is sour grapes – for I admit that it wd. have been great fun to have had a production by the R.B. – though I feel myself that they wd. have made an unholy mess of it with their over-developed calves.
>
>   R.V.W.

Sets for *La Chatte (below)* and for *Le Pas d'Acier (left)*

The geometrical "Constructions" designed for *La Chatte* by the Russian brothers, Gabo and Pevsner, in transparent, light-reflecting materials, against walls in black American cloth, anticipated the vogue brought about by the development of plastics so many years later. So, too, did another Russian designer, Yakoulov, anticipate the age of realism with his pistons and wheels in the set for *Le Pas d'Acier.*

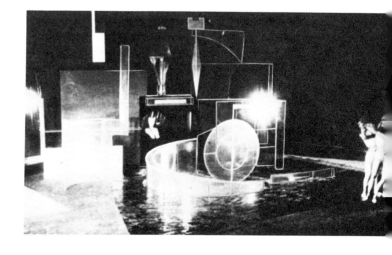

1928

HIS MAJESTY'S THEATRE

JUNE 25th - JULY 28th

FIRST PERFORMANCES IN ENGLAND

June 24th: *Apollon Musagète*
(Stravinsky, Balanchine, Bauchant.)
Paris 12.6.28

July 2nd: *Las Meninās*
(Fauré, Massine; Settings by Socrate, Costumes by Sert.)
San Sebastian, 21.8.16.

July 9th: *Ode*
(Nabokov, Massine, Tchelitchew and Charbonnier.)
Paris 6.6.28

July 16th: *The Gods Go a-Begging*
(Handel, Balanchine; Backcloth – Bakst, *(Daphnis and Chloe,)*
and costumes Braque *(Les Tentations de la Bergère.)*
World Première

REPERTOIRE

L'Après-Midi d'un Faune	*Cimarosiana*	*Le Pas d'Acier*
Aurora's Wedding	*Le Lac des Cygnes*	*Polovtsian Dances*
Barabau	*Les Matelots*	*Pulcinella*
Les Biches	*Midnight Sun*	*Les Sylphides*
La Boutique Fantasque	*Les Noces*	*Le Tricorne*
Le Carnaval	*L'Oiseau de Feu*	*The Triumph of Neptune*
La Chatte		

COMPANY

Branitzka, Chamié, Choulgine, Danilova, Doubrovska, Fedorova A., Grekulova, Ivanova, Klemetska, Maicherska, Markova, Marra, Miklachevska, Nikitina A., Obidenaia, Orlova, Pavlovska, Phillimore, Ross, Savina, Slavinska, Stewart, Sumarakova, Tchernicheva, Vadimova, Zarina.

Balanchine, Borovsky, Domansky, Efimov, Fedorov, Grigoriev, Hoyer I, Hoyer II, Ignatov, Jazwinsky, Katchourovsky, Kotchanowsky, Kremnev, Ladre, Lifar, Lissanevitch, Pavlov, Petrkevitch, Tcherkas, Winter, Woizikowsky, Yovanovitch.

CONDUCTORS

Beecham, Sargent, Desormière.

PIANISTS IN *Les Noces*

Lyell Barbour, Clifford Curzon, Frank Manheimer, Rae Robertson,
(Victor Hely-Hutchinson.)

PROVINCIAL TOUR

Manchester:	12.11.28 – 24.11.28		Edinburgh:	3.12.28 – 8.12.28
Glasgow:	26.11.28 – 1.12.28		Liverpool:	10.12.28 – 15.12.28

APOLLO-ODE

No matter how hilarious, ironic or even scathing some of the critiques of the ballets of the '20's, each new London season was eagerly awaited. Hannen Swaffer was well-known to be by no means a devotee, but on the morning after the opening performance of the 1928 season at His Majesty's Theatre, (to which, despite the fact that Lord Rothermere had suddenly withdrawn his promised support, the company returned, thanks, as has been said, to Lady Juliet Duff,) he reported it in these terms:–

"The Russian Ballet, back for a month's season, proved last night what is always true – that if you give the London public good music you turn away money . . . Daily Express 26.6.28

"His Majesty's could have been filled twice over by lovers of ballet. Even the pit seats, with cushions on, were sold as 24s stalls, and there was scarcely an inch of standing room . . .

"The audience was a remarkable sight. Youth of both sexes predominated in the house . . . A few years ago such a night was impossible. It will be true every night now all through the Russian Ballet's season. Youth will crowd His Majesty's delirious with joy."

As in previous years, *The Times* had already passed on to London its Paris correspondent's report on the reception that city had given to the new ballets. "A new work by Stravinsky is inevitably an event of some importance in the world of music, but the developments of his style are perhaps awaited and discussed with greater interest in Paris than in any other capital. The interest of *Apollon Musagètes* certainly lies primarily in the music, though with the attention half distracted by the colour and movement of the stage it is difficult to appreciate fully the beauties of the score . . . The Times 22.6.28

"It is dancing rather than action or symbolic significance which counts in *Apollo*. The choreography by M. Balanchine is founded no doubt on the steps and movements of the classic school, and, while presenting new elements of striking originality and beauty, avoids the grotesque attitudes which have marked the productions of recent years."

Nicolas Nabokov, whose own ballet was to be produced during the season, recalled that when, earlier in the year, he had arrived in Monte Carlo, he had sat with Diaghilev during a rehearsal of *Apollo*. Pointing at Balanchine, Diaghilev had said to Derain, who was with them, "What he is doing is magnificent. It is pure classicism, such as we have not seen since Petipa." Nabokov p. 83

In order to avoid a "false Hellenism," the costumes and décors had been assigned to a modern French "Primitive" painter, André Bauchant. Beautifully reproduced by Prince Shervachidze, his unorthodox designs were generally liked. Diaghilev had not, however, cared for the classical robes designed for Terpsichore, and had asked his great friend, the dress designer Chanel, to make a "sort of tutu of uneven length, much shorter behind than in front." (In mentioning this, Nikitina made a slip and attributed the discarded design to Rouault, who, in fact, had nothing to do with this ballet.) Nikitina p.91

Stravinsky conducted his own new work on June 25th, Dr. Malcolm Sargent taking *Cimarosiana* and *Firebird*. As one of the reviews refers to the Programme Notes, and as the signature of Igor Stravinsky appears in facsimile below them on the programme, they are here given in full.

SYNOPSIS

Apollo Musagètes is a piece without a plot. It is a ballet whose choreographic action unfolds itself upon the theme Apollo Musagètes, that is to say, Apollo, Leader of the Muses, and inspiring each of them with their art.

The ballet begins with a short prologue representing the birth of Apollo. Leto's divine son leaps into the light. Two goddesses greet Apollo and clothe him in a white robe and a golden girdle. They offer him nectar and ambrosia and lead him to Olympus. End of the prologue and change of scene. Apollo, left alone, dances (Variation.) At the end of his dance appear Calliope, Polymnia, and Terpsichore. Apollo bestows upon each of them a gift (Pas d'action.) This Calliope becomes the Muse of Poetry, Polymnia of Mime, and Terpsichore of the Dance. Each in turn displays her art to turn (Variations). Apollo greets them with a dance in honour of these new-born arts (Variation.) Uniting Poetry and Mime, Terpsichore occupies the place of honour at the Musagètes' side (Pas de deux.) The other Muses join Apollo and Terpsichore in a dance which groups the three of them round their Leader (Coda). These allegorical scenes conclude with an apotheosis in which Apollo leads the Muses, with Terpsichore at their head, to Parnassus, which will henceforth be their home.

The part of Apollo had been created for Serge Lifar. The casting of Terpsichore, however, had caused a quarrel between Balanchine and Diaghilev. Balanchine wanted Danilova to dance it, but Diaghilev insisted that it had to be given to Nikitina. So determined was he on this point that Balanchine had to give way, but a compromise was reached, and Danilova gave the second performance in London. It may be mentioned here that all the memoirs observe that during that winter in Monte Carlo, Diaghilev had frequent fits of sheer bad temper, which were quite unlike him – the company differentiated these from the type of explosion which "gets things done."

In that earlier despatch from Paris, *The Times*' Paris correspondent had said that "M. Lifar is the Etruscan Apollo of Veii come to life . . . He maintains the lines and gestures of archaic sculpture. Compared with the god, the Muses . . . seem strangely 19th century in their formal ballet skirts and tight mauve bodices, but the contrast is not unpleasant, and Mmes. Nikitina, Tchernicheva, and Doubrovska convey with their accustomed grace and beauty the special attributes of each."

The paper's London critic was not so easy to please as his colleague in Paris.

The
Times
26.6.28

"It used to be said that the Russian Ballet would not be much without Stravinsky; his latest production makes us fear that soon it will not be much with him . . . the work was applauded doggedly by a large audience, whose faithfulness was to be rewarded later with the popular *Firebird* . . .

"*Apollo Musagètes* is a very solemn matter. It is not meant to please, like *Cimarosiana*, or to be exciting, like the *Firebird*. It succeeds in avoiding both pitfalls. The music is not even ugly, merely a listless meandering of commonplaces, thickly scored for strings. No percussion, no strident harmonies, no 'Zip!' . . ."

Morning
Post
26.6.28

Francis Toye thought the choreography "extremely ingenious and beautiful at times, particularly as regards some of the held poses, but the whole is too tenuous to hold the attention so long.

"As for the music, Stravinsky seems to have copied another famous composer in searching for progress in the antique, for the influence of Bach and some of the early Italians is strong . . . Further acquaintance will show to what extent the composer has concealed his own personality

Mrs. Maynard Keynes sits
in a box at the ballet and
watches Nikitina, Dou-
brovska, Tchernicheva and
Lifar dancing in Stra-
vinsky's ballet, "Apollo
Musagetes"

(The original caption for this drawing by Cecil Beaton, *Vogue*, 1928.)

underneath this rather obvious surface. Lifar as Apollo and Nikitina as Terpsichore had most of the work to do, and did it notably better than their colleagues."

Richard Capell was present once more, and overheard the comment that *Apollo* was "Quite too *strorrd'nary* for words!" "The *strorrd'nariness* of the new *Apollo*," he said, "lay in no luxury but in the singular austerity of the exercises on Parnassus' top. But first we have a prelude, and the birth of Apollo. He issues – a pretty fancy – from a large hand-painted valentine, signed Bauchant. Daily Mail 26.6.28

"Apollo, whom goddesses unwrap from his swaddling clothes, is a strikingly fit, athletic stripling – none other, of course, than Serge Lifar. He has need of his intensive training, for the choreography (by Balanchine) which he has to undertake looks incredibly difficult. The first curtain goes down on a pose in swimming attitude, Apollo being supported on his stomach by the soles of the goddesses' feet."

When it came to the endowment of the Muses, "Apollo, maintaining the impassiveness of an idol, puts the three through paces which no doubt symbolise the cruel arduousness of the artistic callings . . . The end is Apollo's apotheosis. Lifar deserved it."

Las Meninãs was undoubtedly given as a compliment to King Alfonso and Queen Ena, who were present. Not only were they Diaghilev's greatest reigning-monarch fans, but ever his true friends in adversity. In 1916, inspired by the wonderful country they had come to love, the ballet had created a three-part work, *The Gardens of Aranjuez*, using Gabriel Fauré's *Pavane* for this one section.

In Madrid, Massine had been fascinated by the great Velasquez composition, *Las Meninãs*, in the Prado, in which two tiny girls can be seen, wearing the sumptuous court dresses with the exaggeratedly stiff, wide panniers of the period, and watched by a dwarf. The children, aping their elders in clothes and deportment, were sad little Ladies-in-Waiting – waiting for maturity, whilst childhood passed them by. Massine had moved the scene out of doors, making it a reflective period piece in which the girls had come to adolescence, and had swains. The scenery had been painted by Socrate, and the costumes designed by the "Spanish Grandee" himself, José-Maria Sert.

Daily
Mail
3.7.28
"On a Palladian terrace these stately dames, with their cavaliers, dance a pavane to Gabriel Fauré's sweet and delicate music. The Court Dwarf sidles in and grins in mockery. That is all, except that the dancers' evolutions end in kisses – although one would have said that the formidable fashions of the day would have kept the most pressing of cavaliers at a safe distance." That was all, but it was indeed a charming trifle. ("Blessedly free from any esoteric problems –" *Observer.*)

Richard Capell, who, as has been said, had been attending the *Ballets Russes* ever since their first seasons in Paris, made a few comments which show how the company's own "classics" could pass from one generation of dancers to another and still satisfy. In *Carnaval* – "The Columbine and Harlequin – Mme. Danilova and M. Idzikowski – and the other clever folk had little or nothing to fear from any comparisons –" (which, remembering his earlier raptures over this ballet, was praise indeed.) And again – "In *Aurora's Wedding* . . . Mme. Danilova distinguished herself by her beautiful and cleanly accomplished performance in a type of ballet dancing that insists on grace of style without a flaw," and "Mme. Savina and M. Idzikowski, as the Blue Birds, were again the public's favourites, only rivalled by the Three Ivans (Woizikowsky, Domansky, and Petrkevitch.)"

Anyone who thinks that they can criticise Diaghilev for extravagance ought to look at the programmes for the week beginning Monday, July 9th, 1928. Expenditure, yes, but with programmes planned so as to get full money's worth out of *certain* items, to whit fares and hotel bills. On Saturday, July 7th, the *Daily Mail* announced that "a party of forty Russian singers, soloists and choristers, will be crossing from Paris to England tomorrow to take part in a week of opera-ballets . . ." Diaghilev was packing into one week everything that needed voices: *Les Noces, Barabau, Pulcinella, Midnight Sun,* (which had originally had a lovely little song at the end, later omitted,) and the most controversial new work of this season – *Ode.*

The composer of *Ode*, Nicolas Nabokov, wrote about his ballet in his autobiography, *Old Friends and New Music*, from which excerpts are quoted. If it ended up as a mysterious production, the stages of its transition from a relatively normal inspiration to what finally reached the stage must explain all.

Nabokov was in his early twenties when he arrived in Paris in 1924 with his mother. She was a distant connection of Diaghilev's, whom she lobbied persistently until he agreed to listen to some of her son's music. Diaghilev was at first moderately interested, then became more enthusiastic – and then, as so often, his interest flagged.

In 1927, Nabokov played his ballet, *Ode*, to Diaghilev. "The subject was taken from a poem – an 'ODE TO THE MAJESTY OF GOD ON THE OCCASION OF THE APPEARANCE OF THE GREAT NORTHERN LIGHTS,' by the eighteenth-century court-poet and physicist, Mikhail Lomonosov – ('the father of Russian science.') Written in the flamboyant and archaic Russian of that period, it represents a thinly-veiled allegory on the enthronement of Empress Elizabeth – the Aurora Borealis of the poem."

Though usually quite indifferent to poetry, Diaghilev knew and liked this particular poem. "But chiefly what pleased him in it was its reference to Empress Elizabeth." (Empress Elizabeth, born in 1709, was the daughter of Peter the Great and the Empress Catherine I. She reigned from 1741 until her death in 1762. She built the Winter Palace in St. Petersburg and had many lovers. On her death, no fewer than 15,000 dresses were counted in her wardrobe.) "According to a rumour (which he may well have started himself) Diaghilev was, on his mother's side, a descendant of Elizabeth – a great-great-grandson of one of the Empress's natural children. He was flattered by this illicit relationship to the Imperial house of Russia; it made him a direct descendant of Peter the Great, and gave him a kind of 'morganatic' halo. There was a slight resemblance between him and the puffy-faced daughter of Russia's first Emperor. As for Diaghilev's character, what could be more like that of the dynamic, quick-tempered and despotic Peter?"

Nabokov continued:–

"But quite apart from this, Diaghilev liked the whole idea of a Russian 'period piece.' Boris Kochno and I concocted a two-act ballet libretto, the second act of which was supposed to re-present the 'Feast of the Northern Lights –' in other words, the Coronation of Empress Elizabeth."

The pictorial and decorative potential of baroque Russia may well have appealed to Diaghilev, even if Empress Elizabeth's architect, Rastrelli, had come from Italy. He had found masterpieces of portraiture during his travels throughout "All the Russias" in 1904. Then, again, the mysticism of the Northern Lights presented theatrical possibilities, suggesting a symbolic apotheosis.

Nabokov described the music of *Ode* as "essentially tender, gentle and lyrical, and in its lyricism kin to the music of Russian composers like Glinka, Dargojimsky, and Tchaikowsky, especially to their songs . . ."

After his initial vacillations, Diaghilev suddenly commanded Nabokov to present himself in Monte Carlo, sending him a railway ticket. On his arrival, the composer was asked to re-write some sections. He added that "Diaghilev had been worried about the excessive expense of its production; my score required not only a very large orchestra but also an equally large choir and two soloists besides."

Leaping momentarily from Monte Carlo in April to London in July, (before returning to the stages of creation,) Richard Capell's description will show that considerable changes had been effected in the interim.

"*Ode* can only be compared to a nightmare – but one of the incongruous, not the horrible sort. The subject has a classic simplicity . . . Only the interpretation is odd, – very." Daily Mail 10.7.28

If Diaghilev could be said to have repeated a formula, one might say that it was another "Romeo and Juliet" affair. Inexplicably, he had entrusted the design to a young Russian artist, Pavel Tchelitchew, brilliant, but nearer to the *Surréalists* than to any other group of painters at that time. Tchelichew "had discovered a completely new approach to the problem of stage design – an approach in which light and motion played an unusually important part . . ." Perhaps his new theories about light might accord with a ballet about the Aurora Borealis?

"Tchelichew seemed to like my music, but not the story; he did not like the allegorical allusions to Diaghilev's 'Imperial great-great-grandmother.' He thought the story had nothing to do with what my music was 'really' expressing, and that the whole piece should be treated as a surrealist vision of a mysterious phenomenon of nature, the Aurora Borealis."

By the time Richard Capell saw it, the plot ran like this in the Programme: "Nature expounds her mysteries to a pupil. She exhibits the stars and a river, flowers and bacteria; and finally, 'The master work, the end of all yet done' – Man."

It will be seen from this that Tchelichew had triumphed, and Empress Elizabeth had suffered defeat at his hands.

Fairly early in the proceedings, when Tchelichew's refusal to incorporate Imperial Russia in his designs had become manifest, Diaghilev so lost interest that he refused to have any more to do with the production. Kochno had to act as liaison officer between Massine, Tchelichew, Nabokov, Lifar, and anyone else involved. No one, it would seem, was on speaking terms with anybody else.

If "collaboration" has an antonym, then that is what the creation of *Ode* was.

In Monte Carlo, Diaghilev was tearing about declaring that Massine's choreography was rubbish. The conductor had never seen the score. Tchelichew would not let anyone see his experiments, weakening only once when, needing somebody to help in the timing of some of the film sequences, most reluctantly, he made Nabokov hold the stop-watch. (In this ballet, film projections were being used for the first time.) ("I saw some extraordinary pictures of young men wearing fencing masks and tights, diving in slow motion through what seemed to me to be water. I could not understand what this had to do with my ballet, but I was told by Boris Kochno (Tchelichew wouldn't speak to me,) . . . that this represented 'the element of water.' ")

The company left Monte Carlo for Paris. Three days before the first night, chaos reigned. Nabokov was woken by a telephone call.

"Why are you sleeping when you should be in the theatre? Get dressed right away . . . This mess can't go on any longer. I have ordered a full stage rehearsal at ten, a full orchestra rehearsal at two, a full chorus rehearsal at five, and all evening we will rehearse the lights." Diaghilev had returned to the fray. Diaghilev had spoken.

"Diaghilev had taken over in the fullest sense. From then on *he* gave the orders, *he* made the decisions and assumed the responsibilities. He was everywhere, his energy was limitless . . .

"But above all else he spent two whole nights directing the complicated lighting rehearsals, shouting at Tchelichew – at me when my piano playing slackened – at Lifar when his steps ceased following the rhythm of the music and the changes of the lighting.

"Until the last minute I had been painting the scenery, and had seen Diaghilev leave the theatre an hour before the performance was to begin. He had looked worn, grey and sallow, with a two-day beard. Now he was his usual self again, calm, confident, and resplendent."

That first performance was highly successful.

In Paris, Nature was performed by Mlle. de Beliamina, a niece of Stravinsky's. Finding himself without a "Nature" in London, Diaghilev listened to a suggestion made by Cecil Beaton, who, although he had not yet started to photograph ballet, was always about the theatre. He told Diaghilev that the previous year, he had seen a girl in a revue at the Arts Theatre Club who would look right. Miss Oriel Ross was young, tall, red-headed, and beautiful, and she could dance. In no time at all she was in the Wardrobe, having the dress tried on.

Now the mere sight of this dress appalled her, for it was a white classical column, dead straight from top to bottom, and quilted with cotton-wool stuffing into fluting which, she felt, looked like corrugated iron. Miss Ross asked the Wardrobe if they didn't think it would look nicer if they gave it a little bit "here" (some bosom,) and "there" (some waist.) They, at least, felt some spirit of collaboration, and they pinned and tried. At which moment Diaghilev walked in.

"*Mon dieu! que faites-vous là? Otez tout ça! Enlevez ce buste! Gardez la ligne originale! Ah! ça! par exemple!* . . .

So Miss Ross played Nature in the quilted white columnar costume, dead straight from top to bottom. Massine himself taught her the movements he required. There was a tremendous heat wave, and perspiration poured off her. But she can't have looked like a bit of corrugated iron, (nor, as her ribald friends suggested, a pair of cricket-pads,) for, on the strength of her performance, C.B. Cochran engaged her for the New York edition of his revue, *This Year of Grace*. Diaghilev paid her £50 for all the performances – with which she was well pleased. She does say that all the complicated lighting was, in fact, very beautiful. (Tragically, the material used was such that the film disintegrated.) Tchelichew's name as designer is linked with that of Pierre Charbonnier, an expert in neon lighting, but as this was considered dangerous and forbidden by the fire authorities and police, much of the latter's work may have ended up unused.

The Programme Notes at His Majesty's were, as so often, cryptic, and but little help to comprehension. They were in three parts. "Nature descends from her pedestal, answers her pupil's questions and shows him – The Constellations (nine male dancers, The River (eight female and six male dancers,) Flowers and Mankind (Projections.) M. Serge Lifar appears as The Pupil and The Light Fleck. Then, 'Not satisfied with what he has seen, the pupil begs Nature to show him her Festival.' There are dances, culminating in 'The Aurora Borealis,"

THE MYSTERIOUS TCHELITCHEFF AND CHARBONNIER DECORATIONS OF "ODE": NATURE (MISS ORIEL ROSS) AND THE AURORA BOREALIS IN CRINOLINES AND BLACK GLOVES.

One of the effective moments, scenically, in *Ode*, with Oriel Ross wearing the columnar dress about which she felt dubious.

(Projections and Lights.) Lastly, "Captivated by the beauty of the Festival, the pupil darts forward, enters it and destroys by his presence the vision of the Aurora Borealis. Nature becomes again a statue."

If Capell thought *Ode* rather a nightmare, *The Times*, though perplexed, said that "there are also moments when it achieves a sort of original beauty, which in turn produces a peculiar emotional effect." The Times 10.7.28

The Times was puzzled and asked many questions. "But why these childish figures on the back-cloth, which conveyed no meaning and served only to puzzle? Why these strange antics in white tights? Why the rows of gibbeted dolls? It is this habit of leaving many questions unanswered, in fact of failing to carry through a design, that marks (or mars) too many of the company's new productions."

"The music," said *The Times*, "made little impression on a first hearing . . . The composer employs voices and chorus and, if we were able to understand Russian and hear the words, that might help to elucidate the action."

Morning
Post
10.7.28
Francis Toye's verdict was that "it took a lot of people to make this extraordinary production, of which frankly I could make neither head nor tail. There were cinematographic
squiggles and a long white cord that looked as if it had strayed from the gymnasium of the Bath
Club. There were revolving lime-lights, and a dance of electric lights that carried me back to the
pantomimes of my youth. I gather from the programme that all was part of a lesson given by
Nature to her pupil. It may be that he understood it better than I: at any rate he could not
possibly have understood it less.

"In detail, there was some very good dancing of the typical modern kind. Doubrovska's *pas
seul*, for instance, the duet between Danilova and Massine, and nearly all Lifar's very difficult
contortions. There were even some beautiful effects of light and scenery amidst the general
oddity. I thought the grey crinolines of the figurantes at the end marvellously contrived to show
off the white tights of the principals.

"As for M. Nabokov's music, I thought most of it vulgar, without being funny. At times in
writing for the chorus he shows a certain vigour, but most of the score is redolent of the circus,
whether in straightforward or discordant fashion."

Seeing these grey dresses (which were actually a sort of mauve, made of cheap artificial fur-
nishing silk which gave a mauve-grey shot effect and had the necessary weightiness for the cut)
when they were on display prior to the final Sotheby sale of Diaghilev costumes in March,
1973, their cut seemed less that of a 19th century crinoline than of the panniered style of the
period of Empress Elizabeth. Perhaps she did achieve a passing reference in this aspect of the
design of the ballet.

In spite of the anecdotes with which this account of *Ode* has been peppered, it would be quite
wrong to dismiss it as a joke. It was revolutionary and ahead of its time, most especially in the
work of Tchelitchew and Charbonnier. Back-projection and hectic lighting effects are now the
commonplace of the theatre, and though it would be unwise to claim that this was the first time
such effects were employed in a ballet, most certainly they were used in a novel and beautiful
fashion. (In 1916, Diaghilev had devised a "light" spectacle in Rome, to Stravinsky's early
piece, *Fireworks*. He commissioned the Italian Futurist, Balla, to design a setting consisting of
geometric shapes in transparent coloured materials. Diaghilev placed coloured lights inside
them, and worked out a complicated "plan" to which they played. This setting anticipated by
ten years the Constructivist transparencies of Gabo and Pevsner for *La Chatte*. The models
made in 1966 to recapture it have the shapes made in such crude, hard plastic that one does not
feel they do justice to the gaiety of *Fireworks*.)

The late A.V. Coton, in *A Prejudice for Ballet,* gave (in retrospect, in 1938,) perhaps the most
complete description of *Ode's* lighting effects:–

> "One's strongest remaining impression is of the unearthly beauty created by a revolutionary use
> of light never before seen in any form of Theatre – floods, spots, panoramic effects, projections
> against a screen and great bursts of light suggesting the sudden animation of pyrotechnical
> set-pieces, as the groups of dancers and static figures were bathed in pools of glowing illumina-
> tion swiftly dimmed and flooded again, almost imperceptibly changing colours . . . A projector
> shot enormous blossoms on to the backcloth whilst figures in the foreground complemented the
> pattern in a slow-tempo process referential to the opening and unfolding of flowers seen
> through the agency of the quick-time cinema camera. The final and furthest departure from all
> previous patternings came when a white-clad and masked group danced within a geometric
> limitation of spaces bounded by cords which were passed from hand to hand, creating an infin-
> ite succession of moving, Euclidean forms about which the figures wove a complementary
> notation of space-images, as they joined hands, linked arms, released, extended in slow arabes-
> que and moved silently around this formalized stage-within-a-stage. Throughout certain pas-
> sages a chorus hummed, droned, and intoned an irrelevant accompaniment; never before were
> the senses so delightfully assaulted with unrelated and unrelatable forms of movement, music,
> lighting and colour."

Serge Lifar

Felia Doubrovska

ODE

Pavel Tchelitchew (1898 – 1957) was about
twenty-five when Diaghilev, meeting him in Berlin,
where he painted under "Constructivist" influences in
the early '20's, invited him to create a ballet. By 1928,
when the offer became reality, Tchelitchew's
influences had changed. He had become fascinated
by light. Pierre Charbonnier, (b. 1897,) expert
and experimenter in neon, with whom he had
shared an exhibition in the Galerie Druet in 1926,
became his assistant. Not only on the stage, but also
on the cover of the Souvenir Programme,
Tchelitchew played with his fancies of that time –
multi-images of man, the illumination of man, and
the figure in relation to its own shadow. He borrowed
Leonardo da Vinci's multi-image, and, (regardless of
the expense,) had each cover laboriously pricked with
pins by hand.
Also fascinated by the pictorial imagery created by
light was another Russian refugee, the photographer
George Hoyningen-Huene, (1900 – 1968,) who,
settling in Paris, had been promoted by Condé Nast.
These photographs of *Ode* – so different from those of
the whole stage taken by others—are the first to show
the beautiful lighting effects which had always meant
so much in the success of the ballets. There is no such
pictorial record of the wonders Diaghilev had created
for *Scheherazade*.

The Divine
Comedy of
Pavel
Tchelitchew:
Parker
Tyler
p.329

In 1967, a friend of Tchelitchew's, the American art critic Parker Tyler, disclosed that there was in existence "a complete scenario which will enter a collection at the Museum of Modern Art, New York City, which bears the inscription: 'Scenario by Pavel Tschelistcheff – and dictated to Pierre Charbonnier.' Presumably the handwriting is that of Charbonnier, who was Tchelitchew's technical assistant for the ballet. On the program Kochno is credited with the script of *Ode*, Tchelitchew only with the sets and costumes." Tyler believes that the credits must, in view of the emergence of this scenario, be reoriented. "Tchelitchew is possessed with the most radical and sensational ideas to interpret Lomonosov's poem scenically. For reasons that are about to appear, not all of them will be realized. Yet others replace them." Parker Tyler gives the detailed synopsis of each of the eight tableaux planned, which approximate roughly to an Introduction and the seven Days of Creation. "Nature" is also Isis, and, yet again, represents Empress Elizabeth – who does, therefore, achieve an apotheosis as the ballet ends. In this skeleton is to be found real meaning for some of the effects bespattering the ballet: for example, the huge projected images of seeds and flowers represent growth, germinating and blossoming with magical speed, as in "trick" botanical films to which modern eyes are now accustomed.

How many of these ideas have been used since 1928, not only in ballet, but also, as Mr. Coton put it, in the Theatre? Nabokov complained that the choreography and effects seemed to have little to do with his conception. This allegory of Nature displaying her miraculous creations – showing flowers hugely enlarged, blowing across the simple set – showing her Constellations by using dancers with tiny batteries and lights fitted on the backs of their costumes, so that it appeared as if stars danced – all these and many more devices, the brain-children of Pavel Tchelichew and Pierre Charbonnier – were innovations, and it would appear that they were executed brilliantly and beautifully, and have had many far more puny imitators.

The last new ballet of this season was something entirely different. Sir Thomas Beecham had arranged a charming suite of dances from music by Handel, and there was a comprehensible little plot, and some lovely choreography by Balanchine. The programme did not attribute the scenery and costumes at all – and not one of the critics spotted their origin! The back-cloth from the first part of *Daphnis and Chloe* (designed by Bakst in 1912,) was pressed into service, and all but two of the costumes were those used in *Les Tentations de la Bergère.* (Juan Gris, 1924.)

The
Times
17.7.28

First, let *The Times* describe *The Gods Go a-Begging*: "A *fête champêtre* is in preparation: into the company of noblemen and ladies a shepherd strays; the ladies welcome him to their festivity, but he prefers the simpler charms of a serving-maid. The anger of the company at this rebuff is stilled by the revelation that the two lowly persons are gods disguised as beggars. There is no occasion for far-fetched movements in this artificial but simple design, and there is no straining at the limits of what the human body can express in pure dancing. The choreography (by Georges Balanchine) is not confined to the old 18th-century steps but, like Sir Thomas Beecham's orchestration, is judiciously enriched with the most recent resources of the art. Music, idea, and dancing therefore correspond, and since there is no striving after the unfamiliar we can enjoy one more example of the 18th century seen through the sympathetic spectacles of 20th . . . (Handel's) secular music may be solid, but it is not heavy. Neither was the dancing of the noblemen and ladies, for all their wigs and hooped skirts. Mlle. Alexandra Danilova was nimbleness itself as the serving maid, and when she shed her disguise she was a truly ethereal goddess. The new part, in fact, suits her peculiar, lithe grace even more than the old part of the girl in *Les Matelots*, also revived last night. M. Woizikowsky is by turns an unsophisticated shepherd and a youthful god. The revelation of their divinity makes a picturesque climax to the lines and figure of the concerted dances. The atmosphere is gay with the polite high spirits of Handel's music; the scene is realistic; there is no symbolism; the conventions of the age of reason are well understood; the new ballet is a rest on the arduous road of modern expressionism!"

Daily
Mail
17.7.28

Richard Capell thought it to be "a little allegory told with infinite grace – a sop, no doubt to the conservative part of the public who have not quite caught up with M. Diaghilev's austere new ballets. Only in the duet between the shepherd and the maid does Mr. Balanchine's choreography suggest at moments wife-beating more than love-making.

"The scenery (blue-green elms in a stately park) and the dresses were anonymous. The music was delicious. Sturdy old Handel was represented, in these excerpts from the long-neglected operas, as the most exquisite courtier and gallant. The scoring had been refurbished by Sir Thomas with faultless taste.

"The public approved of the new ballet. The applause amounted to an ovation. The last we saw of Sir Thomas was his trundling a 5 ft. laurel wreath off the stage, like a hoop."

It was a summer of terrific heatwave, but the indefatigable *Lady* managed to fit in plenty of ballet and parties too. On one such evening, "the fun began for me during the last hour of the Russian Ballet, when Lady Juliet Duff and Lady Lavery slipped into seats beside me, the former in a dress borrowed from the wardrobe mistress." (A frequent sight since the Sotheby sales!) "It is sad to think that this is the last week of the ballet. I have so enjoyed it this year, for, although I do not appreciate very well some modern art or modern poetry, I love modern ballet. Last week I was lucky, for I saw *Les Noces*, *Ode*, – which brings back recollections of school-day struggles with right-angled triangles and Euclidean problems and then oddly suggests that geometry and black art are not far apart – and then *Apollo Musagètes*. We were discussing who was the greatest ballet 'fan' of the season. Of course, Lady Juliet Duff has been there most nights and Lady Cunard very often, but then they were guarantors! I think that young Mr. Stephen Tennant and the equally young Lady Seafield probably have it! She has certainly been there every time I have managed to set a seat, always with some odd bit of jewellery to give her modern frock the artistic touch necessary for ballet audiences . . ." (*The Lady* must have seen *La Chatte* as well.)

The Lady 26.7.28

In *Vogue*, Herbert Farjeon turned from the ballerinas to the opposite sex, having observed what he termed "THE RISE OF THE PRIMO BALLERINO."

Vogue July/1 1928

"If any Gibbon of the theatre, prompted by the failure of some of Serge Diaghileff's later productions, should have been busy collecting material for a history of *The Decline and Fall of the Russian Ballet*, he would, I think, be wise to suspend his labours for a while; for the Russian Ballet . . . has recently displayed signs of remarkable vitality. That the dancing of the older ballets is 'not as good as it used to be' must be admitted by all who recall the earlier performances at Covent Garden. But we must remember that it is in the very nature of a revival to be less spirited and sensitive than a production fresh from the creative mint . . . With the flight of time, Hamlets and Petrouchkas must inevitably degenerate, even though at intervals some rare genius may emerge to startle the world with a performance excitingly superior to the performances given by his immediate predecessors. But if we turn our attention to the dancing of the modern ballets, we may not unreasonably ask whether Nijinsky and Karsavina in her prime could have equalled the brilliance of Lifar and of Sokolova in *The House Party* . . . Let us, then, rejoice in *The House Party* while we may, for no matter how skilful the dancers of succeeding generations, it is safe to predict that they will never completely seize the essential spirit of this vivid terpischorean commentary on life, which is at once as witty and satirical and contemporary as a Restoration comedy.

"There is nothing in the execution of *The House Party* more superb than the miming of Sokolova, yet I think the dominant memory of this ballet is the memory of the three magnificent young men who exhibit their masculine splendour as the *prime ballerine* of the past have been accustomed to exhibit their feminine charms, and who are supported by the fluttering admiration of the ladies of the ballet as the ladies of the ballet were formerly supported by the rather flabby admiration of the men. And here we may glimpse the latest and most important phase of the Russian Ballet, which is not its addiction to cubist music and scenery, but its discovery of the fundamental masculine possibilities of the male dancer. In the past . . . he did little more than reflect the *prima ballerina's* feminine grace. He curved, he pirouetted, he gloried in the flesh rather than in the muscle, he did not inspire one with confidence in his virility. And when Mark Perugini, in *The Art of the Ballet*, declared Nijinsky to be so good that 'one's usual objection to the male dancer melted into admiration,' he referred to an objection which was very usual indeed.

"The objection, however, can hardly be brought against the male dancer when he is executing the new style of choreography which seems to have been especially devised to bring out his essentially masculine beauty and which finds its latest expression in such fascinating ballets as *The Cat*. What makes *The Cat* a work of high distinction is not the music or the background of geometrical mica, which has attracted so much attention, but the performance given by Lifar, who may be said not so much to dance as to demonstrate the sublime beauty of strength in a series of brilliantly conceived movements. This new choreography is analytical rather than synthetic. It invites us to admire the machinery by which man achieves the plenitude of power, suggesting rather than materialising the infinite possibilities of which that machinery is capable. It abandons the emulation of the feather, which was an extension of man's pride in being able to walk on two legs instead of four, and it substitutes an aesthetic exultation in the spring, the suppleness, the elasticity, the tension of thews and sinews, which man shares in common with the animals.

"If it is possible to detect anything objectionably unmasculine in this, then lions are effeminate and Hercules was a namby-pamby. Lifar in *The Cat* is one of the finest spectacles the Russian Ballet has yet given us. And if this is considered in connection with the three young men in *The House Party*, of the athletic heroes of *Le Train Bleu* and of the telegraph-boy and the *maître de ballet* in *Romeo and Juliet*, it will be seen that the *primo ballerino* has been given a new lease of life, which is likely, for the time being, to make him not only a more interesting, but a more popular figure than his sister-star."

The
Queen
1.8.28

Towards the end of the season, Sir Richard Terry (as he had become) made an interesting assessment of the last few years.

"The Diaghilev season of Russian Ballet is over, and in taking stock of its achievements a few disturbing reflections present themselves; not about the ballet, but concerning our reception of it.

"Those of us who attended any of the performances could not come away without the conviction that the Diaghileff season was the one live thing in 'musical London' at that time. Hence our surprise at the notices of it which we might happen to read. They ran the gamut from stern disapproval, through the safer channels of patronising tolerance, till they reached the still waters of the non-committal.

"Consequently, the average Londoner who does not attend ballet might well be pardoned for accepting a popular belief . . . that Russian Ballet has now entered on a period of decadence.

"Nothing could be further from the truth, so one is set wondering about the source of this depreciatory criticism of wholly admirable performances of a highly-specialised art-form, the like of which we at least cannot produce in our own country.

"I put it down to the fact that the novelties of 1913 have become the commonplaces of 1928.

"The Russian Ballet of 1913 intrigued us; it gave us thrills and shocks, and its music frequently made us very angry. We get no shocks now, neither do we get angry; *ergo* the thing must have become tamer and duller.

"*O sancta simplicitas!* It isn't that the Russians have become tamer; it is that *they have tamed us*, and made our silly pre-war prejudices look a little foolish. Personally, I find the Russian Ballet not only as good as ever, but in some respects even better . . .

"M. Diaghilev has created a new public . . . The house is always well-filled, which is more than can be said of most other enterprises in 'musical London' at the present time . . ."

Manchester
Evening
News
10.11.28

Manchester
Guardian
13.11.28

A tour was planned for November and December. Two days before the Manchester opening, an article appeared headed "HUSH-HUSH RUSSIAN BALLET," saying that "as late as yesterday morning not a photograph or particle of information, apart from the circularised programme, had been placed in the hands of the manager of the theatre or of the Press."

Not surprisingly, the critic of the *Manchester Guardian* declared himself baffled by *La Chatte*, for which he was totally unprepared. "The present writer found it beyong his powers of comprehension – the pretty fable was easy enough to follow, but what a setting, what choreography! When the lover falls sorrowing to the earth at the loss of his beloved, there is a cortège of squares and circles . . . Had Pavlova fluttered tip-toe across the setting of '*The Cat*' it would have been like a strain of Mozart in a composition by Von Webern."

Unaware, also, of the explanation of *Le Astuzie Femminili* given years before by Diaghileff, he found the interpolation, in *Cimarosiana*, of the "frog-like rhythms of the Russian knee-dance a frank solecisim." He thought the most successful ballet that night had been *The Three-Cornered Hat*, which he found marvellously witty, with scenery and dry irony to match. "The dancing of Leon Woizikowsky and Mme. Tchernicheva was art to wonder at and admire for its mocking point and allusiveness – all based on a sort of rhythmical ground-base, so to speak, relating each movement to the steps of the Fandango."

Apart from a sense of grievance that *Le Carnaval* had not been included in the first week's programme, the *Guardian* was happy to see the "glorified pantomime," as it called *Aurora's Wedding,*and the Corot-ish *Les Sylphides,* "here filled with particular elegance by Mlle. Danilova's beauty of form and movement." The fortnight in the Opera House was a success, and the company moved on to Glasgow.

There, the week passed in a whirl of pleasure and applause. Yet Glasgow gave thought, too, to the inevitable sadness beneath the brilliant parade, since the Russians were exiles from their native land. "At the Parisian sessions it was the Russian nationalism of the exiles that most touched the heart," said William Jeffrey. Possibly cosmopolitan London had come to regard the ballet as such a personal possession that it tended to forget this eternal sorrow. But on this visit, the brilliance of the company, "casting a glamour as of the Opern-platz or the Boulevard des Italiens," had flashed across the northern city, and that city devoutly hoped that it would do so again. *(Glasgow Herald 8.12.28)*

Edinburgh found the ballet magnificent – and Beecham there made his 123rd speech about his Imperial League of Opera!

Liverpool's Lime Street Station had never before seen anything like the Russian Ballet as it arrived, and has probably never seen anything to match it since. Everyone was buried in furs. Diaghilev, who had joined the company late in the tour, told a reporter that "he wondered whether he was really a Russian because he felt so cold. 'O-o-o-er! Your British climate!', he complained, as he pulled his fur collar more closely about his ears. 'You think a Russian should find your cold – how you say it? – easily, yes, no? But it is thirteen years since I was in St. Petersburg, and my skin forgets in so long a time.' Another member of the Ballet was stamping his feet and juggling with a coconut to keep warm. The coconut was required in one of the dances, and it had travelled all over the country with the Ballet. Its owner seemed to treasure it as a pet . . . Two women of the ballet approached Diaghilev. With a charming curtsey they handed him a gorgeous white chrysanthemum from the bouquets they carried. No longer was his head buried in his thick fur collar; he forgot about the cold. With a huge smile he put the great chrysanthemum in his buttonhole, and thanked the women. Quickly he was talking about 'My Ballet,' and there was no mistaking the pride in his voice." *(Liverpool Daily Post 10.12.28)*

There was only thrill, pleasure, delight for the audiences which packed the Empire. To pick one evening only – "To attempt to detail all the felicities on the stage, even excluding those of the Beecham ballet, would be an exhausting task. But even the most cursory review must take note of the amazing *tour-de-force* of the beautiful Danilova and Serge Lifar in their *pas de deux* in *Aurora's Wedding* . . . This was Danilova's evening, for, in addition to her Goddess in *The Gods Go a-Begging*, she was the most provoking of Can-Can dancers in *La Boutique* – provoking only to fall into such pretty pathos later on and make the artificiality of this story almost touching before she left it." *(Liverpool Echo 12.12.28)*

Possibly by coincidence, a ballet item was given prominence in a series of recitals in the music seller's shop of Messrs. Smith and Son, in Lord Street. "Stravinsky has made for the Aeolian Company a series of Duo-Art recordings on the audiographic principle. The rolls have the unique interest that the account of the composer's life is written by himself, and concurrently with each roll there is a self-annotated performance of the *Firebird* music by the composer . . . The story of the ballet is given along with the notes on the orchestration and woodcuts of the Russian Ballet's production by the artist Polunin, who was responsible for the décor." (This will refer to the Gontcharova designs of 1926, which he executed.) *(Liverpool Post and Mercury 15.12.28)*

As this tour ended, the company left for Paris, where it was to spend Christmas and New Year.

1929

ROYAL OPERA, COVENT GARDEN

JUNE 29th – JULY 26th

FIRST PERFORMANCES IN ENGLAND

July 1st:	*Le Fils Prodigue* (Prokofiev, Balanchine, Rouault.) Paris 21.5.1929.
July 8th:	*Le Bal* (Rieti, Balanchine, de Chirico.) Monte Carlo 9.5.1929.
July 15th:	*Le Renard* (Stravinsky, Lifar, Larionov.) Paris, 21.5.1929.

REPERTOIRE

Apollon Musagète	*Contes Russes*	*La Pastorale*
L'Après-Midi d'un Faune	*Les Fâcheux*	*Petrouchka*
Aurora's Wedding	*The Gods go a-Begging*	*Polovtsian Dances*
La Boutique Fantasque	*Le Lac des Cygnes*	*Le Sacre du Printemps*
Le Carnaval	*Les Matelots*	*Les Sylphides*
La Chatte	*Las Meninās*	*Le Tricorne*
Cimarosiana		

COMPANY

Barasch, Branitzka, Chamié, Choulgine, Danilova, Doubrovska, Efimova, Guliuk, Karlevska, Karsavina, Klemetska, Lipkovska, Maicherska, Markova, Marra, Miklachevska, Nemchinova II., Obidennaia, Pavlova (Not Anna), Petrova, Slavinska, Sokolova, Spessiva, Sumarokova, Tarakanova, Tchernicheva, Vadimova.

Balanchine, Bobrov, Dolin, Domansky, Efimov, Fedorov, Grigoriev, Hoyer I., Hoyer II., Ignatov, Jazvinsky, Katchourovsky, Kotchanovsky, Kremnev, Ladre, Lifar, Lissanevitch, Matouchevsky, Pavlov, Petrakevitch, Tcherkas, Woizikowsky, Yovanovitch.

THE ACROBATS IN Le Renard

Bernardo Agustino, Louis Agustino, Adolf Hierlinger

CONDUCTOR:

Desormière.

THE FINAL SEASON

As his 1929 season started, Diaghilev gave an interview once again to the *Observer.*

"I return to Covent Garden with the sentiment of great emotion," he said, "for it was here, at the Command Performance in the year of King George's Coronation, that my Russian Ballet made its first appearance in London.

Observer
30.6.29

"When I came into the theatre," he continued, "the spirit of the Marchioness of Ripon seemed to pervade the place. She was the great friend of the Ballet, the first person in England to love and appreciate our work, and the tradition is still in the family. I am happy to say that her daughter, Lady Juliet Duff, is the principal patron of our present season, which I hope will be not less brilliant than the ones patronised by her mother."

Though he loved nostalgic reminiscence, Diaghilev had a horror of anniversaries. Despite the fact that 1929 would be the twentieth year since his first Paris season, he refused even to consider any special programme or new production to mark the occasion.

After its provincial tour in 1928, the Ballet had given a winter season at the Paris *Opéra,* during which, to everyone's delight, Karsavina had returned to dance some of her most famous rôles.

Massine was no longer with the company. Balanchine's successes entitled him to the major share of the new works, so he was allotted two ballets. Lifar was to be entrusted with one.

The company was to be greatly strengthened by the return of Anton Dolin, who, in March, announced that he had signed a long contract with Diaghilev. Lydia Sokolova, who had suffered both a serious illness and a serious accident which had prevented her dancing for nearly two years, was fit again, so the repertoire could be arranged to include some of her special parts.

Daily
Sketch
19.3.29

During the annual visit to Monte Carlo, a journalist there remarked: "One can see *Jack-in-the-Box* ten times – twenty times – or the *Prince Igor* dances unceasingly, without ever being bored. Could even the finest play . . . hold one's interest ten times?"

Gazette
de Monaco
6.4.29

Before its arrival in London, the company had had the most successful visit of its history to Berlin, given a few performances in Cologne, and then its usual season in Paris.

For the first few nights in London, favourites from the repertoire delighted the "old guard" in the audience, who were thrilled to see Karsavina again in their favourite ballets. Olga Spessiva joined them in London for the first time since *The Sleeping Princess,* this time to dance *Swan Lake.* A glance at the list of dancers is enough to show that the company was in great strength.

The first new ballet was *The Prodigal Son.*

The choice of a New Testament parable as the "book" of a ballet was a striking innovation, the more so as this presented a human family rather than the supernatural element. Diaghilev

had commissioned the music from Prokofiev, the choreography was by Balanchine, and the costumes and *décor* were assigned to an artist quite unlike any to whom Diaghilev had turned previously – Georges Rouault. So often accused of patronising only very youthful artists in the 1920's, Diaghilev had, this time, thought of a man of 58, who for some years had been painting deeply religious themes. His palette was sombre, the effect frequently compared to pictures seen in a dark cathedral, enlivened with gleams of brilliance, as when light strikes through a stained glass window.

Divided into three parts, the ballet followed the Bible story closely – the *ennui* of the boy, bored with his home, the period of dissipation, led astray by debauched companions, including the two friends with whom he had left his family, (Woizikowsky and Dolin,) and a Siren, (wonderfully performed by Felia Doubrovska.)

The
Times
2.7.29
The ballet was an outstanding success for Lifar, as The Prodigal. "M. Lifar, who played the part of the Prodigal Son, was responsible for all the best moments in the ballet. He has developed into a first-class mime, and his technique is now excellent in an individual style," said *The Times*. "He gave to the first and last scenes a Blake-like intensity of gesture and expression, which raised the ballet distinctly above the level of some recent additions to M. Diaghilev's repertory. The moment when the prodigal crept into the bosom of his father was genuinely moving, and the dignified gestures of M. Fedorov as the patriarch contributed a large share to the success of these scenes."

The Times found the choreography original but uneven, and thought that "the stage spectacle would be excellent, for the glowing colours of M. Rouault's *décor*, which are caught up in the velvets of the costumes, provide a fine spectacle, which is marred by a wilful determination to be novel at the expense of meaning."

The
Times
31.5.29
That *The Times* should have described the colours as "glowing" is amusing, for, reporting the *première* in Paris, its own correspondent had said that "the muddy colours which this painter affects are entirely unsuitable to stage decoration. A backcloth, which seems to have been painted in colours mixed with coal-dust and mud, casts a gloom which the most vivid dresses are powerless to dispel. . . . During the banquet offered to the prodigy by his dissolute companions the grouping of the guests in green and white around M. Lifar in brilliant blue is extremely effective."

The reference to Blake must have occasioned sighs of resignation from Ralph Vaughan Williams, Gwen Raverat, and Geoffrey Keynes, for Diaghilev had never returned the etchings of *Job*! Keynes's sister-in-law, Lydia Lopokova, reviewed the new ballets for *The Nation and Athenaeum*, (of which her husband had, for some years, been Chairman, and which, in 1931,

Nerman again made cartoons of the ballet, for *The Tatler,* Lifar and
Doubrovska in *Le Fils Prodigue* attracting his notice.

after amalgamations, turned into *The New Statesman and Nation.*) Entering the lists as a critic,
she said:–

"After the pleasant and delicious, but slight, ballets of last season, the Ballet Russe produced The
Nation &
Athenaeum
6.7.29
on Monday an outstanding work, Prokofiev's *Prodigal Son.* The theme calls for seriousness and
depth, and the three means, choreography, music and décor, joined together to bring out a
corresponding artistic expression . . . The choreographic method was the same which we have
become used to in the earlier ballets of Balanchine. There were the same stylized versions of
acrobatic actions and the same staccato mass movements with a wilful disregard of prettiness.
But his other ballets seemed rather cold and empty and, when one reflected on them, were
about nothing. This time Balanchine seemed to succeed for the first time in using his technique
for the expression of a serious dramatic motif. There is flesh and blood to this ballet, and we
have got back again, as in the earlier ballets, to what the stage can never do without – dramatic
action.

"Lifar is a most poetic Prodigal Son. In the beginning especially, the Jewish gestures were
beautifully done . . . We can rank him now with his predecessors. Doubrovska as an unbe-
lievably fantastic seductress was thin, strong, and enticing. But what would the old ballerinas
have said to anyone who asked them to do with their bodies the things she has to do! She had a
great success – it is a part no one will ever be able to take from her . . . Rouault's scenery was of
great taste and biblical heaviness – all very beautiful and splendid."

Lopokova continued, "I feel that the fashionable audience at the first performance did not
much care about it. They found Prokofiev's rhythms trying and inconvenient, and they did not
easily catch the meaning of Lifar's antics. But if they persevere with it, I think they may find that
this is one of the strong pieces of the new repertoire. M. Diaghilev calls it the '*Parsifal*' of the
Russian Ballet."

The *Daily Sketch*, calling it brilliant, but bizarre, said that there were moments when the Daily
Sketch
3.7.29
audience laughed. However, it also reported that "at last, we learned the meaning of 'riotous
living,' for the Prodigal, . . . acted and danced with great skill by Serge Lifar, enjoyed orgies
that made the wildest of cocktail parties seem tame."

On the whole, it would seem that this ballet met with approbation, and a relatively small
measure of disapproval. On the following Sunday, in the *Observer,* Fox-Strangways said that
"*The Prodigal Son* made an exciting opening . . . As a spectacle it is beautiful at first, and then
startling when Mme. Doubrovska appears with her loud magenta train. The figures of the
dancers are ingenious and diverting, effective in a restless, disjointed fashion. Some of them are
instantly acceptable, others need more than two performances to become familiar, and, after

Prodigal and Siren – Serge Lifar
and Felia Doubrovska.

that, reasonable . . . The dancing of the chorus was highly finished and of an admirable precision."

Richard Capell did not go overboard about this ballet.

Daily
Mail
2.7.29
"The audience went for something new and odd, and they were not deceived . . .

"Among the impressions brought away was that made by Mme. Doubrovska, who played the part of the courtesan in the scene of the orgy. Was there ever woman more strangely serpentine? There was not a hint of voluptuousness in this scene. The prodigal was fascinated by the siren's inhuman contortions, and he joined her in those strained acrobatical feats which characterise M. Balanchine's choreography . . .

"Another impression is that of the returned prodigal, mimed with peculiar intensity, and as though in torture, by young M. Serge Lifar. This scene undoubtedly was, in its strained and fantastic way, beautiful . . .

"And there were other moments in the ballet in which ingenuity came to achievement. Perhaps a full acquaintance with the new Balanchine technics would convince one that the whole thing is a masterpiece; but a casual opinion is that eccentric cleverness has rather outrun the other factors in the case.

"The difficulties and the grotesqueness that are imposed on these lithe creatures, Lifar and Doubrovska, really oppress the spectator (though the dancers do not seem to mind;) and a kind of discomfort, not to say pain, takes the edge from appreciation.

"At the same time, one feels that Balanchine is a serious artist, striving with much intelligence to make new expressive forms out of his long-suffering human material."

Lydia Sokolova and Serge Lifar
in *Le Bal.*

If Capell had not yet come to terms with the newest ideas in choreography, he had most certainly been one of those who, twenty years earlier, had taken instantly to the Fokine innovations. He was probably in some secret heaven on July 3rd.

"It was delightful to see Mme. Thamar Karsavina dancing again with the Diaghilev ballet yesterday afternoon in a part of which she was the 'creator' and in which she has never been surpassed – in *Petrouchka.* Daily Mail 4.7.29

"She played the part (for she is not merely a dancer, but also an actress,) as she first played it 17 years ago – with a touch of pathos, and (yes! although she is but a doll!) of dignity all her own. This was a doll from a princess's nursery.

"The whole ballet – which is Stravinsky's masterpiece and perhaps the high-water mark of all the vast Diaghilev repertory – went well under the conductorship of M. Roger Desormière."

Whether Capell fell ill, or whether he went on leave, one cannot know, but this was the last review of the Diaghilev ballet that he ever signed.

Next came a totally different offering, *Le Bal.* For this Balanchine work, Diaghilev had also turned to a new designer, the painter Giorgio de Chirico, Italian, but a man who had passed most of his working life in Paris, where he was one of the group called "The Surrealists" by Guillaume Apollinaire.

The slender plot was succinctly described in *Telegraph*: "*The Ball* centres round the poignant feelings of a young man who pursues a beautiful lady only to find that wrinkles lie beneath her mask – and then again, after she has turned pursuer, to discover that after all a lovely face is there when the wrinkles themselves have been removed. And M. Anton Dolin, as the young man, exerted all his amazing lissom power to prove how deeply his heart was engaged." Daily Telegraph 9.7.29

That was not quite the whole of the plot – the *Morning Post* added that "he thinks she is only accompanied by a young man disguised, and at the end Number One is left deserted and desolate." This paper said, also, that it "pleased everybody of every section of opinion. It was certainly the most successful novelty of the last few years." Morning Post 9.7.29

Rieti's music and de Chirico's décor were both discussed in *The Times*: "The chief general criticism that is to be brought against Rieti's music is that he mixed his styles. This was even The Times 9.7.29

more noticeable in *The Ball*, which began with the modish sophisticated dissonance of the cosmopolitan modern composer, but as soon as the dance got under way slipped back into familiar tuneful Italian theatre-music. It has, however, the merit of being good for dancing, and as music finds strength in counterpoint of an unacademic kind." *The Times* went on to describe the setting, a stylized Sicilian ballroom. "The ballet is remarkable for the beauty of its décor, for which Signor Giorgio de Chirico is responsible. Under the various pastel shades lies white as a foundation; white often comes to the surface, though the prevailing tone is biscuit brown; elaborate tracery in black adds linear interest. All the dancers wear black and white wigs, looking rather uncomfortably like those convolutions of the brain that are found in text-books of psychology. But their formal significance is greater than their chance representational suggestion, and they help to harmonize the whole scene. The total effect has that touch of the bizarre which is characteristic of modern design, yet is beautiful in the oldfashioned sense of grateful to the eye."

Daily
Mail
9.7.29

"If the dancers in the new Russian ballet, *The Ball*, did not look to be enjoying themselves intensely, that is, after all, how people in everyday life look when they are dancing – solemn, abstracted, almost ritualistic.

"It must not be taken that *The Ball* is a realistic piece. Nothing could be farther from realism than this strange and remote harlequinade . . .

"The whole ballet is like a dream – not a pretty, poetical dream, but a rather uncomfortable, disconcerting one. It is very clever; and the spectacle is strangely beautiful, . . . all in a series of pale buffs and greens and so on, with a rich mythological sea in the background to set off the delicacy.

"The choreography it was that gave the puzzling, dream-like quality to the piece."

Lopokova also reviewed this new work.

The Nation
and
Athenaeum
13.7.29

"After the throbbing *Prodigal Son*, M. Diaghilev has presented us with a sort of *patisserie* in lighter vein. This time I find the ingenuity of M. Balanchine's poses and movements over-startling – there are so many different elements in his composition, steps and positions coming once and never repeated or developed, that they seem, sometimes, to lose significance. The choreography was lively, muscular and pretty, but not inspiring; though the *pas de deux* of

Alexandra Danilova

Dolin and Danilova, who danced very well indeed, and the tarantella of Lipkowska and Lifar were excellent set pieces . . .

"The joy and beauty of this ballet is to be found in Chirico's décor. One could foresee that his talent would be suited to the stage, but the effects surpassed expectation. The vision to the eye is fascinating, *chic* and beautiful at the same time. This is the *smartest* ballet we have seen for many seasons."

The *Saturday Review* remarked that the "men's evening suits are worthy of the attention of our dress reformers!" Saturday Review 17.7.29

Much more detail of the good old balls of the good old days of Imperial ballet was introduced than is realised by those who read only a brief account of this work. The *Telegraph* filled in much of the detail: "The fun begins in the first scene, when we see the guests on their way to the ball. The costumes and scenery convey a plastic, three-dimensional solidity, even to the pilasters painted round the top hats of the men and the architectural designs on the ladies' dresses. We laugh at the odd movements of the guests. When the back-cloth has risen and we watch the chorus indulging in the antics of musical comedy we laugh again . . . But in the interludes *The Ball* begins to be interesting. Mme. Doubrovska has a fine Spanish dance with M. Woizikowsky, always an impeccable artist, and the redoubtable M. Balanchine himself. And the 'Italian entrance' with Mlle. Eugenia Lipkowska – who has the whole front of St. Peter's imprinted on her bodice – and M. Lifar is full of life of the vigorous kind in which that dancer excels.

"And after the guests have gone, sylphides, archaeologists and all, the two door-keepers, in beautiful white tights, upon which fig-leaves have been modestly woven, sweep the floor with delicious grace."

The *Daily Express* liked the work. "M. Anton Dolin carried the honours of this production, and he also carried a great bundle of laurel wreaths at the end. His somersault climax won applause, and generally his youthful vigour formed an agreeable centrepiece." Daily Express 9.7.29

The *Morning Post* said that "*The Ball* pleased every section of opinion. It was certainly the most successful novelty of the last few years . . . Balanchine ingenuity in the construction of dance measures has never been seen to better advantage." Morning Post 9.7.29

Anton Dolin portrayed by Nerman in one of the classical rôles he regularly performed.

After the ballet was over, there was a marvellous party. No one guessed that it would be the last party of Diaghilev's life.

Anton Dolin lived in a studio in Glebe Place, in Chelsea. In his autobiography, he recalled that when Diaghilev accepted his invitation, the question of the piano came into his mind. Dolin possessed an ordinary upright model, which he felt to be unworthy of the occasion, so he dashed off to Harrods, and put down the first payment on a white Blüthner "grand." The great man duly admired it – "You have good taste in pianos, Anton!"

Sunday Dispatch 14.7.29 A reporter arrived early, "to find the guests collected outside the supper-room, the door of which Dolin was guarding, like one of the live white statues in *Le Bal.* 'The ballet,' he said, 'must eat first, they will be so hungry.' And when the ballet arrived, they seemed enchanted with the arrangement. They were all there: Danilova, Tchernicheva with her husband: Nikitina in a tight gold turban: Lifar and Diaghilev, eating sandwiches with Lady Juliet Duff." The *New* N.Y. Times 14.7.29 *York Times* added a few names to the guest-list – Princess Astafieva, (Dolin's teacher,) Lady Hadfield, Rieti, Dorothy Dickson, Anthony Asquith, and a host of composers, authors, and other celebrities. "I never heard so many foreign languages spoken in one place. Even the English people talked French to one another just to show that they could. Then Douglas Byng sang with Ruderich, and Mischa de la Motte and Douglas Byng gave a series of brilliant impersonations. Diaghilev smiled benignly. He could well afford to do so. Mr. Dolin has played the greatest individual part in the success of his present season."

The third new production was to be *Le Renard*, by which Diaghilev set great store, as it would be Lifar's first serious essay in the difficult choreographic art. A double cast had been arranged, following Stravinsky's own "stage directions," which were that it was to be "executed by buffoons, acrobats or dancers." Two days before the *première, The Times* printed a very long (and oft-quoted) letter from Diaghilev, partly to defend this idea in advance, partly to defend his recent ballets, several of which had been attacked on the grounds that they were exhibitions of acrobatics, and partly to introduce his latest *protégé*, a youthful musician, Igor Markevitch.

He started off:–

> "The longer the globe revolves, the less movement we will find on it! Peoples may fight world wars, empires may tumble, a colossal Utopia may be given birth to, but the in-born traditions of humanity remain the same."

The Times 13.7.29

The next paragraph came nearer to his own sphere.

> "Our century . . . interests itself with *'Mouvements mécaniques,'* but whenever new *'Mouvements artistiques'* occur people seem to be more frightened of being run over by them than by a motor-car in the street. For 25 years I have endeavoured to find a new *'Mouvement'* in the theatre. Society will have to recognise that my experiments, which appear dangerous today, become indispensable tomorrow. The misfortune of art is that everyone thinks he is entitled to his own judgment. When a scientist invents an electrical machine it is only experts who assume the right to be competent to criticize, but when I invent my artistic machine, everybody, without ceremony, puts his finger into the most delicate parts of the engine and likes to run it his own way . . .
>
> "The new appreciation of my 'spectacles' of today is a series of exclamations: What an 'Etrange,' 'Extravagant,' 'Repellent' show, and the new definitions of the choreography are 'Athletics' and 'Acrobatics.' I can picture to myself the bewilderment of the people who saw the first electric lamp, who heard the first word on the telephone."

And here Diaghilev proceeded to make one of his most brazen mis-statements in the cause of emphasizing the effect he had had on public taste, for he continued:–

> "My first electric bell for the British public was the *Polovtsian Dances* of *Prince Igor.* The small audience could not then tolerate this eccentric and acrobatic savagery, and they fled. And this only happened in 1911, at Covent Garden."

Diaghilev had most certainly forgotten his own telegram to Astruc! The stampede would seem to have been apocryphal!

Diaghilev continued his letter:–

> "The classical dance has never been and is not today The Russian Ballet. Its birthplace was France; it grew up in Italy, and has been conserved in Russia . . . The coarsest acrobatic tricks are the toe-dancing, the 'Doubles tours en l'air,' next to the 'Pirouettes en dehors,' and the hateful 32 'Fouettés.' That is where acrobatics should be attacked. In the plastic efforts of Balanchine, in *The Prodigal Son,* there are far less acrobatics than in the final classical *pas de deux* of *Aurora's Wedding.*"

The point of his letter really being to smooth the reception of the work of Lifar and Markevitch, Diaghilev added, "The public and the critics will probably be annoyed with my two young friends, but they are both 'débutants,' and they are not afraid of it."

The Times' critic was not slow to hop on to this question of acrobatics – "Does not the word mean 'walking on tip-toe?'" he demanded, having looked it up in the Oxford dictionary. "'If you call my last novelties acrobatic,' he has said in effect, 'what will you call *Renard?*'" The answer is 'a high-class circus.' There is no attempt to express an emotion or to weave a pattern of plastic beauty of line, and the story is consigned to four singers. The piece is prescribed to be played by clowns and acrobats and its aim is to be a grotesque entertainment."

The Times 15.7.29

The Cat   (Jean Hoyer.)

The Goat   (Lissanevitch.)

The Cock   (Efimov.)

Daily
Telegraph
16.7.29

"The scenario," said the *Daily Telegraph*, "is founded by the composer on popular Russian tales, the gist of it being the attempt of the fox to seize the cock, in which design he is frustrated by the cat and the goat. The simple but effective scenery and costumes are by Michel Larionov."

There was a double cast, one of dancers, one of acrobats, identically dressed, so that the trick could be played of having some of them exit right and re-appear left almost simultaneously. It must be acknowledged, however, that though *Renard* amused, it would not appear to warrant the long explanations and justifications: it would have been neither more successful nor less successful had it been shown without a manifesto. The same would seem to go for the Piano Concerto.

The
Queen
24.7.29

Of the music of *Renard*, *The Queen* said that it "belonged to Stravinsky's half-way period between the vigorous iconoclast revealed in *Les Noces*, and the feeble neoclassicist he has lately become in *Apollo Musagètes.*" The *Musical Record* said, "The music is in Stravinsky's Russian manner; it is a sharp sketch from the pen that wrote the elaborate *Sacre* and *Petrouchka*. Be sure the composer has not prettified his farmyard characters. The instruments bark, they worry at short phrases; it is not so much rustic music as rusticity in music, an expression of energetic, brutal, awakening mind too primitive to have a notion of expressing itself. How resourceful, how keen-witted to be so delightfully uncouth! And therein lies the attractiveness of *Renard* to Diaghilev's audience." This writer felt that *Renard* had a "queer poetic value."

All three new ballets this season were successful, the palm being awarded to *Le Bal.*

It is little short of amazing to read through the notices after the revival of Massine's *Sacre du Printemps*, with Lydia Sokolova dancing her exacting rôle as the Chosen Virgin once more. Looking at these calm statements, and turning back to 1913 and even to 1921, one wonders whether it was the same ballet. By 1929, it was completely accepted as "normal." Take this, for example: ". . . the pagan spring rites of peasant Russia, enacted beneath a dome of green and yellow storm-clouds by men in embroidered white tunics, and women with short orange dresses and plaited hair. The group dancing and the background posing for leader dancing were at their best in this richly-coloured ballet, which breathed sunlight and the cornfields. . ." Or this: "The dancing of the ballet was spell-binding. Mlle. Lydia Sokolova, capturing the mood of primitive ecstasy with all her former genius, received an ovation."

Evening News 23.7.29

Daily Express 23.7.29

The season made *The Tatler* nostalgic. "What a bond of friendship this Russian Ballet is! When two enthusiasts discover that they were both in the gallery at the first performance of, say, *Petrouchka*, it is a link almost as abruptly binding as the discovery that they both fought in the same sector during the same offensive in the Great War, or that they were both up at University in the same year. For my own part, I always warm instinctively to anybody who saw Nijinsky in *L'Après-Midi d'un Faune*, and I have a soft spot for those who remember the booing on the first night of *Jeux*, the bizarre lawn-tennis ballet that aroused so many scoffs, when a ball as big as a child's balloon bounded lightly on to the twilit stage. The collector of Russian ballets (for some people collect Russian ballets as others collect postage stamps) may regard *Jeux* as a rare and valuable specimen, for, like *Le Dieu Bleu*, it survived but a few performances. It was condemned as too grotesque, too fidgety, too pettifogging. But if it were revived today it might have had a happier fate. True, we know a great deal more about lawn tennis than we did, and take it in a more grimly realistic spirit." (There had, after all, been Suzanne Lenglen, Helen Wills, Cochet, Borotra, and Tilden, to name but a few, since *Jeux*.) "But we also know a great deal more about the choreographic conventions of which *Jeux* was a pioneer."

The Tatler 17.7.29

Just before the end of the season, *The Times* once again indulged in a summing-up. "The revival of Stravinsky's *Le Sacre du Printemps* was devised, no doubt, to form the climax to the season of the Diaghilev Ballet, which is now nearing its close. It is the charter of the modern ballet. To say that one enjoyed *Petrouchka* more than *Le Sacre* is to confess to old fogeyism, for with *Le Sacre* Stravinsky shed the last remnants of romanticism. . . and subsequently, that is, after its first presentation, Leonide Massine designed a choreography which not only freed it from the vulgarity of story-telling, but even eschewed any recognisable symbolism or 'programme.'

"*Le Sacre* is 'absolute' ballet, and we are assured that it will come to be regarded as having a significance for the 20th century equal to that of Beethoven's choral symphony in the 19th. Well, perhaps; meanwhile there was a rather thin attendance in stalls and boxes last night, but the lovers of true art in the gallery applauded to the echo." (The critic obviously did not have time to notice the other events of the evening, for the absence of many of the usual occupants of stalls and boxes, many of whom had subscriptions, was, in fact, due to a clash with two important political receptions: the house was completely sold out.)

The Times 23.7.29

The season ended, and Diaghilev, as usual, left for the continent, to see his doctor, to hunt antiquarian books, to visit the Salzburg Festival, and to spend his usual holiday on the Lido. The company gave two performances in Ostend, and four in Vichy, and then split up for the annual holidays.

The London papers seemed, more than ever, to regard the Diaghilev Ballet as a possession, and London more and more as "involved." The *Queen*, noting the number of British dancers in the company, said, "This conjures up a vision of a possible all-English ballet that might be rather interesting!" It also said, "All along Diaghilev has been a stimulus to the young creative Russian artist, and through the ballet he has provided an outlet for much modern music that otherwise might have been slow to see the light. One wonders what Stravinsky would have done without Diaghilev . . . Prokofiev is practically only known in England through the *Pas d'Acier*, the *Love of the Three Oranges*, and now the *Prodigal Son* . . .

The Queen 31.7.29

"Vladimir Polunin has an interesting story to tell of his *Seven Years with the Russian Ballet,* from which the figure of Diaghilev emerges as the most irrepressibly dynamic and vital producer in the modern world. Polunin quotes him as saying: " 'There is no interest in achieving the possible. We must aim at the impossible,' – and this was in the difficult days just after the War."

Observer
28.7.29

The *Observer* also came to the "London" theme, after discussing the season which had just ended. This paper thought *Le Renard* the most successful of the three new works. "The tale of the Cock and the Fox is treated so skilfully that, for all the complexity of the steps, and the musical rhythms, the matter is simple to follow and amusing to watch. Children see the points of the tale at once."

The *Observer* continued, "The main part of the programmes has been taken up with increasingly good performances of older ballets. Opinions differ as to the relative worth of these, but no one will seek to depose the de-Falla-Picasso *Three Cornered Hat* from its position as the finest of the modern works, nor refuse a high place to *Aurora's Wedding* among last-century ballets, *Petrouchka* among character ballets, and *The Cat* among the more modern."

The *Observer* had made its own choice, and everyone could argue happily over it. But the paper went on to demonstrate its opinion of the solid appreciation by then apparent in London:

"The audiences at Covent Garden . . . have shown how well-established the ballet of M. Diaghilev is in the esteem of Londoners. The pity of it is that this famous troupe which, criticise it as we may, is the only one that provides spectacles of this excellence, yet has never been offered a permanent home in London, despite the number of wealthy English patrons among its fervent admirers. The warmth of our affection cannot be doubted by M. Diaghilev. What other inducements are needed for him to make London his headquarters it is not possible to guess. But at least it is to be hoped that should the chance happily arise it will not lightly be dismissed. The prestige of London as a capital where art is cherished could not but be increased by the permanent presence of the Russian Ballet."

Just three weeks later, on August 19th, Diaghilev died in Venice.

Hundreds of newspapers throughout the world, in towns and cities which had never even been visited by the company, printed the news, and followed it with long obituary notices. Most of these must have been taken from a handout, and in this his recently-published story of the *Polovtsian Dances* featured prominently. The phrase in that last "notice" in *The Times,* ". . . the Diaghilev Ballet, which is now nearing its close," had proved prophetic.

Diaghilev's vitality had been ebbing away. His friends knew that he suffered from diabetes. Like many hypochondriacs, fussing about the slightest cold, ("it would be pneumonia," said Nabokov,) he ignored the advice of his doctors if it displeased him. He was a prodigious trencherman, who had an arrangement with one of his favourite restaurants in London, which always gave him a double portion at the normal price. Taking a cup of chocolate and pastries at a *confiserie* in Monte Carlo, he pointed one day to his empty plate and said to Nabokov, "This is the way to treat diabetes."

He was buried in the Orthodox section of the cemetery island of San Michele, where the waters of the lagoon lap the wall behind his grave, and where, in 1971, Stravinsky, his first great "discovery," – his "first son" – was to be buried near him.

The Times, of course, did not rely on anything but its own assessments in its obituary notice.

The
Times
20.8.29

"It has been given to few patrons of the arts, for that is essentially what Diaghilev was, to be so much an artist," it said. "If he had been a benevolent millionaire anxious to seek out the finest artists for the pleasure of the capitals of Europe without considering the financial success of their productions, he could not have gathered together more splendid names. Among his musicians were Prokofiev and Stravinsky, among his artists Picasso and Matisse, Derain and Rouault, to mention those names least likely to achieve a popular success. There must be many whose only acquaintance with these uncompromising artists is through Diaghilev's ballet. Of his perfect choice of dancers there is little new to speak. But his productions were not purely benevolent. They had to succeed, and though they often met with opposition and even insult at the beginning, they did succeed . . .

"But such an eclectic yet discriminating taste would have been of little avail if Diaghilev had not been able to combine these arts and produce, by virtue of his extraordinary gift for organization, a perfect whole. Doubtless it was this capacity that in the end ensured the success of his ballets. The most uncompromising art in his hands seemed to serve the ends of yet another art, and thus could be accepted the more readily. His company endured any eccentricities that he might show, since they knew that no one could lead them as he did. He was, it was said, such an artist."

The Lady, lover of the Diaghilev ballet and even of the modern ballet, could not bring itself to write of him after his death, but just before, at the end of the season, had said that "the three novelties manifested that refusal to become enslaved by any particular system which has always been the characteristic of the Diaghilev Ballet and accounts for its unimpaired vitality." The Lady 8.8.29

And that Diaghilev's most adversely criticised experiments were already understood, and his advanced vision appreciated, came out in a tribute in *The Queen*:-

"The Russian Ballet has been the most brilliant feature in every brilliant post-war London Season. It has been the artistic expression of the age, something that was laughed at, was loved, was reverenced later on both by the understanding and the non-comprehending who were afraid of being left behind. It was beyond contemporary thought in many ways, and Diaghilev, by presenting the foretaste of what is to come in so many branches of art, will be understood better later on . . . The Queen 28.8.29

"It is impossible to appreciate adequately his influence on contemporary art. He made the word 'Russian Ballet' almost a fabulous one, so that a Diaghilev first-night was, artistically, a European event.

"He has been called one of the world's half-dozen indispensable men. When unknown people opened their papers one day last week they read of his death. To those who had seen his ballets it was as if the sun had grown cold for a while. They never knew him, but they went about saying, 'Diaghilev is dead.'

"He was to this generation the discoverer of that secret beauty that it could not find alone. His death is the end of an artistic era, and it seems a personal tragedy."

1954

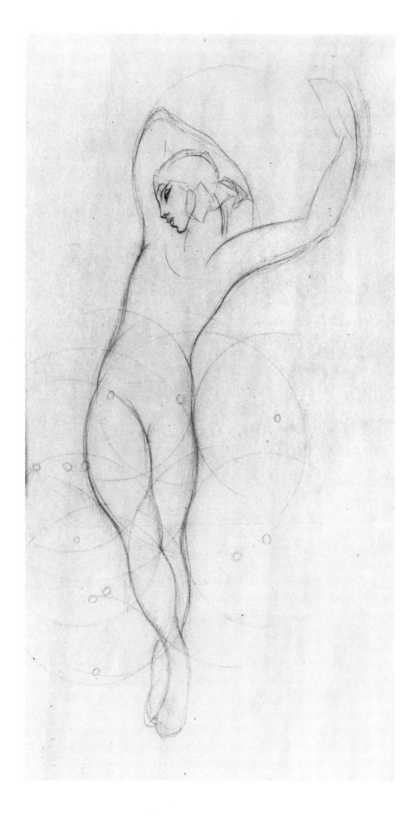

The successes and failures of twenty years are behind. Somehow, the legend remains inviolate, for the legend was, in essence, the truth – the truth of the creation of an amazing array of beautiful, inspiring works of art. Like the Spectre of the Rose, they leapt to view in one bound in 1909; in 1929, they soared from sight.

Every nuance that can be recollected is cherished. Valentine Gross drew the legendary dancers with a hand that gave them motion.

Here, the most beautiful legend of all – the spectre of that rose with which the young girl had danced – is suspended for a moment. Petals lost, carried away by the rush of air his own flight created, remains an exquisite ghost, to which cling a few glistening crystal dew drops to show that once, it was corporeal.

EPILOGUE

In 1930, Karsavina's autobiography, *Theatre Street,* was published, and instantly became a best-seller. The story of an upbringing in the Imperial Ballet School, and of work as a dancer in Russia and in Europe, so delightfully written, remained for long the key with which to unlock the door that led to Diaghilev and the *Ballet Russes.*

Then, in 1954, the Edinburgh Festival decided to mark the twenty-fifth anniversary of Diaghilev's death with an exhibition, and invited Richard Buckle, founder and Editor of the magazine *Ballet,* to mount it.

As far back as 1911, Richard Capell had ended his review on November 15th by saying, "Last night, one wondered if some record of *Scheherazade, Cleopatra,* and the *Carnaval* – sketches and models, for example – could not be made for conservation in a London museum; it would be sad if these performances passed without some visible record of these, the most harmonious and scrupulously artistic stage décors and dresses ever seen in a London theatre."

Buckle sought out original designs – portraits – costumes – and then set out to make the exhibiting of them his own work of art. For this, he did what Diaghilev would have liked – found young artists, and set them to work on the *mise-en-scène.* In Edinburgh, this had "the character of booths at an old Russian fair," said Colette Clark. Of the original designs of Bakst and Benois, she said, "To those who never saw the first productions, their *finesses* and attention to detail may come as a surprise, and they will find a new standard of stage design awaiting them." Punch 10.11.54

In March, Richard Buckle (who was also ballet critic of the *Observer,*) told his readers of three visits he had just paid in Paris, "symbolic of the three periods into which Diaghilev's activity in Western Europe may be roughly divided.

"Alexandre Benois, in his eighties . . . it was he and his learned St. Petersburg friends, the painter Bakst and Somov among them, who 'educated' Diaghilev . . . Benois stands for romantic erudition, for the influence of the French eighteenth century on Peter's capital, and for the Russian *fin de siècle* which was also a *renaissance.*

"What worlds away are the Moscow painters Gontcharova and Larionov! Their sets for *Le Coq d'Or, L'Oiseau de Feu, Les Noces, Soleil de Nuit, Le Renard, Contes Russes,* and *Chout* seemed to bridge in a most daring manner the gap between Russian peasant art and the anarchic experiments of the 'teens and twenties of our century . . . I told Larionov that for our exhibition Leonard Rosoman was creating a huge and fantastic scheme of decoration, 'baroque, but seen through contemporary eyes.' 'Contemporary!' he explained. 'That's the important thing.' He waxed emotional as he described the immensity of Diaghilev's vision.

"The scenery of the last ballets reflected the diversity of the School of Paris; and for these works Boris Kochno wrote nearly all the libretti.

"I watched him pace about his exquisite flat . . . He poured forth treasures from cupboards, drawings by Matisse, Picasso, Tchelitchew, Mirò, Bakst, Laurencin, Pruna, Braque and Sert, marvels which I believe no one has been allowed to look at for years. I gloated at the thought of being able to show them in Edinburgh."

Daily
Telegraph
20.3.54

In Edinburgh, 25,000 people saw the exhibition. Almost by accident, the decision was taken to mount it again in London. Sadly, Richard Capell (who had left the *Daily Mail* some years before) did not live to see it. He died in June. When the announcement about it reached the Press in March, he had said: "Together with Goossens' performance last week of *The Rite of Spring*, this took my mind back to that extraordinary Muscovite and, in particular, to the part he played in the musical life of his time.

"I suppose that never in the history of the theatre has there been another eye-opener so unexpected and so ravishing as the original Diaghilev ballet. A legend has grown to the effect that Londoners were slow to fall for its witchery.

"Quite wrong. The town was captivated from the first. . .

"Diaghilev's devotion to his enterprise was admirable; . . . he thought of nothing else. An incomprehensible character never to be trusted – a streak of treachery in him was hateful . . . All the same, he was a captivating talker. He knew what was going on in Europe in all the arts. In his decline I urged him to put down on paper all his thoughts and experiences.

"He hesitated a moment and then, with characteristic arrogance, said; 'Memoirs? It is a common-place thing to write memoirs.' He felt it his rôle in life to do what had never been done before."

Forbes House, near Hyde Park Corner, stood dark and deserted. Buckle and his friends threw themselves upon it. He would create sympathetic and imaginative settings for the various groups of objects – he would use space in mysterious, theatrical ways, he would drive them all to frenzy, he would coax and cajole and condemn and praise and change his mind, but he would achieve perfection.

"This presentation is dominated by the music, which, relayed throughout the rooms, keeps the atmosphere at a constant pitch of excitement," said Colette Clark in the article already quoted, comparing the two presentations. "New, too, is the air of nostalgia and melancholy lent by the imaginative arrangement of the original costumes themselves which, now limp and faded, recover a little of their former glory . . . Alas! they remind us that the sadly transient nature of ballet is such that although it was his great dancers who made Diaghilev's work famous, they play the smallest part in the exhibition."

Forbes House counted 140,000 visitors to see it.

Diaghilev's career really began in discussions of art over the samovars in the flats of friends in St. Petersburg at the end of the nineteenth century. Let a reporter end this book with the story of a gathering of friends, many of them the dancers, the ephemera of his work, just before Christmas, 1954.

Observer
26.12.54

"An unusually strong gust of nostalgia blew through Forbes House one night last week, when a gathering of celebrities who had worked with Diaghilev sat down to dinner together. At the head of the candle-lit table, Madame Karsavina sipped vodka between Lifar and Grigoriev, the great man's stage-manager – a post none but the most rugged character could have endured.

"In spite of caviare, pickled cucumber, bortsch and a galaxy of Russian name-cards, hardly a word of Russian was spoken; not surprisingly, perhaps, when one considers the good British names hidden behind exotic polysyllables like Markova – de Valois – Sokolova – and Dolin.

"As they emerged into the Hall of the Sleeping Beauty, the company were instantly transformed. The old vitality broke through; Lifar and Tchernicheva were dancing up the stairs, while Sir Malcolm Sargent, tail-coat flying, whirled twinkling-toed Idzikowski round the pillars to the waltz strain of *Le Spectre de la Rose*."

ACKNOWLEDGMENTS AND SOURCES

I wish to express my gratitude to Her Majesty the Queen for her most gracious permission to quote entries from diaries in the Royal Archives.

I have had so much help and interest in the compilation of this book—tips, research, reading, collation, the loan of material and illustrations, work on photographs, the checking of points of detail—that it would be invidious to attempt to make a list in "Order of Merit." So, in addition to the friends named in the Prologue, I would like to thank many individuals, libraries and organisations, authors and publishing houses, and will simply put each group into alphabetical order.

Every possible effort has been made to trace the source or ownership of items quoted or shown. Should any such effort have stopped too soon, sincere apologies are tendered if there is lack of recognition of the author's indebtedness.

Merle Armitage, Lady Ashton (Madge Garland), Mrs. Baker, Miranda Bickford-Smith, Mrs. Humphrey Brooke, Mme. Butsova, G. Cannings, The Hon. Colin Clark, M. Clarke, Dr. Cole, Lady Diana Cooper, Audrey Counsell, Pauline Cox, Norman Crider, Dr. Herbert Curtis, Patience Devas, Angela Dixon, Charles Edridge, Parmenia Ekstrom, Joe Gambone, Madeleine Ginsburg, Renata Gofren, G. Goossens, Miss K. Gordon, C.B.E., Ivor Guest, J. Hart, Mr. and Mrs. Hinderaker, Mrs. Hitchins, Jacqueline Honeyman, Richard Huggett, Ann Jenner, Dean Kortge, Alex Kroll, Professor Dan Laurence, Mr. and Mrs. Lazzarini, Joan Lawson, Philadelphia Lee, Messrs. Lenare, David Leonard, A.F. Lilley, P.W. Manchester, Mr. Marks, Hester Marsden-Smedley, Dr. M. Martin, Leonide Massine, Melissa McQuillan, George Milford-Cottam, Bronislava Nijinska, John O'Brien, Sir Roland Penrose, Lorna and Oleg Polunin, Dame Marie Rambert, John Rogers, Natalia Roslavleva, Oriel Ross, Viscount Shackleton, K.G., Ted Shawn, Baron Thyssen-Bornemisa, Ursula Vaughan Williams, Jennie Walton, Dr. Thomas Walton, Frank Wells and Professor G.P. Wells, Dame Rebecca West, Eric Walter White, John Wiley, Thomas Willis, G.B. Wilson, Dr. M.H. Winter.

LIBRARIES AND INSTITUTIONS

Albany Institute of History and Art
Apollo Magazine
British Library: Reading Room, Newspaper Library
Dansmuseet, Stockholm
Guildhall Library
Guildhall School of Music Library
House of Commons Library
Musée Municipale d'Art Moderne, Paris
National Film Archive

Public Libraries and State Historical Societies in
    Albany (N.Y.), Cleveland (Ohio), Colorado,
    Kansas, Los Angeles, Milwaukee, Pittsburgh,
    and Wisconsin, and Shaker Historical Society
St. Helen's Public Library, Lancs.
Savoy Hotel Press Office
Stock Exchange Library and Yearbook
The Librarian and Archivist of *The Times*
Times Drawing Office

BOOKS TO WHICH REFERENCE IS MADE IN THE TEXT

Armitage, Merle. *Dance Memoranda.* (Duell, Sloan & Pearce)

Benckendorff, Count Constantine, *Half a Life.* (Richards Press)

Beaumont, Cyril. *The Diaghilev Ballet in London.* (A & C. Black)

Bourman, Anatol. *The Tragedy of Nijinsky.* (Robert Hale)

Briggs, John. *Requiem for a Yellow Brick Brewery.* (Little, Brown & Co.)

Buckle, Richard. *In Search of Diaghilev.* (Sedgwick & Jackson)
Nijinsky. (Weidenfeld & Nicholson)

Cochran, C.B. *Cock-a-Doodle-Do.* (J.M. Dent)

Cocteau, Jean (ed. M. Crosland). *My Contemporaries.* (Peter Owen)

Cooper, Lady Diana. *The Rainbow Comes and Goes.* (Rupert Hart-Davis)

Cooper, Douglas. *Picasso: Theatre.* (Weidenfeld & Nicolson)

Coton, A. V. *A Prejudice for Ballet.* (Methuen)

Dent, Alan (Editor). *George Bernard Shaw & Mrs. Patrick Campbell: Their Correspondence.* (Victor Gollancz)

Duke, Vernon. *Passport to Paris.* (Little, Brown & Co.)

Eaton, Quaintance. *Miracle of the Met.* (Meredith)
The Boston Opera Company. (Appleton [Meredith])

Fokine, Michel. *Fokine.* (Constable)

Grigoriev, Serge. *The Diaghilev Ballet 1909–1929.* (1. Constable; 2. Penguin Books)

Guest, Ivor. *The Romantic Ballet in England.* (1. A. & C. Black; 2. Pitman)

Karsavina, Tamara. *Theatre Street.* (Heinemann)

Kennedy, Michael. *The Music of Ralph Vaughan Williams.* (O.U.P.)

Kolodin, Irving. *The Story of the Metropolitan Opera.* (Knopf, N.Y.)

Kschessinska, Mathilde. *Dancing in Petersburg.* (Victor Gollancz)

Ledermann, Minna. *Stravinsky in the Theatre.* (Peter Owen)

Lifar, Serge. *Serge Diaghilev.* (Putnam)

Loguine, Tatiana. *Gontcharova & Larionov.* (Editions Klincksieck)

Mackail, Denis. *The Story of J. M. B.* (1. Peter Davies; 2. Kraus Reprint Corporation in America)

Matz, Mary Jane. *The Many Lives of Otto Kahn.* (Macmillan, N.Y.)

Nabokov, Nicholas. *Old Friends and New Music.* (Hamish Hamilton)

Nijinsky, Romola. *Nijinsky.* (1. Victor Gollancz; 2. Sphere Books)

Nijinsky, Vaslav. *The Diary of Vaslav Nijinsky.* (1. Victor Gollancz; 2. Jonathan Cape)

Nikitina, Alice. *Nikitina by Herself.* (Allan Wingate)

Penrose, Sir Roland. *Picasso: His Life & Work.* (Victor Gollancz)

Polunin, Vladimir & Beaumont, Cyril. *The Continental Method of Scene Painting.* (Cyril Beaumont)

Reid, Charles. *Thomas Beecham: an Independent Biography.* (Victor Gollancz)
Malcolm Sargent. (Hamish Hamilton)

Stilwell, Sir Osbert. *Laughter in the Next Room.* (Macmillan & Co. Ltd.)

Sokolova, Lydia. *Dancing for Diaghilev.* (John Murray)

Steegmuller, Francis. *Cocteau.* (Macmillan & Co. Ltd.)

Stravinsky, Igor. *The Diaghilev I Knew.* (Atlantic Monthly)
Chronicle of My Life. (Victor Gollancz)
Memories and Commentaries (With Robert Craft). (Faber and Faber)

Tyler, Parker. *The Divine Comedy of Pavel Tchelichew.* (Weidenfeld & Nicolson)

Vaughan Williams, Ursula. *R.V.W.* (O.U.P.)

White, Eric Walter. *Stravinsky.* (Faber)

Wilson, A.E. *The Story of Pantomime.* (Home & Van Thal)

Wolkonsky, Prince. *My Reminiscences.* (Hutchinson)

DIAGHILEV PRODUCTIONS

As details of composer, choreographer, designer, and original production, are given on the "Playbill" at the start of each chapter, the ballets are here entered with that page. Each ballet is discussed in the ensuing chapter, and many are mentioned in passing throughout the book. Only key performances, and revival after some years, are given individual pages here.

A = Performed in America   R = Revival   [Illustrations]

NP = Not produced   NPE = Not produced in England by Diaghilev

388

As each ballet is listed on the "Playbill" for the season during which it was first produced in London, composers, choreographers, and designers are listed by that page. Dancers are indexed where they receive an individual notice, as they are listed alphabetically for each season on the playbills.

ff = Discussed in ensuing chapter or pages.   [Illustrations]

Cartoon of Diaghilev on jacket and title-page, by Hyne, 1925. The drawings of Diaghilev, Pavlova, and American critics watching a rehearsal in New York, on pages 1 and 138, and impressions of dancers scattered in the index, are all by Muchette. (*New York Tribune,* British Library.)

OBSERVERS OF THE OBSERVED — SOME CRITICS

RICHARD ALDRICH

HEYWOOD BROUN

GEORGE CALDERON

RICHARD CAPELL

SYDNEY CARROLL

EDWIN EVANS

HERBERT FARJEON

HUBERT GRIFFITH

PERCY HAMMOND

ERNEST J. HOPKINS

HORACE HORSNELL

P. G. KONODY